Baedeker
Czech Republic
Slovak Republic

Baedeker's

CZECH REPUBLIC SLOVAK REPUBLIC

Imprint

262 illustrations, 131 plans and maps, 1 large map of the Czech and Slovak Republics

Original German text: Prof. Erich Bachmann (history of art), Vera Beck (Practical Information from A to Z), Prof. Wolfgang Hassenpflug (Climate), Dr Otakar Mohyla (Sights from A to Z, Practical Information from A to Z), Dr Peter Jordan (Economy), Prof. Ferdinand Seibt (History), Prof. Josef Werdecker (Topography), Dr Florian Zigrai (Ecology)

Editorial work: Baedeker-Redaktion

General direction: Dr Peter Baumgarten, Baedeker Stuttgart

Cartography: Gert Oberländer, Munich; Archiv für Flaggenkunde; Ralf Stelter, Hattingen; Mairs Geographischer Verlag, Ostfildern (large map of the Czech and Slovak Republics)

Source of illustrations: Baedeker-Archiv (2); Baumgarten (5); Bohnacker (4); Cabos (26); Eisenschmidt (1); Gemini (7); Hartl (71); Herold (7); Historia-Photo (13); Karásek (43); Kusak (1); Lade (3); Mohyla (1); Morávek (12); Moravian Museum, Brno (2); Olympia-Archiv (1); Saxon Provincial Library, Dresden (1); Škoda (1); Skupy (40); B. Smettan (6); Stoll (3); Ullstein Bilderdienst (2).

English language edition: Alec Court
English translation: James Hogarth

Following the tradition established by Karl Baedeker in 1844, sights of particular interest are distinguished by either one or two stars.
To make it easier to locate the various sights listed in the "A to Z" section of the Guide, their coordinates on the large map of the Czech and Slovak Republics are shown in red at the head of each entry.

Only a selection of hotels and restaurants can be given: no reflection is implied, therefore, on establishments not included.

The symbol on a town plan indicates the local tourist office from which further information can be obtained. The post-horn symbol indicates a post office.

In a time of rapid change it is difficult to ensure that all the information given is entirely accurate and up to date, and the possibility of error can never be completely eliminated. Although the publishers can accept no responsibility for inaccuracies and omissions, they are always grateful for corrections and suggestions for improvement.
On January 1st 1993 the Czech and Slovak Federative Republic split into two independent states, the Czech Republic and the Slovak Republic. In the "Sights from A to Z" section of this Guide, therefore, there are separate listings for the two countries. In the introductory section, however, it is convenient to consider their geography, history, etc., together. In the Practical Information section there is a single alphabetical listing, with separate information for the two republics within each entry where necessary.
The political developments of recent years have led to many changes in the names of places, streets and institutions within former Czechoslovakia. So far as possible these have been taken account of in this Guide, but the process of change is likely to continue for some time and it is difficult to keep completely up to date.

1st English edition 1994

Prentice Hall General Reference: US and Canadian edition

PRENTICE HALL and colophon are registered trademarks of Simon & Schuster, Inc.

Distributed in the United Kingdom by the Publishing Division of the Automobile Association, Fanum House, Basingstoke, Hampshire RG21 2EA

Licensed user: Mairs Geographischer Verlag GmbH & Co., Ostfildern-Kemnat bei Stuttgart
The name *Baedeker* is a registered trade mark
A CIP catalogue record of this book is available from the British Library

Printed in Italy by G. Canale & C.S.p.A – Borgaro T.se –Turin

ISBN UK 0–7495–0867–1
US and Canada 0–671–89687–3

Contents

The Principal Sights at a Glance: Czech Republic

The Principal Sights at a Glance: Slovak Republic

Preface

This guide to the Czech and Slovak Republics is one of the new generation of Baedeker guides.

These guides, illustrated throughout in colour, are designed to meet the needs of the modern traveller. They are quick and easy to consult, with the principal places of interest described in alphabetical order, and the information is presented in a format that is both attractive and easy to follow.

This guide covers the Czech Republic and the Slovak Republic: that is, the whole territory of former Czechoslovakia. The terms Czech and Slovak Republics are used in default of more "user-friendly" names for both the new states; for although the Slovak Republic is also known as Slovakia (Slovensko) there is no generally acceptable name for the Czech Republic, which includes Bohemia, Moravia and what is known as Moravian Silesia (Moravské Slovácko). The possibility of devising a suitable name has been discussed, but so far no solution has been found – though the term "Czech Lands" (České Země) has come to be used by official bodies.

The guide is in three parts. The first part gives a general account of the two countries, their topography, climate, ecology, population, government and administration, economy, history, famous people, art and culture. A number of suggested itineraries lead in to the second part, in which places of tourist interest are described, first in the Czech Republic and then in the Slovak Republic. The third part contains a variety of practical information. Both the sights and the practical information are listed in alphabetical order.

The new Baedeker guides are noted for their concentration on essentials and their convenience of use. They contain numerous specially drawn plans and colour illustrations; and at the end of the book is a large map making it easy to locate the various places described in the "A to Z" section of the guide with the help of the coordinates given at the head of each entry.

Facts and Figures

General

Geographical situation

The former state of Czechoslovakia, now divided into the **Czech Republic** and the **Slovak Republic**, was a land-locked country extending from west to east in eastern Central Europe, surrounded by Germany in the west, Poland along its whole northern frontier, the Ukraine in the east, Hungary to the south-east and Austria to the south.

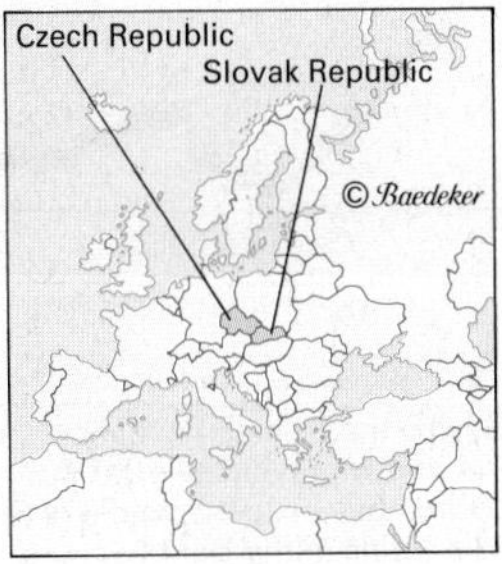

Neighbouring states

The Czech Republic is bounded on the west by the German *Länder* of Bavaria and Saxony, on the north by the Polish voivodates of Jelenia Góra, Wałbrzych, Opole, Katowice and Bielsko-Biała, on the east by the Slovak Republic (central and western Slovakia) and on the south by the Austrian provinces of Lower Austria and Upper Austria.

The Slovak Republic is bounded on the west by the Czech Republic (northern and southern Moravia), on the north by the Polish voivodates of Bielsko-Biała, Nowy Sacz and Krosno, on the east for a short distance by the Ukraine and on the south by the Hungarian counties of Borsod-Abaúj-Zemplén, Nógrád, Pest, Komárom and Győr-Sopron and the Austrian provinces of Burgenland and Lower Austria.

Area

The Czech Republic (the former Imperial Crown lands of Bohemia and Moravia together with small parts of Silesia) has an area of 78,864sq.km/30,449sq.miles, representing 61.66% of the area of former Czechoslovakia. The Slovak Republic (Slovakia) has an area of 49,036sq.km/18,933sq.miles (38.34%).
The total area of the former Czech and Slovak Federative Republic (ČFSR) was 127,900sq.km/49,400sq.miles.

Extent of former ČFSR

The former ČFSR extended for some 765km/475 miles from east to west, with a greatest width from north to south of some 275km/170 miles in Bohemia and 80km/50 miles in eastern Slovakia.

Frontiers of former ČFSR

The total length of the frontiers of the ČFSR was 3553km/2208 miles – 1391km/864 miles with Poland (39.1%), 815km/506 miles with Germany (23%), 679km/422 miles with Hungary (19.1%), 570km/354 miles with Austria (16%) and 98km/61 miles with the Ukraine (2.8%).

Topography

Territory of Former Czechoslovakia

Bohemia, Moravia, Moravian Silesia and Slovakia

The Czech Republic and Slovak Republic are land-locked states in eastern Central Europe.

◄ *A quiet stream in the Jizera Hills*

Territory of former Czechoslovakia

Bohemia, Moravia, Moravian Silesia and Slovakia

The western part of the Czech Republic (Bohemia) is linked with the North Sea by the Elbe (Labe) river system. The central part of the territory (Moravia and Moravian Silesia) has a link with the Baltic by way of the Oder (Odra), but – like the whole of Slovakia – is drained south-eastward by the tributaries of the Danube.
The overseas trade of both the Czech and Slovak Republics necessarily, therefore, passes through the territory of other states.

Form of the territory

The characteristic feature of the territory of former Czechoslovakia is its great extent from east to west. The greater width of Bohemia and the circuit of mountains surrounding it on all sides have made this a heartland, with Prague (Praha) as its centre. Moravia is a land of passage between east and west and between north and south. Slovakia, thanks to the structure of its mountains, has no large central region; its capital, Bratislava, lies on the extreme south-western edge of its territory.

Geomorphological characteristics

The natural structure of Czechoslovakian territory is characterised by the predominance of ancient rocks in the western half and younger folded mountains in the eastern part. The wide distribution of slates, gneisses and granites and the violent disturbances to which the basins of central Bohemia were exposed have given the Bohemian Massif a distinctive unity of its own.

Moravia is mainly occupied by the south-eastern slopes of the Bohemian Massif, but also has a number of ranges of hills belonging to the Western Carpathians – the Little Carpathians (Malé Karpaty), White Carpathians (Bilé Karpaty) and Javorníky – in the region bordering on Slovakia; Slovakia itself is entirely occupied by the folded rock massifs of the Tertiary era. Large areas of the ancient massif were several times exposed to marine transgressions. Thus in northern and eastern Bohemia there are massive deposits of Cretaceous limestones and sandstones: the Bohemian Switzerland (České Švýcarsko), the Teplice and Adršpach Crags (Teplické a Adršpašské Skály) and – the best known region – the Bohemian Paradise (Český Ráj).
The sea of the Miocene period advanced far into Moravia from the Vienna Basin, leaving mostly clayey deposits which then led to the formation of a region of gently rounded hills. The coal measures of the Upper Carboniferous and Middle Tertiary are of economic importance. At the time of the Alpine folding movement differentiated upthrusts of individual ranges within the massif created the main features of the present landscape pattern. At this time too there were volcanic emissions along great fault lines, as in the Bohemian Massif (České Středohoří) and the Doupov Hills (Doupovské Hory).
During this revolutionary geological period the arc of the Western Carpathians which runs through Slovakia and south-eastern Moravia,

continuing the line of the Alps, was formed. The core of the range, in the High Tatras (Vysoké Tatry) on the border with Poland, is mountainous in character. On the inner side, falling down to the Hungarian Basin, is another area of recent volcanism.
There are very considerable variations in altitude in Slovakia. The Gerlachovsky Štít in the High Tatras rises to 2655m/8711ft; the lowest point, on the frontier river Bodrog, is only 94m/308ft above sea level.
Within the Bohemian Massif there are larger areas of low-lying country, but even here the Krkonoše (Riesengebirge) range in the Sudetens (Sudety) reaches a height of 1602m/5256ft in the sharply pointed Sněžka. The lowest area (116m/381ft) is at the point where the Labe (Elbe) leaves Bohemia.

Rivers

The main European watershed runs along the ridges of the Upper Palatinate Forest (known in Bohemia as the Český Les) in the west, then along the Bohemo-Moravian Highlands (Českomoravská Vrchovina) to the Králický Sněžnik, and from there by way of the Eastern Sudetens to the Western Carpathians, continuing east along their northerly ridges.
Bohemia is almost entirely drained by the Elbe (Labe) river system to the North Sea. Moravian Silesia and northern Moravia are drained in part to the Baltic by the Oder (Odra). The rest of Moravia is drained to the Danube (Dunaj) and thence to the Black Sea by the river Morava.
From Slovakia the Váh, the Hron and the Ipel' also flow into the Danube, as do the Tisa, the Hornád and the Ondava. Only the Poprad, coming from the High Tatras, breaks through the northern rim of hills to reach the Dunajec, which drains by way of the Vistula to the Baltic. The Danube itself borders Slovakia for 172km/107 miles, forming the frontier with Hungary and Austria.

Lakes

There are only a few small natural lakes. They are almost all of glacial origin (Bohemian Forest, High Tatras) and are of considerable depth. A much larger area is occupied by a number of artificial lakes formed by damming rivers (Vltava; Orava, Váh).

Ponds

In the southern Bohemian basin there are numerous large fish ponds only a few metres deep: Bezdrev, Hejtman, Rožmberský Rybník, Rybník Svět.

Medicinal springs

The medicinal springs in the spa towns of Karlovy Vary (Karlsbad), Teplice and Janské Lázně in Bohemia and Piešt'any and Sliač in Slovakia have been known since the 11th century. Other important spas in Slovakia are Dudince, Margita-Ilona, Trenčianské Teplice and Vyšné Ružbachy.

The Regions

Bohemia

Mountains and basins

The topography of the Bohemian Massif differs from that of the Carpathians. In Bohemia the enclosing fringe of mountains rises markedly above the central basin and upland regions. This was the territory occupied by the Sudeten Germans.

Bohemian Forest

In the south-west the Bohemian Forest extends for some 220km/140 miles along the frontier between Bohemia and Bavaria. The Domažlice–Furth im Wald depression (alt. 500m/1640ft) dissects it into the lower Český Les (Upper Palatinate Forest), with Mt Čerchov (1039m/3409ft), and the higher Bohemian Forest (Šumava), with the peaks of Plechý (1378m/4521ft), Boubín (1362m/4469ft) and Jezerní Stěna (1343m/4406ft). A series of long parallel ridges, mostly rounded by erosion, give these hills their characteristic tranquil lines. The broad longitudinal valley of the upper Vltava has only a very gentle gradient. In this area is one of the largest artificial lakes in the country, the Lipenská Přehradní Nádrž (Lake Lipno), with an area of

A mountain stream in the Bohemian Forest

48sq.km/18.5sq.miles. Here too many narrow transverse valleys cut through the hills into the foreland region. The corries formed at altitudes of around 1000m/3280ft during the Ice Age and now occupied by dark-hued lakes are a particular attraction of this forest country. On the levelled surfaces of the hills expanses of moorland have been formed. The landscape is still dominated by forests, though large areas of forest have been damaged or destroyed. The trees are predominantly conifers, with great stands of spruce.

(It is planned to combine the Šumava National Park in Czech territory with the Bavarian Forest National Park in Germany into a single nature reserve extending on both sides of the frontier.)

The region was populated by settlers from Bavaria between the 12th and 14th centuries. The peasant villages which were then established, the glassworks and the timber stacks of the woodcutters gave this quiet country its particular character. Only a few small towns developed in the interior of the region on the mountain streams; conditions were more favourable on its borders, where a few larger settlements grew up – Český Krumlov, Prachatice, Vimperk, Sušice, Klatovy and, far to the north, Tachov.

Ore Mountains

The Ore Mountains (Krušné Hory, Erzgebirge) extend in a 130km/80 mile long mountain wall from the Elstergebirge in Germany to the Elbe Sandstone Hills, falling steeply to the Ohře-Bílina rift valley but sloping gradually down to the north-west. The slightly curving ridge line runs at altitudes of between 800m/2625ft and 1000m/3280ft, with the flat-topped Mt Klínovec rising above it to a height of 1244m/4082ft. On the south side, at an altitude of around 600m/1970ft, is a plateau area of varying width, much dissected by tributaries of the Ohře (Eger). The complicated structure of the rocks (micaceous schist, phyllite, granite, gneiss, with recent intrusions of basalt) gave the area rich resources of minerals, which were a major factor in determining the settlement pattern. The mining industry which was formerly so important, however, has now almost died out. The low temper-

Winter landscape on Mt Klínovec in the Ore Mountains

atures and high rainfall, leading to the formation of moorland, have prevented the development of agriculture at the higher levels, which are covered by extensive forests, now suffering from the effects of industrial pollution.

The region was settled, mainly from Saxony, from the 12th century onwards. Villages and mining settlements were established at altitudes of up to 1000m/3300ft; Boží Dar (1028m/3373ft) is the country's highest town. The decline of the mining industry compelled the population to turn to other sources of income (woodworking, textiles).

This was an area of numerous small towns, many of which have declined as a result of the events of the postwar period. Only Jáchymov has maintained its former reputation (silver deposits, radioactive thermal springs; uranium ore mined from the 1950s to the 1980s).

Cheb Region

The Cheb region (Chebsko) is a basin lying at an altitude of 420–500m (1380–1640ft), enclosed by the foothills of the Upper Palatinate Forest, the Fichtelgebirge and the Elstergebirge and by the Císařský Les (Kaiserwald). Favoured by climate and good soil, settlers from northern Bavaria made this a fertile farming region. There are also numerous mineral springs, the result of volcanic activity in geologically recent times. This was the foundation of the prosperity of the spa of Františkovy Lázně (Franzensbad). A good situation from the point of view of communications promoted the growth of the old imperial city of Cheb (Eger) in the centre of the basin and contributed to its historical importance. In the north the textile industry flourished, and downstream on the river Ohře (Eger) the deposits of lignite, clay and kaolin in and around Sokolov (formerly called Falknov) led to the development of busy pottery and chemical industries.

Františkovy Lázně

Císařský Les

To the south of the Ohře rift valley the crystalline rocks of the Ore Mountains outcrop again in an undulating plateau. In the Císařský Les it is built up of slates and granites, rising in the west to 987m/3238ft and sinking in the

Karlovy Vary (Karlsbad)

Doupov Hills

Karlovy Vary

east under the volcanic masses of the Doupov Hills (Doupovské Hory). Numerous streams flow through narrow gorge-like valleys to join the Ohře. The largest of these is the Teplá, on the upper course of which the Premonstratensian abbey of Teplá was founded in 1197. Just before its junction with the Ohře is the famous spa of Karlovy Vary (Karlsbad), with several thermal springs.

Teplá plateau
Mariánské Lázně

On the wooded western edge of the Teplá plateau (Tepelská Plošina), at an altitude of 630m/2070ft, is Mariánské Lázně (Marienbad), famed for its alkaline and acidic springs. In the Doupov Hills massive deposits of lava and tufa have created an upland region rising to heights of up to 932m/3058ft). The lava forced the river Ohře up against the Ore Mountains, through which it then carved a beautiful valley. Here mineral water forces its way up through clefts in the rock (e.g. at the little spa of Kyselka).

Plzeň Basin

In western Bohemia, between the Teplá plateau, the Low Bohemian Forest (Český Les) and the wooded Central Bohemian Hills (Brdy), is an extensive basin, in the centre of which, at an altitude of just over 300m/1000ft, is the city of Plzeň (Pilsen). Here four source streams join to form the river Berounka. In the ancient rocks of the Plzeň basin are deposits of coal. This climatically favoured region offered the necessary conditions for the development of a productive agriculture, and accordingly was settled at a very early period, mostly by Czechs; later German settlers came in from the Cheb region, pushing forward almost to Plzeň. The coalfield and good communications provided the basis for the industrial development of the town of Plzeň, founded in 1272 (Skoda works, producing heavy engineering machinery and installations; breweries, chemical industry, ceramic factories).

Žatec depression

Late Tertiary clays, Cretaceous marls and loess have formed the agricultural character of the fertile Žatec depression on the lower Ohře (Eger), which is known mainly as a hop-growing region. The principal towns are Žatec, Postoloprty and Louny, long a Czech town.

Chomutov-Teplice basin

The long Chomutov-Teplice basin, on the slopes of the Ore Mountains, is bounded on the south-east by the western Bohemian Massif. Now watered by the river Bílina, it was traversed before the later ice age by the Ohře. With fertile clay soil resulting from Tertiary marine deposits, it was settled and brought into cultivation at an early period. The rich deposits of lignite in the subsoil led to the development of a varied range of industry in the 19th century and to the growth of a number of middle-sized towns such as Chomutov, Most, Duchcov, the main centre of opencast lignite working, Litvínov, with its hydrogenation works, and Teplice, a spa famed for its radioactive thermal springs.

Bohemian Massif

The Bohemian Massif (České Středohoří) is a region of denuded volcanic hills in northern Bohemia on both banks of the Labe (Elbe). The different types of rock in this area have produced a variety of landscape forms – conical hills (Milešovka, 837m/2746ft), rocky crags, round-topped hills and jagged ridges, areas of level ground, narrow valleys carved from soft tufas and marls. Still further variety is provided by the valley in which the Labe (Elbe) breaks through the hills.

Long settlement in this area with its mild climate and good weathered soils has led to intensive agricultural development. Many of the sunny hillsides are covered with garden crops. Along the large rivers with their excellent communications have developed busy and prosperous towns like Litoměřice, Ústí nad Labem and Děčín.

Elbe Sandstone Hills

The Elbe Sandstone Hills and the Ploučnice region are given their character by the outcropping of Cretaceous sandstones. At the Nakléřov pass (Nakléřovský průsmyk; 700m/2300ft) the gneisses of the Ore Mountains dip under the sediments over which, east of the Labe (Elbe), the granites of the Lusatian Hills (Lužické Hory) have been thrust upwards. The plateau areas are slashed by valleys and gorges, and weathering and erosion have carved out curious rock formations. In the Děčínský Sněžnik sandstone terraces covered with pine forest and heathland rise to 723m/2372ft. This rocky country has developed into a favourite tourist area.

Ploučnice region

South-east of the Elbe Sandstone Hills, round the river Ploučnice, is a landscape of sandstones traversed by fault lines extending in the direction of the Sudetens. In this area there are a number of volcanoes, such as Ralsko (694m/2277ft) and Bezděz (605m/1985ft). In the Doksy depression a number of large ponds have been formed by damming. This large area is much dissected, with wild gorges (the "Dubá Switzerland"). Until 1946 this was an area of German settlement and, with its natural beauties, a popular holiday region. The natural centre of the area is Česká Lípa. Bor and Kamenický Šenov were centres of the glass industry.

Lusatian Hills

Adjoining the Elbe Sandstone Hills on the east is the granite plateau of the Lusatian uplands, with wide valleys which are drained to the Spree and the Görlitzer Neisse. In population as well as geography this Bohemian outpost is linked with the neighbouring German territory of Saxony. Here the former domestic craft production has developed into considerable industrial activity, with flourishing textile production (Varnsdorf, Rumburk) and metalworking (Mikulášovice).

South-east of these plateaux is the long range of the Lusatian Hills (Lužické Hory). First come a number of Tertiary volcanic cones like Mt Luž (793m/2602ft), rising from a plateau of Cretaceous limestone at altitudes of up to 600m/1970ft, and beyond this, running in the same direction, is the Ještěd range, built up from ancient slates. The quartzite peak of Mt Ještěd (1012m/3320ft) rises impressively above the narrow wooded ridge; famed for the wide-ranging views it offers, it is one of the most popular viewpoints in the country.

Mt Ještěd

Topography

Jizera Hills

The Jizera Hills (Jizerské Hory) form the north-western buttress of the 240km/150 mile long chain of the Sudetens (Sudety), which are divided into the Western and Eastern Sudetens. This granite range, with an average altitude of 850m/2800ft, falls sharply down in the north to the Frýdlant area, and rears above the Liberec basin in the south-west, with long ridges of hill rising out of the wooded plateau. The High Jizera Ridge reaches a height of 1122m/3681ft in Mt Smrk. Numerous streams flow from valley basins covered with moorland towards the young river Jizera.

In the basin to the south-west, traversed by the river Nisa and dominated on the west by Mt Ještěd, the production of textiles developed at an early stage. Liberec, in this area, became one of the leading cloth-making towns in Austria and later, in spite of its inconvenient situation, one of the most important towns in the Sudeten region. The abundance of timber and quartz in the wooded valleys of the Jizera Hills led to the establishment of glassworks, providing the basis for the rise of Jablonec nad Nisou into a town world-famed for its glass jewellery and ornaments and its brassware. In the neighbouring settlements of Tanvald and Polubný these were also produced by craftsmen working at home.

Krkonoše
Sněžka

The Krkonoše range (Riesengebirge) is the highest part of the Sudetens, reaching 1602m/5256ft in Sněžka. It extends for 37km/23 miles between two saddles, the Novosvětské Sedlo (889m/2917ft) and the Libavské Sedlo (529m/1736ft). Below the main ridge on the frontier with Poland are the Bohemian ridges, through which the young Labe (Elbe) cuts its way at the spa of Špindlerův Mlýn. The granite masses are overlaid by hardened mica schists (e.g. in Sněžka). During the Ice Age hills over 1100m/3600ft were covered by ice and glaciers advanced down the valleys to a height of 750m/2480ft, as is shown by moraines at Pec in the Úpa valley. At the south end of the valley is the spa of Janské Lázně with its mineral springs. The area has a real mountain climate (annual average temperature on Sněžka 0°C) which brings the tree-line (spruces) down to 1300m/4265ft. At higher

Sněžka: a peak in the Krkonoše range

levels the strong winds hit vegetation hard. The flatter ridges are covered with mountain pines, mat-grass and moorland. German settlers from Silesia moved into the southern valleys only at a late stage. The high-altitude grassland led to the development of pastoral farming of semi-Alpine type, which has given place in more recent times to tourism and winter sports.

Southern foreland of Krkonoše

Agriculture flourished on the Lower Permian soils in the southern foreland of the Krkonoše range. The towns of Trutnov, Vrchlabí and Hostinné became noted centres of textile production and papermaking. The Kladská Kotlina, a recent collapse basin, is surrounded by ancient rocks which for most of the way mark the Czech-Polish frontier.
Between this area and the main Krkonoše range is the Middle Sudeten Depression, which is filled with strata of the Carboniferous, Lower Permian and Cretaceous. At Žaclér is a disrupted coal seam.

Teplice and Adršpach Crags

The most striking features of this stratified and terraced landscape, formed of Cretaceous rocks eroded by the river Metuje, are the crags of Teplice and Adršpach, which form a rock labyrinth with a mantle of pines. The little town of Broumov, with a Benedictine monastery, was noted for its textiles.

Orlík Hills

Between the Reinerz Saddle (670m/2198ft) and Grulich Pass (534m/1752ft) extend the Orlík Hills (Orlické Hory), a narrow ridge of gneisses and mica schists rising to a height of 1115m/3658ft and draining to the Labe (Elbe). Just to the east of it is the Králický Sněžnik (1422m/4666ft), the first peak in the Eastern Sudetens, which drains to the river Morava. Here too runs the boundary between eastern Bohemia and northern Moravia.

Rychlebské Hory

The wooded ridge of the Rychlebské Hory, rising to 1128m/3701ft, runs south-east to the Ramzovské Sedlo (759m/2490ft). Below the hills, to the north, is a levelled area formed in the Ice Age with good clay soil. This is predominantly farming country, with some granite quarries and lime-kilns.

Jeseníky

From the Ramzovské Sedlo the Jeseníky range, the main ridge of the Eastern Sudetens, formed of gneisses and schists, runs south-east to the

Typical wooden houses in the Krkonoše foreland

1492m/4895ft high peak of Praděd, where it turns sharply, follows a long ridge which climbs above the tree-line in the Vysoká Hole (1464m/4803ft) and then falls steadily down into the Morava depression at Šumperk.

North-east of the Praděd massif (Hrubý Jeseník) a lonely expanse of wooded uplands, with Mt Orlík (1205m/3954ft), extends to the frontier with Poland. To the south-east it falls some 700m/2300ft to the Nízký Jeseník plateau. In the Bílá valley to the north is the little town of Jeseník (formerly called Frývaldov), famed for its linen industry and the spa of Lázně Jeseník. Numerous sawmills and cellulose and papermaking factories exploit the abundance of timber in the great surrounding forests.

Nízký Jeseník (Moravian Uplands)

The Nízký Jeseník plateau (altitude up to 798m/2618ft), formed mainly of Lower Carboniferous schists, falls steeply down on the west side for some 400m/1300ft to the Morava depression. To the north-east it slopes gradually down to the Odra (Oder) plain. The plateau, which is traversed by the rivers Opava and Moravice and the source stream of the Odra, was populated at an early period by German settlers. Most of the forest was cleared, but only the low hilly country on the lower Opava to the south-east is suitable for the highly productive cultivation of wheat and sugar-beet. There are numerous small towns scattered about the upland region. On the east side of the area is Krnov, a noted centre of clothworking and organ-building. On the important railway line to the Ostrava heavy industrial region is the town of Opava, founded about 1200, important as a market town and later as the administrative centre of Austrian Silesia.

Inner Bohemia

Inner Bohemia consists of two regions differing in geological structure and in superficial aspect, the level country of Cretaceous origin and the undulating landscape of the peneplain of crystalline rocks.

Cretaceous tableland

The Cretaceous tableland on the Labe (Elbe), Jizera and lower Vltava can be divided into the sandstone zone and the area of Upper Cretaceous marls. The latter occur more frequently in the south and, with their good soil, are a favoured region for agriculture. To the west of the Vltava-Labe line the Cretaceous terrain is found only in residual patches. The Permian and Carboniferous deposits under the surface can be profitably worked. The productive coal seams have led to the development of important heavy industries at Kladno and Slaný.

Džbán Forest

To the north of Rakovník, a town noted for its ceramic industry, is the Džbán Forest, and at Roudnice nad Labem a rounded basalt hill, the legendary Mt Řip, rises above a great expanse of agricultural land. The plateau with the Labe bend, slashed by numerous valleys, shows many typical Cretaceous sandstone formations in its northern part.

Bohemian Paradise

Thanks to the picturesque landscape forms carved by weathering and erosion the area between Turnov (cutting of semi-precious stones) and Jičín (Wallenstein's palace) is known as the Bohemian Paradise (Český Ráj). The largest town in the area is Mladá Boleslav, on the river Jizera, which has considerable industry (Skoda/Volkswagen cars, textiles).

Labe (Elbe) depression

The excellent soils in the Upper Cretaceous terrain between Hradec Králové and the junction of the Vltava with the Labe at Mělník have led to the extensive development of arable farming. In the Labe depression (Polabí) the principal crops are wheat, barley and sugar-beet. As a result a number of middle-sized towns have grown up, their prosperity also being promoted by their situation on important traffic routes. Notable among the towns in this region of long-established Czech settlement are Hradec Králové, Pardubice, Chrudim, Čáslav, Kolín, Nymburk and the spa of Poděbrady (recommended for heart conditions), situated on a fault line.

Inner Bohemian peneplain

The Inner Bohemian peneplain is a region of undulating landscape left by erosion in central and southern Bohemia. In later upthrusts some sections

A "rock city" at Hrubá Skála in the "Bohemian Paradise"

of the older rocks were left, and these now form basins surrounded by higher ground. Approximately in the latitude of Prague the eroded rocks dip under the Cretaceous sediments.

R. Vltava

The southern axis of the region is formed by the Vltava. During the upthrusts the river and its tributaries were deeply embedded, producing a sharp contrast between the extensive plateau areas and the narrow indented valleys. In these valleys, which are mostly wooded, only a few small settlements have been established. In recent times several dams have been built on the Vltava, creating long artificial lakes in the valley; the largest of these are Lake Orlík (area 27sq.km/10½sq.miles) and Lake Slapy (14sq.km/5½sq.miles). The soils on the plateau are poor, and only undemanding crops can be grown. In consequence there are only a few small towns in this area.

Bohemo-Moravian Highlands

The Inner Bohemian peneplain rises in the Bohemo-Moravian Highlands (Českomoravská Vrchovina) to an altitude of 837m/2746ft at Zd'ár nad Sázavou, in the source area of the river Sázava. From there the Železné Hory (Iron Mountains), given a sharper profile by a later upthrust, extend in the direction of the Sudetens as far as the Labe (Elbe). Among the larger places in this area are Kutná Hora, a former silver-mining town on the edge of the Labe depression, Tábor, on the river Lužnice, and, to the west, Písek on the Otava.

Southern Bohemian Pond Country

The low-lying country of southern Bohemia, to the north of České Budejovice and around Třeboň, has a very distinctive aspect. The subsoil consists of clayey marine sediments of the Middle Tertiary. The country is mainly flat, with expanses of moorland and numerous large ponds. The most important settlement in southern Bohemia is České Budějovice, founded in 1265 at the junction of the Vltava and the Malše, which owed its prosperity to its situation on a good traffic route to Austria and to its active industry.

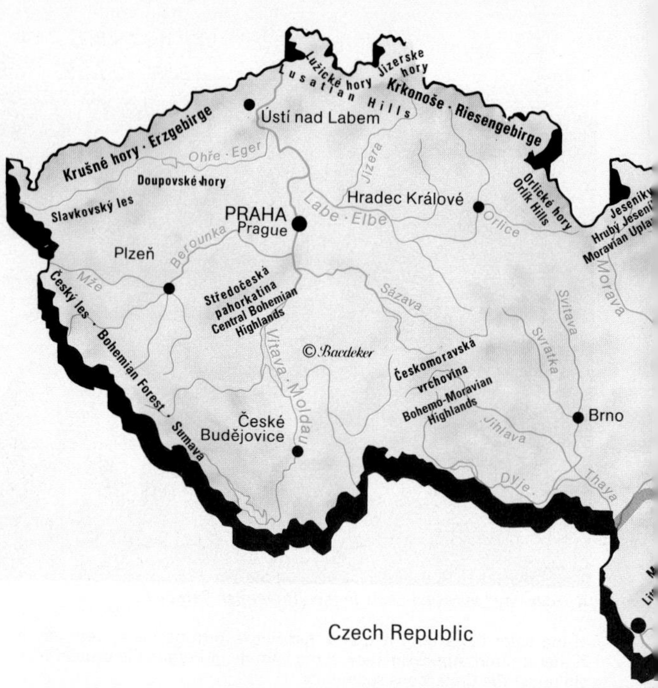

Bohemian Silurian Trough

The most notable feature of the north-western section of the Inner Bohemian peneplain is the Bohemian Silurian Trough (Český Silur). In this geological trough on the strike of the Ore Mountains strata ranging from the Algonkian to the Devonian have been preserved, and as a result of the varying hardness of the rocks have produced sharper landscape forms.

Brdy Forest

Along longitudinal fault lines the Cambrian conglomerates and Silurian quartzites form the long ridges and crests of Brdy Forest (Tok, 865m/2838ft). In the central part of the trough Lower Devonian limestones strike in the direction of the river Berounka, which cuts its way through them in a rocky valley. Here, on a projecting spur, is the historic Karlštejn Castle. The deposits of iron ore on the Zdice–Nučice line were once of economic importance, supplying the ironworks in the industrial town of Králův Dvůr, in the Litavka valley near Beroun. Příbram, to the east of Brdy, was once a considerable silver-mining town.

Prague

At the north-east end of the Silurian Trough, where it meets the Cretaceous tableland, is the Czech capital, Prague, situated in a wide basin in the Vltava valley. The bend in the river, open towards the west, has led to the formation of steeper slopes on the outer bank and gentler ones on the inner side. Thus the mighty Prague Castle, with St Vitus's Cathedral, is built above a steep slope, while opposite it the Old Town and New Town occupy a gently rising site. Here a population of more than 1.2 million lives on an area of just under 500sq.km/190sq.miles. (On the characteristics, history and sights of Prague see the A to Z section of this guide.)

Mountains and Rivers

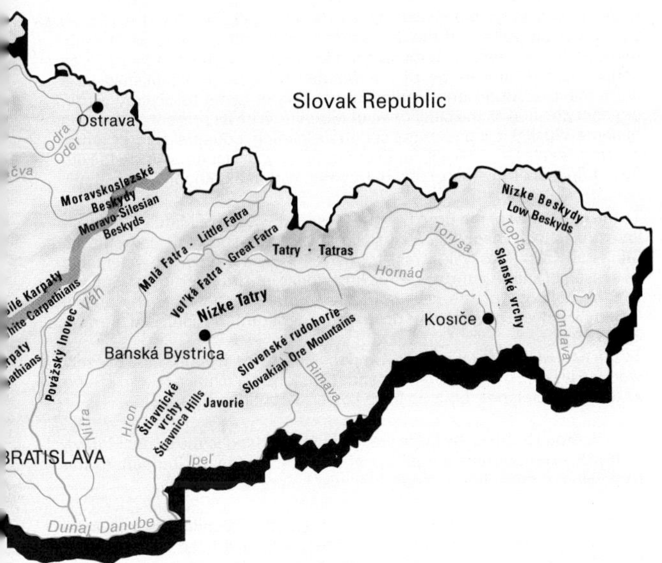

Moravia and Moravian Silesia

Moravian peneplain

The crystalline plateaux of western Moravia give place in the east to the narrow Boskovice Trough in the Lower Permian. Beyond this is the Brno Syenite Mass, and to the north of this the Moravian Karst, with the Haná Uplands bordering the Olomouc basin. The advance of the Miocene Sea played a major part in the formation of the border zone of the massif, giving rise to a series of raised beaches.

The peneplain slopes down gradually south-eastward from a maximum altitude of 837m/2741ft (Javořice) to an abrasion platform up to 40km/25 miles wide at an altitude of around 500m/1640ft. The rivers which drain the peneplain have wide valleys of meadowland in their upper courses and steep-sided wooded valleys lower down. The area is only thinly populated, since the poor soils yield only meagre crops.

At the point where Moravia merges into Bohemia is the hill town of Jihlava, founded by Germans in 1227, which developed into the economic centre of a region extending well beyond this little German linguistic island. On the edge of the massif, near the Czech–Austrian frontier, is the old town of Znojmo (vegetable-growing; ceramics).

At Vranov nad Dyjí, above the town, is a large artificial lake (area 7.2sq.km/2¾sq.miles) formed by damming the river Dyje, here deeply embedded in the abrasion platform.

Topography

Boskovice Trough

The Boskovice Trough is a 5km/3 mile wide depression filled with Lower Permian material. Beginning to the west of Brno, it runs in a gentle arc into the Cretaceous terrain of eastern Bohemia. Its fertile clayey soils have given rise to a productive agriculture. In the border area with Bohemia there was formerly a German linguistic island (1138sq.km/439sq.miles) with a population of over 100,000.

Brno Syenite Mass

The Brno Syenite Mass extends north and west of the Moravian capital. The wooded plateau lying between 400 and 500m (1300 and 1640ft) is slashed by the narrow valleys of the Svitava and the Svratka. The town of Brno, founded by Germans in 1243, lies at the junction of the two rivers in an embayment on the fringe of the wooded hills. Soon established as a cloth-manufacturing and trading town, it later came to occupy a pre-eminent position as the chief town of Moravia. With its present population of some 390,000 it is one of the country's leading industrial centres (engineering, textiles, chemicals, foodstuffs). Its principal landmarks are the old fort of Špilberk (Spielberg) and Petrov Hill, with the Cathedral.

Moravian Karst

To the north-east of the Brno Syenite Mass is a swathe of Middle Devonian limestones with magnificent karstic features. The stalactitic caves in the Moravian Karst (Moravský Kras), formed by the lowering of the water table as a result of sharp upthrusts of the limestones, are on three levels. Following the collapse of the cave roof the funnel-shaped Macocha abyss, 138m/453ft deep, now reaches down to the underground course of the river Punkva.

To the east of the Moravian Karst and the Boskovice Trough is the densely wooded plateau of the Drahan Uplands (Drahanská Vrchovina), also known as the Haná Uplands, built up from Lower Carboniferous schists.

Olomouc basin

The Olomouc basin is the large area of low-lying land in the upper Morava valley. It extends from the inflow of the river Desná at Šumperk to the narrowing of the valley at Napajedla, just before the Beskyds.

Haná

To the south of Olomouc extends a level area 30km/20 mile wide known as the Haná, an ancient area of subsidence which was filled by sediments from the Miocene Sea and later covered by loess and more recent riverine deposits. The excellent soils and favourable climate have promoted the development of intensive agriculture (wheat, sugar-beet, barley for brewing, vegetables). In the centre of the fertile plain, below two rocky hills, is Olomouc, a 13th century German settlement which until 1640 was capital of Moravia. The town, with a population of over 100,000, is now a busy centre of agricultural industries. Other notable towns in the Haná are Prostějov to the west and Přerov, an important road and rail junction, to the east.

Southern Moravian Uplands

The Tertiary uplands of southern Moravia extend south-east from the end of the rump plateau (Znojmo–Brno) to the Morava depression. With its sunny climate and (for the most part) fertile soil the area was intensively cultivated from an early period, with great expanses of arable land and market gardens. The Brno basin, taking in the wide valleys of the Dyje, Jihlava and Svratka, continues to the north-east in the Vyškov depression to the Haná, with the towns of Vyškov and Slavkov u Brna (Austerlitz). Parallel to it extend low ridges of hills, which act as links between the Pre-Alps at Vienna and the foothills of the Beskyds to the south of Přerov.

Pavlov Hills

On the borders of Moravia and Lower Austria the Pavlov Hills (Pavlovské Vrchy) or Pálava, an island of Jurassic limestones, rise to a height of 550m/1800ft, the dry marl hillsides covered with vineyards. Under the south side of the hills is the ancient little town of Mikulov. On the north side is the valley of the Dyje with its riverine woodland and the important prehistoric mammoth-hunters' site of Dolní Věstonice. Beyond this lies the hilly wine-growing region of Hustopeče, once an area of German settlement. The adjoining Ždánický Les consists of Early Tertiary schists and marls. From here extends the densely wooded Chřiby range (Brdo, 587m/1926ft), reaching the river Morava at Napajedla. Between here and the inflow of the Dyje a fan-shaped area of recent alluvial deposits extends along the Morava, much of it covered by dense riverine woodland and expanses of drift sand with heath vegetation and pines. On the important railway line to Vienna are Hodonín and the junction of Břeclav. To the west of this, round Lednice, are large fish-ponds (up to 280 hectares/690 acres) and areas of parkland laid out by the Princes of Liechtenstein.

Ždánický Les

Chřiby range

Beskyd Foreland

The Beskyd Foreland extends below the outermost range of the Western Carpathians in eastern Moravia. It consists of a region of depressions on the Odra (Oder) and Bečva and a stretch of hilly country to the south. The depression known as the Moravian Gate (Moravská Brána) is filled with massive deposits from the Miocene Sea. Round Ostrava these overlie coal measures and are themselves frequently overlaid by loess soils which provide excellent conditions for agriculture in what was once an area of German settlement. The name of "Cow Country" (Kravařsko) given to this area reflects the importance of cattle-farming on the lush meadowland in this damp low-lying region. The chief town in this area is Nový Jičín. To the north-east the Odra valley opens out and finally at the frontier town of Bohumín merges into the Upper Silesian plain.

Moravian Gate

"Cow Country"

Ostrava industrial region

Round the junction of the Ostravice, a south-bank tributary, with the Odra are extensive deposits of coal which have given rise to an industrial region now extending eastward to the river Olše, on the frontier with Poland. The built-up area of Ostrava has now a population of some 330,000, with the workers' suburb of Havířov to the south-east. The communes of Orlová and Karviná are important coal-mining areas. The upland region below the Beskyds is still largely agricultural. The dense forests of the hinterland have

Lysá Hora, in the Beskyds

given rise to a furniture-making industry, e.g. at Valašské Meziříčí. Metalworking industry has also been established in some towns such as Kopřivnice, Frýdek-Místek and Třinec on the upper Olše.
Lower down is Těšín, formerly of importance as the administrative centre of the eastern region of Austrian Silesia but now split in two, with half the former town in Poland.

Moravo-Silesian Beskyds
Jablunka pass

North-east of this the Moravo-Silesian Beskyds, which are higher and have a more varied topography, extend to the important Jablunka pass (Jablunkovský průsmyk (555m/1821ft), south-east of Ostrava. The most northerly forest-covered ridge rises to well over 1000m/3280ft (Radhošt', 1129m/3704ft; Smrk, 1276m/4187ft; Lysá Hora, 1323m/4341ft). Beyond the upper Bečva and Kysuca valleys, on the boundary between Moravia and Slovakia, is the ridge of the Javorníky (1071m/3514ft), extending south to the point where the river Kysuca carves its way through the hills.

Javorníky

White Carpathians

The White Carpathians (Bilé Karpaty) are the range of hills on the borders of Moravia and Slovakia, the watershed between the Morava and the Váh. They are so called because of the light-coloured Jurassic limestones which emerge between the Flysch sandstones. The highest point is the Velká Javorina (970m/3183ft), to the north of the Myjava pass region (Lyský průsmyk).
In the north-western foreland area, in the Dřevnice valley, is the busy shoe-manufacturing town of Zlín (known from 1949 to 1990 as Gottwaldov), base of the large Bat'a business. To the south of this is the popular spa of Luhačovice.

Slovakia

Western Carpathians

Much of Slovakia (Slovensko) is occupied by the mountain ranges of the Western Carpathians. Although they are a continuation of the Alps their structure is very different. The southern edge has been given a complicated pattern by numerous fault movements, and in the interior of the massif the original formations have been much disturbed. As a result the Western Carpathians have been split into many smaller separate ranges.

Beskyds

The peripheral sandstone zone, in contrast to the Alps, is a massive complex, occupying the border area between Slovakia/ Moravia and Poland in a great arc. It consists of a sequence of long ridges, one behind the other, separated by longitudinal valleys in the softer schists. These similarly formed ranges, usually referred to collectively as the Beskyds, have preserved a dense covering of forest. Pastoral farming has been practised on the broad summit plateaux since the 16th century – in the western area by Wallachian shepherds from the Southern Carpathians (Romania), in the centre by Polish Gorals and farther east by Ruthenians.

Slovakian Beskyds

The Slovakian Beskyds (Slovenské Beskydy), along the Slovak-Polish frontier, rise in the Babia Hora to heights of up to 1725m/5660ft. In the Nowy Targ basin and the High Tatras Polish territory reaches far south into the Carpathians.

Low Beskyds

Beyond the valley of the Poprad the sandstone zone reappears on a broad front in the Low Beskyds (Nízke Beskydy). The frontier crossing between Slovakia and Poland at the Dukla pass (Dukliansky priesmyk) is only 502m/1647ft high. From there the wooded hills run eastward along the watershed between the Danube and the Vistula, rising to a height of 1220m/4003ft in the Kremenec area at the point where the frontiers of Slovakia, Poland and the Ukraine meet.

Slovakian Highlands

The mighty belt of sandstones is bounded on the inner side by a zone of superficial deposits at a lower level, an area with lesser forest cover and a denser pattern of settlement. Jurassic limestones and dolomites similar to those of the Calcareous Alps occur in isolated and strikingly shaped formations, eroded out of a covering of soft sediments of the Upper Cretaceous and Early Tertiary. From the Myjava pass region on the south side of the White Carpathians this narrow belt of hills follows the Váh valley to the inflow of the Orava, accompanies this side valley to the Slovak-Polish frontier, turns back in an arc at the Dunajec bend into Slovak territory and then extends along the rivers Poprad and Torysa into the Prešov area in eastern Slovakia.

Váh and Orava valleys

Both the Váh and the Orava cut now into the hard limestones and now into the soft covering sediments, producing a constant variation in the form of the valleys. The chief place in the Váh valley is Trenčín, situated under an old castle on a limestone crag. In a small side valley is the popular spa of Trenčianske Teplice. Other places in the main valley, which is densely populated and now has considerable industry, are Púchov, Považská Bystrica and Žilina. In the middle valley of the Orava, picturesquely situated on a limestone crag, is Orava Castle (Oravský Hrad). Higher up, directly on the Slovak-Polish frontier, is the Oravská Priehrada, a large artificial lake (35sq.km/13½sq.miles). North-east of the High Tatras are the Pieniny Hills, where the Dunajec and the Poprad cut through the limestone rocks in magnificent defiles.

Central zone

The central crystalline zone of the Slovakian highlands is characterised by the contrast between steep-sided hills of varying height and the basins between them. The rivers, flowing in narrow valleys through the hills, link the more densely populated basins and provide transit routes through the whole highland region.

Little Carpathians

Separated from the central zone but associated with it in types of rock is the narrow range of the Little Carpathians (Malé Karpaty), which extends from

Wooden church in the Orava valley

Devín (now incorporated in Bratislava) on the Danube, at the inflow of the Morava, to the Myjava saddle. Immediately above the Váh depression it rises to a height of 768m/2520ft (Záruby). The hills consist of granites, schists and Jurassic limestones. On the lower slopes are orchards and vineyards; elsewhere there is a covering of deciduous woodland.

Bratislava

Under the south side of the Little Carpathians is Bratislava, originally established at a bridge over the Danube, which, thanks to its trade and to the fertility of the surrounding area, developed into an important city. Its importance was further enhanced by its position as an administrative and intellectual centre (University) and by its varied industries. (On the characteristics, history and sights of Bratislava, see the A to Z section of this guide.)

Inovec Hills

The Little Carpathians are continued east of the Váh by the Inovec Hills, which rise to a height of 1042m/3419ft. On the fault line cutting across the river is the spa of Piešt'any (thermal springs; sulphurous water).

Strážov Hills

In the Strážov Hills (Strážovské Vrchy), to the north-east, limestone peaks (Mt Strážov, 1214m/3983ft) rise above the schists. On Mt Strážov rise the source streams of the river Nitra. There was formerly a German linguistic island round Prievidza, in a basin on the upper course of the river. In the lower basin of the Nitra is Topol'čany, chief town of this fertile farming area.

Little Fatra

To the east of the long Žilina-Rajec basin is the Little Fatra (Malá Fatra), a sharply profiled range of hills on both sides of the deeply indented Váh valley. At the south end rises the granitic Vel'ka Lúka (1476m/4843ft); to the north is the dolomitic Velký Kriváň (1709m/5607ft). Above the point where the Váh cuts through the hills (Vrútky) it is joined on the south by the river Turiec, in a large basin devoted to agriculture through which runs the railway line between Wrocław in Poland and Budapest in Hungary. The chief town is Martin (engineering, armaments).

Liptov basin

After the junction with the Orava the Váh, coming from the east, flows through another defile and then through the wide, open Liptov basin, with Ružomberok, formerly an industrial town, and the little country town of Liptovský Mikuláš.

Spiš basin

Going over a watershed at 900m/2950ft (railway line between Ostrava and Košice), we come into the Spiš basin, which is drained by the Poprad to the Baltic and by the Hornád to the Black Sea. This was a prosperous farming area with a number of busy little towns. Kežmarok, Spišská Nová Ves, Levoča and Poprad have remained local centres.

Liptov Alps

Between the Váh and the Orava is the distinctively dolomitic Choč massif (1611m/5286ft), which rises eastward into the Liptov Alps in the Western Tatras (Západné Tatry), reaching a height of 2248m/7376ft in Mt Bystrá.

High Tatras

The High Tatras (Vysoké Tatry) are a magnificent mountain range with a series of peaks, sharply pointed as a result of glacial action, rising to over 2600m/8530ft. The highest point in the range (and in the Western Carpathians) is the Gerlachovský Štít (2655m/8711ft). The trough-like forms of the valleys are very characteristic. Many corries have been filled by small, deep mountain lakes. Since the granitic rocks for the most part directly adjoin the coniferous forests at 1500m/4920ft or the weather-beaten trees at 1700m/5580ft, the zone of Alpine meadows found in the Western Tatras is much reduced. On the south-eastern slopes of the hills, in favoured situations, a number of spas have developed, including Starý Smokovec, Tatranská Lomnica and Štrbské Pleso.

Belianske Tatras

To the north-east is the densely wooded limestone range of the Belianske Tatras (Belianské Tatry), rising to 2152m/7061ft.

In the High Tatras ▶

Topography

Mt Tríbeč

The southern or inner range of hills begins with Mt Tríbeč (829m/2720ft), near the medium-sized town of Nitra on the river of that name.

Great Fatra

The crystalline rocks soon disappear, however, under recent volcanic deposits, re-emerging only in the Great Fatra (Vel'ká Fatra), to the east of the Turiec basin. The highest peak is the rugged Mt Ostredok (1592m/5223ft).

Low Tatras

Beyond this, to the east, are the Low Tatras (Nízke Tatry), between the rivers Váh and Hron. This granite ridge, with great expanses of Alpine meadows, rises in Mt D'umbier to 2043m/6703ft. On the northern edge of the range is a limestone region with numerous caves.

Slovakian Ore Mountains

To the south the Hron valley accompanies the largely wooded uplands, separating them from the Slovakian Ore Mountains (Slovenské Rudohorie), which is also well wooded. Within the range is a rump landscape with ridges averaging 1200m/3940ft in height and areas of plateau which in the source region of the river Slaná rise to over 1400m/4840ft (Stolica, 1476m/4843ft). The ore-bearing ancient schists give place towards the Spiš basin to a zone of limestones and dolomites, with the famous Dobšiná ice cave (Dobšinská ľadová jaskyňa).

Slovakian Karst

The limestone zone on the south side is still further developed. This expanse of the Slovakian Karst (Slovenský Kras) is slashed by gorge-like valleys cut through the rock by the Slaná and Bodva. It falls steeply down to the Rožňava basin. The mining of ores which was begun by German miners in the 14th century has declined sharply; only the working of iron-ore is now of any consequence.

Kremnica Hills

The recent volcanic zone of the Slovakian Highlands is closely linked with the inner central zone at many points. The much dissected and undulating

Úhorná, in the Slovakian Ore Mountains

plateau consisting of the Kremnica Hills (Kremnické Vrchy) and, to the south of the narrow Hron valley, the Štiavnica Hills (Štiavnické Vrchy) extends immediately south of the Great Fatra (Vel'ká Fatra). The ruined lava flows of Mt Sitno rise to 1010m/3314ft. To the east of this is the wooded volcanic stump of Mt Pol'ana (1458m/4784ft), which abuts on the western Slovakian Ore Mountains. Between the rivers Nitra and Hron is the Vtáčnik range, which also belongs to these Late Tertiary formations. The abundance of precious metals led to the early development of a productive mining industry, which in turn promoted the establishment of a number of towns. Banská Štiavnica was founded in the 13th century, and a little later Kremnica, famed for its mint, was established under German law in a side valley of the Hron. On the Hron itself are Zvolen and Banská Bystrica, now market centres and industrial towns of some importance. Similarly the town of Handlová, also a German settlement, grew up in the basin between Mt Vtáčnik and the Kremnica Hills.

Mt Pol'ana
Mt Vtáčnik

Krupina plateau

Andesitic and rhyolitic tuffs are characteristic of the undulating Krupina plateau (Krupinská Vrchovina), which gradually merges into the large Ipel' basin on the Slovak-Hungarian frontier. On the upper course of the Ipel', in soft Tertiary rocks, is another fertile basin centred on the town of Lučenec.

Slanské Vrchy

To the east of the southward-striking fault line on the river Hornád is the wooded ridge of the Slanské Vrchy, built up of andesitic lavas and tuffs. Around the 1092m/3583ft high peak of Mt Šimonka opals are found. At the point where the Hornád emerges from the hills into the southern plain – a situation with excellent communications – is the important commercial and industrial town of Košice (pop. 235,000), originally a German settlement established in the 12th century.

Vihorlat Hills

The last element in the chain of recent volcanic hills on the inner edge of the Slovakian Carpathians is the Vihorlat range (Vihorlatské Vrchy; up to 1076m/3530ft), on the Slovak-Ukrainian frontier. The caldera of a stratovolcano in this area is now occupied by a lake, the Morské Oko (area 14 hectares/35 acres).

Slovakian Lowlands

In western Slovakia the Pannonian lowlands extend far into the mountains in a series of embayments. The tributaries of the Danube, cutting into the hills, have formed an extensive upland region whose covering of loess has given it high fertility. The main centres in this prosperous agricultural area are Trnava, Nové Zámky and Levice.

Žitný Ostrov

This is the case also with the recent alluvial terrain on the Danube below Bratislava. Between the northern arm of the river and the main arm on the Slovak-Hungarian frontier is the Žitný Ostrov, an "island" of fertile agricultural land. A recent controversial project has been the construction of a large hydroelectric power station at Gabčikovo, supplied with water from the Danube by a canal running parallel with the river. At the junction of the two arms of the Danube is the important river port and bridge town of Komárno.

Along the river Bodrog and its tributaries, in the extreme south-eastern corner of eastern Slovakia, the Great Hungarian Plain (Alföld) reaches its most northerly point. Its level terrain and good soil make this a region of highly productive arable farming (wheat, maize, sugar-beet, tobacco). The largest town is Michalovce, with foodstuffs and tobacco industries. Here too, under the south-west side of the Vihorlat range, is a large artificial lake, the Zemplínská Šírava (area 34sq.km/13sq.miles), with several holiday centres.

Climate

General

A zone of transition

The territory of the Czechs and Slovaks lies in the zone of transition between the oceanic climate of Central Europe and the continental climate of

Eastern Europe. In consequence the weather pattern varies from west to east.

Regional differences

Regional differences in climate derive mainly from two factors, situation and relief.

Effects of situation

Situated as it is in the western part of Czech/Slovak territory, Bohemia has a sub-oceanic climate similar to that of Southern Germany. Its characteristics are:

- mild to moderately cold winters, with mean temperatures in the coldest month (January) of about −1°C to −2°C (30–28°F).
- moderately warm to warm summers, with mean temperatures in the warmest month (July) of about 18–19°C (64–66°F)
- a growing period of over 200 days.

Slovakia, situated in the eastern part of the territory, has a sub-continental climate. Its characteristics are:

- cold winters, with mean temperatures in the coldest month (January) below −3°C (26.5°F).
- moderately warm summers, with mean temperatures in the warmest month (July) below 20°C (68°F), except in the lower-lying, warmer south.
- a growing period of 180–210 days.

Effects of relief

Changes of altitude over small areas lead to changing micro-climates.

- The low-lying areas which have the main concentrations of population tend to have continental climatic characteristics, the higher areas oceanic characteristics.
- Depending on altitude, there are warm and moderately warm areas (usually in low-lying country) and cold areas (usually in hill country), which in view of the frequent variations in altitude, particularly in Moravia and Slovakia, are often closely juxtaposed.

A brief description of climatic conditions must necessarily be confined to general characteristics. Since the following account is based on average figures over a long period of years there may be considerable deviations in particular years, perhaps resulting from drought caused by long periods of dry weather in the east, from cool, damp weather in the north-west endangering crops in hill country or from exceptionally heavy rain leading to flooding and landslides.

General characteristics

It is easier to assess local climatic conditions at particular times of year if account is taken of the general climatic rules and characteristics of the country. Among such rules are the following:

- Western weather conditions, with westerly winds, overcast sky, rain-bringing depressions, relatively mild temperatures in winter and cool weather in summer are more frequent in the west.

Eastern weather conditions, with east winds, anticyclones, little cloud cover or rain and cold winters are more frequent in the east.

- Annual and daily variations in temperature increase from west to east, as do the number of "summer days" (i.e. days with maximum temperatures over 25°C/77°F) and days with frost and ice (with minimum and maximum temperatures below 0°C/32°F).
- The windward side of a hill, exposed to rain-bringing winds (mostly from south-west to north-west), has more rain than the sheltered lee side. Low-lying basins are sheltered on all sides and have correspondingly low precipitation.
- On average temperature falls with increasing altitude at the rate of 0.35°C/0.63°F per 100 metres in winter and 0.63°C/1.1°F per 100 metres in summer.

With increasing altitude cloud cover increases and hours of sunshine fall. In winter the phenomenon of temperature inversion may occur, when high ground rises above the layers of fog and cold air in the valleys and basins into clearer air with intense solar radiation.

Climatic Diagrams

Temperature and precipitations

The regional characteristics of the climate of Czech/Slovak territory are illustrated in the diagrams of temperature and precipitations on pp. 32–33. Temperatures are shown in the brown bands, the upper edge of which shows average maximum day temperatures and the lower edge average minimum night temperatures in accordance with the red scale on the right. The width of the band is a measure of daily temperature variations, while its curve reflects annual variations. The blue columns show average precipitations in millimetres month by month in accordance with the blue scale on the right.

Bohemia

Highlands

General

The hills enclosing Bohemia are characterised, above an altitude of around 500m/1640ft, by a cold and damp climate. The prevailing westerly winds bring in moist Atlantic air masses, which are compelled on reaching the hills to rise; they are then cooled, leading to the formation of clouds and to rain. Within Czech and Slovak territory are the inner flanks of the hills, sheltered from the west winds, where the air masses fall again; the air then becomes warmer and the clouds are dispersed. As a result precipitation decreases with decreasing height.

In general temperatures fall by 0.63°C/1.1°F in summer and by 0.35°C/0.63°F in winter for every 100 metres of height, and accordingly are correspondingly lower than in valleys and basins at lower levels. The lower rate of fall in winter is the result of the phenomenon of temperature inversion, in which under the influence of high pressures and the absence of wind cold air accumulates in low-lying areas under a belt of cloud or fog, above which is warmer, dry and clear air exposed to intense solar radiation.
Strong sun and lasting snow cover form the climatic basis for numerous winter sports resorts in the highland regions surrounding Bohemia.

Air pollution

The wooded hills surrounding Bohemia (with the tree-line on the south side of the Sudetens at about 1300m/4265ft) have been particularly exposed since the Second World War to the effects of weather conditions, with easterly winds and little change of air. As a result of intensive industrial development between Prague and the Ore Mountains and Krkonoše range there has been a sharp increase in air pollution over Bohemia. Particularly in the south-eastern foreland of the Ore Mountains large quantities of lignite are mined and consumed in thermal power stations. With little exchange of air, particularly in areas subject to temperature inversion, harmful substances accumulate close to the ground; and the problem is made worse by lack of rain to wash them out. With easterly and southerly winds the air loaded with pollutants is driven towards the surrounding hills, and this has already led to the destruction of considerable areas of forest. This has been demonstrated by numerous satellite photographs showing the clouds and fog impinging on the hills.

Benecko weather station

Benecko (alt. 886m/2907ft), in the Krkonoše range, has an average annual precipitation of 984mm/38in., with a maximum of over 100mm/3.9in. in each of the summer months of July and August and a minimum of 60mm/2.4in. in February and March; the other months have averages of 80mm/3.1in. With increasing altitude the proportion of precipitation falling

Climate

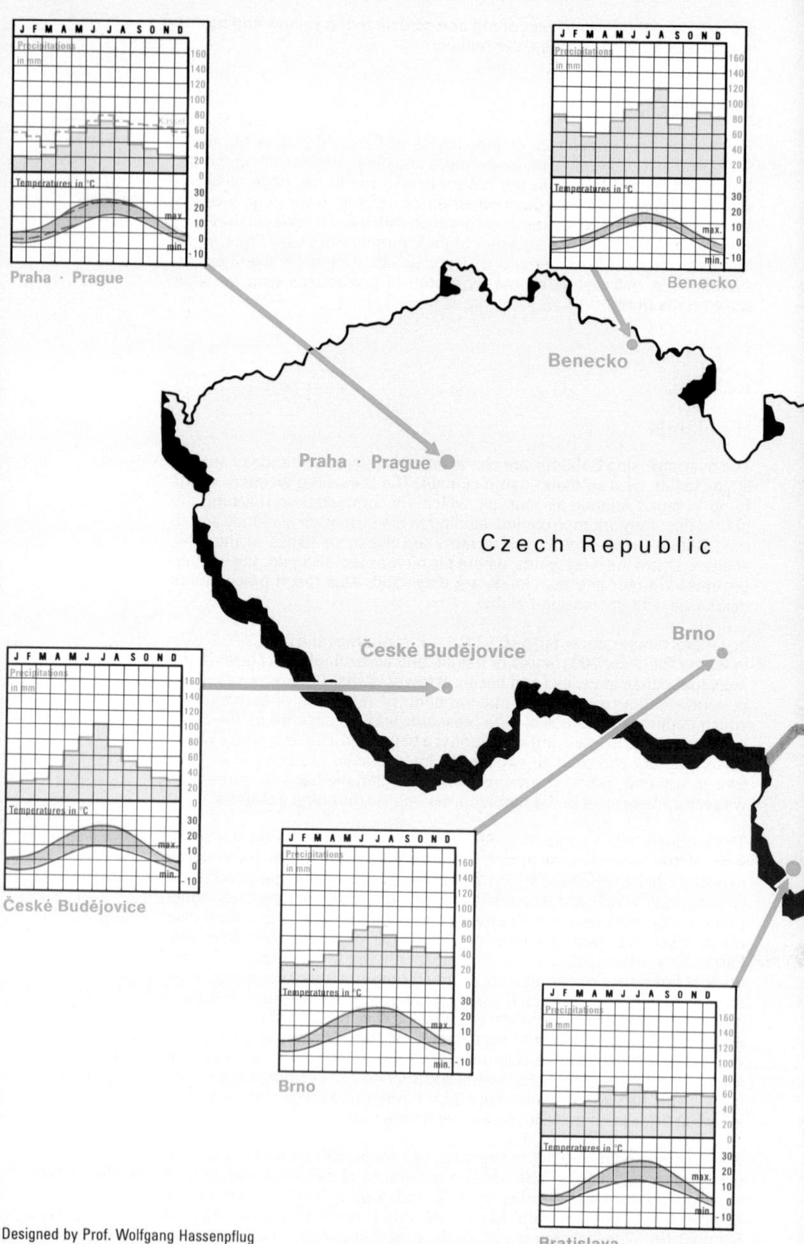

Designed by Prof. Wolfgang Hassenpflug

Nine typical weather stations

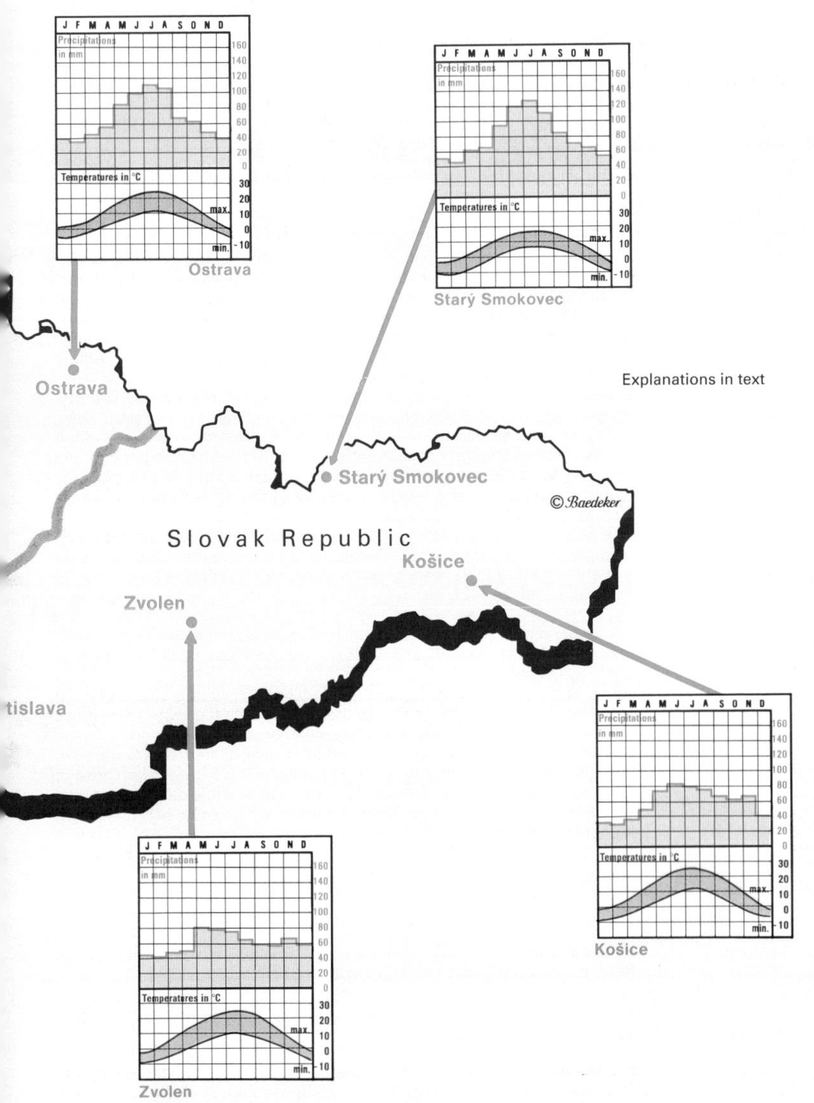

Explanations in text

in the form of snow increases, as does the number of days with full snow cover.

Sněžka

Sněžka, the highest peak in the Krkonoše range (1602m/5256ft), has average annual precipitations of 1227mm/48in., and snow falls on 130 days in the year. The summit region, with long-lasting snow cover, has an average annual temperature of 0.1°C/31.8°F (January −7.1°C/+19.2°F, July 8.3°C/46.9°F).

Lowlands

General

The lowlands of Bohemia within the surrounding hills can be divided, in terms of altitude, temperature and precipitation into the lower-lying, drier and warmer north (Prague weather station), the higher, wetter and cooler regions in the south (České Budějovice weather station) and the hills round the fringes.

Prague weather station

The lowest area round Prague (alt. 263m/863ft) in one of the warmest part of Czech/Slovak territory, with more than 50 "summer days" (i.e. days with maximum temperatures over 25°C/77°F). Average day maxima almost reach the 25°C mark in July and August, cooling down at night to just under 15°C/59°F. In winter the daily temperature variations are markedly lower at 5–6°C/41–43°F. From December to February average daily minima range between −2°C/+28.4°F and −6°C/+21.2°F, while daily maxima remain 1–3°C/1.8–5.4°F above freezing point.

In this low-lying area the precipitation is the lowest in the whole country. Prague has an annual 487mm/19in., falling on 88 days in the year. June, July and August are the months with the highest precipitation (about 60mm/2½in. on 9 days in each month). In spite of this the number of hours of sunshine, at 250 per month from May to August, is high. As a result of the higher temperatures the relative humidity of the air is frequently under 50% in spite of the high rainfall.

The winter months are drier, with the number of days with precipitation falling to 5–7 per month. From December to February there is snow cover on between 7 and 10 days each month. December has the lowest number of hours of sunshine (42).

České Budějovice weather station

The rather higher parts of Bohemia – here represented by the České Budějovice weather station (alt. 383m/1257ft) – show a marked difference from the Prague area.

Annual precipitations are higher (620mm/24in., including 102mm/4in. in July alone; 96 days in the year with precipitation). In the lower-lying areas even relatively low hills show an increase in precipitation.

Southern Bohemia ranks only as a moderately warm area, with fewer than 50 "summer days". Winter minima are some 2°C/3.6°F lower than those of Prague, summer maxima almost 1°C/1.8°F higher, while daily and annual variations are greater. The number of days on which snow falls (34) is two higher than at Prague.

Moravia and Moravian Silesia

A zone of transition

In climatic terms Moravia is a zone of transition between sub-oceanic Bohemia and sub-continental Slovakia (see below).

Northern Moravia

Ostrava weather station

In contrast to inner Bohemia, Northern Moravia is not sheltered by the Sudeten mountains. As a result precipitation is higher, particularly in the

Western Beskyds (Lysá Hora, 1324m/4344ft) – in Ostrava (212m/696ft) 769mm/30in. on 113 days in the year. In this area the annual range of variation in average monthly temperature is 1°C/1.8°F greater than at Prague.

Southern Moravia

Brno weather station

In comparison with other places in the same latitude Southern Moravia has a markedly warmer climate, so that, for example, wine can be grown in this region. In low-lying situations the winters have relatively low temperatures. Autumn is longer and warmer than spring.
Brno weather station lies at an altitude of 223m/732ft.

Slovakia

Characteristics

The climate of Slovakia is sub-continental. This is shown particularly in greater variations in temperature between summer and winter. Spring and autumn are rather shorter than they are farther west, with correspondingly rapid changes in temperature. The continental character of the climate is reflected in the climatic diagrams in the broader and more curving temperature bands. As a result of the varied relief pattern local differences within small areas are particularly great. Thus spring comes to the Danube lowlands some 40 days earlier than in the higher regions of the Carpathians.

Danube Lowlands

Bratislava weather station

The flat Danube region differs in climate from Bohemia particularly in the relatively high summer temperatures which result from the relative absence of cloud cover and the intense solar radiation. In no other climatic diagram is the temperature band so strongly curved as in that for Bratislava (alt. 133m/436ft), which is sheltered on the west by the Little Carpathians (Malé Karpaty). Autumn here is longer and warmer than spring.
Annual precipitations, at 670mm/26in., are higher than in inner Bohemia and are evenly distributed over the year on some 100 days. After a particularly dry winter there may well be water shortages in the following summer.
Annual hours of sunshine are very high (2194). In July, in spite of 9 days with rain, there are 317 hours of sunshine (compared with 265 in Prague).

Eastern Slovakia

Košice weather station

In Eastern Slovakia the winters are markedly colder than in Bohemia. Košice, situated at an altitude of 296m/676ft – only a little lower than Prague – has average minimum and maximum day temperatures in January of −7.4°C/+18.7°F and −0.7°C/+30.7°F. The summers are warmer than in Bohemia. Between the end of April and the end of October average maximum day temperatures are fully 1°C/1.8°F above those for Prague, while average minimum night temperatures are just under 1°C/1.8°F below those for Prague. Extreme minima may sometimes fall below 10°C/40°F, which means that it can feel quite cold.
As a result of the nearness of the hills precipitation (663mm/26in. on 100 days) is not so low as at Prague. Yet the number of hours of sunshine (an annual 2032) is 130 greater than at Prague; in October alone Košice has almost 30 hours more sunshine than Prague (146 against 117).

Highlands

Zvolen weather station

In basin areas – represented by the Zvolen weather station (alt. 299m/981ft) – temperatures are rather more extreme than in Eastern Slovakia. In comparison with valley areas in Bohemia the summer nights are relatively cool. In winter there are frequent temperature inversions, when cold air accumulates in valleys and basins and is covered by a layer of cloud, while the higher ground above the clouds has clear air and intense solar radiation. In the basins there may be minimum temperatures below −30°C/−22°F. In the climatic diagrams this is reflected in the fact that the temperature band for Zvolen is almost 2°C/3.6°F lower in January than that for Košice.

Starý Smokovec

The climatic diagram for Starý Smokovec, situated at an altitude of 1018m/3340ft under the north side of the High Tatras, shows how the character of the climate changes with increasing altitude. The whole of the temperature band is lower down; that is, it is colder over the whole year. Minimum night temperatures are as low as −10°C/+14°F in winter, and summer maxima remain below 20°C/68°F. There may be night frosts in any month except July. In general temperature variations over the day are less than at lower levels – a feature characteristic of an oceanic climate. Precipitations are markedly higher than at lower levels (944mm/37in. on 128 days in the year). During the summer months there are fewer hours of sunshine (207 in August, compared with 255 at Košice), but from December to February there are more (75, 96 and 107 against 55, 66 and 89) – the result of temperature inversion.

Lomnický Štít

On the Lomnický Štít (2655m/8711ft), one of the highest peaks in the High Tatras, there are two or three times as much sunshine in the winter months as at Prague (November to February 131, 129, 137 and 155 hours against 53, 42, 55 and 86 hours).

Ecology

Vegetation

A zone of transition

As explained in the chapter on Climate, the territory of former Czechoslovakia is also a transitional zone as regards the natural plant cover.

Forests

In Bohemia and Northern Moravia and in the highland areas of Slovakia there are great expanses of forest, though in industrial regions the forests have been much damaged by pollution (see Dying of the forests, below). The tree-line lies between 1350m/4430ft and 1400m/4600ft, but in Slovakia it is some 100m/330ft higher and from there up to 1650m/5400ft there are only mountain pines. Above this are alpine meadows with alpine vegetation. Below 1000m/3300ft mixed beech forests predominate.

Upland flora

In the Czech Lands the hill crests, which are frequently flat, are covered with moorland in which Scots pines and birches grow. In clearings in the forests there are upland meadows with a varied flora, including plants of Alpine and Nordic origin which are relics of the Ice Age.

Pannonian/Pontic flora

In the warm, dry territory of northern Inner Bohemia, Southern Moravia and Southern Slovakia a flora of Pannonian/Pontic type is found – open pine and oak woodland, heaths, thorny scrub, steppe grasses and dry grassland. In the valleys of the larger rivers there is riverine woodland, with alders, poplars, ashes and willows.

In general the natural plant formations have been much altered by human activity and have suffered lasting damage from modern industrial development.

Fauna

Animals

In the remoter upland regions at least a relatively rich animal life has survived, and in recent years there has even been some degree of regeneration. This is the case particularly in Slovakia, where wolves, bears, lynxes and wild cats can occasionally be encountered – species which in the first half of the 20th century had seemed to be almost completely extinct. In the Carpathians, in addition to red deer, roe deer, wild pigs and other game there are also otters and martens, and at higher altitudes chamois and marmots, while in the Little Carpathians there are also moufflons. Hares and foxes are found all over the country.

Birds

There are many species and relatively large numbers of birds in Bohemia, and even more in Moravia and the more thinly populated Slovakia. Particularly notable are the numerous waterfowl which inhabit the river basins of Southern Slovakia, the white storks, the great bustards in the Danube depression and the rare golden eagles found in the High Tatras.

Fishes

It is no surprise to find that a country so rich in rivers, lakes and ponds is well supplied with fish. Fish-breeding in special ponds has a long tradition behind it, particularly in Southern Bohemia. The commonest species are carp, trout (several species), Danube salmon, pike and the large catfish – all frequently found on restaurant menus during the season. River eels are also common, particularly in the rivers Hornád and Poprad in Slovakia.

Environmental Problems

The present unsatisfactory ecological conditions in former Czechoslovakia are to a considerable extent the result of the social and political developments of recent decades under the socialist regime, in particular the concentration on heavy industry under the Comecon system. This depended largely on poor-quality sources of energy, particularly in inefficient thermal power stations, which caused serious environmental damage, affecting air, soil, water, flora and fauna. Moreover facilities for the filtration and

Storks

Carp

purification of sewage and effluent and the disposal of waste were inadequate or absent altogether. Agriculture was subjected to excessive concentration and collectivisation, the forests were ravaged for timber, industry and transport had inadequate and antiquated infrastructures and the country's beautiful holiday regions suffered from the effects of organised "social tourism". The main consequences of the lack of concern for the protection of the environment were air and water pollution and the injection of harmful substances into the food chain.

Air

Former Czechoslovakia is one of the countries with the largest emission of harmful substances in the whole of Europe. This is due to the use of poor-quality sources of energy like brown coal and lignite (with a high sulphur content and large ash content) in thermal power stations and heavy industry, inadequate or inefficient filtration plants and antiquated measuring and monitoring installations, as well as the lack of regulations and measures to secure the observance of minimum standards.

Areas of air pollution

As a result of the concentration of power stations, industrial installations and housing areas, combined with the frequent occurrence of temperature inversion in low-lying areas, the following regions in the Czech Lands are particularly subject to air pollution: the Ore Mountains, with the industrial centres of Chomutov, Teplice and Děčín; Central Bohemia, with the Prague conurbation, Kladno, Kralupy and Mělník; the Ostrava–Karviná industrial region; and the cities of Plzeň, Pardubice and Brno.
In comparison with Bohemia, Moravian Silesia and Moravia Slovakia is less affected by air pollution. The main problems are in industrial towns in basins and river valleys subject to temperature inversion with high population density, principally the Bratislava, Prievidza–Nitra, Žiar nad Hronom, Košice and Vajany–Humenné areas.

Effect on health

Thus roughly half the population of Bohemia and Moravia and a third of the population of Slovakia live in areas of air pollution. This is reflected in an increased incidence of diseases of the respiratory tract, latent dust allergies, higher infantile mortality and lower life expectancy.

Water

In view of its particular physical and geographical conditions the territory of former Czechoslovakia is almost entirely dependent on its own, not particularly abundant, resources of surface and ground water. In some areas there is concern about the supply of drinking water: in the Czech Republic in and around Příbram, Tábor, Benešov, Havlíčkův Brod, Brno and Ostrava; in the Slovak Republic in and around Košice, Rožňava, Nitra, Zvolen, Považská Bystrica, Bardejov and Svidník.
Unfortunately these areas threatened with water shortage are also areas of high population density, air pollution and erosion by water and wind. This accumulation of problems not only affects the health of the population but also restricts the scope for economic development.
The situation is complicated by the severe pollution of both surface waters and ground-water by domestic and industrial waste water and by the over-use of fertilisers and intensive stock-farming, which in many areas takes the level of nitrates, phosphates, polychlorinated hydrocarbons, toxic heavy metals and biological contamination well above acceptable limits. Almost half the available water supply falls below proper health standards.

Polluted rivers

Pollution is particularly severe in the rivers Labe (Elbe), Vltava, Berounka, Bílina, Cidlina and Dyje in the Czech Lands and in the Danube (Dunaj), Váh and Hron in Slovakia.

Land

In recent decades urbanisation, industrialisation and the collectivisation of agriculture have led to great changes in the land. The area in agricultural use has been much reduced, with some 10,000 hectares/25,000 acres of arable and fallow land going out of cultivation every year. This loss has

been compensated by increasingly intensive farming methods, which has been accompanied by a disproportionate increase in the size of fields, the over-use of fertilisers, increased use of pesticides and inappropriate change of use of land.
As a result the quality of the soil has suffered – in the whole of the Bohemian Basin, in the Elbe depression and in the Moravian lowlands, but also in the Danube depression in Slovakia and the lowlands of Eastern Slovakia. The leaching out of nutrients, the increased compression and acidity of the soil, changes in soil mechanics, the destruction of the balance of water management and the danger of erosion by wind and water are the most serious consequences of this development.

Vegetation

As a result of the dramatic changes in environmental conditions not only have many species of plants already disappeared or are threatened with extinction but whole plant societies are in danger and many wetland areas have suffered damage. It is estimated that only some 35% of the plant world has remained untouched by human influence.

Dying of the forest

The forests which still cover around a third of former Czechoslovakia, and are important both to the population and the economy, have suffered alarming damage. Air pollution, acid rain, inappropriate changes in land use, the increased planting of conifers as a monoculture, insufficient attention to climate and altitude in afforestation, poor forestry management, over-stocking with game and the effects of mass tourism have caused damage over wide areas: loss of needles in conifers, yellowing of the leaves in deciduous trees, rotting away of branches and thinning of the crowns of trees are unmistakable signs of the "dying of the forest" which is now spreading widely. More than 70% of all living forest trees show signs of damage.
The worst affected forests – in the Ore Mountains, Jizera Hills and Beskyds – are inevitably in the areas surrounding the main sources of air pollution, industrial centres and large concentrations of population.

Emergency measures

The improvement in environmental conditions which is urgently necessary is a major challenge not only to the Czech and Slovak Republics but also to neighbouring countries. An effective cleaning-up of the environment will be possible only with energetic financial, technical and organisational support from outside.
A first step would be the re-structuring and modernisation of energy production and heavy industry. An essential requirement is the introduction of well-conceived legislative measures; but it is no less necessary to make the population as a whole environment-conscious.

Population

Traditionally a multi-national state

From the creation of the first Czechoslovak state in 1918 Czechoslovakia, in spite of its definition as the "state of Czechs and Slovaks", was a multinational state inhabited not only by Czechs and Slovaks but also by many Germans, Hungarians, Ukrainians, Russians and Poles as well as other small minorities.

Population

In 1930 Czechoslovakia had a total population of some 14 million (53% Czechs and 16.4% Slovaks, together with 23.6% Germans, 4.3% Hungarians, 0.8% Ukrainians and Russians, 0.7% Poles and 0.6% Jews). After the Second World War, as a result of losses during the war (including some 350,000 Jews) but mainly of the expulsion of Sudeten Germans and part of the Hungarian population, the figure had fallen to around 12 million (1947). By the early nineties the population of Czechoslovakia had risen to 15.7 million (63.9% Czechs and 30.4% Slovaks; on the minorities see below), fully two-thirds of whom lived in the Czech Lands and one-third in Slovakia.

Population density

This produced a population density of 123 to the sq. kilometre (319 to the sq. mile). In the Czech Lands (with concentrations of population in the

Prague area, the Ostrava industrial region and Northern Bohemia) the density was greater – 132 to the sq. kilometre (342 to the sq. mile), compared with 107 to the sq. kilometre (277 to the sq. mile) in Slovakia.

Social structure

The average rate of population increase between 1980 and 1990 was 0.2% (higher in Slovakia than in the Czech Lands), life expectancy just under 70, the illiteracy rate under 1%. Of the total working population roughly half were employed in industry and only about 10% in agriculture. Employment in the services sector showed a marked increase. Fully three-quarters of the population live in towns, and there is a movement of population away from the land.

Minorities

Since the end of the Second World War the proportion of population represented by minorities has remained below 7%. Even under the communist regime the minority groups (from 1968 including Germans) were granted certain rights, particularly in the cultural field (formation of associations and organisations, publication of their own newspapers, etc.). The largest minority is the Hungarians (some 600,000, mainly in Southern Slovakia), followed by up to 150,000 Germans, some 70,000 Poles (mainly in Moravian Silesia) and 50,000 Ukrainians (predominantly in Eastern Slovakia).

The Romanies (gipsies) who live a nomadic life all over Czech and Slovak territory were formerly excluded from the population statistics and enjoyed no protection as a minority. They are estimated to number at least 500,000 (according to another source more than 800,000). They have recently, following an initiative of their own, been able to take part in political life.

Language

The official languages are Czech and Slovak, two closely related Western Slav tongues. In addition Hungarian, Polish and Ukrainian are spoken in the areas occupied by these minorities, who have a right to be taught in their mother tongue. In these areas signs and notices are often bilingual. Many of the older generation still speak German; among younger people English is more commonly understood.

Religion

Since from 1950 onwards there were no official statistics on the religious affiliations of the population no reliable figures are available. Most believers (an estimated 5 million in 1991) belong to the Roman Catholic church (three provinces). A long way behind come the Czechoslovak Hussite (Catholic) church and the various Protestant denominations (Lutherans,

Presbyterians, Reformed Church), the Hussites and the Orthodox church, as well as Baptists, Bohemian Brethren, Moravian Brethren (Herrnhuters) and Methodists. The number of Jews is estimated at around 15,000.

Government and Administration

Unified state

When the first Czechoslovak state was established after the First World War from parts of the old Austro-Hungarian monarchy it was a unified state of two peoples, the Czechs and Slovaks. After the period of German occupation and the Second World War this continued to exist in the postwar period, from 1945 to 1948, as a pluralist Republic (ČSR). After the communist seizure of power it became, until 1960, a "People's Republic". Under a new constitution introduced in 1960, which nominally permitted non-communist parties, it became a socialist republic on the Soviet model (ČSSR).

Federal state

After the brutal repression of the "Prague Spring" in 1968 the unified centralist state was replaced by a federation of socialist type consisting of the Czech Socialist Republic (ČSR) and the Slovak Socialist Republic (SSR), with separate parliaments and administrations in Prague and Bratislava and a federal parliament and administration in Prague. Finally the "Velvet Revolution" in the crucial year 1989 brought the long-sought democratisation. Czechoslovakia now became the Czech and Slovak Federative Republic (ČSFR), consisting of the Czech Federative Republic (ČFR) and the Slovak Federative Republic (SFR).

Separation

After parliamentary elections in 1992 there was a movement in favour of the dissolution of the federation, and the Czech and Slovak prime ministers then agreed that the dissolution should take place on January 1st 1993, when the Czechoslovak state which had existed for 74 years was divided into two independent states, the **Czech Republic** and the **Slovak Republic**.

Administrative Divisions

Following are the administrative divisions as they were in 1993. A reorganisation of the local government structure is planned in both the Czech and Slovak Republics.

Czech Republic

REGIONS	AREA	CHIEF TOWN
Prague	496sq.km/192sq.miles	Prague
Central Bohemia	11,004sq.km/4249sq.miles	Prague
Western Bohemia	10,876sq.km/4199sq.miles	Plzeň
Northern Bohemia	7808sq.km/3015sq.miles	Ústí nad Labem
Eastern Bohemia	11,241sq.km/4340sq.miles	Hradec Králové
Southern Bohemia	11,343sq.km/4380sq.miles	České Budějovice
Southern Moravia	15,028sq.km/5802sq.miles	Brno
Northern Moravia (with Moravian Silesia)	11,067sq.km/4273sq.miles	Ostrava

Slovak Republic

REGIONS	AREA	CHIEF TOWN
Bratislava	368sq.km/142sq.miles	Bratislava
Western Slovakia	14,513sq.km/5603sq.miles	Bratislava
Central Slovakia	17,976sq.km/6941sq.miles	Banská Bystrica
Eastern Slovakia	16,179sq.km/6247sq.miles	Košice

Bohemia
Čechy

Northern Bohemia
Ústí nad Labem
Hradec Králové
PRAHA
Prague
Eastern Bohemia
Western Bohemia
Czech Republic
Northe
Plzeň
Central Bohemia
Česká Republika
Southern Bohemia
Brno
České Budějovice
Southern Moravia

Coat of arms of former ČSFR

Moravia
Morava

Since Januaury 1st two sovereign states:

Coat of arms of Czech Republic

Czech Republic
Česká Republika

Czech Lands
České země

Nationality plate CZ

Northern Bohemia
Ústí nad Labem
© Baedeker
Hradec Králové
PRAHA
Prague
Eastern Bohemia
Moravian
Western Bohemia
Northern
Silesia
Czech Republic
Ostrava
Plzeň
Central Bohemia
Moravia
Česká Republika
Southern Bohemia
Brno
České Budějovice
Southern Moravia

National flag of Czech Republic

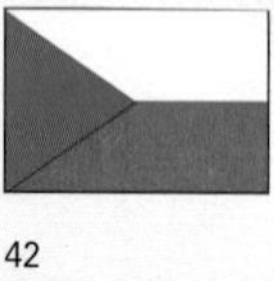

Former Czechoslovakia
Československo

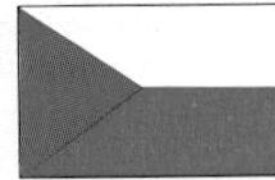
National flag

Czech and Slovak Federative Republic
Česká a Slovenská Federativní Republika · ČSFR
Česká Slovenská Federativná Republika · ČSFR

Nationality plate CS

oravia
Silesia
Ostrava
oravian
Central Slovakia
Eastern Slovakia
Slovak Republic
Slovenská Republika
Košice
Banská Bystrica
estern Slovakia
BRATISLAVA
© Baedeker

Slovakia
Slovensko

Coat of arms
of Slovak Republic

Slovak Republic
Slovenská Republika

Slovakia
Slovensko

SQ Nationality plate

Central Slovakia
Eastern Slovakia
Slovak Republic
Slovenská Republika
Košice
Western
Slovakia
Banská Bystrica
BRATISLAVA
© Baedeker

National flag of
Slovak Republic

These administrative units still reflect the division of the country into regions (*kraj*) under the socialist regime. Although they were theoretically dissolved in 1990 they have remained in existence pending the introduction of a new administrative structure. Within these regions there was a total of 112 districts (*okres),* which in turn were composed of more than 9000 communes (*obec*). The "people's councils" (*národni výbor*) which formerly operated on these various levels have been replaced by district, urban and communal councils (*úřad*) and in the cities by municipal councils.

The new constitutions which are to be introduced in the Czech and Slovak Republics are expected to include provisions for the reorganisation of local government within the two new states. In this connection there has been much discussion in the Czech Republic about whether and in what forms or combinations the historical lands of Bohemia, Moravia and Moravian Silesia – which in recent years have come to be known as the "Czech Lands" (České Země) – should be given a new lease of life.

Parties

The "Velvet Revolution" of 1989 was carried through by the Czech organisation led by Václav Havel which took the name of Civic Forum (Občanské Fórum, OF) and its Slovakian sister organisation People against Violence (Verejnost' proti Násilou, VPN). These two organisations regarded themselves as citizens' movements striving to achieve democracy rather than political parties; but it was not long before large numbers of parties were founded – though after the first free election in 1990 relatively few of them achieved representation in the Czechoslovak parliament. The largest group in the new parliament was the OF/VPN alliance (46.6%), followed by the Communist Party (KPČ; 13.6%), the Christian Democratic Union (KDU; 12%), the Moravian-Silesian Movement (6%), the Slovak National Party (3.6%) and "Coexistence", the party of the national minorities (Hungarian Együttélés; 2.7%), whose greatest strength is among the Hungarians living in Slovakia.

Later the pattern became still more diverse and, particularly for outsiders, difficult to follow. The citizens' movements split into a variety of groupings, there were new divisions and alliances between the existing parties, often under long and complicated names, reflecting the variety of ideas and objectives. In parliamentary elections in 1992 the Citizens' Democratic Party (Občanská Democratická Strana, ODS) in the Czech Republic and the Movement for a Democratic Slovakia (Hnutie za Democratické Slovensko, HZDS) in the Slovak Republic were victorious, and at the end of August their leaders, the Czech prime minister Václav Klaus and his Slovak colleague Vladimir Mečiar, reached agreement that the Czechoslovak Federation should be dissolved on January 1st 1993 and replaced by two independent states, the Czech Republic and the Slovak Republic.

Economy

The political transformation of 1989 led to far-reaching changes in the whole economic structure of Czechoslovakia, the scale of which can be assessed but the full effects of which cannot yet be seen. In such a period of universal change definite facts and figures are lacking and reliable forecasts about the future cannot be made. This is more particularly so in view of the dissolution of the Czechoslovak Federation into the Czech and Slovak Republics on January 1st 1993.

In general terms it can be said that the democratic authorities in both countries are seeking to bring about the introduction of a free market economy, the privatisation of industrial and economic activities (special ministries of the economy, voucher system for the acquisition of shares, investment funds, injection of capital and management participation by foreign firms) and a restructuring of the various branches of the economy. Given the uncertainties of the future, however, the following discussion can be no more than a retrospective survey of the development of the economy down to the recent revolutionary change.

Structure of the Economy

A long established industrial country

Czechoslovakia was a long established and developed industrial country. Among the members of the Eastern bloc's now dissolved Council for Mutual Economic Assistance (Comecon) it had the highest proportion of workers employed in industry and in building and construction (47.5% in 1987), followed by Bulgaria (46.3%), Romania (44.5%) and the German Democratic Republic (44.1%). In 1988 industry contributed 70.3% of the gross national product. Agriculture and the services sector played a relatively minor role, employing 12% and 40.5% of the working population and contributing 6.4% and 23.3% of the gross national product – though in comparison with other members of Comecon these sectors were also well developed.

Integration into Comecon

Until the political and economic turning-point of 1989 Czechoslovakia's foreign trade was closely integrated into Comecon, being exceeded in this respect only by Bulgaria. More than two-thirds of its foreign trade was with other Comecon countries. Its imports from these countries consisted mainly of energy-producing raw materials (the Soviet Union being the main supplier), its exports to them mainly of industrial products. Under the Comecon plan for the division of labour between member states Czechoslovakia was assigned the role of a producer of machinery. However it also exported industrial goods of all kinds, which enjoyed the reputation within Comecon of high quality.

Western trading partners

Until the changes of 1989 Czechoslovakia's principal western trading partners were the German Federal Republic, followed by Austria and Italy. The only Czechoslovak products which could compete successfully in these western markets were motor vehicles; otherwise the pattern of exports resembled that of a developing country (raw materials, semi-finished products).

Change to a free market economy

The reorientation towards a market economy following the political changes of 1989, the dissolution of Comecon and the switch to a hard currency basis for exchanges between the former Comecon countries have led to fundamental changes in earlier economic relationships. In the first place there has been a reduction in foreign trade. The reorientation of the economy has been accompanied by sharp price increases, factory closures and unemployment, but the problems have to some extent been relieved by the high standard of Czechoslovak industry in comparison with other former socialist countries and the relatively low level of foreign debt.

Internal differences in development

The different levels of development and living standards – higher in the Czech regions of Bohemia, Moravia and Silesia, lower in Slovakia – which existed before the First World War and between the wars were largely evened out after the Second World War, mainly as a result of the deliberate policy of industrialisation in Slovakia. With industry in the territories of the present Czech and Slovak Republics contributing respectively 81.2% and 80.4% to the gross national product and average incomes per head of 30.6 and 27.9 crowns (figures for 1988 in both cases), the differences in economic structure and standard of living between the two countries are now relatively small.

Mining and Energy Production

Minerals

The territory of the Czech and Slovak Republics is well supplied with a variety of raw materials.

Well-known exports: Škoda cars . . .

. . . and beer

Among energy-producing raw materials, it is true, oil and natural gas are almost entirely lacking, and the major resource, by a long way, is solid fuel (coal). While the country is self-sufficient in coal, it produces only 0.9% of its oil requirements and 6.3% of its natural gas.

High-quality coal is worked mainly in the Ostrava–Karviná region and in the fifth part of the (mainly Polish) Upper Silesian coalfield which lies within Moravia. The coal is won mainly in open-cast and shallow underground workings. The most important mining areas are Ostrava, Karviná, Havířov and Orlová, with smaller coalfields in the Krkonoše range (Trutnov) and central Bohemia (mainly Kladno).

Like the coal-mines in the Ostrava area, the deposits of brown coal round Duchcov, Most and Chomutov in northern Bohemia have led to the development of an industrial agglomeration. These coalfields, along with the workings at Sokolov in western Bohemia and Handlová in Slovakia, make the territory of former Czechoslovakia one of the largest producers of brown coal in the world. The country's deposits of lignite, however, are small.

In addition to these old-established sources of energy-producing raw materials there are large deposits of uranium in the crystalline rocks of the Bohemian Massif. Uranium is no longer worked in the old mining town of Jáchymov in western Bohemia, and the main supplies now come from Příbram in central Bohemia and Hamr in the Lusatian Hills. Locally produced uranium now fuels a considerable nuclear power industry.

Industrial raw materials

The most important industrial raw materials produced in the territory of former Czechoslovakia are magnesite, kaolin, graphite, lead and zinc. Magnesite working is concentrated in the Slovakian Ore Mountains (Jelšava, Košice-Bankov), kaolin in western Bohemia (Horní Bříza, Kaznějov, Karlovy Vary). There are numbers of graphite mines in the Bohemian Forest and other parts of southern Bohemia. Lead and zinc are mined in central Bohemia (mainly Příbram) and in the Slovakian Ore Mountains. There are only relatively small deposits of copper and iron ore at various points in the Slovakian Ore Mountains and central Bohemia; the only mines of any size now in operation are in the Ore Mountains.

Energy production

Energy production depends to the extent of over 80% on home-produced coal. Nuclear energy contributes some 10%, hydroelectricity less than 2%. Thermal, nuclear and hydroelectric power stations produce respectively 68%, 26% and 6% of the total power supply. The largest thermal power stations are round the large deposits of brown coal in northern Bohemia. The first two nuclear power stations established at Jaslovské Bohunice (1972) in western Slovakia and Dukovany in southern Moravia have antiquated Soviet-made reactors. The power stations at Temelín in southern Bohemia and Mochovce in southern Slovakia were also Soviet-designed. Most of the hydroelectric installations have hitherto been on the rivers Vltava and Váh; there has been much controversy over the establishment of the giant hydroelectric station on the Slovakian island of Žitný in the Danube.

High demand for energy

The high demand for energy (consumption per head of the population 40–50% above the European average) resulting from inefficient use of energy, particularly in industry, can be met only to the extent of two-thirds from home-produced raw materials. Large quantities of oil and natural gas and smaller amounts of electric power must therefore be imported. In recent years they came almost exclusively from the Soviet Union. The Družba (Friendship) pipeline came into operation in 1962 for the conveyance of oil from the Ukraine, at first to a refinery at Bratislava and later to northern Bohemia. In 1979 the Sojuz (Union) pipeline was completed, bringing natural gas from Orenburg via Kiev to Czechoslovakia, with branches to Hungary, Austria, Italy and Germany. Imports of crude oil from the Soviet Union rose eventually to an annual 17 million tons and of gas to 9.5 billion cubic metres (2095 billion gallons), accounting in terms of value for half of all imports from the Soviet Union.
The changed commercial relationships with the successor states to the Soviet Union cast a question-mark over the continuation of these supply arrangements.

Industry

A long established industrial region

Parts of the territory of former Czechoslovakia were among the oldest industrial regions in Europe. Factories began to be built in Bohemia as early as the 17th century. The relatively poor conditions for agriculture, the availability of timber in the forests and the swift flow of the rivers in the hills bordering Bohemia, particularly the Sudetens and the Ore Mountains, gave an early impulse to the development of industry in these regions. In the 18th century they already had a thriving textile industry using locally grown flax and hemp, glassworks and various types of craft production (e.g. glass jewellery and ornaments in Jablonec nad Nisou and toys in the Ore Mountains). Many of these products were made by craftsmen working at home or in addition to some other employment. Frequently Western Europeans were involved as investors or entrepreneurs.
Inner Bohemia and the whole of Moravia, with better land and climate, at first remained more dependent on agriculture, though the Moravian capital Brno developed before 1800 a considerable woollen industry which supplied uniforms for the Austrian army and iron works were established at Blansko in Moravia.

Industry based on coal

The introduction of the steam engine brought a change in conditions for the location of industry, which was attracted to the coal-mining areas producing what was now the most important kind of fuel. Thus in 1826 were established the steelworks at Ostrava which later passed into the hands of the Rothschild family and became the nucleus of one of the most important industrial regions in Czechoslovakia. The steelworks at Vitkovice were also a major factor in the decision to construct the first steam railway in the Austrian Empire, running northward from Vienna (line to Ostrava completed in 1847). The railway, with the lines to Bohemia and Saxony which soon followed (through trains Vienna–Prague–Dresden from 1851), in turn became the axis of further industrialisation. Like the Ostrava coalfield in Moravian Silesia, the Plzeň and Kladno coalfields in central Bohemia soon attracted a concentration of industry.

Parallel development in Bohemia, Moravia and Silesia

The early development of a dense railway network in the second half of the 19th century and the existence of many small and middle-sized towns which could serve as nuclei for the development of industry led before the First World War – in spite of the tendency towards development in the coalfield areas – to a more even distribution of the new industries in Bohemia, Moravia and Silesia than in other parts of Europe. The industries established outside the coalfields and in the larger towns were mainly consumption-oriented, such as brewing (Plzeň, České Budějovice) and the processing of agricultural produce (sugar refineries, steam mills).

Textiles

The old-established textile industry on the northern edge of Bohemia showed very considerable powers of survival in spite of the fact that it had lost its earlier advantages of situation as a result of the switch to imported cotton as raw material and to coal as fuel. Before the First World War the areas in the hills bordering Northern Bohemia had the highest degree of industrialisation in the whole of the Austro-Hungarian monarchy, with up to 48% of the population employed in industry and craft production. There were other less intensive industrial regions in Silesia and northern Moravia, round Brno and in central Bohemia (Plzeň, Kladno, Prague). Their degree of industrialisation was similar to that of Vienna and the southern Vienna basin and the textile region of Vorarlberg, the only comparable industrial regions in the rest of the monarchy. The industrialisation in Bohemia did not extend into Slovakia, which then fell within the Hungarian half of the Empire. The Ore Mountains had a mixed industrial structure, with large chemical works at Ústí nad Labem. The north-eastern edge of Bohemia, Silesia and part of Moravia specialised in the textile and clothing industry. In the coalfield areas the metalworking industries were predominant.

Development after the First World War

When Czechoslovakia became a sovereign state in 1918 it inherited some 65% of the industrial capacity of the Austro-Hungarian Monarchy (against only 20.7% of its area and 27.4% of its population). The textile industry in the hilly northern fringes of Bohemia, Moravia and Silesia, which had long suffered from disadvantages of situation, were now thrown into crisis. The metalworking and engineering industries in the industrial agglomerations and towns of Bohemia, on the other hand, were offered new possibilities of development. The industrial development of Slovakia made little progress, and something like 90% of the country's industrial capacity was concentrated in Bohemia.

Second World War

During the period of German occupation and the Second World War the German armaments industry initiated new patterns in the location of industry which were taken over and continued by postwar Czechoslovak governments.

Communist industrial policy

From 1948 onwards communist industrial policy brought a second great wave of industrialisation which changed both the types and the location of industry.

Heavy and capital goods industries

Under this new policy heavy industry and the production of capital goods were promoted at the expense of the consumption goods industries. Large steelworks were built all over the country, particularly in Slovakia (Košice), using iron ore from the Ukraine. Particular emphasis was placed on the development of the engineering industry. With the beginning of the "Prague Spring" (1966 onwards) a brake was put on the development of heavy industry and attention was now concentrated on the chemical industry, light engineering, instrument-making and the production of consumption goods and foodstuffs.

Development in Slovakia

In the location of industry the most notable feature, apart from the establishment of small factories in almost every commune in the country, was the way in which Slovakia now began to catch up with the rest of the country. Within 40 years it was transformed from a poor agricultural region into an industrial country which could stand beside the old-established industrial regions of Bohemia, Moravia and Silesia. The main industrial areas in Slovakia are now Bratislava with its hinterland to the east, the middle Váh valley (Trenčín, Dubnica, Púchov, Považská Bystrica, Žilina, Martin), the valleys of the Slovakian Ore Mountains (Partizánske, Podbrezová) and Košice in eastern Slovakia.

Industrial products

Before the recent political changes much the most important branch of industry, measured by the number of workers employed, was engineering, with 39% of the total industrial work-force. It was followed, far behind, by the foodstuffs industry and the still shrinking textile industry (each 7%) and by the ironworking and chemical industries (each 6%).
Among the principal industrial products were tools, locomotives, weapons, motor vehicles, plastics, cellulose, crude steel, rolled steel products, tractors, goods waggons, cine-cameras, washing machines, refrigerators, canned fruit and beer. The quality of such products, however, will have to be improved to enable them to compete in western markets.

Conversion to market economy

The move towards a market economy in both domestic and foreign trade has created major problems for the many "politicat" factories, the establishment and location of which was frequently determined more by ideological factors than by economic considerations. This is true both of the large primary industries and of small factories in what were formerly rural communes. The main assets in the present reorientation of industry are the high educational level of the employees and the high standard of technical and scientific research.

Agriculture

Although agriculture plays a smaller part in the economy than industry it is still of great importance not only in providing basic foodstuffs for the population but in supplying raw materials for industry and in its effects on the countryside. Industry was already exerting a strong influence on the landscape in Bohemia in the 19th century, when industrialists acquired land in the country, raw materials for industry (sugar-beet, hops) were produced and the rural population were being attracted off the land to the industrial centres. The efficient and well organised agriculture of Bohemia now produced a high proportion of total Austro-Hungarian production of sugar-beet, rye, barley, oats, potatoes and hops.
In Slovakia, however, agriculture remained backward as a result of the continued fragmentation of holdings in successive generations of families which were mostly large. Some improvement resulted from the introduction of "urbariates" – associations of peasant farmers for the cooperative acquisition of villages and land, with provisions preventing individual members from obtaining a majority holding; the system was given legal force in 1899.

Land reform in the interwar period

The land reform of the interwar period was designed mainly to promote an ethnic mix in the minority regions of the new state (Sudetenland, southern Slovakia), but had little effect on social conditions in rural areas.

Communist collectivisation

The collectivisation of agriculture after the communist seizure of power in 1948 was carried through in three phases. The first phase, from 1949 onwards, concentrated on the land abandoned by Sudeten Germans and Hungarians on the fringes of Bohemian territory and in southern Slovakia; after the second phase, around 1960, more than 90% of the country's agricultural land had been collectivised; and in the early seventies only a relatively small area remained to be taken over. Immediately before the political changes of 1989 the only land in private occupation consisted of holdings worked part-time along with some other employment (mainly in the Slovakian hills), land held by members of agricultural production co-operatives and what were called "subsidiary personal holdings". The majority of agricultural land (an average of 63% over the country as a whole) belonged to cooperative organisations, and some 32% was in state farms and farms run by public bodies. This last form of ownership was predominant in the former Sudetenland. Thus in completeness of collectivisation Czechoslovakia was surpassed among the socialist countries only by Albania. With the combination of the former small holdings into large agricultural units collectivisation made a fundamental change in field patterns, the more so because the farming units, particularly on the state farms, were larger than in neighbouring countries; the largest of all were in the former German settlement areas of southern Bohemia, southern Moravia and northern Bohemia, with farms of between 8000 and 15,000 hectares (20,000 and 37,500 acres).

Privatisation of agriculture

After the political revolution of 1989 the privatisation of agriculture was slow to get under way. After decades of industrialisation and urbanisation the population who had become unaccustomed to rural life were reluctant to take to farming again.

Four main production zones

In the agricultural and forest land of former Czechoslovakia four main production zones can be distinguished, depending on climate, soil and altitude.

Maize zone

The most productive of these is the maize zone, in areas with a warm, dry climate (average annual temperature 9°C/48°F, annual rainfall 500–600mm/20–24in.), black and brown earth soils and altitudes below 200m/650ft. This zone takes in the Morava basin and the low-lying parts of southern and eastern Slovakia. In addition to maize the crops include tobacco, sunflowers, wheat, wine, fruit and vegetables. Yields of wheat per hectare are higher than in the neighbouring regions of Austria and Hungary, thanks to intensive use of fertilisers, but yields of maize are lower.

Sugar-beet zone

Lying between 200m/650ft and 350m/1150ft, the sugar-beet zone has a rather cooler and wetter climate. The soils are mainly brown earth, black earth and podzol. To this zone belong the Labe (Elbe) basin in central and eastern Bohemia, the middle and lower Ohře valley, the upland regions of Moravia and Silesia and the fringe zone to the south of the Carpathians. The characteristic crop of this zone is sugar-beet, but wheat, barley, fodder plants, sunflowers, fruit and vegetables are also grown. Yields of sugar-beet per hectare are below those of comparable areas in Austria and Bavaria.

Potato zone

The potato zone occupies the largest part of the country's agricultural land and arable land. It lies between 350m/1150ft and and 600m/1970ft, with podzolic soils and a cooler, wetter climate. In addition to large areas in western and southern Bohemia and the Bohemo-Moravian Highlands it includes valley areas in the Carpathians. Some 60–70% of agricultural production is accounted for by stock-farming (cattle, pigs), compared with 40–50% in the maize zone. Other crops grown in this zone are fodder plants, potatoes and the less demanding types of grain (barley, rye).

Hill farming zone

At altitudes above 600m/1970ft, in areas of podzolic soil with cool temperatures (annual average below 6.5°C/43.7°F) and annual rainfall over 800mm/31in. hill farming predominates, with large areas of forest, stock-farming and crops of potatoes, rye, oats and flax sufficient only to meet local needs. The main hill farming areas are at higher altitudes in the fringing hills of Bohemia and in the Carpathians.

Hops

The growing of hops has a long tradition in Bohemia, being referred to as early as the 12th century. Among the main growing areas are the zone of low rainfall (under 450mm/18in. annually) around Žatec in the middle Ohře valley and the Labe (Elbe) valley between Mělník and Litoměřice.

Fish-farming

Fish-farming (carp) is also long established. It is concentrated in the basins of southern Bohemia with their numerous ponds.

Wine

Viniculture is also of some importance, covering roughly a quarter of domestic wine consumption. The main vine-growing areas are southern Moravia (a continuation of that of Lower Austria) and southern Slovakia, in particular the south-eastern fringe of the Little Carpathians north-east of Bratislava.

There are also small areas of vines on the loess terraces of Mělník in the middle Labe (Elbe) valley and round Litoměřice.

Services Sector

Transport

Thanks to its geographical situation Bohemia has potentially a central position in the transport system of Central Europe. The low hills surrounding the region offer no serious obstacles to traffic, and the Moravian Gates have from time immemorial formed a link between the northern lowlands and the Danube and Mediterranean region: this was the route followed by the "amber road" from the Baltic to the Adriatic.

Railways

The industrial structure of the Bohemian lands (Bohemia, Moravia and Silesia) led to the development of a dense railway network during the 19th century, beginning with the line between Vienna and Brno constructed in 1839 and extended to Olomouc in 1841. Before the First World War this area had the highest railway density in continental Europe after Germany. With good connections to Vienna (Prague to Vienna in 7 hours), to Dresden and Berlin, to Galicia (Cracow, Lvov) and Prussian Silesia (Breslau), the Bohemian lands played a central role in the railway system of Central Europe. Railway development in Slovakia came later and was less comprehensive: its system was directed mainly southward towards the then capital, Budapest, apart from a line between Košice and Starý Bohumín opened in 1872. During the interwar period the problem facing the new state of Czechoslovakia was first to link the Bohemian lands with Slovakia and then to construct new lines in Slovakia for east–west traffic.

After the Second World War the demand for goods transport increased sharply as a result of the breakneck speed of industrialisation in all parts of the country. The modernisation of the railway system, however, made relatively slow progress. The first important main line (Prague–Košice, 700km/435 miles) was electrified only in 1957. Only Slovakia had a younger railway system which was in line with modern requirements.

Bus services

In order to make the railway available for goods traffic the government adopted a policy of developing bus services to carry passenger traffic. Between 1937 and 1974 the proportion of passenger traffic carried by the railways fell from 49.3% to 11.3%, while the proportion carried by buses rose from 14.1% to 43%. Czechoslovakia then had not only the densest railway network in Europe but also one of the densest networks of bus services. Bus traffic per head of population in Czechoslovakia was six times as high as in Austria.

Private cars

As in the other socialist states, private car ownership in Czechoslovakia was far below the level in western Europe, but in this as in other respects

Czechoslovakia took a leading place among the countries of the Eastern bloc.

Roads

The country's low level of car ownership was matched for many years by the inadequacy of the road system, which is less dense in Slovakia than in Bohemia and Moravia. In recent years, however, considerable progress has been made. There is now a motorway between Prague, Brno and Bratislava, with a number of side branches. This stretch of motorway was planned in 1977 as a section of the ring motorway in the Comecon countries, with continuations to Berlin and Budapest.

Inland shipping

The territory of former Czechoslovakia has some 475km/295 miles of inland waterways for goods transport. In addition to the Danube (Dunaj; 172km/107 miles) sections of the Labe (Elbe; from Chvaletice, *c.* 1995 from Pardubice) and the Vltava (between Slapy and Mělník) are used by freight barges. An important type of freight carried on the Labe is brown coal, which is transported by water from the Northern Bohemian coalfield to the Mělník thermal power station and to other power stations in eastern Bohemia. With the opening of the Main–Danube Canal, the last link in the Rhine–Main–Danube waterway from the North Sea to the Black Sea, there is again much discussion of the old project of a Danube–Oder canal, with a link to the Elbe.

The inland state of former Czechoslovakia depended for its overseas traffic on ports in the northern Adriatic (mainly Rijeka, Koper and Trieste) and on German and Polish ports in the Baltic (mainly Szczecin with its free port). Hamburg, still a port of great importance for inland shipping on the lower Elbe (with the extra-territorial Vltava/Moldau port there), is likely in future to handle a larger proportion of the country's overseas trade.

Domestic trade

From the 1950s until 1989 all shops and restaurants in Czechoslovakia were in the public sector. The standard of retail shops and restaurants during this period was similar to that of neighbouring socialist countries, though their numbers in relation to population, at least in the larger towns, particularly in Bohemia and part of Northern Moravia, were higher than, for example, in Poland or Hungary; but southern Moravia and Slovakia, particularly in the south, were no better off than these other countries. From the beginning of 1991 publicly owned shops and restaurants were offered for sale to private persons – though shortage of capital has hampered any rapid or large-scale transfer of retail trade to private ownership.

Trade fairs

In former Czechoslovakia, as in other socialist countries, trade fairs were concentrated in a few towns. The one with the longest tradition was Brno. With its shows devoted to capital goods and consumption goods and numerous specialised exhibitions (chiefly foodstuffs, the restaurant trade, transport, the environment) Brno is one of the leading trade fair towns in Central Europe. Also of some importance are the Chemical Fair in Bratislava and smaller specialised fairs in Prague and Ostrava.

Higher education

The higher educational system is one of the assets inherited from the communist era. Prague had had the Charles University since 1348, but until the communist takeover in 1948 the only universities in Czechoslovakia were those of Brno, Bratislava, Ostrava and Olomouc. Thereafter, particularly during the 1950s, there was a considerable expansion, with the establishment of 18 new universities and colleges of university status. Particular attention was given to Slovakia, which before 1948 had only a university and a college of technology in Bratislava and now has ten universities and colleges of university standard in five different towns. Prague, however, with some 60,000 students in its various higher educational establishments, still occupies a leading place, followed by Bratislava with 40,000 students and Brno with 25,000. These cities are also important centres in the cultural field (theatres, opera houses, concert halls) and in the provision of health services.

Tourism
Spas

What would now be called tourism developed in Czechoslovakia at an early stage and to a high standard. Before the First World War Karlovy Vary (Karlsbad), Mariánské Lázně (Marienbad) and Františkovy Lázně (Franzensbad) in north-western Bohemia were spas with an international reputation. Karlsbad was the largest spa in the Austro-Hungarian monarchy. There were also popular spas at other places in the Ore Mountains (e.g. Teplice) and Krkonoše range (e.g. Špindlerův Mlýn). Visitors to the spas in the "Bohemian triangle" came mainly from Germany and from Vienna. There were also a number of much visited smaller spas in Slovakia: thus the spa towns in the Váh valley, in particular Piešt'any, and the summer resorts at the foot of the High Tatras were favourite resorts of the Hungarian upper classes and the best people from Vienna.
In the interwar period the spas in both Bohemia and Slovakia preserved their attraction, but as a result of the redrawing of political boundaries the Slovakian resorts were now visited mainly by Czechs rather than Hungarians. A busy traffic of one-day excursionists, in both directions, also developed over the German and Austrian frontiers.

Hotel provision

After the communist takeover in 1948 most hotels in Czechoslovakia, as in the other socialist countries, were converted into rest and holiday homes for workers in factories and public organisations. During this period the influx of foreign visitors dried up, replaced by "sociat" and low-price tourism. It was only during the destalinisation and liberalisation of the early sixties that foreign visitors began to return to the famous Czechoslovak spas, at first coming almost entirely from other socialist states. During the seventies and eighties Czechoslovakia thus became the favourite holiday area for visitors from the Eastern bloc, particularly from the German Democratic Republic, Poland and Hungary. By this time there had developed, in addition to the traditional holiday resorts and winter sports areas in the north of Bohemia and the High Tatras, new holiday regions, for example around the numerous new artificial lakes that had been created.
In the early eighties, following a relaxation of frontier formalities and a certain amount of publicity designed to attract bringers of hard currency, the numbers of visitors from the West began to increase, though they were still small in comparison with the great though financially unrewarding influx of visitors from other socialist countries.

Tourist boom since 1989

Following the political transformation of 1989 Czechoslovakia was able to return to its earlier role as one of the main holiday areas in Central Europe. Its great asset, in addition to its scenic beauty and variety, is the rich and relatively well preserved cultural heritage (cities, palaces, castles); its handicaps are the still inadequate tourist infrastructure and the ecological damage it has suffered. Nevertheless a total of 66.2 million foreign tourists visited Czechoslovakia in 1991, almost half of them from Germany.

Privatisation and restitution:
see end of Czech Republic A to Z.

History

Historical Regions

In order to understand the history of the territory of the Czech and Slovak Republics it is advisable to consult a map showing the different regions of which it is made up: see the small-scale map on p. 10.

Czech Lands
Bohemia, Moravia and Moravian Silesia

Slovakia

From west to east three natural geographical units can be distinguished, which as historical regions gave the modern state of Czechoslovakia its name: in the west the Czech Lands (České Země) of Bohemia (Čechy) and Moravia (Morava; including Moravian Silesia) and – sharply divided from the other two regions by the arc of the Carpathians – Slovakia (Slovensko). Each of these areas has its particular form and its own history; and each of them has expanses of agricultural land which have been cultivated since time immemorial and mineral resources (iron, copper, silver, gold) which made them in medieval times the richest regions in Europe. In the 19th and 20th centuries a textile industry based on old hand-weaving traditions and deposits of coal and iron fostered in Bohemia and Moravia an astonishingly well developed industrialisation; and after the Second World War, under the socialist regime, much effort was devoted to enabling Slovakia to achieve a similar level of industrialisation.

Historical Development

Since the old-established city of Prague played a major part in the history of what became Czechoslovakia, further information about the historical development of the country as a whole will be found in the A to Z (Czech Republic) section of this guide under the heading Prague, History. Information about the recent history of Slovakia will be found in the A to Z (Slovak Republic) section under the heading Bratislava, History.

Prehistory

250,000 B.C.

The earliest human remains found on the territory of Czechoslovakia are believed to date from a quarter of a million years ago. With an alternation between the ice ages and periods of subtropical climate in prehistoric Europe, there was no continuous settlement.

30,000 B.C.

It was only in the Late Palaeolithic that Moravia developed into a land of mammoth-hunters, evidenced by finds of carved or inscribed cult objects (female figures and the animals which were the hunters' prey, found at Věstonice, Mikulov, Předmostí near Přerov and other sites).

5000 B.C.

Continuity of settlement, with the first primitive forms of agriculture, is found from the Mesolithic period onwards in three unforested low-lying areas with good soil: on the middle Labe (Elbe) in northern central Bohemia, in the Morava and Dyje valleys in southern Moravia and in the Nitra and Váh valleys in southern Slovakia. The further development of each of the three large historical regions started out from these areas.

2nd millennium B.C.

The areas of settlement gradually extended farther up the river valleys and into western and southern Bohemia in the Berounka and Vltava valleys,

25,000 years old: the Venus of Věstonice ▶

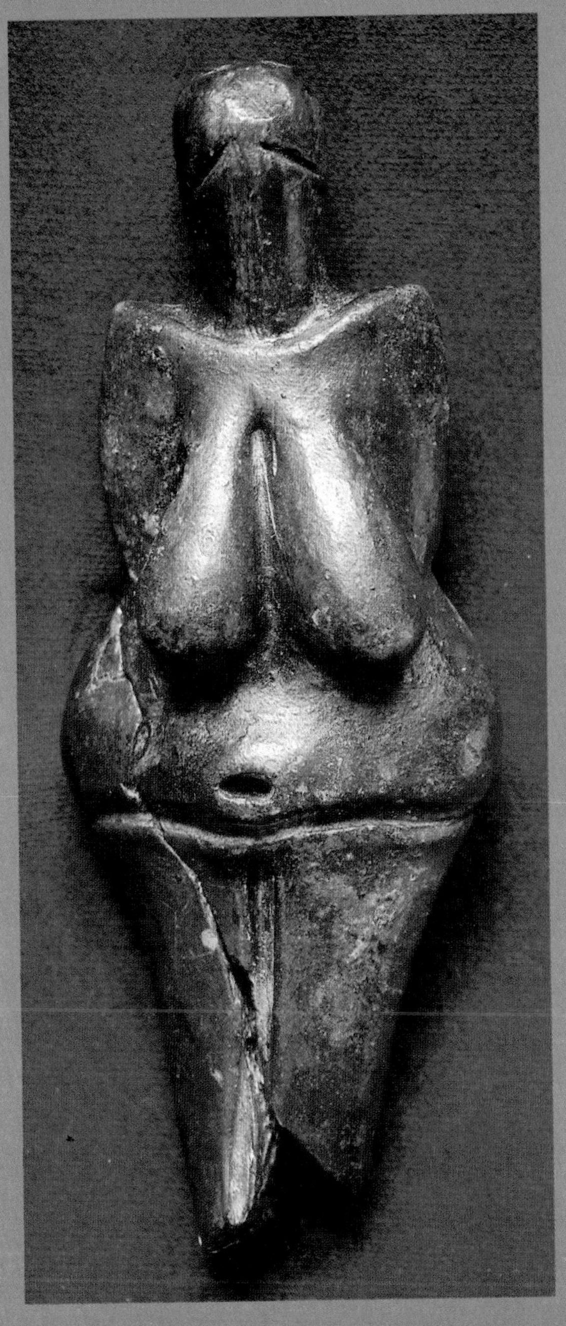

into central Moravia in the valleys of the Morava and its tributaries and into central Slovakia in the valleys of the Váh, Nitra and Hron.

1700–400 B.C. These three regions, extended in this way, evolved a rich culture within the context of developments in Central Europe during the Bronze Age and Early Iron Age, evidence of which has been found on burial sites and in the remains of settlements.

Antiquity and the Age of the Great Migrations

400–100 B.C. At a later stage the peoples who produced these remains can be identified as Celts; that is, members of the great linguistic group which achieved a remarkable degree of economic and political organisation in the last pre-Christian centuries in Western and Central Europe and brought the territories they occupied in Ireland, Britain, France, South Germany, Austria and Czechoslovakia almost to the level of the advanced cultures of the Mediterranean countries. River names of Celtic origin, such as the Isère in France, the Isar in Bavaria and the Jizera in northern Bohemia, still bear witness to this wide spread of a common culture. The name of Bohemia itself comes from a Celtic tribe, the Boii. The Celtic culture of the Vltava and Berounka valleys and other areas, with its fortified strongholds and settlements of urban type, is a special field of study for Czech prehistoric archaeologists.

9 B.C. to A.D. 19 Just before the beginning of the Christian era the Celts were overcome by the Roman advance from the south and pressure from Germanic peoples in the north. In Bohemia and Moravia a great Germanic empire was established, controlled by a league of Germanic chieftains and their followers, known collectively as the Marcomanni, headed by Marbod, who had been educated and trained by the Romans.

1st–5th C. A.D. Even after Marbod's fall the Marcomanni remained a powerful tribe, in partial dependence on Rome. Their areas of settlement in Bohemia and Moravia coincided with those of the earlier culture. They lived side by side with other Germanic tribes, perhaps only as a political ruling class in a process of gradual intermingling and fusion with the Celts. It is not clear why they left these territories; the older theory that they migrated into Bavaria has never been satisfactorily established.

6th century In 527 Slav tribes began to attack the Roman frontier on the Danube, and in the course of the 6th century they moved into the territory of former Czechoslovakia, evidently also coming from the north. This is reflected in the archaeological record, which shows a completely fresh beginning in house types, burial rites and pottery forms ("Prague ware"). Slavs, evidently dependent on the Avars, who were then building up a large empire in south-eastern Europe, also pressed into Slovakia and Moravia from the south-east.

By the end of the 6th century there must have remained in these areas only scanty remnants of Germanic peoples living as peasant farmers, who had little cultural influence on the Slavs and have left little evidence in the form of place-names.

7th century Between 623/624 and 660 a Frankish caravan trader named Samo, probably helped by a defeat inflicted on the Avars by Byzantine forces, gained control of the Slav tribes in Bohemia and part of Moravia. The site of his capital, known in German as Wogastisburg, has never been established – whether in Moravia or, more probably, in Bohemia, or perhaps even in northern Bavaria, in Slav territory in the upper Main and Pegnitz valleys.

Early Middle Ages

8th–9th centuries
791–803 The final entry of these territories into the political world of the Middle Ages was brought about by Charlemagne's policy of conquest.

Charlemagne drove back the Avars and compelled the numerous petty lords in Bohemia to pay tribute, thus preparing the ground for their political amalgamation and Christianisation. The Christian mission in those days always began at the top, with the rulers and their immediate followers. An important advance was made in 845, when fourteen petty Bohemian princes were baptised at Regensburg. 805

Great Moravian Empire 833–906

But even before the Bohemian tribes were brought together in a more powerful whole by one of their petty princes (Mojmir I) the Moravians had already achieved unification and established a large empire. The amalgamation of the tribes of Moravia was followed by the incorporation of Slovakia and then Bohemia, the upper Vistula valley and perhaps also Lusatia. In constant rivalry with the Byzantine Empire, Great Moravia, as it was later called by a Byzantine historian, was finally able to assert its position as an independent political force.
The Moravian Prince Rastislav demonstrated his political mastery in 863 when he summoned two Byzantine scholars, Cyril and Methodius, to organise an independent Moravian church which was also to include the Slavs in Upper Hungary and the Southern Slavs in Slovenia and Croatia; but this first attempt at Ostpolitik, which had Papal support, was unsuccessful, leaving as its only result the use of a Slav language in worship – though not in Czechoslovak territory but among the Bulgarians and in Russia, where it was to be of great cultural importance.

10th century

The Moravian empire, whose remarkable abundance of stone-built churches and large fortified settlements in southern Moravia and southern Slovakia has been revealed in recent years by large-scale excavation, was finally overthrown by the Magyars (Hungarians) in 907. It is not known how much of its cultural and political achievement was preserved in later centuries under Hungarian rule. Thereafter Slovakia remained until 1918 within the Hungarian state which developed from the 10th century onwards.

Přemyslids in Bohemia and Moravia

Following the decline of the Moravian empire Bohemia went its own way, under some influence from its western neighbours. The Czechs, one of the small tribes in the region, contrived, in a development of which nothing is known, to gain control of the whole country under the dynasty of the Přemyslids and to give it their name (Čechy, the Czech name for Bohemia). In the 10th century Prague became the ruler's residence, and its castle, the Hradčany, ranks as one of the oldest princely residences in Northern Europe. During the reign of Boleslav II, in 972–973, Prague Castle also became the seat of a bishop; but here, in contrast to the West, the church long remained in dependence on the Duke.
After alternating expansion plans between Bohemia and Poland Moravia was finally brought under Přemyslid rule, though it soon developed a life of its own under a bishop in Olomouc and Přemyslid collateral lines in Brno, Olomouc and Znojmo.
Political relationships with the German Empire which had just developed out of the Frankish state of the Carolingians varied from time to time according to changes in the balance of power and can be understood only in the light of contemporary conceptions of international law. Strivings for political independence lay behind a family dispute which led to the death in 921 of Ludmilla, mother of the reigning Duke, who soon came to be revered as the country's first Christian martyr. Thereafter her grandson Wenceslas (Václav) allied himself closely with the German kingdom, but also fell victim to anti-German feelings and was murdered by his own brother in 929. After his death he was recognised as the country's patron saint, giving his name to the royal Crown of St Wenceslas which is still preserved in St Vitus's Cathedral in Prague.

Slovakia becomes Hungarian

During the 10th century the Árpád dynasty of Hungary, like the Přemyslids in Bohemia, established a centrally controlled kingdom of which Slovakia became part. At first in southern Slovakia and later in the hilly northern part of the country a closer connection developed with the Magyar kingdom, which, with its own king and its own archbishop, enjoyed a much greater degree of independence from the German Empire than the Bohemian lands. In the struggle with the Pechenegs, a people of Tatar origin, and the White Cumans Slovakia served as a frontier stronghold and an area of settlement for prisoners. After a period of fighting on the frontier Slovakia's western border with Moravia was established only in the 12th century.

11th century

From the 11th century onwards, beginning with the union of Moravia with Bohemia by Duke Břetislav in 1029, the Přemyslids rose steadily from mere tributary princes to the leading place among the princes of the Empire, while maintaining their independence of the German king in domestic policy. Their political dependence as vassals of the German king (1085, Vratislav II crowned by Emperor Henry IV in Mainz as first king of Bohemia) guaranteed an undivided succession for their dynasty in Bohemia and thus saved the country from the fate of Poland in the High Middle Ages. From the 13th century until 1806 the king of Bohemia was an Elector of the Holy Roman Empire.

Foundation of monasteries

An important factor in the development of the country was the foundation of numerous monasteries. The first Benedictine houses were established around the turn of the first millennium, some of them by Italian but most by German monasteries (Sázava, Břevnov, Ostrov, Rajhrad, Klášterní Hradisko, Kladruby). During the 12th and 13th centuries the Benedictines were followed by the "forest-clearing" orders, the Cistercians and Premonstratensians (Strahov, Sedlec, Plasy, Teplá, Zlatá Koruna, Vyšší Brod, etc.).

High Middle Ages

12th–14th centuries

Of decisive importance to the development of the country was a massive increase in economic strength in Western, Central and Northern Europe – an agricultural revolution which has been compared with the industrial revolution of modern times. The old settlement areas were extended into the upper valleys of the rivers and the forests began to be cleared for cultivation. The task soon became too much for native population resources, and experienced agricultural workers seeking land and employment were brought in from both the neighbouring and more distant regions of Germany. The new economic boom promoted the growth of a money economy and the division of labour, while the payment of money rents made land development attractive to noble and ecclesiastical landowners. The dynamic of this early money economy was displayed in many forms. The new settlers were granted special privileges (the Germans in 1173 by Soběslav II) which were later gradually extended to the whole country. The settlers were allowed to establish their own settlements of craftsmen and traders with charters as independent communities, and Bohemia and Moravia were dotted with little towns.

The increased density of population led to a higher cultural level, and by around 1350 Bohemia and Moravia were at least equal in this respect to their immediate neighbours. The earlier tendency towards a decline in cultural achievement from west to east was thus no longer in evidence. Bohemia and Moravia now became bilingual (Czech and German). The bringing into cultivation of the less rewarding land in the peripheral wooded hills and the organisation of urban life were predominantly the work of German settlers (1198–1230, foundations of towns in the reign of Otakar I; from 1241, settlements in the Špis area in Slovakia).

The German Emperors had repeatedly recognised the Přemyslid rulers' right to the title of king, and in 1212 this was formally confirmed.
The Bohemian kings drew rich revenues from the country's silver-mines, particularly those at Jihlava and later at Kutná Hora. This wealth enabled

Otakar II (1251–78) to extend Přemyslid rule southwards. For 25 years he ruled Austria, and for part of that period Styria, Carinthia and Carniola as far as the Adriatic; then in 1278 he was killed at Dürrnkrut in Lower Austria in a battle with rebellious nobles, the Hungarians and the German king Rudolf of Habsburg. For five years Otakar's son Wenceslas (Václav) II ruled Poland as well, and his grandson Wenceslas (Václav) III was seeking to gain the Polish crown when he was assassinated and the dynasty unexpectedly became extinct (1306).

End of Přemyslid dynasty (1306)

Luxembourg dynasty

Bohemian ambitions for expansion were soon afterwards pursued by the Luxembourg dynasty (1310–1437), a noble family from western Germany who ruled Bohemia for over a century (Kings John, Charles IV, Wenceslas IV and Sigismund). From 1346 they were also kings of Germany and from 1387 kings of Hungary.

The Luxembourg rulers added Silesia to their Bohemian territories, and in the middle of the 14th century Charles IV made Prague a capital city of European standing. The "golden city", now the see of an archbishop (1344) and the seat of the first university in Central Europe (1348), became one of the most beautiful cities of its time, with magnificent works of Gothic architecture (St Vitus's Cathedral, Charles Bridge with its towers; Karlštejn Castle in surrounding area), painting (panel paintings, frescos in Karlštejn Castle, etc.) and sculpture (busts in triforium of St Vitus's Cathedral, St George Fountain).

Development in Slovakia

The extension of settlement was also of great importance for the development of Slovakia. It began in the 10th century with the withdrawal into the mountain valleys in face of the Magyar advance and was carried on in the 12th century by settlers from neighbouring countries, including many Germans.

The great Tatar incursion in 1241–42 hit Slovakia particularly hard, after the invasion the development of the country was actively pursued, with the same organisational forms as in the rest of eastern Central Europe. Here too a considerable network of towns was built up along the old trade routes to the south-east. The German mining towns with special privileges supplied most of Hungary's output of gold, which far exceeded that of all other European countries. In parallel with Bohemia under the Luxembourg dynasty, Hungary under its Angevin kings enjoyed an economic and cultural upsurge, and the Slovakian towns, which soon became centres of attraction for ambitious Slovak settlers, produced a great flowering of Late Gothic art.

15th–16th centuries

Hussite wars (1419–35)

The Hussite revolution in Bohemia arose out of a European movement for the reform of the wealthy Church and for the participation of ordinary citizens in the country's political life, hitherto dominated by the nobility. Jan Hus, Rector of Prague University and a popular preacher who had been influenced by the views of the English reforming theologian John Wycliffe, was condemned by the Council of Constance in 1415 to death at the stake for his reforming zeal. Four years later a movement aimed at the improvement of the world by violent means, starting from Prague and the densely populated region of southern Bohemia, spread throughout the country. In fifteen years of bitter fighting for freedom of conscience, the right of resistance in matters of faith, the participation of the lower orders in political activity and the fraternal equality of all men, but also for the unity of the Czech nation, this brought up for the first time the question of differences of belief within the Roman Catholic church. In spite of all the suffering and devastation, this period ranks, in virtue of its objectives, as a heroic age in Czech history. Recent Czech research has laid emphasis on the chiliastic attitudes and communistic ideals of the members – mostly small peasant farmers – of the brotherhoods and military "field communities" who developed under the leadership of Jan Žižka into a formidable

military force based in the newly-founded town of Tábor (named after the Biblical Mount Tabor). Similar views were given wide circulation by the writer Alois Jirásek (1851–1930) in his novels and chronicles.
The Hussite revolution is of particular importance in a European context as the first revolution in class-based western society, the beginning of a revolutionary chain which was continued, with variations reflecting different historical conditions, in Germany (1519), the Netherlands (1578), Britain (1649) and France (1789).
The Hussite movement brought losses to the Germans in Bohemia; but in general the conflict was mainly over religious rather than national interests, and there were active German Hussites both inside and outside Bohemia. Only certain parts of Moravia were affected, and the movement was brought to Slovakia only at a later stage by scattered survivors from the Hussite wars.

After an agreement with the Church at the Council of Basle (1436) which was not ratified by the Pope George of Poděbrady (Jiří z Poděbrad), a Czech noble who was leader of the Utraquists (a Hussite sect), sought to restore the power of the monarchy, first as Governor and Regent for the heir to the throne, the Habsburg prince Ladislas (1439–58), and later as king (1458–71).

Habsburg rule

After George's death the crown fell by election to the Jagiellonian dynasty of Poland, which also acquired Hungary, and then to the Habsburgs. As a result Austria, Bohemia, Moravia and Hungary were united for the next 400 years in a single great empire.

Secularisation

The Hussite revolution, which had been little felt in the Poohří region around Cheb, the Plzeň area (Plzeňsko) and other frontier territories, led for the first time in Europe to the confiscation of Church property by the civil authorities, the rise of the lesser nobility, the burghers of the towns and the peasantry, the development of utopian ideas on social organisation and the transformation of strivings for necessary reform, in the absence of any political solution, into fierce revolutionary tensions. While after the revolution the idea of the "new class" was established, at the end of the day the higher nobility of Bohemia and Moravia remained in control. Whether Hussite or Catholic, they gained from the secularisation of Church property and strengthened their hold on the election of the king. From 1526 (Ferdinand I), however, they came up against the power of the Habsburg empire.

Art and culture

During the early part of the 15th century, as a result of war and economic recession, Bohemian art suffered a decline. At the same time there was a shift of interest to literature, in forms which served the purposes of the revolution (series of pictures, journalism in Latin and Czech, popular songs). The period of consolidation in the second half of the century found expression in the patronage of art by kings, nobles and wealthy burghers, who commissioned work by Matthias Rejsek and the two South German artists Benedikt Ried and Hans Spiess (completion of St Barbara's Church in Kutná Hora, Powder Tower and Vladislav Hall in Prague Castle).

Slovakia

Around the turn of the 15th century Slovakia was affected by social unrest in the kingdom of Hungary which can be compared in some respects with the Hussite revolution. A marshalling of forces for a crusade against the Turks developed into a peasant war (1514) directed against the high nobility and the prelates, and a decade later the men of the Slovakian mining towns rose in a rebellion associated with the rise of Lutheran doctrines and the peasant war in Germany. During this conflict, which was aggravated by the unresolved struggle for power between the lesser nobility, the high nobility and the monarchy, there occurred the long awaited Turkish advance, in the course of which the young king and most of the nobility of his Hungarian kingdom were killed. Slovakia became a place of refuge for some of the Hungarian nobles, and thereafter was the heartland of Hungary until the lost territory was recovered by the Habsburgs at the end of the 17th century.

Rise of Protestantism

Meanwhile in Bohemia there had come into being around a lay hermit called Petr Chelčický, quietly and unobtrusively, a community derived from the Hussite reform movement which sought to live on the pattern of Early Christian communism, in total brotherly love. It organised itself and grew into the Community of Bohemian-Moravian Brethren (1447–58), which was tolerated in eastern Bohemia and Moravia, mainly by noble landowners; indeed members of the community, with a reputation as reliable workers, were encouraged by landowners to settle on their land. The Community of Brethren and the Utraquist beliefs (communion in both kinds, liturgical texts in Czech, priests without possessions) which had become established since the Compact of Basle in 1436 soon became associated with Lutheranism, which was brought into the country by the influx of new settlers from Saxony and the establishment of new mining towns in the Ore Mountains, notably Jáchymov (St Joachimsthal), whose silver coins (Joachimsthaler, or thaler for short; hence the word dollar) had a European reputation. The Bohemian towns sided with the German Protestants in the War of the League of Schmalkalden (1547), and as a result were punished and lost their influence and economic power.

Early Modern Times

Rudolphine period

The Emperor Rudolph II (1576–1612) once again moved the capital to Prague, where it remained for thirty years. This Rudolphine period, though of great importance in the history of art (the "Bohemian Renaissance": palaces of nobility, imperial collections, Jewish Town Hall, etc.), was a time of political apathy which led to a further Bohemian revolution – the rising of 1618, sparked off by the famous "defenestration" of imperial officials. The freedom of worship enjoyed by the Protestants was the occasion for the resistance of the nobility; but the nobles lacked the support of the towns, which they had themselves treated as rivals, and the help of the great mass of the population. The attempt to form an alliance with German Protestantism and with Britain by the election as king of Frederick, Elector of the Palatinate (the "Winter King", 1619), who had married the daughter of James I of England and VI of Scotland, was a failure. The revolution was defeated by Habsburg forces and the army of the German Catholic princes in the battle of the White Mountain outside Prague in 1620.

Defenestration of Prague (1618)

Thirty Years' War (1618–48)

This led in Germany to the Thirty Years' War and in Bohemia to the violent Catholic Counter-Reformation and the victory of the centralist Habsburg kingdom. The social consequences were far-reaching – the destruction of the power of the nobility, the confiscation of two-thirds of landed property in Bohemia and half in Moravia, the emigration of 30,000 Protestant families). Thereafter Bohemia declined from a kingdom into a province. Against this background two figures stand out all the more prominently: the educationist and philosopher of the State Jan Amos Comenius (Komenský; 1592–1670), bishop of the Moravian Brethren in Poland, Germany and, in exile, the Netherlands; and his fellow-countryman Albrecht von Wallenstein (Waldstein, Valdštejn; 1583–1634): see Famous People.

The Age of Absolutism

17th century

Czech historians refer to the Baroque period, considered from nationalist, Habsburg or anti-ecclesiastical points of view, as a period of darkness (*Temno:* cf. the novels of Alois Jirásek). But this is a very one-sided judgment. During this period Bohemia, like most other countries in Western and Central Europe, was going through a phase of royal absolutism without which the maturity of modern society and the rational organisation of government would have been inconceivable.

Counter-Reformation

The Counter-Reformation was accompanied by a flowering of aristocratic and ecclesiastical art and architecture in the style known as Bohemian Baroque which has left a magnificent legacy in towns, palaces and pilgrimage churches throughout the country; and the hymns and religious writings of the period show no decline in literary skill.

After the loss of more than a third of the population as a result of war and plague the economy began to revive in the second half of the century thanks to an influx of craftsmen from neighbouring German lands and to agricultural redevelopment. For the peasant farmers at the bottom of the social structure, however, this was a bad time, though there were regional differences. The new landed nobility, many of them of foreign origin, actively pursued the trend which had begun to develop in the 16th century towards the establishment of large farms on which the peasants were tied to the land; and a wave of peasant risings around 1670 calling for the Emperor's protection against the landlords altered nothing.

18th–19th centuries

The 18th century gradually began to relieve the peasants' lot, partly through the Emperor's concern with population policy, partly as a result of economic development. "Manufactories" (large workshops, still without steam power) making textiles, glass, porcelain and other products formed the basis of a typical industrial landscape, particularly in the wooded and over-populated border areas. The abolition of serfdom in 1780 gave the rural population freedom of movement and thus enabled them to seek employment in the new manufactories.

During the reign of Maria Theresa, who was crowned as Queen of Bohemia in Prague in 1743, the loss of almost the whole of Silesia (1745) after 400 years in the Austrian Empire greatly increased the importance of Bohemia and Moravia to the industrialisation of Austria. Around 1900 some 60% of the country's output of steel came from Bohemia and Moravia, which also had some 80% of its mechanical looms, most of Austria's glass production, much of its engineering industry and most of its brown coal and hard coal. By 1910 only 36% of the working population of Bohemia and Moravia were employed in agriculture – a proportion found at that time only in highly industrialised countries – while in Slovakia the position was exactly reversed, with only 35% of the population not employed in agriculture.

Battle of Austerlitz (1805)

The "Battle of the Three Emperors" at Austerlitz (Slavkov u Brna) in southern Moravia on December 2nd 1805 ended in Napoleon's victory over the allied armies of the Austrian Emperor Francis I and the Russian Tsar Alexander I. The subsequent armistice negotiations led to the Peace of Pressburg (Bratislava) on December 26th 1805.

Slovakia

Slovakia as a whole suffered from the general Hungarian economic backwardness, due partly to the Habsburg economic policy of "internal colonialism" and partly to the greater economic immobility of the large Hungarian estates. The only progressive element in the economy, and that only in a small area, was the mining industry of Slovakia. As late as the first half of the 19th century the despair of the peasants led to risings (1831). As a result the process of political democratisation in more recent times followed a different course in Slovakia than in Bohemia and Moravia.

Awakening of national consciousness among Czechs and Slovaks

The awakening of national consciousness among Czechs and Slovaks occurred within the context of a general European movement, but it gave rise to problems quite different from those of Western Europe. The linguistic nation was not formed by the state, as it was, for example, in France, but had to develop in opposition to the state. Moreover the growth of national feeling meant the end of a centuries-old community of existence with Germans and Hungarians, now felt to be representatives of an alien national state with a policy of Germanisation or Magyarisation (1876, abolition of self-government in the German-speaking towns of the Spiš area in eastern Slovakia). In contrast to Poland and Hungary the national movement of the Czechs and Slovaks developed without the help of an

aristocratic upper class: the impetus came from the educated middle classes. As a result it was much slower to develop in Slovakia with its predominantly peasant population.
The creation of a national consciousness in Bohemia and Moravia developed out of the supra-national and largely German-influenced educational programme of the Enlightenment (K. H. Seibt, A. G. Meissner, F. Kindermann) by way of a "patriotic" school of historians (G. Dobner, A. Voigt), the philological restoration of the Czech language (J. Dobřovský') and literary achievement (K. H. Mácha) – a powerful impulse being given to the process by the work of the great Czech historian František Palacký – to achieve its first political expression in the 1848 revolution.
The Austrian constitution of 1848 guaranteed all peoples within the state the "inviolability of their nationality and language".

Consequences of the 1848 revolution

Over the next fifty years there developed, amid much intellectual discussion, a remarkable disengagement of economic and cultural ties between Germans and Czechs, particularly marked in Bohemia but also observable in Moravia with its much more mixed population. A treaty providing for electoral reform with equality of rights did not bring about the desired effect, but later offered a model for the minority problems of other states. Domestic policy in Bohemia was powerless to deal with the new national consciousness of the different groups. Both sides now embarked on a massive effort of political education, using the press, literature, the theatre and economic organisations for the first time to bring about a wide public interest in political matters.
The Slovak national movement now also came to the fore for the first time as a political force. The decision was now taken to take the Central Slovak dialect as the future linguistic standard (L'udovít Štúr), following earlier contributions to Czech literature by the Slovaks Ján Hollý and Ján Kollár. The Protestant middle classes and the Catholic clergy formed an educated upper class of the nationalist movement – a role which they continued to perform into recent times.
In spite of the first strikes and attempts to organise the workers in the years before 1848 the revolution did not become involved in the social problems of the industrial proletariat. A land reform law was introduced for the benefit of the peasants, but in general the political programme was one of middle-class liberalism. In the 1860s, however, a workers' movement came into being among German textile workers in the industrial region in northern and western Bohemia, and a little later there were the first beginnings of what became the Christian Social movement. Both of these continued to influence the wider workers' movement under the Austro-Hungarian Dual Monarchy which was established in 1867. The Social Democratic party, which after the introduction of universal suffrage in 1907 developed out of these first beginnings into the strongest political party, was unable to settle the problem of nationalities. In both nations "bourgeois" nationalism remained predominant (Pan-Slavist movement, Pan-German League).

Battle of Königgrätz (1866)

In the Austro-Prussian War the Austrians were decisively defeated by the Prussians in the battle of Königgrätz (Hradec Králové) on July 3rd 1866, and Austria left the German Confederation.

Division of Prague University

The Charles University was now divided into a Czech and a German half.

Czechoslovakia in the 20th Century

First World War (1914–18)

During the First World War the Czech population in general took an opportunist line, in spite of individual acts of resistance and the formation of a Volunteer Legion supporting Russian, French and Italian forces.
The formation of an independent state in historical Bohemian territory, combined with the ethnically related region of Slovakia (1916, establishment of a Czechoslovak National Council) and a small area in the western

Ukraine ("Carpatho-Russia") was achieved during the final phase of the war by Tomáš Garrigue Masaryk (1850–1937) and Edvard Beneš (1884–1948), then in exile in the West. Under the treaty of Pittsburgh (May 30th 1918) the Slovaks were promised self-government within the Czechoslovak state which was now to be founded (though they did not in fact achieve it). The Czechoslovak National Council in Paris formed a government with Masaryk as President and Benes as foreign minister (October 14th 1918).

First Czechoslovak Republic

On October 28th 1918, in Prague, Masaryk was proclaimed President of the first Czechoslovak Republic (ČSR). A German protest demanding self-determination, initiated by the German Social Democratic party, was forcibly repressed (March 4th 1919; 54 dead). Nevertheless the new Republic made a promising start and contrived, in spite of some measures showing national partiality (land reform, 1919; language law, 1926), to overcome the mistrust of the German parties by its economic achievements, and brought into the government members of the Christian Social party, the Farmers' League and later the Social Democratic party. In face of these active policies the representatives of a narrow nationalist programme remained in a minority in the German population. Finally the Roman Catholic Slovak People's Party also joined the government. For a time, therefore, under a government led by Antonín Švehla, there were prospects of a détente in the nationality problem. But Švehla, a powerful personality and a prudent politician, was compelled by a severe illness to retire from political life in 1929, and thereafter the world economic crisis plunged Czechoslovakia into an insoluble complex of national and social problems.

In a predominantly lower middle class country, however, these problems led to disputes between the different nationalities rather than to class war. The Communist Party of Czechoslovakia (KPČ), led from 1929 by Klemens Gottwald, gained only 10% of the votes in elections in 1929 and 1935. Instead there were signs of right-wing dissatisfaction with the state, less marked in a Czech Fascist movement but stronger among the Slovaks and Germans. Although the dangerous pan-German policies of the German National Socialist Workers' Party had been banned in 1932, before Hitler's seizure of power, the hostility to the Czechoslovak state of the German population – who, partly because of their industrial structure, had a higher rate of unemployment than the Czechs (18% against 3%) – was reflected in the flood of new recruits to Konrad Henlein's Sudeten German Heimatfront (which in 1935 became the Sudeten German Party). By 1935 it had become, by a small margin, the largest party in the country, with some two-thirds of all German votes. In spite of the financial help it received from Nazi Germany it seems to have begun to accept Hitler's policy directives only towards the end of 1937.

In 1937 Czechoslovakia, with Milan Hodža, a Slovak, as prime minister and Edvard Beneš, a Czech, as President, missed a final opportunity to legitimise the younger generation of leaders of the three German parties which accepted the Czechoslovak state (G. Hacker, W. Jaksch, H. Schütz) by political successes. Czech foreign policy also foundered on the nationality problem, in which Hitler saw a basis for political expansion, unimpeded by the appeasement policy of the western powers.

Munich agreement (1938)

After the Munich agreement (September 29th 1938) providing for the incorporation of the German-populated border areas of Czechoslovakia in the Nazi Reich, Hitler forcibly established a German "Protectorate" in the remaining territory of Bohemia and Moravia, while Poland and Hungary "corrected" their frontiers with Czechoslovakia.
Some 2000 émigrés from Germany who had sought refuge in Czechoslovakia and in spite of the absence of any formal right of asylum had found help there (leaders of the German Socialist Party; Otto Strasser; Thomas Mann; Theodor Lessing, murdered in Marienbad in 1933; Jewish refugees; German communists) were able for the most part to escape to the West, and

some 5000 Sudeten Germans, mostly Social Democrats, also went into exile. They were unable, however, to induce President Beneš, who had emigrated to the United States in 1938, to take part in constructive cooperative action.

Slovakia, which had been since October 6th 1938 a self-governing state within Czechoslovakia, now broke away and, as a separate state under German protection, achieved a limited degree of independence under the leadership of the Catholic prelate Jozef Tiso (March 14th 1939).

Second World War (1939–45)

In the "Reich Protectorate of Bohemia and Moravia" established on March 15th 1939, after the carefully planned repression of the Czech intelligentsia, with the eventual objective of assimilating the Czechs in accordance with Nazi race policy, and the deportation or killing of "inferior" races, resistance had grown, particularly following the brutal measures carried out by the "Reich Protector" Reinhard Heydrich. The killing of Heydrich by a Czech émigré on May 26th 1942 was followed by the Lidice massacre on June 10th 1942.

Partisan activity had significant effects only in Slovakia (autumn 1944). Altogether a total of probably more than 30,000 Czechs and Slovaks fell victim to political persecution or lost their lives in the resistance movement and some 200,000 Czech, Slovak and German Jews, after being herded together in the Theresienstadt ghetto, were murdered in the Nazi extermination camps.

In London during the Second World War Edvard Beneš formed the Czechoslovak National Committee (autumn 1939), secured the abrogation of the Munich agreement by Parliament (1942), achieved British recognition of his government in exile and finally, under an agreement with Stalin, obtained Soviet support for the re-establishment of Czechoslovakia within its old frontiers (1943). At the end of the war he gained the assurance that none of the great powers would oppose the mass expulsion of Germans from Czechoslovak territory.

Postwar period (1945–48)

In April 1945, Edvard Beneš, with the advancing Red Army in Košice (Eastern Slovakia), took over the government of the restored Czechoslovak state, with a cabinet under the strong influence of the Czech and Slovak communists (proclamation of the Košice Programme, April 5th 1945). In subsequent months an estimated 2.5 to 3 million Germans were expelled to Germany, frequently involving outrages which cost many thousand lives.

After careful preparation the Communist Party succeeded by the threat of civil war in forming a cabinet majority just before a general election. A few days later, in mysterious circumstances, the foreign minister Jan Masaryk, the popular son of the first President of the Republic, fell to his death from the window of his office. Thereafter President Beneš retired into the background, resigned his office and died a few months later.

People's Republic (1948–60)

Under the constitution of May 9th 1948 the Czechoslovak Republic became a "unified people's democratic republic". Thousands of "unreliable" officials were dismissed (a quarter of a million of them are said to have spent some time in "re-education camps"), industry was transferred to state ownership, and in subsequent years almost the whole of agriculture was collectivised (state farms, agricultural production cooperatives).
Nominally non-communist parties were permitted under the 1948 and 1960 constitutions to exist, but after the reshaping of the parliamentary system on the Soviet model power lay with the Communist Party of Czechoslovakia (KPČ). Many Czechs and Slovaks now began to leave the country and seek refuge in the West.

ČSSR (1960–68)

The new constitution of 1960 transformed the people's republic into a socialist republic, the Czechoslovak Socialist Republic (ČSSR). Under the new regime the Catholic church was treated more harshly than the smaller Protestant groups; parish priests were required to take an oath of loyalty, while the higher clergy were mostly imprisoned or put under house arrest, monasteries and convents were dissolved and their members interned.

At first many of the Czech and Slovak intelligentsia and party members worked willingly, and indeed with enthusiasm, in the building of socialism. In spite of the low level of trade in the economically important sectors and the defects of economic planning there were some successes in the building up and redirection of industry, even in the former German-populated areas. Finally, however, the low standard of living and the distortion of the economy to meet Soviet economic needs drove Czechoslovakia, a country with the capacity for high economic achievement, to look for a new way forward. The mood for change was also felt by the more open-minded people who realised that the creation of a "new socialist man" was a utopian ideal.

Intimations of a political thaw (1961 onwards)

The Soviet destalinisation of 1956 had only rhetorical effects, but only five years later there were intimations of a certain political "thaw", which did not amount to a rejection of Marxism but sought to reform it. Criticism of the older generation of party functionaries and a rebellion against any doctrinaire approach initiated a development which under the leadership of Alexander Dubček, a Slovak party official, sought after two decades of class struggle to offer all citizens equal rights and security under the law: this was to be "socialism with a human face". The aim was also to reduce the country's ideological, economic and political dependence on the Soviet Union. Soon wide circles of the population, stimulated by writers, artists, historians and journalists, threw off the political apathy in which they had been sunk for so many years.

Crushing of the **"Prague Spring" (1968)**

These new beginnings were crushed when Czechoslovakia was invaded by Warsaw Pact forces on August 20th and 21st 1968. The capitulation of the Czechoslovak President, Ludvik Svoboda, in Moscow (August 26th–27th), the replacement of Alexander Dubček by Gustav Husák and the tightening-up of party discipline, however, did not at once produce the desired "normalisation". But intellectual life was crippled, and the rebellious intellectuals who were now deprived of employment were not replaced by a new generation.

Federative state (from 1969)

In spite of the removal of the reformers the constitutional results of the Prague Spring were preserved for reasons of domestic policy. The centralised Republic now became a Federation (October 27th 1969) consisting of a Czech federative state (ČSR: Bohemia and Moravia) and a Slovak federative state (SSR), each with its own parliament and government in Prague and Bratislava, with a federal parliament and government in Prague. A further constitutional reform (December 20th 1970), however, still showed centralising tendencies.
In 1968 the change to a "state for the whole people" was proclaimed. This implied that there would be no further discrimination against the "bourgeois" population and that the Communist Party's monopoly of power was ended – though in theoretical discussions the necessity of the "dictatorship of the proletariat" was still stressed.

Charter 77

A group concerned with citizens' rights of which the writer Václav Havel was a leading member published their "Charter 77" on January 1st 1977, calling in particular for the right to freedom of opinion which was guaranteed in the current constitution. Thereafter those who signed the Charter were subjected to relentless persecution by the all-powerful state apparatus.

Recent Developments in Headlines

(For details see Prague and Bratislava, History)

First demonstrations critical of the regime. 1988

After the brutal repression of demonstrators by state security forces Civic Forum, an organisation aimed at securing democracy, is founded (November 19th 1989), under the leadership of Václav Havel. **1989**
The Velvet Revolution leads to the formation of a "government of national understanding" (December 9th 1989) in which, for the first time, the communists are in a minority. "Velvet Revolution"
After the retirement of Gustav Husák Václav Havel is elected President (December 29th 1989).

The ČSSR is renamed the Czechoslovak Federative Republic (ČSFR; March 29th 1990), a name which is soon afterwards changed, on the insistence of the Slovaks, to the Czech and Slovak Federative Republic. **ČSFR** (1990)
Free parliamentary elections (June 8th 1990) are won in both the Czech and Slovak Republics by the civic rights parties, who form the core of the new "Government of National Sacrifice" (June 27th 1990).
The Federal Assembly of the ČSFR re-elects Václav Havel as President (July 5th 1990).

In elections on June 7th the Democratic Citizens' Party (ODS) in the Czech Republic and the Movement for a Democratic Slovakia (HZDS) in Slovakia win most votes. In the Presidential election (July 3rd) Václav Havel fails to win a majority and resigns (July 20th). 1992
On August 27th the Czech prime minister and his Slovak counterpart agree on the dissolution of the Czechoslovak Federation into two independent states on January 1st 1993. There is much controversy in both the Federal Parliament and the Czech and Slovak parliament about the arrangements for the separation.
On November 7th Alexander Dubček (b. 1921), a leading figure in the Prague Spring, dies from injuries received in a traffic accident.
The Federal Parliament passes the controversial law on the splitting-up of the Federation at its third attempt (November 25th), avoiding the necessity of a referendum on the division of the country. It signals the dissolution of the Czechoslovak state founded in 1918 in the clause: "The Czech and Slovak Federative Republic will cease to exist after December 31st 1992".

With effect from January 1st 1993 the Czech and Slovak Federative Republic gives place to the Czech Republic and the Slovak Republic (Slovakia). **1993 Establishment of Czech and Slovak Republics**
On January 26th Václav Havel is elected first President of the Czech Republic in Prague, and on February 15th Michal Kováč is elected first President of the Slovak Republic.

Famous People

This section contains brief biographies of notable people who were born, lived or died in Bohemia, Moravia, Moravian Silesia or Slovakia.

Tomáš Bat'a
Industrialist
(1876–1932)

The Bat'as were a family of shoemakers who had been settled in Zlín since 1580. Tomáš Bat'a, son of Antonín Bat'a (1844–1905), attended the local school and then learned the shoemaker's trade, starting from the bottom, as an apprentice in his father's workshop. After taking over the family business he set about enlarging and developing the original small workshop. A brief period of work in the United States introduced him to American methods of working and the use of machinery. After his return he sought to enlist the cooperation of his work-force in reducing production costs by the application of rational methods of production and – for the first time in Europe – the participation of the workers in profits. As a result the factory in Zlín grew in the course of time to become the largest of its kind in Europe, eventually employing some 20,000 workers. The town of Zlín now enjoyed an economic boom, with modern factories and new housing developments. In the years before the First World War and in the early postwar years Bat'a built factories and shops in many countries throughout the world; in Europe the main concentration was in Switzerland.
When the Bat'a factories and shops in Czechoslovakia were nationalised after the communist takeover in 1948 Tomáš Bat'a's son Tomáš J. Bat'a continued to run the company's other operations from Canada. The firm is now headed by his grandson Thomas G. Bat'a.

Ralph Benatzky
Composer
(1884–1957)

The well-known operetta composer Ralph (Rudolph) Benatzký was born in Moravské Budějovice, the son of a conductor. He studied in Munich, and later lived and worked in Berlin and Vienna. In 1938 he emigrated to Switzerland and in 1940 moved to Hollywood, from which he returned to Switzerland in 1948.
Ralph Benatzký was famed in particular for his pop and satirical songs, which showed a masterly command of melody and rhythm. His popular stage works – more than a hundred in all, together with music for films – ranged from the traditional operetta to revues and musical comedies, and helped to form the musical taste of the period.
Ralph Benatzký died in Zurich in 1957.

Edvard Beneš
Politician
(1884–1948)

Edvard Beneš, born in Kožl'any in 1884, was one of the dominant figures in the Czechoslovak Republic and also one of the most tragic, exerting an influence on the development of Czechoslovakia which extended beyond the bounds of the country.
In 1909 Beneš became professor of political economy in Prague University, where along with Tomáš Garrigue Masaryk (see entry), whose closest collaborator he became, he worked for the establishment of a Czechoslovak state. In 1917–18 he was Secretary-General of the Czechoslovak National Council in Paris, which on September 28th 1918 was recognised by the Allies as the provisional government of the Czechoslovak Republic. After the foundation of the new state Beneš became foreign minister, a post he retained until 1935. During the peace negotiations in Paris he was his country's chief delegate. As foreign minister (and in 1921–22 as prime minister) he sought to defend the new order in Central and South-Eastern Europe created by the peace treaties through a close relationship with France, the "Little Entente" (an alliance between Czechoslovakia, Yugoslavia and Romania, 1921–22) and an alliance with the Soviet Union (1935). Beneš belonged to the left-wing Czechoslovak National Socialist Party (Československá Národní Socialistická Strana, ČNSS), which was represented in all governments between 1918 and 1938. After the death of

Masaryk in 1935 Beneš succeeded him as President of Czechoslovakia. Under the Munich agreement of 1938 Czechoslovakia was compelled to cede its German-speaking border territories to Germany, whereupon Beneš resigned (October 5th 1938) and soon afterwards went into exile. After the outbreak of the Second World War he formed the Czechoslovak National Committee in London, and on July 23rd 1940 this was recognised by the Allies as the provisional government of Czechoslovakia. On December 11th 1940 Beneš appointed a State Council to serve as a parliament in exile. This was accompanied by the formation of a government in exile, which organised Czechoslovak forces to fight alongside the Allies.
After the defeat of Germany Beneš resumed his office as President of Czechoslovakia. He was unsuccessful, however, in preventing the takeover of power by the Communist Party and was compelled in 1948 to resign. Thereafter he lost all influence on political events in his country. He died on September 3rd 1948 at Sezimovo Ústí.

Tycho Brahe
Astronomer
(1546–1601)

The famous Danish astronomer Tycho (Tyge) Brahe was born in Kastrup, in what was then the Danish province of Skåne in southern Sweden. In 1567 King Frederick II of Denmark enabled him to build two observatories on the island of Ven in the Sound, where for 20 years he observed and studied the planets and fixed stars. In 1572 he discovered a new star (a "nova") in the constellation of Cassiopeia. In 1599 the Emperor Rudolph summoned him to the post of court astronomer in Prague, where he was able by improved methods of observation to increase the accuracy of his measurements. Brahe ranks as the leading astronomer of the period before the invention of the telescope. His observations of the positions of planets and in particular his observations of Mars prepared the way for the work of Johannes Kepler, whom he induced to come to Prague in 1600 and to whom he bequeathed his notes on the laws governing the orbits of the planets.
Tycho Brahe died in Prague on October 24th 1601. His tomb is in the Týn Church.

Čapek brothers:
Josef Čapek
Painter and writer
(1887–1945)

The brothers Josef Čapek (born in Hronov) and Karel Čapek (born in Malé Svatoňovice) originally worked together as writers. Later Josef illustrated books, particularly for his brother Karel, producing work which set the standard for modern book illustration. Among Josef Čapek's writings were the deeply pessimistic novel "Shadow of the Ferns", "Insect Life" (written jointly with his brother Karel), essays and articles. As a painter he was at first under the influence of Expressionism and Cubism, and later painted genre scenes of city life with a strong social commitment. As a confirmed pacifist and opponent of the German occupation he produced political caricatures and pictures and, after he was sent to Belsen concentration camp, pictures of life in the camp. He died in Belsen in April 1945.

Karel Čapek
Writer
(1890–1938)

After the early books written jointly with his brother, Karel Čapek developed into a successful writer of works of social criticism who depicted in his essays and novels, with delicate irony and grotesque invention, the world of the "little man". All his work is imbued with the spirit of humanism and with warnings of the rise of fascism. Karel Čapek also wrote plays, travel books, books about animals, children's books and much journalism. His reputation was also enhanced by his biography of Masaryk.
Karel Čapek died in Prague on December 25th 1938.

Giacomo Girolamo Casanova
Adventurer and writer
(1725–98)

The Italian adventurer and writer Giacomo Girolamo Casanova, who granted himself the noble title of Chevalier de Seingalt, was born in Venice. He travelled widely throughout Europe in the service of various masters, spending some time at the courts of Frederick the Great, the Emperor Joseph II and the Empress Catherine II. His irregular wandering life brought him into contact with many of the great figures of his day, including Voltaire and the Swiss physician and writer Albrecht von Haller; but since he was constantly involved in quarrels and disputes he was frequently compelled to move on. While in Venice in 1755 he was accused of atheism and thrown into prison, from which he made a spectacular escape in the following year.

Giacomo Casanova

J. A. Comenius

Antonín Dvořák

In 1785 Casanova took up a post as librarian to Count Wallenstein (Valdstejn) in his castle at Duchcov in Bohemia, where he wrote in French his famous memoirs, "Histoire de ma Vie", describing his various amorous adventures – one of the most important source books on the cultural history of his age. Many of his statements have been confirmed by later research. Casanova also wrote a utopian novel, "Edward and Elizabeth, or A Journey to the Centre of the Earth", 1787), as well as historical and mathematical works, and left an extensive correspondence.
Casanova died in Duchcov Castle on June 4th 1798.

Charles IV
King and Emperor
(1316–78)

Charles IV (originally Wenceslas) of the House of Luxembourg, born in Prague, the son of King John of Bohemia (1310–46) and the Přemyslid princess Elizabeth, daughter of Wenceslas II of Bohemia (1278–1305), was one of the greatest monarchs of the late Middle Ages.
From 1323 he lived at the court of the French king Charles IV, whose niece Blanche he married (d. 1348). In 1333 he returned to Prague as Margrave of Moravia and representative of his father. After his father's death in 1346 he became king, and in 1349 defeated Günther von Schwarzburg, who had been elected king in opposition to him. In January 1355 he became king of Italy, and in April of the same year was crowned as German Emperor in Rome. By a shrewd policy of marriages and treaties he contrived to add extensive territories to his dynastic possessions, including parts of Silesia, Lusatia, Brandenburg and the Upper Palatinate. His sons married Bavarian and Hungarian princesses, and he himself, in his fourth marriage with Elizabeth of Pomerania (1347–93), established links with the Hanseatic League. In 1364 he concluded a testamentary contract with the House of Habsburg.
As a result of Charles's policies the centre of gravity of the Empire moved eastward, and he promoted the political, economic and cultural development of Bohemia, which thus became the central region of the Empire. He made his capital, Prague, an intellectual and spiritual centre by the construction of the New Town, St Vitus's Cathedral, Karlštejn Castle and the Charles Bridge, the rebuilding of Prague Castle, and much else besides. In 1344 he made Prague the see of an archbishop; in 1348 he founded the Charles University in Prague, the first university in Central Europe; and he introduced a new code of laws for Bohemia, the "Majestas Carolina". He attracted to his court great artists, architects, sculptors and painters, like Peter Parler and Theoderich of Prague, and scholars like Johannes von Neumarkt who brought early humanist culture to Bohemia, and maintained relations with leading figures of the Early Renaissance in Italy like Petrarch and Cola di Rienzo. In 1356 Charles promulgated the first constitution of the Empire, the Golden Bull. In 1378 he secured the election of his son Wenceslas (1378-1400) as German king. All these extensions to his

power, however, were in practice negatived by the division of his possessions in 1377 between his sons Wenceslas, Sigismund and John; and since he was unable to settle the conflict between the estates of the realm all his achievements had little effect on posterity.
Charles spoke German, Czech, French and Latin and was also a writer. Among his works was an autobiography, the "Vita Caroli Quarti". He died in Prague on November 29th 1378.

Jan Amos Comenius Theologian and educationist (1592–1670)

The theologian and educationist Jan Amos Comenius (Komenský), perhaps the greatest representative of Czech culture, spent most of his full working life abroad. Born in Nivnice (southern Moravia), he studied Protestant theology and after working for some time as a teacher became a preacher in 1616. Between 1618 and 1621 he worked in Fulnek, near Opava, and elsewhere. The Thirty Years War compelled him to leave Moravia and he moved to Poland, where he became a bishop and director of education in the community of Bohemian Brethren. He travelled widely, to England, Hungary, Sweden and Holland, finally settling in Amsterdam in 1656. His books and writings found a wide audience throughout Europe, and the followers whom he attracted during his travels looked forward to achieving the union of Christendom through the bringing together of all knowledge of God and the world in the "Pansophia" which he preached – a doctrine which it was hoped would point the way towards a world-wide realm of scholarship and peace.
Comenius advocated compulsory schooling for children. His modern-seeming ideas looked far into the future, and his ideas on education influenced the schoolbooks and schools of his century.
He died in Amsterdam on November 15th 1670; his grave is in Naarden.

Dientzenhofer family

The Dientzenhofers were a family of architects of the 17th and 18th centuries who stemmed from Aibling in Bavaria and were active in Franconia and Bavaria during the last phase of Baroque church architecture. Christoph Dientzenhofer and his son Kilian Ignaz Dientzenhofer rank among the leading architects of the Late Baroque period in Bohemia.

Christoph Dientzenhofer (1655–1722)

Born in St Margarethen (Bavaria), Christoph Dientzenhofer was one of the first German architects to be influenced by the Late Baroque style of Guarino Guarini and Francesco Borromini. He appears in the records in Prague from 1685 onwards, building fortifications and churches in the style known as "radicat" Baroque. He took over from Guarini the idea of transverse arches dividing up the vaulting. He died in Prague on June 20th 1722.

Kilian Ignaz Dientzenhofer (1689–1751)

Kilian Ignaz Dientzenhofer, son and pupil of Christoph Dientzenhofer, was born in Prague. He trained under Lucas von Hildebrandt and Johann Bernhard Fischer von Erlach in Vienna and after long periods of travel and study in Italy and Paris settled in Prague in 1720. He is regarded as the outstanding architect of the Late Baroque period in Bohemia. He built numerous villas and churches in Bohemia, Moravia and Silesia, seeking in his churches to achieve new architectural forms in a combination of longitudinal and centralised structures. It is not always clear, however, what part he actually played in the design of the buildings attributed to him.

Antonín Dvořák Composer (1841–1904)

Antonín (Leopold) Dvořák, born in Nelahozeves, near Prague, studied music at the Organ School in Prague and thereafter played in various orchestras, including the orchestra of the Interim Theatre under Bedrich Smetana (see entry), as a viola player (1862–81). Through the mediation of his patron and, later, friend Brahms and the music critic Eduard Hanslick he was awarded a state grant in 1874. From 1884 onwards he paid several visits to Britain for performances of his works. In 1890 he became professor of composition at the Prague Conservatoire. From 1892 to 1895 he was in the United States, where he became director of the National Conservatory in New York and strongly influenced the younger generation of musicians. He gave expression to his impressions of America in his ninth and last symphony, the "New World" (1893), in which he incorporated melodies of the

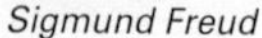

Sigmund Freud

Jaroslav Hašek

Jan Hus

North American Indians and blacks as well as Bohemian songs and dance tunes. After his return to Europe, in 1901, he became director of the Prague Conservatoire.

Dvořák's early work was at first influenced by the Viennese classical school and later by Schumann, Liszt and Wagner; in later years the influence of Brahms and Smetana can also be detected. The whole of his creative work, derived from Bohemian and Moravian folk music, displays vigorous popular elements and markedly Czech characteristics. He and Smetana rank as the supreme representatives of Czech music. He wrote ten operas (including "Rusalka", 1900), choral works with orchestra both secular and religious ("Stabat Mater", 1877; "Requiem", 1890; "Te Deum", 1892), nine symphonies and five symphonic poems, as well as instrumental concertos, chamber music, lieder and dances.

Dvořák died in Prague on May 1st 1904 and was buried in the Vyšehrad cemetery.

Sigmund Freud
Doctor and psychologist
(1856–1939)

One of the greatest and best-known sons of Czechoslovakia is undoubtedly the psychiatrist and neurologist Sigmund Freud (originally Sigismund Schlomo Freud: he altered his first name to Sigmund in 1877), born in Příbor (northern Moravia), the son of a Jewish merchant. When the father retired in 1860 the family moved to Vienna, where Sigmund attended the Gymnasium (grammar school) from 1865, passing his "Abitur" (the university entrance qualification) in 1873 with high honours ("summa cum laude"). He began his medical studies in that year, took his doctorate in 1881 and practised from 1886 as a neurologist and hypnotherapist, while at the same time lecturing on neuropathology. From 1902 until he was compelled because of his Jewish descent to move to London in 1938 Freud was a professor in Vienna, ranking as the founder of theoretical and practical psychoanalysis.

Freud extended his psychological theory into all the intellectual, cultural, religious and social areas of life. His doctrines – often rejected, opposed or misinterpreted – had world-wide influence not only on medicine and psychology but also on philosophy, art and literature: indeed on the whole consciousness of our century. In December 1933 his works were banned by the Nazi authorities in Germany and publicly burned in Berlin.

Sigmund Freud died in London on September 23rd 1939, having suffered from cancer of the lips since 1929.

Jaroslav Hašek
Writer
(1883–1923)

The well-known Prague-born writer Jaroslav Hašek made his name by the numerous satires and humorous tales directed against the Austro-Hungarian monarchy in its final phase ("Of Divorces and Other Comforting Matters", "The School of Humour", "The Traitor's Confession"), but he achieved world fame with his satirical novel "The Adventures of the Good

Soldier Schwejk in the Great War" (1921–23). Schwejk, the typical anti-hero, became a symbolic figure: the "little man" who with his pretended denseness, his phlegmatic disposition, his guile and a touch of cynicism defeats the apparently all-powerful militarism of his superiors.
Hašek died in Lipnice nad Sázavou (eastern Bohemia) on January 3rd 1923, leaving "The Good Soldier Schwejk" unfinished; it was published posthumously by Karel Vaněk.

Jan Hus
Reformer
(*c.* 1370–1415)

The Reformer Jan Hus, born about 1370 in Husinec (Southern Bohemia), the son of a peasant (or according to other sources a carrier), is one of the outstanding personalities of world history.
After attending the Latin School in Prachatice he began in 1380 to study the "seven liberal arts" at Prague University, where he took his bachelor's degree in 1393 and his master's in 1396. In 1398 he became acquainted with the revolutionary religious and social doctrines of the Oxford theologian John Wycliffe. Adopting them as his own, he began to attack, in less radical form, the many abuses in the Church. He also took over from Wycliffe the doctrine of predestination. In 1400 Hus was ordained as a priest and began to study theology. He gave lectures on philosophy in Prague University, and in 1401 was appointed dean of the faculty of philosophy. In 1402 he became a professor and in 1409–10 Rector of the University, while at the same time preaching in the Czech language in the Bethlehem Chapel. He supported Wycliffe's ideas on reform, attacked trends towards secularisation in the church and in monasteries, rejected various church dogmas and promoted the use of the Czech language. He thus became the real originator of the idea of a Czech national church. Hus's great historical achievements, however, were the Czechisation of Prague University and the fostering of the ecclesiastical and national independence of the Czechs by the creation of a unified Czech written language, the standardisation of its orthography and the establishment of a Czech literature. In protest against these developments the German professors and students of the University left Prague in 1409 to found a new university in Leipzig. Hus also wrote many religious works and numerous polemical and edifying works in the Czech language.
In 1410 a Bull issued by the anti-Pope Alexander V in Prague promulgated a variety of measures against the "Wycliffites". Their books were burned; in July 1410 Hus was excommunicated; and in 1411, when he announced a number of lectures defending Wycliffe's doctrines, the Archbishop of Prague put him under an interdict (i.e. banned him from speaking). After the death of Pope Alexander V in 1410 another anti-Pope, John XXIII (not now accepted by the Roman Catholic church), was elected. Hus still, however, remained in favour with King Wenceslas IV of Bohemia (1378–1419) and was able to continue his opposition to the calls by John XXIII for a crusade against Ladislas of Naples and for the sale of indulgences to finance it. Then in 1412 the faculty of theology of Prague University came out against him and he was excommunicated by the Pope. In the same year there were riots in Prague against the sale of indulgences and King Wenceslas had three apprentices executed. Hus said masses for them as martyrs, and wrote an "Appeal to Christ" which he caused to be posted up near the Archbishop's Palace. In 1413 he was compelled to flee from Prague to southern Bohemia, where he wrote his principal work, "De Ecclesia", a sharp attack on the hierarchical structures of the Roman Catholic church based on references to Biblical texts.
The Council of Constance (1414–18), summoned by anti-Pope John XXIII on the initiative of King (from 1433 Emperor) Sigismund, called on Hus to renounce his doctrines and invited him to appear before the Council to justify himself, with a written guarantee of safe conduct by King Sigismund. In spite of this guarantee Hus was arrested on his arrival in Constance, and when he refused to give up his doctrines he was condemned to death at the stake (July 6th 1415).
Thanks to his upright bearing and resolute appearance before the Council and to the broken promise of safe conduct, which Hus's supporters and

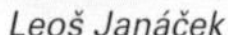

Leoš Janáček

Franz Kafka

Charles IV

many Czechs saw as a deliberate provocation, Hus became a martyr and the national hero of the Czech people and the Czech nation. His death at the stake in Constance sparked off the Hussite wars of subsequent decades.

Hviezdoslav (Pavol Országh)
Poet
(1849–1921)

Pavol Országh, known as Hviezdoslav, born in Vyšný Kubín (central Slovakia), was originally a lawyer and a judge but is now known as the greatest Slovak lyric poet. He began by translating great works of world literature, including Shakespeare, Goethe, Schiller and Pushkin, into Slovak. With his creation of new words and numerous formal innovations and neologisms he created a Slovak literary language richer in forms and nuances. In his popular lyrics and verse epics on themes from Slovak life he glorified the strength and morality of the Slovak people. His cycles of poems, usually centred on particular themes, in which he shows himself a master of nature poetry and thoughtful lyrism, represent a high point in 19th century Slovak poetry.
Pavol Országh died in Dolný Kubín on November 8th 1921.

Leoš Janáček
Composer
(1854–1928)

Leoš Janáček, one of the greatest Czech composers and one of the best known internationally, was born in Hukvaldy (Moravia), the son of a musically gifted teacher. After studying at the Organ School in Prague and the Leipzig and Vienna Conservatoires he worked as an organist in Brno in 1881 and later, until 1886, was conductor of the Brno Philharmonic Society. In 1919 he was appointed professor of composition in the master classes of Prague Conservatoire. His work was strongly influenced by Moravian folk music and Czech declamation, and developed a very distinctive musical style. In his nine operas he sought to develop the musical structure out of the melody and rhythm of the Czech language. His very personal expressive power, however, was slow in achieving recognition. It was only with the revival in Vienna in 1916 of his opera "Jenufa" (first performed in Brno in 1904) that his reputation spread beyond the bounds of his homeland. With "Kat'á Kabanova" (1921), the comic opera "The Naughty Little Vixen" (1924) and "From the House of the Dead" (first performed posthumously in 1930), based on Dostoevský's work, he achieved world fame. In addition to operas Janáček wrote orchestral works, much chamber music, numerous works for piano and choral works, edited several collections of Moravian folk songs and wrote on musical theory. Janáček died in Ostrava on August 12th 1928. The Janáček Quartet, founded in Brno in 1947, devotes itself particularly to works by Czech composers. Its distinctive feature is that it plays without the score.

Alois Jirásek
Writer
(1851–1930)

Alois Jirásek, born in Hronov (Southern Bohemia), became one of the most popular Czech writers thanks mainly to his masterly historical novels and tales, particularly those set in the time of the Hussite wars, published in

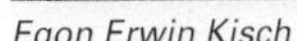

Egon Erwin Kisch

Tomáš G. Masaryk

Gregor Mendel

1904 under the title "The Chod Freedom Fighters". Other notable works include his plays "Jan Žižka" (1903) and "Jan Hus" (1911). As a member of parliament Jirásek was an enthusiastic supporter of republican ideas. He died in Prague on March 12th 1930.

St John of Nepomuk
Patron saint of Bohemia
(*c.* 1350–93)

St John of Nepomuk, patron saint of Bohemia, was born in Nepomuk (western Bohemia) about 1350. After being ordained as a priest in 1380 he studied law at Prague and Padua Universities and in 1389 became Vicar-General of the archbishopric of Prague. Legend has it that King Wenceslas IV tried unsuccessfully to get John to reveal the secrets of the confessional: at any rate he was arrested on the orders of the king, tortured and finally drowned in the Vltava on March 20th 1393.
John was much loved by the people of Bohemia, as is shown by the pictures, spiritual songs and popular plays devoted to his memory and by the legends which were later associated with him. After a statue of the saint was set up on the Charles Bridge in Prague in 1683 he became the patron saint of the bridge. His feast-day is May 16th.

Franz Kafka
Writer
(1883–1924)

Franz Kafka, born in Prague to an old-established and respected family of Jewish merchants, studied German language and literature at the German University in Prague (1901-06) and went on to study law. In 1906 he took his doctorate in law, and after a brief period of court work joined the staff of a Prague insurance company (1908–23). From 1911 he devoted himself to an intensive study of Judaism and the Hebrew language. In 1917 he fell gravely ill with tuberculosis, and a series of summer journeys to Italy, France and Switzerland and courses of treatment at Zürau, Merano, Špindlerův Mlýn and Müritz failed to effect a cure. In 1923 he gave up his job with the insurance company and lived as a writer in Berlin. In 1924 the writer Max Brod took him back to Prague. Finally he was admitted to a sanatorium at Kerling, near Vienna, where he died of tuberculosis of the larynx on June 3rd 1924.
Kafka was by nature a loner, though in his youth he formed friendships with the writers Max Brod, Franz Werfel and Johannes Urzidil and the theologian Martin Buber. He owed no allegiance to any particular literary movement, though he showed a leaning towards Expressionism. His first prose tales were published in 1909 in the Munich journal "Hyperion", and these were followed by "The Judgment" (1913), "The Administration" (1915) and "In the Penal Settlement" (1919). The works left unfinished on his death – "The Triat" (1925), "The Castle" (1926) and "America" (1927) – were, contrary to his instructions in his will, edited by his friend Max Brod and published posthumously.
Kafka's fundamental theme was the vain and hopeless struggle of the individual with the anonymous forces, hidden but always present, which

oppose him. This passive and resigned mood is the basic element in his work. Often described as surrealist and written in precise and objective language, it prefers grotesque and sinister subjects and introduces visionary elements into a basically realist action.
Kafka is buried in the Jewish cemetery in Prague-Žižkov.

St Ludmilla
Patron saint of Bohemia
(*c.* 860–921)

Ludmilla, wife of the Christian Duke Bořivoj, was the first Christian princess of Bohemia, having been baptised by Methodius, first archbishop of Moravia and Pannonia. She brought up her son Wenceslas (Václav), later Duke of Bohemia and a saint, in the Christian faith. She was murdered by her pagan enemies at Tetin, near Beroun, on September 15th 921 and was later canonised. Her feast-day is September 15th.

Gustav Mahler
Composer and conductor
(1860–1911)

Gustav Mahler, born in Kaliště (Moravia), began his musical studies with Robert Fuchs at the Vienna Conservatoire and was also taught privately by Anton Bruckner. After working in Hall (Upper Austria), Ljubljana (Slovenia), Olomouc, Vienna and Kassel he was appointed assistant kapellmeister of the German Theatre in Prague in 1885. In 1886 he moved to the Leipzig Opera House, in 1888 he became musical director of the Budapest Opera and in 1891 he was appointed chief kapellmeister of the Municipal Theatre in Hamburg. He was also guest conductor in Poland, Russia and elsewhere. From 1897 to 1907 he was kapellmeister (and later director) of the Vienna Court Opera, from 1898 to 1901 director of the Vienna Philharmonic Orchestra, in 1907 guest conductor of the New York Metropolitan Opera and in 1908 director of the New York Philharmonic Society.
Mahler was celebrated for his strict orchestral discipline. He was an outstanding and influential interpreter of Beethoven, Wagner, Weber and Mozart, and had no scruples about retouching in his own fashion works by such composers as Beethoven and Weber – a procedure which on occasion incurred sharp criticism.
Mahler's work, which broadly followed the Romantic school, was concentrated mainly on symphonies and lieder. It represented a synthesis of the classical Viennese symphony, Romantic lieder and folk songs. He gave these traditional elements fresh effect and significance by his unconventional use of them and anticipated many modern compositional techniques.
Mahler died in Vienna on May 18th 1911.

Tomáš Garrigue Masaryk
Statesman and philosopher
(1850–1937)

The great statesman Tomáš Garrigue Masaryk, one of the founders of the first Czechoslovak Republic, celebrated as the "Liberator President", was born in Hodonín, near Brno. From 1882 to 1914 he was professor of philosophy and sociology at the Czech University in Prague, enjoying a great scholarly reputation. In politics he was a pragmatist, rejecting the view of Czech nationalism based on a mystical view of history and looking to the realisation of the Czech national idea in the first place within the Habsburg monarchy along with the Germans. As a scholar, a politician and a writer Masaryk was against the pan-Slavist trends in the Czech national movement, against clericalism, the nobility and the House of Habsburg and against the increasingly evident efforts by the Germans and Magyars to achieve predominance.
Masaryk was a member of the Austrian Reichsrat from 1891 to 1893 as a representative of the "Young Czechs", who demanded self-government for their country, and from 1907 to 1914 was a representative of the liberal Czech Progressive Party, which he had founded and of which he was president, in the Reichsrat in Vienna, where he occupied a moderate position between the National Democrats and the Marxists. In 1914 he left the country and went to London, where in 1915, along with Edvard Beneš (see entry), he called for the dissolution of the Habsburg monarchy and an independent Czech state and, in order to achieve these aims, established a Czech National Council. In 1917 he organised the formation of a Czech Legion in Russia composed of Czech émigrés and prisoners of war which fought on the side of the Allies against the Central Powers. After the United

States entered the First World War (1917) Masaryk reached the "Pittsburgh agreement" with Czech and Slovak émigrés in America, calling for the establishment, after the dissolution of the Habsburg monarchy, of a Czechoslovak Republic bringing Czechs and Slovaks together in an independent state but leaving each of them with certain rights of self-government within the state. The Allied powers recognised the Pittsburgh agreement and declared their acceptance of it.
After the foundation of the Czechoslovak Republic on October 28th 1918 Masaryk became its first President. In his foreign policy he looked towards the West and in domestic policy sought to achieve a balance between the Czechs and Slovaks and the German population. His commanding personality and his cautious and moderate policies brought him the respect of all classes of the population and earned him the style of "Liberator President". He was re-elected President in 1920, 1927 and 1934. In 1935 he resigned on grounds of age and retired to Lány Castle near Prague, the summer residence of the President. He died there on September 14th 1937 and was buried in the cemetery.

Jan Masaryk
Politician
(1886–1948)

Jan Masaryk, Tomáš Garrigue Masaryk's son, entered the diplomatic service and from 1925 to 1939 was Czechoslovak ambassador in London. During the Second World War he was foreign minister of the government in exile in London, and after the restoration of the Czechoslovak Republic in 1945 remained foreign minister in Prague. After the communist takeover, on March 10th 1948, he fell to his death in mysterious circumstances from the window of his office. Like his father, he was buried in the cemetery at Lány.

Gregor Mendel
Botanist
(1822–84)

Gregor (originally Johann) Mendel, renowned for his research in genetics, was born in Hynčice, near Odry (northern Moravia). In 1843 he entered the Augustinian monastery in Brno, taking the name of Gregor (Gregory), and in 1854 became teacher of natural history and physics in Brno secondary school.
From 1856 onwards he devoted himself to botanical studies, carrying out experiments in hybridising peas and beans in the monastery garden and producing some 13,000 hybrid varieties by artificial fertilisation. The results of his experiments enabled him to formulate the Mendelian laws on the inheritance of simple characteristics – in which the learned world of the day showed little interest (they were rediscovered only around 1900). Mendel was also interested in bee-keeping and meteorology.
Gregor Mendel became prior of his monastery in 1868 and died there on January 6th 1884.

Otakar I
Přemysl
King of Bohemia
(*c.* 1155–1230)

Otakar I Přemysl, son of Vladislav II, was granted the duchy of Bohemia by the Emperor Henry VI in 1197. By repeatedly changing sides in the conflict between the Hohenstaufens and the Guelphs for the imperial throne he secured recognition of his hereditary kingdom of Bohemia by the German king, Philip the Fair of Swabia, in 1198, by Pope Innocent III in 1203 and by the Emperor Frederick II in 1212 and fostered the settlement and cultural development of his country. From 1228 onwards he ruled jointly with his son Wenceslas (Václav) I (see entry), whom – in pursuit of his skilful marriage policy – he had married to the Hohenstaufen princess Kunigunde, daughter of the German king Philip of Swabia.

Otakar II
Přemysl
King of Bohemia
(*c.* 1233–78)

Otakar II Přemysl, grandson of Otakar I and son of Wenceslas I and Kunigunde, became king of Bohemia in 1253. His father Wenceslas I refused in 1247 to recognise him as joint ruler, and he then took advantage of the interregnum in the German Empire to build up his power over a territory extending from the Adriatic to the Ore Mountains. His marriage with Margarete (d. 1267), sister of the last Duke of Austria of the Babenberg line, gave him possession of the Duchy of Austria; in 1260 he acquired Styria and in 1266 the Egerland (Cheb region); and in 1269 he inherited Carinthia, Carniola and the Wendish March (Lower Carniola). He undertook two crusades in support of the Teutonic Order, then hard pressed by Prussian tribes, and in 1255 took part in the foundation of Königsberg, which was so named in his honour. In 1261 he married Kunigunde of Hungary. His attempts to secure the crown of Germany and later of Hungary were unsuccessful. He opposed the election as German king of a rival candidate, Rudolph of Habsburg, and refused to do homage to him. Rudolph thereupon contested his claims to the additional territories he had acquired and in 1276 compelled him to give up Austria, Styria and Carinthia. During an attempt to recover these territories Otakar's army was defeated in the battle of the Marchfeld (Lower Austria) and he himself was killed by personal enemies on August 26th 1278 at Dürnkrut while fleeing from the battlefield. His son Wenceslas (Václav) II (see entry) retained possession only of the ancestral lands of Bohemia and Moravia.

Within Bohemia and Moravia Otakar consolidated his power, developing the country's resources by bringing in German peasant farmers and miners and introducing a centralised administration on the Sicilian model. He was also able to win the support of the towns by supporting them against the nobility.

František Palacký
Historian and politician
(1798–1876)

The Czech historian František Palacký, born in Hodslavice, near Český Těšin (Moravia), was appointed historiographer and archivist of Bohemia in Prague in 1839. As a Czech of firm nationalist convictions he refused in 1848 to take part in the German National Assembly in Frankfurt and instead presided over the Slav Congress in Prague. In the Diet of Kroměříž (1848–49), at which the Austrian parliament, meeting there instead of in Vienna during the Counter-Revolution, gave the Austro-Hungarian Monarchy a new constitution, Palacký represented the interests of the Slav Party. From 1861, as leader of the "Pan-Czechs" in the upper house of the Austrian parliament and in the Bohemian Diet in Prague, he devoted himself entirely to current politics. Originally he advocated equality of treatment for Slavs within the Habsburg monarchy ("Austro-Slavism"), but later, disillusioned by the Austrian policy on nationalities, moved increasingly towards Pan-Slavist ideas.

Under the influence of the German philosopher J. G. von Herder (1744–1803) and the historian Heinrich Luden (1778–1847) Palacký wrote his six-volume "History of Bohemia" (1836–67), which laid the foundations for a Czech national school of history. In his "Documentary Contributions to the History of the Hussite War" (1872–74) he declared the Hussite period to be the central epoch in Czech history.

František Palacký died in Prague on May 26th 1876.

Pavol Jozef Šafárik
Literary historian and Slavist
(1795–1861)

The Slovak scholar Pavol Jozef Šafárik, famed for his pioneering philosophical work on Slav antiquities and ethnography, was born in Kobeliarovo (Slovakia). Appointed to a professorial chair in Prague in 1848, he became the founder of scientific Slav archaeology. In 1826 he published his "History of Slav Language and Literature in All Dialects", in 1843–44 his "Slav Antiquities" (in German) and various writings on Slav ethnography. He was also a great collector of Slav folk songs.

He died in Prague on May 26th 1861.

Jaroslav Seifert
Writer
(1901–86)

The Czech writer Jaroslav Seifert, a native of Prague, began his career on the staff of various left-wing newspapers, at first writing "proletarian" lyrics; but he soon abandoned the dogmas of Socialist Realism and turned to "Poetism", a form of poetry without logic or particular themes, a mere playing with words and impressions. Later he wrote melancholic light poetry, children's books and journalism, as well as translations of Aleksandr Blok and Guillaume Apollinaire. Among his published works were two volumes of poetry, "Darkness in the Mirror" (1982) and "Halley's Comet" (1986) and a collection of stories, "A Heaven Full of Ravens" (1985). In 1968 he was one of the signatories to the "Manifesto of 2000 Words", and as a result was banned from practising his profession. In 1969 he became

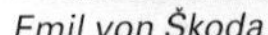

Emil von Škoda

Bedřich Smetana

Adalbert Stifter

President of the Czech Writers' Union. In 1984 he was awarded the Nobel Prize for Literature.
Seifert died in Prague on January 10th 1986.

Emil Ritter von Škoda
Industrialist
(1839–1900)

The great industrialist Emil von Škoda, nephew of the well-known physician Joseph Škoda (1805–81), was born in Cheb (western Bohemia). In 1866 he became director and in 1868 owner of the Count Valdštejn Engineering Works (founded 1859) in Plzeň, which he developed into the largest and most important plant in the Austrian armaments industry. He died in Plzeň on August 8th 1900.
In 1906 the Škoda works also began to produce cars, and in the 1920s and 1930s it was one of Europe's leading industrial firms. During the years of German occupation (1939–45) the factory was taken over by German armaments firms, and after the re-establishment of the Czechoslovak Republic and the communist takeover it was nationalised. The Škoda works in Plzeň now manufacture locomotives, rolling mills, and machine tools, while the works in Mladá Boleslav produce private cars (recently in cooperation with Volkswagen).

Bedřich Smetana
Composer
(1824–84)

The great Czech composer Bedřich (Frederick) Smetana, son of a brewer in Litomyšl, was born in the old brewery, in a room which is shown to visitors. He made his first public appearances as a pianist at the early age of six. After studying music in Prague he founded a music school there in 1848, remaining director until 1856. He then spent five years as director of subscription concerts with the Harmoniska Sällskapet in the Swedish city of Gothenburg. In 1861 he returned to Prague, where at first he worked as a choirmaster and musical critic; then in 1866 he became kapellmeister of the Czech National Theatre and in 1872 its artistic director. In 1874, however, he was compelled to give up his work because of his steadily increasing deafness, and in 1882 appeared the first symptoms of the mental illness of which he died on May 12th 1884.
Smetana is regarded as the founder of a distinctively Czech musical style both in opera and in symphonic writing. His music, with its passionate warmth and artistic balance, combines Czech folk music with the symphonic expressiveness of a Liszt and the dramatic power of a Wagner. His first world success was his comic opera "The Bartered Bride", first performed in 1866. In "Dalibor" (1868) and "Libuše" (1881) he turned to heroic and patriotic grand opera. After he became completely deaf he composed light operas ("The Kiss", 1876; "The Secret", 1878) which were enthusiastically received. His six-part symphonic cycle "My Fatherland" (1874–79; including "The Vltava") was a magnificent act of homage to his country. His other works included a symphony (1854), overtures, chamber music

(including the string quartet in E minor, with an over-long E in the finale which marks the beginning of his deafness), choral works and lieder.

L'udovít Velislav Štúr
Philologist, writer and politician
(1815–56)

L'udovít Velislav Štúr, born in Uhrovec, near Trenčín (western Slovakia) was a remarkable personality who inspired in the young people of Slovakia an enthusiasm for their national culture. From 1840 to 1843 he taught in the Protestant grammar school in Bratislava. A respected philologist, he worked for the development of the Middle Slovak dialect into a written language, and with the introduction of a new phonetic orthography founded the literary Slovak language, which was approved in 1851 by leading representatives of the nation, including the Catholics. The religious barrier was thus removed and Slovakia was united in language, culture and nationality. In 1847 Štúr was elected a member of the Slovak Diet, in which he committed himself to the defence of Slovak rights against the Hungarians. A year later he was the organiser and one of the leaders of the Slovak fight for freedom. In 1867, influenced by the German Romantic movement and Pan-Slavism, Štúr wrote "Slav Culture and the World of the Future" and a number of patriotic poems. He also collected and published Slav folk songs and fairytales.
Štúr lived in Modra, near Bratislava, where he died on January 12th 1856 and was buried in the local cemetery.

Ludvík Svoboda
Officer and politician
(1895–1979)

One of the leaders of the "Prague Spring" was Ludvík Svoboda, a native of Hroznatín in Moravia. In 1944 he was commander of a Czechoslovak army corps in the Soviet Union which took part, along with the Red Army, in the "liberation" of Czechoslovakia in 1945. As minister of defence and supreme commander of the armed forces he cooperated with the takeover by the Communist Party in 1948. In 1951 he became a member of the governing Presidium, but later in the year was relieved of all his functions. He was rehabilitated in 1955, and in the following year became Commander of the Military Academy. In March 1968 he was elected President of the Republic by the reformers under Alexander Dubček's leadership. As head of state he at first supported the reforming ideas of the "Prague Spring", but after the entry of Warsaw Pact forces in August 1968 adapted to the new situation and sought to act as a moderating influence.
In May 1975 he was compelled to resign, and thereafter he lived in retirement in Prague, where he died on September 20th 1979.

Jozef Kajetán Tyl
Actor and dramatist
(1808–56)

The Czech actor and dramatist Jozef Kajetán Tyl, born in Kutná Hora, was the author of romantic and historical dramas, plays drawn from everyday life, comedies in the style of Iffland and Kotzebue, fairytale plays with themes and characters from Czech legend ("The Piper of Strakonice", 1847) and patriotic novels ("Rosina Ruthard", 1838). After the foundation of the first Czechoslovak Republic in 1918 a song from his popular comedy "Fidlovačka" ("The Fiddle Festivat", 1834), "Kde domov můj?" ("Where is my home?"), became the first (Czech) verse of the Czechoslovak national anthem.
Tyl lived in Plzeň, where he died on July 11th 1856. His grave is in St Nicholas's Cemetery.

Vladislav Vančura
Writer
(1891–1942)

The Czech doctor and writer Vladislav Vančura, born in Háj, near Opava (northern Moravia), was one of the country's leading prose writers of the interwar period, whose style, with its delight in experiment and its rich vocabulary of metaphors, archaisms and hyperboles, became the model for modern Czech prose. In his novels he frequently depicted the life of outsiders ("Jan Marhoul the Baker", 1924), but he also dealt with national and historical themes ("Marketa and Miklas", 1931; "Ballade of the Robbers", 1970).
During the German occupation (1939 onwards) Vančura was an active member of the Resistance, and after the attack on Reinhard Heydrich was executed in Prague on June 1st 1942.

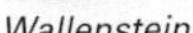
Wallenstein

Franz Werfel

Jan Žižka

Albrecht Eusebius Wenzel von Waldstein (Wallenstein) General (1583–1634)

Albrecht Wenzel (Václav) von Waldstein (Wallenstein), a general in the Imperial service during the Thirty Years' War, was born in Heřmanice (eastern Bohemia), a scion of the noble Valdštejn family. Brought up as a Protestant, Wallenstein took service in the Habsburg army in 1604, and in 1606 became a Catholic. In 1617 he supported Archduke Ferdinand with his own troops against the Venetian Republic, and after the end of hostilities was rewarded by appointment as an Imperial aide-de-camp and elevation to the dignity of count. Through his marriage in 1609 to Lucrezia von Witschkow he gained rich estates in Moravia; then in 1623 he married Isabella Katharina von Harrach, daughter of an intimate of the Emperor Ferdinand II. Wallenstein took no part in the rising of the Bohemian Estates at the beginning of the Thirty Years' War, but after the defeat of the rising he acquired over 50 properties confiscated from rebels who had been expelled from the country. These huge possessions were erected by the Emperor Ferdinand II in 1624 into the Duchy of Friedland (Frýdlant), making Wallenstein a Prince of the Empire.

In 1625, when the Emperor was hard pressed by the League of Lower Saxony, Wallenstein put his own mercenary army of 40,000 men at his disposal, supplying and paying them at the expense of the conquered territories. In return he was appointed commander-in-chief of all Imperial forces. In 1625 he defeated Ernst II von Mansfeld and, together with General von Tilly, drove the Danish king Christian IV out of North Germany. In 1622 Wallenstein received from the Emperor the Duchy of Sagan and in 1628 the Duchy of Mecklenburg and the title of "General of the Oceanic and Baltic Seas".

Wallenstein's plans for a reform of the Empire and further military action were turned down by the Emperor. In 1630 the Emperor, under pressure from his political opponents, was compelled to dismiss him; but in 1632 he was reappointed commander-in-chief and granted special powers. He now drove the Swedes out of South Germany and after his victory at Lützen (November 16th 1632) over the Swedish king Gustavus II Adolphus withdrew to his estates in Bohemia. Thereafter his unauthorised and devious negotiations with Sweden, Brandenburg and Saxony aroused the Emperor's increasing mistrust, and his autocratic behaviour and method of conducting the war provoked opposition. In 1634, therefore, Wallenstein required the officers of his army to swear an oath of unconditional loyalty to himself. An Imperial patent was then issued (February 22nd 1634) accusing him of high treason and calling for his capture, either dead or alive. Then on April 25th, while Wallenstein was in Cheb considering the possibility of an understanding with the Swedes under Duke Bernhard of Saxe-Weimar, he and three of his officers were murdered in the Town House by an Irish captain in the Imperial service named Devereux. Wallenstein's

body was taken to his estate of Mnichovo Hradiště and buried in St Anne's Chapel in the castle church.
History's judgment of Wallenstein is divided. Some see him as an idealist who sought to bring peace to the country and recognise his military genius and his political far-sightedness; others condemn his boundless striving for power, his unrestrained ambition and his constant desire to enrich himself.

St Wenceslas
Patron saint of Bohemia
(*c.* 903–939)

Wenceslas (Václav), grandson of Duchess (St) Ludmilla (see entry), became Duke of Bohemia about 921, but until 922 was under the tutelage of his mother Drahomira. He sought to achieve the incorporation of his duchy in the German Empire and also its Christianisation, opposition to which was led by his brother Boleslav. On September 28th 929 Boleslav had him murdered in Brandýs nad Labem. Wenceslas, the first Duke of Bohemia of the Přemyslid dynasty, is revered as a saint and martyr and is the patron saint of Bohemia. His feast-day is September 28th.

Wenceslas I
King of Bohemia
(1205–53)

Wenceslas (Václav) I, son of King Otakar I (see entry), became king of Bohemia in 1230. Although he was a son-in-law of the German king Philip of Swabia he was frequently an antagonist of the Hohenstaufens. With his son Otokar II (see entry) he conducted successful wars in 1239 and 1250 for the inheritance of the Babenberg dynasty in Austria. He favoured the German settlers in his country and was a patron of the minnesingers and of art and learning. Wenceslas died in Beroun on September 23rd 1253.

Wenceslas II
King of Bohemia and Poland
(1272–1305)

Wenceslas (Václav) II, son of King Otakar II (see entry), became king of Bohemia in 1278. At the beginning of his reign he had difficulty in asserting his authority against the resistance of the nobility. He married Guta, a daughter of Rudolph I of Habsburg, who granted him Bohemia and Moravia as an Imperial fief and in 1289 secured for him the dignity of Elector. In 1300 he had himself crowned as king of Poland in Gniezno. He consolidated the royal power in his ancestral lands and in 1300 reformed the coinage. When the Árpád dynasty died out in Hungary he claimed the Hungarian crown for his son, later Wenceslas III, and had him crowned as king of Hungary in 1302. This brought him into conflict with the German king Albert I, but he died in Prague on June 21st 1305 before the dispute was finally settled.

Wenceslas III
King of Bohemia and Hungary
(1289–1306)

Wenceslas (Václav) III, son of Wenceslas II (see entry), became king of Hungary in 1302 and in 1305, after the death of his father, king of Bohemia. In 1305, however, he renounced the Hungarian crown. During an attempt to assert his right to the Polish crown he was murdered at Olomouc, on his way to Poland, on August 4th 1306. On his death the Přemyslid dynasty of Bohemia died out in the male line.

Jan Žižka z Trocnova
Hussite leader
(*c.* 1370–1424)

Jan Žižka, the most important military leader of the Taborites, the radical and social revolutionary wing of the Hussites, was born around 1370 in Trocnov, near České Budějovice. A skilled organiser, he contrived to unite the two more moderate groups in the Hussite movement, the Utraquists and the Calixtines, under his command. Although blinded in one eye, he won a brilliant victory over the Emperor Sigismund's forces on Mt Vítkov, in the Žižkov district of Prague, on July 14th 1420. During an assault on Rabí Castle, perched on a 520m/1705ft high rocky hill south-west of Horazd'ovice (near Sušice in Western Bohemia) and hitherto deemed impregnable, he lost his second eye. Though now completely blind, he won another overwhelming victory at Havlíčkův Brod on January 8th 1422.
From 1421 Jan Žižka was a representative of the people in the assembly of the Estates, meeting in the church of SS. Peter and Paul in Čáslav, which denied the Bohemian crown to the Emperor Sigismund. He died on October 11th 1424 at Přibyslav and was buried in the church; but in 1623, on the orders of the Emperor Ferdinand II, his remains were removed and his tomb destroyed.

Art and Culture

Art and Architecture in Bohemia, Moravia and Moravian Silesia

Prehistory and early historical period

The lozenge-shaped basin of Inner Bohemia, formed by remains of an ancient mountain range dating from the earliest period of the earth's history, has been continuously occupied by man since the third millennium B.C.

Venus of Věstonice

One of the earliest works of art found in the territory of former Czechoslovakia is the "Venus of Věstonice" (Věstonická Venuše), a small archaic figurine of fired loess with strongly marked female characteristics found at Dolní Věstonice (north of Břeclav in Moravia) which is dated to about 25,000 years ago; it is now in the Moravian Museum in Brno.

In the Neolithic era the Bohemian lands belonged to the Danubian cultural province (linear and stroke-ornamented pottery, in Moravia painted pottery). In the Chalcolithic period, as often in later times, they accommodated a whole range of cultures, showing variations which were no doubt sometimes ethnically based (the Corded Ware people, the Bell Beaker people, etc.); and the situation was similar in the Early, Middle and Late Bronze Age (1700–900 B.C.: Úňetice culture, Lusatian culture, etc.).

In the period of transition between the Bronze and Iron Ages the Hallstatt culture of the eastern Alpine region (900–450 B.C.) came to Bohemia, probably brought by Illyrians. They were followed at the beginning of the La Tène period (450 B.C. to the beginning of the Christian era) by the Boii, probably a Celtic people, who gave their name to Bohemia (settlements of urban type, trade, gold coins). The last century B.C. saw the arrival of Germanic tribes – the Marcomanni in Bohemia, the Quadi in Moravia – who established a large kingdom under King Marbod around the beginning of the Christian era. From A.D. 166 to 180 the Marcomanni were at war with Rome. Shortly before the turn of the 6th–7th century came the peaceful immigration of the Slavs, who for a time were overlaid by the Avars. Under a merchant named Samo (623–658), who was probably of Frankish origin, a great Slav kingdon was established. This was followed by the kingdom of Great Moravia, on the eastern frontiers of the Carolingian empire, which for a time had links with the Byzantines (mission of Cyril and Methodius, the Apostles of the Slavs, 863–885). The Christianisation of the Bohemian lands, however, began before the Byzantine mission, initiated by missionaries from Bavaria (Passau, Regensburg).

Pre-Romanesque and Romanesque periods

The earliest stone-built Christian churches, dating from the middle and second half of the 9th century, have been excavated at Mikulčice in southern Moravia, Pohansko (near Břeclav), Staré Město u Uherského Hradiště and Prague (Levý Hradec, Hradčany). From the 10th century there is evidence of the Prague principality of the Přemyslids. The dukes and (from the 12th and 13th century) kings of Bohemia were Princes of the Empire (Electors), and as such were several times elected Emperor. For something like a thousand years Bohemia was part of the Holy Roman Empire.

The most important religious buildings erected in the pre-Romanesque and Romanesque periods were the Rotunda (a round building with four apses; 926–930) and Basilica (with two choirs, a west transept and two crypts, like St Emmeram's in Regensburg; *c.* 1060) of St Vitus, both of which are preserved in the foundations of St Vitus's Cathedral in Prague Castle. Characteristic of the Bohemian lands are the aisleless round churches known as "Bohemian rotundas" (St Martin's, Vyšehrad, Prague). Otherwise the church architecture of Bohemia was little different either in spatial form or in ground-plan from that of Central Europe.

The most important surviving monuments of the Romanesque period are St George's Basilica in Prague Castle, the Benedictine church of Třebič in southern Moravia and the Premonstratensian churches of Milevsko and particularly Teplá (consecrated 1232), the first hall-church on Bohemian soil.
Other notable works of Romanesque art are the monumental sculpture of St James's Church, Kutná Hora (1165); the wall paintings of Stará Boleslav and the Rotunda in Znojmo (1134); and the illuminations of the Codex Vyšehradiensis (1086; National Library, Prague).

Gothic

Gothic architecture was introduced in the second quarter of the 13th century by the Cistercians and the mendicant orders, most of whose churches were destroyed during the Hussite wars, like the hall-choirs of Mnichovo Hradiště, Zbraslav (Royal Hall) and the Cathedral choir of Sedlec. Among surviving buildings of this period are the Cistercian churches of Vyšší Brod and Tišnov and a number of churches of the mendicant orders in Prague, České Budějovice and Jihlava. Under the last of the Přemyslids, who died out in 1306, as under the last Hohenstaufens, the emphasis was on secular architecture. Notable buildings of this period were the double chapel in the Imperial stronghold in Cheb, the royal castles of Zvíkov, Písek and Bezděz and the castle of the bishops of Prague at Horšovský Týn. In the reign of Otakar II Přemysl (d. 1278 in the battle of the Marchfeld), who made Bohemia the leading power in Central Europe and came near to election as Emperor, many towns were founded by German settlers with charters on the model of Nuremberg or Magdeburg. There are fine town churches in Transitional style in Kolín (St Bartholomew's), Kouřim and Písek; and to this period also belongs the Old-New Synagogue in Prague's Josefov district.

Late Gothic

Under the Emperor Charles IV, who spoke German, French, Czech and Latin, the art and architecture of the Bohemian lands took a leading place in Central Europe and the Late Gothic style came in. Prague, the capital city and the see of an archbishop (from 1344), grew considerably in size and became the seat of the first university in Central Europe. With the rebuilding in Gothic style of St Vitus's Cathedral, begun in 1344 by Matthias of Arras (d. 1352) and continued by Peter Parler and his sons, Prague became the leading centre of architecture and sculpture in Central Europe, whose influence extended as far afield as Italy (Milan Cathedral) and Spain. The Parlers also built the choirs of Kolín and Kutná Hora cathedrals.
The art of Charles IV's reign anticipates some of the results of the Renaissance: the earliest net vaulting and sacred images in Central Europe, the first free-standing equestrian statue since antiquity (St George in Prague Castle, by the brothers Martin and Georg von Klausenburg).
In painting a new style grew out of a synthesis of French and Italian elements and found expression in all genres. Characteristic of this period are the "Bohemian Madonnas" (half-length figures of the Virgin and Child). Among leading artists were the Master of Vyšší Brod, Nikolaus Wurmser of Strasbourg, Tomaso da Modena, Master Theoderich and the Master of Třeboň. The finest examples of the art of this period are the altars and panel paintings to be seen in the National Gallery in Prague, the wall paintings in the Emmaus Monastery, Prague, and above all in Karlštejn Castle, built by the Emperor to house the Imperial jewels and sacred relics.
Magnificent work was also done in book illumination (e.g. the splendid manuscripts of King Wenceslas in the National Library in Vienna). Other manuscripts were commissioned by the great humanist Johannes von Neumarkt from Silesia, under whose aegis the German written language began to be formed in the Imperial Chancery in Prague.
After the death of Charles IV (1378) and Peter Parler (1399) a decline set in. King Wenceslas was deposed as Emperor in 1400 and the centre of gravity moved to Vienna. One of the principal works of the over-refined art of

◀ *The Powder Tower, on the edge of Prague's Old Town*

The Emperor Charles IV and his wife Anna

around 1400 is the "Beautiful Madonna" from Český Krumlov (Museum of Art, Vienna; replica in National Gallery, Prague).

Increasing religious, social and national tensions, stirred up by the preaching of the great Czech Reformer Jan Hus in the Bethlehem Chapel in Prague (demolished in the 18th century, rebuilt since the last war), finally led in 1409 to the departure of the German students and professors of Prague University for Leipzig, and the outbreak of the Hussite wars in 1410 put an end to this, the greatest flowering of culture in the history of Bohemia.

After the Hussite wars the character of Bohemian (now almost purely Czech) art remained until the end of the century conservative and eclectic. The most notable Czech architect of this period was Matthias Rejsek (Powder Tower, Prague, 1478; vaulting of choir in St Barbara's Church, Kutná Hora, 1489–99).

In the reign of Vladislav II (1490–1516) some of the leading architects in Central Europe were summoned to Bohemia, like Jakob Haylmann of Schweinfurt (hall-choir of town church, Most) and above all Benedikt Ried (Beneš z Loun) of Piesting (Vladislav Hall in the Royal Palace in Prague, 1493–1502, one of the most magnificent secular buildings of its period; nave of St Barbara's Church, Kutná Hora, with what is perhaps the finest net vaulting of the final phase of Gothic).

Sculpture and painting show the influence of almost all the major schools and trends of the Dürer period, particularly the work of Hans Leinberger, Tilman Riemenschneider, Lucas Cranach and the Danube school. Notable among native painters is the Master of the Litoměřice Altarpiece, who also worked on the paintings in St Wenceslas's Chapel in St Vitus's Cathedral, which are among the finest examples of the monumental wall painting of the period in Central Europe.

Renaissance

The art of the Italian Renaissance probably came to Bohemia at an earlier stage than to anywhere else in Central Europe apart from Hungary. The Belvedere Palace in Prague (designed by Paolo della Stella), built for Ferdinand I in 1534, is one of the purest examples of Renaissance architecture north of the Alps. The unusual Star Palace (Hvězda) on the outskirts of Prague, on a star-shaped ground plan, was built by Italians on the basis of an idea of Archduke Ferdinand's. In the second half of the 16th century the leading architect in Bohemia was the Imperial court architect Bonifaz Wohlmut of Überlingen (Ball Game Hall in Prague Castle, 1568; organ gallery in St Vitus's Cathedral; net vaulting in the Hall of the Diet, Prague Castle; dome of Karlov Church, with net vaulting, 1575).
Another centre of Renaissance art was the territory of the powerful Lords of Rosenberg (z Růže) in southern Bohemia and Moravia (Jindřichův Hradec). Characteristic of this area are palaces with arcaded courtyards (Bučovice, 1567–83; Rosice, etc.).

Mannerism

Under the Habsburg Emperor Rudolph II (1576–1612) Prague again became an Imperial residence and one of the cultural centres of Europe, this time with the international art of Mannerism. The Emperor drew artists of all nations to Prague – Adriaen de Vries, Bartholomäus Spranger, Jan ("Velvet") Brueghel, Arcimboldi, Savery, Sadeler, Hans of Aachen, Hufnagel, Gundelach, Heintz, Rottenhammer, Benedikt Wurzelbauer and many others – though no new and enduring traditions were established in Bohemia.
Two Bohemian artists who attained international reputation were the Czech engraver Wenceslas (Václav) Hollar (1607–77) and the still-life painter Georg Flegel (1568–1638) from Olomouc in Moravia.
There were also a number of notable post-Gothic churches, both Catholic and Protestant, in Prague (St Salvator's, St Roch's).

Baroque

The victory of the Catholic party in the battle of the White Mountain outside Prague (1620) marked the beginning of half a century of predominantly Italian architecture in Bohemia. Building operations were almost completely monopolised by organised associations of Italian craftsmen and building workers. The main architectural activity in the 17th century was the construction of palaces. The principal builders among the Bohemian magnates were Albrecht von Wallenstein (Valdštejn Palace in Prague, 1623–28), Count Humprecht von Czernin (Czernin Palace in Prague, 1669–92), Prince W. E. von Lobkowitz (palace in Roudnice, *c.* 1665) and Prince K. E. von Liechtenstein (Plumlov Palace in Moravia, 1680–85).
Church-building was much influenced by the Jesuit churches, the most fertile practitioners of the style in Bohemia being Carlo Lurago (St Ignatius's in Prague, 1665–78; Březnice, begun 1640; Hradec Králové) and Orsi dei Orsini (Klatovy). Some churches, however, showed a continuance of older native traditions (the hall-church with galleries, the pilaster-walled church), for example in St Salvator's, Prague, and Kralovice.
Unlike architecture, sculpture and painting continued to be dominated by artists from Bohemia and neighbouring countries. The leading sculptors in the second half of the 17th century were Jan Jiří Bendl (St Salvator's and Týn Church in Prague) and Hieronymus Kohl. The most notable painters were Karel Škréta (1610–74), a scion of a noble Czech family who left the country on religious grounds and returned as a convert (National Gallery, Prague), and Michael Willmann (1630–1706), a Silesian who worked in Bohemia (Sedlec).

Late Baroque

The Baroque of Bohemia, Moravia and Silesia reached its peak in the early decades of the 18th century, artistically the most fertile period in these lands since the time of Charles IV. The link with developments in Europe was provided by Jean-Baptiste Mathey (*c.* 1630–95), a Frenchman who had been trained in Rome (represented in religious architecture by the Augustinian church in Prague, 1679–89, and in secular architecture by the Troja Palace, 1679–85). The hegemony of the Italians was now broken and the

Baroque stucco cartouches in the Church of the Assumption, Prague

leading place was taken by native artists. The Late Baroque art of Bohemia cannot be understood without reference to the art of Austria and Bavaria, more particularly because all the great architects of these countries created masterpieces in the Bohemian lands: for example Fischer von Erlach (Clam-Gallas Palace in Prague, Vranov Palace in Moravia), Lucas von Hildebrandt (St Lawrence's in Jablonné v Podještědí) and Christoph Dientzenhofer (1655–1722), a member of the great Bavarian family of architects, who spent most of his life in Bohemia. Together with his son Kilian Ignaz Dientzenhofer (1689–1751) and Giovanni Santini-Aichel, an Italian who settled in Germany, he ranks as one of the three leading architects in Bohemia in the Late Baroque period. In Bohemia and Franconia the Dientzenhofers achieved a synthesis between the old Bavarian pilastered wall structure and the baldachin principle of Guarino Guarini and thus prepared the way for the last and finest period of church-building in Central Europe, represented by the work of Balthasar Neumann (1687–1753), a native of Cheb, in Germany (Neresheim, Vierzehnheiligen) and of Kilian Ignaz Dientzenhofer in Bohemia and Silesia. The work of the elder Dientzenhofer, Christoph, is inadequately documented: Smiřice, 1699; Oboriště, begun 1702; St Clare's in Cheb, 1707–11; St Margaret's in the Břevnov district of Prague and St Nicholas's in the Lesser Quarter, one of the most important Late Baroque churches in Central Europe for its place in the development of architecture and town-planning. Of the many buildings by his son Kilian Ignaz Dientzenhofer, without which it is impossible to imagine either the townscape of Prague or the Baroque cultural landscape of the rest of Bohemia, only one or two can be mentioned – St Nicholas's in the Old Town of Prague, St John on the Rock in the New Town and churches in Opařany and Karlovy Vary.

Giovanni Santini-Aichel (1677–1723), who rebuilt some of the monastic churches destroyed by the Hussites in fantastic pseudo-Gothic forms (Sedlec, near Kutná Hora; Kladruby; Zelená Hora, near Zd'ár nad Sázavou), and Ottavio Broggio (1670–1742), another Italian who had settled in Ger-

many, were the main creators of Bohemian "popular Baroque", seen at its purest in numerous pilgrimage churches (Loreto and the White Mountain in Prague and the sacred mounts of Svatá Hora near Přibram, Svatý Kopeček near Olomouc and Zelená Hora near Zd'ár nad Sázavou). Other notable Baroque architects were the Czech František Maximilian Kaňka (1674–1766), who occasionally also worked in Germany, Pavel Ignác Bayer of Jihlava (1656–1733) and the Italians G. B. Alliprandi (1665–1720; Liblice Castle, Piarist church in Litomyšl), M. Canevale (1652–1711) and G. B. Allio. Among sculptors working in Prague and the provinces around 1700 were Johann Georg and Paul Heermann from Dresden (entrance staircase of Troja Palace, Prague), Václav Jäckel (1655–1738), the Italian Ottavio Mosto (1659–1701) and Franz Preiss (1666–1712), a native of Prague. Then Bohemian Baroque sculpture reached its high point with the work of Ferdinand Maximilian Brokoff (1688–1731) and the Tirolean sculptor Matthias Bernhard Braun von Braun (1684–1738), who brought the Berninesque manner to Bohemia. The main works of most of these sculptors are to be seen on the Charles Bridge in Prague.
The leading Czech fresco painter of the Late Baroque period was Václav Vavřinec Reiner (1689–1743), a native of Prague, whose work can be seen in Prague (Loreto, Czernin Palace) and Zbraslav (Royal Hall). In addition all the great fresco painters of Austria (Rottmayr, Troger, Gran, Maulpertsch), Bavaria (Otto Hiebel, Cosmas Damian Asam, Johann Adam Schöpf, Anton Scheffler) and Silesia (Franz Xaver Palko) are represented in Bohemia by major works. The leading practitioner of panel painting was Petr Brandl of Prague (1668–1735), of portrait painting the refugee Czech Jan Kupecký (1667–1740), who was a master of psychological characterisation; there are pictures by him in the National Gallery in Prague.

Rococo

Many artists worked in the Rococo style in Bohemia, but no distinctive local variant of the style developed as it did in Bavaria and Franconia and at Potsdam. Building work in Prague Castle (1756–74) was directed by the chief court architect Baron von Pacassi, on the Archbishop's Palace in Prague (1764–65) by Johannes Josef Wirch. The Estates Theatre in Prague was designed by Count Künigl and built by Anton Haffenecker (1781–83). The leading sculptors of the late 18th century in Prague were Johann Anton Quittainer (1709–65), Ignaz Platzer the Elder (1717–87; St Nicholas's Church in Prague, Teplá Abbey, etc.) and Richard Prachner (1705–82); in western Bohemia there was Jakob Eberle (Decanal Church, Karlovy Vary), in eastern Bohemia František and Jirí Pacák. The reputations of Ferdinand Dietz and the delicate painter Norbert Grund extended well beyond the bounds of Bohemia.

Neo-classicism

Unlike Baroque, to which Bohemia probably held longer than most other countries in Central Europe, neo-classicism was of subordinate importance, at any rate in the arts. Nevertheless the Kačina Palace, near Kutná Hora (by the Dresden architect C. F. Schuricht, 1802–22) and the Custom House in Prague with its Empire façade (by Georg Fischer, 1800–11) are among the finest creations of the period.

Romanticism

The art of the Romantic period flourished in Bohemia after Herder's ideas led to the revival of a consciousness of Czech nationhood. The Czechs' rise to cultural independence, however, was accompanied by the decline of supra-national Bohemian art, which in the second half of the 19th century increasingly developed into separate Czech and German components.
Among leading Romantic and post-Romantic painters were the Nazarenes Josef von Führich (1800–76) and the Czech František Tkadlík, the Czechs Josef Mánes (1820–71) and Mikoláš Aleš (1852–1913), Gabriel Max (a pupil of the Munich painter Ferdinand Piloty) and Václav Brožík. More important than the neo-Gothic architects Josef Kranner and Josef Mocker (work on St Vitus's Cathedral) was the Czech Josef Zitek (1832–1909), a pupil of Gottfried Semper (Czech National Theatre, designed 1866, and Rudolfinum in Prague; Mühlbrunnen Colonnade, Karlovy Vary). Bohemian artists now

The "Sacred Mount" near Olomouc

made their way not only to Munich and Vienna but also to Paris. The landscapists Wilhelm Riedel, Franz Rumpler and the Czech Antonín Chitussi were influenced by the Barbizon school, Antonín Slaviček by the Impressionists. Czech artists also, however, came under the influence of Feuerbach (Vojtěch Hynais) and Art Nouveau (Jan Preisler).

In sculpture Josef Václav Myslbek (1848–1922; St Wenceslas in Wenceslas Square, Prague; Schwarzenberg tomb in St Vitus's Cathedral) founded a school, influenced by his French contemporaries, to which such notable sculptors as Jan Štursa (1880–1925), Bohumil Kafka (1878–1942) and Otto Gutfreund (1889–1927) belonged.

Many German sculptors (Metzner, Lederer, Hanak) and architects (Josef Olbricht, Josef Hofmann) worked outside Bohemia, in Germany or Austria, making important contributions to the Vienna school and the Sezession.

Modernism

One of the fathers of modern architecture was Adolf Loos (1870–1933), who worked mainly in Vienna and very little in Prague. After the First World War the Czech architect Josef Gočár (1880–1954) completed the transition to modern architecture. The leading representative of Czech Functionalism was Bohuslav Fuchs (1895–1972).

The conservative schools of art also remained active, represented by the important Czech painter and illustrator Max Švabinský (1873–1962), the portrait painter Vratislav Nechleba and Heinrich Hönich, a pupil of Wilhelm Leibl.

Expressionism and Cubism had some outstanding representatives, the former more among the Germans (Oskar Kokoschka, Alfred Kubin, Josef Hegenbarth), the latter among the Czechs (Emil Filla, Václav Špála). Adolf Hölzel of Olomouc was one of the founders of abstract painting.

Art and Architecture in Slovakia

General

Slovakia, lying on the southern slopes of the Carpathians, opens through its river valleys into the Pannonian plain. Although the country belonged for nine centuries (until 1918) to the kingdom of Hungary, it was more closely associated in the development of art with the Alpine and Danubian regions of Austria, although it also received important impulses from Hungary and from Bohemia, Silesia and Poland (particularly Cracow).

Prehistoric and early historical periods

Traces of human settlement from the Stone Age onwards have been found in both western and eastern Slovakia (Šarovce, Barca). The large Celtic fortified camps, some of which had a double ring of ramparts up to 4m/13ft high, still served as refuges a thousand years later, during the Mongol incursions. In the first century A.D. the Celts were followed by two Germanic peoples, the Quadi and the Bastarnae, against whom the Romans built a chain of fortified bridgeheads on the north bank of the Danube (Stupava, Devín, Bratislava, Komárno). Roman forces advanced up the Váh valley as far as Trenčín (Roman memorial tablet, A.D. 179). After the withdrawal of the Germanic tribes from the 6th century onwards the Slav immigration began.

Pre-Romanesque and Romanesque periods

The Christianisation of Slovakia was begun by missionaries from Salzburg, who anticipated the Byzantine mission of Cyril and Methodius. In 833 Archbishop Adalram of Salzburg consecrated a church dedicated to St Emmeram in Nitra, the political centre of western Slovakia. In the 9th century western Slovakia was part of the Great Moravian Empire; thereafter it belonged briefly to the kingdoms of Bohemia and Poland, and in the 11th century it was incorporated in Hungary. Of the pre-Romanesque buildings of which there is documentary evidence none have survived, and the earliest Romanesque buildings date from the 12th century. They are of

St James's Church, Levoča . . .

. . . and its high altar

the usual Central European types: three-apsed basilicas with (usually) twin towers on the west front (Diakovce, Hronský Beňadik, Janošovce, Bíňa, Ilija, Krupina, Dobrá Niva), chapels with west galleries built by noble families, apsed aisleless churches of Mediterranean type (Dražovce, Pominovce), rectangular churches with choirs of North-Western European type and churches on a centralised plan (charnel-houses of Alpine type; Bohemian rotundas, as at Sjalica and Dechtice; tetraconchal churches, as at Chrast' nad Hornádom). There are churches at Ilija and Malá Bíňa with Late Romanesque doorways of Danubian type.

Gothic

After the Mongol invasion in the 13th century German settlers established numerous towns in central and eastern Slovakia, either on the East German model with a rectangular square and a regular street grid or of South German type with a winding market street. This period saw the foundation of the hill towns of central Slovakia with charters based on German law, particularly in the Spiš region centred on Levoča, at the foot of the High Tatras. In the early 14th century the Hungarian kings of the Angevin dynasty renewed the privileges of the settlers in charters written in German.
New architectural types now came into Slovakia through Austria, like the three-aisled hall-church (Levoča, Gelnice, Spišská Kapitula, Košice, Bratislava, Hronský Beňadik, Kežmarok, Okoličné, Spišské Vlachy, Spišská Nová Ves, Prešov-Solivar, Banská Štiavnica, etc.). Two-aisled hall-churches and single-pier churches are particularly common in the Spiš region (Lubica, Vrbov, Veľ'ká Lomnica, Javorina-Ruskinovce, Lendak, Spišská Sobota, Žehra, Danišovce).

Late Gothic

The Late Gothic of the Parler family came to Slovakia from Vienna rather than Prague. The most important example of church architecture in Slovakia, St Elizabeth's Church in Košice, however, has a radial rather than the usual cathedral plan, after the pattern of Braisne, Trier, Xanten or Ahrweiler, with twin subsidiary chapels. The two-storey palace chapel finally reached Slovakia by way of Vienna with a certain time-lag (Bratislava, Spišská Kapitula, Spišský Štvrtok). In this peripheral region of eastern Central Europe, the frontiers of which were pushed far to the east during the Gothic period, the building of fortified castles played a prominent part (Bratislava, Zvolen, Lietava, Trenčín, Strečno, Krásna Hôrka and, in a magnificent scenic setting, Spišský Hrad).

Gothic sculpture received impulses from Schwäbisch Gmünd in Swabia (Košice) and from the Parlers in Prague (Town Hall, Bratislava). In painting the influence first came from Italy (Spišská Kapitula, "Coronation of Robert of Anjou", 1317) and later from the Bohemian painters in the time of the Emperor Charles IV and from Austria. During the Hussite wars many towns were destroyed.
Jakob Kassai, one of the leading sculptors in Central Europe in the second third of the 15th century, emigrated to Vienna and Freising in Bavaria. Around 1500 there was a great flowering of art in Slovakia under the influence of German art – in painting Dürer, Cranach and Altdorfer, in sculpture Veit Stoss. Master Pavol of Levoča was one of the leading artists of the Dürer period, though only one of his numerous works, the high altar of St James's Church in Levoča, has a firm documentary attribution. The churches of the hill towns and the Spiš region were filled with altars, sculpture, pictures and other furnishings, many of which are now in museums in Košice, Bratislava, Prague and Budapest.

Renaissance

The Renaissance, brought by Italian artists at the Hungarian court, came to Slovakia earlier than to Bohemia or Austria (town halls in Banská Bystrica, Bardejov, Levoča, etc.). After the Turkish invasion (battle of Mohács, 1526) numerous fortified castles and defensive structures were built, as at Banská Štiavnica (Old and New Castles), Bytča, Bratislava, Fričovce, Strážky and elsewhere.
Characteristic of the Slovak Renaissance are the free-standing bell-towers to be seen, for example, at Poprad, Spišská Sobota, Vrbov and Kežmarok.

Also typical (probably introduced from Silesia) are the crenellations and ornamental cornices with blind arcading (e.g. on Fričovce Castle).
Much of the sculpture and painting was influenced by the Reformation art of the Netherlands and Germany (epitaphs in churches at Bratislava, Levoča and Košice). The Roland Fountain (1572) in Bratislava was the work of Andreas Luttringer. The main centres of the goldsmith's art which flourished during this period were Kremnica (Christian Füssl, Wolfgang Roll, Achaz Thundl, Joachim Elsholtz, etc.) and Košice (Jakob Pinder). Examples of the Herrngrund miners' cups which were a particular speciality can be seen in the Eastern Slovakian Museum in Košice.

Baroque

The Baroque style which came in with the Counter-Reformation affected the west much more strongly than the Protestant towns of central and eastern Slovakia. Large numbers of artists now emigrated – Johann Spillenberger to Augsburg, Jakub Bogdan to England, Samuel Gottlieb Hanrits (Heinrich) to Berlin, Adám Mányoki to Dresden, Johannes Brokoff to Bohemia, Adam Friedrich Oeser (the teacher of Winckelmann and Goethe) to Leipzig.

Against this, many Austrian artists worked in Slovakia. Bratislava became an important centre of the Imperial Baroque of Vienna (Esterházy, Jesenák, Appónyi, Mirbach and Grassalkowich Palaces). Bohemian and Franconian Baroque was also influential (Balthasar Neumann's designs for Munkacs). Large country palaces were built at Dolná Mičiná, Markušovce, Bernolákovo (formerly Čeklís), Bijakovce, Holíč and Král'ova.

A number of important churches were built during this period in Bratislava (Elizabethine and Trinity Churches, by Anton Pilgram), Trnava (University Church, by P. Spazzo), Trenčín (Piarist Church) and the Premonstratensian monastery of Jasov in eastern Slovakia (Anton Pilgram). The Protestant churches did not confine themselves to the standard types, mostly introduced from Silesia, but on occasion adopted some features of Catholic

Synagogue, Trenčín

church-building (pilastered walls in Levoča, domed church on oval groundplan in Banská Štiavnica). The Protestant church in Bratislava was built by Mathias Walch, the wooden church in Kežmarok by Müttermann.
The victory of the Counter-Reformation was marked by the erection of Marian and Trinity Columns in many towns (Bratislava, Nitra, Prešov, Žilina, Trnava, Trenčín, Vrbov, Kremnica, Banská Štiavnica).
Of the great Austrian Baroque artists the sculptor Raphael Donner worked for more than a decade in Bratislava (St Martin's Altar in the Cathedral), the fresco painter Franz Anton Maulbertsch in Trenčín-Bohuslavice, Paul Troger and F. X. Palko in Bratislava (Elizabethine and Jesuit Churches) and Johann Lukas Kracker in Jasov. The goldsmith's art received new impulses from Transylvania as well as from Augsburg and Nuremberg; among leading exponents of the art were Peter Kecskemeti, Paul Nonnert and the Szilassi brothers, who founded a school.

Neo-classicism

Unlike Baroque, the neo-classical style was practised particularly in eastern Slovakia. In Košice there are a number of fine palaces and burghers' houses (Luženský, Dessewffy, Csáky, etc.) dating from this period. A notable architect of the period was Josef Ballagh (1781–1869), who paraphrased ideas taken from Schinkel and Klenze. His pupils turned to Romanticism and Historicism. Josef Fischer built a neo-Gothic palace in Košice, while Emmerich Henszlmann was a pioneer in the conservation of ancient monuments in Hungary and Slovakia.
The leading neo-classical sculptor in Hungary and Slovakia was Stefan Ferenczy (1792–1856), a pupil of Thorvaldsen and Canova. Notable painters were Josef Czauczik, Karol Tibély and Karol Marko (1791–1860), a landscape painter of international reputation who spent the decisive years of his life in Italy.

Romanticism

As in Bohemia and Hungary, the Romantic period led in Slovakia to a new realisation of nationhood. Slovak and Czech artists in Munich formed the Škréta artists' union, whose aim was the creation of a national Slav art on the basis of traditional folk art. The leading personality of this generation was the architect Dušan Jurkovič.
Slovakia still preserves a rich treasure of folk art. Although much has been lost in recent years as a result of rapid industrialisation, there are still surprisingly large numbers of fine Baroque and even Gothic wooden churches, for example at Tvrdošín (late 15th c.), Trnové (*c.* 1500), Točany (16th c.), Hervartov (1593), Bodružal (1658), Paludza (17th c.), Hronsek (1725), Mirol'a (1770) and Zboj (1776).

Music

Czech lands

The Czechs are often spoken of as a "people of musicians", and there is no doubt that music, and in particular music-making, is a favourite activity in the Czech lands. A distinctive tradition of folk music developed in Bohemia and Moravia at an early stage, and as early as the 16th century Bohemian musicians were famed in many European countries.
At first Czech composers were influenced mainly by German music (J. V. A. Stamic, 1717–57), but in the 19th century Bedřich Smetana (see Famous People) established a national romantic musical tradition which was carried on by Antonín Dvořák (see Famous People) and Zdeněk Fibich (1850–1900). The favourite genres were operas, symphonies and ballet music.

Among leading Czech composers of the 20th century are Josef Suk (1874–1935), Jan Kubelik (1880–1940) and the operatic composer Leos Janáček (see Famous People), whose late works belong to the New Music school. The outstanding representatives of this school were the neo-classical composer Bohuslav Martinů (1890–1957) and Alois Hába (1893–1973), with his unconventional system of very short intervals. Representatives of the modern generation of composers include Václav Dobiáš (1909–78), Zbyněk

Vostřák (1920–85), Rudolf Komorous (b. 1931), Marek Kopelent (b. 1932), Luboš Fišer (b. 1935) and Petr Kotík (b. 1942), who experiments with unusual sound-producers.
The country's best known orchestra is the internationally renowned Czech Philharmonic (founded 1894), the director of which since 1968 has been the well-known conductor Václav Neumann.

In addition to Bohemian folk music, which is also popular beyond the bounds of Bohemia, there has developed in recent years a considerable jazz and light music scene, which – like almost all fields of cultural life – was exposed to fierce persecution under the communist regime.

Slovakia

As in Bohemia and Moravia, the basis of the musical tradition is the country's folk music. Here too an independent national tradition emerged only in the 19th century, when Ján Levoslav Bella (1843–96) made his name as a composer.
The most important Slovak composers of the 20th century are Mikuláš Moyzes (1872–1944), his son Alexander Moyzes (1906–84) and Eugen Suchoň (b. 1908), whose operas are well known outside Slovakia.

Folk Traditions

Since the development of the territory of former Czechoslovakia during the period of Austrian rule into an industrial country with numerous towns the native folk traditions – old habits and customs, costumes, folk music, country architecture – are now to be found only in areas remote from the larger towns.

Bohemia

In Bohemia, subject to the influence of the old cultural centre, Prague, and to a consequent trend towards uniformity, distinctive local traditions have

Lace-maker

Girl in traditional costume

been preserved only in the region around Domažlice in southern Bohemia which has been occupied since the Middle Ages by the Chods, traditionally responsible for guarding the frontier.

Moravia

In Moravia, on the other hand, folk traditions are very much alive, particularly in the Haná plain around the old Moravian capital of Olomouc, in Moravian Slovakia (Moravské Slovácko), where the Slovaks settled at an early stage, and in Moravian Wallachia (Moravské Valašsko) with its rich folk art and its two local centres, Valašské Meziříčí and Rožnov pod Radhoštěm (Wallachian Open-Air Museum).

Moravian Silesia

Attempts are being made in Moravian Silesia, particularly since the overthrow of the communist regime in 1989, to revive the traditions of this very individual region, which once formed part of the Austrian crown land of Silesia.

Slovakia

Old customs and lively folk traditions are active and distinctive in the highland regions of Slovakia, notably in the High Tatras. Traditional practices (costumes, wooden houses, fortified farmsteads) are maintained with particular fervour by the Gorals (highlanders with an infusion of Polish blood) living around the village of Ždiar. There are numerous little wooden churches in the most easterly region of eastern Slovakia, where Carpatho-Ukrainian influence is evident. The towns and villages originally founded by German settlers in the Spiš region (below the south-east side of the High Tatras), the Štiavnica and Kremnica Hills bear witness in their layout and style of building to the way of life of their original inhabitants. Equally evident is the Magyar influence of the large Hungarian minority in Slovakia, which until the end of the First World War, as "Upper Hungary", was part of the Austro-Hungarian dual monarchy.

Suggested Routes

The routes suggested in this section are designed to help visitors travelling by car to plan their trip, while leaving them free to vary the routes according to their particular interests and the time available.
The suggested routes take in all the main tourist sights in the Czech and Slovak Republics; but not all the places of interest described in this guide lie directly on the routes, and to see some of them it may be necessary to make detours or side trips from the main routes. The descriptions in the A to Z sections of the guide, therefore, contain numerous suggestions and recommendations for detours and excursions to see these other sights.
The suggested routes can be followed on the map enclosed with this guide, which will help with detailed planning.
In these routes the names of places which are the subject of a separate entry in the A to Z sections of the guide are given in **bold** type.
All the places mentioned – towns, villages, regions, hills, rivers, isolated features of interest, etc. – are included in the Index at the end of the guide, making it easy to find the description of any notable sight.
The figures given in brackets at the head of each route are rounded figures for the main route. The additional distances involved in the various detours and excursions are indicated in each case.

Czech Lands

1. From Berlin (Germany) via Dresden to Prague (330km/205 miles)

Main route

From Berlin the A 13 autobahn runs south through Brandenburg and western Upper Lusatia to Dresden, on the Elbe, from which the route continues in hilly country, but without unduly steep gradients, through the eastern Ore Mountains to enter the Czech Republic (Bohemia). Beyond **Teplice** it runs through the beautiful Bohemian Massif (České Středohoří) to rejoin the Elbe (known in the Czech lands as the **Labe**) at Lovosice, briefly follows the course of the river Ohře, cuts through the Central Bohemian uplands, crosses the Vltava and comes to **Prague**, the magnificent capital of the Czech Republic.

Detours and walks

From Cinovec there is an attractive drive (8km/5 miles) along the ridge of the Ore Mountains (Krušné Hory) to the Komáří Hůrka, a hill commanding extensive views.
There is also a rewarding walk (1–1½ hours) from Bílka or Velemín to Mt Milešovka (835m/2740ft), the highest peak in the Bohemian Massif, with magnificent views. Another easy climb is the ascent (1 hour) of Mt Lovoš from Bílinka or Lovosice.
Shortly before **Terezín** (Theresienstadt; concentration camp memorial) a road branches off to the interesting town of **Litoměřice** (2.5km/1½ miles).
From Straškov it is a short drive (6.5km/4 miles) up Mt Říp (459m/1506ft), which is associated with the legend of Čech, the legendary ancestor of the Czech people.
Shortly before Veltrusy a side road (2km/1¼ miles) goes off to Nelahozeves, with the birthplace of the composer Antonín Dvořák.

2A. From Nuremberg (Germany) via Cheb and Karlovy Vary (Karlsbad) to Prague (340km/210 miles)

Main route

From Nuremberg the A 9 autobahn crosses over the hilly plateau of the Franconian Switzerland and then cuts through the Fichtelgebirge. On the frontier with the Czech Republic the road passes through the Chebsko area,

bounded by the Ore Mountains (Krušné Hory) and the Slavkov Forest (Slavkovský Les), with its old-world capital **Cheb**.
The route then continues by way of the world-famous spa of **Karlovy Vary** (Karlsbad), past the Doupovské Hory and through the featureless landscape of central Bohemia and the Kladno coalfield to **Prague**.

Detours and variants

From Cheb it is only 5km/3 miles to the well-known spa of **Františkovy Lázně** (Franzensbad). To Mariánské Lázně (Marienbad): see Route 3A.
From Sokolov a detour (25km/15 miles) can be made into the western Ore Mountains to Kraslice. From Karlovy Vary it is 18km/11 miles to Nejdek. To Jáchymov, Boží Dar and Mt Klínovec: see Route 3B.
From a road intersection half way between Karlovy Vary and Prague it is possible either to turn north by way of the hop-growing town of Žatec to the brown coal region around Most or south to Plzeň, continuing from there to Prague.

2B. From Prague via Plzeň to Nuremberg (290km/180 miles)

Main route

From **Prague** the route runs through central Bohemia and at Beroun cuts across the Berounka valley, which is of interest for its limestone formations. It then continues to **Plzeň**, the economic and administrative centre of western Bohemia. Beyond Plzeň the road broadly follows the course of the river Mže and then climbs into the western Bohemian Forest (Český Les), where it leaves the Czech Republic.
After crossing the frontier the route crosses the plateau of the Upper Palatinate Forest, runs through the Franconian Alb and then down the beautiful Pegnitz valley to Nuremberg, the second largest city in Bavaria.

Detours and variants

From Beroun there are attractive drives through the Berounka valley to **Karlštejn Castle** (14km/8½ miles), **Křivoklát Castle** (27km/17 miles) and the caves of Koněprusy (7km/4½ miles), in the Bohemian Karst (Český Kras).
Plzeň to České Budějovice and the Bohemian Forest: see Routes 6A and 6B.
From **Stříbro** a rewarding detour (4km/2½ miles) can be made to Kladruby Monastery.

The Spas of Western Bohemia and the Bohemian Ore Mountains (Krušne Hory)

3A. From Cheb via Mariánské Lázně (Marienbad) to Karlovy Vary (Karlsbad) (75km/45 miles)

Main route

From the old imperial city of **Cheb** the road runs between the wooded hills of the western Bohemian Forest (Český Les) and Slavkov Forest (Slavkovský Les) to the world-famed spa of **Mariánské Lázně** (Marienbad). It then continues through the western foothills of the Teplá Uplands (Tepelská Plošina) and the beautiful Teplá valley, mostly well wooded and at times narrow, to the well-known spa of **Karlovy Vary** (Karlsbad).

Variant and detour

Beyond Dolní Žandov it is possible to branch off the direct road and continue to Mariánské Lázně by way of the little spa of Kynžvart with its castle. Just beyond Mariánské Lázně a rewarding detour can be made to the Premonstratensian abbey of Teplá with its striking church and valuable library.

3B. From Karlovy Vary (Karlsbad) to Teplice (105km/65 miles)

Main route

From **Karlovy Vary** the route crosses a plateau, with expanses of bog, between the Ore Mountains (Krušné Hory) and the Doupov Hills and then

◀ *Panská Skála: a basalt crag in the "Bohemian Switzerland"*

continues through the picturesque valley of the Ohře into northern Bohemia.
Thereafter the road runs immediately below the southern slopes of the Ore Mountains and along the northern edge of the extensive brown coal region by way of the industrial towns of **Chomutov** and Litvínov to the well-known spa of **Teplice**, in the valley between the Ore Mountains and the Bohemian Massif (České Středohoří).

Detours

From a road junction beyond Ostrov a worthwhile detour (13km/8 miles) can be made by way of the spa of **Jáchymov** to Boží Dar on the crest ridge of the Ore Mountains, from which there are easy climbs up Mt Plešivec and Mt Klínovec.
From Vernéřov it is only 3km/2 miles to the old-world little town of **Kadaň**, which is well worth a visit for the sake of the historic old buildings round its market square.
From Osek (Cistercian abbey) a short detour (5km/3 miles) can be made to **Duchcov** with its castle containing mementoes of the 18th century adventurer Casanova.

3C. From Teplice via Děčín to Liberec (110km/70 miles)

Main route

From the spa of **Teplice**, in the valley between the Ore Mountains and the Bohemian Massif, the route runs below the southern slopes of the Ore Mountains and then the **Elbe Sandstone Hills** (Labské Pískovce) to the town of Děčín, beautifully situated in the valley of the **Labe** (Elbe). It then continues through constantly changing scenery in the southern **Lusatian Hills** (Lužické Hory).
Below the north-western slopes of the Ještěd range the road joins the valley of the Lužická Nisa, which it follows to the important industrial town of **Liberec** in northern Bohemia.

Detours

Just beyond Chlumec (the scene of a French defeat in 1813), at Varvažov, a road goes off on the left to Nakléřov Hill (6km/4 miles), from which there are extensive views.
From Libouchec a detour (3km/2 miles) can be made to the unique "rock city" of the Tiské Stěny.
From Jílové it is a 4km/2½ mile drive and a half-hour climb to the summit of the Děčínský Sněžník, the highest peak in the Elbe Sandstone Hills.
A particularly attractive excursion from Děčín is along the **Labe** (Elbe) valley to Dresden (62km/39 miles). A detour not to be missed is from Hřensko (12km/7½ miles from Děčín) to the Dolní Soutěska and Divoká Soutěska, two gorges carved out by the river Kamenice, and the magnificent Pravčická Brána.
From Česká Kamenice a drive (11km/7 miles) can be made to Jetřichovice, a good base for walks and climbs in the Bohemian Switzerland (České Švýcarsko).
Those who have sufficient time at their disposal can make an interesting excursion from a road junction beyond Česká Kamenice or from Svor through the western **Lusatian Hills** (Lužické Hory) to the Lusatian Uplands (Lužická Pahorkatina) and Rumburk.

3D. From Děčín via Ústí nad Labem to Litoměřice (50km/30 miles)

Main route

This attractive route ascends the valley of the **Labe** (Elbe), which between Lovosice and **Děčín** pursues a picturesque and winding course through the dark basalt of the Bohemian Massif (České Středohoří), the rounded summits of which are forest-covered, while the lower slopes, particularly towards the south, are covered with orchards and vineyards.

From Děčín the best route is along the west bank of the Labe to **Ústí nad Labem**, the economic and administrative centre of northern Bohemia and an important river port.

The route continues along the right bank of the river, passing Střekov Castle on its rocky crag. Then follows a beautiful stretch of road (in the last section sometimes at some distance from the river) to the old episcopal city of Litoměřice, situated on the edge of the wide Labe/Elbe depression opposite the junction of the Ohře with the Labe.

Excursions

From Neštědice it is a 45 minutes' climb to the summit of the Kozí Vrch, from which there are extensive views.

Possible excursions from Ústí nad Labem are a trip to the ruins of Střekov Castle and the ascent of the Vysoký Ostrý.

4. From Prague via České Budějovice to Linz (Austria) (250km/155 miles)

Main route

From **Prague** the route passes through central Bohemia, traversing the Central Bohemian Highlands (Středočeská Vrchovina) and continues through southern Bohemia to the old Hussite stronghold of **Tábor**, in the valley of the Lužnice.

The road then climbs the Lužnice valley. Beyond Veselí nad Lužnicí, where a side road branches off on the left, running via **Třeboň** to Vienna (see Route 7A), the main route continues on the old trade route linking Bohemia with Upper Austria to **České Budějovice**, capital of southern Bohemia, and then up the Malše valley into Upper Austria and down to Linz in the Danube valley.

Detours and branch routes

From Benešov u Prahy there are attractive detours to the much visited castles of **Konopiště** (2km/1¼ miles) and Jemniště (10km/6 miles).

From Tábor there are two attractive branch routes. A road runs west by way of the Orlík Dam (Orlická Přehradní Nádrž), near which are **Orlík** and Zvíkov Castles, and the beautiful Brdy Forest to **Plzeň**, from which it is possible to continue to Nuremberg or return to Prague (see Route 2B). The other road turns east through the south-western Bohemo-Moravian Highlands (Českomoravská Vrchovina) via the old town of **Pelhřimov** to **Jihlava**, from which it is possible either to continue to Vienna or to return to Prague (see Route 7B).

From Soběslav the moorland area (Blata) south-west of the little town can be seen in an attractive round trip of 20km/12½ miles.

10km/6 miles beyond České Budějovice a road branches off to **Český Krumlov**. Shortly before the Czech–Austrian frontier, at Dolní Dvořiště, another road branches off to **Vyšší Brod** and the Lipenská Přehradní Nádrž (Lake Lipno), a large artificial lake formed by a dam on the Vltava.

5. From Regensburg (Germany) through the Bohemian Forest to Plzeň (155km/95 miles)

Main route

From the old imperial city of Regensburg on the Danube the route leads through Eastern Bavaria and the Furth depression, on the line of an important medieval trade route into Bohemia, to enter the Czech Republic, running between the main crests of the Upper Palatinate Forest and the Bavarian Forest, followed by the Bohemian Forest (Šumava), into the Chod country (Chodsko).

The route then continues through the hilly foreland of the Bohemian Forest, down the Radbuza valley into the heavily industrialised Plzeň basin (Plzeňská pánev) and comes to **Plzeň**, the economic and administrative centre of western Bohemia, famed particularly for its beer.

Climb

From Česká Kubice it is a 3-hour climb to the summit of Mt Čerchov, the highest peak in the Bohemian part of the Upper Palatinate Forest (Český Les).

Detour

From Draženov it is 7.5km/4½ miles by way of Klenčí pod Čerchovem, a Chod village which still preserves its old traditions, to a fine viewpoint (Výhledy).

6A. From Plzeň via Písek to České Budějovice (140km/85 miles)

Main route

From **Plzeň** the route runs between the Brdy Forest and the foreland of the Bohemian Forest (Šumavské Podhůří) and through Nepomuk, birthplace of St John of Nepomuk, to the Southern Bohemian town of Blatná with its handsome moated castle.

The route then continues to the old gold-panning town of **Písek**, on the river Otava, and through the Budějovice basin (Budějovická pánev) to **České Budějovice**, capital of southern Bohemia, at the junction of the river Malše with the Vltava.

Detour and variants

From a road junction beyond Losiná a short detour (7km/4½ miles) can be made to Kozel Castle, an old hunting lodge.

From Písek it is possible to take a road which leads north-east to **Tábor** and continue from there to České Budějovice, or alternatively to return to Plzeň.

From Opařany, on the Písek–Tábor road, a detour (11km/7 miles) can be made to the spa of **Bechyně**, picturesquely situated on the river Lužnice.

Just before České Budějovice the castles of Kratochvíle, **Hluboká nad Vltavou** and Ohrada can be visited.

6B. From Plzeň through the Bohemian Forest (Šumava) to České Budějovice (270km/170 miles)

Main route

From **Plzeň** the route follows the valley of the Úhlava and beyond **Klatovy** runs through the wooded hills of the Bohemian Forest (Šumava).

Beyond this, in southern Bohemia, is the source area of the **Vltava**. The road descends the Vltava valley, passing the large artificial lake formed by the Lipno Dam (Lipenská Přehradní Nádrž) and through the picturesque little town of **Český Krumlov**, to reach **České Budějovice**, capital of southern Bohemia.

Variants and detours

From Klatovy it is possible either to turn west for **Domažlice** and return from there to Plzeň or to make straight for České Budějovice by way of **Strakonice** and Vodňany. From Horažd'ovice, between Klatovy and Strakonice, a detour (10km/6 miles) can be made to Rabí Castle.

From Běšiny, on the road running south from Klatovy, a side road (9km/5½ miles) runs east to the imposing ruins of Velhartice Castle.

From **Železná Ruda**, near the Czech–German frontier to the south of Klatovy, a minor road goes north-west to Domažlice. On this road is the little summer resort of Špičák, from which there are pleasant walks (½–1 hour) through unspoiled natural forest to the Devit's Lake (Čertovo Jezero) and the Black Lake (Černé Jezero). From a road junction after the bridge over the Otava beyond Dolejší Krušec a short detour (7km/4½ miles) can be made to **Sušice**.

Also worth a visit is the old town of **Vimperk**, which can be reached either from the Otava valley by way of Kašperské Hory or by a diversion (12km/7½ miles) from Horní Vltavice.

From Kvilda it is a 1½ hours' walk to the source of the Vltava.

Volary is a good base for walks and climbs in the area around Mt Plechý, the highest peak in the Bohemian Forest. From Volary it is also possible to take a road by way of the charming little town of **Prachatice** to Vodňany and from there direct to České Budějovice.

Instead of continuing along the whole length of Lake Lipno it is possible to turn off at Černá v Pošumavi into a road which leads direct to Český Krumlov by way of Hořice nad Šumavě, formerly famous for its Passion play. From a road junction beyond Český Krumlov it is 8km/5 miles to a chair-lift up Mt Klet', the highest peak in the Blanský Les.

1km/¾ mile from Rájov is the Cistercian monastery of Zlatá Koruna.

7A. From Prague via Tábor and Třeboň to Vienna (315km/195 miles)

Main route

From **Prague** as in Route 4 to beyond Veselí nad Lužnicí; then on through the Southern Bohemian pond country and its chief town, **Třeboň**. The route continues into Lower Austria and follows the Danube down to Vienna.

Detours

See Route 4

7B. From Vienna via Jihlava to Prague (300km/185 miles)

Main route

From Vienna the route ascends the Danube valley and leads through Lower Austria into the Czech Republic.
Within the Czech Republic it crosses the Dyje valley and, in southern Moravia, runs through the Bohemo-Moravian Highlands (Českomoravská Vrchovina), which extend into the south-western part of eastern Bohemia, cutting across the valleys of the Jihlava and the Sázava.
In central Bohemia the route enters the wide basin of the **Labe** (Elbe) and comes to **Prague**, on the Vltava.

Detours and variants

From a road junction beyond **Znojmo** a very rewarding detour (16km/10 miles) can be made into the wild Dyje valley, which forms an attractive contrast with the rather featureless landscapes of the rest of southern Moravia. Here can be seen Vranov Castle, the beautiful Vranov Lake formed by a dam on the Dyje (Vranovská Přehradní Nádrž) and Bitov Castle.
From Moravské Budějovice there are possible detours to Jaroměřice nad Rokytnou (8km/5 miles) or to the old-world little town of Dačice (33km/20 miles) and **Slavonice** (37km/23 miles).
From a road intersection between Moravské Budějovice and Jihlava detours can be made to the interesting towns of **Třebíč** and **Telč**.
From a road junction beyond **Jihlava** there is a good connection to the Moravian capital, **Brno**. From this road detours can be made to the little towns of Náměšť nad Oslavou and Kralice.
From Jihlava a road runs south-west via **Jindřichův Hradec** and **Třeboň** to České Budějovice.
From **Havlíčkův Brod** a road leads east into northern Moravia, with the interesting town of **Žd'ár nad Sázavou**. There is also a possible excursion from Havlíčkův Brod to Lipnice nad Sázavou, once the home of the well-known writer Jaroslav Hašek.
Within easy reach of Čáslav are the castles of Žleby and Žehušice.
4km/2½ miles from Malín is the Empire-style castle of Kačina.

One excursion from Malín that should not be missed is to the interesting and attractive town of **Kutná Hora** (4km/2½ miles).
Also worth seeing are **Kolín** with its cathedral and Kouřim, still surrounded by its old walls (5km/3 miles).

8. From Prague via Hradec Králové and Brno to Vienna (375km/235 miles)

Main route

From **Prague** the route passes through the wide **Labe** (Elbe) basin in Central Bohemia and continues through eastern Bohemia to its capital, the important town of **Hradec Králové**.
It then traverses the north-eastern part of the Bohemo-Moravian Highlands (Českomoravská Vrchovina), crosses the old boundary between Bohemia and Moravia and comes into the Hřebečsko district. Thereafter it continues through southern Moravia to its economic and administrative centre, **Brno**.
Beyond Brno is the vine-growing region of southern Moravia, with the Pavlov Hills (Pavlovské Vrchy). The route then continues over the historic Marchfeld into the Danube valley and so to Vienna.

Detours and variant

From Lipůvka it is 11km/7 miles to Blansko, a good base from which to visit the magniificent caves of the **Moravian Karst** (Moravský Kras). Another rewarding trip from Lipůvka is to Tišnov (10km/6 miles), with the Porta Coeli monastery, and from there up the Svratka valley to the large castle of **Pernštejn** (26km/16 miles).

From Brno there is an attractive route by way of **Uherské Hradiště** and through Moravian Slovakia (Moravské Slovácko) to **Trenčín** in the Slovak Republic and from there through the Váh valley to **Bratislava**.

From Brno the castle and battlefield of **Slavkov u Brna** (Austerlitz) can be visited.

Within easy reach of Uherské Hradiště (all within 5km/3 miles) are Buchlov Castle, the monastery of Velehrad and the archaeological site of Sady. The spa of **Luhačovice** is only 11km/7 miles away.

From **Mikulov** a road runs east via the wine-growing town of Valtice to **Břeclav**, near which are the important archaeological sites of Pohansko and Mikulčice. To the east of Mikulov is **Lednice**, in an extensive area of parkland and ponds, with numbers of castles.

9A. From Prague via Mladá Boleslav and Turnov to Wrocław (Poland)

(280km/175 miles)

Main route

From **Prague** the route passes through the wide basin of the **Labe** (Elbe) and up the Jizera valley, below the western foothills of the Jičín Uplands (Jičínská Pahorkatina). Then, in northern Bohemia, it cuts through the Krkonoše foreland (Krkonošské Podhůří) between the **Jizera Hills** and the **Krkonoše** range and crosses the Jakobstal pass (889m/2917ft) to enter Polish Silesia (Śląsk).

It then continues down the beautiful Szklarska valley, through the Bober-Katzbach Hills and over the Central Silesian plain to Wrocław (formerly Breslau).

Detours and variants

From **Mladá Boleslav** it is 18km/11 miles to Jabkenice, where the composer Smetana lived for some time.

From **Mnichovo Hradiště** the ruins of Valečov Castle, partly hewn from the local sandstone, and the rock formations on the slopes of Mt Mužský can be visited.

From **Turnov** a road runs north to **Liberec**. Just off this road (1.5km/1 mile) is Sychrov Castle.

From Turnov a road runs south-east via **Jičín** to **Hradec Králové**, from which it is possible to continue (as in Route 9B) to Wrocław. Beyond Turnov the road traverses the beautiful **Bohemian Paradise** (Český Ráj), with its extraordinary rock formations and picturesque ruined castles. At Hradec Králové is the battlefield of Königgrätz.

From Polubný there is an attractive road through the lonely forest-covered **Jizera Hills** (now damaged by pollution) to **Frýdlant**.

9B. From Prague via Hradec Králové and Náchod to Wrocław (Poland) (275km/3170 miles)

Main route

From **Prague** as in Route 8 to **Hradec Králové**.

The route then continues through eastern Bohemia along the **Labe** (Elbe) and into the Úpa valley. Just before the Czech–Polish frontier it crosses the river Metuje.

Within Poland (Wałbrzych) the route runs through the Kłodzko Uplands into the valley of the Nysa Kłodzka, and so to Wrocław.

Detours and variants

From Jaroměř it is 7km/4½ miles to **Kuks**, notable for the fine Baroque statues by Matthias Bernhard Braun von Braun.

3km/2 miles from Česká Skalice, in the Úpa valley, is Ratibořice Castle, with mementoes of the Czech poetess Božena Nemcová.

From a road junction a few kilometres before **Náchod** a road goes south-east to Svitavy, passing through a number of interesting places and of-

fering attractive detours: from **Nové Město nad Metují** to Slavoňov with its wooden church (4km/2½ miles); from Dobruška to Opočno (5km/3 miles), with a handsome castle set in a beautiful park; from **Rychnov nad Kněžnou** to the holiday resort of Rokytnice (18km/11 miles), in the **Orlík Hills**; from Vamperk to the castles of Doudleby nad Orlicí (2km/1¼ miles), Kostelec nad Orlicí (6km/4 miles) and Častolovice (8km/5 miles); from Ústi nad Orlicí to the summer resort of Letohrad (12km/7½ miles) or to Brandýs nad Orlicí (12km/7½ miles), once the headquarters of the Bohemian Brethren.
From Náchod it is an easy climb (¾ hour) to the summit of Mt Dobrošov (622m/2041ft; wide views).
From a road junction a short distance before the Czech–Polish frontier a beautiful road leads into the Broumov Uplands (Broumovská Vrchovina). **Broumov** is a good base from which to explore the "rock city" of the Broumov Crags (Broumovské Stěny).
For the Teplice and Adršpach Crags (Tepličko-Adršpašské Skalý) see Route 10.
Near the Polish spa of Kudowa Zdrój, in the village of Czermna, is an interesting "Chapel of Skulls".

10. From Liberec via Tanvald and Trutnov to Náchod (130km/80 miles)

Main route

From the industrial town of **Liberec** with its many handsome buildings the route runs through northern Bohemia along the southern fringe of the **Jizera Hills**, up the valley of the Nisa (Neisse) to the watershed between the Odra (Oder) and the Labe (Elbe) and then down into the valley of the Kamenice.
Now in eastern Bohemia, it follows the winding and sometimes narrow valley of the Jizera and then skirts the **Krkonoše** range, passing through its southern foothills and crossing the valley of the **Labe** (Elbe).
Then on through the southern foreland of the Krkonoše (Krkonošské Podhůří) and down the Úpa valley.
The route ends at the frontier town of **Náchod**, in the valley of the Metuje.

Detours into the hills

From Jablonec nad Nisou there is a pleasant excursion (6km/4 miles) to the Černá Studnice, from which there are far-ranging views.
6km/4 miles north of Jablonec is the village of Janov, a good base for walks and climbs in the hills.
A side road in the Jizera valley leads to the holiday resort of Rokytnice nad Jizerou (3km/2 miles).
From Hrabačov a hill road (23km/14 miles) goes up to the Zlaté Návrší (Golden Hill), from which there is a rewarding walk to the Labe Falls (Vodopád Labe), the Labská Studánka (Spring) and Mt Kotel.
Vrchlabí is the starting-point of a road through the Labe valley (15km/9 miles) to Špindlerův Mlýn, a popular holiday centre in the Krkonoše range from which there are numerous footpaths into the hills. From Špindlerův Mlýn a road climbs up (8km/5 miles) to the Špindler pass (Špindlerovka), on the Czech–Polish frontier.
At Čistá a country road (9km/5½ miles) goes off to the spa of Janské Lázně.
From the near end of Mladé Buky a road ascends to Pec pod Sněžkou (15km/9 miles), starting-point for the ascent of Mt Sněžka, the highest point in the Krkonoše range; from the summit there are superb panoramic views.
From **Trutnov** one excursion is highly recommended – to the **Teplice and Adršpach Crags** (Teplicko-Adršpašské Skály; 18–24km/11–15 miles), between which is the Wolf's Gorge (Vlčí Rokle).

11. From Prague via Pardubice and Olomouc to Ostrava (365km/225 miles)

Main route

From **Prague** the route runs through central Bohemia and then, in eastern Bohemia, reaches the **Labe** (Elbe), which is crossed at **Pardubice**.

It continues by way of Svitavy and through the Hřebečsko area and the Zábřež Uplands (Zábřežská Vrchovina) in northern Moravia into the Morava valley. Then over the fertile Haná plain to **Olomouc**, formerly capital of Moravia.
Beyond this the route leads into the Bečva valley and through the Moravian Gate (Moravská Brána) into the wide valley of the Odra (Oder), between the Odra Hills (Oderské Vrchy) and the **Moravo-Silesian Beskyds** (Moravskoslezké Beskydy). The route ends in the coal-mining and industrial region of **Ostrava**, on the Czech–Polish frontier.

Detours and variants

From Chrudim it is 4km/2½ miles to Slatiňany Castle, which houses the Horse Museum. – From Mohelnice it is 8km/5 miles to Úsov Castle, with the Hunting and Forestry Museum. – It is a rather longer trip (74km/46 miles) to Jeseník, but a very rewarding one, with the opportunity of exploring the remote fastnesses of the Hrubý Jeseník range. – From Loštice it is 6km/4 miles to the mighty Bouzov Castle. – Shortly before Nasobůrky a road goes off to the stalactitic caves of Javoříčko (10km/6 miles). – From Olomouc a beautiful road goes to Staré Mešto u Uherského in Moravian Slovakia (Moravské Slovácko). From Hulín on this road a detour can be made to the attractive town of **Kroměříž** (6km/4 miles). From Otrokovice-Kvítkovice a road runs via the shoe-manufacturing town of **Zlín** (10km/6 miles) to Vizovice (16km/10 miles), which has a fine castle.
An alternative to the direct road from Olomouc to Ostrava or Český Těšín is the detour (9km/5½ miles longer) through the **Moravian Uplands** (Nízký Jeseník), with the possibility of an excursion (15km/9 miles) from Šternberk to Sovinec Castle, another from **Opava** via Krnov (25km/15 miles) to the Hrubý Jeseník hills (see above), or a return via Hradec nad Moravicí (8km/5 miles) to the main route at Fulnek.
From Lipník nad Bečvou it is 4km/2½ miles to the ruins of Helfštýn Castle. – Near Hranice is the little spa of Teplice nad Bečvou, with an interesting aragonite cave. From Hranice there is an attractive trip (85km/53 miles), first in the Bečva valley through Moravian Wallachia (Valašsko) and then through the wooded Javorník hills to Bytča in the Váh valley (Slovakia). From a road junction beyond Rožnov pod Radhoštěm a hill road (8km/5 miles) leads to the holiday resort of Pustevny in the Western or Moravo-Silesian Beskyds, from which there is a ridge walk (1 hour) to the legendary Mt Radhošt'. – Beyond **Nový Jičín** a side road branches off to the picturesque little town of Štramberk, from which it is a 15-minute walk to the Šipka Cave. – From **Příbor** it is 5km/3 miles to Kopřivnice, famed as a car-manufacturing town and as the birthplace of the great runner Emil Zátopek. The Municipal Museum displays Zátopek's sports trophies and the products of the Tatra car plant. – From Rychaltice a country road (3km/2 miles) goes off to the large ruined castle of Hukvaldy.

Slovakia

Prague to Bratislava by motorway, 313km/195 miles
D 1 Prague–Brno, 196km/122 miles, D 2 Brno–Bratislava, 117km/73 miles

1. From Vienna to Bratislava (65km/40 miles)

Main route

From Vienna the route runs through Lower Austria at some distance from the Danube basin with its marshland and riverine woodland, through a rather featureless landscape in which the patterns of settlement show the transition to the Hungarian puszta.

The frontier of the Slovak Republic is crossed just before its capital, **Bratislava**, whose massive castle can be seen from a great way off.

The main feature of interest on this short route is the site of Roman Carnuntum (Archaeological Park near Petronell and Bad Deutsch Altenburg), which is easily accessible on the main road.

2. From Bratislava via Piešt'any and Žilina to Poprad (345km/215 miles)

Main route

From the Slovak capital of **Bratislava** on the Danube (Dunaj) the route runs through the vine-growing region bordering the **Little Carpathians** (Malé Karpaty) into the valley of the Váh. It then ascends the valley by way of the well-known spa of **Piešt'any**, passing between the White Carpathians (Bilé Karpaty) and the Inovec Hills (Povazšký Inovec) and then between the Javorník Hills and the upland region of Stražovská Hornatina.

A few kilometres before **Žilina** the road turns east and passes through the **Little Fatra** (Malá Fatra) in the Strečno defile.

At **Ružomberok** the road enters the Liptov area, the upper valley of the Váh, which is enclosed on the north by the Choč Hills (Chočské Pohorie) and the Western Tatras (Západné Tatry), on the south by the **Low Tatras** (Nízke Tatry). It then crosses the watershed between the Váh and the Poprad and comes to the town of **Poprad** in the **Spiš** region, where the **High Tatras** (Vysoké Tatry) rear steeply up.

Detours and variants

From Bernolákovo it is 3km/2 miles to the village of Chorvátsky Grob, which is famed for its folk arts and crafts.

From **Trnava** it is 12km/7½ miles to Dolná Krupá, where Beethoven frequently stayed.

Beyond Trnava a road goes off on the right to Hlohovec (8km/5 miles), on the left bank of the Váh.

From Nové Město nad Váhom it is 7km/4½ miles to the romantic ruined castle of Čachtice.

The well-known spa of Trenčianské Teplice lies a short distance off the road through the Váh valley in a beautiful setting of wooded hills (6km/4 miles from Trenčianská Teplá; tram service).

Beyond Beluša there is a rewarding detour (10km/6 miles longer) on a side road which runs close to the river (dam) to Považská Bystrica.

From Považská Teplá the wild Manín Gorge (Manínska Úžina) can be visited (3km/2 miles).

Beyond Predmier there is an attractive detour (6km/4 miles) to the extraordinary "rock city" of Súl'ovské Skaly.

From Žilina, an important road junction, a number of interesting excursions are possible. A beautiful hill road (39km/24 miles) ascends into the Strážovská Hornatina and the south-western Little Fatra (Lučanská Fatra), ending at the village of Čičmany, which preserves many old customs. There is a particularly attractive trip (33km/20 miles) into the beautiful Vrátna valley, the main tourist region in the north-eastern Little Fatra (Krivánska Fatra; chair-lift to the Snilovské Sedlo, 1520m/4987ft). A road runs north over the Jablunka Pass (Jablunkovský Průsmyk; 553m/1814ft), in the territory of the Czech Republic, into the Těšinské Slezsko district on the river Olše, which shows Polish influence.

4km/2½ miles south of Priekopa, on the road up the Hron valley, is the town of **Martin**, which has played an important part in the cultural and political life of Slovakia, with the Slovak National Museum and the well-stocked National Library.

Kral'ovany is the starting-point of an attractive detour (58km/36 miles) up the beautiful Orava valley to Lake Orava (Oravská Priehradná Nádrž), formed by a dam on the river.

The peak of Vel'ky Choč (1611m/5286ft; fine views) is best climbed from the little spa of Lúčky, reached on a road (10km/6 miles) which branches off on the left just beyond Ružomberok. 10km/6 miles farther east, on the northern shores of the recently formed artificial lake of Liptovská Ondrašová, is a large recreation area.

From **Liptovský Mikuláš** there is a particularly attractive drive up the Demänova valley (Demänovská dolina), with an ice cave and a stalactitic cave, into the pretty Jasná valley (Jasná dolina), below the crest ridge of the **Lower Tatras** (Nizké Tatry; chair-lift up Mt Chopok, 2024m/6641ft). Continuation into Bystrá valley: see Route 5.

3. From Poprad into the High Tatras (Vysoké Tatry)

(round trip, about 100km/60 miles)

Main route

From **Poprad**, the "gateway of the Tatras", the route leads north-east down the Poprad valley through the **Spiš** region to **Kežmarok**, an old town which is the chief place in the Upper Spiš area.

Thereafter the road turns west and heads for the **Belianske Tatras**. Below these hills is the starting-point of a route (electric railway) along the south-eastern edge of the mountains which offers less scenic variety but is an excellent means of access to the **High Tatras** (Vysoké Tatry). Along this road are the main tourist centres on the Slovak side of the hills and numerous little altitude resorts. From the end of this road, on the Štrbské Pleso (Lake), a winding road descends to rejoin the main road to Poprad.

Detours, walks and climbs

Before taking the road running along the south-east side of the Belianske Tatras it is worth making a detour to the Belianské jaskyňa (stalactitic cave; 1km/¾ mile and a 20-minute walk) and the interesting Goral village of Ždiar (9km/4½ miles).

Tatranské Matliare is the starting-point of a mountain walk (about 2¼ hours) to the Green Lake (Zelené Pleso), enclosed by steep-sided crags.

From **Tatranská Lomnica** a cableway almost 6km/4 miles long runs up the Lomnický Štít (2632m/8636ft).

From **Starý Smokovec** there are rewarding walks (up to 3 hours) into the long Vel'ka Studená dolina (valley) and to the Five Spiš Lakes (Pät'Spišských Plies), continuing to the morainic wall of Mt Hrebienok (1280m/4200ft; funicular).

From Tatranská Polianka the Velická dolina goes north. From this valley it is possible to climb the Gerlachovský Štít (2655m/8711ft; 7 hours), the highest peak in the High Tatras.

From the **Stŕbské Pleso** a rewarding path runs up the beautiful Mengusovská dolina to the magnificently situated Lake Poprad (Popradské Pleso), from which Mt Ostrva (1984m/6510ft; 1½ hours) and Mt Rysy (2499m/8199ft; 3 hours) can be climbed. From the Stŕbské Pleso it is a 5–6 hours' climb up Mt Kriváň.

4. From Poprad via Prešov to Košice (120km/75 miles)

Main road

From **Poprad**, the "gateway of the Tatras", on the river Poprad, the route traverses the historic **Spiš** region to **Levoča**, its old capital, situated between the Levoča Hills (Levočské Pohorie) and the upper valley of the river Hornád. It then continues by way of the picturesque little town of Spišská Kapitula and past the massive ruins of Spiš Castle (Spišský Hrad), which gave its name to the region.

Thereafter the road runs through the wooded Branisko Hills into the Šariš region and the Šariš Uplands (Šarišská Vrchovina) to the chief place in this area, Prešov, where the Carpatho-Ukrainian element in the population is unmistakable.

The route now continues through the broad valley of the Torysa, which is bounded on the east by the Slanské Pohorie, to **Košice**, on the river Hornád, the chief town in eastern Slovakia.

Detours and variants

From Levoča a country road (10km/6 miles) runs south to Spišská Nová Ves, from which the **Slovak Paradise** (Slovenský Ráj) with its karstic gorges can be visited. 6km/4 miles from Spišská Nová Ves is Markušovce Castle, which contains a collection of keyboard instruments.

Beyond Spišské Podhradie a side road (4km/2½ miles) goes off to Žehra, with a Gothic church in which wall paintings of the 13th–15th centuries have been discovered. Those who prefer to head direct from Prešov to Rožňava rather than continue to Košice can take the beautiful road (90km/56 miles) through the **Slovakian Ore Mountains** (Slovenské Rudohorie), passing the hill towns of the Lower Spiš area, once a German linguistic island in the Hnilec and Smolník valleys.

5. From Košice via Banská Bystrica to Bratislava (425km/265 miles)

Main route

From **Košice** the route passes through eastern Slovakia and the upland region of the **Slovakian Karst** (Slovenský Kras) to the old town of **Rožňava**. It then continues through the **Slovakian Ore Mountains** (Slovenské Rudohorie), first in the Slaná valley and later in the romantic upper valley of the Hnilec. Most of the route is through the valley of the Hron, the upper section of which, below the south side of the **Low Tatras** (Nizké Tatry), is particularly beautiful.

From **Zvolen** the route still follows the Hron valley, between the Kremnica and Štiavnica Hills. At Hronský Beňadik it leaves the valley and continues through western Slovakia with its great expanses of arable land to the lively town of **Nitra** on the river Nitra, once an important centre of missionary activity in Great Moravia.

Beyond this the road cuts across the wide valley of the Váh and comes to **Bratislava**, capital of the Slovak Republic, situated on the Danube (Dunaj) below the **Little Carpathians** (Malé Karpaty). The last section of the road is described in Route 2.

Detours and variants

From Dvorniky it is 1km/¾ mile on a hill road to the entrance to the karstic canyon of Zádielská dolina.

From Rožňava there is a road through the south-western part of the Slovakian Karst (Slovenský Kras) by way of **Lučenec** to Zvolen. From this road there are attractive detours to a stalactitic cave at Gombasek (Gombasecká jaskyňa; 1.5km/1 mile); to an ice gorge at Silica (Silická l'adnica; 7km/4½ miles and ½-hour walk); and to the Domica Cave (Domica jaskyňa; 10km/6 miles; in summer underground boat trips to Aggtelek Cave in Hungary).

Within easy reach of Lučenec are Halič Castle (7km/4½ miles) and the old-world little town of Fil'akovo (15km/9 miles). Beyond Kriván a side road (3km/2 miles) branches off to the hill village of Detva, on the edge of the volcanic uplands of Pol'ana, which has preserved old folk traditions.

In the upper Hnilec valley is the Dobšin Ice Cave (Dobšinská l'adová jaskyňa; ½-hour walk on a beautiful forest track).

From Brezno there are two roads (each 13km/8 miles) to the entrance to the beautiful Býstra valley, in which a road (11km/7 miles) runs by way of the holiday settlement of Tále to just below the main ridge of the **Low Tatras** (Nizké Tatry; chair-lift up Mt Chopok, 2024m/6641ft). Beyond this into the Jasná valley: see Route 2.

Another road (9km/6 miles) runs up from Brezno into the **Slovakian Ore Mountains** (Slovenské Rudohorie) and to the hill village of Čierny Balog, where old traditional costumes are still worn.

The well-known spa of Sliač Kúpele is only 2km/1¼ miles off the main road. A rewarding detour (20km/12½ miles) is to **Banská Štiavnica**, a town of great importance in the Middle Ages. From here it is an easy climb (2 hours) up Mt Sitno (1009m/3311ft), the highest peak in the Štiavnica Hills.

From a road intersection near the ruined Šášov Castle two important roads branch off. A hill road runs north (11km/7 miles) by way of the interesting town of **Kremnica**, which had a mint in the Middle Ages, into the wide Turiec basin (Turčianska Kotlina), which extends into the Váh valley. Another road runs west via Handlová and Prievidza to **Trenčín** (103km/64 miles), also in the Váh valley.

5km/3 miles from Zlaté Moravce, which lies some distance off the route, is the handsome Topol'čianky Castle, set in a large game reserve, with bison as well as many species of game. An attractive excursion (1½ hours) from **Nitra** is to Mt Zobor (588m/1929ft; extensive views). It is also possible to continue south from Nitra by way of Nové Zámky to the river port of **Komárno** on the Danube (road bridge to Komárom on the Hungarian bank). Some 55km/34 miles north-west, on the Žitný Ostrov, a large island in the Danube, is the controversial Gabčikovo hydroelectric station, which is supplied with water from the Danube in a canal 30km/19 miles long.

Sights from A to Z: Czech Republic

Bechyně D 3

Region: Southern Bohemia
District: Tábor
Altitude: 406m/1332ft
Population: 6000

*Situation and characteristics

The little town of Bechyně in southern Bohemia, picturesquely situated above the river Lužnice, is a popular spa (carbonated mineral springs; mud baths). It is noted for its pottery industry, and has a well-known ceramic college.

Sights

Castle

Bechyně's handsome Renaissance castle, originally a fortified Gothic castle, was enlarged in the 16th and 18th centuries. Most of it is now occupied by a rest home.

Churches

On the Lužnice is a former Minorite friary (15th c.); the church has fine Gothic diamond vaulting. In the town's main square is the Decanal Church, built in 1615 and remodelled in Baroque style in 1740.

Town walls
Bridge

Other features of interest are the town walls (with four bastions) and the reinforced concrete road and rail bridge, built in 1928, which crosses the Lužnice at a height of 50m/165ft. The first electrified railway line in Austria-Hungary, between Bechyně and Tábor (24km/15 miles), was opened in 1904. There are a local museum and a firefighting museum (Hasičské Muzeum).

Firefighting Museum

Surroundings of Bechyně

Židova Strouha

2km/1¼ miles south is the romantic rocky valley of Židova Strouha.

Příběnice

3km/2 miles north of Bechyně, in a bend on the Lužnice, are the picturesque ruins of the Early Gothic castle of Příběnice (founded in 13th c.; destroyed 1437).

Dobronice

5km/3 miles north of Bechyně can be seen the ruins of Dobronice Castle (originally 14th c.); fine views.

Bernartice

10km/6 miles north-west of Bechyně is Bernartice (alt. 463m/1519ft), with a church which was originally Gothic (now altered except for the choir). The village was once famed for the making of pipes and cigarette-holders (a cottage industry). In the nearby forest is a prehistoric burial site. During the Second World War the Benartice area suffered heavy damage.

Bohemian Paradise / Český Ráj D/E 2

Regions: Northern and Eastern Bohemia
Area: about 125sq.km/48sq.miles
Altitude: 400–500m/1300–1640ft

◀ *Český Krumlov, a picturesque town in Southern Bohemia*

An idyllic scene in the "Bohemian Paradise"

Situation and characteristics

The Bohemian Paradise (Český Ráj), the oldest nature reserve in the Czech Lands (established 1955), lies in the well wooded Jičín Uplands (Jičínská Pahorkatina) on the borders of northern and eastern Bohemia, between the towns of Turnov, Mnichovo Hradiště and Jičín (see entries).

*Rock formations
*Castles

With its innumerable bizarre rock formations, "rock cities" and rock labyrinths and its many castles the Bohemian Paradise is a popular recreation area for walkers and rock-climbers. Its most notable landmark is the striking silhouette of the ruined Trosky Castle (see below). The chief place in the Bohemian Paradise and a good base from which to explore it is the town of Turnov, on the northern edge of the area.

Sights in the **Bohemian Paradise

Valdštejn Castle

3km/2 miles south-east of Turnov, in a forest setting in the north of the Bohemian Paradise (alt. 389m/1276ft), are the ruins of Valdštejn, an Early Gothic castle partly built into the rock which was the ancestral seat of the Valdštejn (Wallenstein) family. Part of the castle has been rebuilt in neo-Gothic style.

Sedmihorky

4km/2½ miles south-east of Turnov lies the summer resort of Sedmihorky (alt. 270m/886ft), formerly a spa. It is a good base for excursions to the "rock cities" and the castles of Hrubá Skála and Valdštejn.

Hrubá Skála

5km/3 miles south-east of Turnov is Hrubá Skála (alt. 287m/942ft), with a medieval castle (alt. 367m/1204ft) which belonged to the Aehrenthal family, rebuilt in its present form in the 19th century.

To the west of the little town is the "rock city" of Hrubá Skála (Hruboskalské Skalní Mešto), the largest of the kind in the Bohemian Paradise, with 220 sandstone crags and pinnacles known under a variety of picturesque names (the "Dragon Walls", the "Dragon's Tooth", the "Conductor", the "Conductor's Baton", etc.).

Rovensko pod Troskami

8km/5 miles south-east of Turnov is the summer resort of Rovensko pod Troskami (alt. 306m/1004ft; pop. 1300). The Gothic church has a wooden bell-tower (1630), with bells hanging upside down ("rebel bells"). There is a handsome bridge in Empire style (1847).

***Kost Castle**

10km/6 miles south of Turnov, on the southern edge of the Bohemian Paradise, stands Kost Castle (Hrad Kost; alt. 274m/899ft). The core of this Gothic castle dates from the 14th century; the Schellenberg Building is Late Gothic; and the Biberstein Wing (destroyed during the Second World War) was added in the 16th century. Within the castle are St Anne's Chapel (Gothic) and an old alchemists' kitchen. There is an exhibition of Late Gothic art.

***Trosky Castle**
(Plan p. 114)

10km/6 miles south-east of Turnov, on two rugged basalt crags known as the Panna (Maiden; 57m/187ft) and the Baba (Grandmother; 47m/154ft), can be found the romantic ruins of Trosky Castle (alt. 488m/1601ft; the name means "rubble"), founded in 1380, which dominates the surrounding country, affording wide views.

Libuň

14km/8½ miles south-east of Turnov is the village of Libuň (alt. 320m/1050ft), with a Gothic church (remodelled in Baroque style in 1771) and a Gothic presbytery.

Vyskeř

6km/4 miles south of Turnov we come to the village and viewpoint of Vyskeř (alt. 372m/1221ft).

Sobotka

13km/8 miles south of Turnov, on the southern edge of the Bohemian Paradise, is the little town of Sobotka (alt. 305m/1001ft; pop. 2500), a good starting-point for walks through the romantic Plakánek valley (sandstone crags) and to Kost Castle. Sobotka has a number of handsome examples of traditional architecture. To the north of the town is a Baroque hunting lodge, Humprecht (1666–72), on an oval ground-plan. It now houses art exhibitions. Fine views.

Kost Castle

(14th c.; restored in 20th c.)

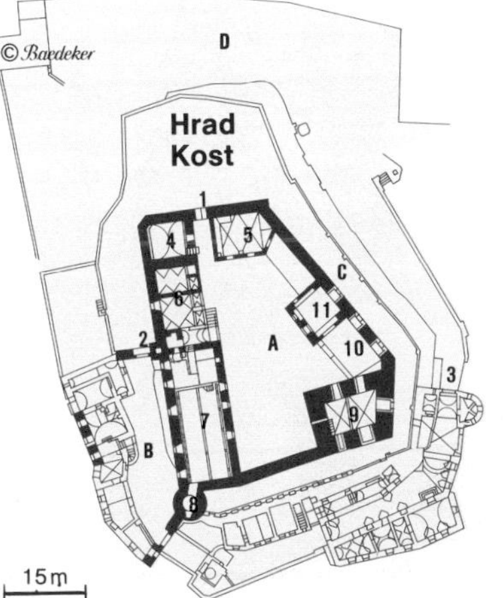

A Inner Ward
B Biberstein Wing (16th c.)
C Moat
D Outer Ward

1 First Gate
2 Second Gate
3 Third Gate
4 Gate-Tower
5 Chapel (Gothic)
6 New Palace (Schellenberg Building, Late Gothic)
7 Old Palace (Gothic)
8 Round Tower (Gothic)
9 White Tower (Gothic)
10 Sala terrena (Early Baroque, unfinished)
11 Early 16th century building

Hrad Trosky

Trosky Castle ruins

A Outer ward (moat)
B Second outer ward
C Working quarters
D Inner ward
E Gothic Palace
F Staircase (early 19th c.)
G "Panna" Tower (maiden)
H "Baba" Tower (grandmother)

© Baedeker

Příhrazy

8km/5 miles south-west of Turnov lies the village of Příhrazy (alt. 288m/945ft), a good base for walks and climbs among the rocks and crags in the surrounding area.

Drábské Světničky

9km/5½ miles south-west of Turnov are the Drábské Světničky (alt. 380m/1247ft) – seven great blocks of sandstone in which six passages and 18 rooms have been hewn. In the early 15th century this was a Hussite stronghold.

Valečov

11km/7 miles south-west of Turnov are the ruins of Valečov Castle (alt. 236m/774ft), a Gothic rock stronghold dating from the 14th century.

Mt Mužský

In the west of the Bohemian Paradise is a basalt hill, Mt Mužský (463m/1519ft), from which there are far-ranging views.

****Prachov Crags**

The Prachov Crags (Prachovské Skály, 430–450m/1410–1475ft) are a landscape reserve (area about 3sq.km/1.2sq.miles) in the south-east of the Bohemian Paradise.

Rock city

Here too are bizarre rock formations, a "rock city" with some 80 towers and 200 flights of steps (prehistoric settlements).

Three waymarked paths, with railings and ladders to provide security, lead through these bizarre sandstone formations (towers, pillars, pinnacles, passages, caves, etc.) to the best viewpoints and into deep, narrow gorges. The most picturesque of these is the Emperor's Gorge (Císařská Chodba), named after Emperor Francis II of Austria, who visited the rock city in 1813. In the centre of the Prachovské Skály is a small rest-house (*turistická chata*).

Prachov Crags

Jinolice

On the north-eastern edge of the Prachov Crags, around the village of Jinolice (alt. 325m/1066ft), is an area much visited for its three ponds, the largest of which is the Oborský Rybník (11 hectares/27 acres).

Prachov

On the south-eastern edge of the rock city is the village of Prachov (alt. 265m/869ft), from which the crags take their name.

Pařez Castle

On the north-western edge of the Prachov Crags are the ruins of the small medieval castle of Pařez (alt. 360m/1181ft), which is partly hewn from the sandstone.

Brandýs nad Labem · Stará Boleslav D 2

Region: Central Bohemia
District: Praha-Východ
Altitude: 169m/554ft
Population: 16,000

Situation and characteristics

The towns of Brandýs nad Labem (on the left bank of the Labe/Elbe) and Stará Boleslav (on the right bank), some 20km/12½ miles north-east of Prague, were combined in 1960 into a double town.

Sights

Brandýs nad Labem

The town of Brandýs nad Labem was founded in the 14th century. Its most notable feature is the Renaissance castle (16th c.), once the summer residence of the Emperor Rudolph II, situated on higher ground on the north-eastern edge of the town.

Stará Boleslav

In the early Middle Ages Stará Boleslav was a place of importance, a residence of the rulers of Bohemia. On the spot where according to legend Duke Wenceslas (Václav), the future St Wenceslas, was murdered in 929 by his brother there now stands the richly furnished St Wenceslas Chapel (originally 11th c.; rebuilt in 15th c. in Gothic style and remodelled in Baroque style in 1740), with a Romanesque crypt. Nearby is the little St Clement's Church (12th c.; renovated in 17th and 19th c.). The Early Baroque Church of Our Lady (formerly a pilgrimage church) was built in 1617–27 and restored in the 18th century. There are remains of the 14th century town walls; town gate, rebuilt in Baroque style, with museum.

Surroundings of Brandýs nad Labem and Stará Boleslav

Přerov

12km/7½ miles east, on the left bank of the Labe, is Přerov nad Labem (alt. 178m/584ft; pop. 1000), with an open-air museum of traditional architecture.

Lysá nad Labem

16km/10 miles east lies the town of Lysá nad Labem (alt. 175m/574ft; pop. 10,000), with a large castle (rebuilt in Baroque style in 17th c.) and a beautiful park.

Benátky nad Jizerou

17km/10½ miles north-east, on the Jizera, is the little town of Benátky nad Jiserou (alt. 225m/738ft; pop. 7000; manufacture of abrasive materials), with a 16th century Renaissance castle which was enlarged in the 17th century. The astronomers Tycho Brahe and Johannes Kepler lived here in 1599–1601, and Tycho Brahe died here. Other residents were, in the 18th century, the Benda family of musicians, and in the 19th century the young Bedrich Smetana (see Famous People).

Plan of inner city

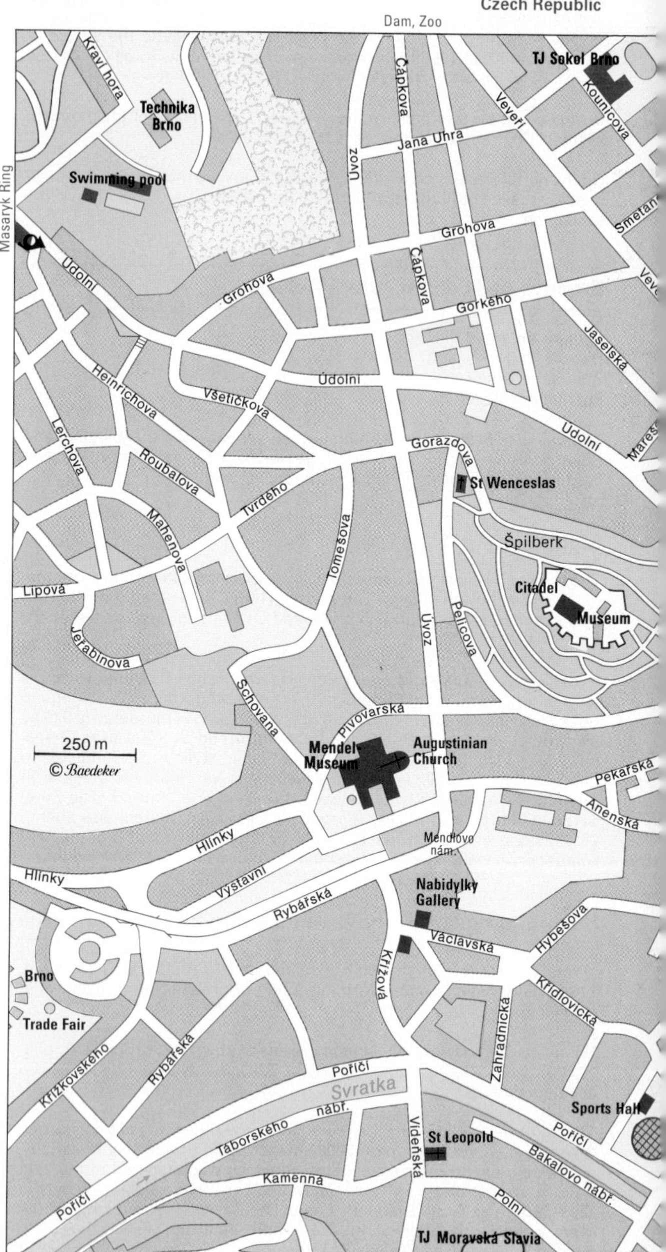

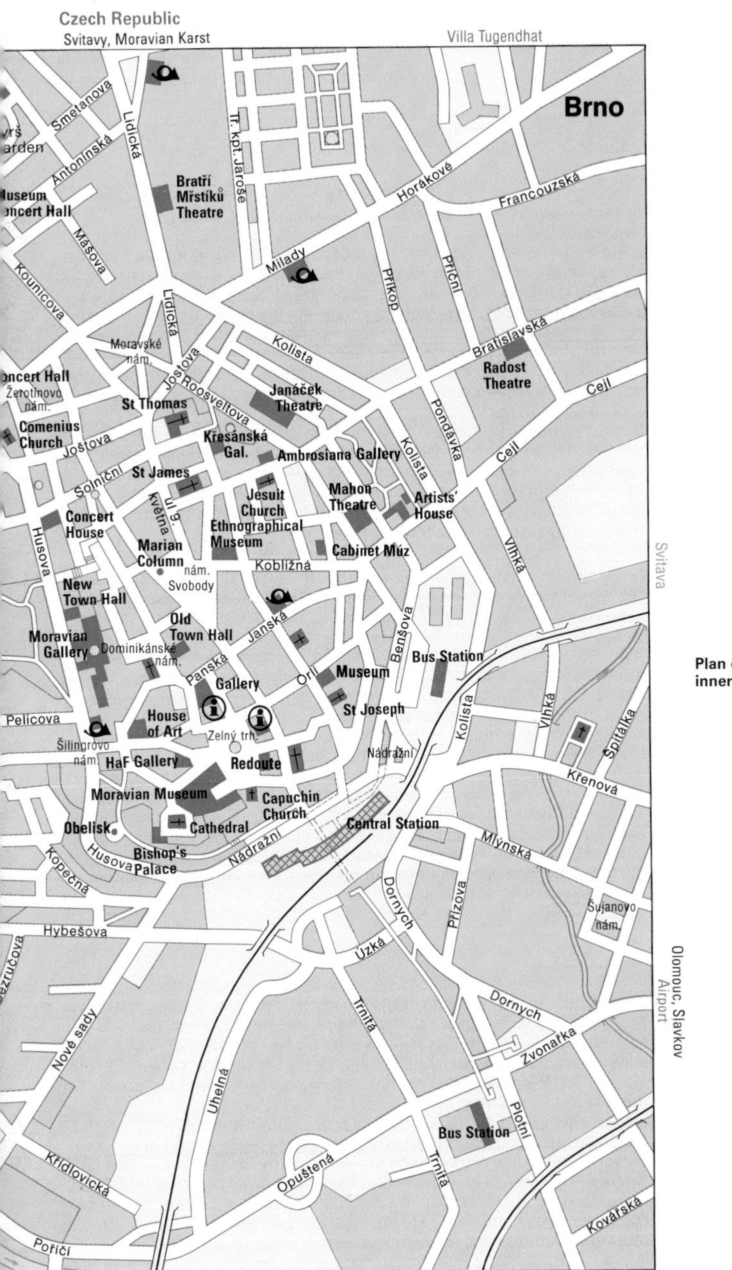

Plan of inner city

Brno

F 3

Chief town of Moravia
Region: Southern Moravia. District: Brno
Altitude: 216m/709ft. Population: 390,000

Situation and characteristics

Brno, chief town of Moravia, the see of a bishop, the seat of a university, a technical college and a college of agriculture, the second largest city in the Czech Republic (airport; motorways to Prague and Bratislava), with several theatres and museums, lies at the foot of the Špilberk in the basin of the rivers Svratka and Svitava, which join here. The old town is surrounded by a ring of gardens and streets, replacing the old fortifications which were pulled down in 1861, and round this again are the city's extensive suburbs. Brno is also one of the country's most important industrial and commercial towns (particularly textiles, engineering, leather goods, papermaking, chemicals and electrical engineering). Most of the factories are in the southern and eastern suburbs. The Brno International Fair is the country's most important trade fair.

Since the political changes in 1989 there has been increased building activity in Brno. The huge Boby Centre, at present under construction, will have an area of some 30,000sq.m/36,000sq.yd, with a department store, a hotel, restaurants and cafés and a variety of leisure facilities. An international architectural competition is being held for the construction of a modern office complex near the University.

History

Brno, whose name originated, in the form Brynn, from the Celts who settled here, was where a type of Palaeolithic man (Homo fossilis) dating from about 30,000 B.C. was found. It first appears in the records in A.D. 1091 as a Slav stronghold on Petrov Hill, in the territory of the Margraves of Moravia. In 1243 the town was granted a charter on the South German model by King Wenceslas I. In the 14th and 15th centuries the castle on the Špilberk was the seat of the Margraves of Moravia. In 1348 Charles IV granted the town important privileges as a trading centre. It withstood sieges by the Hussites in 1428 and 1430 and by King George of Poděbrady in 1464. Important churches were built during this period. In 1641 Brno became capital of Moravia. After the troubles of the Thirty Years' War (during which the town was besieged by the Swedes in 1643 and 1645) and Tatar and Turkish incursions (1663 and 1683) Brno was surrounded by massive fortifications (demolished in 1861 and now replaced by parks and gardens). In the 18th and particularly in the 19th century major industries (textiles, engineering) developed in the town, exploiting the resources of the region (sheep-farming, coal).

Sights

Freedom Square

The hub of the city's traffic is the triangular Freedom Square (Náměstí Svobody), which is surrounded by shops and offices. From this square, formerly known as the Lower Market (the lower of the town's two main squares), radiate the three main streets of the old town – to the north 9th May Street (Třída 9. Května), to the south Victory Street (Třída Vítězství), to the east Kobližná Street.

In the centre of Freedom Square is a Marian Column erected in 1680. At No. 15 is the neo-Renaissance Klein Palace of 1847–48. At the south-west corner of the square can be found the House of the Lords of Lipá, a late 16th century Renaissance building with a fine doorway by G. Gialdi (1589). On the east side, at the corner of Kobližná and Mozart Streets, is the old Noblewomen's Foundation (1679), now occupied by the Ethnographical Museum (Národopisné Muzeum), with rich collections of arts and crafts (Moravian rural house interiors, pottery, glass, etc.).

Ethnographical Museum

Dietrichstein Palace, Brno

Vegetable Market

A little way south of Freedom Square is the Zelný Trh (Vegetable Market), the upper of the old town's two main squares. In the centre of the square are the Parnassus Fountain (by J. B. Fischer von Erlach, 1693–95) and a Trinity Column (by A. Schweigl, 1729–33). On the south side of the square, to the left, stands the 18th century Reduta, the town's oldest theatre (now used for operettas and musicals). To the right is the former Dietrichstein Palace (17th c.). This palace and the adjoining Old Bishop's Palace (15th–16th c.; Gothic chapel, beautiful arcaded courtyard with a Baroque fountain of 1693) now house the Moravian Museum (Moravské Zemské Muzeum; 1818), with large collections of material on natural history (Moravian fauna, insects from all over the world, mineralogy, etc.) and archaeology. An item of outstanding importance is the "Venus of Věstonice" (*c.* 25,000 years old), the oldest known statuette of artistic quality.

***Moravian Museum**

At Nos. 12 and 13 is the Malý Špalíček, an architecturally uniform block of two houses which have preserved their medieval cores.

Capuchin Square

In Capuchin Square (Kapucínské Náměstí), immediately south-east of the Vegetable Market, stands the Capuchin Church (Kapucínský Kostel), originally belonging to a Capuchin friary (1656), which has a 15th century Gothic Madonna. In the burial vault are the remains of Colonel von der Trenck (d. 1749: see below), in a glass coffin, and 50 mummies, naturally dried, of Capuchin friars and notable citizens of Brno.

Petrov Hill
*Cathedral

To the south-west, on Petrov Hill (fine views of the town), is the Cathedral of SS Peter and Paul (Dóm na Petrově), which occupies the site of an old Slav stronghold and an 11th century Romanesque basilica. Originally Gothic (15th c.), the Cathedral was rebuilt in Baroque style after its destruction during the Swedish siege of 1645. In 1904–11 the exterior was restored in Gothic style and the two towers were built. It contains a stone Madonna of around 1300 and modern Stations of the Cross. The high altar is neo-Gothic.

Cathedral of SS Peter and Paul

Bishop's Palace

Facing the Cathedral, to the west, is the Bishop's Palace (1751–54), and adjoining this are canons' residences.

Farther south-west, in the Denisovy Sady (Gardens), rises a 20m/65ft high marble obelisk erected in 1818 to commemorate the end of the Napoleonic wars. Here too are remains of medieval and Baroque town walls and bastions.

Old Town Hall

To the north of the Vegetable Market is the Old Town Hall (Stará Radnice), originally built in 1311 but much altered in later centuries. It has a richly decorated Late Gothic doorway (probably by Master Pilgram; 1511) and a Renaissance loggia in the courtyard (early 16th c.). In the arched passageway to the rear is the "Dragon of Brno", actually a stuffed crocodile presented to the town in 1608 by an Oriental potentate.

Dominican Square
St Michael's Church

Dominican friary

To the north, in Dominican Square (Dominikánské Náměstí), stands St Michael's Church (Chrám Sv. Michala; begun 1655), with a rich Baroque interior. On the terrace is a gallery of stone sculptures dating from before the mid 18th century. Adjoining to the north is the former Dominican friary, with a Romanesque and Gothic cloister (13th–15th c.) and a Gothic refectory. The refectory, remodelled in Baroque style, served as the House of the Estates; it is now, with 19th century additions, the New Town Hall (Nová Radnice). It has a magnificent Renaissance staircase and contains a number of handsome rooms decorated with frescoes, including the Knights' Hall (now the Marriage Hall), the Hall of the Diet and the Hall of Records. To the north of the New Town Hall stands the massive International Hotel, the main entrance to which is in Hus Street (see below).

From Dominican Square Dominican Street (Dominikánská Ulice), with the House of the Lords of Kunštát (exhibition rooms; concerts and theatrical performances in courtyard), leads south-west to Šilingrovo Náměstí, the Augustinian Monastery (Mendel Museum) and the Trade Fair Grounds (see below).

Villa Tugendhat

To the north-east, outside the old town, is the Villa Tugendhat (45 Černopolní St), built in 1928–30 by Ludwig Mies van der Rohe – his last important work in Europe. Here in August 1992 the decision was taken to dissolve the Czechoslovak Federation.

Špilberk
Citadel

From Šilingrovo Náměstí Hus Street (Husova Třída) runs north below the east side of the Špilberk. From this wide street paths run up through the gardens to the Špilberk (Spielberg), a conical hill 56m/184ft high (288m/945ft above sea level). On top of the hill is the Citadel (Hrad) of Špilberk, originally dating from the 13th century, which was altered and enlarged as a fortress in the 17th and 18th centuries. From 1349 to 1411 it was the residence of the Margraves of Moravia. From 1621 to 1858 it was an Austrian state prison for common criminals and more particularly for enemies of the Habsburg monarchy, including many Italians and Poles. Among the prisoners confined here were the pandour commander Baron von der Trenck (1746–49) and the Italian poet and Carbonaro Silvio Pellico (1822–30), who described his stay here in "Le mie prigioni".

Interior

The Citadel is now a museum, in which visitors can see the casemates, with portraits of interesting prisoners, the various prison cells and a special section devoted to resistance fighters against the Nazis (in the former chapel and other rooms). Recently collections of material from the Brno Municipal Museum (Muzeum Města Brna; temporarily closed) have also been displayed here. A notable feature is a 114m/374ft deep well.
There is an attractive walk round the hill below the Citadel, with fine views.

Mendel Square

Church of Assumption

From Šilingrovo Náměstí Bakers' Street (Pekařská Třída) leads west below the south side of the Špilberk, passing the large University Hospital (on left), to Mendel Square (Mendlovo Náměstí), in which is the fine Gothic Church of the Assumption (14th c., rebuilt 1740).

View towards Špilberk

Augustinian monastery (Mendel Museum)

Here too is the Augustinian monastery (now the Mendel Museum), in which between 1858 and 1868 the Augustinian monk and Gregor Mendel (1822–84: see Famous People) carried out his experiments in hybridisation, particularly of peas and beans, and discovered the fundamental laws of genetics. Facing the Augustinian church, to the south, is a monument to Mendel (by Charlemont, 1910).

Trade Fair Grounds

1km/¾ mile west of Mendel Square lies the large Pisárky Park, most of which (the eastern part) is occupied by the extensive grounds (76 hectares/188 acres) of the Brno International Fair (Mezinárodní Veletrh Brno). The largest Foreign Trade and Engineering Fair in the country is held annually in the exhibition halls (total area 100,000sq.m/120,000sq.yd) and a glass viewing tower, mainly built by Czech architects in 1926–28 and between 1958 and 1973.

Mitrovský Palace

In the adjoining Křížovský Street are the little pleasure palace (late 18th c.) of the Mitrovský family and the Voroněž Hotel.

Velodrome

Views

To the south of the Trade Fair Grounds is an oval Velodrome (cycle-racing stadium). Farther west is the Myslivna restaurant (forester's house), from the terrace of which there are extensive views of the whole city.

*Anthropos Museum

At the north end of the park the Anthropos Pavilion houses the Anthropos Museum, established in 1965, which, like the Musée de l'Homme in Paris, illustrates the development of man since his earliest beginnings, with particular regard to the rich prehistoric material found in the Brno area (see Moravian Karst). Notable items are the exact reproductions of the prehistoric cave paintings of Altamira in northern Spain and Lascaux in south-western France.

Bohemian Street

From Freedom Square Česká Ulice (Bohemian Street), the principal street within the pedestrian zone, runs north-west, lined by fine old houses (Nos.

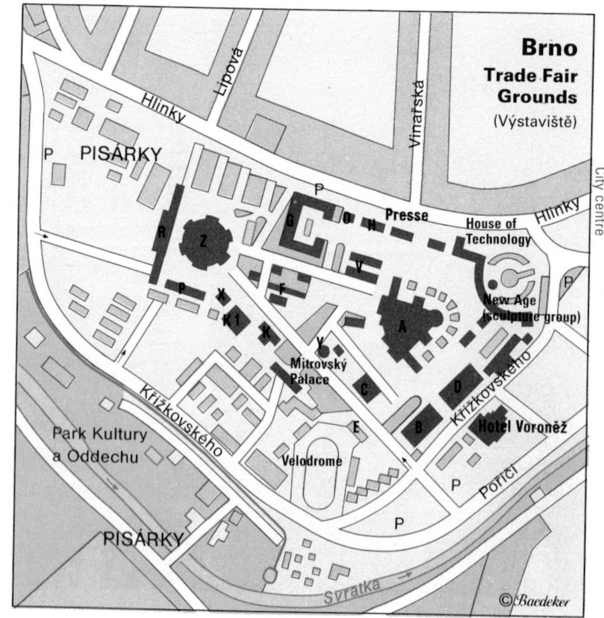

Exhibition buildings in the Trade Fair Grounds

5, 6, 8). At No. 20 is the Avion Hotel, an example of Constructivist architecture.

***St James's Church**

To the north of Freedom Square, in 9th May Street, stands St James's Church (Chrám Sv. Jakuba), a Late Gothic hall-church, originally dating from the 13th century, rebuilt in the 16th century and restored by Ferstel in 1874–79, with a 92m/302ft high tower. The harmonious interior has fine net vaulting. Behind the high altar is the tomb (cast by Kerker in 1722) of Raduit de Souches (d. 1683), who defended Brno in 1645 against the Swedes. The stone pulpit dates from 1525. In the modern cloister are two Late Gothic reliefs. On the outer wall can be seen a 14th century wooden cross.

St Thomas's Church

To the north of St James's Church stands St Thomas's (14th c., restored in 17th c.). On the Baroque high altar is a painting by Maulpertsch, and the church also has a 14th century stone Pietà.

Moravian Square

Lužánky

Farther north, in the ring of gardens round the old town, is the large Moravian Square (Moravské Náměstí), on the east side of which is the Liberation Monument (Památnik Osvobození). Farther north lies the Lužánky, a popular park with numbers of old trees.

***Jesuit Church**

To the east of St James's Church by way of St James's Square (Jakubské Náměstí) is Jesuit Street (Jezuitská Ulice), on the right of which is the Jesuit Church of the Assumption, built in 1598–1602 on the site of an earlier Gothic church. This is Brno's finest Baroque church, with a sumptuously furnished interior (magnificent ceiling paintings).

Janáček Theatre

Mahen Theatre

To the north-east, in Roosevelt Street (Rooseveltova Třída), stands the Janáček Theatre (Janáčkovo Divadlo; opera and ballet), opened in 1965. South of this is the Mahen Theatre (Mahenovo Divadlo), built by the Viennese architects Fellner and Helmer in the second half of the 19th

Artists' House
Central Station

century. This was the first theatre in Europe to be lit by electricity. Facing it, to the east, is the Artists' House (Dum Umení; 1911).
From here Beneš Street (Benešova) runs south to the Central Station (Hlavní Nádraží). A short distance west, at the corner of Minorite Street (Minoritská Ulice) and Eagle Street (Orlí Ulice), is the Museum of Technology (Technické Muzeum).

Museum of Technology

Měnín Gate

To the east of the Museum of Technology, on the north side of Eagle Street, the Měnín Gate (Měnínská Brána) is Brno's only surviving town gate.

Minorite Church
Head Post Office

To the north of the Museum, in Minorite Street, is the Minorite Church of St John (1729–33). Still farther north, in Post Street (Poštovská Ulice), on the right, is the Head Post Office (Poštovní Úrád Brno 1). From here Gagarin Street, on the left, returns to Freedom Square.

Surroundings of Brno

Zoo

7km/4½ miles north-west of the city centre, in the suburb of Bystrc, is Brno's Zoo (Zoologická Zahrada).

Brno Dam

8km/5 miles north-west of the city can be found the Brno Dam (120m/130yd long, 34m/112ft high; hydro-electric station), forming an artificial lake which extends north-west for some 9km/5½ miles in a beautiful wooded setting. The dam was built in 1936–40 to regulate the flow of the river Svratka and to provide electric power, and is now a popular recreational area (bathing facilities, water sports, boating; restaurants, camping site).

Veveří Castle

From the little harbour near the dam excursion boats sail over the lake to Veveří Castle (13th c., enlarged in 16th and 17th c.; not open to public), which can also be reached on a road (6km/4 miles) running along the south-western shore of the lake.

***Masaryk Ring**

15km/9 miles west of Brno, near Kývalka, is the Masaryk Ring, a motor-racing circuit newly laid out in the 1980s to meet modern requirements and named after the first President of the Czechoslovak Republic, Tomáš Masaryk (see Famous People).
The difficult original circuit, almost 30km/19 miles long, was the venue of important Grand Prix races in the 1930s. The new circuit is just over 5km/3 miles long and is equipped with all the technical facilities required for car and motorcycle racing.

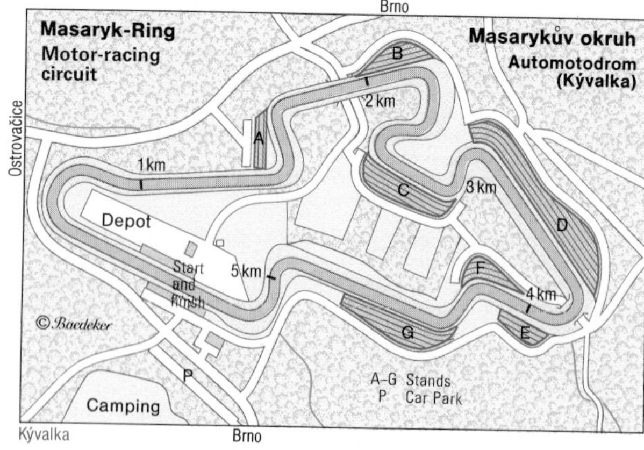

Ivančice

21km/13 miles south-west of Brno is the industrial town of Ivančice (alt. 210m/689ft; pop. 7500), which has a number of handsome Renaissance houses, remains of its Gothic town walls, a Gothic church remodelled in Baroque style and a large Jewish cemetery with old gravestones (the oldest dating from the 15th century). Ivančice was the birthplace of the painter Alfons Mucha (1860–1939).

Oslavany

23km/14 miles south-west of Brno is the mining town of Oslavany (alt. 230m/755ft; pop. 5000). It has an old 13th century nunnery which was converted (1583 onwards) into a Renaissance palace with arcading.

Rajhrad

12km/7½ miles south of Brno, in Rajhrad (alt. 193m/633ft; pop. 3000), can be found a former Benedictine monastery founded in the 11th century. The church was rebuilt in the 18th century in magnificent High Baroque style.

Židlochovice

18km/11 miles south of Brno is Židlochovice (alt. 190m/623ft; pop. 3000), on the river Svratka, with an old castle (rebuilt in the 18th and 19th centuries) and a large hunting reserve (particularly pheasants). Between the two world wars Židlochovice was the summer residence of the President of the first Czechoslovak Republic.

Austerlitz

See Slavkov u Brna

Broumov F 2

Region: Eastern Bohemia. District: Náchod
Altitude: 405m/1329ft. Population: 8200

Situation and characteristics

The little town of Broumov in eastern Bohemia earned a place in history in 1618, when an order by the abbot to close the Protestant church led to violent disturbances and finally to a rising in Prague which sparked off the Thirty Years' War. Textile industry.

Sights

Benedictine abbey

Broumov's Benedictine abbey, founded in the 14th century, was at one time a dependency of Břevnov Monastery in Prague. It has a fine church, rebuilt by Martin and Johann Allio between 1683 and 1694. The conventual buildings, by Kilian Ignaz Dientzenhofer, date from 1735.

Cemetery

In the town cemetery can be seen a wooden church of 1450, the oldest of its kind in Bohemia.

Surroundings of Broumov

Broumovské Stěny

South-west of Broumov, in the Broumov Uplands (Broumovská Vrchovina), are the Broumovské Stěny (Broumov Crags), which extend for some 10km/6 miles from north-west to south-east and are continued beyond the Czech-Polish frontier. This area is a nature reserve; good walking country.

Křinice

3km/2 miles south-west of Broumov, on the edge of the Broumovské Stěny, is the village of Křinice (alt. 395m/1296ft), with some fine old peasant houses; the oldest (No. 152) dates from 1792.
Křinice is the starting-point of a 2-hour walk through the Broumovské Stěny to the former pilgrimage chapel of Hvězda (see below) and the entrance to the Křinice "rock city" (Kovářova Rokle; a walk through it takes 2 hours).

Hvězda

3km/2 miles west of Křinice, on the ridge of the Broumovské Stěny, is the former pilgrimage shrine of Hvězda (alt. 674m/2211ft), from which there are superb views. The Baroque chapel (1733) was the work of Kilian Ignaz Dientzenhofer. The inn (1854), in the Swiss style, was originally a pilgrim hostel.

Police nad Metují

14km/8½ miles south-west of Broumov is the picturesquely situated little town of Police nad Metují (alt. 441m/1447ft; pop. 4200), with textile and engineering industries. Police is a good starting-point for walks and climbs in the Broumovské Stěny, to the north-east, and to the tabular hill of Ostaš (700m/2300ft), 3km/2 miles north-west.
Features of interest in Police itself are the former Benedictine monastery (13th c.), which was remodelled in Baroque style by Kilian Ignaz Dientzenhofer, the Baroque Town Hall (1718) and a number of burghers' houses of the Baroque period (two-storey wooden building, the Old School, 1785). The Cemetery Church (13th c.), originally Gothic, was remodelled in Baroque style in the early 18th century.

Česká Lípa

D 2

Region: Northern Bohemia
District: Česká Lípa
Altitude: 250m/820ft
Population: 40,000

Situation and characteristics

The Northern Bohemian district town of Česká Lípa lies in a beautiful setting on the river Ploučnice. Its industries include textiles, engineering, the production of accumulators (recently in association with the German firm Varta), and the manufacture of rolling-stock and musical instruments. Features of interest are the "Red House" (Červený Dům), a small Renaissance palace of 1583 (restored in 19th c.; now a museum); the Church of St Mary Magdalene (originally 13th c.; rebuilt in 16th and 18th c.); the Church of the Holy Cross (16th c.; re-Gothicised in late 19th c.); the Baroque St Mary's Church (1714); and All Saints Church, with a former Augustinian monastery founded by Wallenstein in 1627.

Surroundings of Česká Lípa

Zákupy

7km/4½ miles east of Česká Lípa is Zákupy (German name Reichstadt; alt. 271m/889ft; pop. 2500), with a large castle (originally in Renaissance style; altered *c.* 1680), at one time an imperial residence, and a Late Gothic church. In 1818 Napoleon's son was granted the title of Duke of Reichstadt (though he never visited the town).

Horní Police

11km/7 miles west of Česká Lípa lies Horní Police (alt. 252m/827ft; pop. 750), with a beautiful Baroque church of 1723 (renovated 1968; richly furnished interior) which is surrounded by a covered ambulatory.

Mt Ralsko

15km/9 miles north-east of Česká Lípa is a prominent basalt hill, Mt Ralsko (696m/2284ft), with the remains of a 12th century castle.

Lake Mácha

25km/15 miles south-east of Česká Lípa lies Lake Mácha (Máchovo jezero; alt. 266m/873ft), originally known as the "Great Pond". It was formed in 1366 by Emperor Charles IV, and in the 19th century it was given its present name in honour of the Czech Romantic poet Karel Hýnek Mácha (1810–36). With an area of 278 hectares/687 acres (originally 350 hectares/865 acres), it is now a popular recreational area, with two small islands, bathing beaches and facilities for water sports. On the south side of the lake is the summer resort of Doksy (alt. 275m/900ft; pop. 5000), on the north-western shore Staré Splavy (alt. 290m/950ft).

Jestřebí

8km/5 miles north-west of Lake Mácha is Jestřebí (alt. 260m/855ft; pop. 1500), with the ruins of a Gothic castle and a Baroque church of 1780.

Mt Bezděz

9km/5½ miles south-east of Lake Mácha is Mt Bezděz (604m/1982ft), with the ruins of an Early Gothic castle built in 1264–78 by Přemysl Otakar II. The chapel is a jewel of architecture in the typical local style; other features are the 20m/65ft high Devil's Tower and the Great Tower, which is more than 30m/100ft high.

Bělá pod Bezdězem

13km/8 miles south-east of Lake Mácha is Bělá pod Bezdězem (alt. 301m/988ft; pop. 4600), with a Renaissance castle, remains of town walls and one surviving town gate (Česká Brána).

České Budějovice

D 3/4

Region: Southern Bohemia
District: České Budějovice
Altitude: 385m/1263ft
Population: 95,000

Situation and characteristics

České Budějovice (German name Budweis), chief town of its district and the industrial and cultural centre of southern Bohemia, lies some 130km/80 miles south of Prague at the outflow of the river Malše into the Vltava (on which there are a number of dams to the north of the town). České Budějovice has expanded greatly since the Second World War and now has a variety of industry in the newer districts, including engineering, enamel production, woodworking and paper products (Hardtmuth's Koh-i-noor pencils have been made here since 1874) and foodstuffs. The town is also noted for its beer – Budvar (the original Budweiser beer) and Samson – which has been brewed here since 1894. České Budějovice is the see of a Catholic bishop and has a college of agriculture, a teachers' training college and several museums and theatres.

History

České Budějovice was founded by Otakar II in 1265, when it was fortified and given a charter on the German model. It enjoyed a period of prosperity in the 16th century (fish-breeding, brewing, the salt trade; mint). The old town, surrounded by beautiful parks and gardens, has many handsome old buildings, mostly dating from the Renaissance and Baroque periods. Until the 19th century the population was predominantly German. The first horse-drawn railway in Europe, between České Budějovice and Linz in Austria, began to operate in 1828.

Sights

***Přemysl Otakar II Square**

In the centre of the old town, which is surrounded by parks and gardens, particularly on the east and north sides, is Přemysl Otakar II Square (Náměstí Přemysla Otakara II), surrounded by arcades. Measuring 133m/436ft each way, it is one of the largest town squares in Bohemia.

*Samson Fountain

In the centre of the square is the handsome Baroque Samson Fountain (by Josef Dietrich, 1727).

Town Hall
Bishop's Palace

At the south-west corner of the square stands the Baroque Town Hall (Radnice), with three towers, built by the Italian architect Martinelli in 1727–30 on the site of an earlier Renaissance building. Adjoining it on the right is the 18th century Bishop's Palace.

***Cathedral**

North-west of Přemysl Otakar II Square is the Baroque Cathedral of St Nicholas (Chrám Sv. Mikuláše), built in 1649 on the site of an earlier Gothic church, with a separate bell-tower, the "Black Tower" (Černá Věz; 1572) 72m/236ft high. From the gallery with Tuscan columns (360 steps) there are magnificent views, extending in clear weather to the Bohemian Forest and the Alps. Behind the Cathedral, to the east, is a detached chapel (1731).

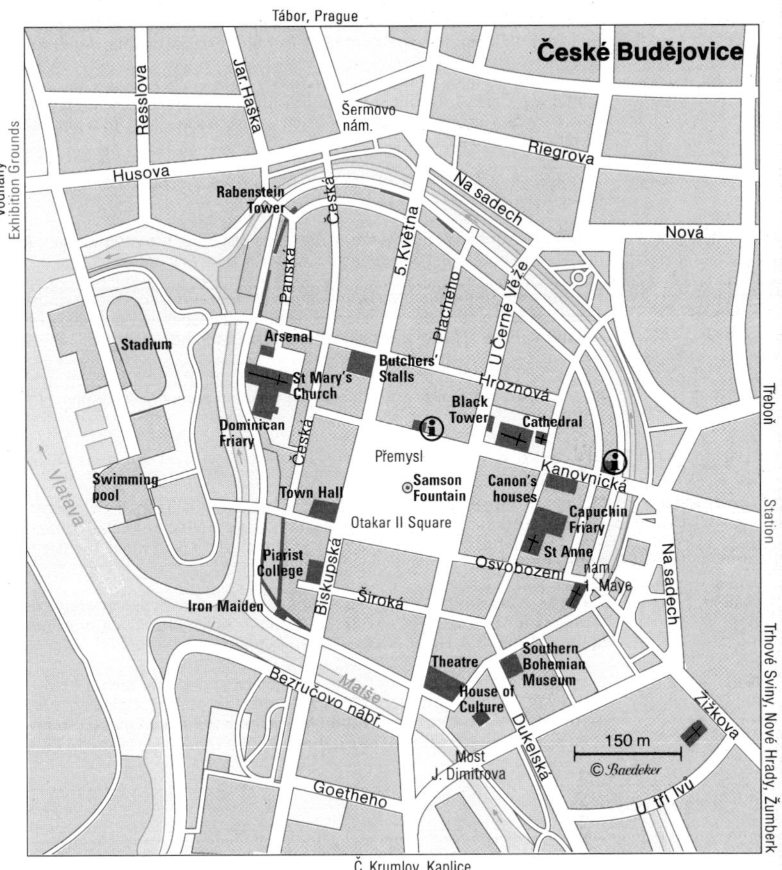

From the Cathedral Canons' Street (Kanovnická) runs east, crossing the Mill Canal (Mlýnská Stoka), to the railway station.

Burghers' houses

In the old-world little streets, some of them flanked by arcades, round Přemysl Otakar II Square are many charming Baroque and Renaissance houses, including the sgraffito-decorated Kneisl House (Kneislův Dům; 16th c.). In the picturesque arcaded street (Kněžská Ulice) which runs past the east end of the Cathedral is a former Capuchin friary (now a teachers' training college), with the Church of St Anne (1615–21), now also used as a concert hall.

St Mary's Church

North-west of Přemysl Otakar II Square is the Gothic Church of St Mary (or Piarist Church; 1265), which belonged to a Dominican friary (now occupied by a school) founded by Otakar II at the time of the town's foundation; the cloister has been partly restored.

◀ *Samson Fountain, České Budějovice*

Salt Store

Facing St Mary's Church, to the north, can be seen the former Salt Store (Solnice), with a stepped gable of 1531. It originally served as the municipal arsenal.

Butchers' Stalls

A little way east of the Salt Store, in Hroznová Ulice, are the Masné Krámy (Butchers' Stalls; 1560), which have been occupied since 1953 by a popular restaurant and beer hall.

Rabenstein Tower

Some 200m/220yd north of the Salt Store rises the Rabenstein Tower (Rabenštejnská Věž; 14th–15th c.).

Iron Maiden

South-west of the main square is the "Iron Maiden" (Železná Panna), a tower (with wall-walk) which formed part of the town's defences.

Southern Bohemian Museum

The Southern Bohemian Museum (Jihočeské Muzeum), south-east of the square at Dukelsa Třída 1, has collections of old Bohemian painting and sculpture, natural history, local history and culture and weapons.

Exhibition Grounds

North-west of the town centre are the Exhibition Grounds (32 hectares/80 acres), where a large agricultural show is held annually in August.

Surroundings of České Budějovice

Trhové Sviny

20km/12½ miles south-east of České Budějovice is Trhové Sviny (alt. 458m/1503ft; pop. 5000), with the beautiful Late Gothic St Mary's Church and a magnificent Baroque pilgrimage church (by KIlian Ignaz Dientzenhofer, 1708–10).

Žumberk

27km/17 miles south-east of České Budějovice lies the medieval village of Žumberk (alt. 541m/1775ft), with fortifications which are now a museum (painted furniture). Nearby is the Žárský Rybník pond.

Nové Hrady

34km/21 miles south-east of České Budějovice is the little town of Nové Hrady (alt. 541m/1775ft; pop. 2300), with a Gothic castle (originally 1279; rebuilt in 15th and 16th c.; exhibition of Southern Bohemian glass). South-west of Nové Hrady is the nature park of Terčino Údolí (established 1756).

Český Krumlov

D 4

Region: Southern Bohemia
District: Český Krumlov
Altitude: 492m/1614ft
Population: 14,000

*Situation and **townscape

The Southern Bohemian district town of Český Krumlov is beautifully situated on both banks of the upper Vltava, which here follows a winding course under the south side of the Blanský Les, an outlier of the Bohemian Forest. Like Kutná Hora (see entry), Český Krumlov has preserved an unusually complete medieval townscape, with winding lanes and many old buildings. The silver-mining industry which flourished in the 14th century is now extinct and the modern town's economy depends on light industry.

History

From its foundation in the mid 13th century until 1302 Český Krumlov, with its castle commandingly situated above the town, was held by the noble family of Vítkovci; thereafter it passed to the Rožmberks, under whom the old fortified castle became a magnificent Renaissance palace; from 1622 it belonged to a German noble family, the Eggenbergs; and after their line became extinct it passed to the Princes Schwarzenberg.

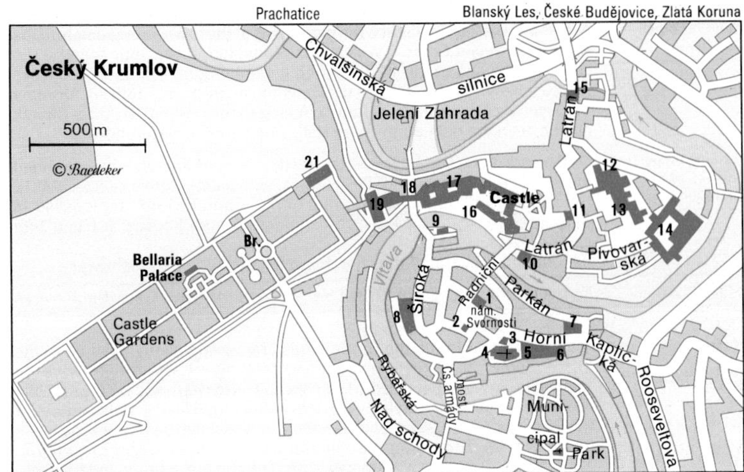

1 Town Hall
2 Plague Column
3 Chaplaincy
4 St Vitus's Church
5 Prelature
6 Jesuit College
7 Jesuit Seminary
8 Municipal Brewhouse
9 Arsenal
10 St Jost's Church
11 Red Gate
12 Convent of Poor Clares
13 Minorite Friary
14 Rožmberk Brewhouse
15 Budějovice Gate
16 Mint
17 Upper Castle
18 Three-tiered bridge
19 Baroque Theatre
20 St Martin's Church
21 Riding School

Sights

Old Town Square

In the centre of the Old Town, which is enclosed within a loop on the Vltava, is the main square, surrounded by handsome Renaissance houses, with a tall Plague Column (by Matthias Jäckel, 1716).

Town Hall

On the north side of the square stands the Town Hall (Radnice), with Gothic arcades, a rich Renaissance frieze and large coats of arms of Bohemia, the town and the noble families of Eggenberg and Schwarzenberg.

Chaplaincy
Prelature
Jesuit College

From the square Horní Ulice (Upper Lane) runs east, passing on the right the oriel-windowed Chaplaincy (1514–20). Beyond this is the Prelature, which has an arcaded Rococo staircase in the courtyard. Farther along is the former Jesuit College (by Baltasar Maio da Vomio, 1586–88), which in 1773 became a barracks and in 1878 a hotel.

Theatre
Museum

Beyond the Jesuit College is the Theatre, built in 1613 as a Jesuit theatre. On the opposite side of the street the former Jesuit Seminary (1650–62) now contains the District Archives and an interesting local museum (fine collection of Gothic art).

St Vitus's Church
Latin School

To the south of the Chaplaincy, rising above the Vltava, stands the Late Gothic church of St Vitus, founded in 1309 and completely rebuilt between 1407 and 1439. It has a 16th century high altar, frescoes of 1420 (in north aisle) and a Late Gothic crypt. On the south side of the church is the old Latin School (1554), now a school of traditional crafts.

Renaissance houses

To the west of the main square, running roughly parallel to the Vltava, is Široká Ulice (Broad Street), with a number of particularly fine Renaissance houses, some of them with fresco decoration.

Bridge

From the square Radniční Ulice (Town Hall Street) leads north to a bridge over the Vltava.

Latrán
St Jost's Church
Brewhouse

On the far side of the river, in what was originally the lower ward of the castle, lies the Latrán district, the oldest part of the town. Immediately to the right is St Jost's Church, which was renovated in the 16th century and closed at the end of the 18th. Beyond it, on the right, a street called Nové Město ("New Town") leads to the Brewhouse (originally 16th c.), formerly the arsenal of the Rožmberk family. A little to the north of St Jost's Church can be seen the old Latrán Town Hall, with sgraffito decoration.

Minorite Friary
Convent of Poor Clares

To the east of the Latrán Town Hall are the former Minorite Friary, founded in 1350, and the Convent of Poor Clares, with a Late Gothic cloister (1491). Here too can be found the Corpus Christi Church (1357; remodelled in Baroque style in 17th c.), which belonged to both houses; it has a 14th century Pietà.

Beyond the east end of the church is a bastion with a round tower.

Budějovice Gate

To the north of the Latrán Town Hall is the Budějovice Gate (Budějovická Brána; 1598).

***Castle**

From St Jost's Church the Castle Steps (Zámecké Schody) lead up to the Castle (Zámek; the largest in Bohemia after Prague Castle), high above the Vltava. It originally dated from the 13th and 14th centuries but was mostly rebuilt in Renaissance style by William of Rožmberk in the 16th century. At the lower gate, the Latrán Gate, is a moat in which live bears are kept. In the lower courtyard (cannon) are the entrances to the massive Keep (by B. Maio da Vomio, 1580; wide views from top), the rich Library and the State Archives.

The Castle, with some 300 rooms laid out round four courtyards, is lavishly furnished with furniture, tapestries, pictures and porcelain. Particularly notable are the Picture Gallery; the Hall of Masks (1748), with lively trompe-l'oeil paintings; the Chinese Cabinet; the Great Chapel (15th c.); and the Little Chapel (18th c.). The high Plášt'ový Most, a bridge with three tiers of arches, leads to the Rococo Theatre (1765–66), with rich painted decoration, which still preserves the original stage machinery (in course of restoration).

*Castle Gardens

The uppermost corridor of the bridge leads to the Castle Gardens. Immediately on the right can be seen the Winter Riding School (1745). In the centre of the gardens is the little Bellaria Palace (1706–08). Here too is an open-air theatre (1958), with a rotating auditorium seating 500. At the south-west end of the gardens is a fish-pond formed in 1686.

Surroundings of Český Krumlov

Blanský Les

To the north of Český Krumlov lies the Blanský Les (Forest), the highest point in which is Mt Klet' (1083m/3553ft; chair-lift from Krasetín). On the summit are a mountain hut, outlook tower, radio mast and observatory.

***Zlatá Koruna**

7km/4½ miles north-east of Český Krumlov is the fortified Cistercian monastery of Zlatá Koruna (alt. 473m/1552ft), founded by King Otakar II in 1263, built between 1300 and 1370 and dissolved in the 17th century. There remain the large Gothic church (fine interior; cenotaph of Otakar II in choir) and the well preserved Chapterhouse (late 13th c., remodelled in Baroque style in 17th and 18th c.; museum).

Dívčí Kámen

10km/6 miles north-east of Český Krumlov is the Dívčí Kámen, a hill topped by the ruins of a mid 14th century castle.

Kájov

6km/4 miles west of Český Krumlov is Kájov (alt. 540m/1772ft; pop. 1000), which has a fine Gothic pilgrimage church (14th c., rebuilt 1471–83) with a Late Gothic Madonna (*c.* 1500).

Větřní

6km/4 miles south of Český Krumlov we come to Vetrní (alt. 592m/1942ft; pop. 3500), which has one of the largest papermaking factories in the country (established 1870).

Český Šternberk D 3

Region: Central Bohemia
District: Benešov
Altitude: 310m/1017ft
Population: 300

Situation

The village of Český Šternberk lies some 45km/28 miles south-east of Prague in the valley of the Sázava. It is dominated by the massive bulk of Šternberk Castle, one of the best preserved castles in the Czech Lands.

*Šternberk Castle

History

Thanks to its excellent situation on a narrow spur of rock above the left bank of the Sázava on the edge of an extensive area of forest the castle long remained impregnable. It was built by Zdeslav von Divišov about 1240, in the reign of King Wenceslas (Václav) I, and apart from a brief interval in the 18th and 19th centuries remained in the possession of the noble Šternberk family until the mid 20th century. One notable member of the family was the scientist Kašpar Maria Šternberk, one of the co-founders of the National Museum in Prague in 1818.

In the reign of King George of Poděbrady the castle was captured and badly damaged; then in 1479 it was renovated in Late Gothic style and reinforced by the construction of massive bastions. After the Thirty Years' War it was altered and enlarged in Early Baroque style. From that period date the interior of the Great Hall with its richly decorated Baroque chimneypieces and decorative stucco reliefs.

Museum

The castle contains large collections of weapons, 17th century graphic art and period furniture.

Český Šternberk Castle

Surroundings of Český Šternberk

Rataje nad Sázavou

4km/2½ miles north-east of Český Šternberk, in the romantic valley of the Sázava, lies the summer resort of Rataje nad Sázavou (alt. 383m/1257ft; pop. 800), with remains of the Gothic castle of Pirkštejn and a Renaissance palace remodelled in Baroque style.

Sázava

8km/5 miles north of Český Šternberk, in the Sázava valley, is the little town of Sázava (alt. 312m/1024ft; pop. 3500), another popular summer resort, with a glassworks (laboratory and optical glass). It grew up round a Benedictine monastery founded in 1032 by Prince Oldřich which was converted into a residence at the end of the 18th century. The building now houses a collection of material on Slav Sázava and a museum of technical glass. To the north of the church are the foundations of a Romanesque building.

Vlašim

13km/8 miles south of Český Šternberk the industrial town of Vlašim (alt. 365m/1198ft; pop. 13,000; manufacture of stockings and shoes) has a Baroque castle set in a large English-style park.

Mt Blaník

20km/12½ miles south of Český Šternberk, rising out of the typical rolling landscape of Central Bohemia, is Mt Blaník (638m/2093ft), the scene of many legends. The surrounding area is now a landscape reserve.

Cheb B 2

Region: Western Bohemia
District: Cheb
Altitude: 460m/1510ft
Population: 31,000

Situation and characteristics

Cheb (German name Eger), chief town of its district, is an important traffic junction and industrial centre (textiles, foodstuffs, bicycles, mechanical engineering) in the Chebsko district (Egerland), situated near the Czech–German frontier on a terrace on the right bank of the river Ohře (Eger). The chief tourist attraction of Cheb, which suffered serious damage during the Second World War only in the station district to the south-east, is the old medieval core of the town, which is well preserved and restored, particularly round the market square.

History

Cheb, which first appears in the records in 1061, grew up round a castle belonging to the Margraves of Vohburg. In the reign of King Conrad III it passed by marriage to the Hohenstaufens and became a free imperial city; then in 1167 it became the property of the Emperor Frederick II Barbarossa, who had married Countess Adelheid of Vohburg in Cheb in 1149.
In 1265 the Chebsko district came into the hands of King Otakar II of Bohemia. In 1277 it returned to the German Empire, but in 1315 it was mortgaged by Ludwig the Bavarian to Bohemia, whose destinies it has continued to share down to the present day. King Rudolph of Habsburg granted it a special municipal charter in 1279, and in 1355 Charles IV gave it the right to coin money. In 1634 Wallenstein (see Famous People) was murdered in Cheb, and in 1687 the famous Baroque architect Balthasar Neumann was born here (d. 1753 in Würzburg). The town's fortifications, built between 1675 and 1700, were demolished in the early 19th century.

Sights

***Market square**

In the centre of Cheb is the long market square with its fountains, King George of Poděbrady Square (Naměstí Krále Jiřího z Poděbrad), surrounded by handsome old houses.

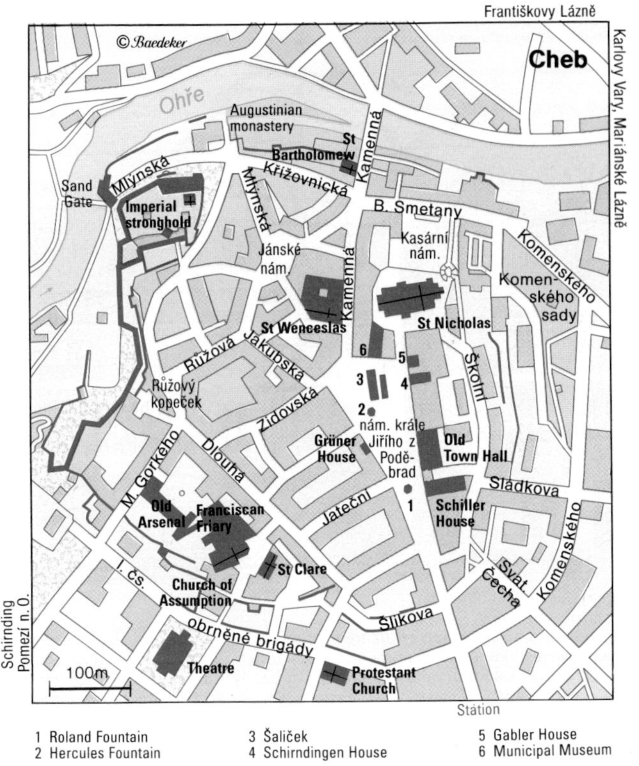

Old Town Hall

On the east side of the square is the Baroque Old Town Hall (Radnice; by Giovanni Battista Alliprandi, 1722–28), now occupied by the Municipal Art Gallery (Gallery of 20th Century Bohemian Art). To the right of this can be seen the Schiller House, in which the German dramatist Friedrich Schiller lived when writing his drama "Wallenstein".

Schiller House

Schirndingen House

At the north-east corner of the square is the Schirndingen House (originally 15th century), with a high Gothic gable and a beautiful arcaded courtyard.

Gabler House

The Gabler House, to the left of this, has a fine Rococo façade (tablet commemorating a visit by Goethe in 1821).

Špalicek

At the lower end of the market square is the Špalicek, a group of eleven houses dating from the 13th century, originally occupied by Jewish merchants. In front of the houses is the Hercules Fountain (16th c.).

Town House

Immediately north of the Špalicek stands the former Town House, built in the early 17th century by Burgomaster Pachelbel, in which Wallenstein was murdered on February 25th by an Irishman named Devereux, acting on the orders of Emperor Ferdinand. In the handsome courtyard are old German gravestones and a charming wooden gallery.

Municipal Museum

In the Town House is the Municipal Museum (Chebské Muzeum), which gives an excellent survey of the history, ethnography and traditions of Cheb and the Chebsko district. It contains a historical model of Cheb and

18th century houses in the market square

plans for the restoration of the town after 1945, interiors of typical burghers' houses, domestic equipment, embroidery, weapons and religious art, including an altar frontal with 13th century bead embroidery, together with archaeological and scientific collections. On the first floor is the room in which Wallenstein was killed (also containing a collection of pewter and ivory miniatures).

St Nicholas's Church

North-east of the Town is the Gothic church of St Nicholas (1230–70; restored in 15th c.), the oldest parts of which date from the Romanesque period (west doorway and lower part of east towers, damaged in 1945; Early Gothic choir, after 1270).

Dominican Church

To the west of St Nicholas's is the former Dominican Church (1674–88). The monastery is now a cultural centre.

Imperial stronghold

North-west of the Dominican Church, on a crag on the banks of the Ohře which was formerly occupied by a fortified Celtic settlement, can be seen an early 12th century Vohburg castle which was enlarged and strengthened by the Emperor Frederick I Barbarossa between 1167 and 1175. After Wallenstein's murder in 1634 it was uninhabited, and in 1743 it was destroyed by the French. To the left of the entrance, surrounded by casemates, is the 21m/69ft high Black Tower, a keep built of lava blocks which is a relic of the Vohburg castle, with a brick-built superstructure of the 15th century; from the top of the tower there are fine views.

**Double Chapel

To the right of the entrance is the Double Chapel of St Erhard (12th–13th c.), with a very plain exterior. The lower chapel has Romanesque vaulting pierced by an octagonal opening; the upper one (1215–22) has Gothic vaulting borne on four slender marble columns. In the choir is a column of white marble with zigzag ornament.

Palace

Beyond the chapel is the palace built by Frederick I in the late 12th century. In the banqueting hall, now roofless, Wallenstein's four generals were

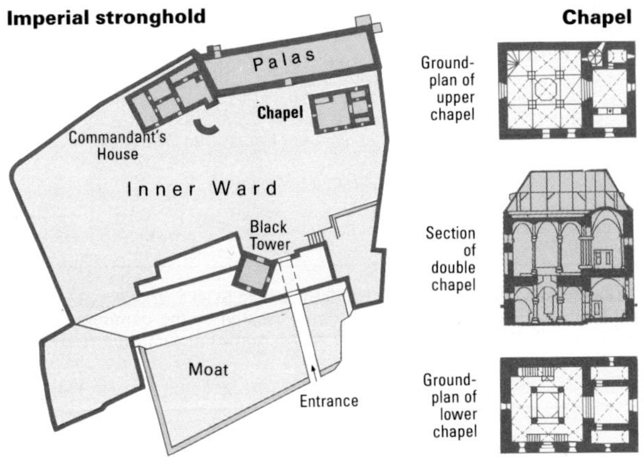

killed shortly before his murder. In the side wall of the hall are three arched Romanesque windows separated by four columns. There is an interesting lapidarium.

Viewing terrace

From the terrace, 25m/80ft above the Ohře, there are fine views.

Augustinian monastery

To the north-east of the imperial stronghold, also rising above the Ohře, is a monastery of Augustinian canons, with St Bartholomew's Church (1414), now housing the Municipal Art Gallery's collection of Gothic sculpture.

Imperial stronghold

Roland Fountain

Franciscan Church

South-west of the market square, in Franciscan Square, stands the former Franciscan Church (1285). The friary to which it belonged, with a beautiful cloister (open to public), is now occupied by the museum administration.

St Clare's Church

Facing the Franciscan Church, to the east, is the beautiful Baroque church of St Clare (1707–11), probably designed by Christoph Dientzenhofer. The church is now a concert hall. The convent houses the District Archives.

Bicycle Museum

Also in Franciscan Square is the Bicycle Museum.

Surroundings of Cheb

Artificial lakes

To the west of the town is the 8km/5 mile Lake Skalka, and 7km/4½ miles east is Lake Jesenice, 8km/5 miles long, created by the damming of the Ondrava. Both lakes have excellent recreational facilities (bathing, boating).

Chomutov C 2

Region: Northern Bohemia
District: Chomutov
Altitude: 340m/1115ft
Population: 50,000

Situation and characteristics

Chomutov, an old-established industrial centre (brown coal mining, ironworks, engineering) and chief town of its district, lies 14km/8½ miles north-east of Kadaň (see entry) in Northern Bohemia, at the foot of the Ore Mountains (Krušné Hory), on the old road to Saxony.

Market square, Chomutov

Sights

In the market square, which is surrounded by arcaded houses, are, side by side, the Gothic St Catherine's Church (13th c.) and the Castle (1520), now housing municipal offices and a museum. Also in the square is the parish church (16th c., rebuilt in 17th and 18th).

Market square
Castle
Parish church

To the north-west is the Municipal Park.

Municipal Park

On the northern outskirts of the town lies the Alum Lake (Kamencové Jezero), which has an area of 16,000sq.m/19,000sq.yd (bathing beach and camping site). The lake contains a percentage of aluminium sulphate and accordingly harbours no living creatures.

Alum Lake

Děčín D 2

Region: Northern Bohemia
District: Děčín
Altitude: 135m/443ft. Population: 56,000

Situation and characteristics

This district town in Northern Bohemia, known until 1945 as Děčín-Podmokly, lies 12km/7½ miles south of the Czech–German frontier on both banks of the river Labe (Elbe), here flanked for part of its course by rocky hills, at the inflow of the Ploučnice, between the Elbe Sandstone Hills (see Labské Pískovce) to the north and the Bohemian Massif (České Středohoří) to the south. Děčín has an important river harbour on the Labe.

Sights

Old Town
Market square

In the centre of Děčín's Old Town on the right bank of the Labe, which preserves a number of Renaissance and Baroque houses, is the market

Děčín Castle

square, with a fine fountain of 1906. A little way north stands St Wenceslas's Church.

Holy Cross Church

To the south of the market square is Holy Cross Church (Kostel Sv. Kříže; 1691, Baroque), with a fine interior and wall paintings of 1792.

Castle

From Castle Square (Zámecké Náměstí), south-east of Holy Cross Church, a street cut through the rock runs up to the Castle (not open to the public), on a sandstone crag 50m/165ft above the Labe (Elbe). Built in 1786–99 on the site of an earlier Gothic stronghold, it formerly belonged to the Counts of Thun. On the east side of the castle is a beautiful rose-garden (Růžová Zahrada), with picturesque Baroque flights of steps (views).

*Gothic bridge

Some 500m/550yd south of the Castle on the Litoměřice road, immediately on the right (concealed under a modern street intersection), is the Gothic Stone Bridge (Kamenny Most; 1564–69) over the river Ploučnice.

Tyrš Bridge

From the market square Town Hall Street (Radniční Třída) runs south. Off this street on the right is Tyrš Street, which leads to the Tyrš Bridge (Tyršův Most), built in 1933 on the site of the older Chain Bridge. The bridge is named after Miroslav Tyrš (1832–84), founder of the Sokol gymnastic movement, who was born in Děčín.

Podmokly

On the left bank of the river extends the Podmokly district. From the west end of the bridge the Labe Embankment (Labské Nábřeží) runs south below the Shepherds' Wall (Pastýřská Stěna: see below, Surroundings) to the railway station (Hlavní Nádraží), on a parallel street.

Hus Square

To the west of the station lies Hus Square (Husovo Náměstí), the main square of the Podmokly district. 500m/550yd beyond this is the little Sheep's Bridge (Ovčí Müstek) over the Jílovský Potok, which dates from the 1620s.

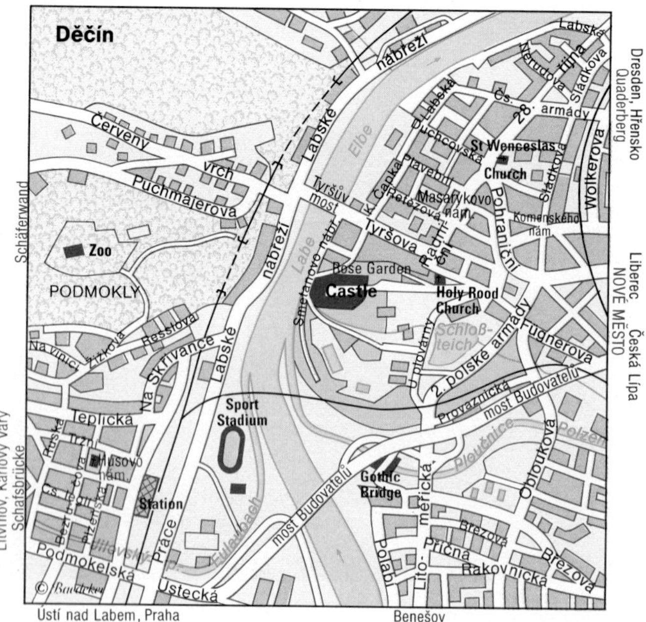

Surroundings of Děčín

***Stoličná Hora**

From the market square there is a rewarding climb (½–¾ hour) up the Stoličná Hora (289m/948ft), from which there are fine views of the town and the Labe.

Dečínská Výšina

A 15-minute walk to the north-east leads to the Dečínská Výšina (292m/958ft) and the Labská Vyhlídka, a viewpoint from which there is a magnificent prospect, downstream, of the Labe.

*Shepherds' Wall

From Hus Square in Podmokly it is a half-hour walk to the wooded hill known as the Shepherds' Wall (Pastýřská Stěna; 288m/958ft) which rises steeply to the north (lift; restaurant at top), also affording magnificent views.

Benešov

8km/5 miles south-east of Děčín is Benešov nad Ploučnicí (alt. 210m/690ft; pop. 8000), which has a busy textile industry. Features of interest are the Upper Castle (Horní Zámek, 1522–24), originally a medieval stronghold, and the Lower Castle (Dolní Zámek; 1540–44, restored 1973), both in Renaissance style. Adjoining the Gothic parish church is the Salhausen Chapel (*c.* 1550), with Renaissance grave slabs. Of the same period are two houses (Nos. 51 and 52) in Zámecká Ulice (Castle Street). In the sloping market square is a large Marian Column (1742). There are remains of the town's fortifications.

Domažlice B 3

Region: Western Bohemia
District: Domažlice
Altitude: 428m/1404ft. Population: 12,000

Situation and characteristics

The district town of Domažlice, some 50km/30 miles south-west of Plzeň near the Czech–German frontier and the chief place in the Chod country (Chodsko), is famed for its folk art (woodcarving, pottery) and folk songs, its beautiful local costumes and its old customs (bagpiping, etc.).

History

Domažlice was given the status of a royal town by King Otakar II Přemysl around 1260. In 1431 there was an important battle near the town in which

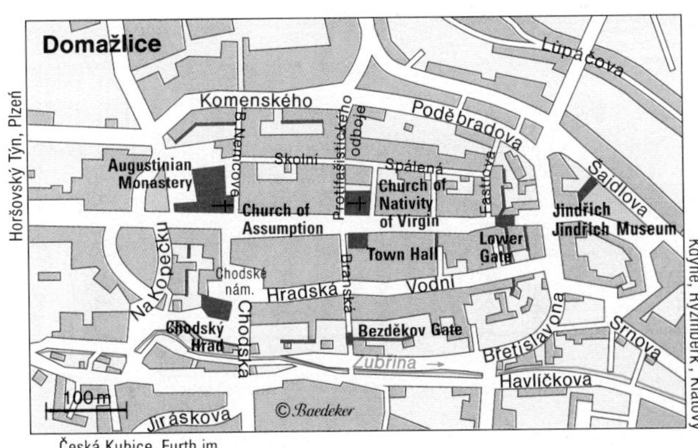

the Hussite army defeated the knights of the Teutonic Order. At that period the Chods were given responsibility for guarding a 30km/20 mile section of the frontier. The Chods, a free people, were known as the "Dogs' Heads", from the dog's head on their banner. After the Thirty Years' War they lost their privileges and rose in rebellion. The rebellion was crushed and the Chod leader, Jan Sladký-Kozina, was executed in 1695.

Sights

***Market square**
Church of Nativity of Virgin

In the centre of the town is the long market square, on the north side of which stands the Church of the Nativity of the Virgin (Kostel Narození Panny Marie; also known as the Cathedral), originally dating from the 13th century but rebuilt in Baroque style by Kilian Ignaz Dientzenhofer in 1747 after a devastating town fire. It has a leaning bell-tower (13th c.; wide views from top), formerly also used as a watch-tower, and a Gothic south doorway, now under a Baroque porch decorated with statuary. It has a richly furnished interior with fine frescoes.

Arcaded houses

The market square, which divides the picturesque old town for almost its whole length into a northern and a southern half, is lined with charming old arcaded houses in Renaissance, Baroque and Empire style.

Town Hall

On the south side of the market square, opposite the church, is the neo-Renaissance Town Hall (1891).

Augustinian monastery

At the north-west corner of the market square can be found a former Augustinian monastery, with a church which was originally Gothic but was rebuilt after the town fire; it contains a Gothic Madonna.

***Chodský Hrad**

Museum

A little way south of the Augustinian monastery is the Chodský Hrad (Chod Castle), with a massive tower. Originally dating from the 13th century, it was later rebuilt in Renaissance style. It contains an interesting local museum with rich collections of material on the history (including the

The arcaded market square of Domažlice

privileges of the Chods), ethnography and art of the Chod country and a valuable hoard of 2700 silver coins dating from the 14th–17th centuries which was hidden during the Thirty Years' War and rediscovered in 1963.

Lower Gate

At the east end of the market square the Lower Gate (Dolní Brána; *c.* 1270) is one of the two surviving town gates (the other being the South Gate). Near the gate, on the left of the street, is the Jindřich Jindřich Museum, with another fine collection of the folk art of the Chod country assembled by the composer Jindřich Jindřich (born in Domažlice in 1876), an enthusiastic collector. Farther east the little Gothic church of All Saints (Kostel u Svatých; 14th–15th c.) has a pulpit of 1562. Annually in August a Chod Festival is held here.

Jindřich Museum

Surroundings of Domažlice

Trhanov

6km/4 miles south-west of Domažlice is the village of Trhanov (Chod castle; alt. 450m/1475ft), with a Baroque palace (gallery of works by the Chod country painter Josef Špillar).

Babylon

7km/4½ miles south-west of Domažlice, in beautiful forest country, is the summer holiday resort of Babylon (alt. 460m/1510ft), with a bathing pond (area 13 hectares/32 acres) and a camping site.

Klenčí pod Čerchovem

8km/5 miles west of Domažlice is Klenčí pod Čerchovem (alt. 493m/1618ft), a little town with a Baroque church (St Martin's) and the Old Post House of 1546. The birthplace of the Chod writer Jindřich Šimon Baar (1869–1925) is now a museum. A short distance away is a viewpoint, Výhledy (705m/2313ft), with a monument commemorating Baar.

Kdyně

10km/6 miles south-east of Domažlice the little town of Kdyně (alt. 450m/1475ft; pop. 3500) has a church, originally Gothic, which was remodelled in Baroque style in 1763. To the north-east is the ruined castle of Nový Herštejn (alt. 682m/2238ft) and to the east Mt Koráb (773m/2536ft), with an outlook tower.

Nový Herštejn

Mt Koráb

Česká Kubice

Mt Čerchov

11km/7 miles south-west of Domažlice is Česká Kubice (alt. 550m/1805ft), at the foot of Mt Čerchov (1039m/3409ft), the highest peak in the Bohemian Forest (Český Les), the Bohemian part of the Upper Palatinate Forest.

Duchcov

C 2

Region: Northern Bohemia
District: Teplice
Altitude: 201m/659ft
Population: 10,000

Situation and characteristics

The old town of Duchcov is the chief place in the important Northern Bohemian coalfield, where lignite has been worked since the first half of the 18th century. In addition to the mines the town has engineering, glass and porcelain factories.
Tradition has it that the German minnesinger Walther von der Vogelweide came from Duchcov.

Sights

Castle

In the 18th century castle of the Valdštejn (Wallenstein) family (open April to October) the Italian adventurer Casanova (see Famous People) worked as librarian from 1785 until his death in 1798. His famous memoirs, the

Duchcov Castle

"Histoire de ma Vie", were written while he was living in the castle. There are mementoes of Casanova in the rooms which he occupied. The castle also contains fine sculpture by Matthias Bernhard Braun von Braun, a collection of furniture and a picture gallery. A fresco by V. V. Reiner formerly in the castle has been transferred to a modern pavilion in the gardens.

Barbara Pond

In the eastern part of the town, surrounded by gardens, is the Barbara Pond (Rybník Barbora; boating).

Surroundings of Duchcov

Most

See entry

Chomutov

See entry

Bílina

6km/4 miles south of Duchcov, on the river Bílina, we come to the town of Bílina (alt. 214m/702ft; pop. 17,000), with a Baroque palace which belonged to the Counts Lobkowitz (1675–82; not open to public). Excavations in the park have revealed remains of a Slav stronghold of the 10th century.

In the Kyselka district is an acidic mineral spring (spa treatment).

Litvínov

9km/5½ miles west of Duchcov is the industrial town of Litvínov

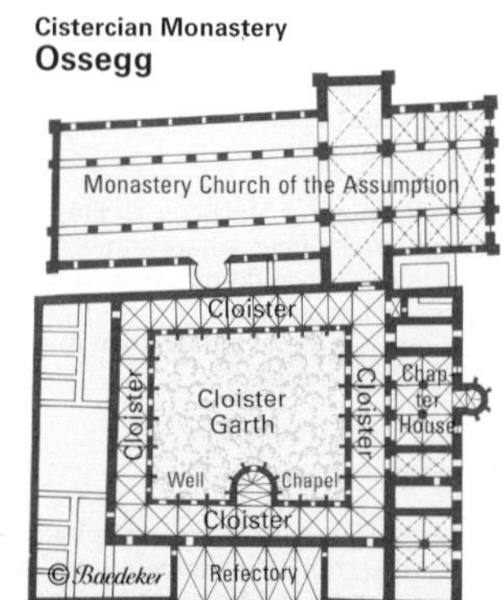

Osek Monastery

(alt. 338m/1109ft; pop. 29,000; lignite workings, chemical industry), with a fine Baroque castle (1732) which belonged to the Valdštejn (Wallenstein) family.

Osek
*Monastery

5km/3 miles north-west of Duchcov is the little mining town of Osek (alt. 307m/1007ft; pop. 5000), with a famous Cistercian monastery founded in the 12th century. The conventual buildings and the church, originally 13th century, were remodelled in Baroque style in the 18th century. The chapterhouse dates from around 1240, the choir ambulatory from the first half of the 14th century. Richly furnished interior. The monastery is surrounded by terraced gardens.

Rýzmburk

North of Osek are the ruins of a castle founded in the 13th century, the Rýzmburk (alt. 561m/1841ft; not open to public).

Františkovy Lázně / Franzensbad B 2

Region: Western Bohemia
District: Cheb
Altitude: 442m/1450ft
Population: 5000

Situation and characteristics

*Medicinal springs

The spa of Františkovy Lázně (German name Franzensbad) situated 5km/3 miles north-west of Cheb on the plateau between the foothills of the Bohemian Forest, the Fichtelgebirge and the Ore Mountains and surrounded by beautiful parkland, was founded in 1793, in the reign of the Emperor Francis I, and the first Kurhaus was built in 1828. The 24 medicinal

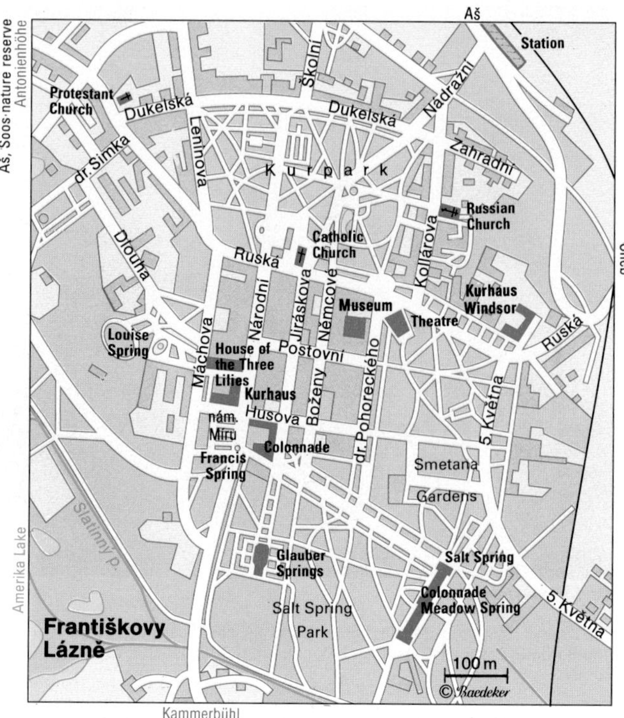

springs (alkaline Glauber salt, acidic ferruginous, sulphurous and chalybeate springs; 10.1–12.5°C/50.2–54.5°F), used in both drinking and bathing cures, together with ferruginous mud baths, carbonated baths and radioactive gas baths, are particularly recommended for the treatment of gynaecological disorders, heart conditions, rheumatism and anaemia. The springs of Františkovy Lázně were already famed in the 12th century. In the 18th century the water was despatched to all parts of the Austro-Hungarian monarchy, and it is still an important table water.

Sights

Kurhaus

The life of the spa centres on Peace Square (Náměstí Míru), with the Kurhaus (Společenský Dům).

Francis Spring

On the south side of the square rises the Francis Spring, the principal source of water for drinking cures, housed in a rotunda of 1832. Close by is the popular statue of "Little Francis", which has become the emblem of the town.

Glauber Springs
Sprudel

Beyond the Francis Spring are the Glauber Springs (in use since 1920) and the Sprudel Spring.

Bath-House I
Louise Spring

To the west of the Kurhaus is Bath-House I (Lázně I), built in 1827, and to the north of this, housed in a rotunda surrounded by columns, is the Louise Spring, which was discovered in the early 19th century.

Glauber Springs, Františkovy Lázně

Salt Spring
Meadow Spring

500m/550yd south-east of the Kurhaus are the Salt Spring and the Meadow Spring, with Bath-House II to the north-east and Bath-House III to the south.

Town centre

From the Francis Spring National Street (Národní Třída), the town's wide main street, runs north through the regularly laid out town centre. In this street is the oldest surviving boarding-house in the town, "At the Sign of the Three Lilies".
On the east side of the town centre are the Smetana Gardens (Sady Bedřicha Smetany), with the Goethe Fountain to the east. At the north-west corner of the gardens are the Municipal Theatre (1906) and the Municipal Museum.

Surroundings of Františkovy Lázně

Komorní Hůrka

2km/1¼ miles south-west of Františkovy Lázně the Komorní Hůrka (503m/1650ft), a 30m/100ft high volcanic cone, rises above the road on the right.

America Lake

2km/1¼ miles west of Františkovy Lázně lies America Lake (Jezero Amerika; water sports, camping site).

Aš

16km/10 miles north-west of Františkovy Lázně is the town of Aš (pop. 12,000; textiles, porcelain), in the centre of an industrial area. The little Zedwitz Palace now houses a museum.

Mt Háj
*View

Half an hour's walk north of Aš rises Mt Háj (758m/2487ft), a hill built up of mica schists, topped by an outlook tower with fine panoramic views: to the west the Franconian Forest, to the south-west the Fichtelgebirge, to the south-east the Chebsko district, to the east the Ore Mountains and to the north the Vogtland area.

Soos nature reserve

Skalná

6km/4 miles north of Františkovy Lázně is the old village of Skalná (alt. 465m/1525ft), with a castle of the Late Romanesque period (*c.* 1200; well preserved tower).

***Soos Nature Reserve**

6km/4 miles north-east of Františkovy Lázně, at Hájek, extends the Soos Nature Reserve, an area of marshland and peat bogs almost 2km/1¼ miles long and 1km/¾ mile across, of great interest and charm with its numerous springs of carbonated water, its geysers, its mud volcanoes and its unique flora of salt-loving bog plants (moorland trail).

Frýdek-Místek H 3

Region: Northern Moravia
District: Frýdek-Místek
Altitude: 300m/985ft
Population: 64,000

Situation and characteristics

The double town of Frýdek-Místek, which is divided by the river Ostravice into a Moravian and a Silesian half, is a rising district capital with textile, woodworking and heavy industry (rolling mills).

Sights

Frýdek

Frýdek, on the east bank of the Ostravice, is dominated by the prominent tower of a Baroque palace (17th–18th c.; museum of Wallachian folk art) which developed out of a medieval castle. Other features of interest are the twin-towered Baroque parish church (18th century, with 14th century foundations), the little church of St Jobst (16th c.), with a wooden tower, and the Old Town Hall (early 17th c.).

Místek

Místek, on the west bank of the river, has a fine market square surrounded by arcaded Renaissance and Baroque houses. The church, in Late Baroque style, dates from 1763–67. Místek also has a number of 18th century wooden buildings.

Surroundings of Frýdek-Místek

Olešná Dam

2km/1¼ miles south-west of Frýdek-Místek is the Olešná Dam.

Sedliště

4km/2½ miles north-east of Frýdek-Místek is Sedliště (alt. 330m/1085ft), with a wooden church of 1447, rebuilt in 1624.

Žermanice

7km/4½ miles north-east of Frýdek-Místek lies a recreational area round the Žermanice Dam (area 250 hectares/620 acres; water sports).

Frýdlant nad Ostravicí

The industrial town of Frýdlant nad Ostravicí (alt. 357m/1171ft; pop. 14,000), 10km/6 miles south of Frýdek-Místek, has an ironworking tradition going back to the middle of the 17th century. The town is a good base for walks and climbs in the Moravo-Silesian Beskyds (see entry).

Ostravice

14km/8½ miles south of Frýdek-Místek is Ostravice (alt. 415m/1362ft; pop. 2500), the largest holiday resort in the Ostrava industrial region. South of the town is the Šance Dam (reservoir).

Kunčice pod Ondřejníkem

16km/10 miles south of Frýdek-Místek we come to the summer resort of Kunčice pod Ondřejníkem (alt. 395m/1295ft; pop. 2000), with a small wooden church moved to its present site in 1931 from Carpatho-Russia (which was the most easterly part of the Czechoslovak Republic from 1920 to 1938).

Morávka

15km/9 miles south-east of Frýdek-Místek is the holiday resort of Morávka (alt. 520m/1705ft; pop. 5000), with some remains of traditional architecture and a reservoir formed by a dam.

Jablunkov

35km/22 miles south-east of Frýdek-Místek, at the junction of the river Lomná with the Olše, the town of Jablunkov (alt. 386m/1266ft; pop. 10,000; light industry, woodworking) is a good base for a visit to the Jablunka Hills, an area with old folk traditions. Here, annually in August, is held a folk festival of the Gorals, the highlanders of the Beskyds.

Goral festival

Jablunka pass

6km/4 miles south of Jablunkov is the Jablunka pass (Jablunkovskýprůsmyk; 553m/1814ft), an important means of passage through the Western Beskyds, between the Moravo-Silesian Beskyds in the west and the Silesian Beskyds (Beskid Śląski), which are for the most part in Polish territory, to the east. A 670m/735yd long railway tunnel now runs under the pass.

Jablunka Entrenchments

South-west of the pass are the Jablunka Entrenchments (Jablunkovské Šance), the remains of Renaissance fortifications of 1578 directed against the Turks; they were given their present form at the beginning of the 18th century.

Copper Road

Near the Jablunka Entrenchments ran the old Copper Road (Měděná Cesta) which linked the mining region of Central Slovakia with Silesia.

Carpathian Forest

8km/5 miles south-west of Jablunkov Mionší (alt. 883m/2897ft) are remains of the old Carpathian Forest, now a nature reserve (area 170 hectares/420 acres; admission only with official guide).

Třinec

24km/15 miles east of Frýdek-Místek is Třinec (alt. 300m/985ft; pop. 46,000), with an ironworks founded in 1838.

Guty

6km/4 miles south-west of Třinec is the village of Guty, with a little church which is one of the oldest wooden churches in the Czech lands (1656).

Český Těšín

24km/15 miles east of Frýdek-Místek, on the Czech–Polish frontier, is the industrial town of Český Těšín (alt. 270m/885ft; pop. 29,000; printing and textiles), the Czech part of the Polish town of Cieszyn (alt. 270m/885ft; pop. 25,000). Český Těšín was once the chief town of a duchy.

Frýdlant E 2

Region: Northern Bohemia
District: Liberec
Altitude: 308m/1011ft
Population: 6200

Situation and characteristics

The old-world little town of Frýdlant (German Friedland) lies in the hilly foreland of the Jizera Hills in northern Bohemia, on the banks of the river Smědá. It has preserved its original layout and some remains of its old town walls. It has some industry (textiles, papermaking).

Sights

Market square
Town Hall

In the market square, which is surrounded by handsome gabled houses, is the Town Hall (1897; local museum).

Decanal Church

The Rädern Chapel in the Gothic Decanal Church (originally 13th century; rebuilt in 15th–16th centuries) contains the fine monuments of Friedrich von Rädern (d. 1564) and Melchior von Rädern (d. 1600) and his family, with bronze figures of the dead (by the Dutch sculptor C. G. Heinrich, 1610). Behind the high altar is the Gothic monument of the Biberstein family.

***Castle**

On a basalt hill (352m/1155ft) to the south of the square, approached by a winding road, is the imposing Castle, with a 60m/200ft high cylindrical keep

Frýdlant Castle

known as the Indica. Built in the 13th–16th centuries and set in a beautiful park, it was held from 1278 to 1551 by the Biberstein family and later by the Barons von Rädern. From 1622 to 1634 it belonged to the celebrated Albrecht von Wallenstein (Valdštejn: see Famous People), who was granted the title of Duke of Friedland. Later it passed into the hands of the Counts Gallas and in 1759 to their heirs the Counts Clam-Gallas.
The castle contains period furniture and collections of ceramics and glass, weapons, portraits (including a likeness of Wallenstein, 1626) and a picture gallery with works by the Baroque painters Petr Brandl, V. V. Reiner and Karel Škréta.
From the keep there are fine views of the Jizera Hills (see entry).

Surroundings of Frýdlant

Hejnice

10km/6 miles south-east of Frýdlant, beautifully situated in the wooded valley of the river Smědá, is the little town of Hejnice (alt. 370m/1215ft; pop. 2500; textile industry). The large Baroque monastic church, a great pilgrimage church, was built to the design of J. B. Fischer von Erlach in 1722–29 and rebuilt after a fire in 1761. On the high altar is a carved wooden image of the Virgin, and in a chapel in the north transept are a winged altar (15th c.) and the tomb of Count Clam-Gallas. The conventual buildings of the former Franciscan friary date from the end of the 17th century.

Lázně Libverda

7km/4½ miles south-east of Frýdlant lies Lázně Libverda (alt. 400m/1310ft), a spa (alkaline earthy springs and springs containing arsenium and iron) recommended for the treatment of gynaecological disorders, heart conditions, diseases of the metabolism, etc.
The popular Obři Sud restaurant is housed in a giant cask.

Havlíčkův Brod

E 3

Region: Eastern Bohemia
District: Havlíčkův Brod
Altitude: 422m/1385ft
Population: 25,000

Situation and characteristics

The old mining town of Havlíčkův Brod (formerly called Německý Brod) in eastern Bohemia, chief town of its district and a railway junction, is beautifully situated on the banks of the Sázava in a well wooded region in the Bohemo-Moravian Highlands. The town was founded in the 13th century by German miners who settled here to work the rich deposits of silver ore which then existed in the area. Havlíčkův Brod now has textile, engineering, foodstuffs and chemical industries.
The town featured in history as the scene of the Hussite leader Jan Žižka's victory over the Emperor Sigismund in 1422. Its present name commemorates the Czech journalist Karel Havlíček Borovský (1821–56).

Sights

Market square
Old Town Hall

Havlíčkův Brod has a handsome market square traversed diagonally by the main street, with interesting gabled houses and the Old Town Hall (originally 15th c.; rebuilt in Renaissance style in 16th c.).

Decanal Church
Havlíček House

Other features of interest are the Decanal Church, built by the Teutonic Order in the 15th century and altered in the 17th (old bell in tower), and the Havlíček House (Havlíčkův Dům; with round oriel window), in which the journalist and poet Karel Havlíček Borovský was arrested on political grounds in 1851 (Museum).

Market square, Havlíčkův Brod

Malina House

In an old burgher's house at No. 50, the Malina House, is an Art Gallery (graphic art and book illustration).

Surroundings of Havlíčkův Brod

Lipnice nad Sázavou

12km/7½ miles west of Havlíčkův Brod is the village of Lipnice nad Sázavou (alt. 590m/1935ft; pop. 1000), with the ruins of a Gothic castle which has preserved the characteristic features of 14th century military architecture. The chapel has wall paintings of the same period. The Old Palace also dates from the 14th century, the New Palace from the 16th.
Jaroslav Hašek (see Famous People), author of "The Good Soldier Schwejk", lived in the village and died there. A festival of satire and humour is held here annually in his memory. Hašek's house is now a memorial museum; his grave is in the village churchyard.

Světlá nad Sázavou

14km/8½ miles north-west of Havlíčkův Brod we come to the industrial town of Světlá nad Sázavou (alt. 400m/1310ft; pop. 5000). The main local industries are stonemasonry and crystal manufacture ("Bohemia" crystal). The town has an early 19th century castle set in a park and a Late Gothic church.

Ledeč nad Sázavou

The town of Ledeč nad Sázavou (alt. 353m/1158ft; pop. 5500), 24km/15 miles north-west of Havlíčkův Brod, in the Sázava valley, has engineering and shoe-manufacturing industries. In the market square is a Baroque Plague Column (1715). Above the right bank of the river is a medieval castle which was enlarged in 1556, with later alterations. Above the left bank is an aisled Gothic church.

Chotěboř

15km/9 miles north-east of Havlíčkův Brod is the old mining town of Chotěboř (alt. 515m/1690ft; pop. 8500; engineering industry), with a Baroque castle (1701–02) and a beautiful park.

12km/7½ miles east of Havlíčkův Brod lies Přibyslav (alt. 475m/1560ft; pop. 5000; foodstuffs industry), which owed its foundation in the mid 13th century to the deposits of silver ore in the area. The Castle (1560), now housing a Firefighting Museum, occupies the site of an earlier castle of the Gothic period. **Přibyslav**

During a siege of the town in 1424 the famous Hussite leader Jan Žižka (see Famous People) died in the neighbouring village of Žižkovo Pole, renamed in his honour.

Humpolec (alt. 527m/1729ft; pop. 11,000), 19km/12 miles south-west of Havlíčkův Brod, has a long tradition of cloth-manufacture and flax-growing. The Decanal Church, originally Gothic, was remodelled in Baroque style and again altered in recent times. By the cemetery is a neo-classical church. Humpolec was the birthplace of the Czech anthropologist Aleš Hrdlička (1869–1943), and the local museum has a special exhibition on modern anthropology. **Humpolec**

Hluboká nad Vltavou D 3

Region: Southern Bohemia
District: České Budějovice
Altitude: 394m/1293ft
Population: 3400

Situation and characteristics

Hluboká nad Vltavou, 10km/6 miles north of České Budějovice, is mainly known for its large castle. The town also has fish-farming and woodworking industries.

© Baedeker

30 m

Hluboká nad Vltavou
Ground plan of Castle
Frauenberg

*Hluboká Castle

History

On a rocky hill, 83m/272ft above a bend in the Vltava, rises the massive bulk of Hluboká Castle, which belonged to the Princes Schwarzenberg. Originally built in the 13th century, it was much altered in later centuries and finally rebuilt in its present form, with eleven towers and several bastions, on the model of Britain's Windsor Castle, between 1840 and 1871.

*Art collections

The castle is now a museum, displaying in its more than 140 rooms rich collections of pictures, porcelain, glass, tapestries, furniture, hunting trophies, arms and much else besides.

The mid 19th century riding school is now occupied by the Aleš Gallery (1952–55), named after the Czech painter Mikoláš Aleš (1852–1913), with a large collection of pictures and sculpture by Southern Bohemian artists from the Middle Ages (particularly the Gothic period) to the present day.

A beautiful park, with a game preserve surrounds the castle.

Hluboká Castle

Surroundings of Hluboká nad Vltavou

Ohrada Castle

1km/¾ mile south-west of Hluboká nad Vltavou, on the southern shore of the Munický Rybník (fish-pond), stands the Baroque Ohrada Castle, built in 1707–18 as a hunting lodge. It now houses a Museum of Fishing, Hunting and Forestry. Near the castle is a small zoo.

Bezdrev Pond

5km/3 miles west of Hluboká nad Vltavou lies Bezdrev Pond, the second largest natural lake in the Czech lands (520 hectares/1285 acres; bathing).

Plástovice

The village of Plástovice, situated in marshland (Blata) 9km/5½ miles west of Hluboká nad Vltavou, has a number of interesting 19th century houses in the style known as rustic Baroque.

Horšovský Týn B 3

Region: Western Bohemia
District: Domažlice
Altitude: 377m/1237ft
Population: 4100

Situation and characteristics

The little town of Horšovský Týn (formerly also known as Horšův Týn) is charmingly situated on the river Radbuza in the Chod country, 16km/10 miles north of Domažlice (see entry).

Sights

***Castle**

The Castle, with four ranges of building round a central courtyard, was built in the 16th century on the site of a 13th century castle of the bishops of

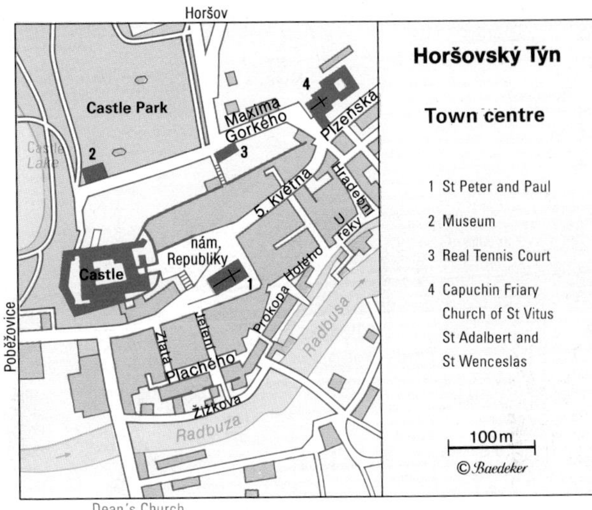

Prague and rebuilt in the 19th century. It formerly belonged to the Counts of Trauttmannsdorff.

Art collections

The Castle has interesting decoration and furnishings and contains a variety of collections, including 17th century paintings and East Asian porcelain. It has a large park.

Republic Square

In the centre of the town is Republic Square (Náměstí Republiky), surrounded by old gabled houses. In the square is the Church of SS Peter and Paul (13th century; remodelled in Baroque style in the early 18th century).

Decanal Church

On the right bank of the Radbuza stands the Decanal Church (1260–70).

Town walls

On the north side of the town there are some remains of its 16th century walls.

Surroundings of Horšovský Týn

Horsov

3km/2 miles north of Horšovský Týn lies the old-world village of Horšov (alt. 387m/1270ft), with a late 12th century galleried church (partly remodelled in Baroque style in the 18th century) and an 18th century hunting lodge.

Poběžovice

10km/6 miles west of Horšovský Týn is Poběžovice (alt. 431m/1414ft; pop. 1500), with a Baroque castle (originally Gothic) set in a park.

Hradec Králové / Königgrätz

E 2

Region: Eastern Bohemia
District: Hradec Králové
Altitude: 224m/735ft
Population: 100,000

Situation and characteristics

Hradec Králové (German Königgrätz), situated at the junction of the river Orlice with the Labe (Elbe), is the economic and cultural centre of eastern

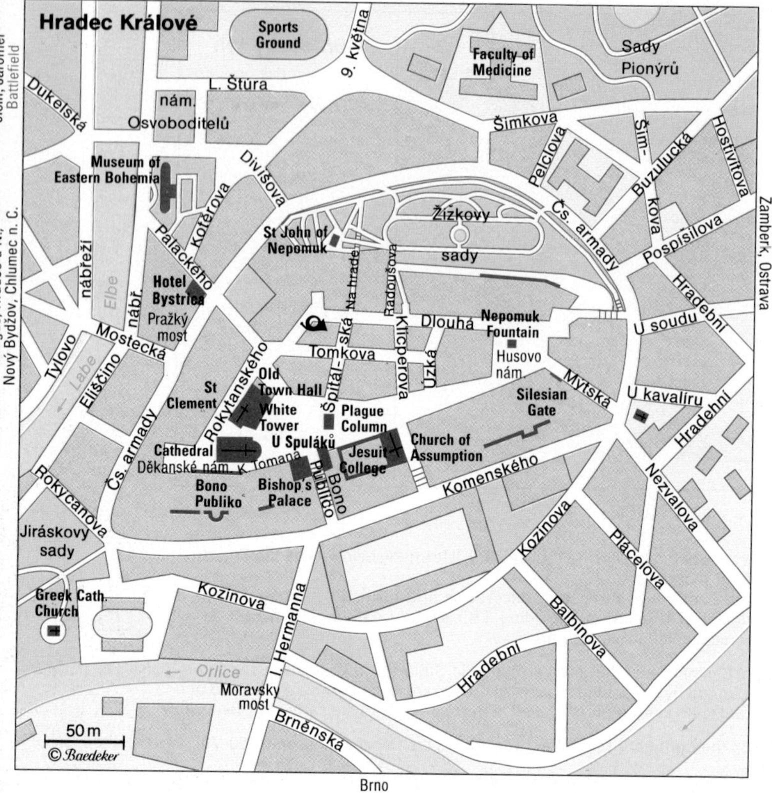

Bohemia, an important traffic junction and industrial town: manufacture of diesel engines, distillery, sugar-refinery, musical instruments (Petrof pianos). It has a theatre, a teachers' training college, a medical school and a college of pharmacy.

History

The town's name is derived from the castle (*hradec, grätz*) of the Bohemian queens who resided here in the 14th century. During the 15th century the town was a stronghold of the Hussite movement. The old town, situated on higher ground, was surrounded between 1766 and 1789 by massive fortifications which hampered its further development. It was only after the demolition in 1893 of these fortifications (of which some remains survive) that Hradec Králové was able to expand in all directions – though most of the new town, much of it laid out in considerable style, lay to the west of the Labe, extending to the railway station. Two leading Czech architects, Jan Kotěra and Josef Gočár, were involved in the new developments.

In the hilly country to the north-west of the town, on July 3rd 1866, was fought the decisive battle of Königgrätz in the Austro-Prussian war for predominance in Germany.

Church of the Assumption and Plague Column, Hradec Králové ▶

Sights

***Market square**

The central feature of the old town is the triangular market square (Žižkovo Náměstí, Žižka Square), with a 19m/62ft high Plague Column (1717). The west side of the square is dominated by five towers: to the left the twin-towered Cathedral, in the centre the White Tower, to the right the Old Town Hall. The best view of the towers is from the arcades on the north side of the square.

Cathedral

The brick-built Early Gothic Cathedral of the Holy Spirit (Katedrála Sv. Ducha; early 14th c.), with its tall choir facing the market square, has a beautiful tabernacle of 1492, a pewter font of 1407, a 15th century winged altar and a painting of St Anthony by Petr Brandl.

St Clement's Chapel

Immediately north of the Cathedral can be found St Clement's Chapel (Baroque), built in 1716 on the site of an earlier Gothic church.

White Tower

Adjoining is the 68m/223ft high White Tower (Bílá Věž; 1574–89), with the 10-ton bell known as Agustín (cast 1509).

Old Town Hall

On the north side of the White Tower stands the Old Town Hall (Stará Radnice), a Renaissance building (16th c.; restored around 1850) with two towers.

Church of Assumption
Jesuit College

On the south side of the market square is the Baroque Church of the Assumption, a Jesuit church (by Carlo Lurago, 1654–66) with a richly furnished interior (including paintings by Petr Brandl). Next to the church is the former Jesuit College (*c.* 1720), which since 1773 has been a barracks.

Bono Publiko
Bishop's Palace

To the west, at the corner of the stepped street called Bono Publiko, can be seen the Baroque Špulak House (U Špuláků). Still farther west is the Bishop's Palace (Biskupská Residence), rebuilt in Baroque style around 1780. It contains an interesting gallery of 20th century Bohemian painting (E. Filla, B. Kubišta, J. Preisler).

Little Square

To the west of the Cathedral is the Little Square (Malé Náměstí), with handsome arcaded houses and old-world little lanes opening off the square. Here too are a number of old canons' houses.

Castle Square
Episcopal Seminary
St John of Nepomuk

A little way north of the market square, in the picturesque Castle Square (Náměstí na Hradě), are the former Episcopal Seminary and the Church of St John of Nepomuk, two Baroque buildings erected between 1710 and 1720 on the site of the old castle of the Bohemian queens and the later Burgrave's House (16th c.; remains of sgraffito decoration).

Museum

On the west side of the old town, bordering the Labe, is the Museum of Eastern Bohemia, an Art Nouveau building (by Jan Kǒtera, 1909–12), with a historical section, a collection of applied art, a lapidarium and a library.

Jirásek Park
Wooden church

To the south of the Museum, in Jirásek Park (Jiráskovy Sady), at the junction of the Orlice with the Labe, stands the Greek Catholic church, a little wooden church (1759) which was brought here from Malá Pol'ana in eastern Slovakia.

Surroundings of Hradec Králové

Hrádek u Nechanic

12km/7½ miles west of Hradec Králové is Hrádek u Nechanic, a Tudor-style castle (1839–54) containing valuable furniture (glass, picture gallery, library). It is surrounded by an English-style park with a game enclosure.

Novy Bydžov

The town of Novy Bydžov (alt. 232m/761ft; pop. 7000) 22km/13½ miles west of Hradec Králové on the river Cidlina, has a Gothic church dating from the first half of the 14th century (partly rebuilt in Baroque style), a neo-Gothic Town Hall (1862–65) and an old Jewish cemetery (1520).

Chlumec nad Cidlinou Karlova Koruna

28km/17 miles west of Hradec Králové is Chlumec nad Cidlinou (alt. 223m/732ft; pop. 5000). Prominently situated on a hill, the domed Baroque castle of Karlova Koruna ("Charles's Crown") houses an interesting collection of Bohemian Baroque art. The castle is set in a beautiful park with old trees (protected).

Smiřice

10km/6 miles north of Hradec Králové, on the Labe, we come to the little town of Smiřice (alt. 240m/785ft; pop. 3200). It has a Baroque castle with arcades and a park (17th c.) and a large Baroque chapel (1699–1706) with fine pictures (Petr Brandl) and ceiling paintings.

Třebechovice pod Orebem

13km/8 miles east of Hradec Králové is Třebechovice pod Orebem (alt. 243m/797ft; pop. 5500). In the Museum is the famous Třebechovice Crib (Nativity group), with 400 carved wooden figures (late 19th or early 20th century).

Battlefield of Königgrätz

Access

The battlefield of Königgrätz (Bojište u Hradec Králové) is reached by taking the Jičín road, which runs north-west and comes in 10km/6 miles to a side road on the right signposted to Chlum. A short distance along this road, on the right, can be seen a low obelisk topped by an eagle commemorating the dead of the First Army Corps of the Imperial army. In 1km/¾ mile the road

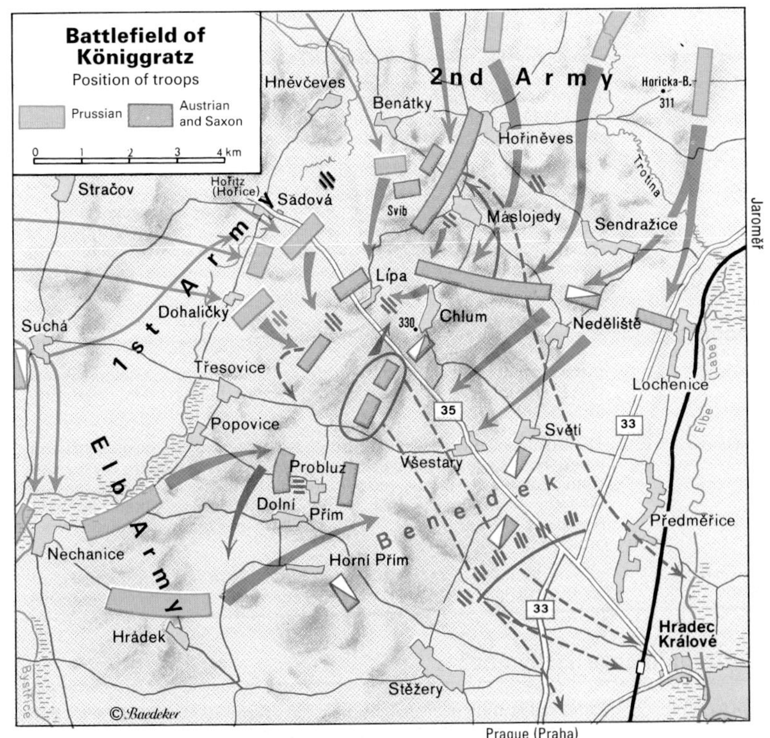

reaches the village of Chlum, where a road goes off on the left beyond the church, signposted to the Ossuary. After passing a Prussian military cemetery and the Ossuary (both on the left) it comes in 750m/800yd to the Museum (Válečni Muzeum 1866), with a viewing platform (alt. 330m/1080ft).

Museum

The Museum contains a collection of historical documents and displays, uniforms, arms, etc.

From the viewing platform there is an excellent view of the battlefield. The various monuments can be seen on signposted tracks in 2–3 hours. A complete tour of the battlefield would take a whole day, and is not particularly rewarding.

Battle of Königgrätz

The battle of Königgrätz or Sadowa, one of the greatest battles of the 19th century and the decisive engagement in the Austro-Prussian War, was fought on July 3rd 1866 in the hilly terrain north-west of Hradec Králové between the Bystřice and the Labe. The victorious Prussian army lost just over 9000 officers and men, the Austrians and their Saxon allies (including prisoners) just over 41,500.

Jáchymov B 2

Region: Western Bohemia
District: Karlovy Vary
Altitude: 635–780m/2085–2560ft
Population: 5000

Situation and characteristics

The old mining town of Jáchymov (German St Joachimsthal) in western Bohemia straggles along a narrow valley below Mt Klínovec in the Ore Mountains. It has highly radioactive thermal springs (average temperature 28°C/82°F), rising in the pitchblende-uranium mines, which are recommended for the treatment of nervous and rheumatic diseases.

History

Jáchymov owed its foundation in 1516 to the rich deposits of silver ore which were worked down to the end of the 19th century. Here about 1820 Count Schlick began to mint the gold coins which became known, after the German name of the town, as Joachimsthaler: hence the word thaler or dollar. In 1898 Pierre and Marie Curie discovered the element radium in the Jáchymov pitchblende-uranium ore (which had been used before then in the manufacture of glass and porcelain).

Sights

The spa

In the southern part of the town lies the spa district, with the Radium Palace (1911) and other treatment facilities, including the new Běhounek Sanatorium (1975).

Old town

The old mining town occupies the higher northern part of the present town. In the market square, which slopes down towards the south, are the Late Gothic Town Hall (16th c.), the town church (1876; originally 16th c.) and the Museum (history of coining, radioactive minerals, balneology, etc.). Nearby is the old Mint (1534–36) in which the original "dollars" were produced.

Freudenstein Castle

Above the town to the west (half-hour walk) are the remains of Freudenstein Castle (alt. 814m/2671ft; panoramic views), built by Count Schlick in 1517.

Surroundings of Jáchymov

Boží Dar

5km/3 miles north of Jáchymov, near the Czech–German frontier, lies Boží Dar (alt. 1028m/3373ft), the country's highest town. A mining town from the

Jáchymov

late Middle Ages, it is now a popular winter sports resort. To the west of the little town is a peat-bog, with characteristic vegetation.

Mt Klínovec

5km/3 miles north-east of Jáchymov is Mt Klínovec (1244m/4082ft), the highest peak in the Ore Mountains. On the summit are an inn, an outlook tower (fine views, particularly towards Bohemia) and a weather station. On the west side of the hill are a chair-lift and a good skiing piste.

Ostrov

7km/4½ miles south of Jáchymov, at the foot of the Ore Mountains, which here rear steeply up, is the old mining town of Ostrov (alt. 400m/1310ft; pop. 21,000), with engineering, textile and woodworking industries; in the postwar years uranium was also mined here. St James's Church (1226) has a Romanesque doorway and Gothic vaulting. There is a Baroque castle (1690), set in a magnificent park with a Baroque pavilion (art gallery).

Mt Plešivec

6km/4 miles west of Jáchymov rises Mt Plešivec (1027m/3370ft), a basalt hill with fine panoramic views from an outlook tower on the summit.

Abertamy

8km/5 miles west of Jáchymov, in an interesting moorland area, is Abertamy (alt. 850m/2790ft; lace-making and glove manufacture).

Jeseníky (Hrubý Jeseník and Nízký Jeseník) F/G 2/3

Region: Northern Moravia
Districts: Šumperk and Bruntál

Situation and characteristics

The Jeseníky (= the Jeseníks) nature reserve, with an area of 740sq.km/285sq.miles, takes in almost the whole of the Hrubý Jeseník massif and part of the Nízký Jeseník (Moravian Uplands) in north-western Moravia.

View towards the Hrubý Jesenik range

Hrubý Jeseník

The Hrubý Jeseník or Praděd range is the second highest in the Sudeten mountain system. The central ridge, much of it bare of vegetation, ranges in height between 1000m/3280ft and 1492m/4895ft (Mt Praděd, the highest peak in the Eastern Sudetens). The range, 40km/25 miles long, is much indented and broken up, with romantic valleys and numerous waterfalls between its often rocky summits.

Nízký Jeseník

South-east of the Hrubý Jeseník extends the Nízký Jeseník or Moravian Uplands, a plateau (about 800m/2625ft) out of which rise numerous basaltic hills.

Jeseníky Nature Reserve

Topography

This upland region is almost completely covered with forests of spruce, with only occasional patches of mixed woodland. On the high plateaux are some interesting expanses of peat-bog. The best known of these is the Rejvíz nature reserve (alt. 757m/2484ft), 7km/4½ miles east of Jeseník, with the Little and the Large Moss lakes (5.5km/3½ mile long nature trail).

Ridge walk

The Hrubý Jeseník ridge walk begins at the Ramzovské Sedlo (759m/2490ft) or, for a shorter walk, Mt Šerák (1351m/4433ft; chair-lift). The section from Mt Šerák to Mt Keprník (1423m/4669ft) climbs at a moderate gradient, and the route then runs down by way of the Červená Hora, with the Vřesová mountain hut, to the Červenohorské Sedlo (1013m/3324ft); walking time about 3½ hours. The route then climbs to the Švýcárna hut and the summit of Praděd with its tall television tower (2½ hours). From there the bare ridge path continues by way of the Petrovy Kameny (1446m/4744ft) and Vysoká Hole (1464m/4803ft) to the Skřitek saddle, with a peat-bog (877m/2877ft; 4 hours).

Television tower on Mt Praděd ▶

North-west of the Hrubý Jeseník is the rarely visited Králický Sněžník massif (1423m/4669ft).

Winter sports

The Jeseníky area offers excellent winter sports facilities: langlauf trails at Ovčárna, downhill pistes at Ramzová, Ovčárna and Karlov pod Pradědem.

Places of Interest in the Jeseníky Nature Reserve

Jeseník

In a valley basin below the north-east side of the Hrubý Jeseník is the spa of Jeseník (alt. 440m/1445ft; pop. 14,000), formerly called Frývaldov. Behind the 15th century parish church (R.C.) is the Castle (Late Gothic), which now houses a local museum. In the Municipal Park can be seen a monument to Vinzenz Priessnitz (1799–1851), who devised the cold-water method of spa treatment. In 1826 he opened his own sanatorium at the altitude resort of Lázně Jeseník (632m/2074ft), 2km/1¼ miles north-west.

Lipová Lázně

5km/3 miles west of Jeseník we come to Lipová Lázně (alt. 530m/1740ft; pop. 2500), a spa recommended for the treatment of metabolic disorders and skin diseases.
Some 2km/1¼ miles north is the karstic cave Na Pomezí.

Vidnava

Vidnava (alt. 240m/785ft; pop. 2500) 18km/11 miles north of Jeseník has remains of its Gothic town walls, a Gothic church and a number of Renaissance burghers' houses of similar design, including the old Governor's House.

Javorník

24km/15 miles north-west of Jeseník is Javorník (alt. 250–350m/820–1150ft; pop. 4500), with the large Baroque mansion of Jánský Vrch, built on the site of an earlier Gothic castle. It has a richly furnished interior (gallery; collection of pipes) and a large park. The house was occupied from 1769 to 1794 by the German composer Karl Ditters von Dittersdorf (1739–99). There is also a Romanesque and Gothic cemetery church.

Karlova Studánka

In the south of the Jeseníky nature reserve (15km/9 miles north-west of Bruntál) lies the trim little spa of Karlova Studánka (alt. 775m/2545ft), situated on the Bilá Opava amid magnificent forests on the eastern slope of the hills, with chalybeate springs which are recommended for disorders of the respiratory tract (also drinking cures for the treatment of anaemia, carbonated baths and mud baths).

There is a rewarding excursion (2 hours) up the Bilá Opava valley, passing many waterfalls, by way of the Ovčárna ("Sheepfarm"; 1260m/4135ft; mountain inn; bus to this point) to Mt Praděd (1492ft/4895ft).

Malá Morávka

10km/6 miles north of Rýmařov, on the river Moravice, is the holiday centre of Malá Morávka (alt. 660m/2165ft; pop. 1000). As well as several hotels it still has a few examples of traditional local architecture. Malá Morávka is a good base for walks and climbs in the Velká Kotlina nature reserve, which has preserved a rare Ice Age flora.

Jičín

E 2

Region: Eastern Bohemia
District: Jičín
Altitude: 290m/950ft. Population: 17,000

Situation and characteristics

The old-world town of Jičín in eastern Bohemia, chief town of its district, lies on the Cidlina, a right-bank tributary of the Labe (Elbe). It is a good centre from which to explore the Bohemian Paradise (see entry). The town has some industry (foodstuffs, agricultural machinery).

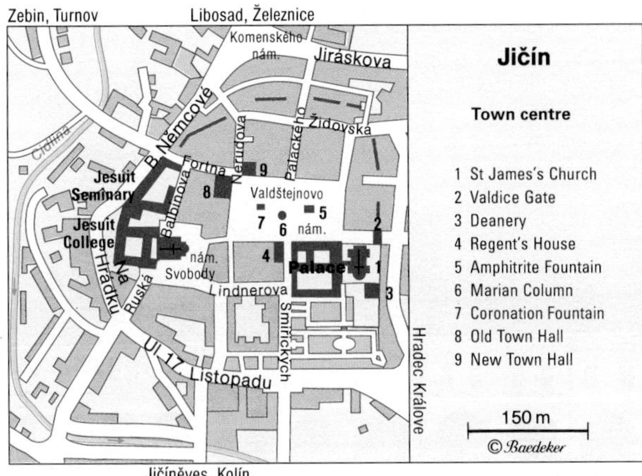

History

The town, founded in 1300, enjoyed only a brief period of prosperity in the time of Wallenstein (see Famous People), the great general of the Thirty Years' War, who as Duke of Friedland (from 1627) made Jičín the political, economic and cultural centre of his new duchy, even establishing a university as well as a mint. After Wallenstein's murder at Cheb (see entry) in 1634 Jičín was left only with its fine buildings (mostly the work of Italian architects) as reminders of past glory.

Jičín was the birthplace of the writer and critic Karl Kraus (1874–1936).

Sights

Wallenstein Palace

Wallenstein's palace, a Renaissance building which was enlarged in Early Baroque style and given its present aspect in 1830–60, dominates the south side of the spacious rectangular market square, which is lined by Baroque and Empire arcaded houses. To the rear of the palace are beautiful gardens.

Picture Gallery

The palace now houses the Municipal Picture Gallery. On the first floor is the conference room in which the Holy Alliance against Napoleon was formed between the Emperors Frederick William III of Prussia, Francis I of Austria and Alexander I of Russia in 1813.

St James's Church

Immediately east of the palace stands the towerless Early Baroque St James's Church (1627), with a richly furnished interior (altarpieces and trompe-l'oeil paintings in dome by J. Kramolín). Adjoining is one of the old town gates, the 52m/170ft high Valdická Bráma (1568–78; enlarged in 1768 and 1840); from the wall-walk there are wide views.

Jesuit Church

Near the south-west corner of the market square is the Jesuit church of St Ignatius (originally 14th century, with much later alteration). In the centre of the square are the Amphitrite Fountain (1835), a Baroque Plague Column of 1702 and the Coronation Fountain (Korunovační Kašna), in the unusual form of a Greek temple (1836).

Surroundings of Jičín

Libosad

From Jičín an avenue lined by four rows of old lime-trees runs 2.5km/1½ miles north-east to Wallenstein's pleasure garden of Libosad (summer palace with loggia, 1632–34).

Arcaded houses in the market square, Jičin

Zebín — Conspicuously situated on a basalt cone a little to the north-west of the gardens is the Zebín chapel (*c.* 1700).

Železnice — 5km/3 miles north of Jičín lies the little spa of Železnice (alt. 321m/1053ft; pop. 1000). The centre of the town is in Empire style. There are a number of fine old wooden houses in the lane called Na Zámkách.

Bradlec
Kumburk — 9km/5½ miles north-east of Jičín are two ruined Gothic castles, Bradlec (alt. 557m/1828ft) and Kumburk (642m/2106ft), both built in the 14th century and destroyed in the 17th.

Jičiněves — 8km/5 miles south of Jičín, in the village of Jičiněves (alt. 254m/833ft), is a Baroque mansion with an English-style park.

Staré Hrady — 11km/7 miles south-west of Jičín stands the Renaissance castle of Staré Hrady (1573), which now houses literary archives.

Bohemian Paradise — See entry

Jihlava E 3

Region: Southern Moravia
District: Jihlava
Altitude: 520m/1705ft
Population: 54,000

Situation and characteristics — Jihlava, chief town of a district in southern Moravia, lies near the Bohemian border in the heart of the Bohemo-Moravian Highlands (Českomoravská Vrchovina). It takes its name from the river Jihlava. The principal industries

of this former royal mining town are the manufacture of motor vehicle parts, mechanical engineering, textiles, leather goods, glass and woodworking. Jihlava has a well preserved old town, but in recent times has extended beyond its historic centre with the development of new housing districts.

History

The market village on this site founded by German settlers first appears in the records in 1233. Before the discovery of silver at Kutná Hora (see entry) Jihlava was the most important silver-mining town in Central Europe after Freiberg in Saxony. The charter of mining laws granted to the town by King Wenceslas (Václav) II about 1300 was for many years a model for all German mining towns between the Sudetens and the Carpathians; it was imitated in many other European countries and in the 16th century, by way of Spain, reached as far afield as Latin America. In the 13th century coins were minted in Jihlava; but at the beginning of the 14th century Wenceslas II concentrated the minting of his coinage in Kutná Hora and the mining industry of Jihlava declined.

In 1436 the Emperor Sigismund swore in Jihlava to observe the Compact of Prague (1433, at the end of the Hussite wars) under which the Czech people were permitted to receive communion in both kinds.

Towards the end of the Middle Ages the town was an important centre of cloth manufacture. Relics of this period are the "covered courtyards", the vaulted tower-like rooms to be seen in the houses of well-to-do cloth-merchants. The Thirty Years' War (1618–48) put an end to the town's prosperity, and it was only in the 18th century that it began to revive. Thereafter, until the 19th century, the town's cloth-making craftsmen were able to compete successfully with the industrially produced textiles of Brno and Northern Bohemia.

The famous conductor and composer Gustav Mahler (see Famous People) lived in Jihlava as a child.

Until the Second World War Jihlava was the chief place in a German linguistic island, roughly half of the 80 communes in which had a German majority.

Sights

***Masaryk Square**

In the centre of the picturesque old town is the town's long main square, Masarykovo Náměstí, one of the largest of its kind in the country.

Town Hall

On the east side of the square, which slopes down towards the south, stands the Town Hall (Radnice), which was originally Gothic but was rebuilt and enlarged in the 16th and 18th centuries; it has a Baroque façade (with turret) built in 1786. The town's archives, preserved here, include in addition to other valuable documents a law book (with illuminations) written by Johann von Gelnhausen in 1389.

Catacombs

In the Town Hall can be seen the entrance to an immense labyrinth of underground passages, the "Catacombs", which were hewn from the rock in the 14th–16th centuries to serve as store-rooms and during the Thirty Years' War provided shelter for the defenders of the town against the Swedes. The Catacombs are not at present open to the public.

Plague Column

At the north end of Masaryk Square is a Plague Column (1690).

Jesuit Church

Facing the column on the east is the Jesuit church of St Ignatius (Kostel Sv. Ignáce), built by an Italian architect, Jacopo Brasca, in 1680–89 and remodelled in Baroque style in 1760. The richly furnished interior has sumptuous ceiling paintings and several pieces of Gothic sculpture (including a Pietà and the "Přemyslid Cross", both dating from the 14th century).

To the left of the church stands the former Jesuit College (1699), now occupied by the Municipal Library.

Masaryk Square, Jihlava

At the north-west corner of the square, housed in two handsome Renaissance houses (16th century), is the Regional Museum. In two other Renaissance buildings at 10 Komensky Street is the Art Gallery of the Bohemo-Moravian Highlands.

Museums

At the north-east corner of Masaryk Square is Křížová Ulice (Cross Street), the main street in the northern part of the old town. In this street, on the right, stands the former Dominican church of Church of the Holy Cross (Kostel Povýšení Sv. Kříže; 14th c.), now a Protestant church.

Dominican Church

Mint Street (U Mincovny), which leaves Masaryk Square on the south side of the Town Hall, is believed to have been the site of the town mint (see History).

Mint Street

The next street to the south is Farní Ulice, which leads east to the twin-towered Gothic parish church of St James (Kostel Sv. Jakuba; 13th–14th c.), with a fine main doorway of 1260. The church has Baroque altars, some notable pieces of Gothic sculpture and a Renaissance font of 1599. A Baroque chapel built on to the church in the 18th century has a magnificent grille.

Parish church

From the west side of Masaryk Square Mother of God Street (Ulice Matky Boží) leads to the Minorite Church (Minoritský Kostel). Originally built in the 13th century, it has a Baroque façade (18th c.), a Late Gothic choir (1499–1508) and old wall paintings.
The adjoining Minorite friary has a fine cloister.

Minorite Church

Just to the west of the Minorite church can be seen the Mother of God Gate (Brána Matky Boží; 14th and 16th c.), the only one of the town's five gates to survive and now one of the landmarks of Jihlava.

Mother of God Gate

Between the Mother of God Gate and Znojemská Ulice (Znojm Street), which runs south from the main square, as well as farther to the east and north, there are remains of the medieval town walls (14th–15th c.) in the gardens which have taken their place.

Town walls

Surroundings of Jihlava

Brtnice

12km/7½ miles south-east of Jihlava lies Brtnice, with a castle, originally Gothic, which was converted into a Renaissance palace towards the end of the 16th century. Other notable features of the town are the Renaissance Town Hall, Renaissance and Baroque burghers' houses and two Baroque bridges decorated with figures.
Brtnice was the birthplace of the architect Josef Hoffmann (1870–1956), a leading representative of the Viennese Art Nouveau movement known as the Sezession.

Polná

14km/8½ miles north-east of Jihlava is the little town of Polná (alt. 490m/1610ft; pop. 4000), with an Early Gothic castle which was rebuilt as a Renaissance palace in the 16th century. It now houses a branch of the Museum of the Bohemo-Moravian Highlands. Renaissance and Baroque burghers' houses in the market square; remains of the old Jewish ghetto.

Rokštejn Castle

10km/6 miles south-east of Jihlava are the ruins of the 13th century Gothic castle of Rokštejn.

Stonařov

13km/8 miles south of Jihlava is Stonařov, which has a Gothic church (1598, with later alterations) with a Renaissance tower. Adjoining the church is a Romanesque charnel-house (13th c.).

Třešt'

Třešt', 14km/8½ miles south-west of Jihlava has a Renaissance castle (second half of 16th c.) remodelled in Baroque style in 1660, two Gothic churches and a synagogue.

Třešť' was the birthplace of the economist Joseph Alois Schumpeter (1883–1950).

Jindřichův Hradec D/E 3

Region: Southern Bohemia
District: Jindřichův Hradec
Altitude: 478m/1568ft
Population: 22,000

Situation and characteristics

The Southern Bohemian town of Jindřichův Hradec lies 15km/9 miles north of the Czech–Austrian frontier on the river Nežárka and Lake Vajgar, a small lake 1km/¾ mile long. Its main industries are woodworking, textiles and foodstuffs; a local speciality is the weaving of tapestries.

History

The town grew up round the castle (*hradec*) founded by Jindřich z Vitkovicû about 1200.

Sights

Market square

In the centre of the old town, which slopes gently upwards from Lake Vajgar, is the triangular market square, with a number of burghers' houses of the Renaissance, Baroque and neo-classical periods. In the square is a tall Trinity Column with numerous figures (by M. Strhovský, 1764).

Town Hall

On the north side of the square stands the Town Hall (Radnice; originally Gothic, rebuilt 1801–07).

Church of St John the Baptist

To the north is the town's principal church (Gothic, 14th–15th c.), dedicated to St John the Baptist (Kostel Sv. Jana Křtitele), which has fine 14th–15th century wall paintings.

Minorite Friary

Adjoining the church can be seen the former Minorite friary (13th and 15th c.), now a hospital. In the cloister are 14th century frescoes.

Jesuit College
Museum

The former Jesuit College (Stará Jesuitská Kolej; 16th–17th c.), with the 17th century church of St Mary Magdalene and a pillared courtyard con-

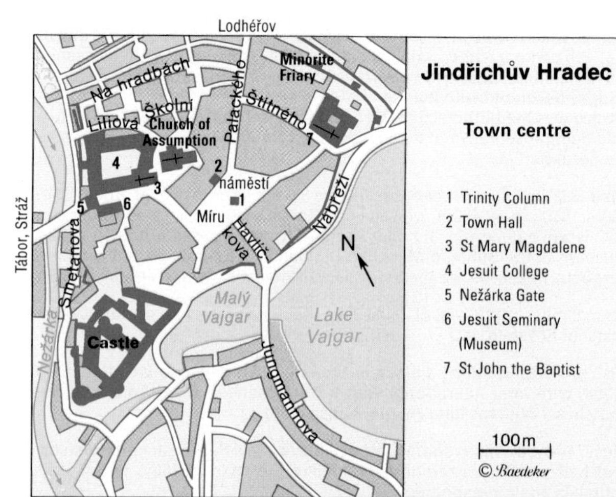

taining a fountain, which now houses the Municipal Museum. This displays in its 25 rooms a large collection of material on local history and traditions, including Christmas cribs (Nativity groups).
Next the Museum is the Nežárka Gate.

***Castle** (in course of restoration)

On the west side of the old town, on the edge of a fish-pond, towers the mighty Castle (Zámek), which last belonged to the Counts Czernin. The oldest part of the structure, built between the 13th and the 15th century after the demolition of the original castle, was partly rebuilt in the 16th century by Italian architects and enlarged by the addition of a large Renaissance wing (burned down 1773). Particularly notable are the three courtyards, the largest of which has a beautiful wrought-iron fountain and three-storey Renaissance arcades.
In the Gothic part of the castle are a chapel with paintings of the legend of St George (*c.* 1340) and valuable archives (including a large collection of autograph manuscripts). In the Renaissance wing, which is decorated with fine wall paintings, are a picture gallery (pictures by the Baroque painters Karel Škréta and Petr Brandl; the "Madonna of Hradec", painted on wood) and a museum (furniture, china, etc.).
There is an attractive 16th century garden pavilion with rich carved decoration.

Surroundings of Jindřichův Hradec

Excursions

A number of places in the surrounding area offer facilities for bathing and water sports: 8km/5 miles east the Ratmirovský Rybník (fish-pond); 14km/8½ miles east the Komorník pond at Strmilov (alt. 545m/1788ft); 16km/10 miles south-east the Osika pond, near Albeř (alt. 629m/2064ft) and Klášter (alt. 655m/2149ft), with a fine Baroque church; 6km/4 miles south-west the Dřevo pond at Horní Pěna (alt. 473m/1552ft).

Jindřichův Hradec Castle (to left, garden pavilion)

Červená Lhota Castle

Devil's Stone
*View

12km/7½ miles north of Jindřichův Hradec, rearing above the village of Lodhéřov, is the Devil's Stone (Čertův Kámen; 659m/2162ft), with magnificent views of the surrounding pond district.

***Červená Lhota Castle**

7km/4½ miles north-west of Lodhéřov lies Deštná, from which it is 4km/2½ miles south-west to the little moated castle of Červená Lhota, picturesquely situated in a pond surrounded by forest and approached by an old stone bridge. The original Gothic castle on the site was replaced in the mid 16th century by a Renaissance castle which was remodelled in Baroque style between 1658 and 1678; the interior was restored in the 19th century and again a few years ago. The castle contains a fine collection of furniture. It was occupied for a time by the 18th century musician and composer Karl Ditters von Dittersdorf.

The castle is surrounded by a beautiful park.

Stráž nad Nežárkou

10km/6 miles south-west of Jindřichův Hradec is Stráž nad Nežárkou (alt. 450m/1475ft; pop. 1700), with a Baroque castle which was originally Gothic. The castle (not open to the public) was from 1915 to 1930 the home of the Czech singer Ema Destinnová (1878–1930).

Jizera Hills (Jizerské Hory) E 2

Region: Northern Bohemia
Districts: Liberec and Jablonec nad Nisou
Altitude: 700–1124m/2300–3688ft

Situation and
*topography

The Jizerské Hory are a range of hills in northern Bohemia, much visited by tourists and holidaymakers, with great areas of plateau at altitudes of between 700 and 900m (2300 and 2950ft), dense forests of spruce (dam-

aged by pollution) and expanses of peat-bog (nature trails). The range extends for more than 40km/25 miles, with a breadth of about half that. Above it rise the peaks of Mt Jizera (1122m/3681ft; rocks, remnants of natural forest) and Mt Smrk (1124m/3688ft). There are numerous outlook towers and mountain inns. On the north the hills fall steeply down to the plain, with height differences of as much as 500m/1650ft and numerous waterfalls. In the southern part of the range twelve dams have been built (at Josefův Důl, Souš, Bedřichov, etc.), mainly serving for the storage and supply of drinking water.
The Jizera Hills and surrounding area have an old-established tradition of glass manufacture (Jablonec nad Nisou, Desná, Železný Brod, Nový Bor, etc.). The textile industry also developed in the 19th century, e.g. at Liberec (see entry), Jablonec nad Nisou and Tanvald.

Features of Interest in the Jizera Hills

Bedřichov

The hill village of Bedřichov (alt. 680m/2230ft) to the north of Liberec is a popular summer resort but also enjoys a considerable reputation as a winter sports centre (several ski-lifts; langlauf trails).

Mt Bukovec

Mt Bukovec (1005m/3297ft), which rises above the village of Jizerka on the eastern edge of the Jizerské Hory, is one of the highest basalt cones in Central Europe. With its rare flora it is known as the "garden of the Jizera Hills".

Černá Studnice

Černá Studnice (869m/2851ft) is the highest peak in the southern range of hills (mountain hut, outlook tower).

Jizerka

Jizerka (alt. 860m/2820ft), situated on the little river Jizera from which it takes its name, is the highest town in the Jizera Hills. From the 15th century it was populated by Czech charcoal-burners; in the 16th century it attracted gold-miners and prospectors for precious stones; and in the 19th century it was a town of glass-makers and woodcutters. It is now mainly a holiday resort.

Kristiánov

Kristiánov (alt. 815m/2674ft), to the east of Bedřichov, was once a hill farm. There is an interesting Glass-Making Museum.

Nová Louka

To the north of Bedřichov is the Nová Louka peat-bog (alt. 770m/2525ft). In a large meadow can be seen a timber hunting lodge built in the mid 19th century by Count Clam-Gallas.

Smědava

4km/2½ miles south-west of Mt Jizera is the Smědava saddle (847m/2779ft), with an inn.

Tanvaldský Špičák

Tanvaldský Špičák (alt. 808m/2651ft; outlook tower), on the south-eastern edge of the Jizera Hills, is a favourite skiing centre.

Kadaň C 2

Region: Western Bohemia
District: Chomutov
Altitude: 300m/985ft
Population: 18,000

Situation and characteristics

The old-world little town of Kadaň, a royal foundation of about 1260, lies in the foreland area of the Ore Mountains (Krušné Hory) on the left bank of the river Ohře, between Karlovy Vary (Karlsbad) and Chomutov (see entries). It has a ceramics industry, and round the town are extensive deposits of lignite worked by opencast methods and a number of large thermal power stations.

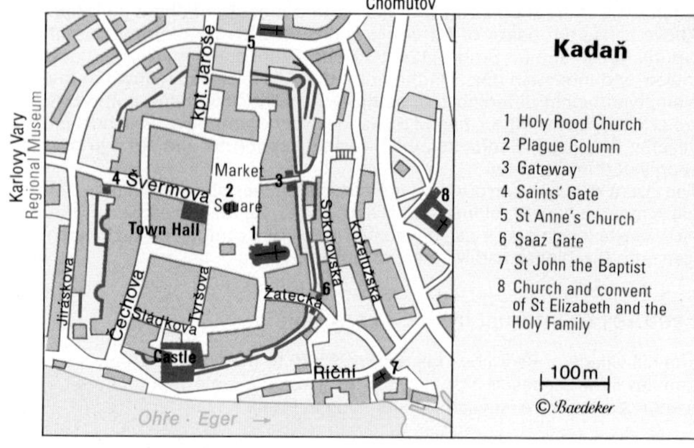

Sights

Market square The most striking feature of the large trapezoidal market square is the Town Hall (originally a Gothic building of the second half of the 14th century, rebuilt in 1811), with a massive tower which dominates the town. In the square is an 18th century Plague Column with numerous figures, and adjoining this is one of the old town gates, the Svatá or Mikulovická Brána (Sacred Gate or Mikulovice Gate). There is another town gate dating from 1458, the Žatecká Brána (Žatec Gate). The town preserves a number of Gothic, Renaissance and Baroque houses. On the east side of the market square is Hangman's Lane (Katovská Ulička), with a Gothic doorway.

Franciscan friary (Museum) In the western outskirts of the town a former Franciscan friary (now the District Museum, with a lapidarium) has a Late Gothic church (15th c.). The cloister has fine cellular vaulting, the oldest in Bohemia.

Near here is Mt Stražiště (401m/1316ft), from which there is a panoramic view of the Ohře valley.

Surroundings of Kadaň

Hasištejn Castle 8km/5 miles north of Kadaň are the ruins of Hasištejn, a Gothic castle which was restored in the late 19th century. There are good views from the tower.

Klášterec nad Ohří 8km/5 miles west of Kadaň is Klášterec nad Ohří (pop. 16,000; porcelain and cork industries), prettily situated on the Ohře. It takes its name from a 12th century monastery (*klášter*) which once stood here. Porcelain has been made here since 1794 in a manufactory originally established by the Count of Thun. The Castle (originally 17th c., restored in 19th c.) now contains a Porcelain Museum; the park has rare species of trees. There are alkaline carbonated mineral springs.

Karlovy Vary / Karlsbad B 2

Region: Western Bohemia. District: Karlovy Vary
Altitude: 374m/1227ft. Population: 58,000

*Situation and **characteristics Karlovy Vary (more familiar in the past in its German form, Karlsbad), the leading Czech spa, straggles along the beautiful narrow valley of the Teplá at its junction with the Ohře. (The main spa area is closed to traffic.)

Market square, Kadaň (p. 174)

History

Karlovy Vary was probably founded in 1348 by the Emperor Charles IV, who is said to have discovered the hot springs while hunting in the area; in fact, however, there is evidence that the springs were already known. Until the early 16th century the water was used only for bathing; thereafter it was also used for drinking. The first bath-house of some size was built in 1762. Karlsbad became, particularly during the 19th century, a fashionable resort frequented by an international clientele, including many famous figures.

The *springs

Karlovy Vary owes its international fame to its mineral springs. Altogether there are about 60 springs, but only twelve of them (with a daily flow of 6 million litres/1.3 million gallons of alkaline water containing Glauber salt) are used. The springs differ only in temperature (ranging from 42°C/108°F to 73°C/163°F) and in their greater or lesser content (depending on temperature) of free carbonic acid. The powerful healing effect of the water is the result of the high concentration (7 grams per litre/491 grains per gallon) of 32–35 different minerals in solution. The water is drunk in association with diet and exercise regimes and is used for bathing. It is particularly effective in the treatment of disorders of the liver and gall bladder and diseases of the stomach and intestines.

The springs emerge from the ancient granite rocks of the Teplá valley; the Sprudel spring comes from a layer of sinter, into which several bore-holes (which must be re-bored every year because of incrustations deposited by the water) reach down to a depth of only a few metres.

Events

For the entertainment of its visitors Karlovy Vary has a theatre and a well-known orchestra which plays in an annual musical festival mainly devoted to Dvořák, the Karlovy Vary Autumn. There is an international festival in alternate years and an annual festival of tourist films (Tourfilm).

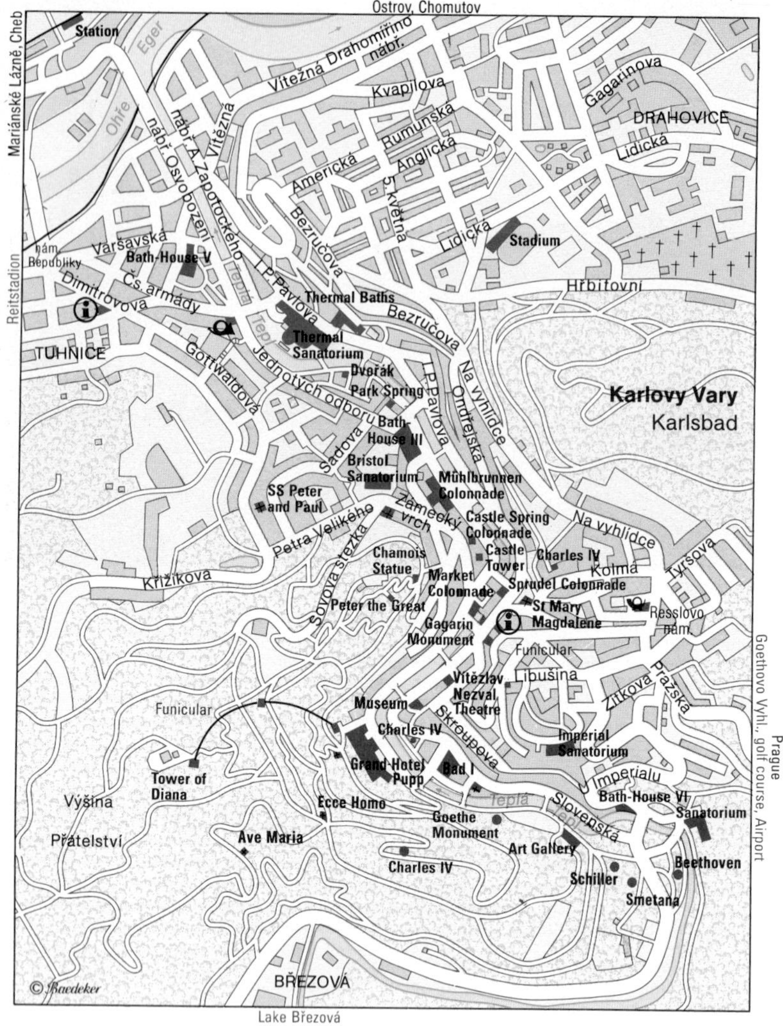

Sights

Mühlbrunnen Colonnade

Spa life centres on the Mühlbrunnen Colonnade (Mlýnská Kolonáda) on the left bank of the Teplá. This is a long hall lined by Corinthian columns (by Josef Zítek, 1872–81) containing the Rose Spring (Rusalčin Pramen), the Prince Wenceslas Spring (Pramen Knízete Václava), the Libussa Spring (Libusin Pramen) and the Mill Spring (Mühlbrunn, Mlynsky Pramen). The temperature of these springs ranges between 42°C/108°F and 60°C/140°F.

Karlovy Vary (Karlsbad)

After the last war a large open space was created by bridging over the Teplá.

Bath-House III

At the north end of the colonnade, beyond the Rock Spring (Skalní Pramen), is Bath-House III, the old Kurhaus of 1867.

Market

From the Mühlbrunnen Colonnade the Mlýnské Nabřeží (Mill Embankment) leads south to the Market (Tržiště), in which is the Market Colonnade (Tržní Kolonáda, 1883, a wooden structure with carved decoration), with the Castle Tower (Zámecká Věž, 1608) rearing above it. In this colonnade are the Charles IV Spring (Pramen Karla IV) and the Market Spring (Tržní Pramen). At the south end of the Market can be seen a Baroque Trinity Column (1776). Higher up are the two Castle Springs: in a grotto on the lower terrace the Lower Castle Spring (Dolní Zámecký Pramen, 62.3°C/144.1°F), with an Art Nouveau figure of the "Protector of the Springs" and a statue of the goddess Hygieia; in a rotunda (1913) on the upper terrace the Upper Castle Spring (Horní Zámecký Pramen, 49.8°C/121.6°F; lift).

Castle Square

To the north-west is Zámecké Náměstí (Castle Square).

Municipal Museum

Farther north-west, on Zámecký Vrch (Castle Hill), is the Municipal Museum (Městské Muzeum), with interesting material on the history of the town. Beyond it are the Museum Gardens (Muzejný Sady).

Sprudel Colonnade
*Sprudel

From the lower end of the Market a bridge leads over the Teplá to the Sprudel Colonnade (Vřídelní Kolonáda), with the Sprudel (Vřídlo), the oldest and hottest (73°C/163°F) of the springs of Karlovy Vary. This is a geyser-type spring which propels a stream of water as thick as a man's arm to a height of up to 12m/40ft. There are between 40 and 60 bursts of varying strength every minute, with a total daily flow of 3 million litres/660,000 gallons. The water is also used to produce natural Karlsbad Sprudel salt.

Church of St Mary Magdalene

In Náměstí Svobody (Freedom Square), above the Colonnade to the east, stands the Church of St Mary Magdalene (Kostel Sv. Maří Magdaleny), a twin-towered domed church (by Kilian Ignaz Dientzenhofer, 1733–36) with a picturesque interior.

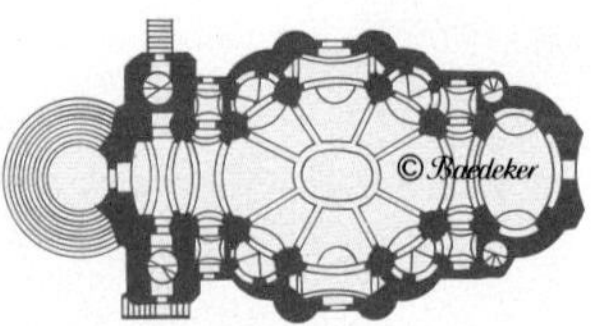

Municipal Park

Higher up (reached by way of Školní Ulice and a street to the left) is the Municipal Park, with a statue of the Emperor Charles IV (by Josef Max, 1858).

Stará Louka

To the south of the Market, extending along the Teplá, is the Stará Louka (Old Meadow), a tree-lined promenade with many shops which is particularly lively in the evenings.

At the south end of the Stará Louka is Goethe Square, with the Grand Hotel Pupp. From here a funicular ascends up Výšina Přatelství (Friendship Hill). From the hotel Puškinova Stezka (Pushkin Way) runs south-east, passing the old Imperial Baths, Bath-House I (Lázně I) and the Protestant church (both on the right bank of the Teplá), and comes in some 500m/550yd to the Art Gallery (Galerie Umění), with works by modern Czech and Slovak painters and sculptors. Beyond this is the Posthof (1791), an old centre of musical life in Karlovy Vary.

Bath-House VI

Opposite the Art Galltery, on the right bank of the Teplá, is the new Bath-House VI (Lázně VI).

Park

To the east of the Art Gallery, in a loop of the river, lies a beautiful park, with monuments commemorating famous visitors to Karlovy Vary, including Beethoven and Smetana.

Grand Hotel

Richmond Sanatorium

To the north-east, on the right bank of the Teplá, is the Richmond Sanatorium (formerly a hotel), an annexe of the Imperial Sanatorium (see below).

Nová Louka

Running parallel with the Stará Louka (see above), on the right bank of the Teplá, is the Nová Louka (New Meadow), at the east end of which we come to the semicircular Theatre Square, laid out in gardens. On the south side of the square stands the Municipal Theatre (Divadlo Vitězslava Nezvala; by Fellner and Helmer, 1886).

Imperial Hill

From the north-east side of the square a funicular (Lanovka) ascends Imperial Hill (Vyšina Imperiál) in a tunnel. On top of the hill, dominating the town, rises the massive bulk of the Imperial Sanatorium. Another funicular descends the south side of the hill to Slovenská Třída (Slovak Street), opposite the Art Gallery.

Park Spring

North-west of the Mühlbrunnen Colonnade and Bath-House III, housed in a colonnade, can be found the Park Spring (Sadový Pramen).

Church of SS Peter and Paul

Near here is Sadová Třída (Park Street), which leads up south-west to the Russian church of SS Peter and Paul (by Wiedemann, 1897). The church, built at a time when the spa was much frequented by the Russian nobility, was modelled on a church at Ostankino (Moscow). In the lower part of the church, behind a grille, can be seen a monument to Peter the Great. The entrance to the church is 5 minutes' walk higher up, in Třída Krále Jiřího (King George Street).

Dvořák Park

North-west of the Park Spring, between Zahradní Třída and the river, is the beautiful Dvořák Park (Dvořákovy Sady). Farther to the north-west, beyond the Head Post Office (Pošta 1), lies Smetana Park (Smetanovy Sady), with Bath-House V (Lázně V). Between the two parks, on the right bank of the Teplá, are the 16-storey Thermal Hotel (1976; thermal baths) and the Festival Cinema.

Sprudel

Astoria Hotel, in Art Nouveau style

1km/¾ mile north-west of Dvořák Park, beyond the junction of the Teplá with the Ohře, in the industrial district of Rybáře, is the main railway station (lines to Prague and Cheb).

Rybáře

A variety of industries have been established in the Rybáře district to the north of the Ohře – glass manufacture (Moser), porcelain (since the 18th century) and other ceramic products (based on the deposits of kaolin in the surrounding area), the manufacture of gloves and wafers, Sprudel salt and the herb liqueur becherovka (since 1805).

Museums

In the Dvory district on the west side of the town can be found the Glass-making Museum (Moser glass), and in the southern district of Březová the Porcelain Museum.

Surroundings of Karlovy Vary

***Petrova Výšina**

Above the Market, to the west, rises the Petrova Výšina (Peter's Hill) or Výšina Petra Velikého (Peter the Great's Hill), which commemorates a visit by Peter the Great to Karlsbad. The hill can be climbed either from the north end of the Stará Louka on a steep path by way of the Jelení Skok (Stag's Leap) or by an easier path from the south end (20 or 30 minutes). Funicular: see below. On the rocky summit of the hill is the Jelení Skok restaurant, with extensive views to the north, extending as far as the Ore Mountains. A little way south of the restaurant is the highest point on the hill, from which there is a fine view of the spa district of the town. By the little viewing terrace can be seen a bust of Peter the Great. Below the terrace is a pavilion which also offers a magnificent view.

Stag's Leap

5 minutes' walk to the east, below the Stag's Leap, is a crag crowned by the figure of a chamois. Legend has it that while the Emperor Charles IV was hunting in this area a stag leapt from this crag into the hot springs, leading to their discovery by the Emperor. From the crag there is a more restricted but picturesque view of the Imperial Sanatorium.

From Peace Square a funicular (lower station Stará Louka, 381m/1250ft) ascends in 6 minutes via the intermediate Jelení Skok station (8 minutes' walk to Stag's Leap) to the upper station (555m/1821ft) on Friendship Hill (Výšina Přatelství, 585m/1919ft), with an outlook tower and the Diana restaurant.

25 minutes' walk south-east (or a half-hour climb from Peace Square) we come to Charles IV Hill (Vyhlídka Karla IV, 507m/1663ft), which also has an outlook tower.

***Goethe Viewpoint**

From Hřbitovní Třída (Cemetery Street), on the right bank of the Teplá, the Gogol Path (Gogolova Pěšina) climbs up by way of the Hill of the Three Crosses (U Tři Křížů, 551m/1808ft), with three large crosses and a viewing platform, to the Goethe Viewpoint (Goethova Rozhledna, 636m/2087ft; about 1¼ hours), with a 30m/100ft high outlook tower (180 steps) from which there are superb panoramic views. It is also possible to reach this point by car (4km/2½ miles), leaving on the Prague road (No. 6) by way of Hůrky and then turning left into a narrow but perfectly negotiable road up the hill.

Andělská Hora

6km/4 miles south-east of Karlovy Vary on the Andělská Hora (Angel Hill, 665m/2182ft) can be seen a ruined castle which was originally Gothic, later became a Hussite stronghold and was reduced to ruin in 1718.

***Svatošské Skály**

8km/5 miles south-west of Karlovy Vary, above the Ohře valley, are the Svatošské Skály (432m/1417ft), a group of bizarrely shaped granite rocks which are supposed to represent a petrified wedding procession.

Kyselka

10km/6 miles north-east of Karlovy Vary lies the spa of Kyselka (alt. 358m/1175ft), with mineral springs (Mattoni's table water) and spa establishments dating from the second half of the 19th century.

Karlštejn

D 3

Region: Central Bohemia
District: Beroun
Altitude: 319m/1047ft

Situation and characteristics

Karlštejn Castle (formerly called Karkův Týn), the most famous castle in Bohemia and a scheduled National Monument, rears above the little vine-growing village of Karlštejn (alt. 245m/805ft; pop. 900), 18km/17 miles south-west of Prague.

Approach

From the car park at the entrance to the village an uphill walk of some 2km/1¼ miles brings us to the castle, which stands to the north of the village on a rocky hill overlooking a side valley of the Berounka.

History

The castle was built in a relatively short period (1348–57) in the reign of Charles IV as a repository for the crown jewels of the Holy Roman Empire, the Bohemian royal insignia and numerous sacred relics. It was probably designed by a French architect, Matthias of Arras. The castle was partly rebuilt in the 15th and 16th centuries and was restored between 1887 and 1899, with many alterations, by Friedrich Schmidt and Josef Mocker.

**Karlštejn Castle

The castle

The castle is entered through two gateways 100 metres apart. The second gateway leads into the Burgrave's Court (Purkrabský Dvůr), which is now fitted out as an open-air theatre. Here from May to August or September Jaroslav Vrchlický's farce "Noc na Karlštejně" ("A Night in Karlštejn") is performed (Sat. and Sun. 7–11pm). Conducted tours of the castle also start here.

On the south side of the court stands the four-storey Burgrave's House (Purkrabství), the lower parts of which date from the 15th century. At the western tip of the castle are domestic offices and the Well Tower, with a 90m/300ft deep well and a large wheel for drawing water.

From the Burgrave's Court a large gateway leads into the narrow Main Court (Hradní Nádvoří).

Imperial Palace

To the right is the Imperial Palace (Císařský Palác); a staircase (far right) leads up to the first floor. Documents, pictures and models illustrating the history of the castle are displayed in two rooms of the palace. At the east end is St Nicholas's Chapel (not open to the public).
Of the imperial apartments on the second floor only the Emperor's study, with fine panelling, is preserved. The original half-timbered top storey, in which were the women's apartments, was replaced during the 19th century restoration by a wooden wall-walk.

St Mary's Tower and Church

To the north of the palace is St Mary's Tower (Mariánská Věž). On the second floor (reached by a staircase within the walls) can be found St Mary's Church, with a painted beamed ceiling and partly preserved 14th century wall paintings (themes from the Apocalypse, representations of Charles IV, etc.). At the south-west corner of St Mary's Tower is the vaulted St Catherine's Chapel. It was originally decorated with wall paintings, but Charles IV had these replaced by large plaques of semi-precious stones let into the walls.

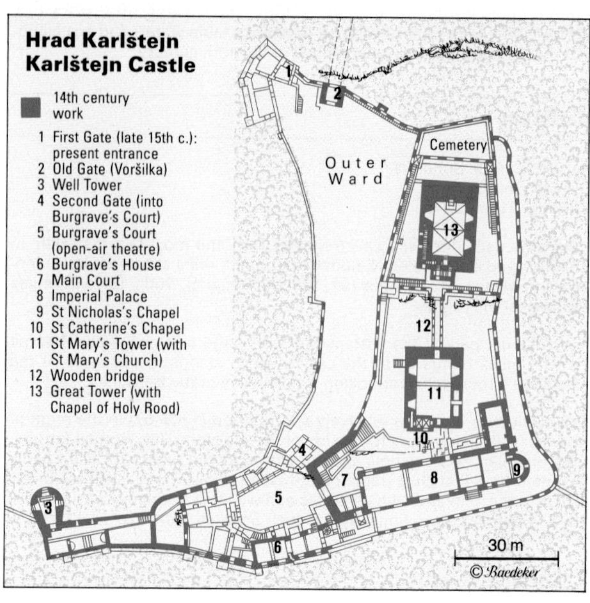

Great Tower

On the highest part of the site is the mighty Great Tower (Velká Věž), 37m/121ft high, which is linked with St Mary's Tower by a wooden bridge. On the second floor is the Chapel of the Holy Rood (Kaple Sv. Kříže), which was consecrated about 1360. It is divided into two by a gilded iron screen which closes the sanctuary to the public. The vaulting, which comes down low on the walls, is completely gilded and studded with glass stars. On the walls, above the candle stands (for 1330 candles), are more than 2200 precious stones set in gilded plaster and 127 painted panels by Master Theodoric (1348–67), behind which there were originally relics. Behind the altar is a recess in which the Imperial crown jewels (now in the Hofburg in Vienna) and the Bohemian royal insignia (now in St Vitus's Cathedral in Prague) were formerly kept.

Surroundings of Karlštejn

Tetín

7km/4½ miles west of Karlštejn is Tetín, one of the oldest towns in Bohemia, the site of a castle in the 9th–10th century. It has two churches which were originally Romanesque.

Beroun

10km/6 miles north-west of Karlštejn, at the junction of the Litavka with the Berounka, lies Beroun (alt. 225m/740ft; pop. 18,000), chief town of its district, which is steadily joining up with the industrial town of Králův Dvůr (ironworks, cement factories). It was founded in the 13th century by settlers from Switzerland or Italy, and its name is alternatively derived from Berne or from Verona. The old town preserves two town gates (Plzeňská Brána, the Plzeň Gate, and the Pražská Brána, the Prague Gate), some remains of early 14th century walls, a number of Renaissance and Baroque houses and two churches, originally Gothic, which were remodelled in Baroque style in the 18th century.

Karlštejn Castle

*Koněprusy Caves

6km/4 miles south of Beroun are the stalactitic caves of Koněprusy, the largest in Bohemia, which were discovered only in 1950. Excavations in the caves brought to light human and animal bones dating from the Palaeolithic. Also of great interest is the reconstruction of a 15th century coiner's (counterfeiter's) workshop.

Točník and Žebrák Castles

22km/14 miles south-west of Beroun are the prominently situated ruins of Točník Castle, which has preserved a Gothic palace of the 15th century (restored), and the remains of Žebrák Castle (13th c.), once the summer residence of King Wenceslas (Václav) IV.

Hořovice

Hořovice (alt. 375m/1230ft; pop. 7000; mechanical engineering, manufacture of instruments), 24km/15 miles south-west of Beroun, has an 18th century Baroque castle which belonged to the Princes of Hanau (collection of porcelain; beautiful gardens).

Kladno D 2

Region: Central Bohemia
District: Kladno
Altitude: 380m/1245ft
Population: 73,000

Situation and characteristics

Kladno, 25km/15 miles north-west of Prague, prospered around the middle of the 19th century after the discovery of a rich coalfield in the area. The development of mining and ironworking can be studied in the museum now housed in the Baroque castle, which since 1985 has also included an art gallery (periodic exhibitions).

Surroundings of Kladno

Smečno

7km/4½ miles north-west of Kladno is Smečno (alt. 372m/1221ft; pop. 1800), with a castle, originally Gothic, which was rebuilt in Renaissance style around 1586.

Okoř

10km/6 miles east of Kladno are the ruins of the Gothic castle of Okoř (alt. 275m/900ft).

Budeč

14km/8½ miles north-east of Kladno is Budeč, the site of a 9th century Slav stronghold, with a Romanesque rotunda of the 10th century.

Lidice

6km/4 miles east of Kladno lies Lidice (alt. 343m/1125ft; pop. 500), a mining village which on June 10th 1942 became a symbol of the fight against fascism. On that day the village was razed to the ground by the SS in reprisal for the assassination of the Nazi "Protector" of Bohemia and Moravia, Reinhard Heydrich. All the 173 male inhabitants over the age of 15 were shot (the place of execution is now marked by a simple wooden cross), and the 196 women and 105 children were separated from one another and carried off to concentration camps. All the buildings were set on fire and the whole village destroyed. Immediately after the end of the Second World War a beginning was made with the building of a new Lidice, a modern village which can now be seen a short distance away from the old one.

National Memorial

In the National Memorial Museum is a room dedicated to the victims of National Socialism, and in the Garden of Friendship and Peace are roses from all over the world. A sculpture by B. Stefan, "Gloria", marks the position of the mass grave. On the site of the priest's house can be seen a monument by K. Lidický.

Wooden cross marking the site of the Lidice massacre

Klatovy

C 3

Region: Western Bohemia
District: Klatovy
Altitude: 405m/1330ft
Population: 23,000

Situation and characteristics

Klatovy, chief town of its district, lies in a beautiful setting under the north side of the Bohemian Forest, just to the east of the river Úhlava. Founded in the 13th century, it is now an important centre of light industry and floriculture (particularly carnations).

Sights

Decanal Church

The town's principal monument is the Gothic Decanal Church (13th–16th c.), with its free-standing White Tower (1581; rebuilt 1758).

Jesuit Church

In the market square stands the twin-towered Jesuit Church (17th c.; rebuilt in 1717 by Kilian Ignaz Dientzenhofer), with a beautiful doorway. In the crypt are mummified bodies. Under the church are catacombs (entrance on north side of church) in which members of the Jesuit order were buried.

Old Town Hall
*Black Tower

Adjoining the church is the Old Town Hall (16th c.), with the Black Tower (76m/249ft; viewing platform).

Museum
Pharmacy

In the market square are an interesting Museum and a Baroque pharmacy "At the Sign of the White Unicorn", with its original fittings (first half of 18th c.). In the square and the adjoining streets can be seen a number of Gothic, Renaissance and Baroque houses.

Klatovy

Town walls

Round the historic centre are some remains of the old town walls.

Surroundings of Klatovy

Švihov

9km/5½ miles north of Klatovy is Švihov (alt. 374m/1227ft; pop. 1500), a friendly little place on the river Úhlava. In meadowland bordering the river is an old moated castle (Late Gothic, 1480–1510) which in the 18th century was used as a grain store (restored in the 1950s). Two residential wings enclose a courtyard and are protected by the park walls. The chapel has a fine wall painting of 1515.

Chudenice

Chudenice (alt. 488m/1601ft) 12km/7½ miles north-west of Klatovy has a Gothic church (wall paintings), the Empire-style castle of Lázeň, an English park and an arboretum (American Garden; established 1842). On a nearby hill (584m/1916ft) is the Bolfánek outlook tower.

Bezdékov

5km/3 miles west of Klatovy, Bezdékov (alt. 412m/1352ft), has a neo-Romanesque castle (after 1855) set in a park. On Mt Římek is a Baroque chapel. In the churchyard is a monument to the Romantic writer Christian Spiess (1755–99).

Janovice nad Úhlavou

6km/4 miles south-west of Klatovy is Janovice nad Úhlavou (alt. 410m/1435ft), which has an Early Gothic church (late 13th c.) which was remodelled in Baroque style in 1764; it preserves some Gothic paintings (after 1320).

Klenová

8km/5 miles south-west of Klatovy is Klenová (alt. 485m/1590ft), with the ruins of a Gothic castle of the 13th century. In the outer ward is a Renaissance mansion with an art gallery (19th and 20th century Bohemian painting and sculpture).

***Velhartice Castle**

17km/10½ miles south-east of Klatovy can be found Velhartice Castle, an imposing Gothic stronghold of the 13th–14th century. A particularly notable feature is the four-arched 14th century bridge borne on stone piers which links two towers. The tract of buildings along the castle wall dates from the 17th century (in course of restoration).

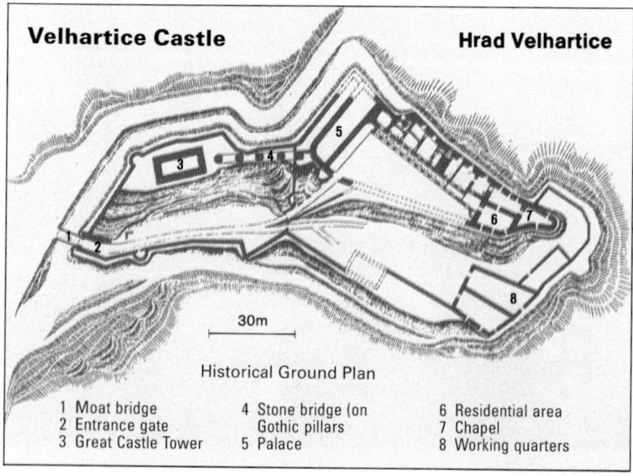

Kolín

E 2

Region: Central Bohemia
District: Kolín
Altitude: 225m/740ft
Population: 31,000

Situation and characteristics

The old Central Bohemian district town of Kolín lies on both banks of the Labe (Elbe), on the southern edge of the fertile river basin. It is an important railway junction and industrial town (foodstuffs, chemicals, mechanical engineering, graphic trades).

Sights

Old town
*St Bartholomew's Church

The old town (founded 1257) on the right bank of the Labe is dominated by St Bartholomew's Church (Chrám Svatého Bartoloměje), a hall-church in Transitional style (second half of 13th century) with two west towers and a choir (by Peter Parler, 1360–78) in the richest Gothic style. Beside the church rises a free-standing bell-tower (1504).

Old Town Hall

On the north side of the main square are the two adjoining buildings of the Old Town Hall (sgraffito decoration).

Zálabí

In the Zálabí district are the Gothic tower known as the Práchovna, St Vitus's Church (14th c., rebuilt in 18th c.) and the old Jewish Cemetery (15th c.).
A brass band festival, Kmochův Kolín ("Kmoch's Kolín", after the 19th century Kolín composer and kapellmeister of that name) is held in Zálabí annually in June.

Surroundings of Kolín

Křečhoř

6km/4 miles west of Kolín, just off the E 15 to Prague, can be found the village of Křečhoř. Near here on June 18th 1757 was fought the battle of Kolín, in which Austrian forces led by Field-Marshal von Daun defeated Frederick the Great's Prussian army. From the hill called Friedrichsberg (alt. 278m/912ft) Frederick watched the battle, which is commemorated by a column erected in 1842.

Kouřim

16km/10 miles west of Kolín is the old-world little town of Kouřim (alt. 268m/879ft; pop. 2000), ringed by well-preserved old town walls, with the Prague Gate (13th–15th c.). It has an Early Gothic church with a 13th century crypt.
South-east of the town are the extensive excavations of an old Slav settlement (Stará Kouřim).

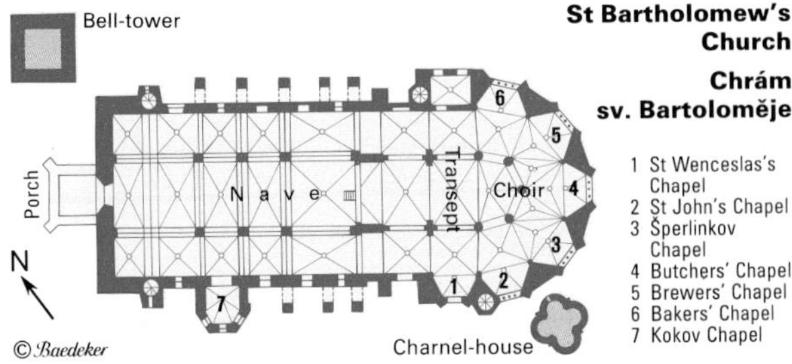

St Bartholomew's Church

Chrám sv. Bartoloměje

1 St Wenceslas's Chapel
2 St John's Chapel
3 Šperlinkov Chapel
4 Butchers' Chapel
5 Brewers' Chapel
6 Bakers' Chapel
7 Kokov Chapel

Old Town Hall, Kolín

On the Ždánický Potok, a small stream, is an open-air museum of Central Bohemian village architecture.

Lipany

20km/12½ miles west of Kolín, on a hill near the village of Lipany, stands a monument commemorating the battle in 1434, during the Hussite wars, in which the moderate Utraquists defeated the radical Taborites.

Český Brod

Český Brod (alt. 219m/719ft; pop. 7000), an industrial town with agricultural colleges 26km/16 miles west of Kolín, has a church, originally Gothic (14th c.), which was remodelled in Baroque style in the 18th century and a Renaissance bell-tower (end of 16th c.). There are remains of the town walls and one of the old town gates, the Kouřimská Bráma (Kouřim Gate).

Tismice

3km/2 miles south-west of Český Brod is the village of Tismice, with a small Romanesque basilica (13th c.; partly altered in Baroque style).

Konopiště D 3

Region: Central Bohemia
District: Benešov
Altitude: 375m/1230ft

Situation

Konopiště Castle (Zámek Konopiště) lies 40km/25 miles south-east of Prague near the district town of Benešov (see Surroundings).

*Konopiště Castle

Approach

From the car park below the castle it is a 10-minute walk to the entrance in the East Tower. The first courtyard is entered through a Baroque doorway by F. M. Kaňka with sculpture by M. B. Braun von Braun (1725).

Zámek Konopiště

Konopiště Castle

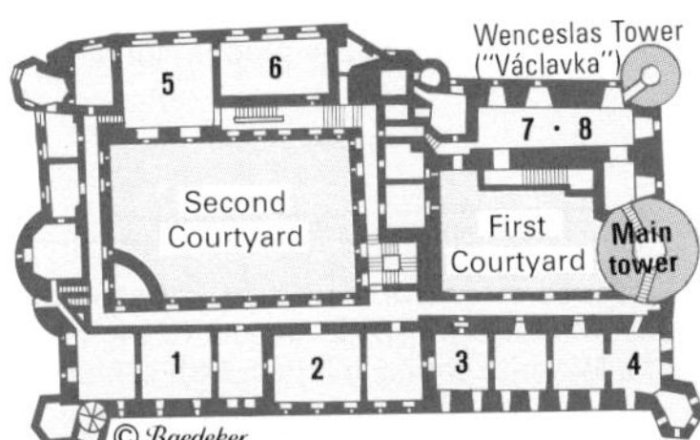

FIRST FLOOR
1 Pillared Salon
2 Lobkowitz Hall
(grand dining-room)
3 Tirpitz Salon
4 Vrtbh Salon

SECOND FLOOR
5 Smoking salon
6 Library
7 Chapel

THIRD FLOOR
8 Armoury

History

The original Gothic castle (13th–14th c.), a square structure on the French model with four towers, was rebuilt in Late Gothic style in the early 16th century and enlarged at the beginning of the 17th century by the building of a Renaissance palace; some Baroque features were added in the 18th century.
In 1887 Konopiště passed into the hands of Archduke Francis Ferdinand of Este, the heir to the Austrian throne whose assassination in Sarajevo in 1914 sparked off the First World War. He had the castle remodelled by Josef Mocker between 1889 and 1894 as a splendidly appointed palace.

**Collections

The sumptuous interior of the castle, including the works of art in the museum devoted to St George (paintings, figures and other representations of the saint), dates from the time of Archduke Francis Ferdinand. The large collection of arms and armour (most of it from the Este family's collections in Modena) is one of the finest in Europe, with almost 5000 exhibits (including 15th and 16th century tournament armour and valuable swords and guns). There are also great numbers of hunting trophies and

Konopiště Castle

Park

other mementoes (pictures, porcelain, tapestries, etc.) brought back by the Archduke from his world travels.

Near the castle is an English-style park with a rose-garden containing statuary brought from Italy.

Surroundings of Konopiště

Benešov

2km/1¼ miles east of the castle is the chief town of the district, Benešov (alt. 360m/1180ft; pop. 15,000; foodstuffs industries). North-east of the main square can be seen the ruins of a Minorite church (Gothic, 14th century).

Chvojen

2km/1¼ miles south-west of Konopiště is Chvojen (alt. 407m/1335ft), with a commandingly situated little church dating from the second half of the 13th century (altered in early 20th c.; wall paintings). In the churchyard are the graves of men who took part in the peasant rising of 1775.

Poříčí nad Sázavou

Poříčí nad Sázavou (alt. 284m/932ft; pop. 1000) 6km/4 miles north of Konopiště has two Romanesque churches. The older of the two is the cemetery church of St Peter (end of 11th c.), with a gallery and remains of Gothic paintings. The other, St Gall's, dates from the early 13th century but was remodelled in the 17th and 19th centuries (fine crypt).

Týnec nad Sázavou

8km/5 miles north-west of Konopiště we come to the little industrial town of Týnec nad Sázavou (alt. 281m/922ft; pop. 6300), which has a Romanesque rotunda (late 11th c.) with a prismatic tower and a museum of earthenware.

Jemniště

9km/5½ miles south-east of Konopiště is Jemniště (alt. 440m/1445ft), with a Baroque castle (1717–25). The castle contains a remarkable cartographic collection, the Theatrum Mundi (Dutch maps, town plans, vedute by 17th century Amsterdam cartographers, etc.).

Křivoklát

C 2

Region: Central Bohemia
District: Rakovník. Altitude: 250m/820ft

Situation and characteristics

Křivoklát Castle, one of the oldest surviving fortified castles in Bohemia, is commandingly situated on a rocky hill above the village of Křivoklát, on a tributary of the Berounka, 45km/28 miles west of Prague.

*Křivoklát Castle

History

The royal stronghold of Křivoklát first appears in the records at the beginning of the 12th century. Towards the end of the 14th century it was enlarged and fortified, and a century later was rebuilt in Gothic style. In the reign of Otakar II (1252–78) it became a summer residence of the Přemyslids, and Charles IV and Wenceslas (Václav) IV used it as a hunting lodge. Under the Habsburgs Křivoklát declined in importance, and later it was owned by various noble families. Around 1920 the castle was extensively restored. There are

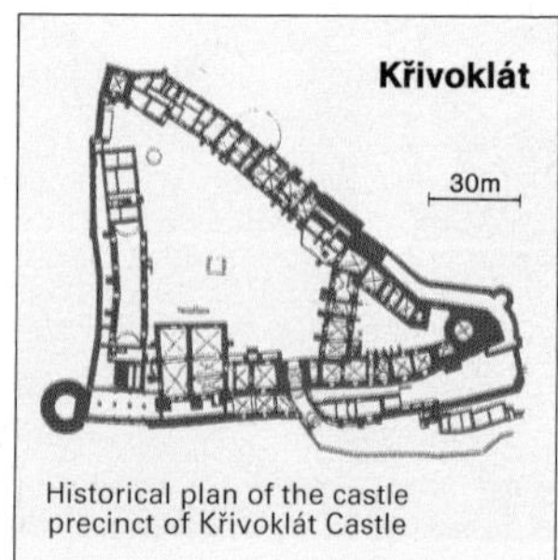

Historical plan of the castle precinct of Křivoklát Castle

Křivoklát Castle

some remains of the Late Romanesque royal stronghold and the single-storey palace of Otakar II's time.

Chapel

Particularly fine is the chapel, in High Gothic style, with a valuable winged altar and carved figures of apostles and saints.

Events

Concerts of classical music and dramatic performances take place in the castle every summer.

Surroundings of Křivoklát

Křivoklátsko nature reserve

The extensive forests (63,000 hectares/156,000 acres) between Beroun, Zbiroh and Rakovník are now included in UNESCO's MAB ("Man and the Biosphere") programme. Areas scheduled under the programme are protected eco-systems representative of the biosphere in which research projects (e.g. on measures for protecting the environment) are carried out.

Lány

12km/7½ miles north of Křivoklát is Lány (alt. 421m/1381ft), with a castle which is the summer residence of the President of the Republic and a deer park on the northern edge of the nature reserve. In the cemetery can be seen the grave of Tomáš Garrigue Masaryk, first President of the Czechoslovak Republic (see Famous People).

Rakovník

12km/7½ miles north-west of Křivoklát, surrounded by forests and hop-fields, is Rakovník (alt. 322m/1056ft; pop. 17,000), a town (now chief town of its district) founded in the 13th century, with an old-established brewery (founded 1460), engineering plants and factories producing ceramics and chemicals (soap, fats). Of the old town walls there survive two Late Gothic gate-towers (early 16th c.), the Pražská Brána (Prague Gate) and the Vysoká Brána (High Gate). The Baroque Town Hall dates from 1734–38, the Gothic St Bartholomew's Church from the 14th century.

Krakovec

16km/10 miles west of Křivoklát lies the village of Krakovec (alt. 395m/1295ft), with the ruins of a Gothic castle (in course of reconstruction) in which the Czech Reformer Jan Hus (see Famous People) lived in 1414. In that year he left here to appear before the Council of Constance.

Týřov

9km/5½ miles south-west of Křivoklát are the ruins of Týřov Castle (alt. 320m/1050ft), one of the oldest of the Czech castles in the Berounka valley. Fine views from the top.

Zbiroh

20km/12½ miles south-west of Křivoklát is Zbiroh (alt. 425m/1395ft; pop. 3500), a little industrial town and altitude resort on the edge of the Křivoklátsko nature reserve. Above the town is an old castle, much altered, in which the great Czech Art Nouveau painter Alfons Mucha (1860–1939) lived and worked (no admission).

There are interesting examples of traditional local architecture in some of the surrounding villages, for example at Jablečno (3km/2 miles north), Ostrovec (12km/7½ miles north-west; mill) and Lhota pod Račem (4km/2½ miles south-west).

Krkonoše E 2

Region: Eastern Bohemia
Districts: Semily and Trutnov
Altitude: 800–1600m/2625–5250ft

Situation and *topography

The Krkonoše (the "Giant Mountains", German Riesengebirge) is the finest range of hills in Bohemia and in the whole Sudeten mountain system. Ranging in height between 800 and 1600m (2625 and 5250ft), it extends over an area of some 40 by 20 kilometres (25 by 12½ miles), once covered by forest but now largely bare and treeless. Its two main ridges follow the Czech–Polish frontier; the one actually on the frontier is the higher and less broken-up of the two. The highest peak is Sněžka (1602m/5256ft).

The Krkonoše shows the clearest traces in the Bohemian lands of the activity of a Scandinavian glacier which once extended to this region. The mightiest ice masses were in the Labský Důl and the Obří Důl, through which now flow the two main rivers in the range, the Labe (Elbe) and the Úpa.

***National Park**

Now strictly protected as a National Park, the Krkonoše is the most visited mountain region in Bohemia. It is relatively well equipped with accommodation and catering facilities and has good access roads and several chair-lifts, so that less experienced walkers and climbers can reach the highest points and the finest views without difficulty. All the footpaths and trails are well marked.
Characteristic of the Krkonoše are massive granite crags like the "Maiden Stones" (Dívčí Kameny) and "Men's Stones" (Myžské Kameny) on the frontier ridge. In some parts of the range there are expanses of peat-bog, and in the corries gouged out by the glaciers rare mountain plants are to be found. The trees (predominantly spruce), however, have been badly damaged by industrial pollution.

Exploring the *Krkonoše

Špindlerův Mlýn

Founded in the second half of the 18th century as a mining settlement, Špindlerův Mlýn (alt. 714–850m/2343–2789ft; pop. 1400), 17km/10½ miles

Moorland in the Krkonoše range ▶

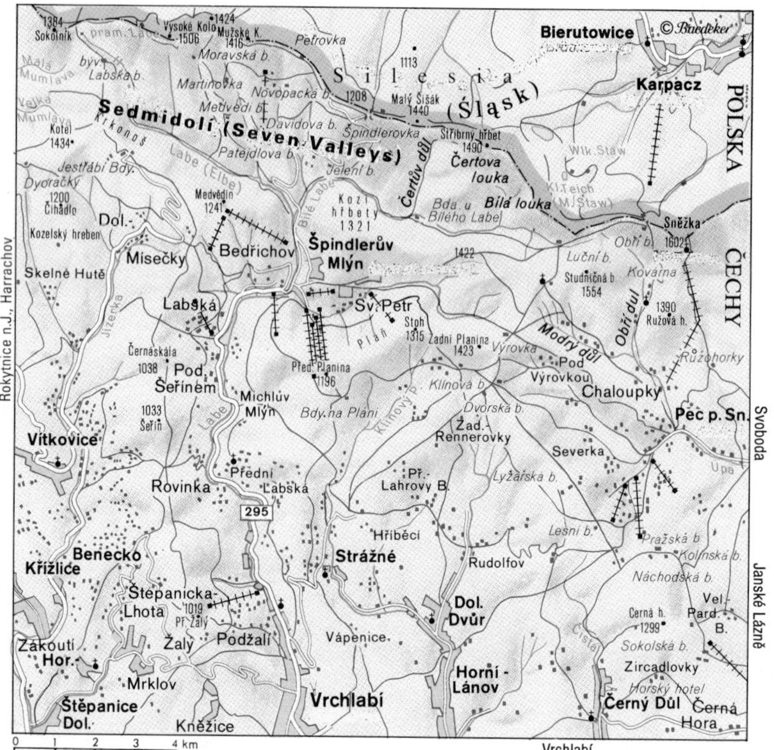

north of Vrchlabí (see entry), is now the largest holiday and sport centre in the Krkonoše. Its principal sight is St Peter's Chapel (early 16th c.).

Walks

From Špindlerův Mlýn there are attractive routes to the source of the Labe (Elbe) or, in the opposite direction, Sněžka. These and other ridge walks can be done either entirely on foot or with the help of two chair-lifts, up Mt Medvědín and Mt Pláň. From Medvědín the summit of Mt Krkonoš (formerly called Zlaté Návrší, Golden Hill; 1412m/4633ft) can be reached in an hour. From there it is a 40 minutes' walk north-west to the Labe mountain hut and the Labe Falls (Vodopád Labe; alt. 1248m/4095ft), a 40m/130ft high waterfall on the young Labe. It is a further 20 minutes' walk north-west to the Labe Spring (Labská Studánka; alt. 1384m/4541ft), the source of the Labe/Elbe (wellhead with coats of arms of towns on the river), in an expanse of marshy meadowland.

Half an hour's walk west of Mt Krkonoš rises Mt Kotel (1434m/4705ft), the highest peak in the western Krkonoše, with superb views in all directions.

Špindler pass

From Špindlerův Mlýn a road (buses only) runs 8km/5 miles north-east, first along the left bank of the Labe to U Dívčí Lávky, then crosses the Bilé Labe and winds its way up the wooded slopes of the Sedmidolí (Seven Valleys) to the Špindler pass (Špindlerovka, 1208m/3963ft), on the Czech–Polish frontier.

Svaty Petr

The magnificently situated village of Svaty Petr is the oldest settlement in the region, originally established here because of the silver and copper mines in the area, which were closed down in 1630. This is the starting-point of the chair-lift up Mt Pláň (1196m/3924ft), which has the best skiing pistes and ski-jumps. From here there is a walk (3–4 hours) by way of the Keil mountain hut, the Geiergucke (viewpoint) and the Wiesenbaude (mountain hut) to Mt Sněžka.

Pec pod Sněžkou

Pec pod Sněžkou (alt. 769m/2523ft; pop. 600), in the eastern part of the Krkonoše, is a summer and winter sports resort in the narrow, forest-fringed valley of the Velká Úpa, at the point where a beautiful side valley comes in from the south-west.

Sněžka

To the north of Pec rises Sněžka (1602m/5256ft), the highest peak in the Krkonoše: a bare conical hill strewn with boulders and scree. On the summit, over which the frontier with Poland runs, are a round chapel (1681) and a mountain restaurant on the Polish side and, on the Czech side, the Česká Bouda restaurant. A project by a group of Czech architects (SIAL) in 1976–78 to construct a cableway up Sněžka and a large multi-functional building on the top came to nothing.

**View

The views from the summit of Sněžka are famous, both for their extent and for their variety. To the west, beyond the rounded summits of the Krkonoše, can be seen Mt Ještěd, Mt Milešovka and other peaks in the Bohemian Massif; to the north-west is the Landeskrone (near Görlitz in south-eastern Germany); and to the north and north-east, beyond the Bober-Katzbach range, is a view of the broad Silesian plain in Poland. The prospect to the east is particularly varied, with the wide Landshuter Pforte ("Landshut Gate"), bounded on the left by the conical peaks of the Waldenburg uplands and the ridge of the Eulengebirge and on the right by the striking sandstone hills of the Heuscheuer range and the Orlík Hills (see entry), beyond which, in the distance, are the Kralický Sněžník and Praděd. To the south the Krkonoše falls down in broad wooded ridges into Bohemia, with views which in clear weather extend as far as Hradec Králové (see entry) and the White Mountain (Bilá Hora) in Prague.

Pomezní Boudy

6km/4 miles east of Sněžka, in a saddle at the east end of the Krkonoše range, are the Pomezní Boudy (alt. 1050m/3445ft; mountain huts on the frontier with Poland).

Rokytnice nad Jizerou

Rokytnice nad Jizerou (alt. 500–800m/1640–2625ft; pop. 4000; textile industry) is an increasingly popular summer and winter resort which straggles along the Jizera valley for some 6km/4 miles to the foot of Mt Kotel and the slopes of the Lysá Hora (1344m/4410ft; skiing).

Harrachov

The little town of Harrachov (alt. 660–720m/2165–2360ft; pop. 1500) lies – only 3km/2 miles south of the road crossing into Poland – in the charming Mumlava valley, below the beautifully wooded western slopes of the Krkonoše. It is a popular resort both in summer and for winter sports (chair-lift, five ski-jumps). It has a long glass-making tradition (first glassworks established 1713), which is illustrated in a small museum (with sales point for glass products). Harrachov is also a good base for walks and climbs in the eastern part of the Jizera Hills (see entry).

Benecko

Benecko (alt. 850m/2790ft; pop. 3000), a little town to the north of Vrchlabí (see entry) which has been known since the 17th century, is the place with the greatest amount of sunshine in the whole region, making it particularly suitable for family holidays.

Horní Mísečky

Horní Mísečky (alt. 1100m/3610ft), a little town founded in 1642, is now an important winter sports centre (particularly langlauf skiing) in the western

Winter in Harrachov

Krkonoše. It can also be reached by road from the town of Jilemnice. In summer there is a bus service to the Vrbatova Chata (alt. 1396m/4580ft), a mountain hut on Špindlerův Mlýn.

Kroměříž

G 3

Region: Southern Moravia
District: Kroměříž
Altitude: 201m/659ft
Population: 29,000

Situation and characteristics

The Southern Moravian district town of Kroměříž lies 40km/25 miles south of Olomouc (see entry) on the right bank of the Morava (see entry) in the south-eastern part of the fertile Haná plain. It is a market centre and industrial town (manufacture of engines, foodstuffs) and has a Cereal-Growing Research Institute.

History

From its beginnings Kroměříž was held by the bishops (from 1107) and archbishops (from 1778) of Olomouc, who after the town was burned down by the Swedes in 1643 rebuilt it as their magnificent summer residence. In 1848–49 the Austrian Parliament (with the participation of Czech politicians) met in the Archbishop's Palace and gave the Habsburg monarchy a new constitution.

Sights

Main square

The hub of the town's life is the main square (Velké Náměstí), which is surrounded by charming arcaded houses. In the square are a Baroque

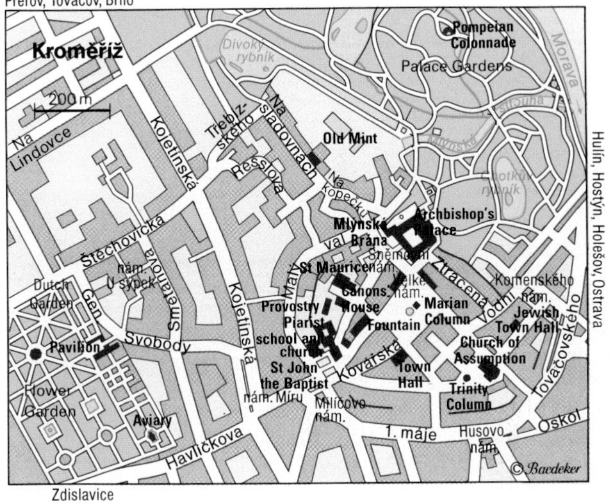

Marian Column and the beautiful Triton Fountain. On the south side stands the Town Hall (16th–17th c.).

***Archbishop's Palace**

At the north-west corner of the square is the Baroque Archbishop's Palace, built by Bishop Liechtenstein-Castelcorno in 1664–95 on the site of an earlier castle and restored after a fire in 1752.

**Collections

The palace, richly appointed and decorated with frescoes, contains a fine library (some 40,000 volumes, including valuable early medieval manuscripts) and archives (including musical archives), with a number of documents almost a thousand years old and a collection of coins and medals (particularly coins minted between 1608 and 1760 in Kroměříž itself). Its great glory, however, is the picture gallery, the finest in the country after the National Gallery in Prague. Among its principal treasures are paintings by Titian ("The Flaying of Marsyas by Apollo"), Anthony Van Dyck ("Charles I and Queen Henrietta"), Lucas Cranach the Elder ("Beheading of John the Baptist", "Martyrdom of St Catherine"), Jan and Pieter Brueghel, Veronese, Bassano, etc. There is also a collection of graphic art, including notable works by Max Švabinský (1873–1962). The Fief Hall has ceiling frescoes by F. A. Maulpertsch and J. Stern (1758–60).

Palace gardens

On the north and west sides of the palace are the beautiful palace gardens (Podzámecká zahrada), laid out in the English style in the 16th century, with Empire-style pavilions, ponds and the Pompeian Colonnade (with antique statues from Pompeii; 1795). The gardens also contain some remains of the old town walls, with the Mlýnská Brána (Mill Gate) of 1585.

Mint

Farther north can be seen the former episcopal Mint (Baroque, 1665).

Parish church

To the east of the main square is the Baroque parish church of St Mary (1724–36).

St Maurice's Church

To the south of the Archbishop's Palace stands the town's principal church, St Maurice's (Kostel Svatého Mořice), a Gothic church completed in 1260 but much altered in later centuries. In a Baroque chapel built on to the church are the tombs of bishops of Olomouc.

Main square, Kroměříž

Piarist school and church

Farther south are the former Piarist grammar school (18th c.) and the Baroque Piarist church dedicated to St John the Baptist (Chrám Jana Křtitele; 1737–68), with a massive fresco-decorated dome.

***Flower Garden**

Some 500m/550yd south of the Piarist church, beyond the Kovářská Brána (Smiths' Gate), on right, lies the Flower Garden (Květná Zahrada; also known as Libosad, the Pleasure Garden; festival in summer), an area measuring 485 by 300m (530 by 330yd) laid out in the manner of Versailles, with grottoes, mazes and artificial hills which can be climbed on spiral paths. In the centre of the garden is an octagonal pavilion (17th c.).

Colonnade

The whole of the west side of the garden is occupied by a 233m/255yd long colonnade built in 1675, in the time of Bishop Liechtenstein-Castelcorno.

Surroundings of Kroměříž

Přerov

16km/10 miles north of Kroměříž, on the Bečva, a left-bank tributary of the Morava, is Přerov (alt. 212m/696ft; pop. 48,000), chief town of its district and an important rail and road junction (also an airport), with considerable industry (optical apparatus, chemicals, engineering, foodstuffs, etc.). Its most notable features are the parish church (originally Gothic; remodelled in Baroque style in 18th c.), a Renaissance palace (originally a medieval castle) in the Upper Square (Comenius Museum; collections of archaeological material and insects), remains of the town walls and bastions (14th–15th c.) and a number of Renaissance houses.

Předmostí

In the Předmostí district can be found an archaeological site dating from the time of the mammoth-hunters, some 20,000 years ago.

Mt Hostýn

22km/14 miles north-east of Kroměříž is Mt Hostýn (735m/2412ft), with the former monastery and the well-known pilgrimage church (1721–48) which have given their name to the wooded hills in the surrounding area, the Hostýnské Vrchy (Kelčský Javorník, 865m/2835ft).

Tovačov

Tovačov (alt. 197m/646ft), 17km/10½ miles north-west of Kroměříž on the river Morava, has a castle which has been much altered and rebuilt. The doorway of the 96m/315ft high tower is one of the earliest Renaissance works in Moravia. The castle now houses a Haná Folk Museum. In the surrounding area are a number of ponds with facilities for bathing.

Hulín

6km/4 miles east of Kroměříž is Hulín (alt. 196m/643ft; pop. 6000), a small industrial town (sugar-refinery, engineering, brickworks). It has a Late Romanesque church (13th c.), remodelled in Baroque style in 1750–55, with a beautiful doorway and tower of 1583.

Holešov

8km/5 miles east of Kroměříž, below the west side of the Hostýnské Vrchy, is Holešov (alt. 232m/761ft; pop. 14,000; woodworking and foodstuffs industries).

Its main features of interest are its Early Baroque castle (museum, with exhibition of locally made furniture), a former monastery (mid 18th c.) and a synagogue of 1560 (permanent exhibition on "Jews in Moravia"). At Holešov is the regional airport for Zlín (see entry).

Zdislavice

12km/7½ miles south-west of Kroměříž, between the Chřiby Hills to the south-east and the Litencice Hills to the north-west, is the village of Zdislavice (alt. 318m/1043ft), birthplace of the German writer Marie von Ebner-Eschenbach (1830–1916).

Kuks E 2

Region: Eastern Bohemia
District: Trutnov
Altitude: 298m/978ft
Population: 500

Situation and characteristics

Kuks is a village in the Labe (Elbe) valley where between 1694 and 1724 the self-willed Count Anton von Sporck built a mansion (of which only a few remains survive), a bath-house at the mineral springs on the left bank of the river and a hospital and church (by G. B. Alliprandi) on the right bank, together with a large number of expressive Baroque statues (1715–18) by the Innsbruck sculptor Matthias Bernhard Braun von Braun.

Sights

***Baroque statues**

The principal sight of Kuks is the profusion of allegorical statues of the Virtues, the Beatitudes and the Vices on the hospital terrace.

Pharmacy

In the hospital building can be seen a Baroque pharmacy of 1730–40.

Burial vault

Under the church is the burial vault of the Sporck family.

Surroundings of Kuks

Bethlehem

3km/2 miles west of Kuks, at the village of Stanovice, a series of Biblical scenes were carved from the local sandstone (some now badly weathered) by Matthias Bernhard Braun von Braun. Among them is a Nativity scene, which has earned the site the name of Betlém (Bethlehem).

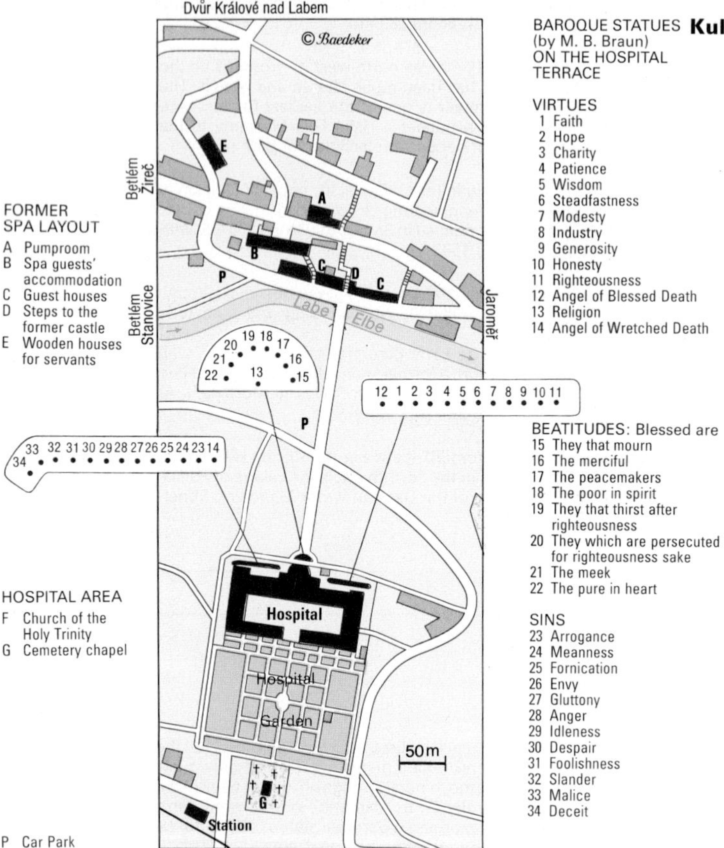

Dvůr Králové nad Labem

6km/4 miles north-west of Kuks is Dvůr Králové nad Labem (alt. 283m/929ft; pop. 18,000; textile industry), once the jointure of the queens of Bohemia. The main feature of interest is the 16th century Renaissance Town Hall, with sgraffito decoration. The new municipal Zoo (area 100 hectares/250 acres) is notable particularly for its African big game (safari park); rhinoceroses are bred here.

"Devils' Castles"

3km/2 miles south-west of Dvůr Králové, at Lipnice, are the massive sandstone formations known as the "Devils' Castles".

Mt Zvičina

15km/9 miles north-west of Kuks is Mt Zvičina (671m/2202ft), the highest peak in the Krkonoše foreland area. On the summit are a Baroque church, a mountain hut and an outlook tower.

Pecka

22km/14 miles north-west of Kuks lies Pecka (alt. 497m/1631ft; pop. 1000), a popular summer resort with a Baroque church and a number of wooden houses (e.g. the Dresler House). In the market square is a beautiful Baroque fountain of 1634. Above the town are the ruins of a castle (originally Gothic, 14th–15th c.; enlarged in 16th–17th c.). The only part of it that can be visited is the Harant Palace, with a local museum and an exhibition of sculpture by Bohuslav Kafka (1878–1942).

Nová Paka

28km/17 miles north-west of Kuks is the industrial town of Nová Paka (alt. 422m/1385ft; pop. 9000). In the market square are a Plague Column of 1716 and a fountain of 1814. The office of the Communal Council, also in the square, contains a collection of semi-precious stones. The Baroque church, with a wooden staircase of 1737, has a Gothic Madonna of about 1500.

Smiřice

11km/7 miles south of Kuks, on the Labe, we come to Smiřice (alt. 240m/785ft; pop. 3200). The castle has a Baroque chapel (1696–99) with fine pictures and beautiful ceiling paintings.

Jaroměř

6km/4 miles south-east of Kuks is Jaroměř (alt. 254m/833ft), an old town situated at the junction of the Metuje and the Úpa with the Labe (Elbe) with active leatherworking and textile industries. Notable features of the town are the Gothic St Nicholas's Church (14th c.; Baroque interior), the Late Gothic St James's Church and a number of Renaissance houses. The south-eastern part of the town is occupied by the old fort of Josefov, with fortifications (mostly well preserved) built by the Emperor Joseph II in 1780–87 but never used, underground passages and an Empire-style church of 1810.

Hořice

17km/10½ miles west of Kuks the little town of Hořice (alt. 311m/1020ft; pop. 7500) has textile, foodstuffs and engineering industries and an old school of stonemasonry and sculpture (two galleries displaying Czech and international sculpture). The Baroque castle, on the site of a medieval castle, dates from the 18th century. There is a fine Baroque church by Kilian Ignaz Dientzenhofer (1741–44), with superb stonework. The neo-Gothic Town Hall was built in 1872.

Lázně Bělohrad

22km/14 miles west of Kuks lies Lázně Bělohrad (alt. 291m/955ft; pop. 3500), a little spa recommended for the treatment of rheumatic conditions. On the south-eastern outskirts of the town is a beautiful English-style park (60 hectares/150 acres).

Kutná Hora E 3

Region: Central Bohemia
District: Kutná Hora
Altitude: 273m/896ft
Population: 21,000

Situation, history and characteristics

The old mining town of Kutná Hora (German Kuttenberg), charmingly situated above the valley of the little river Vrchlice, 65km/40 miles east of Prague, was the second largest town in Bohemia in the Middle Ages and for a time the residence of the Bohemian kings, then among the richest monarchs in Europe. The prosperity of the town came from the silver mined in this area between the 13th and the 18th century, which provided the raw material for the famous Bohemian silver groschens (or Prague groschens) minted in Kutná Hora. The Kuttenberg Decree (1409) altering the statutes of the Charles University of Prague in favour of the Czechs led the University's professors and students to move to other universities, principally to Leipzig. As a result of antiquated working methods in the local mines and competition from newer silver-mines in the 16th century, and even more so after the Thirty Years' War, the prosperity of Kutná Hora declined. The Bohemian groschens were minted here for the last time in 1547, and in 1726 the mint was closed down.

The famous Baroque painter Petr Brandl died in Kutná Hora in 1735. Josef Kajetán Tyl (see Famous People), founder of the modern Czech theatre and author of the Czech national anthem, was born here in 1808.

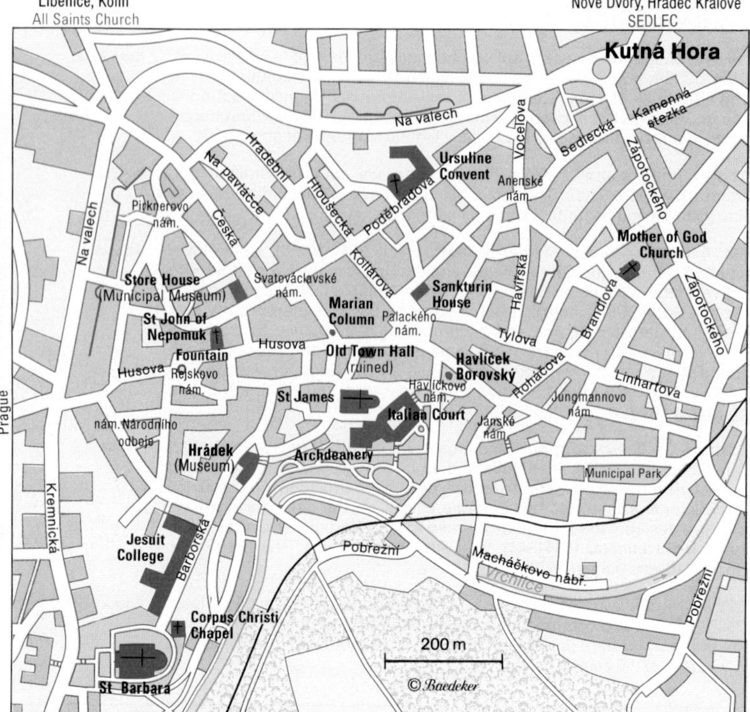

The modern town, now expanded far beyond its old boundaries, has a variety of industry (chocolate and tobacco manufacture, large engineering plants).

**Townscape

In spite of all modern developments Kutná Hora has preserved the medieval aspect of the old town centre almost intact, making it one of the most rewarding tourist destinations in the country.

Sights

***Palacký Square**

In the centre of the town is Palacký Square (Palackého Náměstí), surrounded by charming Renaissance houses. On the south-west side of the square are the ruins of the Old Town Hall.

Šultys Square

A little way to the west is Šultys Square (Šultysovo Náměstí), with a tall Plague Column (by F. Baugut, 1713–15) commemorating a plague in 1713. From here Šultys Street (Šultysova Třída) leads north to St Wenceslas Square (Svatováclavské Náměstí).

***Stone House** (Municipal Museum)

In the narrow western part of St Wenceslas Square, on the right, is the Stone House (Kamenný Dům; 1485–95), with an oriel window and rich sculptural decoration, which now houses the Municipal Museum (Městské Muzeum).

Kutná Hora

Ursuline Convent

North-east of St Wenceslas Square, in George of Poděbrady Street (Třída Jiřího z Poděbrad), is the Baroque Ursuline Convent (Klášter Uršulinek), built in 1733–43 to the design of Kilian Ignaz Dientzenhofer.

Hus Street

From Šultys Square Hus Street (Husova Třída) runs west, passing on the right a 17th century Baroque church.

Mint Street

On the left is Mint Street (Mincířská Ulice), a short street with flying buttresses. Farther along Hus Street, on the right, stands the beautiful Baroque church of St John of Nepomuk (Kostel Svatého Jana Nepomuckého; by F. M. Kaňka, 1734–50), with ceiling paintings of 1752.

***Stone Fountain**

Hus Street, climbing gently, runs into Rejsek Square (Rejskovo Náměstí), in the centre of which is the Late Gothic Stone Fountain (Kamenná Kašna; 1493–95).

Marble House

At the south-west corner of the square is the Marble House (U Marmorů), with a magnificent Renaissance doorway.

***St James's Church**

To the east of Rejsek Square by way of Comenius Square (Komenského Náměstí) lies Italian Court Square (U Vlašského Dvora), on the right of which is the Gothic St James's Church (Chrám Svatého Jakuba; 1330–1420), with an 82m/270ft high tower. It has a richly furnished interior, with a magnificent high altar of 1678 and fine paintings (including works by Petr Brandl and Karel Skréta).

Archdeanery

Immediately south of St James's Church can be seen the Archdeanery, once the residence of the Mint Master.

***Italian Court**
(Museum)

Adjoining the Archdeanery on the east is the Italian Court (Vlašský Dvůr), built shortly before 1300. This was the royal Mint (named after the first coiners, who came from Florence) and for many years a residence of the Bohemian kings. In the picturesque courtyard, which is entered from the

east side, is the Gothic St Wenceslas's Chapel (on right), with a fine oriel window; it has a carved and painted altarpiece (Death of the Virgin).
The building now houses a museum, with old coining apparatus and pictures by the local painter Felix Jennewein (1857–1905).
From the terrace on the south side of the Italian Court there is a charming view of the town, in particular of St Barbara's Church.

Hrádek (Museum)

South-west of St James's Church, in St Barbara Street (Barborská Ulice), stands the Hrádek (Fort), built in the 15th century as a royal stronghold (replacing an earlier timber structure of the 14th century), which soon after its completion served as a second Mint. It now houses a museum illustrating the history of silver-mining and coining. The Gothic Knights' Hall has fine 15th century wall paintings; two chapels in oriels.

Jesuit College

Farther along St Barbara Street, on the right, can be seen the imposing bulk of the former Jesuit College (Jesuitská Kolej; by Domenico Orsi, 1626–67), which was used for many years as a barracks. On the balustrade flanking the street on the left are thirteen Baroque statues by F. Baugut (1703–16).

****St Barbara's Church**

At the south end of St Barbara's Street is the Late Gothic St Barbara's Church (Chrám Svaté Barbory), dedicated to the patron saint of miners. Begun by Peter Parler in 1388, it was later continued by Benedikt Rieth and Matthias Rejsek and completed in 1565; it was carefully restored and the façade was completed between 1884 and 1905. It has a striking exterior, with three tent-like pointed towers over the

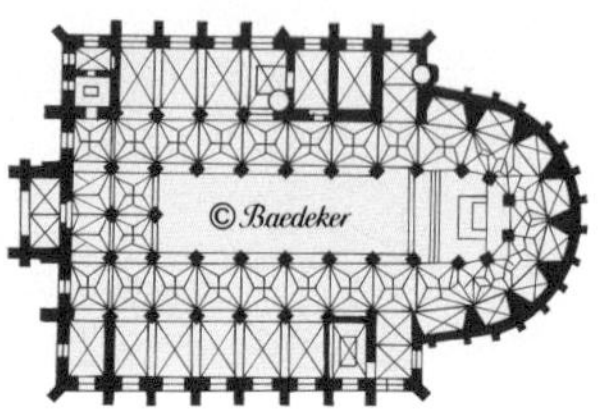

Net vaulting . . .

. . . in St Barbara's Church, Kutná Hora

nave and a range of richly ornamented flying buttresses. The impressive and spacious interior – five-aisled, with an ambulatory and ring of chapels round the choir – is roofed with fine net vaulting which already shows Renaissance influences, with numerous coats of arms. Notable features are the beautiful Gothic choir-stalls in the north aisle, the frescoes in the choir chapels, the Renaissance pulpit (1566), the carved high altar (1903) and paintings by Karel Skréta and Petr Brandl.

*Net vaulting

From the church there are fine views of the town and the deeply indented valley of the Vrchlice. In the parvis in front of the church are stalls selling souvenirs (including reproductions of coins minted in Kutná Hora).

*View

Church of the Mother of God

To the east of Palacký Square, on the edge of the old town, can be found the 14th century Church of the Mother of God (Matka Boží or Kostel Panny Marie na Náměti), with beautiful Gothic vaulting and a pulpit of 1520. In the church is the tomb of Petr Brandl (d. 1735).

Surroundings of Kutná Hora

Sedlec

Some 3km/2 miles north-west of the town centre is the district of Sedlec. Here, in a street on the right leading to Malín, is St Mary's Church (Chrám Panny Marie), a five-aisled Gothic church built between 1290 and 1330 which was partly remodelled in Baroque style by J. Santini in 1699–1707. As a result it shows a curious mingling of Gothic and Baroque forms, particularly in the ceiling paintings by J. Steiner; there are also paintings by Petr Brandl. The church originally belonged to a Cistercian monastery which is now a tobacco factory.

Ossuary Chapel

400m/440yd north of St Mary's Church, in the cemetery, is the 12th century Gothic Ossuary Chapel. It is a double chapel, in the lower part of which all the furnishings (altar, chandeliers, coats of arms, etc.) are made from countless human bones, the remains of some 10,000 bodies. In the cemetery can be seen a statue of St John of Nepomuk (1704).

Kačina

5km/3 miles north-east of Kutná Hora is Kačina Castle (1802–22), the purest example of an Empire-style castle in Bohemia, with a library, a theatre, an agricultural museum and an English-style park.

Žehušice

10km/6 miles east of Kutná Hora is the Early Baroque castle of Žehušice, later remodelled in Empire style. It has a deer park with some 40 white deer.

Čáslav

9km/5½ miles south-east of Kutná Hora, in a fertile agricultural region, lies the town of Čáslav (alt. 231m/758ft; pop. 11,000), which was founded in the 13th century (foodstuffs industry, engineering). In the Church of SS Peter and Paul (originally 12th c., with alterations in 14th and 15th c.) was held the meeting of the Estates in 1421 which deposed the Emperor Sigismund from the throne of Bohemia. Jan Žižka (see Famous People), one of the representatives of the people at that meeting, was buried in the church; but in 1623, on the orders of the Emperor Ferdinand II, his remains were removed and the tomb destroyed. Other features of interest in the town are the Baroque Town Hall (18th c.) and the remains of the town's fortifications (Žižka Gate, Otakar Bastion).

Žleby

16km/10 miles south-east of Kutná Hora is the Gothic castle of Žleby, which was rebuilt in neo-Gothic style in the 19th century. Interesting interior furnishings of the 16th and 17th centuries.

River Labe / Elbe — C–E 1/2

General

A Central European river and international waterway
Name: Czech Labe, German Elbe (a name probably of Germanic origin), Latin Albis (perhaps connected with *albus*, "white").

Course in Czech Republic: through Eastern, Central and Northern Bohemia,
Source: in Krkonoše range (alt. about 1400m/4600ft).
Mouth: at Cuxhaven (North Germany), into North Sea.
General direction of flow: from south-east to north-west.

Course of the Labe in the Czech Republic

Source in *Krkonoše

The Labe (Elbe), one of the principal rivers of Central Europe, rises on the Bohemian side of the Krkonoše range (National Park), near the Czech–Polish frontier. It is formed from a number of small streams flowing from springs in the upland meadowland, much of which is marshy.

The main source streams of the Labe are the Bílé Labe (White Labe), which rises in the Bílá Louka (White Meadow) at an altitude of 1400m/4600ft, near Mt Sněžka, and the Labe Brook, which rises in the Labská Louka (Labe Meadow) – the "official" source is the Labe Spring (Pramen Labe) at 1346m/4416ft – and plunges down 40m/130ft in the Labe Falls (Labský Vodopád) into the deep Labe Gorge (Labský Důl), one of the Seven Valleys (Sedmidolí). The two source streams join at an altitude of 780m/2560ft to form a torrential mountain stream, now called the Labe, which cuts through the southern ridge of the Krkonoše in a valley which for most of the way is extremely narrow.

The river then flows through the popular altitude resort and winter sports centre of Špindlerův Mlýn, below which is a small dam, the Labská Přehrada, and continues south through a defile, the Labská Soutěska, to the old mining town of Vrchlabí. It then turns south-east, is joined by the Malé Labe (Little Labe), flows past Hostinné, Dvůr Králové and Kuks (see entry) and comes to the historic old town of Jaroměř, where two tributaries come in on the left, first the Úpa and then the Metuje.

Bohemian Basin

Beyond the old stronghold of Josefov, now a south-eastern district of Jaroměř, the Labe pursues a more tranquil south-south-westerly course through flat country to Hradec Králové (see entry), where the Orlice comes in on the east. It then flows south to enter the Bohemian Basin and continues through this fertile plain to its junction with the Vltava at Mělník (see below).

The Labe now flows round the Kunětická Hora (300m/985ft), crowned by its castle, in a wide eastward bend, is joined by the Loučná, coming from the east, and reaches Pardubice (see entry), noted among other things for its annual steeplechase, where another tributary, the Chrudimka, comes in on the left.

Polabí

At Pardubice the Labe turns sharply west and, in the Polabí depression, flows past Přelouč and Kladruby nad Labem and comes to Chvaletice. From this point the river is navigable by vessels of up to 1000 tons, which supply the Chvaletice thermal power station with lignite from Northern Bohemia. Beyond this it reaches the most southerly point in its course, and soon afterwards comes to Kolín (see entry), one of the oldest royal towns in Bohemia, situated at a ford on the Labe.

The river then flows north-west, is joined on the left by the Cidlina (near the mouth of which are the remains of the early medieval stronghold of Libice) and comes to the spa town of Poděbrady, where the Bohemian king George of Poděbrady (Jiří z Poděbrad, 1420–71) is believed to have been born.

At Nymburk the Labe turns west again and follows a winding course past Kostomlátky (to the north), Lysá nad Labem (to the north), Přerov nad Labem and Čelákovice (both to the south).

Junction with Jizera

Soon afterwards come the junction with the Jizera (from the north) at the little spa of Toušeň (on the left) and then the double town of Brandýs nad Labem–Stará Boleslav. Thereafter the river again turns north-west through

The Labe (Elbe) at Mělník ▶

the Polabí depression and at Kostelec nad Labem comes within 20km/12½ miles of Prague. It then flows past Neratovice and Obříství, which in the days of the Austro-Hungarian monarchy was the terminus of a boat service to Dresden.

Junction with Vltava

After the junction with the Vltava and soon afterwards with the Vltava Lateral Canal, which both come in from the south-west, the Labe, now considerably wider, flows past the wine-producing town of Mělník (on the high north bank) and continues north-west past Liběchov (on right, at the mouth of the romantic Liběchov valley) and Štětí, and after a wide bend to the south-west reaches the Northern Bohemian industrial town of Roudnice nad Labem. To the south-east is Mt Říp (456m/1496ft), to which the legendary founder of the Czech nation, Čech, is said to have led his people so that they might settle in the surrounding area.

Junction with Ohře

The next place of any size is the historic old town of Litoměřice (see entry), on the north bank of the Labe opposite the inflow of the Ohře. A short distance up the Ohře valley is the old fortified town of Terezín (see entry), which during the period of German occupation gained melancholy fame as the site of the Theresienstadt concentration camp.

Bohemian Massif

*Porta Bohemica

At the industrial town of Lovosice the Labe turns north-east in a sharp bend and cuts its way through the Bohemian Massif (České Středohoří) in a narrow winding valley, accompanied by a road and railway on either side. After its breakthrough at Mt Lovoš (572m/1877ft), a prominent basalt hill, the river flows through the beautiful valley scenery of the Porta Bohemica (Bohemian Gate). In the course of a long programme of river regulation works (1933–51) a hoard of Early Bronze Age material (weapons, tools, jewellery, etc.) was dredged from the river at Velké Žernoseky.

Since the construction of the large dam on the Labe (with locks and a hydro-electric station; 1928–36) below the ruins of Střekov Castle on its 85m/280ft high crag of phonolite little is left of the idyllic landscape which was celebrated in the painting and poetry of the Romantic period. Around Ústí nad Labem, on the eastern edge of the lignite region of northern Bohemia, where the Bílina flows into the Labe from the south-west, the landscape is dominated by blocks of flats of questionable architectural merit and huge industrial buildings. With its extensive port installations Ústí nad Labem is the largest port on the Labe/Elbe after Hamburg.

At this point the Labe turns north-east and becomes rather wider, still following a winding course and still accompanied by roads and railways on both sides.

Below Boletice nad Labem (to the right), at the junction with the Ploučnice, is the town of Děčín (see entry), dominated by its imposing Baroque castle. Děčín itself is on the right bank of the river, with the district of Podmokly on the left bank, above which the Pastýřská Stena ("Shepherds' Wall"; 282m/925ft) rears steeply up.

***Elbe Sandstone Hills**

At Děčín begins what is perhaps the most beautiful part of the whole Labe valley within Bohemia. The river now cuts its way through the Elbe Sandstone Hills (see Labské Pískovce), which begin here. On the left bank is the main railway line to Dresden, on the right bank the road. The steep slopes on both sides of the valley are covered with forest, and the striking sandstone formations which have given the range its name appear with increasing frequency.

Bohemian Switzerland

Near the frontier town of Hřensko (alt. 116m/381ft), at the inflow of the Kamenice on the right, the Czech–German frontier extends for some 4km/2½ miles along the middle of the Labe. This is the area known as the Bohemian Switzerland (České Švýcarsko), which is continued on the German side of the frontier as the Saxon Switzerland.

Labské Pískovce / Elbe Sandstone Hills D 1/2

Situation and *topography

The Elbe Sandstone Hills (Labské Pískovce) are a nature reserve which extends to the east and west of Děčín (see entry). They are composed of massive expanses of sandstone which outcrop in the deeply indented valley of the Labe (see entry) and its tributary the Kamenice. The largest and most impressive of these "rock cities", the Tiské Stěny (Tisá Walls), lies to the west of Děčín. This region, also known as the Bohemian or Bohemian-Saxon Switzerland, is a favourite area with large numbers of walkers and climbers in summer.

Access

From Děčín there is a good road (the Dresden road) running north along the right bank of the Labe to Hřensko, the most popular excursion centre in Bohemia, and the Czech–German frontier.

Exploring the *Elbe Sandstone Hills

Děčínský Sněžník

*View

6km/4 miles north-west of Děčín rises the Děčínský Sněžník (726m/2382ft), the highest peak in the Elbe Sandstone Hills. From the outlook tower on the summit plateau (2km/1¼ miles long by 700m/770yd across) there are wide panoramic views.

Hřensko

10km/6 miles north of Děčín is the charmingly situated little town of Hřensko (alt. 130m/425ft), which straggles up the Kamenice valley from the Labe for 1.5km/1 mile.

*Gorges

A very rewarding excursion from Hřensko is to the Dolní Soutěska (Low Gorge; there and back, including boat trip, 2½ hours; including Wild Gorge 3½ hours). From the road running along the bank of the Labe take a side

Pravčická Brána, a natural bridge in the Elbe Sandstone Hills

road on the right and drive for 1km/¾ mile along the Kamenice, between sheer sandstone walls, to the inflow of the Belá. From here follow a signpost on the right to the gorges, through which the Kamenice pursues a winding course between rugged rock faces to which cling trees and ferns. The continuation of the Low Gorge eastward is the equally fine Wild Gorge (Divoká Soutěska).

**Pravčická Brána

3km/2 miles east of Hřensko is the largest natural rock bridge in Central Europe, the Pravčická Brána (alt. 447m/1467ft), a sandstone arch 15m/50ft long and 3m/10ft thick.

Jetřichovice

15km/9 miles east of Hřensko, in a wide basin, is the holiday resort of Jetřichovice (alt. 232m/761ft), a good base for walkers and climbers, with sheer rock pinnacles rearing above the town on the north-east. 4km/2½ miles north-west of Jetřichovice are the ruins of Šaunštejn Castle (alt. 340m/1115ft; 14th c.), which is partly hewn from the rock.

Česká Kamenice

18km/11 miles north-east of Děčín, on the river Kamenice, lies Česká Kamenice (alt. 317m/1040ft; pop. 7000; papermaking, textiles). The Castle, which belonged to the Princes Kinsky, was originally built in the 16th century, in Renaissance style, but was Baroquised in the 17th century. Other features of interest are the Town Church (15th and 16th c.) and St Mary's Chapel (Baroque; 1739).
South-east of Česká Kamenice is a basalt hill, the Zámecký Vrch (Castle Hill; 544m/1785ft), with a ruined castle and an outlook tower.

Lednice

F 4

Region: Southern Moravia
District: Břeclav
Altitude: 172m/564ft
Population: 2100

Situation

The little town of Lednice in southern Moravia lies on the river Dyje, a tributary of the Morava. At the beginning of the 19th century the meadows bordering the river between Lednice and Břeclav (see Surroundings) were laid out as an expanse of parkland and ponds which in recent years has been declared a bird sanctuary.

*Parkland

Sights

***Castle**

On the northern outskirts of Lednice stands the large Castle of the Princes of Liechtenstein, built between 1846 and 1856 on the site of earlier castles, very much in the spirit of the Romantic movement: a neo-Gothic building complete with pointed arches and battlements. The interior, in the same style, has richly carved wooden ceilings and contains valuable old furniture, as well as collections of weapons, porcelain and hunting trophies.
The old stables on the west side of the castle were an early work by J. B. Fischer von Erlach (1688–90).
The domestic offices are now occupied by the faculty of horticulture of the Brno College of Agriculture ("Mendeleum"; greenhouse of 1845, with lush tropical vegetation). Part of the castle is an Agricultural Museum, with four permanent exhibitions (Parks and Gardens, Fruit-Growing, Vegetable-Growing, Hunting).

Romantic buildings in park

To the north of the castle, on the banks of a pond, rises the 63m/207ft high Oriental Tower or Minaret (1797), from the top of which there are fine views.
Scattered about the park are numerous other Romantic buildings of the 19th century.

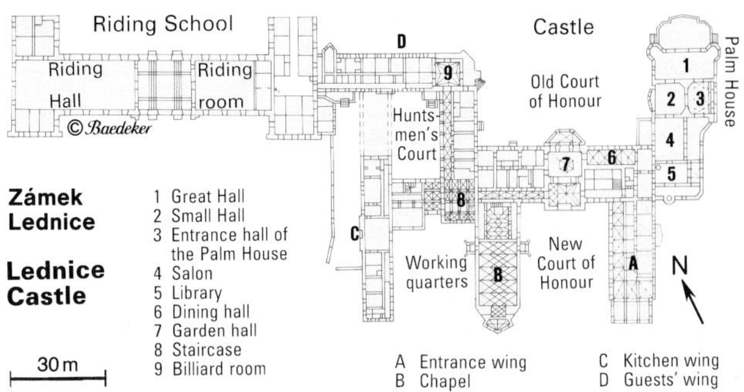

Avenue

A charming avenue 7km/4½ miles long runs south-west to Valtice (see Surroundings).

Surroundings of Lednice

Valtice

7km/4½ miles south-west of Lednice is the little town of Valtice (alt. 187m/614ft; pop. 3000), with large wine-cellars, a fine Baroque parish church (1631–71) and another massive Liechtenstein castle (1670–1725), with magnificent state apartments in which a festival of music and culture is held annually in summer.

Břeclav

8km/5 miles south-east of Lednice, on the river Dyje, lies the district town of Břeclav (alt. 159m/522ft; pop. 25,000), an important railway junction with a

Lednice Castle

variety of industry (rubber, plastics, ceramics, maltings, sugar refineries). To the west of the town is a Renaissance castle (16th c.; restored in 19th c.), set in a park.

Pohansko

3km/2 miles south of Břeclav, at the old Empire-style hunting lodge of Pohansko, excavations from 1959 onwards have yielded important material dating from the time of the Great Moravian Empire (9th c.).

Lanžhot

The village of Lanžhot (alt. 164m/538ft), 6km/4 miles from Břeclav at the south-eastern tip of Moravia, has preserved old local traditions and customs.

Mikulčice

20km/12½ miles east of Lednice is the village of Mikulčice (alt. 165m/540ft; pop. 2000), near which, on the right bank of the Morava, is the most important Slav stronghold and occupation site in the territory of former Czechoslovakia. Excavations carried out here from 1954 brought to light the remains of a princely residence. This area was part of the first league of Slav tribes (the kingdom of Samo, mid 7th c.), but more importantly of the Great Moravian Empire (9th–10th c.). Visitors can see the foundations and other remains of eleven churches, together with a variety of small finds (jewellery and ornaments, everyday objects) displayed in the small site museum.

Liberec

E 2

Region: Northern Bohemia
District: Liberec
Altitude: 340–413m/1115–1355ft
Population: 104,000

Situation and characteristics

Liberec, situated on the Lužická Nisa between the Jizera Hills (see entry) and Mt Ještěd (see below, Surroundings), is the chief town of its district and a major centre of the textile industry in Bohemia, with a University of Textile Technology; its other industries include motor vehicles and chemicals.

History

Until the end of the Second World War Liberec, under its German name of Reichenberg, was the largest town in the Sudeten German border areas of Czechoslovakia, and it is still the centre of the textile industry (manufacture of cloth and wool) which has flourished in this area since the late medieval period.

Trade Fair

The products of the region are displayed in the Liberec Trade Fair (Liberecké Výstavní Trhy, LVT; held in alternate years) for textiles, glassware, jewellery, porcelain and furniture and furnishings.

Sights

***Town Hall**

The hub of the town's life is Dr Beneš Square (Náměstí Dr E. Beneše; pedestrian zone), with a number of 18th century burghers' houses and the imposing Town Hall (Radnice) in Flemish Renaissance style (by Franz von Neumann, 1888–93). From the 65m/215ft high central tower there are extensive views.

Municipal Theatre

Behind the Town Hall, to the north, is the Municipal Theatre (Severočeské Divadlo F. X. Šaldy; by Fellner and Helmer, 1883). It bears the name of the writer and critic František Xaver Šalda (1867–1937), a native of Liberec.

Town hall, Liberec ▶

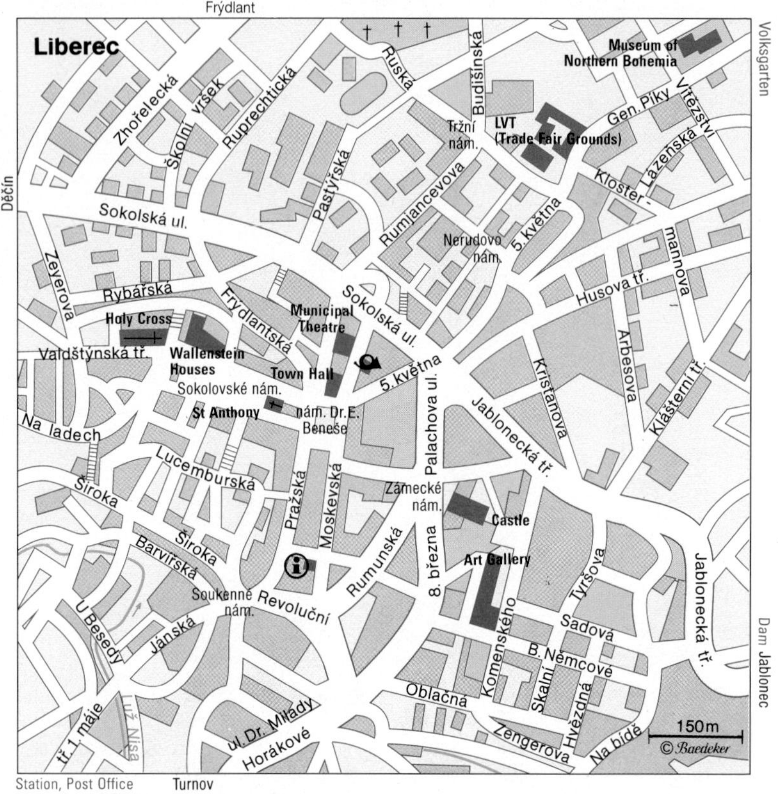

Sokolov Square

To the west of Dr Beneš Square, beyond the Archidecanal Church (originally 16th c.; rebuilt in neo-Gothic style in 1879), is Sokolov Square (Sokolovské Náměstí), with several houses in Empire style.

Větrná Ulička

In Větrná Ulička (Windy Lane), a short street opening off the north-west corner of the square, are a number of half-timbered houses known as the Wallenstein Houses.

Holy Cross Church

At the west end of Větrná Ulička stands Holy Cross Church (built 1695, renovated 1756), with a beautiful Baroque interior. On the first altar on the left is a painting (St Anne with the Virgin and Child) ascribed to Dürer. Beyond the church is a Plague Column of 1719.

Šalda Square

A short distance east of Dr Beneš Square lies Šalda Square (Náměstí F. X. Šaldy), from which six streets radiate.

Castle

To the south of Šalda Square is the Castle (built 1582–86, enlarged in 1779 and 1850) of the Counts of Clam-Gallas. In the castle chapel (1604–06) are a carved high altar of the Late Renaissance and an oratory of 1606.

Art Gallery

The Art Gallery (Galerie Výtvarných Umění), south-east of the Castle, houses works by Bohemian, French and Dutch painters.

500m/550yd west of the Art Gallery is Soukenné Náměstí (Cloth Square), the town's business centre.

Soukenné Náměstí

From Šalda Square Třída 5. Května (5th May Street) runs north-east, passing the Trade Fair Grounds (LVT) on the left, to the Museum of Northern Bohemia (Severočeské Muzeum; 1897–98), which offers an excellent survey of the economy and culture of Northern Bohemia (including the development of the textile and glass industries; also old Flemish tapestries).

Trade Fair Grounds
***Museum**

North-east of the Museum lies the large People's Park (Lidové Sady Petra Bezruče). Near the entrance is the little Swan Lake (Labutí Jezero), and to the north of this is the beautiful Botanic Garden (Botanická Zahrada; rich collections of orchids and cactuses). To the east of this is the Zoo (Zoologická Zahrada), the oldest in the country (founded 1906). Still farther east is an open-air theatre (Letní Divadlo), with seating for 3000 spectators.

People's Park
Swan Lake
Botanic Garden
Zoo
Open-air theatre

In Hus Street (Husova Třída), one of the streets leading from Šalda Square, is a museum devoted to the German occupation of 1938–45.

Museum

Some distance south of Hus Street is the 700m/770yd long Harcov Dam (Harcovská Přehrada; 1904), with an open-air swimming pool.

Dam

Surroundings of Liberec

6km/4 miles south-west of the town centre rises Mt Ještěd (1012m/3320ft), the summit of which can be reached on a cableway 1183m/1294yd long (constructed 1932–33) from Horní Hanychov (7km/4½ miles from town centre; tram service); the ascent takes 5 minutes. On the summit is an extraordinary conical tower topped by an aerial mast (total height 92m/302ft) which accommodates a hotel and restaurant as well as a tele-

***Mt Ještěd**

Jablonec nad Nisou

communications, radio and television relay station. From the top there are far-ranging panoramic views of the Krkonoše and Jizera Hills, the Zittau Hills in Germany, the Bohemian Massif and the Bohemian Basin. Mt Ještěd is also a popular winter sports area, with skiing pistes and a toboggan run.

Vratislavice nad Nisou

5km/3 miles south-east of Liberec we come to Vratislavice nad Nisou (alt. 376m/1234ft; pop. 6000), a small industrial town (acidic chalybeate spring; carpet factory, brewery) on the river Nisa (Neisse). This was the birthplace of Ferdinand Porsche (1875–1951), the automobile constructor who conceived the idea of the original Volkswagen (1934).

Jablonec nad Nisou

15km/9 miles south-east of Liberec, below the south side of the Jizera Hills, is Jablonec nad Nisou (alt. 495m/1625ft; pop. 45,000), chief town of its district and the main centre of the Northern Bohemian jewellery and brassware industry (artificial precious stones, earrings, necklaces, beads, buttons, etc.). The imposing Town Hall was built in 1931–32; from the tower (open to the public) there are extensive views. The parish church, on higher ground, is in Constructivist style (by J. Zasche, 1929–33). The National Museum of Technology has a permanent exhibition of glassware (imitation precious stones, etc.).

Lidice

See Kladno, Surroundings

Lipník nad Bečvou G 3

Region: Northern Moravia
District: Přerov
Altitude: 245m/805ft
Population: 11,000

Situation and characteristics

Lipník nad Bečvou is an industrial town (mechanical engineering, manufacture of matches, foodstuffs, printing) on the river Bečva, at the Moravian Gate (see below).

Sights

Castle

In the old part of the town can be found its Baroque Castle (16th c.; altered in 19th c.).

Parish church

The parish church (originally 15th c.; remodelled in Baroque style in 1765–66) has a fine interior and a Renaissance bell-tower of 1609.

Synagogue

The former Synagogue (Late Gothic) has belonged since 1950 to the Czechoslovak Church.

Other features of interest are an Early Baroque monastery, remains of the town's 15th and 16th century fortifications (watch-towers) and the Záhoří District Museum.

Surroundings of Lipník nad Bečvou

Helfštýn Castle

4km/2½ miles south-east, in the village of Týn nad Bečvou, are the ruins of Helfštýn Castle (alt. 406m/1332ft), the largest castle in Moravia. Built in the 13th–15th centuries, it was demolished in 1656. There are now plans to rebuild it.

Moravian Gate

The Moravian Gate (Moravská Brána) lies in the depression formed by the valleys of the Bečva and the Odra (Oder) between the Sudeten Mountains to the north-west and the Carpathians to the east. It is the watershed (alt. 310m/1015ft) between the Baltic and the Danube river system which drains to the Black Sea.

Potštát

12km/7½ miles north of Lipník nad Bečvou is the little town of Potštát (alt. 502m/1647ft), which has a castle in Empire style. In the market square is a clock-tower (Hodinová Věž) dating from the 16th and 18th centuries. There are a number of Baroque houses and works of sculpture.

Hranice

10km/6 miles north-east of Lipník nad Bečvou is Hranice (alt. 255m/835ft; pop. 19,000), an old-world town on the river Bečva with some industry (building materials). Notable features are the Renaissance Castle (16th–17th c.; arcaded courtyard), the Baroque Town Church (1754–63) and the Old Town Hall (1544). The former synagogue is now a museum with a fine ceramic collection (including faience formerly produced in Hranice). There are some remains of the 14th–15th century town walls.

Teplice nad Bečvou

12km/7½ miles east of Lipník nad Bečvou on the left bank of the Bečva, surrounded by forest, we come to the little spa of Teplice nad Bečvou (alt. 333m/1093ft), with acidic chalybeate springs used in the treatment of vascular and cardiac diseases.

*Karstic formations

In this area there are numerous karstic formations, including a very interesting aragonite cave formed by the action of mineral water (Zbrašovské aragonitové jeskyně). On the right bank of the Bečva is the Hůrka (about 350m/1150ft), a karstic ridge with interesting rock formations and caves (nature reserve). There is a fine view into the Bečva valley from the crags at the tall Baroque column with a figure of St John of Nepomuk (Svatý Jan). In this karstic region can be found the deepest abyss in the country, the Kranická Propast (244m/801ft deep, including 175m/574ft under water).

Litoměřice D 2

Region: Northern Bohemia
District: Litoměřice
Altitude: 171m/561ft
Population: 25,000

Situation and characteristics

Litoměřice lies on the right bank of the Labe (Elbe; bridges, river port) opposite the inflow of the Ohře, in a fruit- and vine-growing region on the southern fringes of the Bohemian Massif. It is a major centre of the foodstuffs industries (refrigeration plants). The "Garden of Bohemia" fruit, vegetable and flower show is held here annually in September.

Garden Show

History

In the 9th century this was the site of a Slav stronghold, and in 1227 Litoměřice became a royal town. The town was devastated during the Thirty Years' War. The see of a bishop since 1655, it has a number of magnificent churches, many of them built or rebuilt by the well-known architect Ottavio Broggio, who was born in Litoměřice. A seminary for the training of priests and a faculty of theology were also established in the town.

Litoměřice was the home of the Slavist Josef Jungmann (1773–1847), the Czech Romantic poet Karel Hynek Mácha (1810–36) and the Austrian graphic artist Alfred Kubin (1877–1959).

Sights

*Town Square

In the centre of Litoměřice lies the spacious Town Square, surrounded by Gothic, Renaissance, Baroque and Empire houses, with a Plague Column of 1681.

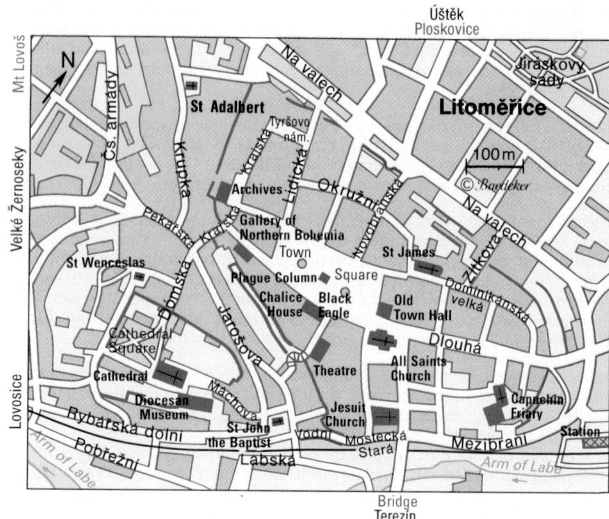

Gallery of Northern Bohemia

To the west is the Gallery of Northern Bohemia (Bohemian art since the 12th century; naïve art).

Old Town Hall

At the east end of the square stands the Old Town Hall (originally Gothic; rebuilt in Renaissance style 1737–39), with arcading and a Roland Column (1539) at the left-hand corner.

District Museum

The Old Town Hall is now occupied by the District Museum (paintings, sculpture, ceramics, etc.). Its greatest treasure is a Utraquist hymn-book (1520–30) with superb illuminations.

Town Church

On the right of the Old Town Hall is the Town Church (All Saints), originally dating from 1235, it was rebuilt by Ottavio Broggio between 1704 and 1731 in rich Baroque style and has a beautiful Baroque façade and a sumptuous interior (including a panel painting by the Master of Litoměřice). The square tower is a relic of the town's 13th century fortifications.

***Chalice House**

On the south side of the square can be seen the Chalice House (Mrázovský Dům; also known as Pod Báni, "Under the Dome"), built by a Utraquist burgher in 1584 as a salt-store. The chalice-shaped tower, believed to be a reference to the Last Supper, has become the emblem and landmark of the town.

Black Eagle House

Adjoining the Chalice House is the Black Eagle House (Černý Orel; Renaissance), with fine sgraffito decoration.

Jesuit Church

To the south of All Saints Church, near the 550m/600yd long bridge over the Labe, stands the Baroque Jesuit Church (1701), with a magnificent doorway and a richly furnished interior (massive high altar). Adjoining is the former Jesuit College.

***St Stephen's Cathedral**

On a hill sloping down to the Labe in the western part of the town, near the railway station, is St Stephen's Cathedral, built in 1663–81 by Giulio Broggio and other architects on the site of an earlier church, with a separate bell-tower in neo-Renaissance style. It has a richly furnished interior (paint-

Town Square and Chalice House, Litoměřice

ings by Karel Škréta, J. P. Molitor and the school of Cranach, etc.); the famous Litoměřice Altarpiece is now in the National Gallery in Prague.

Diocesan Museum

The 17th century Bishop's Palace to the east of the Cathedral now houses the Diocesan Museum.

St Wenceslas's Church

A little way north-west of the Cathedral is the little Baroque church of St Wenceslas (by Ottavio Broggio, 1714–16), with a picturesque interior.

St James's Church

Notable among the town's other fine churches is the Baroque St James's Church (by Ottavio Broggio, 1730–40), which originally belonged to a Dominican friary.

Surroundings of Litoměřice

Mt Mostka

To the north of the town is Mt Mostka (272m/892ft), from the top of which there are extensive views.

Ploskovice

5km/3 miles north-east of Litoměřice can be seen the Baroque castle of Ploskovice (alt. 238m/781ft), which was altered in 1850–53 to make a summer residence for ex-Emperor Ferdinand I.

Velké Žernoseky

The village of Velké Žernoseky (alt. 151m/495ft; pop. 1000) 5km/3 miles west of Litoměřice has the most northerly vineyards in Bohemia (large wine-cellars in the Late Gothic castle).

Lovosice

7km/4½ miles south-west of Litoměřice is Lovošice (alt. 153m/502ft; pop. 12,000), a town on the left bank of the Labe (lock, bridges, river port) with large industrial installations (synthetic fibres, fertilisers, foodstuffs) and intensive fruit-growing in the surrounding area. The Castle of the Princes Schwarzenberg, originally Renaissance, was rebuilt in Baroque style in the 19th century. St Wenceslas's Church dates from 1733–48. There is a local museum.

Mt Lovoš

North-west of Lovošice rises Mt Lovoš (570m/1870ft; far-ranging views). To the west is Mt Boreč (446m/1463ft), which emits warm air in winter and cold air in summer ("ventaroles"). To the south-west are the ruins of the Gothic castle of Košt'álov (alt. 481m/1578ft; extensive views).

Doksany

10km/6 miles south of Litoměřice, at Doksany (alt. 156m/512ft; pop. 500), is a Premonstratensian monastery founded in 1144–45, with a fine church (large pillared crypt).

Třebenice

12km/7½ miles south-west of Litoměřice is Třebenice (alt. 228m/748ft; pop. 2800), with the Museum of Bohemian Garnets (semi-precious stones), founded in 1872.

Úštěk

The little town of Úštěk (alt. 240m/785ft; pop. 3000), 16km/10 miles north-east of Litoměřice, has preserved its medieval aspect. In the market square are Gothic and Renaissance houses with arcades and handsome gables. Other features of interest are a fine Late Baroque church (1764–72) with valuable furnishings; remains of the town's Late Gothic fortifications, with the Picards' Tower (1428); and the "birds' houses" (*ptačí domky*) clinging to a rocky hillside, constructed by Italian workers who were brought in to build the railway in the 19th century.

Theresienstadt

See Terezín

Litomyšl F 3

Region: Eastern Bohemia
District: Svitavy
Altitude: 330m/1085ft
Population: 10,000

Situation and characteristics

The old-world Eastern Bohemian town of Litomyšl lies on the river Loučná, on a site which was occupied by a fortified castle in the 10th century. It played an important part in the revival of Czech national feeling in the 19th century. It has chemical industries (including the manufacture of synthetic fibres).

Operatic festival

Litomyšl was the birthplace of the composer Bedřich Smetana (see Famous People); the room in which he was born can be seen in the former brewery. An operatic festival, "Smetana's Litomyšl", is held here annually in July, a musical festival of youth in September.

Sights

Castle

The Renaissance-style Castle was built by G. Avostalis in 1568–73, with beautiful sgraffito decoration. It has a fine theatre (1796–97).

Market square

In the long, straggling market square (Náměstí) are numbers of well preserved old houses with fine gables and arcades.

Town Church

The Gothic Town Church (originally 14th c.; rebuilt in early 17th c.) has valuable furnishings.

Museum

The Baroque Piarist Church (by G. B. Alliprandi) was built between 1714 and 1726. The adjoining Piarist College (17th c.) now houses the Municipal Museum; among its principal treasures is a rare gradual (book of plainsong) of 1563.

Surroundings of Litomyšl

Ústí nad Orlicí

12km/7½ miles north of Litomyšl is Ústí nad Orlicí (alt. 340m/1115ft; pop. 16,000), chief town of its district, with large engineering and textile plants. It

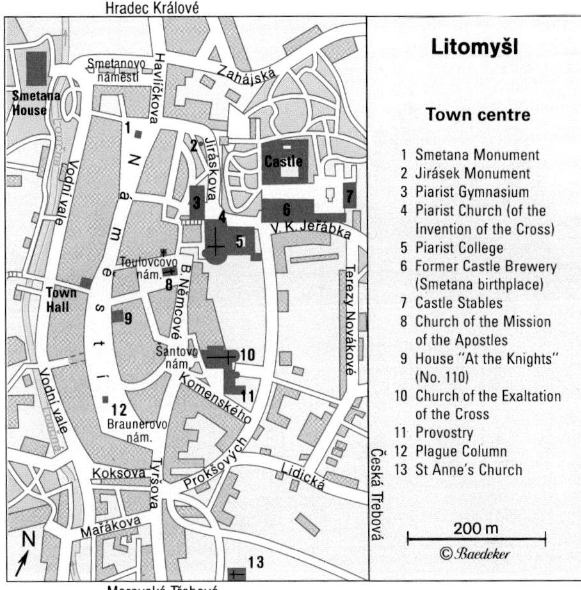

has a beautiful Baroque church (1770–76), with valuable furnishings; the local Christmas cribs (Nativity groups) are famous.

Česká Třebová

9km/5½ miles north-east of Litomyšl lies Česká Třebová (alt. 375m/1230ft; pop. 18,000), a railway junction and industrial town (engineering, textiles). In the cemetery (now disused) is a Romanesque rotunda (13th c.; rebuilt in 16th and 18th c.).

Nové Hrady

13km/8 miles west of Litomyšl is the Rococo country house of Nové Hrady (1773–78; fine furniture), set in a park (1791–1807).

Brandýs nad Orlicí

15km/9 miles north of Litomyšl, with a ruined castle looming over it, is Brandýs nad Orlicí (alt. 305m/1000ft; pop. 1500), once a stronghold of the Bohemian Brethren. Here from 1622 to 1625 Jan Amos Comenius (see Famous People) worked on his "Labyrinth of the World and Paradise of the Heart". There are a small Baroque mansion (17th c., with much later alteration) and a Baroque church (1778–87).

Vysoké Mýto

15km/9 miles north-west of Litomyšl is Vysoké Mýto (alt. 284m/932ft; pop. 11,000), an industrial town (coach-building) on the river Loučná, with well preserved Gothic town walls (three gates) and a twin-towered Gothic church (14th c.; rebuilt 1875–1904). In the main square are a number of historic old burghers' houses.

Choceň

16km/10 miles north-west of Litomyšl we come to Choceň (alt. 290m/950ft; pop. 9500), a small industrial town (textiles, engineering) with a 16th century castle which belonged to the Kinský family, set in a park. There is a beautiful Baroque church with a Rococo interior.

Svitavy

15km/9 miles south-east of Litomyšl, on the upper course of the river Svitava, is the district town of Svitavy (alt. 435m/1425ft; pop. 17,000), with

Litomyšl Castle

some industry (textiles, engineering). There are a number of fine Renaissance houses in the market square.

Lanškroun

22km/14 miles north-east of Litomyšl is Lanškroun (alt. 373m/1224ft; pop. 11,000), a town founded by German settlers in 1241, with a Renaissance Town Hall (1581–82) and several wooden buildings.

Loket B 2

Region: Western Bohemia. District: Sokolov
Altitude: 427m/1401ft. Population: 3000.

*Situation

Loket is a picturesque little town situated on a granite crag encircled by a bend on the river Ohře (the name Loket means "elbow").

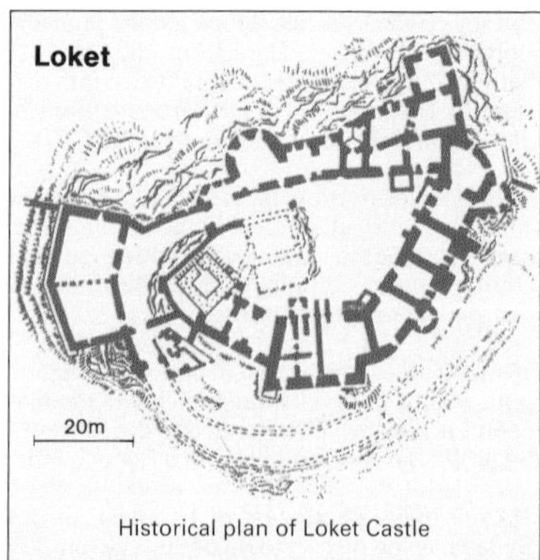

Historical plan of Loket Castle

Sights

***Castle**

The town is dominated by the massive castle built in the 13th century to protect the western frontier of Bohemia and much altered in later centuries. From the keep there are far-ranging views.

Margrave's House

The Margrave's House is now a museum, with col-

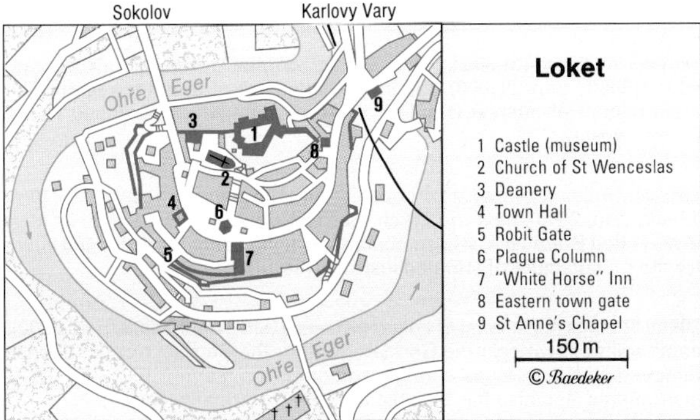

lections of glass and porcelain (mainly of Bohemian origin), old documents, etc. It is at present closed for renovation.

St Wenceslas's Church

St Wenceslas's Church (originally Late Gothic, remodelled in 18th c.) has a fine 15th century Madonna.

Market square

In the market square are a number of historic old houses, the Early Baroque Town Hall (1682–87) and a Plague Column of 1718.

Bridge

The Ohře is spanned by a modern bridge (1935).

Porcelain manufactories

There are several porcelain manufactories in the Ohře valley (first established in 1815) producing well-known makes of tableware.

Loket Castle

Surroundings of Loket

Sokolov

7km/4½ miles south-west of Loket lies Sokolov (formerly Falknov; alt. 400m/1300ft; pop. 25,000), the industrial centre of a lignite region. The main feature of interest is a 17th century castle which belonged to the Counts Nostitz.

Luby

25km/15 miles north-west of Loket is the little town of Luby (alt. 518m/1700ft; pop. 2500), near the Czech–German frontier. The German frontier town is Bad Brambach, whose inhabitants have been famed for 400 years for the manufacture of stringed instruments.

Kraslice

28km/17 miles north-west of Loket is Kraslice (alt. 514m/1686ft; pop. 7500), another little town near the German frontier; the German frontier town is Klingenthal. Kraslice has a long tradition in the manufacture of musical instruments, and also has a textile industry (principally lace).

Louny C 2

Region: Northern Bohemia
District: Louny
Altitude: 185m/605ft
Population: 23,000

Situation and characteristics

The Northern Bohemian district town of Louny lies on a terrace above the river Ohře in a hop-growing region. It is an important regional centre, with railway workshops, engineering plants, sugar refineries and a brewery.

History

The town, originally founded by German cloth-makers, was granted a municipal charter in 1260 and was at once fortified. During the 15th century wars of religion Louny was on the Hussite side. In 1517 the town was almost totally destroyed by a devastating fire; the rebuilding was carried out by the celebrated architect Benedikt Ried or Rieth (known in Czech as Beneš z Loun).

Sights

St Nicholas's Church

Louny's finest church is St Nicholas's, which was renovated before 1540 in the "Vladislavian Gothic" style. It has a striking tripartite tent-roof and a battlemented tower with a spire flanked by four pinnacles; from the wall-walk there is a fine view of the town. Notable features of the interior are the fine ribbed vaulting, the 16th century stone pulpit and the beautiful Baroque woodcarving (for example on the high altar).

Other churches

Other notable churches are the 16th century Church of the Mother of God and St Peter's Church and the Cemetery Church (1713).

Burghers' houses

In the main square is a Renaissance house with an oriel window (Daliborka), from which sentences of death were announced. There are other Late Gothic and Renaissance burghers' houses elsewhere in the town.

Žatec Gate
Bridge over Ohře

The Žatec Gate (Žatecká Brána) dates from 1500, the bridge over the Ohře from 1462.

St Nicholas's Church, Louny

Surroundings of Louny

Citoliby

3km/2 miles south of Louny lies the little town of Citoliby (alt. 236m/774ft; pop. 1000), with a Baroque castle and a Baroque church containing sculpture by M. B. Braun von Braun and paintings by V. V. Reiner. In the second half of the 18th century Citoliby was one of the centres of Czech Baroque music.

Peruc

10km/6 miles east of Louny, Peruc (alt. 335m/1100ft; pop. 800) has a Rococo castle on the site of a medieval stronghold. In the castle is a museum commemorating the Czech painter Emil Filla (1882–1953). Below the castle is the ancient Oldřich Oak, under which the Bohemian Prince Oldřich is said to have met his future wife Božena (early 11th c.).

Házmburk Castle

17km/10½ miles north-east of Louny, commandingly situated on a basalt crag, are the ruins of Házmburk Castle (alt. 418m/1371ft; Gothic), with the remains of its two towers. From the castle there are extensive views.

Libochovice

18km/11 miles east of Louny is Libochovice (alt. 166m/545ft; pop. 3700), with an Early Baroque castle (1683–90) in which the Czech physiologist Jan Evangelista Purkyně (1787–1869) was born.

Luhačovice G 3

Region: Southern Moravia. District: Zlín
Altitude: 250–300m/820–985ft. Population: 6000

Situation and characteristics
Mineral springs

The Southern Moravian spa of Luhačovice, founded in 1789, lies on the Horní Olšava in the wooded setting of the Vizovice Hills (Vizovické Vrchy). It is famed for its brine springs containing iodine and bromine, used in the treatment of disorders of the respiratory passages and alimentary tract and diabetes.

Sights

Sanatoria

Several sanatoria (Janův Dům, Slovensky Dům) were built in uniform style by the Slovak architect Dušan Jurkovič (1868–1947), following Wallachian architectural traditions. The old Vila Lipová sanatorium now houses a folk museum.

Castle

The Baroque Castle dates from 1738.

Surroundings of Luhačovice

White Carpathians

South-east of Luhačovice, along the Slovak frontier, are the White Carpathians (Bilé Karpaty), a range of forest-covered hills which extends for some 90km/55 miles, with an average breadth of 20km/12½ miles, between the wide valleys of the Morava and the Váh. The highest peak is the Velká Javorina (970m/3183ft).

Starý Hrozenkov

17km/11 miles south-east of Luhačovice we come to the village of Starý Hrozenkov (alt. 378m/1240ft), where a folk festival is held annually in summer. The village is a good base for walks and climbs in the White Carpathians.

Uherský Brod

11km/7 miles south-west of Luhačovice is Uherský Brod (alt. 238m/781ft; pop. 18,000), an old town on the Olšava with a variety of industry (foodstuffs, woodworking, engineering, manufacture of sporting guns). Features of interest are the old town walls, some stretches of which are well

Fountain, Luhačovice

preserved, two Baroque churches (17th and 18th c.) and a 16th century castle.
Uherský Brod and the little town of Nivnice, 6km/4 miles south, contend for the honour of being the birthplace of the preacher and educationist Jan Amos Comenius (see Famous People), mementoes of whom, together with rare editions of his works (including the "Orbis Pictus"), are displayed in the Comenius Museum, housed in a former stable complex known as the Baraník.

Lusatian Hills / Luzické Hory D/E 1/2

Region: Northern Bohemia
Districts: Děčín, Česká Lípa and Liberec
Altitude: up to 793m/2602ft

Situation and topography

The Lusatian Hills (Luzické Hory), which extend along Bohemia's northern frontier with Germany, consist of a series of rounded basaltic and phonolitic hills (Luž, 793m/2602ft; Jedlová, Klič, Hvozd) and sandstone formations. Throughout the region, which is densely wooded, can be seen the typical "log cabin" type of house.

In the Lusatian Hills

Cvikov

Cvikov (alt. 357m/1171ft; pop. 5000) has a 16th century Gothic church which was remodelled in Baroque style in 1726.
3km/2 miles north are the remains of the medieval castle of Milštejn (alt. 535m/1755ft; fine views).

Hrádek nad Nisou

The industrial town of Hrádek nad Nisou (alt. 270m/885ft; pop. 4500) lies near the point where the Czech, Polish and German frontiers meet. St Bartholomew's Church, originally built in 1486, was later altered in Renaissance style. There are some fine examples of traditional local architecture.
2km/1¼ miles east are Grabštejn Castle (alt. 330m/1085ft; originally Early Gothic, later rebuilt in Renaissance style) and a castle in Empire style (no admission).

Jablonné v Podještědí

Jablonné v Podještědí (alt. 315m/1035ft; pop. 4000) lies 26km/16 miles west of Liberec (see entry). Its most notable feature is the massive monastic church of St Lawrence (1729; crypt open to public).
3km/2 miles south-east, on a wooded hill (352m/1155ft), stands Lemberk Castle (originally 13th c., rebuilt in 17th c.), with a fine Renaissance tower. It now houses a museum of domestic living (Gothic period to end of 19th c.). In the Hall of Fables are a painted coffered wooden ceiling and scenes from Aesop's fables (no admission).

Nový Bor

The town of Nový Bor (alt. 365m/1200ft; pop. 12,000) is one of the main centres of the Bohemian glass industry (production of artistic and everyday glassware; Glass Museum), with several Baroque and Empire houses and a Late Baroque church (18th c.).
3km/2 miles south-east the village of Sloup (alt. 292m/958ft) has the romantic remains of a castle partly hewn from a monumental sandstone boulder (alt. 318m/1043ft; early 14th c.). There are other bizarrely shaped sandstone and basalt rocks in the neighbourhood.
3km/2 miles north-east is the village of Klič (alt. 760m/2495ft), with wide-ranging views.

Panská Skála

5km/3 miles west can be seen the well-known Panská Skála, a gigantic rock organ created by the cleavage of the basalt (see illustration, p. 98).

Rumburk

Rumburk (alt. 387m/1270ft; pop. 10,000) is an industrial town near the Czech–German frontier, with a Baroque castle (second half of 18th c.), a Gothic church (early 16th c., later remodelled) and a former Capuchin friary (late 17th c.) with a church and Loreto Chapel (1704–05). Wooden houses of traditional type in Šmilovského Ulice.

Tolštejn Castle

8km/5 miles south-west are the extensive ruins of Tolštejn (alt. 670m/2200ft), a 14th century Gothic castle which was burned down by the Swedes in 1642. It was much visited and admired by the 19th century Romantics (superb views).

Mariánské Lázně / Marienbad B 3

Region: Western Bohemia
District: Cheb
Altitude: 600m/1970ft
Population: 15,000

Situation and *characteristics

Western Bohemian town of Mariánské Lázně (more familiar in its German form, Marienbad), charmingly situated on the southern edge of Slavkov Forest (Slavkovský Les), south-east of Cheb (see entry), is one of Europe's most celebrated spas. It has 40 springs similar to those of Karlovy Vary (Karlsbad), though colder (9–12°C/48–54°F). The waters of Mariánské Lázně – mostly acidic, containing Glauber salt – are particularly recommended for the treatment of obesity and disorders of the stomach and intestines, the gall bladder, the kidneys and bladder, the skin, the respiratory tract and the nerves. There are also alkaline chalybeate springs and muds containing iron sulphate.

History

The springs of Mariánské Lázně had long been known and used, but the spa in its modern form was founded in 1808 by Teplá monastery, under Abbot Karl Reitenberger, which owned the site (then partly marshland). It owed its rise to popularity and success to the efforts of Dr Josef Nehr (d. 1820), the doctor attached to the monastery and to the spa, who with the help of Václav Skalník, a gardener who later became mayor of the town, had the marshy ground transformed into beautiful parks and gardens and the first bath-houses built.

Numerous plaques and monuments in Mariánské Lázně commemorate famous visitors to the spa, among them Goethe, Chopin, Tsar Nicholas II and King Edward VII.

Sights

***Park**

Mariánské Lázně's main street (Hlavní Třída) runs the length of the town from south to north. From the north end of the street the beautiful Skalník Park (Skalníkovy Sady) extends eastward, rising to Goethe Square (Goethovo Náměstí).

Town Hall

In Ruská Třída (Russian Street), which branches off the west side of the main street, is the Town Hall. From here a path leads up to a street on a higher level in which are the small Anglican Church and the Russian Orthodox Church of St Vladimir.

Peace Square

At the north end of the main street is Peace Square (Mírové Náměstí), with a fountain (by Dietrich, 1913), a number of large hotels and the Protestant church (Bohemian Brethren).

Theatre

To the west, in Třebízský Street (Třebízského Ulice), is the Municipal Theatre.

Forest Spring

Some 250m/275yd farther north, in a recently laid out park, can be found the Forest Spring (Lesní Pramen).

Cross Spring

A little way east of Peace Square, at the north end of Skalník Park, is the Cross Spring (Křížový Pramen), under a columned rotunda (1819). In front of it is a bronze bust of Dr Josef Nehr.

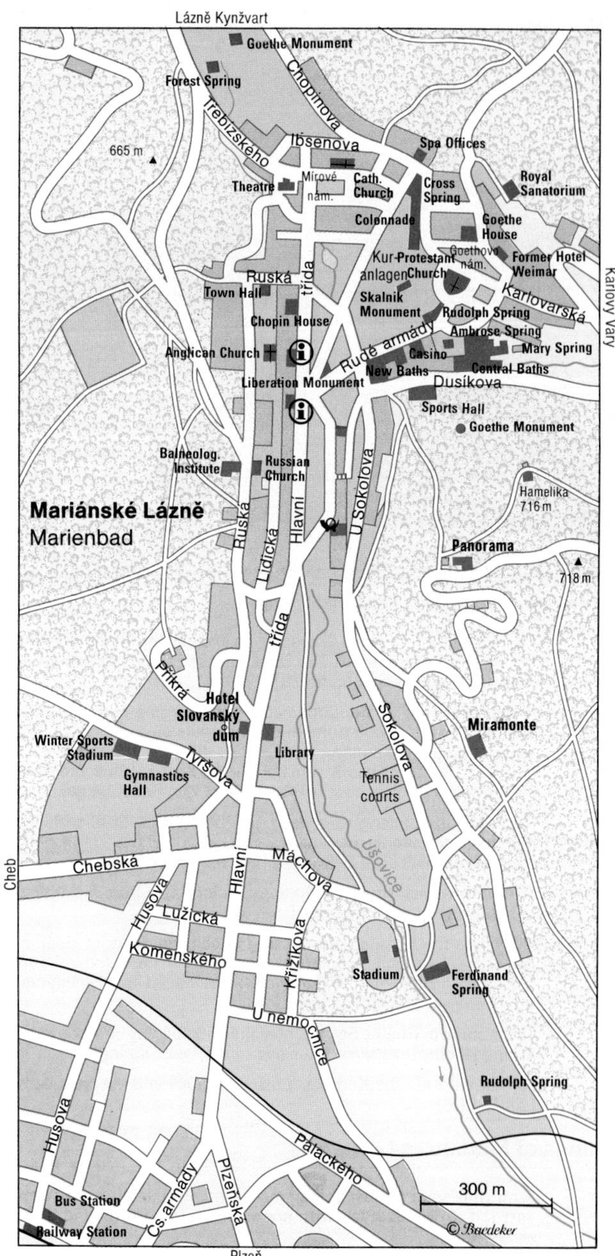
Lázně Kynžvart
Goethe Monument
Forest Spring
Chopinova
Třebízského
665 m
Ibsenova
Spa Offices
Royal Sanatorium
Theatre
Mírové nám.
Cath. Church
Cross Spring
Colonnade
Goethe House
Goethovo nám.
Former Hotel Weimar
Kur-anlagen
Protestant Church
Ruská
Town Hall
třída
Karlovarská
Karlovy Vary
Skalnik Monument
Rudolph Spring
Chopin House
Ambrose Spring
Anglican Church
Rudé armády
Casino
Mary Spring
New Baths
Central Baths
Liberation Monument
Dusíkova
Sports Hall
Goethe Monument
Balneolog. Institute
Russian Church
U Sokolova
Hamelika 716 m
Mariánské Lázně
Marienbad
Ruská
Lidická
Hlavní
Panorama
718 m
třída
Příkrá
Hotel Slovanský dům
Sokolova
Miramonte
Winter Sports Stadium
Library
Tyršova
Gymnastics Hall
Tennis courts
Úšovice
Chebská
Hlavní
Máchrova
Cheb
Husova
Lužická
Komenského
Křižíkova
Stadium
Ferdinand Spring
U nemocnice
Rudolph Spring
Husova
Palackého
Čs. armády
Plzeňská
300 m
Bus Station
Railway Station
© Baedeker
Plzeň

Colonnade containing Rudolph and Ferdinand Springs

Colonnade Immediately south of the Cross Spring extends the long Colonnade (1889) fronting the pump-rooms. This is the main rendezvous and promenade for visitors taking the cure (concerts).

*Singing Fountain At the south end of the Colonnade is the Singing Fountain, 18m/60ft in diameter, which at odd-numbered hours puts on a display with hundreds of jets leaping and soaring in time with different programmes of music; after dark the fountain is illuminated. To the west, in front of the Colonnade, can be seen a bronze bust (1879) of Abbot Karl Reitenberger.

Rudolph Spring
Ferdinand Spring Farther south, under a colonnade, are the Rudolph Spring (Rudolfův Pramen; diuretic) and the Ferdinand Spring (Ferdinandův Pramen), the actual sources of which are 1.5–2km/1–1¼ miles farther south.

Catholic church To the north-east, above the Rudolph Spring, is the Roman Catholic Church of the Assumption, a rotunda.

Goethe Square Higher up the hillside, laid out in gardens, we come to Goethe Square (Goethovo Náměstí), with large hotels and the house (now the Municipal Museum) in which the 74-year-old Goethe stayed in 1824, infatuated with the 19-year-old Ulrike von Levetzow.

Ambrose Spring To the south of Goethe Square, near the Rudolph Spring, rises the Ambrose Spring (Ambrožův Pramen; an acidic chalybeate spring).

Kurhaus Farther west are the Kurhaus (Casino) of 1901 and the New Baths (Nové Lázně; 1896).

Surroundings of Mariánské Lázně

Lázně Kynžvart 5km/3 miles north-west of Mariánské Lázně is the little spa of Lázně Kynžvart (alt. 673m/2208ft), with six chalybeate springs and a children's sanatorium.

Singing Fountain

Kynžvart Castle (1833–39), in a large and beautifully laid out English-style park (100 hectares/250 acres), was once the residence of the Austrian Chancellor Prince Metternich. It contains large collections of manuscripts, curios, etc., but is not open to the public.

Above the 19th century house are the ruins of the original Gothic castle.

Planá

11km/7 miles south of Mariánské Lázně lies Planá (alt. 507m/1663ft; pop. 4000), an old town which has preserved its medieval core.

Mnichov

12km/7½ miles north-east of Mariánské Lázně is Mnichov (alt. 725m/2380ft), with a Town Hall of around 1730, in front of which is a pillory, and a Baroque church (1719–25) with a fine interior.

Teplá

*Basilica

12km/7½ miles east of Mariánské Lázně we come to the little town of Teplá (alt. 657m/2156ft; pop. 2000). South-east of the town is the Premonstratensian monastery of Teplá, founded in 1193, with a twin-towered fortified Romanesque basilica which was later rebuilt in Gothic and Baroque style (restoration planned).
The conventual buildings date from 1685–1721; they include an Old and a New Library (80,000 volumes, including many manuscripts and incunabula).

Tachov

20km/12½ miles south-west of Mariánské Lázně is Tachov (alt. 504m/1654ft; pop. 13,000), chief town of its district, which has well preserved 14th century town walls, a Gothic church (remodelled in neo-Gothic style) and, in the market square, several 17th century burghers' houses. Baroque castle, recently rebuilt; old monastery, now a museum. Tachov has a large riding school, established in 1857.

Teplá Monastery

Interior of church

Bečov nad Teplou

25km/15 miles north-east of Mariánské Lázně is Bečov nad Teplou (alt. 492m/1614ft), an ancient little town in a beautiful setting, with a 14th century castle (enlarged in 16th and 18th c.) looming over it.

Úterý

25km/15 miles east of Mariánské Lázně is the medieval mining town of Úteřy (alt. 513m/1683ft), in an area where gold and silver were mined from the 13th to the 15th century. In the market square are half-timbered houses of the late 17th century, often concealing earlier structures of the late medieval period. On the façade of the Town Hall can be seen the town's coat of arms (1561). The Early Baroque parish church (1689) and the cemetery church (1747) were the work of the Dientzenhofers; both have fine interiors.

Mělník D 2

Region: Central Bohemia
District: Mělník
Altitude: 222m/728ft
Population: 20,000

*Situation and characteristics

Mělník, chief town of its district, lies 38km/24 miles north of Prague on the vine-clad right bank of the Labe (Elbe), opposite the inflow of the Vltava. The town's origins go back to the 10th century, when there was a Slav stronghold on the site, and it received its municipal charter in 1274. The Emperor Charles IV caused the first Burgundian vines to be planted on the slopes above the Labe and the Vltava – the first beginnings of viniculture in Bohemia, of which Mělník is now the main centre.

A large vintage festival is held here annually on the last weekend in September. The town's well-known Ludmila wine commemorates the country's first martyr and patron saint.

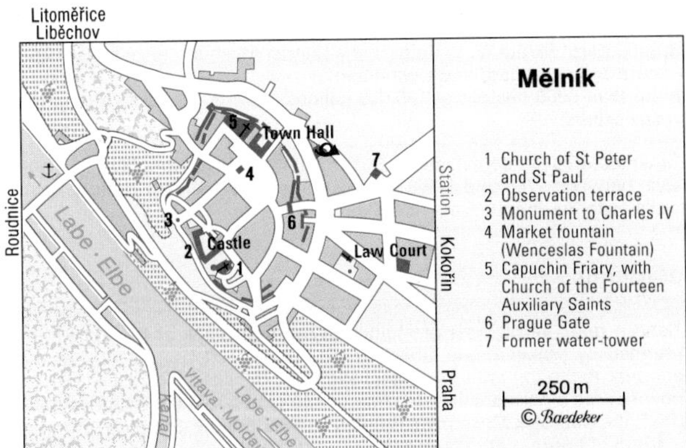

Sights

Church of SS Peter and Paul

The town's skyline is dominated by the Gothic Church of SS Peter and Paul (15th c.) with its tall tower and by the massive bulk of the Castle, originally founded in the 14th century.

From the viewing terrace in front of the church there is a charming prospect of the vineyards on the banks of the Labe, the bridge over the river (below, to the right) and the junctions (to the left) of the Vltava Canal (in the foreground; to the south is an old lock) and the Vltava itself with the Labe.

Mělník: Castle and Church of SS Peter and Paul, above the Labe (Elbe)

Castle

The Renaissance castle of the Princes Lobkowitz (16th c.; in course of renovation) now houses a valuable collection of Baroque pictures (Petr Brandl. Karel Škréta, V. V. Reiner), the District Museum (local history and culture, vine-growing) and a wine bar.
More than 6000 hectolitres/130,000 gallons of wine can be stored in the castle cellars.

Town Hall
Town walls
Prague Gate

Other features of interest are the Old Town Hall (14th c.; rebuilt in Baroque style between 1765 and 1793) and the remains of the 13th century town walls, with the Prague Gate (*c.* 1500).

Surroundings of Mělník

Liběchov

7km/4½ miles north-west of Mělník on the right bank of the Labe, surrounded by vineyards, is Liběchov (alt. 163m/535ft; pop. 1100), at the entrance to the romantic Liběchov valley. The Renaissance Castle (16th c.) now houses a permanent exhibition on the cultures of the Asian peoples (from the Náprstek Museum in Prague). In the Baroque gardens (18th c.) is a group of figures carved from the living rock (19th c.).

Mt Říp

14km/8½ miles north-west of Mělník is Mt Říp (456m/1496ft), an isolated basalt hill, partly wooded, which is crowned by the Romanesque St George's Rotunda (with St George's Tower, 1126). Mt Říp – which has recently again become a place of pilgrimage – plays an important part in Czech mythology: according to an old Slav legend the forefather of the Czech people, Čech, led his tribe here so that they might settle in Bohemia (Čechy).

Veltrusy

14km/8½ miles south-west of Mělník the village of Veltrusy (alt. 175m/575ft; pop. 1700) has a Rococo castle of the Counts Chotek. The castle has a richly appointed interior (furniture, mirrors, tapestries, porcelain).
In the large and beautiful English-style park (mid 18th c.) are a number of romantic buildings. Here in 1754 was held the "Great Market of the Products of the Kingdom of Bohemia", an early trade fair.

Kokořín Castle

17km/10½ miles north-east of Mělník, above the beautiful Kokořín valley, in which the river Pšovka carves its way through rugged limestone rocks, and surrounded by dense forest, stands Kokořín Castle, a fine example of the romantic neo-Gothic style of the early 20th century. The castle was originally built in the 14th century but was badly damaged during the Hussite wars and was completely rebuilt in 1911–18.

Nature reserve

In the nearby Kokořínsko nature reserve are interesting rock formations and sandstone valleys.

Nelahozeves

18km/11 miles south-west of Mělník is Nelahozeves (alt. 185m/605ft; pop. 1500), with a Renaissance castle (1553–93) containing a collection of European art from the Gallery of Central Bohemia. The birthplace of the composer Antonín Dvořák (see Famous People) is now a museum.

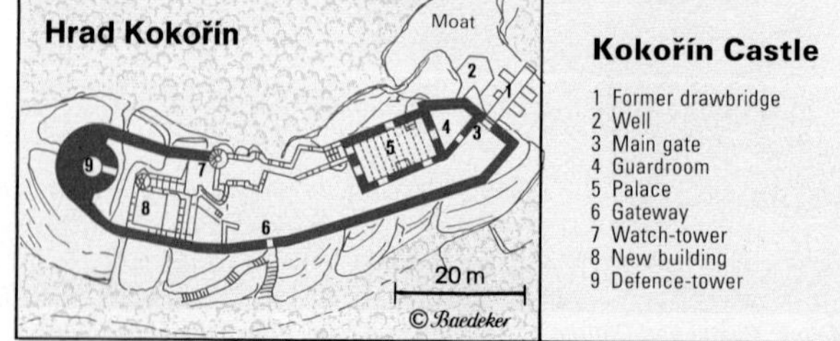

Roudnice nad Labem

20km/12½ miles north-west of Mělník is Roudnice nad Labem (alt. 195m/640ft; pop. 15,000), an old town on the left bank of the Labe with engineering and foodstuffs industries. The monumental Lobkowitz Palace (17th c.) in the market square is now occupied by an academy of military music and a picture gallery (works by modern Czech painters). Within the precincts of the palace can be found a former Capuchin friary with a church of 1615–28. To the west of the town are a former Augustinian monastery (Gothic), with a 14th century church (remodelled in Baroque style in 1725–34 by the Litoměřice architect Ottavio Broggio), and a Baroque chapel dedicated to St William (1726).

Mikulov F 4

Region: Southern Moravia
District: Břeclav
Altitude: 248m/814ft
Population: 7500

*Situation and characteristics

The Southern Moravian town of Mikulov, beautifully situated below the south side of the Pavlov Hills (Pavlovské Vrchy), is the chief town in a productive vegetable-, fruit- and vine-growing region (large wine cellars; giant cask of 1643 with a capacity of 1000 hectolitres/22,000 gallons). Among distinguished pupils of the Gymnasium (grammar school) have been the Czech scientist Jan Evangelista Purkyně (1787–1869), the Austrian President Karl Renner (1870–1950) and Adolf Schärf (1890–1965).

Sights

***Castle**

The town is dominated by the massive Baroque castle of the Princes Dietrichstein (originally a medieval castle of 1322; rebuilt and enlarged in 17th and 18th c.; restored after wartime destruction in 1945). Here on July

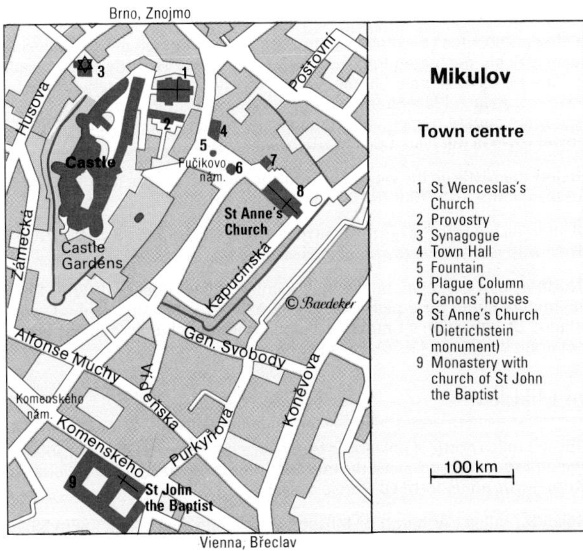

Mikulov Castle

26th 1866 was signed the preliminary peace treaty which ended the Austro-Prussian War.

Museum

The castle contains an interesting museum on the history of wine-production.

Churches

Other notable features are the Late Gothic parish church of St Wenceslas, with a richly decorated Rococo interior; the heavy High Baroque façade (1704–10) of St Anne's Church, whose original choir was rebuilt in neo-classical style in 1844–56 as a burial church; and a Trinity Column of 1723 in the main square, which is surrounded by handsome old houses. In the lower town is the Piarist Church (Baroque, 17th c.).

Jewish quarter

Below the castle on the west lies the former Jewish quarter (cemetery, with graves of the 17th–19th c.).

Kozí Vrch

A short distance to the north of the main square is the rocky Kozí Vrch (Goat Hill), with a medieval tower (extensive views).

Mt Kopeček

North-east of the town, on the bare summit of Mt Kopeček (363m/1191ft; 45-minute climb on a path lined by 18th century Stations of the Cross), stands St Sebastian's Church, a domed Baroque church (17th c.) with a separate bell-tower (1636). Far-ranging views.

Surroundings of Mikulov

Hustopeče

15km/9 miles north of Mikulov is Hustopeče (alt. 193m/633ft; pop. 3000), a wine-producing town since the mid 14th century. In the northern district of Kurdějov is a fine fortified Gothic church.

Velké Pavlovice

14km/8½ miles north-east of Mikulov is Velké Pavlovice (alt. 182m/597ft; pop. 3000), in one of the most important vine- and fruit-growing regions in southern Moravia. It was the birthplace of the famous philosopher and writer Rudolf Kassner (1873–1959).

Pavlov Hills

The Pavlov Hills (Pavlovské Hory) are an expanse of karstic terrain 30km/19 miles south of Brno (see entry) and just north of the Czech–Austrian frontier; the highest point is Mt Děvín (550m/1805ft). They consist of a series of sharp ridges with a rich steppe flora, the haunt of moufflon. The hills are crowned by the ruined castles of Divčí Hrady and Sirotčí Hrádek.
On the north side of the hills is a new system of reservoirs formed by dams, Nové Mlýny. Near here is the important mammoth-hunters' occupation site of Dolní Věstonice, where Stone Age material dating back 25,000 years has been found. There is a site museum; the famous "Venus of Veštonice" is now in the Moravian Museum in Brno.

Mladá Boleslav D 2

Region: Central Bohemia
District: Mladá Boleslav
Altitude: 235m/770ft
Population: 44,000

Situation and characteristics

The Central Bohemian district town of Mladá Boleslav, 55km/34 miles north of Prague (No. 10 motorway), has extensive industrial installations.
The Laurin and Klement car factory was established in Mladá Boleslav in 1905. It was succeeded in 1925 by the Škoda automobile plant, which since 1990 has been operating in association with Volkswagen.

Sights

Old town

The old town of Mladá Boleslav lies on a rocky hill above the river Jizera. The site was occupied in the 10th century by a castle which was rebuilt in Renaissance style in the 16th century and from the 18th century until 1953 served as a barracks; it is now occupied by the District Museum. In Old Town Square are the Old Town Hall (1559) and the Town Church (15th c., remodelled in Baroque style in the early 18th c.). The church of the Bohemian Brethren (mid 16th c.) is now an art gallery.

Surroundings of Mladá Boleslav

Kosmonosy

4km/2½ miles north is the industrial town of Kosmonosy, now part of Mladá Boleslav. Features of interest are the castle and monastery (both 17th c.) and a Baroque pilgrimage chapel (Loreto; early 18th c.).

Jabkenice

Jabkenice (alt. 230m/755ft), 12km/7½ miles south of Mladá Boleslav, boasts a Baroque forester's house in which the great Czech composer Bedřich Smetana (see Famous People) lived and composed from 1876 to 1884. In front of the house, which is now a museum, is a monument to Smetana. Nearby is a game park.

Mnichovo Hradiště D 2

Region: Central Bohemia
District: Mladá Boleslav
Altitude: 240m/785ft
Population: 7000

Situation and characteristics

The little Central Bohemian town of Mnichovo Hradiště, on the left bank of the Jizera, is a good centre from which to explore the Bohemian Paradise

Chapel containing Wallenstein's tomb, Mnichovo Hradiště

(see entry). It is an important centre of the automobile industry, producing the LIAZ lorries (now in association with Mercedes-Benz).

Sights

Castle

The early 17th century Renaissance castle of the Wallenstein family, remodelled in Baroque style in 1700, has a richly furnished interior. Of particular interest are the library, the Empire-style theatre and the collections of porcelain and weapons.

***Park**

In the castle's English-style park is a charming sala terrena.

Wallenstein's tomb

In the Baroque chapel of St Anne in the castle church can be seen the tomb of Albrecht von Wallenstein (see Famous People), the great general of the Thirty Years' War.

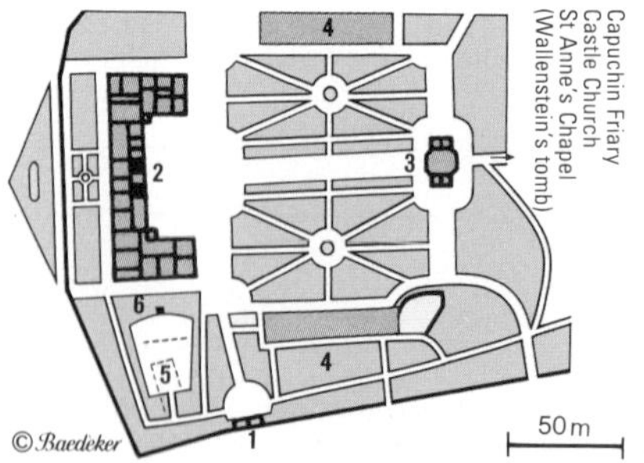

Mnichovo Hradiště

Zámecký park
Castle Park

1 Main entrance
2 Castle
3 Sala terrena
4 Domestic offices
5 Remains of Gothic church
6 Monument of Václav Budovec z Budova

Adjoining the park, on the right bank of the Jizera, is a former Capuchin friary (17th c.).

Surroundings of Mnichovo Hradiště

Mochelnice nad Jizerou

4km/2½ miles north of Mnichovo Hradiště, Mochelnice nad Jizerou (alt. 232m/761ft) has a Romanesque church of around 1260 (restored 1876).

Valečov

4km/2½ miles south-east of Mnichovo Hradiště are the ruins of Valečov Castle (alt. 355m/1165ft; 14th c.), which is partly hewn from the local sandstone.

Mt Mužský

5km/3 miles north-east of Mnichovo Hradiště is Mt Mužský (463m/1519ft; extensive views), a basalt hill – the most westerly outpost of the Jičín Uplands (Jičínská Pahorkatina) – on the slopes of which are interesting "rock cities" and archaeological sites.

Příhrazy

12km/7½ miles north-east of Mnichovo Hradiště lies Příhrazy (alt. 288m/945ft), a holiday resort with a camping site picturesquely situated in a rocky recess: a good base from which to explore the Bohemian Paradise (see entry).

Moravian Karst / Moravský Kras F 3

Region: Southern Moravia
Districts: Blansko and Brno-Venkov
Altitude: up to 600m/1970ft

Situation and morphology

Some 20km/12½ miles north-north-east of Brno (see entry) are the Drahan Uplands (Drahanská Vrchovina), an offshoot of the Bohemo-Moravian Highlands with peaks up to 735m/2412ft high. The central feature in this region is the Moravian Karst (Moravský Kras), a tract of Devonian limestones averaging 400–600m (1300–2000ft) in height which is bounded on the west by the river Svitava and dissected by its tributaries, some of them flowing underground.

*Stalactitic caves

*Macocha abyss

In the northern part of this karstic area (some 25km/15 miles long by 6km/4 miles across), which is furrowed by valleys (often dry) and patterned by dolines, gullies and extraordinary rock formations, are several magnificent stalactitic caves, in which palaeontologists have made important finds, and the mighty Macocha abyss.

Prehistoric finds

In the southern part of the karstic area traces of prehistoric man have been found in a number of caves, notably at Adamov in the Svitava valley (the "Bulls' Rock", Býčí Skála) and at Ochov u Brna in the Řička valley (the "Swedes' Table", Švédův Stůl, and the "Bakery", Pekárna). Finds from these sites can be seen in the Anthropos Museum in Brno.

Tour of the **Moravian Karst

(about 35km/22 miles; visits to caves 6–7 hours)

Starting point: Blansko

A good starting-point for a tour of the cave country is the district capital, Blansko (alt. 276m/906ft; pop. 20,000), which is easily reached from the main road from Brno to Svitavy (No. 43). Blansko has been an iron-working town since the Middle Ages; in its Renaissance castle is the Museum of the Moravian Karst.
From the railway station take Road 380, which runs south, crossing the river Svitava; then in 1.5km/1 mile, at the junction of the Punkva with

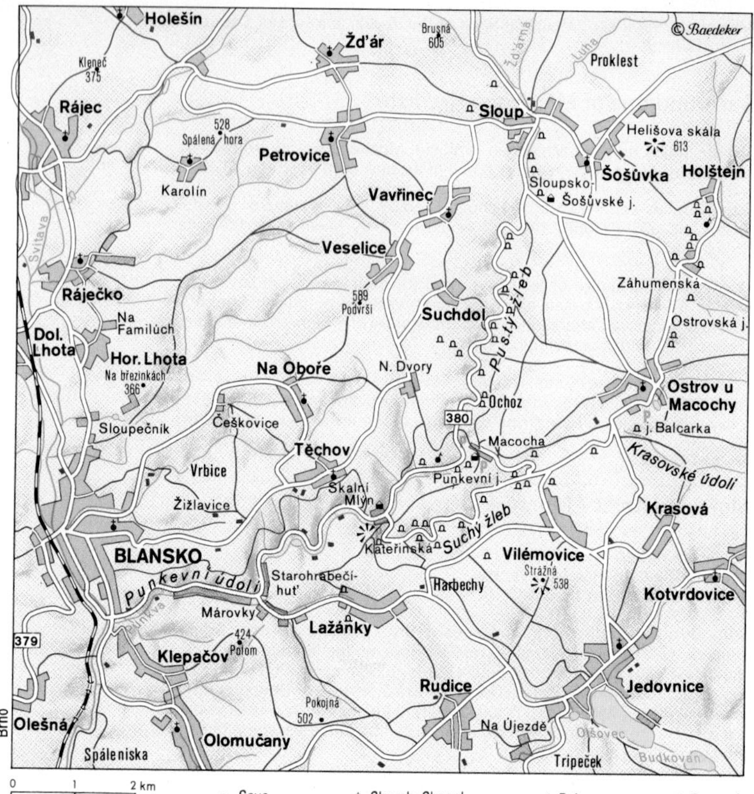

Moravian Karst

Moravský kras

the Svitava, turn left into a road up the Punkva valley (Punkevní Údolí) on the right bank of the river, passing the Blansko ironworks. In another 5.5km/3½ miles the road comes to the Skalní Mlýn inn, where the Suchý Žleb (Dry Valley) comes in on the right. 500m/550yd up this valley is the Catherine Cave (see below). The road continues up the Punkva valley. In another 1.5km/1 mile, below the road on the right, the river emerges from a 3m/10ft high opening in the rock after its underground passage through the Punkva caves. On the hill to the left are the ruins of Blansek Castle (13th c.; destroyed 1432).

***Punkva Caves**

Soon after the emergence of the Punkva, at the foot of the cliff on the right, is the entrance (alt. 370m/1214ft) to the extensive Punkva cave system (Punkevní jeskyně), a labyrinth of chambers and passages with a profusion of stalactites and stalagmites. The tour of these caves, which are also linked with the Catherine Cave, is a fascinating experience. Since many of the caves are filled with water from the Punkva, which flows through them, most of the trip has to be done by boat. It ends at two small lakes in the Macocha Abyss and, including the return to the entrance, takes two hours.

In the Punkva Caves

From the entrance to the Punkva Caves the road runs north-east in the direction of Sloup, following a winding course through the waterless Pustý Žleb (Empty Valley). In 6km/4 miles a country road – to be followed on the return journey – goes off on the right to Ostrov u Macochy. The main road continues into the fertile Sloup valley, which is bounded on the east by whitish-grey limestone crags 40–50m/130–165ft high, the upper slopes of which are wooded. On the right, at the foot of the crags, is the yawning entrance to the tunnel-shaped Kůlna ("Shed") cave, a prehistoric occupation site.

Farther on, also on the right, is the Hřebenáč or "Devil's Rock", an isolated crag, 76m/250ft in girth and 20m/65ft high, separated from the rest of the limestone massif by erosion. Near here the Sloup stream disappears underground.

Sloup and Šošůvka caves

Beyond this (500m/550yd from the turn-off for Ostrov) is the entrance to the Sloup and Šošůvka caves (Sloupsko-Šošůvké jeskyně), a system of parallel passages interrupted by chasms and gullies and of spacious chambers, with a great variety of stalactites and stalagmites. The system has a total length of more than 4km/2½ miles, of which 3km/2 miles are accessible. The tour of the accessible parts takes about 1½ hours.

Sloup

1km/¾ mile north is the village of Sloup (alt. 471m/1545ft; pop. 700), with a beautiful Baroque pilgrimage church of 1750 (frescoes).

To continue the round trip, turn back at Sloup and return along the same road. In 1km/¾ mile, where a road (No. 380) goes off on the right into the Pustý Žleb, take the road on the left, which passes through a field of dolines and comes in 3.5km/2 miles to the village of Ostrov u Macochy (alt. 485m/1590ft; pop. 1400), where the Holštejn valley comes in on the left. 3km/2 miles along this valley, in which are numerous caves and gullies, is the village of Holštejn.

Balcar cave

1km/¾ mile south-west of Ostrov u Macochy the road circles round the Balcar Crag (on left), at the foot of which is the entrance to the Balcar Cave (Jeskyně Balcarka), opened up between 1923 and 1935. A special feature of this cave system, which is on two levels, is the occurrence of translucent coloured stalactites and stalagmites. The tour of the caves takes about an hour.

From the Balcar Cave continue south-west, past some curious karstic formations on the right, and in 1.5km/1 mile turn off the road (which leads into the Suchý Žleb) into a road on the right which climbs up fairly steeply, with many bends, and traverses forest country.

****Macocha Abyss**

In another 1.5km/1 mile the road ends at a large car park near a mountain inn, the Chata na Macoše. From here it is only a few yards to the Upper Gloriette (490m/1610ft), a small viewing platform immediately above a rock face which plunges vertically down for 138m/453ft into the wild Macocha Abyss. The Macocha ("Stepmother"), a vast cavity 281m/307yd long by 126m/137yd across, was formed by the collapse of the roof of a karstic cave. At the bottom are two small lakes and an entrance to the Punkva Caves (see above). A winding path (waymarked) leads down from the Upper Gloriette by way of the Lower Bridge (442m/1450ft; good view into the abyss) to the bottom; the walk takes about half an hour.

After seeing the Macocha return to the car park and follow the same road back for 1.5km/1 mile; then turn off into a road on the right which follows a winding course through the Suchý Žleb (Dry Valley), which at some points is extremely narrow.

Catherine Cave

In 2.5km/1½ miles the road comes to a pointed arch in the rock (on the right) which is the entrance to the Catherine Cave (Kateřinská Jeskyně), a drip-

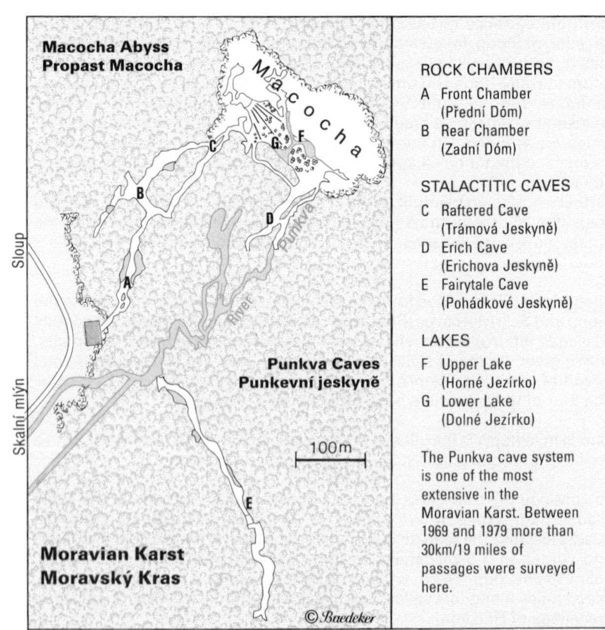

stone cave with three large chambers in which the bones of a prehistoric cave bear were found. The most striking feature of this cave is the "Stalagmite Forest", with large numbers of remarkably thin stalagmites up to 4m/13ft high. The visit takes about half an hour.

500m/550yd beyond this is the Steinmühle inn, where the road crosses the Punkva. The return to the starting-point of the tour at Blansko is on Road 380, following the right bank of the river.

Rájec

The tour can be rounded off by a visit to the little town of Rájec (alt. 295m/970ft; pop. 3000), 6.5km/4 miles north of Blansko, with an elegant Rococo castle (1763–69) which belonged to the Princes of Salm and is set in a charming English-style park. It has a fine picture gallery (in particular works by 17th century Dutch masters).

Other Places Around Blansko

Jedovnice

7km/4½ miles east of Blansko is Jedovnice, a popular summer resort with the large Olšovec pond (42 hectares/104 acres).

Vranov

Vranov (alt. 465m/1525ft), 7km/4½ miles south of Blansko, has a Baroque pilgrimage church, a Baroque monastery and the burial vault of the Liechtenstein family, in Empire style (1819–22).

Bořitov

8km/5 miles north-west of Blansko is Bořitov (alt. 305m/1000ft), with a church (originally Romanesque but rebuilt before 1500) containing Romanesque and Gothic frescoes.

Křtiny

In Křtiny (alt. 417m/1368ft), 10km/6 miles south-east of Blansko, can be seen a Baroque pilgrimage church with a fine interior (frescoes) and a Baroque castle (1660, with later alterations).

Lysice

14km/8½ miles north-west of Blansko is Lysice (alt. 362m/1188ft). Features of interest are the Castle (Renaissance, with alterations in Baroque and Empire style) and the Empire colonnade in the castle gardens (fine interiors).

Moravo-Silesian Beskyds / Moravskoslezské Beskydy H 3

Region: Northern Moravia
Districts: Frýdek-Místek and Vsetín

Situation and *topography

The picturesque Moravo-Silesian Beskyds (Moravskoslezské Beskydy) consist of a northern part with a number of short ridges ranging in height between 1100m/3600ft and 1325m/4350ft (Radhost', 1192m/3911ft; Smrk, 1276m/4187ft; Lysá Hora, 1323m/4341ft), the Vsetín Hills (Vsetínské Vrchy) to the south and the eastern ranges – the Zadní Hory (Bilý Kříž) and the Javorníky – which form the frontier with Slovakia.

Rivers

The most important river in this area is the Ostravice, a right-bank tributary of the Odra (Oder). The Bečva, flowing south, is a left-bank tributary of the Morava. There are a number of artificial lakes formed by dams – Bystřička, Horní Bečva, Olešná, Žermanice – which provide facilities for recreation. The Ostravice and Morávka reservoirs supply drinking water to the Ostrava industrial region.

Tourist attractions

The hills are densely wooded, and there are some tracts of primeval forest. There are numerous attractive viewpoints, on the lower ridges as well as on the highest peaks.

The area offers excellent scope for ridge walks and winter sports (particularly langlauf skiing, for example. at Pustevny).

Moravská Třebová F 3

Region: Eastern Bohemia
District: Svitavy
Altitude: 408m/1339ft
Population: 12,000

Situation and characteristics

Moravská Třebová, 55km/34 miles west-north-west of Olomouc (see entry), was founded in the 13th century and laid out on a regular grid plan centred on the large market square which has largely preserved its medieval aspect. The old town centre is now a conservation area. The town has some industry (engineering, silk-weaving).

Sights

Castle

At the south-east corner of the old town is the Castle, a Late Renaissance building with three wings enclosing a central courtyard; it was built in 1612–18, during a period of prosperity, on the site of an earlier medieval castle. The gate is earlier (1493), and indeed is the earliest Renaissance structure in Moravia. The whole castle is in course of restoration.

***Market square**

On the south side of the market square, which is surrounded by Late Gothic and Renaissance burghers' houses, stands the Town Hall (originally Gothic; rebuilt in Renaissance style 1560–65). In the centre of the square is a Plague Column (1717–20).

Parish church

To the south of the Town Hall is the parish church of the Assumption (altered and enlarged in Baroque style from 1726 onwards), with rich fresco decoration and fine Baroque paintings.

Piarist College

At the north-east corner of the old town is the former Piarist College (Baroque, 18th c.).

Town walls
Municipal Park

At several points around the old town there are remains of the old town walls. In the Municipal Park can be seen busts of Smetana and the German poet and dramatist Friedrich Schiller.

Surroundings of Moravská Třebová

Zábřeh

18km/11 miles north-east of Moravská Třebová is Zábřeh (alt. 285m/935ft; pop. 15,000), an industrial town in a beautiful setting on the north side of

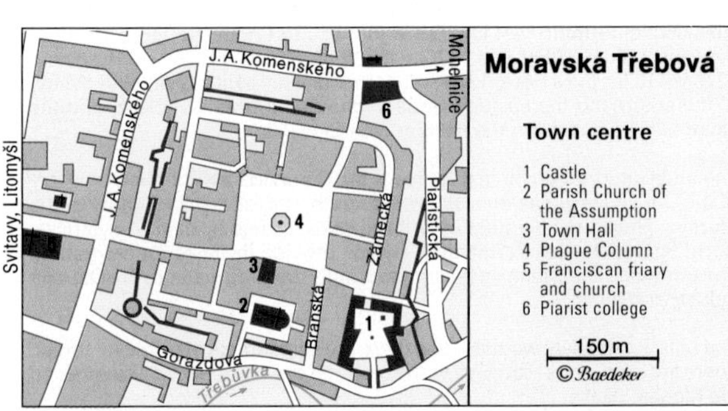

the Zábřeh Highlands (Zábřezšká Vrchovina). It preserves a Renaissance house (1581) in which the young Comenius (see Famous People) lived for a time and found his wife.

Mohelnice

18km/11 miles east of Moravská Třebová is Mohelnice (alt. 275m/900ft; pop. 7000), an old town with remains of Gothic fortifications and a town gate of 1540. The Gothic Decanal Church (early 15th c.) has a tall tower which dominates the town. Numerous traces of Neolithic settlement have been found in the surrounding area (museum in square outside church).

Úsov

8km/5 miles east of Mohelnice, in the village of Úsov (alt. 285m/935ft), is an Early Baroque castle (17th c.) which belonged to the Liechtenstein family; it now houses an old hunting and forestry museum.

Mladeč

24km/15 miles east of Moravská Třebová is Mladeč (alt. 242m/794ft). Near the village are caves formed during the Ice Age in which important archaeological discoveries were made.

Bouzov

The village of Bouzov (alt. 366m/1201ft), 16km/10 miles south-east of Moravská Třebová, has a massive 14th century castle (rebuilt around 1900) which belonged to the Teutonic Order. It has a richly appointed interior in neo-Gothic style; in the chapel are the tombs of Masters of the Order.

Javoříčko

18km/11 miles south-east of Moravská Třebová is the village of Javoříčko, which was destroyed on May 5th 1945 and later rebuilt. There is a monument commemorating the event.
In the karstic terrain above the village are a number of dripstone caves.

Bilá Lhota

20km/12½ miles south-east of Moravská Třebová is Bilá Lhota (alt. 287m/942ft), with a Baroque castle and an interesting park (arboretum laid out for purposes of study).

Most C 2

Region: Northern Bohemia
District: Most
Altitude: 245m/805ft
Population: 70,000

Situation and development

The Northern Bohemian district town of Most, on the river Bílina, is an industrial centre which owes its importance to the rich seams of lignite in the area and to its chemical plants.
In the 1960s and 1970s the whole of the old town centre and some of the surrounding housing areas were pulled down to allow the deposits of lignite under the town to be worked and were replaced by huge blocks of modern flats on the outskirts. As a result Most is now a faceless and rather depressing industrial town, and the site of the old town is a huge hole in the ground from which the lignite is extracted by opencast methods. Of the old buildings only the church has been preserved.

Church of the Assumption

The fine old Late Gothic hall-church of the Assumption which once stood on the south side of the market square was built between 1517 and 1549 to the design of Jakob von Schweinfurt and renovated in the 18th century.

The decision was taken in 1964 to move the church to a new site outside the area of the coal workings, and the immense operation was carried through in October 1975. The main part of the church, measuring 57m/157ft by 28m/92ft and weighing something like 12,000 tons, was supported on 53 cradles and transported to its new site, 841 metres (over half a mile) away, at the rate of 1–3 centimetres a minute (2–6 feet an hour). The church's 16th century tower was taken down and rebuilt stone by stone. Restoration work on the church was still continuing in 1993.

The old town of Most before its demolition (centre, the Church of the Assumption)

The Church of the Assumption now stands by itself among old factory buildings on the edge of the coal workings. In a two-storey substructure under the church are displays illustrating the archaeological investigation of the church, its history and furnishings and the technique used to move it to its new site.

Castle Hill

From the old outlook tower on Castle Hill (411m/1348ft), south-west of the town, there is a extensive view of the industrial landscape, devastated by opencast mining.

Opencast coal workings on the site of the old town

Surroundings of Most

Motor-racing circuit

South-west of the rebuilt town of Most, near the intersection of Roads 15 and 27, is a racing circuit for motorcycles and sports cars (4.15km/2.6 miles long, with ten bends), which has recently been modified to bring it up to modern requirements.

Náchod F 2

Region: Eastern Bohemia
District: Náchod
Altitude: 350m/1150ft
Population: 22,000

Situation, characteristics and history

The Eastern Bohemian district town of Náchod, on the river Metuje, is an industrial centre of some importance (textiles, chemicals, construction of engines). It was the scene of a battle in 1866, during the Austro-Prussian War, in which the Prussians defeated the Austrians, enabling the Prussian army to enter Bohemia.

Sights

***Castle**

Above the town rears the Castle (Zámek), which once belonged to the Princes of Schaumburg-Lippe. In was built between 1556 and 1614 on the site of a medieval frontier fort (13th c.), from which a round tower survives, and enlarged in 1650–59 by Carlo Lurago. It contains a rich collection of pictures, Dutch tapestries, etc., and there is fine stucco decoration in the chapel. From the terrace there are extensive views.

St Lawrence's Church

In the centre of the town's main square is the Gothic church of St Lawrence (14th c., with 16th c. alterations in Renaissance style). It has two domed wooden towers, popularly known as Adam and Eve.

New Town Hall

The New Town Hall (1902–04) has sgraffito decoration by Nikoláš Aleš.

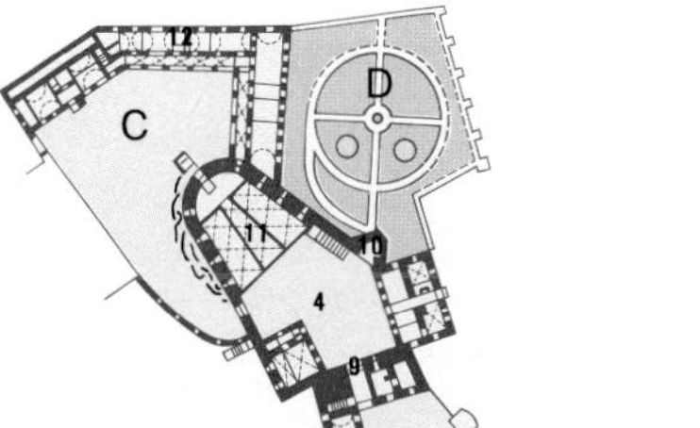

Náchod · Náchod
Zámek · Castle

A Old Castle of the Lords of Smiřice
B Piccolomini Building
C 18th c. addition
D French Garden

1 First courtyard
2 Second (upper) courtyard (arcades on two sides)
3 Third (lower) courtyard
4 Fourth courtyard
5 Great Tower (remains of a medieval Gothic castle)
6 Small Tower
7 Circular bastion
8 Chapel (Lady-chapel, with early Baroque stucco doors)
9 Piccolmini Portal
10 Garden pavilion
11 "Turion" Bastion (inside are original stables; above a later theatre)
12 North portal (*c.* 1730)

Surroundings of Náchod

Běloves 3km/2 miles north-east of Náchod, at a frontier crossing into Poland, is the little spa of Běloves (alt. 352m/1155ft). The well-known Ida mineral water is bottled here.

Mt Dobrošov 3km/2 miles south-east of Náchod is Mt Dobrošov (624m/2047ft), with the Jirásek mountain hut and an outlook tower from which there are views of the Orlík Hills (see entry) and the Glatz uplands in Poland. A short distance away are remains of fortifications built before the Second World War.

Rozkoš 7km/4½ miles south-west of Náchod the small artificial lake of Rozkoš (10sq.km/4sq.miles), formed in 1972, has facilities for bathing and water sports on its north side.

Česká Skalice 8km/5 miles south-west of Náchod is the town of Česká Skalice (alt. 284m/932ft; pop. 5000), in which the Czech writer Božena Němcová (1820–62) spent her early years. Notable features of the town are the Baroque church (fine carved altar), the neo-Gothic Town Hall (19th c.) and a 19th century fountain.

Ratibořice 8km/5 miles west of Náchod is Ratibořice Castle, built in 1708. Here in 1813 King Frederick William III of Prussia, Tsar Alexander I of Russia and the Austrian Chancellor Prince Metternich met, as guests of Princess Zaháňská, to discuss common action against Napoleon. Božena Němcová immortalised the castle and surrounding area in her novel "Babička" ("The Grandmother"), and as a result this much visited part of the Úpa valley (now a nature reserve) is known as Grandmother's Valley (Babiččino Údolí). The buildings mentioned in the novel (Staré Bělidlo, Old Bleach-Field) have been restored and are open to the public. Near the castle (chestnut avenue) is a piece of sculpture by O. Gutfreund (1922), "Grandmother and Children".

Náchod Castle rising above the houses of the town

Červený Kostelec

12km/7½ miles north-west of Náchod is the industrial town of Červený Kostelec (alt. 414m/1358ft; pop. 8500), with a Gothic church remodelled in Baroque style.

Rtyně v Podkrkonoší

The little mining town of Rtyně v Podkrkonoší (alt. 405m/1330ft; pop. 3000), 16km/10 miles north-west of Náchod, has an Early Baroque church (1679) with a wooden bell-tower (16th c.) and a memorial to the peasant rising of 1775.

Malé Svatoňovice

20km/12½ miles north-west of Náchod is the summer resort of Malé Svatoňovice (alt. 441m/1447ft; pop. 1500), with the birthplace of the writer Karel Čapek (1890–1938), a museum devoted to the brothers Karel and Josef Čapek (see Famous People) and a Baroque pilgrimage church.

Nové Město nad Metují F 2

Region: Eastern Bohemia
District: Náchod
Altitude: 332m/1089ft
Population: 10,000

*Situation and characteristics

The Eastern Bohemian town of Nové Město nad Metují, founded in 1501, is picturesquely situated on a rocky hill enclosed within a bend on the river Metuje, under the north-west side of the Orlík Hills (see entry).

Sights

Market square

The rectangular market square is lined with 16th century arcaded houses. On the north side of the square stands the Town Hall. In the centre of the square are sculptures of the Virgin and the Holy Trinity.

Castle

The Renaissance castle (16th c.; remodelled in Early Baroque style in 17th c.; renovated about 1910) has a striking cylindrical tower. It contains a permanent exhibition on the Antarctic.

Park

In the park surrounding the castle (replanned at the beginning of the 20th century) are some fine pieces of Baroque sculpture.

Parish church

Near the south end of the market square is the Late Gothic parish church of the Holy Trinity (1523).

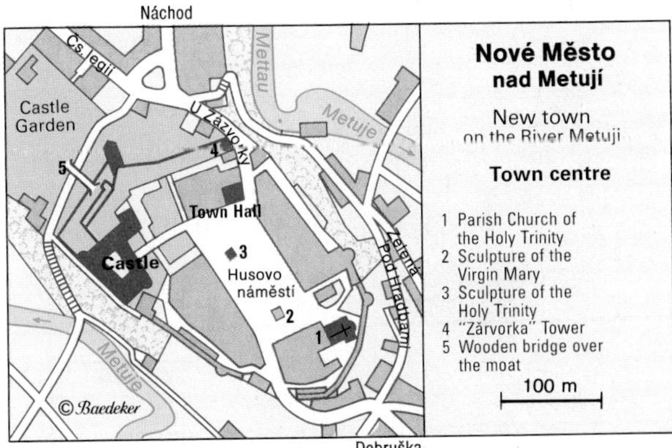

Town walls

There are considerable remains of the old town walls.

Surroundings of Nové Město nad Metují

***Metuje valley**

The beautiful rocky and deeply indented valley of the Metuje, north-east of the town, offers the possibility of attractive excursions.

Slavoňov

4km/2½ miles east of Nové Město nad Metují in the village of Slavoňov can be seen a fine wooden church of 1553 with a separate bell-tower.

Dobruška

7km/4½ miles south-east of Nové Město nad Metují is Dobruška (alt. 287m/942ft; pop. 7000), a small town with engineering and textile industries which at the turn of the 18th–19th centuries was an important centre of the Czech revival movement. In the market square is the Renaissance Town Hall (second half of 16th century), with a tall tower which dominates the town.

Opočno

11km/7 miles south of Nové Město nad Metují is Opočno (alt. 292m/958ft; pop. 3000), with a large Renaissance palace which belonged to the Counts Colloredo, built in 1560–67 on the site of a medieval castle. It contains valuable collections of pictures, weapons, etc. In the park is a Renaissance church (altered in 1716).
In 1813 the treaty establishing the coalition of Russia, Prussia and Austria-Hungary against Napoleon was signed in Opočno.

Nový Jičín

G/H 3

Region: Northern Moravia
District: Nový Jičín
Altitude: 285m/935ft
Population: 29,000

Situation and characteristics

The Northern Moravian district town of Nový Jičín is an industrial centre with an old-established hat factory; also textiles, cigarette manufacture and engineering.

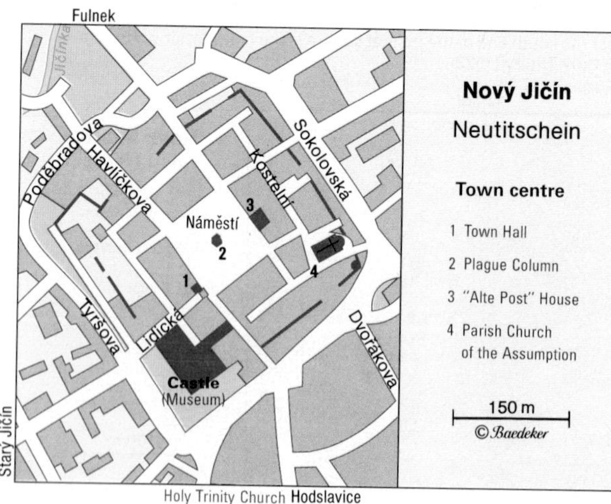

Market square, Nový Jičín

Nový Jičín, which obtained its municipal charter and the right to levy tolls in 1313, is the chief place in the Kravarško district ("Cow Country"), a cattle-farming area which extends along the upper course of the Odra (Oder) to Fulnek (see Ostrava, Surroundings). From the 11th century until the end of the Second World War this was a German linguistic island.
The famous Hückel hat factory was established in Nový Jičín in 1799 and in the course of the 19th century developed into one of the largest hat factories in the world. Nový Jičín is still known as a hat-making town.

Sights

***Market square**

In the market square, which is surrounded by charming arcaded houses, are a Plague Column of 1718 and the amusing Peasants Fountain (by F. Barwig, 18th c.). At the south corner of the square stands the Town Hall, on the north-east side the Old Post-House (Stará Pošta, 1563).

Castle

At the south end of the old town is the Castle (Zámek; 16th–17th c.), which contains a number of very different special collections. The Hat Museum illustrates and explains the local hat-making industry; another museum is devoted to car lights and radiators; and there is also a folk museum.

Parish church

The parish church of the Assumption, at the east end of the old town, dates in its present Baroque form from 1729–36; the tower is Renaissance.

Town walls

Around the old town centre are considerable stretches of the old town walls.

Surroundings of Nový Jičín

Starý Jičín

4km/2½ miles south-west of Nový Jičín, below the ruins of a Gothic castle (alt. 485m/1590ft; 13th c., destroyed in 17th c.), lies the little town of Starý

Jičín (alt. 374m/1227ft; pop. 2000), built between the 15th and 17th centuries.

Sedlnice

8km/5 miles north-east of Nový Jičín is the village of Sedlnice (alt. 254m/833ft), with a Baroque castle (now a House of Culture) in which the German Romantic poet and writer Joseph von Eichendorff (1788–1857) frequently stayed.

Hodslavice

8km/5 miles south of Nový Jičín we come to Hodslavice (alt. 337m/1106ft; pop. 2000), with a wooden church of 1551 and the birthplace of the leading Czech historian František Palacký (see Famous People).

Olomouc

G 3

Region: Northern Moravia
District: Olomouc
Altitude: 221m/725ft. Population: 106,000

Situation and characteristics

The Northern Moravian city of Olomouc (German Olmütz) is beautifully situated in the fertile Haná plain on both banks of the river Morava at the inflow of the Bystřice and the Střední Morava (Middle Morava). It is a university town and the see of a Roman Catholic archbishop, with three theatres and a well-known symphony orchestra. Among its principal industries are foodstuffs and engineering.

With its many beautiful churches, handsome palaces and fountain-decked squares Olomouc is one of the most attractive tourist destinations in the Czech Republic.

History

The town first appears in the records in 1055. In 1063 it became the see of a bishop and in the 13th century a residence of the Přemyslid kings and capital of Moravia. Thereafter, with the influx of German settlers, the town enjoyed a period of prosperity during which numerous churches and religious houses were built. In the Hussite wars Olomouc was on the Catholic side. A Jesuit school founded in 1566 became in 1573 Olomouc University. In 1778 the University was transferred to Brno (although the Olomouc faculty of law continued to exist until 1855), but in 1946 it reopened in Olomouc as the Palacký University. During the period of Swedish occupation (1642–50) in the Thirty Years' War most of the town's Gothic and Renaissance buildings were destroyed, and in 1642 Brno displaced Olomouc as capital of Moravia. In the 18th century, during the reign of the Empress Maria Theresa, a splendid new Baroque town came into being on

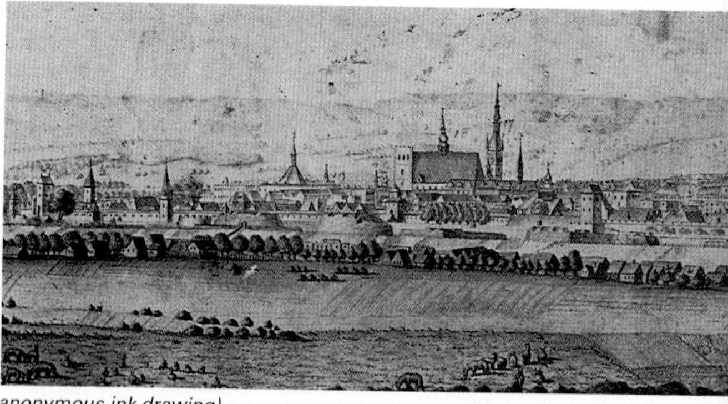

Olomouc in 1756 (anonymous ink drawing)

the medieval site. The fortifications built in 1742–54, which hampered the expansion of the town, were pulled down in 1888 and replaced by parks and gardens. In 1778, when the University moved to Brno, the southern part of the diocese of Olomouc was transferred to the newly created bishopric of Brno, and Olomouc became the see of an archbishop. During the revolutionary events of 1848 the Austrian imperial family fled from Vienna to Olomouc; the Emperor Ferdinand abdicated in favour of Francis Joseph, who took over in Olomouc as the Emperor Francis Joseph I. Until the First World War Olomouc was a predominantly German town.

Sights

***Upper Square**

In the centre of the city is the Upper Square (Horní Náměstí). Among the finest houses in the square are the Petráš Palace and the House at the Sign of the Golden Stag.

***Town Hall**

The Town Hall in the centre of the square was built between 1378 and 1607. Originally a merchant's house standing on the site of an earlier Gothic building of 1261, it has a 70m/230ft high tower from the top of which there are extensive views. On the north side of the Town Hall is a large astronomical clock (1420–22) which was destroyed at the end of the Second World War and restored in the 1950s to the design of Karel Svolinský. On the east side, rising above a flight of steps, is a loggia in Late Renaissance style (1564). Under the steps can be found a magnificent Renaissance doorway (1592).

Inside the Town Hall a fine Renaissance staircase leads up to the Gothic Knights' Hall (15th c.).

A notable feature of the interior is St Jerome's Chapel (*c.* 1550), the small Late Gothic choir of which forms an oriel on the south side of the Town Hall.

***Trinity Column**

At the north-west corner of the square a 32m/105ft high Trinity Column (by Render, Zohner and Scherauf, 1754) is the largest and most magnificent in the country, with 18 gilded copper statues.

Hercules Fountain

Farther east is the Hercules Fountain (1668–87).

Caesar Fountain

At the south-east corner of the Town Hall is the Caesar Fountain (1715–25), with an equestrian statue of Caesar and his dog. (There is a legend that Olomouc was founded by Caesar).

Theatre

On the west side of the Upper Square stands the Theatre (Divadlo O. Stibora; by the Viennese architect Kornhäusel, 1830), where the conductor and composer Gustav Mahler (see Famous People) and the actor Max Pallenberg (1877–1934) began their careers.

Lower Square
Neptune Fountain
Marian Column
Jupiter Fountain

To the south of the Upper Square is the triangular Lower Square (Dolní Náměstí), with two beautiful fountains: to the north the Neptune Fountain (1695), to the south the Jupiter Fountain (1707). Between the two can be seen a Marian Column (1716–26).

Haunschild House

Among the finest buildings in the square are the Haunschild House (late 16th c.), with a richly decorated Renaissance doorway and oriel, and the house at No. 174.

Capuchin Church

On the south side of the square are the Capuchin Church, with a plain and modest façade, and the former conventual buildings.

Žerotín Palace

A little way north of the Lower Square the Žerotín Palace now houses a section of the Municipal Museum (see below).

Salesianum

Still farther north, in Žerotín Square (Žerotínovo Náměstí), is the Salesianum, formerly an archiepiscopal seminary for the training of priests and now the Educational Institute of the University.

Dominican friary

To the left of the Salesianum stands a former Dominican friary, with a large neo-classical portico.

***St Michael's Church**

Immediately adjoining the Dominican friary is St Michael's Church (Kostel Svatého Michala; originally Gothic; remodelled in Baroque style 1674–1700), with three striking domes and a richly furnished interior.

***St Maurice's Church**

To the north of the Upper Square, in St Maurice's Square, can be found St Maurice's Church (Kostel Svatého Mořice; 15th–16th c.), a massive Gothic hall-church with unfinished towers (fine views from top). Notable features of the spacious interior are a superb Late Gothic pulpit and a large Baroque organ from the workshop of the Breslau organ-builder Engler.

Mercury Fountain

The charming Mercury Fountain (1730) lies a little way west of St Maurice's Church

Republic Square

From St Maurice's Church Pekařská Ulice (Bakers' Lane) and Denisova Ulice, one of the town's principal streets, lead to the triangular Republic Square (Náměstí Republiky), with the beautiful Triton Fountain (1707–08).

***Church of Our Lady of the Snows**

At the near end of the square, on right, is the large Baroque church of Our Lady of the Snows (Kostel Panny Marie Sněžné), built by the Jesuits in 1712–19 on the site of an earlier church, with a richly decorated doorway and brilliantly coloured ceiling paintings.

***Municipal Museum**

On the north side of Republic Square, housed in a former Convent of Poor Clares and its large church, is the Municipal Museum (Městské Muzeum), with rich mineralogical, botanical, zoological (particularly insects), Egyptological, numismatic and ethnographic collections, a large herbarium with some 70,000 plants from all over the world and a collection of graphic art.

Head Post Office

At the south-east corner of Republic Square stands the Head Post Office.

University

From the Head Post Office Křížkovský Lane (Ulice Křížkovského) runs south-east between old canons' houses to the main building of the University, refounded in 1946 as the Palacký University (Palackého Universita), and the Faculty of Philosophy. From here Wurmova Ulice (fine doorways) leads north, passing on the right the State Archives (Statní Archiv), to Bishop's Square (Biskupské Náměstí). On the east side of this square the Archbishop's Palace (1664–74) also houses a gallery of European art.

Arsenal

On the south side of Bishop's Square is the Arsenal (Zbrojnice), built in 1771.

From here Wurmova Ulice continues north, crosses 1st May Street (Třída Prvního Máje), which runs south-west to Republic Square, and joins

Trinity Column in Olomouc's Upper Square ▶

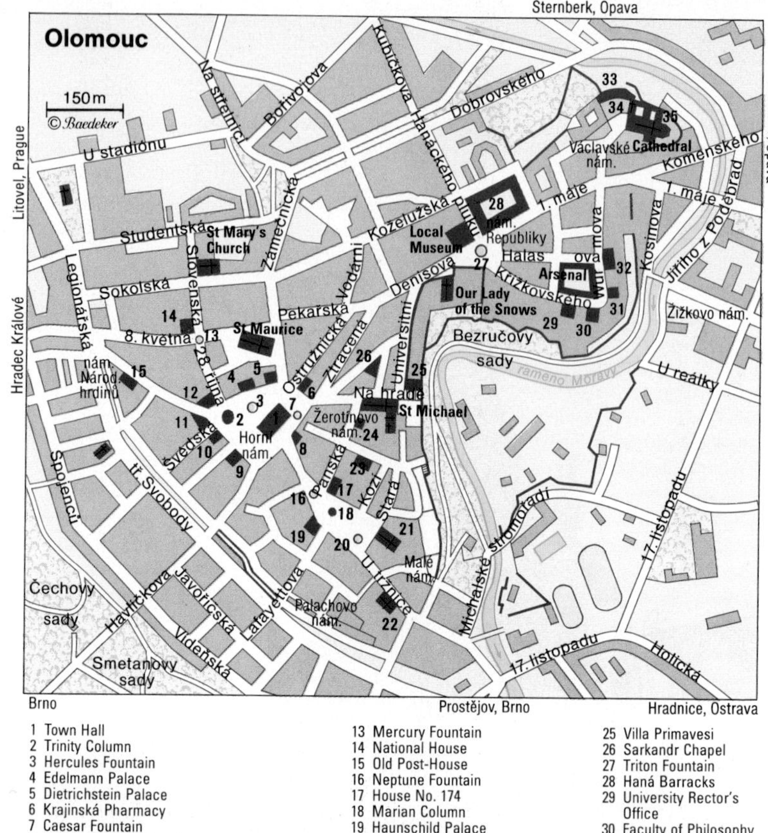

1 Town Hall
2 Trinity Column
3 Hercules Fountain
4 Edelmann Palace
5 Dietrichstein Palace
6 Krajinská Pharmacy
7 Caesar Fountain
8 House At the Golden Stag
9 Oldřich Stibor Theatre
10 Baroque palace
11 Petráš Palace
12 Salm Palace
13 Mercury Fountain
14 National House
15 Old Post-House
16 Neptune Fountain
17 House No. 174
18 Marian Column
19 Haunschild Palace
20 Jupiter Fountain
21 Capuchin Church
22 St Catherine's Church
23 Žerotin Palace
24 Faculty of Education
25 Villa Primavesi
26 Sarkandr Chapel
27 Triton Fountain
28 Haná Barracks
29 University Rector's Office
30 Faculty of Philosophy
31 State Archives
32 Archbishop's Palace
33 Former Deanery
34 St Anne's Chapel
35 Přemyslid Palace

Domská Ulice (Cathedral Lane), leading to Wenceslas Square (Václavské Náměstí), which with the Cathedral and surrounding buildings occupies the site of an old Slav stronghold on a hill falling steeply down to the Middle Morava.

***Cathedral**

On the east side of Wenceslas Square is the Gothic Cathedral of St Wenceslas (Chrám or Dóm Svatého Václava), originally a Romanesque basilica, built in 1107–31, in the time of Bishop Jindřich Zdík, altered and rebuilt in Gothic style in the 13th, 14th and 16th centuries and restored in the neo-Gothic manner in 1883–90, with a 100m/330ft high east tower, two neo-Gothic west towers and some remains of Romanesque work. The interior of the Cathedral is impressive, with a neo-Gothic altar, richly carved choir-stalls, bishops' tombs and a famous and valuable treasury.

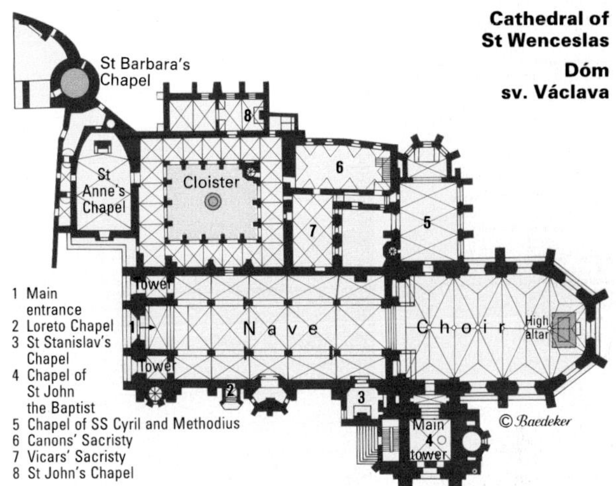

St Anne's Chapel, to the left of the west front, is where the bishops of Olomouc were formerly elected. Beyond it is a round tower, originally part of the Romanesque fortifications, containing St Barbara's Chapel.

St Anne's Chapel
St Barbara's Chapel

On the east side of St Anne's Chapel is the Gothic Cloister (Křížová Chodba; 14th c.), with fine ceiling paintings of around 1500. On its north side can be seen the chapel of St John the Baptist (Kaple Svatého Jana Křtitele).

Cloister

On the east side of the cloister stands the Sacristy, which is built into the Romanesque Přemyslid palace. High up on the wall is a Romanesque double window from the old palace (*c.* 1200).

Sacristy

On the north side of Wenceslas Square is the Deanery (now a University institute), in which Mozart lay ill with smallpox for six weeks in 1767.

Deanery

1km/¾ mile north of the Cathedral, beyond the river Morava, is the Baroque Hradsko Abbey (Klášter Hradsko; 17th and 18th c.). Originally a Benedictine house, it was taken over by the Premonstratensians, and later became a hospital. It contains fine ceiling paintings and sculpture.

Hradsko Abbey

To the south of the Upper Square, in the broad Třída Svobody (Freedom Street), is the Theresa Gate (Terezská Brána; 18th c.), a relic of the old fortifications which were pulled down in 1886.

Theresa Gate

Still farther south, on the south side of the old town, lies the large Smetana Park (Smetanovy Sady), in which (along with other parks in the town) the Flóra garden show, with international participation, is regularly held.
In the southern part of the park are a large palm house and other hothouses.

Smetana Park

Surroundings of Olomouc

7km/4½ miles north of Olomouc the "Sacred Mount", Svatý Kopeček (412m/1352ft) the most southerly outlier of the Jeseníky (see entry), is topped by a large and conspicuous 17th century pilgrimage church (interior remodelled in 18th c.).

Mt Kopeček

Art Nouveau decoration in Prostějov

Plumlov Castle

Ústín

7km/4½ miles west of Olomouc in the village of Ústín (alt. 238m/781ft) can be seen some fine examples of the traditional architecture of the Haná plain, including a farmhouse with arcades (now occupied by the Communal Council), the Baroque "Swan" inn ("U Labutě") and a 17th century stone bridge.

Příkazy

10km/6 miles north-west of Olomouc is the village of Příkazy (alt. 226m/742ft), where an open-air museum of the traditional architecture of the Haná plain is in course of development.

***Šternberk**

16km/10 miles north of Olomouc, beautifully situated on the south-western edge of the Moravian Uplands (see Jeseníky, Nízký Jeseník), is Šternberk (alt. 238m/781ft; pop. 17,000). Above the town stands a castle which belonged to the Princes of Liechtenstein; originally built in the 13th century (with only one round tower dating from that period), it was rebuilt and restored in the 16th and 19th centuries. It contains fine art collections (sculpture, faience, Czech Gothic art, Dutch and Italian painters of the 15th and 17th centuries, historic old stoves). In the barbican is a watch and clock museum (the Prim watch factory is in Šternberk).
Near the castle is a former Augustinian monastery, with a church remodelled in the 18th century (fine Baroque interior).

Prostějov

The district town of Prostějov (alt. 223m/732ft; pop. 48,000), lying 16km/10 miles south-west of Olomouc, is an industrial centre (textiles, agricultural machinery). It has a handsome Town Hall of 1521 (collection of historic old clocks), a castle of 1526, the Holy Cross Church (originally 14th c., with much later alteration) and an 18th century Baroque church. There are some remains of the medieval town walls.
Prostějov was the birthplace of the philosopher Edmund Husserl (1859–1938), founder of phenomenology, and the Czech poet Jiří Wolker (1900–24).

Plumlov Castle

7km/4½ miles west of Prostějov, on the edge of the Drahan Uplands (Drahanská Vrchovina) and above a small dam on the river Hloučela, can be seen Plumlov Castle (17th c.).

Náměšť na Hané

18km/11 miles west of Olomouc, under the east side of the Drahan Uplands, which bound the fertile Haná plain on the west, is Náměšť na Hané (alt. 247m/810ft), with the Late Baroque Upper Castle (1760–63), a beautiful park and a collection of historic coaches belonging to the bishops and archbishops of Olomouc. The well-known Hannaki harvest festival (Hanácké dožinky) is held here annually in autumn.

Litovel

19km/12 miles north-west of Olomouc lies the little town of Litovel (alt. 250m/820ft; pop. 10,000), an old settlement of the Hannaki (people of the Haná plain), with remains of its 15th century town walls, St Mark's Church (originally Gothic, rebuilt in 17th c.), a Plague Column in the market square and a number of historic old houses. The Municipal Museum has collections of ethnographic and archaeological material (including finds from the Mladeč caves).

Uničov

20km/12½ miles north of Olomouc is Uničov (alt. 242m/794ft; pop. 13,000), one of the oldest towns in the country (founded 1213), with remains of its Gothic town walls and two old town gates, the Medlovská Brána and the Vodní Brána. The church, originally Gothic, was later rebuilt in Baroque style. Other features of interest are the fine Baroque Marian Column (1743), a Baroque fountain and the local museum.

Sovinec

26km/16 miles north of Olomouc in the village of Sovinec (alt. 486m/1595ft) can be found a large 13th century castle (much altered in later centuries) in which French officers were interned during the Second World War. The castle was burned down in 1945 and has recently been restored.

Opava G 3

Region: Northern Moravia (Moravian Silesia). District: Opava
Altitude: 257m/843ft. Population: 63,000

Situation and characteristics

The old town of Opava (German Troppau) lies on the river Opava, a tributary of the Odra (Oder), at a road junction in fertile upland country, near the Czech–Polish frontier. It is a district capital and industrial town (chemicals, pharmaceuticals, engineering). It is also an important Moravian cultural centre, with the Silesian University (founded 1990) and the Silesian Theatre.

History

Opava was the old capital of the duchy of Troppau and from 1849 to 1918 chief town of the Austrian crown land of Silesia (Slezsko). In the closing days of the Second World War the old town centre suffered heavy destruction.
Opava was the birthplace of the Czech poet Vladimir Vašek (alias Petr Bezruč; 1867–1959), who described the life of the miners of his native country in his "Silesian Songs".
Gregor Mendel (see Famous People), founder of modern genetics, and the architect Joseph Maria Olbrich (1867–1908), one of the founders of the Viennese Art Nouveau school, the Sezession, were pupils of the local Gymnasium (grammar school).

Sights

Upper Square
Town Tower
Old Town Hall
Parish church

The most prominent feature in the Upper Square (Horní Náměští) is the handsome 72m/236ft high Town Tower (1618) of the much rebuilt Old Town Hall. Opposite it is the Bezruč Theatre. To the south of the theatre stands the brick-built Gothic parish church (1360–70), with a domed Baroque tower.

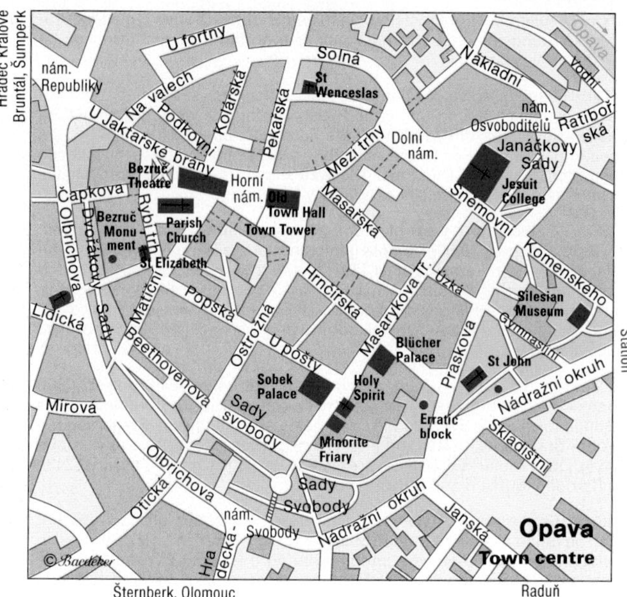

Lower Square
Jesuit College

In the Lower Square (Dolní Náměstí) can be seen the Jesuit College, in which the Silesian Diet used to meet.

Minorite Friary

The Minorite Friary (originally 13th c.) was the meeting-place of the Estates from the 16th century. Here in 1820 the leaders of the Holy Alliance met to discuss the political future of Italy.

Other churches

Other notable churches are St Wenceslas's (13th c.; due to become a concert hall), the Church of the Holy Spirit (also 13th c.) and St John's Church (14th c.; rebuilt in 18th c.).

Palaces and burghers' houses

Of particular interest are the Blücher and Sobek Palaces and a number of old burghers' houses in Masaryk Street (Masarykova Třída).

Modern architecture

Modern architecture is represented by St Hedwig's Church (1935–38) in St Hedwig's Square, the Prior department store (1927–28) and the Koruna Hotel in Republic Square.

Silesian Museum

The Silesian Museum in Comenius Street (Komenského Ulice) has rich collections of applied art, historical material and natural history. There is also a room commemorating the poet Petr Bezruč (see History). In the nearby park is the largest erratic block (travelled boulder) in the country.

Chapel of the Holy Cross

In the north-western suburb of Kateřinky is the Gothic Chapel of the Holy Cross (late 14th century; wall paintings).

Surroundings of Opava

Raduň

6km/4 miles south-east of Opava is Raduň (alt. 284m/932ft; pop. 1000), which has a 16th century church (with later alterations). There is a castle in

Parish church, Opava

Silesian Museum

which collections from Hradec Castle (see below) are temporarily housed. The castle is set in an English-style park containing a number of small lakes.

Kravaře

7km/4½ miles east of Opava we come to Kravaře (alt. 250m/785ft), with a Baroque castle which belonged to the Eichendorff family, set in a large park.

Hradec nad Moravicí

Hradec nad Moravicí (alt. 277m/909ft; pop. 6000) lies 8km/5 miles south of Opava. The castle and park once belonged to the Princes Lichnowsky. The "White Castle" (Bilý Zámek), now a House of Culture, originated as a medieval fortified castle, which was rebuilt in Renaissance style and later remodelled in Empire style at the end of the 18th century. The old stable block was converted into the "Red Castle" (Červený Zámek), which now contains a collection of pictures and mementoes of distinguished visitors to the house (Beethoven, Liszt, Paganini, etc.). The castle is at present closed for major renovation, and part of the collection is housed in Raduň Castle (see above). Around the castle is a large park (130 hectares/320 acres).

Nový Dvůr

10km/6 miles west of Opava in Nový Dvůr (alt. 325m/1065ft) stands a small neo-Renaissance castle. Attached to it is an arboretum (27 hectares/67 acres) with over 2000 species of trees, both native and foreign, and 1200 tropical plants.

Hlavnice

12km/7½ miles west of Opava is the village of Hlavnice (alt. 338m/1109ft), with a small castle in Empire style. To the east, at Choltice, can be seen an old windmill which has been brought back into operation.

Bruntál

33km/21 miles west of Opava, Bruntál (alt. 547m/1795ft; pop. 18,000), an old town founded in 1223, is beautifully situated on the Černý Potok (Black Stream), with textile, woodworking and foodstuffs industries. Notable features are a castle which belonged to the Teutonic Order (originally 15th c.;

rebuilt in Baroque style in 1766–69) and the Late Gothic parish church (15th c.).
2km/1¼ miles south-west, on a basalt hill, the Uhlířský Vrch (672m/2205ft), is a beautiful pilgrimage church.
5km/3 miles south-west is the Venušina Sopka ("Venus's Volcano"; 655m/2149ft).

Krnov

25km/15 miles north-west of Opava is Krnov (alt. 317m/1040ft; pop. 26,000), a charmingly situated town near the Polish frontier, mostly on the left bank of the river Opava. It has textile and engineering industries and a well-known organ-building firm (founded 1873). Its most notable buildings are the twin-towered Late Gothic parish church of St Martin (1559; rebuilt in late 18th c.); a castle, with arcades, which belonged to the Liechtenstein family (1552; remodelled in Baroque style 1799); and a former Minorite friary (14th c.; rebuilt in Baroque style 1720–30), now the Morava Hotel.

South of the town the Castle Hill (45 minutes' climb) is crowned by a Baroque pilgrimage church (18th c.), from which there is a view of Mt Praděd (see Jeseníky). Farther south-east are the ruins of Cvilín Castle (13th c.), which has remained desolate since the Thirty Years' War.

Orlík

D 3

Region: Southern Bohemia
District: Písek
Altitude: 385m/1265ft

Orlík Castle

Orlík Castle, recently restored to the Schwarzenberg family, was originally a royal stronghold founded in the second half of the 13th century. It was much rebuilt and enlarged in subsequent centuries and was given its present neo-Gothic form in 1849–60.

Until the damming of the Vltava (see below) the castle was commandingly situated above the deeply indented valley of the river; it is now on the shores of the artificial lake formed by the dam.

The castle is entered over a bridge spanning the moat. To the left is a 14th century round tower, straight ahead the oldest part of the royal palace and to the right the chapel.

*Collections

The richly appointed apartments – the Hall of the Hunt, Knights' Hall, Museum, Library and Chinese Saloon – have beautiful carved ceilings and contain fine period furniture, arms and armour, hunting trophies, pictures, porcelain, etc.

Park

In the large and well cared for park (143 hectares/353 acres) is the mausoleum of the Princes Schwarzenberg.

Boat service

From the castle there is a regular boat service to Zvíkov Castle (see Surroundings).

*Orlík Dam

12km/7½ miles north of Orlík Castle is the Orlík Dam (Orlická Přehrada), one of a series of dams harnessing the power of the Vltava and its tributaries. The dam, completed in 1961, is 550m/600yd long and 92m/300ft high. The artificial lake formed by the dam has an area of some 26sq.km/10sq.miles.

Zvíkov Castle

Inner courtyard

High-level bridge

The Žd'ákov Bridge (named after a village now submerged by the lake) over the Vltava was completed in 1967. It spans the river at a height of 50m/165ft in a single arch 360m/395yd long borne on two concrete piers and has a total length of 541m/592yd.

Surroundings of Orlík

Paštik

2km/1¼ miles north-east of Orlík is the village of Paštik (alt. 465m/1525ft), with a beautiful Baroque church (the last work of Kilian Ignaz Dientzenhofer, 1747–53).

Mirovice

The little town of Mirovice (alt. 433m/1421ft), 9km/5½ miles west of Orlík, has a 14th century Gothic church which was remodelled in Baroque style in 1724, a Plague Column of 1717 and a castle, originally Gothic, which was rebuilt in Renaissance style in the 16th century.

Mirotice

13km/8 miles south-west of Orlík lies Mirotice (alt. 412m/1352ft), with a 12th century church rebuilt in 1870–72. In the little town are memorials to the painter Mikoláš Aleš (d. 1913) and the puppet-master Matěj Kopecký (d. 1847).

Milevsko

15km/9 miles south-east of Orlík the industrial town of Milevsko (alt. 460m/1510ft; pop. 9000) has two notable Romanesque monuments – a cemetery church remodelled in Baroque style and a former Premonstratensian monastery.

***Zvíkov Castle**

15km/9 miles south of Orlík (boat service), on a rocky hill above the junction of the Otava with the Vltava, stands Zvíkov Castle (alt. 395m/1295ft). The castle, which first appears in the records in 1234, is one of the most celebrated and best preserved royal seats in Bohemia. Originally a 13th

century fortified castle in Early Gothic style, it was transformed into the present palatial building in the 16th century. From the 32m/105ft high tower there are extensive views. Among its most notable features are the arcaded courtyard and the 15th and 16th century frescoes in the chapel, jewels of Bohemian Early Gothic art.

Březnice

16km/10 miles north-west of Orlík, in the Skalice valley, is the little town of Březnice (alt. 485m/1590ft; pop. 3000), with a Baroque Jesuit church (1642–50; richly furnished interior) and a Renaissance (originally Gothic) castle.

Blatná

22km/14 miles south-west of Orlík in the valley of the Lomnice (a left-bank tributary of the Otava) is Blatná (alt. 440m/1445ft; pop. 7500), famed as a rose-growing centre.

*Moated castle

At Blatná is a large moated castle (originally 13th c., but much altered and enlarged in the 15th, 16th and 19th centuries) with fine interior furnishings. Of the original 13th century castle only the remains of a Gothic chapel survive. The massive keep (15th c.) has fine Gothic paintings. The castle is surrounded by a beautiful park.
In the market square of Blatná is a notable Gothic church (15th c.) with a separate bell-tower.

Lnáře

30km/19 miles south-west of Orlík is Lnáře (alt. 445m/1460ft), with an Early Baroque castle and the Trinity Church of 1706 (fine interior).

Orlík Hills / Orlické Hory F 2

Region: Eastern Bohemia
Districts: Náchod and Rychnov nad Kněžnou
Altitude: up to 1115m/3658ft

Situation and characteristics

The Orlík Hills (Orlické Hory), largely forest-covered, extend for some 40km/25 miles from north-west to south-east along the Czech Republic's north-eastern frontier with Poland, with only small variations in height. The highest peak in this upland region (much of it now a nature reserve) is the Velká Deštná (1115m/3658ft).

Holiday Resorts in the Orlík Hills

Jablonné nad Orlicí

Jablonné nad Orlicí (alt. 421m/1381ft; pop. 3000), 11km/7 miles south-east of Žamberk, lies in the most southerly part of the range. A notable feature is the traditional "log cabin" style of architecture.

Suchý Vrch

North-east of the little town is the Suchý Vrch (995m/3265ft), with an outlook tower and a mountain hut.

Divoká Orlice

7km/4½ miles east of Žamberk, at Pastviny (alt. 469m/1539ft), extends the Divoká Orlice ("Wild Eagle") reservoir (area 110 hectares/272 acres), which cuts through the hills in a romantic valley known as the Zemská Brána.

Rokytnice v Orlickych Horách

Rokytnice v Orlickych Horách (alt. 580m/1905ft) is a popular resort both in summer and for winter sports.

Šerlich

From the mountain hut of Šerlich (alt. 1019m/3343ft), on the crest ridge 3km/2 miles north-east of Deštné, there are far-ranging views.

Říčky

Říčky (alt. 635m/2085ft) lies 5km/3 miles north of Rokytnice. One of the attractions of the village is the traditional timber-built houses, many of which can be rented for family holidays. There is good skiing on Mt Zakletý (991m/3251ft).

Zdobnice

The village of Zdobnice (alt. 605m/1985ft), 10km/6 miles north-west of Rokytnice, also has typical examples of the traditional local architecture.

◄ Orlík Castle

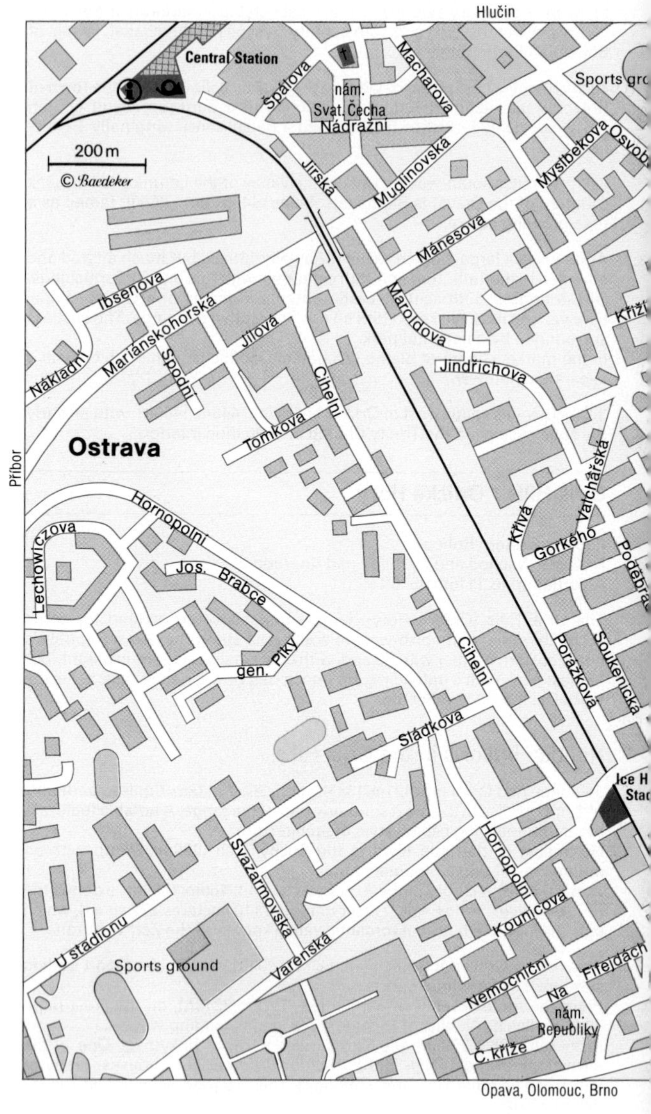
Hlučin
Central Station
Sports gr
Špálova
nám.
Svat. Čecha
Nádražní
Macharova
200 m
© Baedeker
Jirská
Muglinovská
Myslbekova
Osvob
Mánesova
Ibsenova
Mariánskohorská
Jílová
Maroldova
Křiži
Náklad[n]í
Spodní
Cihelní
Jindřichova
Tomkova
Ostrava
Příbor
Hornopolní
Lechowiczova
Jos. Brabce
Křivá
Vaicharská
Gorkého
Poděbra
gen. Piky
Cihelní
Porážková
Soukenická
Sládkova
Ice H
Stad
Svazarmovská
Hornopolní
Kounicova
U stadionu
Sports ground
Varenská
Nemocniční
Fifejdách
Na nám. Republiky
Č. kříže
Opava, Olomouc, Brno

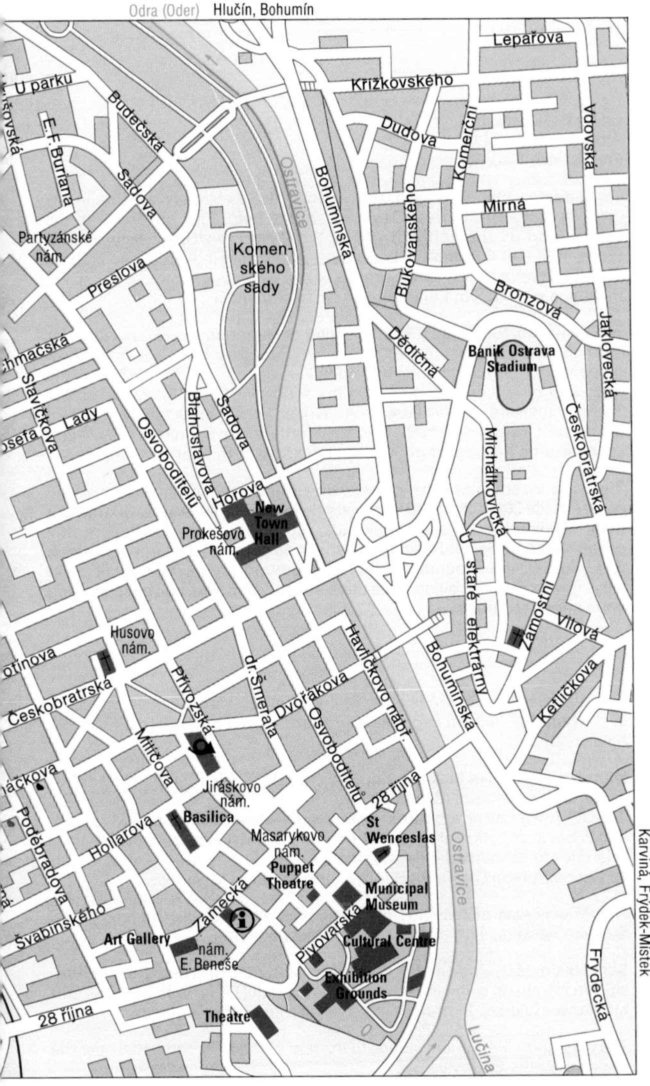
Odra (Oder)
Hlučín, Bohumín
Lepařova
Křižkovského
U parku
Budečská
Dudova
Komerční
Vdovská
E.F. Buriana
Sadova
Ostravice
Bohumínská
Bukovanského
Mírná
Partyzánské nám.
Komenského sady
Preslova
Bronzová
Jaklovecká
Dědičná
Baník Ostrava Stadium
Stavičkova
Lady
Blahoslavova
Sadova
Osvoboditelů
Českobratrská
Michálkovická
Horova
New Town Hall
Prokešovo nám.
U staré elektrárny
Zámostní
Vilová
Husovo nám.
Havlíčkovo nábř.
Bohumínská
Ketlicova
Českobratrská
Přívozská
dr. Šmerala
Dvořákova
Osvoboditelů
Milíčova
Jiráskovo nám.
28 října
Basilica
Podébradova
Hollarova
Masarykovo nám.
St Wenceslas
Puppet Theatre
Municipal Museum
Ostravice
Karviná, Frýdek-Místek
Zámecká
Švabinského
Art Gallery
nám. E. Beneše
Pivovarská
Cultural Centre
Exhibition Grounds
Frýdecká
28 října
Theatre
Lučina

Deštné

Deštné (alt. 649m/2129ft), 3km/2 miles west of the Velká Deštná, has a large Baroque church (1723–26).

Ostrava

H 3

Region: Northern Moravia
District: Ostrava
Altitude: 217m/712ft
Population: 330,000

Situation and characteristics

The industrial city of Ostrava (known until 1945 as Moravská Ostrava) lies on both banks of the river Ostravice shortly before its junction with the Odra (Oder), at the northern end of the "Moravian Gate" between the Sudeten Mountains and the Beskyds. It is the chief industrial and cultural centre of northern Moravia, with a College of Mining, an old-established theatre, a well-known Philharmonic Orchestra and a Zoo.

History

The town was founded by Bishop Bruno of Olomouc in 1267 as a frontier stronghold and later prospered as a cloth-making town. Its real development into an industrial town, however, began only in 1763 with the discovery of rich seams of coal on the south-western edge of the Upper Silesian coalfield. The Witkowitz ironworks, in the south-western part of the present town, brought the first blast furnace into operation in 1830 and soon became the largest ironworks in the Austro-Hungarian monarchy.

The various settlements which grew up around the mines joined up in the course of the 20th century to form a single town. The landmarks of a mining area, winding-towers and slag heaps, are to be found even in the city centre. After the Second World War large new suburbs, the largest of which is Havířov (see Surroundings), grew up around the town. In addition to large ironworks and rolling mills there are coking plants and chemical and engineering factories.

Sights

Masaryk Square

The central feature of the old part of the town is Masaryk Square (Masarykovo Náměstí), laid out in gardens and surrounded by modern offices and flats.

Old Town Hall

On the south side of Masaryk Square is the Old Town Hall (Stará Radnice; 1556), with a Baroque tower of 1687.

Municipal Museum

The Old Town Hall now houses the Municipal Museum (Městské Muzeum), which has a collection of material on the history of the town, with particular reference to its industrial development.

Exhibition Grounds

To the rear of the Old Town Hall are the Exhibition Grounds.

St Wenceslas's Church

A little way east of the Old Town Hall is St Wenceslas's Church (Kostel Svatého Václava; 13th c.), the town's oldest building.

New Town Hall

Some 500m/550yd north of St Wenceslas's Church, in Prokeš Square (Prokešovo Náměstí), is the massive New Town Hall (1930), with an 85m/280ft high tower (views). In front of it is a small tree-planted square.

Liberation Monument

The Liberation Monument stands to the rear of the New Town Hall near the bridge over the Ostravice.

Comenius Park

To the north of the New Town Hall the charming Comenius Park (Komenského Sady) extends along the banks of the Ostravice.

Castle

On the right bank of the river are the ruins of a Renaissance castle (originally a 13th century fortified castle).

Antonín Dvořák Theatre, Ostrava

Wooden church, Hrabová

In the southern suburb of Hrabová is a fine 16th century wooden church.

Surroundings of Ostrava

Recreation areas

The main recreation areas around Ostrava are the Moravo-Silesian Beskyds (see entry) to the south, the Hrubý Jeseník range (see Jeseníky) to the north-west and the beautifully wooded Oderské Vrchy (up to 680m/2230ft) to the south-west.

Ostrava industrial zone

Ostrava and a number of other towns in the surrounding area combine to form the Ostrava industrial zone, an area in which much of the landscape has been spoiled by industrial development.

Bohumín

10km/6 miles north of Ostrava, on the Czech–Polish frontier, is Bohumín (alt. 198m/650ft; pop. 25,000), a railway junction, with an ironworks and a wire factory.

Orlová

14km/8½ miles east of Ostrava is Orlová (alt. 220m/720ft; pop. 34,000), and 8km/5 miles beyond this the district capital of Karviná (alt. 252m/722ft; pop. 69,000), a coal-mining town.

Darkov

2km/1¼ miles south of Karviná lies the little spa of Darkov, with springs containing iodine and bromine.

Havířov

16km/10 miles south-east of Ostrava we come to Havířov (from *havíř*, "miner"), a town formed in 1955 by the amalgamation of several smaller settlements, with a total population of almost 100,000, providing accommodation for the industrial workers in the area in large blocks of flats.

Vratimov

Vratimov (alt. 250m/820ft; pop. 9000) is situated 7km/4½ miles south of Ostrava close to the town's New Ironworks.

Fulnek, in the "Cow Country"

Studénka

15km/9 miles south-west of Ostrava is Studénka (alt. 239m/784ft; pop. 11,000), with a large wagon-building works.

Fulnek

"Cow Country"

25km/15 miles south-west of Ostrava is the old-world little town of Fulnek (alt. 284m/932ft; pop. 8000; textile industry), charmingly situated on the north-western edge of the "Cow Country" (Kravarško), a cattle-farming region in the Odra (Oder) depression (see Nový Jičín). It has a 17th century castle (originally a medieval fortified castle) and a Late Gothic parish church (*c.* 1407; altered in 17th and 18th c.) of the Bohemian Brethren with a memorial to Jan Amos Comenius (see Famous People), who preached here in 1618–21. Other features of interest are the Trinity Church (1760) and the Gothic presbytery.

Pardubice E 2

Region: Eastern Bohemia
District: Pardubice
Altitude: 218m/715ft
Population: 94,000

Situation and characteristics

Pardubice, chief town of a district in north-eastern Bohemia, lies in the fertile plain of the Labe (Elbe) – which from 1995 is expected to be navigable from this point – at its junction with the Chrudimka. It has a College of Chemical Technology and a variety of active industries – chemical products, foodstuffs (including a popular kind of gingerbread), radio and television sets, etc.

*Townscape

The old town of Pardubice, laid out on a regular plan, on Gothic foundations, by the noble Pernštejn family in the 16th century, has preserved the

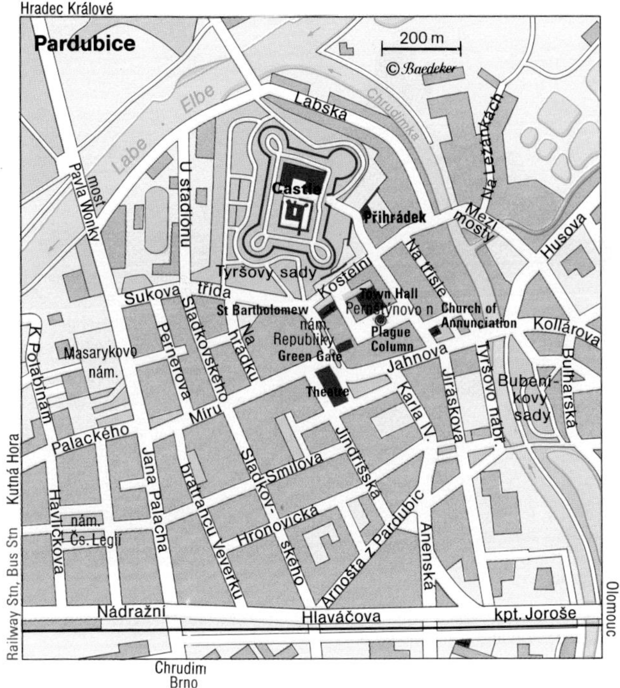

aspect of a Renaissance town in spite of having been set on fire by the Swedes in 1645. The area round Pernštejn Square is protected as a national monument.

Events

The great event of the sporting year in Pardubice is the Grand Pardubice Steeplechase, one of the most difficult in Europe (7km/4½ miles long, with 39 obstacles, including a jump almost 10m/33ft long). Another annual attraction is the Golden Helmet motorcycle race.

Sights

Republic Square

The hub of the city's traffic is the large Republic Square (Námeští Republiky), surrounded by shops and offices, from which Peace Street (see below) runs west.

St Bartholomew's Church

At the north end of Republic Square stands St Bartholomew's Church (Sv. Bartoloměje), the town's principal church, originally built in the 13th century, rebuilt in Late Gothic style about 1514 and soon afterwards remodelled by Italian builders in Renaissance style. It has a beautiful Gothic doorway and a free-standing bell-tower.

Theatre

At the south end of Republic Square is the Municipal Theatre (Městské Divadlo), in Art Nouveau style.

***Green Gate**

On the east side of Republic Square, opposite the end of Peace Street, is the Green Gate (Zelená Brána; 1507–34, restored 1886), formerly known as the

Municipal Theatre, Pardubice

Prague Gate (Pražská Brána), from the gallery of which there is a good view of the town and surrounding area.

Pernštejn Square

To the east, through the Green Gate, lies Pernštejn Square (Pernštýnovo Náměští), which is surrounded by fine Renaissance houses. Laid out in 1507, this is the main square of the old town, bounded on the north by the castle gardens, on the south by Jahn Street (Jahnova Třída) and on the east by the Chrudimka, and has largely preserved its old-world character.

*Plague Column

In the centre of the square can be seen a Baroque Plague Column of 1680, richly carved with numerous figures.

Town Hall

On the north side of the square is the Town Hall (Radnice), in German Renaissance style (1894), with sgraffito decoration by Mikoláš Aleš.

Burghers' houses

Particularly fine examples of burghers' houses are Nos. 77 and 78 on the west side of the square; the Werner House (Wernerův Dům, No. 116) and the Wenceslas House (No. 3, to right of Town Hall) on the north side; No. 60 on the south side; and the Gothic Jonas House (U Jonáše, No. 50) and No. 51 (a pharmacy) on the east side.

Church of Annunciation

South-east of Pernštejn Square, in Klášterní Ulice, is the Church of the Annunciation (Zvěstvování Panny Marie; 16th c.).

From the north-east corner of the square Pernštejn Street (Pernštýnská Ulice), lined with old burghers' houses, runs north. 100m/110yd along this street, on the left, is the old-world Church Lane (Kostelní Ulice), which runs alongside the old moat (now filled in). In this street can be found the

Archdeanery

Archdeanery, which until 1532 was a Minorite friary.

Castle

Castle Lane (Zámecká Ulice) continues north from Pernštejn Street into a small square and beyond this to the Castle (Zámek), a four-square structure in Renaissance style, built between 1519 and 1543 on the site of a Gothic moated castle, with a richly decorated doorway (1529) and a handsome courtyard surrounded by two tiers of arcades. Notable features of the interior, which is decorated with wall paintings, are the Gothic chapel and the local museum (with a large collection of birds among much else). The fortifications on the moat date from the Renaissance.

Castle Gardens

To the west of the castle are the Castle Gardens (Tyršovy Sady).

Sports stadiums

Still farther west are two sports stadiums.

Peace Street

From Republic Square Peace Street (Třída Míru), the town's principal shopping street, leads west, passing the Head Post Office (on right), to the Church of St John the Baptist (*c.* 1515) and the main railway station (Hlavní Nádraží).

Surroundings of Pardubice

Kuněticka Hora

6km/4 miles north-east of Pardubice is the Kuněticka Hora (294m/965ft), a basalt hill topped by the imposing ruins of a Hussite castle (built 1421–23; destroyed by the Swedes 1645; partly restored *c.* 1930).

Chrudim

7km/4½ miles south of Pardubice, under the north-east side of the Železné Hory (Iron Mountains), on the river Chrudimka, lies the town of Chrudim (alt. 265m/870ft; pop. 24,000; engineering), which was founded in 1263. Features of interest are the Gothic Church of the Assumption (14th c.; restored in 19th c.), the Town Hall (originally Renaissance, remodelled in Baroque style in 1721; Empire façade) and a number of old burghers' houses, notably the three-storey Mydlář House (1573–77; interesting Puppet Museum), with arcades and a minaret-like tower. An annual Puppet Festival is held here.

Chrudim was the birthplace of Josef Ressel (1793–1857), an engineer who invented the ship's screw (patented 1827).

Lázně Bohdaneč

8km/5 miles north-west of Pardubice is the little spa of Lázně Bohdaneč (alt. 246m/807ft; pop. 2000), with an alkaline thermal spring (21°C/70°F) and mud baths. Notable features of the little town are a Baroque church (fine interior) and an English-style park.

Hrochův Týnec

10km/6 miles south-east of Pardubice is Hrochův Týnec (alt. 241m/791ft), with a plain Baroque castle and a church of the same period.

Slatiňany

In Slatiňany (alt. 268m/879ft; pop. 4000), 11km/7 miles south of Pardubice, can be found a Renaissance castle (altered in 18th and 19th c.) containing an interesting Horse Museum (Hippologické Muzeum). Horse races are regularly held here.

Kočí

13km/8 miles south-east of Pardubice is the village of Kočí, with a small Gothic church (1397; ceiling paintings in popular style), with a wooden bell-tower (1666); it is approached by a wooden bridge (1721).

Holice

Holice (alt. 244m/801ft; pop. 7000), 16km/10 miles east of Pardubice, has a museum containing the collection assembled by the Czech African explorer Emil Holub (1847–1902).

Lake Seč

25km/15 miles south-west of Pardubice extends the artificial lake of Seč (alt. 500m/1640ft; area 215 hectares/530 acres), formed by a dam constructed in 1934.

Seč is a popular holiday resort in summer. Above it are the ruins of Oheb Castle (14th c.), with remains of the living quarters and the keep.

Pelhřimov

E 3

Region: Southern Bohemia
District: Pelhřimov
Altitude: 494m/1621ft
Population: 17,000

Situation and characteristics

The Southern Bohemian town of Pelhřimov is a district capital in the western part of the Bohemo-Moravian Highlands (Českomoravská Vrchovina), with extensive parks and gardens. The local industries include the manufacture of agricultural machinery, knitwear, bags, etc.

Sights

Market square

The market square (officially Peace Square, Mírové Náměští), in the western half of the oval-shaped old town, is surrounded by well preserved gabled houses of the Renaissance and Baroque periods.

Castle (Museum)

On the western edge of the old town is the 16th century Castle, which later served as the Town Hall and now houses the District Museum.

St Bartholomew's Church

North-east of the Castle stands St Bartholomew's Church (13th c.), with a 60m/200ft high tower.

Town gates

Pelhřimov has preserved two old town gates (originally Gothic but later Baroquised) – on the south side the Upper Gate (Horní or Rynárecká Brána), on the east the Lower Gate (Dolní or Jihlavská Brána) – which formed part of the town's fortifications, some stretches of which are preserved.

Churches

On the north side of the old town is St Vitus's Church (Kostel Svatého Víta); outside the town on the south is the Baroque St Mary's Chapel (18th c.).

Surroundings of Pelhřimov

Mt Křemešník

10km/6 miles south-east of Pelhřimov is the finely wooded Mt Křemešník (767m/2517ft), with a Late Gothic chapel which in the 18th century attracted many pilgrims. This is now a popular winter sports area.

Kamenice nad Lipou

The holiday resort of Kamenice nad Lipou (alt. 563m/1847ft; pop. 4000), 16km/10 miles south-west of Pelhřimov, has a castle which was much

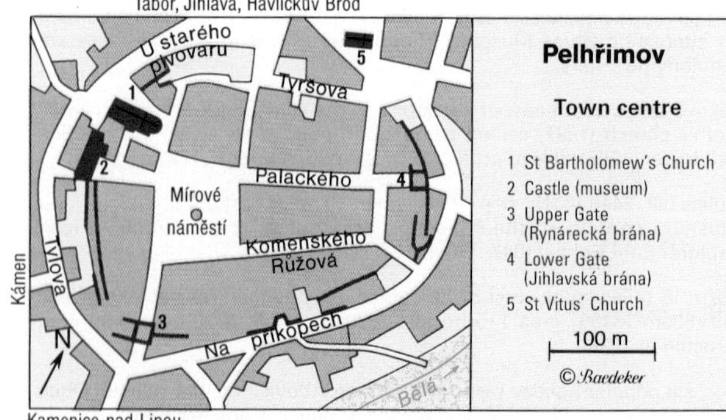

Market square, Pelhřimov

altered and rebuilt in the course of its history, most recently in 1806–11; it is now a children's holiday home. In the castle park is an ancient lime-tree: hence the "nad Lipou" ("by the lime-tree") in the place-name.

Kámen

16km/10 miles west of Pelhřimov at Kámen (alt. 585m/1919ft) is a 12th century castle rebuilt in Baroque style in the 17th century. The museum in the castle has a collection of historic two-wheeled vehicles.

Pernštejn F 3

Region: Southern Moravia
District: Žd'ár nad Sázavou
Altitude: 365m/1200ft

*Pernštejn Castle

Situation and history

Pernštejn Castle, 40km/25 miles north-west of Brno, is one of the largest and best preserved fortified castles in the Czech Republic. From 1285 to 1596 it belonged to the Moravian noble family of Pernštejn. The keep dates from the second half of the 13th century, but as a result of alterations and additions in the 15th and 16th centuries the castle, which was regarded as impregnable, increasingly took on the form of a noble Renaissance palace, with towers, gates and oriel windows.

Inner castle

The rooms in the inner castle, as remodelled in the 18th and 19th centuries, are furnished in contemporary style (period furniture, picture galleries, a library) and display a collection of weapons.

Towers of Pernštejn Castle

Surroundings of Pernštejn

Doubravník

4km/2½ miles south of Pernstejn, on the river Svratka, lies the village of Doubravník (alt. 313m/1027ft), with a Late Gothic marble church (Baroque tower; fine interior).

Tišnov

14km/8½ miles south-west of Pernštejn is the industrial town of Tišnov (alt. 253m/830ft; pop. 11,000; mechanical and electrical engineering, textiles).

*Porta Coeli

On the right bank of the Svratka, in the Předklášteří district, is the former Cistercian abbey, in Transitional style, of Porta Coeli ("Gate of Heaven", Brána Nebes), founded in 1233. Particularly notable features are the richly sculptured west doorway of the church, the cloister and the chapterhouse.

All the carving and sculpture dates from the mid 13th century. The abbey now houses the Museum of the Foreland of the Bohemo-Moravian Highlands, with collections of historical material.

Vítochov

In a Romanesque church at Vitochov (alt. 592m/1942ft), 15km/9 miles north of Pernstejn, can be seen interesting Gothic frescoes.

Kunštát

16km/10 miles north-east of Pernštejn is Kunštát (alt. 445m/1460ft; pop. 2000), with a pottery workshop. Features of interest are the Renaissance castle (originally Gothic; rebuilt in 17th and 19th c.; now a museum) and the monument to King George of Poděbrady (Jiří z Poděbrad), who is believed to have been born here.

Boskovice

23km/14 miles north-east of Pernštejn is the town of Boskovice (alt. 381m/1250ft; pop. 13,000; woodworking, textiles, manufacture of sewing-machines). Features of interest are the large Castle (19th c.; richly appointed interior in Empire style), the Town Church (14th c.; Renaissance monuments) and the local museum. On a hill to the south of the town are the ruins of a Gothic castle (14th c.).

Písek D 3

Region: Southern Bohemia
District: Písek
Altitude: 398m/1306ft
Population: 29,000

Situation, history and characteristics

The Southern Bohemian district town of Písek lies on both sides of the Otava, a left-bank tributary of the Vltava, surrounded by beautiful forest country. Once a stronghold of the Hussites, the town takes its name from the gold-bearing sand (*písek*) of the Otava as gold was formerly panned here. It now has a variety of industry – metalworking, woodworking, textiles (Jitex) and foodstuffs.

Sights

***Stag Bridge**

The Stag Bridge over the Otava (13th c.) is believed to be the oldest stone bridge in Bohemia (older than the Charles Bridge in Prague). The sculptured figures on the bridge date from 1754–57.

Church of Nativity of Virgin

The Gothic Church of the Nativity of the Virgin (13th c.; rebuilt in Renaissance style after a fire; restored in Gothic style in 1886) has a 74m/243ft

Stag Bridge and old town, Písek

high tower with sculptural decoration. The church has a Gothic panel painting of the Madonna of Písek, Gothic frescoes on the central piers and a pewter font of 1587.

Other churches

Other notable churches are the Baroque St Wenceslas's Church (1636–99) and the cemetery Church of the Holy Trinity (1549–76), which has a marble doorway (Renaissance) and a fine pulpit.

Old Town Hall

Museum

In the courtyard of the twin-towered Old Town Hall (Baroque, 1740–65; tower clock, town's coat of arms, allegorical sculpture) is the Gothic hall of the old royal castle (13th–15th c.; burned down 1532; groin vaulting), which now houses the Municipal Museum.

Burghers' houses

In the market square are a number of fine old burghers' houses.

Town walls

There are some remains of the old town walls (15th–16th c.), including the Putim Gate (Putimská Brána).

Surroundings of Písek

Putim

5km/3 miles south of Písek is Putim, a typical Southern Bohemian village with farmhouses in "rustic Baroque" style.

Kestřany

6km/4 miles south-west of Písek near Kestřany are two Gothic fortified castles and a 17th century Baroque castle.

***Bridge over Vltava**

A 510m/560yd long bridge with a 150m/165yd arch, the Podolský Most (1939–43), spans the Vltava 10km/6 miles north-east of Písek; the river is dammed at this point (see Orlík).

Sudoměř

10km/6 miles south-west of Písek is Sudoměř (alt. 383m/1257ft), with a monument to Jan Žižka (see Famous People) on the site of a Hussite victory in 1420. There are some charming examples of traditional Bohemian architecture in the village.

Albrechtice nad Vltavou

Albrechtice nad Vltavou (alt. 428m/1404ft), 12km/7½ miles south of Písek, has a Romanesque church dating from before 1200 (Romanesque wall paintings).

Protivín

12km/7½ miles south-east of Písek, on the river Blanice, is the little town of Protivín (alt. 383m/1257ft), with a 17th century castle occupying the site of a 14th century fortified castle. The Baroque church dates from the 17th century. There are some remains of town walls.

Temelín

At Temelín, 25km/15 miles south-east of Písek, the largest nuclear power station in the country is under construction.

Týn nad Vltavou

25km/15 miles south-east of Písek is Týn nad Vltavou (alt. 362m/1188ft; pop. 6000), one of the oldest settlements in southern Bohemia. Features of interest are the local museum, a Baroque castle, the Renaissance Town Hall and an Early Gothic church (altered 1560–67).

Plzeň / Pilsen C 3

Region: Western Bohemia
District: Plzeň
Altitude: 322m/1056ft
Population: 175,000

Situation and characteristics

Plzeň (more familiar in the German form Pilsen), the largest city in Bohemia after Prague and an important industrial and economic centre (brewery established 1842, Škoda works 1869), lies in the flat Plzeň basin at the junction of the rivers Mže, Radbuza, Úhlava and Úslava to form the Berounka, the valley of which opens the way to Prague. An important cultural centre, it has several higher educational establishments and a well-known theatre.

History

The town founded and fortified by King Wenceslas (Václav) II in 1295 between the rivers Mže and Radbuza was known as New Plzeň to distinguish it from the older settlement of Starý Plzenec (Old Plzeň) 10km/6 miles south-east in the narrow valley of the Úslava.
Situated at the junction of the trade routes from Regensburg, Nuremberg and Saxony to Prague, the town soon prospered. After the Hussite wars, during which it was several times besieged, it developed with great rapidity (in 1468 the first Czech book, the "Trojan Chronicle", was printed here), but a series of fires, particularly in the early 16th century, brought setbacks. During the Thirty Years' War Plzeň was stormed by Count Mansfeld, and at the turn of the year 1633–34 it was Wallenstein's headquarters. At this period the town's population was reduced by half.
From the mid 19th century Plzeň developed into a major industrial centre, known worldwide for its beer. After the Second World War the city expanded, mainly to the east (Doubravka district) and south (Slovany district).

Sights

Republic Square

In the centre of the old town, which is laid out on a regular plan in a square measuring roughly 500m/550yd each way, is Republic Square (Náměstí Republiky). This is lined, particularly on the east and south sides, by handsome Renaissance and Baroque houses (Emperor's House, 1606; Valdštejn House, Chotěšovský House). Measuring 193m/211yd by 139m/152yd, this is the largest square in Bohemia, with ten streets opening off it.

***St Bartholomew's Church**

In the northern half of the square is the large Gothic church of St Bartholomew (Sv. Bartoloměje), the city's principal church, begun in 1297 and completed at the end of the 15th century. Its massive tower has the tallest steeple in the country (103m/338ft). From the gallery at the top of the tower there are fine views.

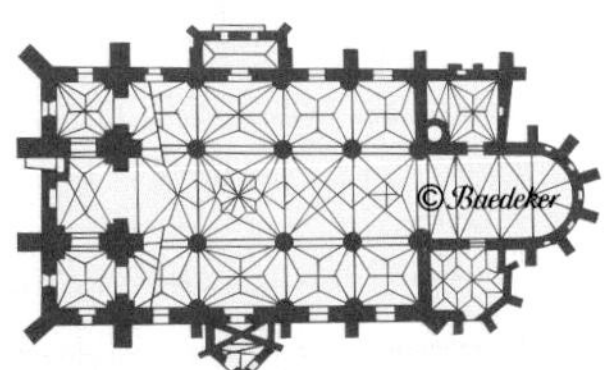

The interior of the church is impressive, with magnificent stellar vaulting. On the high altar is the Plzeň Madonna (*c.* 1390), a superb example of Gothic sculpture. Other notable features are a Calvary of about 1460 and the early 16th century Sternberk Chapel on the south side of the choir.

Archdeanery

Facing St Bartholomew's Church on the west side of the square is the Archdeanery, a handsome Baroque palace by J. Auguston (1710).

***Town Hall**

On the north side of Republic Square stands the Town Hall (Radnice; by the Italian architect Giovanni de Stazio. 1554–59), a notable example of Bohemian Renaissance architecture, with rich sgraffito decoration.

Plague Column

Between the Town Hall and St Bartholomew's Church can be seen a Plague Column of 1681.

Franciscan Church

In Františkánská Ulice (Franciscan Street), which runs south from the south-east corner of Republic Square, is the Franciscan Church (Františkánský Kostel, *c.* 1340; Baroque façade), with the former friary, a beautiful

Plan of city centre

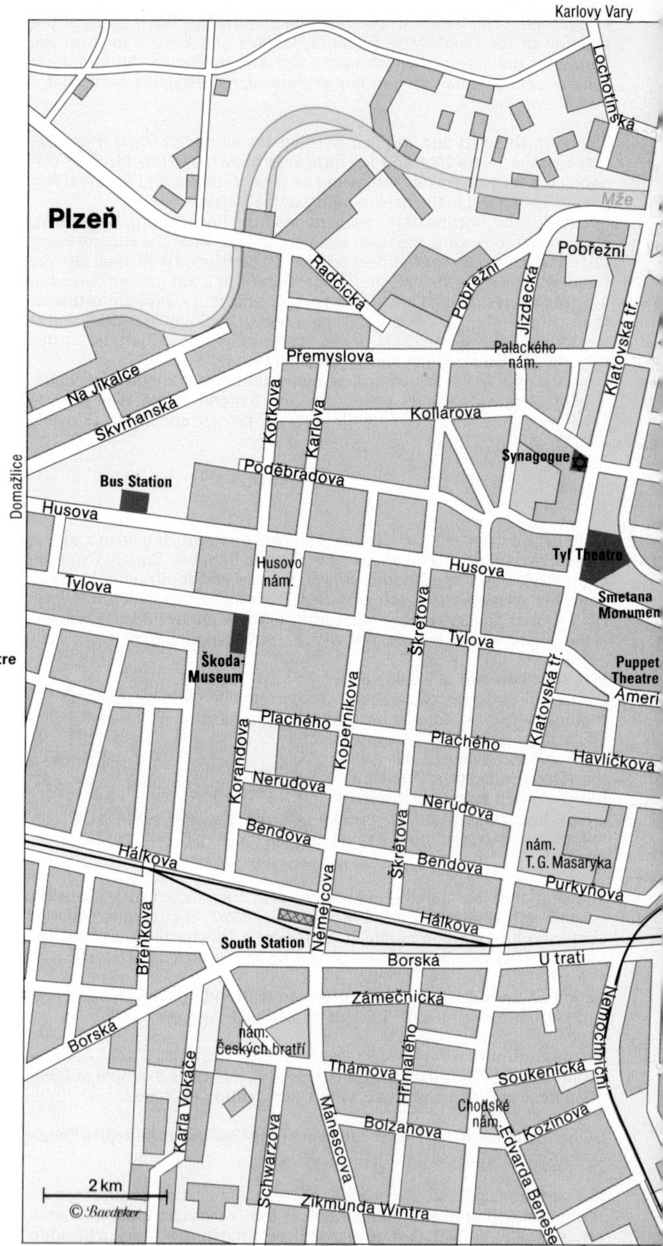

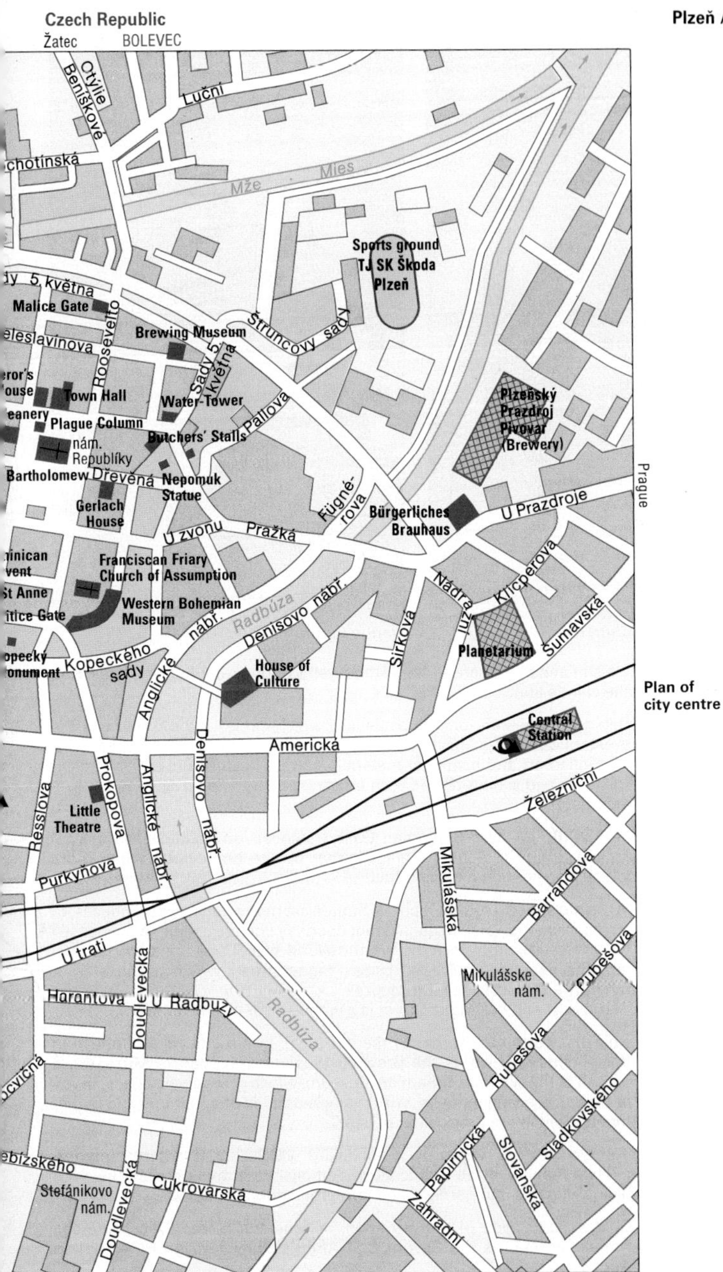
Žatec
BOLEVEC
Otýlie
Beniškové
Luční
Mže
Mies
Sports ground
TJ SK Škoda
Plzeň
5. května
Malice Gate
Roosevelto
Brewing Museum
Štruncovy sady
Sady 5. května
Town Hall
Water-Tower
Pallova
Plague Column
nám.
Republiky
Butchers' Stalls
Dřevěná
Nepomuk
Statue
Gerlach
House
Fügnerova
Bürgerliches
Brauhaus
U Prazdroje
Plzeňský
Prazdroj
Pivovar
(Brewery)
Prague
U zvonu
Pražká
Franciscan Friary
Church of Assumption
Western Bohemian
Museum
Radbúza
Denisovo nábř.
Nádražní
Klicperova
Šumavská
Planetarium
Sirkova
House of
Culture
Kopeckého
sady
Anglické nábř.
Americká
Central
Station
Plan of
city centre
Železniční
Prokopova
Resslova
Little
Theatre
Denisovo nábř.
Purkyňova
Mikulášská
Barrandova
U trati
Haranfova
U Radbuzy
Doudlevecká
Radbúza
Mikulášske
nám.
Rubešova
Stefánikovo
nám.
Cukrovarská
Papírnická
Slovanská
Sladkovského
Zahradní

St Bartholomew's Church

Plague Column and Town Hall

cloister and St Barbara's Chapel (fine wall paintings, *c.* 1460, of scenes from the saint's life).

***Western Bohemian Museum**

Behind the church, on the boulevard which circles the old town, is the Western Bohemian Museum (Západočeské Muzeum), with rich collections of applied art and historical material and the Western Bohemian Gallery (pictures and sculpture by Czech artists from the Middle Ages to the present day).

Part of the Western Bohemian Gallery's collection is housed in the old Masné Krámy (Butchers' Stalls) farther up the boulevard to the north, which also contain a concert hall.

Renaissance houses

In the old streets around Republic Square are many Renaissance houses, of which frequently only a magnificent doorway survives. Most of the houses have been restored since the Second World War. There are some particularly fine examples in Pražská Ulice (Prague Street), which goes east from the north-east corner of the square.

Water-tower

At the east end of Prague Street is a water-tower of about 1550.

Brewing Museum

Near the north-east corner of the old town, in a medieval malthouse in Veleslavínova Ulice, is the Brewing Museum (Pivovarské Muzeum), a branch of the Western Bohemian Museum, which gives an excellent survey of Plzeň's brewing industry, with many examples of apparatus and implements used in the production of beer.

Boulevard

The old town is ringed by a boulevard which, under different names, follows the line of the fortifications demolished in the 19th century, with beautiful parks and gardens and numerous public buildings.

St Anne's Church

On the south side of the old town, in Smetana Street (Ulice Bedřicha Smetany), stands the Baroque St Anne's Church (18th c., by Jakob Auguston).

Klatovská Třída

Along the west side of the old town runs Klatovská Třída, with a long strip of gardens and a large twin-towered synagogue. In Klatovská Třída and even more in Nerudova Ulice, which branches off it farther south, are many houses with sgraffito and fresco decoration by the Czech painter Mikoláš Aleš (1852–1913).

Tyl Theatre

At the south end of the gardens in Klatovská Třída is the Tyl Theatre (Velké Divadlo J. K. Tyla), named after the distinguished actor and dramatist Josef Kajetán Tyl (see Famous People), who is buried in St Nicholas's Cemetery, south-west of the main railway station.

Gardens

To the east of the Tyl Theatre, on the south side of the old town, are the Smetana Gardens (Smetanovy Sady) and the Kopecký Gardens (Kopeckého Sady).

Little Theatre

On the south side of the Kopecký Gardens can be found the Little Theatre (Malé Divadlo J. K. Tyla).

Americká Třída

To the south of the Smetana and Kopecký Gardens, parallel with them, is Americká Třída, one of the city's principal streets, which leads east from Klatovská Třída, crosses the Radbuza and leads to the main railway station.

Planetarium

To the north of the railway station is the Plzeň Planetarium.

Plzeň Brewery

Farther north is the Plzeň Brewery, the old Bürgerliches Brauhaus (Měst'anský Pivovar) founded in 1842, the oldest and largest of Plzeň's breweries (open to visitors; samples).

Prazdroj Restaurant

On the ground floor of the administrative block, by the massive entrance gate, is the popular Prazdroj (Pilsner Urquell) Restaurant, in which the world-famed light-coloured 12° beer is served. There is also a stall selling a variety of souvenirs.

Tyl Theatre

Brewery gate

In the sandstone rock under the brewery is a 9km/5½ mile long labyrinth of fermentation rooms and store-rooms.

Gambrinus Brewery

In the adjoining Gambrinus Brewery the dark Diplomat beer is made.

Zoo

Some 2km/1¼ miles north of Republic Square, beyond the river Mže in the Lochotín district, can be found a large park (fine views of the town), the beautiful Botanic Gardens (Botanická Zahrada), the Zoo and an open-air theatre with seating for 20,000.

Škoda Works

In the west of the city are the huge Škoda Works (known from 1952 to 1990 as the V. I. Lenin Works), founded in 1866 by Emil von Škoda (see Famous People), which produce steel, engines, motor vehicles, locomotives and arms.

Bus station

To the north of the Škoda Works is a large bus station.

Surroundings of Plzeň

Radyně

8km/5 miles south-east of Plzeň are the ruins of Radyně Castle (alt. 569m/1867ft), built in the 14th century by the Emperor Charles IV.

Kozel

12km/7½ miles south-west of Plzeň the late 18th century neo-classical hunting lodge of Kozel (alt. 362m/1188ft) has a richly appointed interior (murals) and beautiful gardens.

Rokycany

Rokycany (alt. 362m/1188ft; pop. 16,000), 16km/10 miles east of Plzeň, is the chief town of a district, with an old-established ironworks and engineering and foodstuffs factories. The town's principal church, originally Gothic, was remodelled in Baroque style. In the market square are a number of handsome Renaissance and Baroque buildings.

Přeštice

20km/12½ miles south of Plzeň we come to Přeštice (alt. 350m/1150ft; pop. 5000), a little town on the river Úhlava with a conspicuous twin-towered church. Přeštice was the birthplace of the composer Jakub Jan Ryba (1765–1815), author of the Czech Christmas Mass, and the architect Josef Hlávka (1831–1908), who worked on several buildings in Vienna, including the Opera House.

Dobřív

In the village of Dobřív (alt. 417m/1368ft), 22km/14 miles east of Plzeň, can be seen a 19th century water-driven hammer mill (small museum).

Plasy

24km/15 miles north of Plzeň, at Plasy (alt. 350m/1150ft; pop. 2500), is a large Baroque monastery (1701–40), now a museum and art gallery. Nearby is the burial vault of the Metternich family, in Empire style.

Nepomuk

32km/20 miles south-east of Plzeň is Nepomuk (alt. 450m/1475ft; pop. 2500), with a fine Baroque church (by Kilian Ignaz Dientzenhofer, 1733–38), traditionally believed to occupy the site of the house in which the popular Bohemian saint, John of Nepomuk (see Famous People), was born.

1km/¾ mile north, commandingly situated, is Zelená Hora ("Green Hill"), a Baroque castle which belonged to the Colloredo family.

Manětín

34km/21 miles north-west of Plzeň lies the little town of Manětín (alt. 413m/1355ft), with a Baroque castle and much fine 18th century sculpture.

Poděbrady E 2

Region: Central Bohemia
District: Poděbrady
Altitude: 187m/614ft
Population: 14,000

Situation and characteristics

The attractive spa town of Poděbrady, situated on the young Labe (Elbe) in Central Bohemia, has 13 alkaline and carbonated thermal springs which have been used since 1907 in the treatment of cardiac and vascular diseases. Here too is the Bohemia glassworks (producing lead crystal glass).

Sights

Castle

In the town's main square stands the Castle (originally a 13th century fortified castle, altered in the 16th, 18th and 19th centuries), with a cylindrical tower ("Hláska"). Part of the building is occupied by Prague's Charles University.

*Statue of George of Poděbrady

In front of the Castle is an equestrian statue of the Bohemian king George of Poděbrady (Jiří z Poděbrad), who is believed to have been born here.

Churches

Two notable churches are the Town Church (originally Gothic, 16th c.; later remodelled) and the little Miners' Church on the left bank of the Labe.

Museum

There is an interesting Municipal Museum.

Surroundings of Poděbrady

Nymburk

10km/6 miles north-west of Poděbrady, on the Labe, is the district town of Nymburk (alt. 193m/633ft; pop. 14,000), an important railway junction (railway workshops) with a fine 14th century Gothic church, a circuit of 13th–14th century town walls (six bastions) and moats, and a water-tower (the "Turkish Tower") of 1597.

PRAVDA PÁNĚ VÍTĚZÍ
SLAVNÉMV·BOHATÝRV
JIŘÍMV
KRÁLI·ČESKÉMV·1458-14
PODĚBRADY

21km/13 miles west of Poděbrady in Přerov nad Labem (alt. 178m/584ft; pop. 1000), is a museum of the traditional architecture of the Polabí area (the Labe depression). In the centre of the village is a much rebuilt Renaissance castle.

Přerov nad Labem

Prachatice

C/D 3

Region: Southern Bohemia
District: Prachatice
Altitude: 560m/1835ft
Population: 11,000

Situation and history

Prachatice is a charming little town in the foreland of the Bohemian Forest (Šumava), situated in a basin surrounded by wooded hills. It was once an important salt-trading town, the terminus in Bohemia of the "Golden Road" which appears in the records as early as 1010 – a mule track, protected by a series of castles, from the Bavarian town of Passau on the Danube on which, until the end of the 17th century, salt was carried from Bavaria to Bohemia and malt was transported in the opposite direction. The bell which used to be rung to guide merchants to the town is still rung every evening at 10 o'clock.

*Townscape

The town, which was rebuilt after a devastating fire in 1507 and thereafter passed into the hands of the Rožmberk family, has retained its old-world aspect and is one of the best preserved Renaissance towns in Bohemia. Many buildings in the picturesque town centre, which is now a conservation area, have been restored in the last few years.

Sights

St James's Church

The three-aisled Gothic church of St James (14th–15th c.), with its high, steep roof and its tall tower (the second tower was left unfinished), is the dominant landmark of the town. The Late Gothic high altar (1563) incorporates reliefs and figures from a considerably older altar.

Town Halls

In the market square are the Old Town Hall of 1571, with sgraffito decoration (Biblical and antique subjects and scenes from Holbein's "Dance of

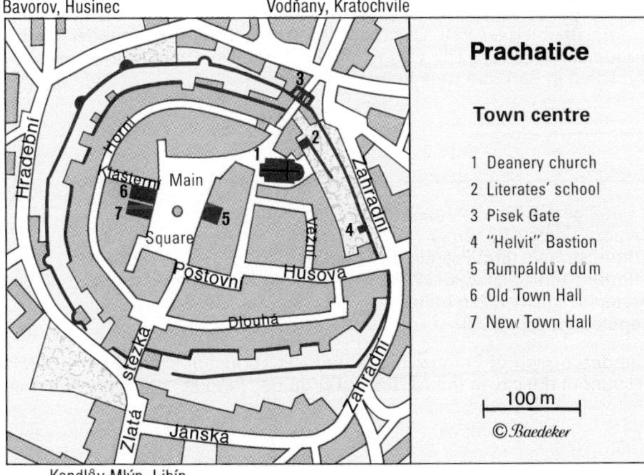

◀ *Statue of King George, Poděbrady*

Death"), and the neo-Renaissance New Town Hall built at the beginning of the 20th century.

Burghers' houses
Literary School

There are numbers of old burghers' houses with sgraffito decoration, such as the Rumpálův Dům (the old salt-store) and, most notably, the Literary School or Heydlův Dům (16th c.), with figural decoration on the attic and battlements.

Town walls
Písek Gate
Helvít Bastion

There are well preserved remains of the old town walls (gardens), including the sgraffito-decorated Písek Gate (1527; interior Gothic) and the Helvít Bastion.

Surroundings of Prachatice

Kandlův Mlýn

2km/1¼ miles south-east of Prachatice lies Kandlův Mlýn, a small holiday resort with a swimming pool.

Mt Libín

Mt Libín (1096m/3596ft), 5km/3 miles south of Prachatice, is topped by a 27m/89ft high observation tower.

Křišt'anovický Rybník

7km/4½ miles south-west of Prachatice is the Křišt'anovický Rybník (alt. 750m/2460ft), with a camping site and good bathing facilities.

Husinec

5km/3 miles north of Prachatice we come to Husinec (alt. 504m/1654ft), birthplace of Jan Hus (see Famous People), who is commemorated by a museum and a monument.

Kratochvile

Kratochvile, a Renaissance castle with fine stucco decoration and wall paintings (permanent exhibition on puppets and animated cartoons), lies 13km/8 miles north-east of Prachatice.

Bavorov

17km/11 miles north of Prachatice is Bavorov (alt. 446m/1463ft; pop. 2500), with a beautiful two-aisled church in Southern Bohemian Gothic style (1370–89; altered 1652–54; re-Gothicised 1905–08).

Vodňany

24km/15 miles north-east of Prachatice we find the small town of Vodňany (alt. 398m/1306ft; pop. 6300) with textile and engineering industries and a fish-breeding school. Features of interest are the Gothic church (13th c.; restored 1894–96), with paintings to the design of Mikoláš Aleš, and the old town walls (end of 14th c.).

Chelčice

3km/2 miles south of Vodňany lies the village of Chelčice, birthplace of the Hussite theologian Petr Chelčický (1390 to after 1492), founder of the Bohemian Brethren. The village church, originally Romanesque, was remodelled in Baroque style in the 17th century.

Prague / Praha D 2

Capital of the Czech Republic
Region: Central Bohemia
Administrative unit: Prague City Region
Altitude: 180–391m/590–1283ft
Area: 497sq.km/192sq.miles
Population: 1,212,000

N.B.

The description of Prague in this guide is abridged, since there is a full account of the city in the AA/Baedeker guide "Prague".

General

Status

Until the dissolution of the Czechoslovak Federation Prague (Czech Praha) was by far the largest city and the metropolis, predominant in every respect, of the whole of Czechoslovakia; capital both of the Czech and Slovak Federative Republic (ČSFR) and of the federative Czech Republic (ČR). Since the Czech Republic became an independent sovereign state Prague has remained capital of the Republic and administrative centre of the Prague City Region.

Situation

Situated at the north-eastern end of the Silurian basin of Bohemia, in latitude 50°5′ north (roughly the same as the southern tip of Cornwall, Frankfurt am Main in Germany, Kharkov in the Ukraine and Winnipeg in Canada) and longitude 14°25′ east, Prague lies in a wide basin in the valley of the Vltava (a left-bank tributary of the Labe/Elbe), which flows through the city for a length of 28km/17 miles, with a breadth of up to 300m/330yd, and is spanned by 16 bridges. The bend in the river, open to the west, has led to the formation of a higher bank on the outer side of the bend and a lower one on the inner side. Thus the part of the city around Prague Castle, the Hradčany, stands high above the river on the steeply sloping left bank, while the Old Town and New Towm rise only gradually up from the right bank.

Extent

The modern city has expanded in all directions on to the surrounding plateaux. Since its most recent enlargement in 1974 it has a total area of 497sq.km/192sq.miles.

**Townscape

The historic core of "Golden Prague" (Zlatá Praha) clusters round a bend in the Vltava and with its countless towers and domes, the river spanned by its handsome bridges and the tremendous silhouette of the Hradčany and St Vitus's Cathedral offers a spectacle of unique beauty.

Protection of monuments

The Old Town (Staré Město), along with Vyšehrad and part of Josefov (Josefstadt), the Lesser Quarter (Malá Strana), much of which is still medieval, and the Hradčany with its outlying districts – some 800 hectares/2000 acres in all – have been declared a conservation area. This was reinforced by UNESCO's decision at the beginning of 1992 to add Prague to the list of the world's cultural monuments which must be protected. But with the city's abundance of characteristic medieval and Baroque buildings (over 2000 individual monuments) the work of conservation and restoration will inevitably take many years.

Reflecting this concern for maintaining the harmony and balance of Prague's townscape, new buildings have been carefully adapted in height and style to their surroundings (e.g. the Federal Assembly Building, the Inter-Continental Hotel, the reconstruction of the Central Station, various office blocks and department stores) or have been sited outside the historic centre (high-rise flats in Kačerov, headquarters of the Motokov foreign trading company in Pankrác, Palace of Culture at the south-west end of the bridge over the Nusle valley). The new television tower in the eastern district of Žižkov, however, has added a modernist accent to the city's skyline which some may find annoying rather than interesting.

Economy

Prague's economic standing depends on its importance as a centre of commerce, banking and insurance as well as an industrial city (in particular the construction of engines and motor vehicles, metal-processing, chemicals and pharmaceuticals, papermaking, rubber, clothing and foodstuffs, including several breweries).

Transport and tourism

Prague is an important traffic junction, with its international airport at Ruzyně, six main railway lines and several important trunk roads, including the motorway running via Brno to the Slovak capital of Bratislava and shorter stretches of motorway running south-west to beyond Zdice in the direction of Plzeň and north-east to Poděbrady. There are also shipping services down the Vltava to its junction with the Labe (Elbe) at Mělník and from there down the Elbe to Hamburg (with a traditional extra-territorial

harbour for Czech freighters), as well as excursion boats along the Vltava to Lake Slapy.
Prague is one of Europe's favourite tourist cities: every year an estimated 12 million foreign tourists visit the Golden City.

Music and theatre

As a musical and theatrical city Prague can look back on a glorious past. It has a Conservatoire with a long tradition behind it, three outstanding symphony orchestras and numerous well-known chamber music ensembles, some of them specialising in the playing of medieval music. Modern music too, as well as jazz and light music, also have excellent interpreters. In over 30 theatres and some 20 music theatres (including two opera-houses) all dramatic genres from opera to farce are presented, while the "little theatres" (mime, cabaret, puppets) and the combined film and stage shows of the Laterna Magika are distinguished by their originality. The high point of the city's musical and dramatic life is the "Prague Spring" (Pražské Jaro) festival, held annually from mid May to the beginning of June, during which both Czech and foreign orchestras and soloists of international reputation perform not only in concert halls but also in churches (St Vitus's Cathedral, St George's Basilica, St Nicholas's in the Lesser Quarter, Týn Church, St James's Church, etc.), museums, aristocratic palaces and Baroque gardens.

Film

The main base of the internationally renowned Czech film industry (feature films, television films, short films, puppet films, animated cartoons) is the studios on Barrandov Hill.

Science and culture

In the field of science and culture Prague has, in addition to the ancient Charles University (the oldest university in Central Europe), a major Academy of Art, numerous teaching and research institutions in many different specialities, a wide range of libraries and archives, laboratories, museums (over 20) and art collections.
Since the return to democracy the city's traditionally lively literary and artistic life is no longer subject to any state control.

Administration

From 1960 to 1990 the territory of Prague was divided for administrative purposes into ten wards. The first of these, Praha 1, corresponded to the city's historic core, taking in the Old Town (Staré Město), the Lesser Quarter (Stará Strana), the Hradčany, Josefov (Josefstadt, the old Jewish quarter) and part of the New Town (Nové Město).

After the free local government elections of 1990 the old ward structure was abolished and the socialist administrative authority replaced by a democratic council of 76 members presided over by a *primator*.

Population

In the 14th century, during the reign of Charles IV, Prague was one of the largest towns in Central Europe, with a population of some 60,000. It suffered severely during the Thirty Years' War, losing much of its population, which at the end of the 17th century was still only 40,000, and began to recover only in the 18th and 19th centuries with the establishment of its role as a royal residence. Further stimulus was given by increasing industrialisation from the 1870s onwards, and by the end of the century the population had passed the 200,000 mark. Thereafter there was a period of rapid development, which was reinforced by the incorporation of outlying districts. By 1930 the population had reached 849,000.
After the Second World War the upward trend continued, and by 1960 Prague had a population of a million. In the mid 1960s the demographic curve began to flatten, and in the last few years the population has been only slowly approaching the figure of 1,300,000.
The largest population group in Prague has traditionally been the Western Slavs, in particular the Czechs. In the Middle Ages there was a substantial German minority, but by the 19th century it had fallen to a small proportion of the population.

◀ *Town Hall of Prague's Old Town*

The Hradčany, rising above the Lesser Quarter

In the course of its history Prague acquired a considerable Jewish population, earning it the name of the Jerusalem of Europe.

Religion

The majority of those among the citizens of Prague who profess a religion have traditionally been Roman Catholics. After a period during which the archdiocese of Prague was headed by an apostolic administrator an archbishop was appointed in 1978.
The second largest denomination is the Hussite Church, which was founded in 1919 and is represented in Prague by a Patriarch. Another important Protestant community is the Evangelical Church of the Bohemian Brethren. The Jewish community, once very large, now numbers only about 1000 members.

History of Prague

Prehistory and early historical period

Prague lies in an area of very ancient settlement, for Bohemia has been inhabited by man since early Stone Age times. At least as early as the warmer period between the second and third ice ages the hills above the Vltava were occupied by Palaeolithic man.

During the Bronze Age the density of settlement increased and the area grew in importance as a centre of trade, since here, at a ford on the Vltava, the important north–south trade routes (the Salt Road and the Amber Road) crossed other routes running from east to west.
At the beginning of the Late Iron Age (the La Tène culture) a Celtic tribe, the Boii, moved into the area and gradually gained mastery over the native population (large Celtic oppidum on Mt Závist, on the southern outskirts of Prague).
During the Roman period the Boii came under the rule of the Marcomanni (probably with a Germanic ruling class).
During the great migrations the area of present-day Prague was settled by Western Slavs. Fortified homesteads were established on the Hradčany and in the Lesser Quarter.

Libussa

Legend has it that Prague (Praha) was founded by Libussa (Libuše), a princess with prophetic powers. She had a vision of a city whose fame should one day reach to the stars, and, as she had foretold, her followers found the site of the city at the spot where a man was constructing the threshold (*práh*) of his house. When, after some years, her people were dissatisfied with female rule Libussa sent her companions to the river

Bílina, where they encountered at Stadice, as she had again foretold, a young ploughman, Přemysl Oráč, her future husband and first prince of the Přemyslid dynasty.

Přemyslids
Borivoj

The first Přemyslid ruler for whom there is historical evidence is Bořivoj (*c.* 850–894), who subjugates the Czech tribes, moves his residence to Prague at the end of the 9th century and gradually makes Prague Castle (the Hradčany) the centre of government and administration for the whole of Bohemia. After becoming a Christian (probably baptised by Methodius, the Apostle of the Slavs) he builds within the castle, at some time before 894, a church dedicated to the Virgin, a small rotunda.

Ludmilla

Bořivoj's widow Ludmilla (Ludmila), also a Christian, is murdered in the course of a family quarrel and soon comes to be revered as the country's first Christian martyr.

St Wenceslas, patron saint of Bohemia

Around 922 Ludmilla's grandson Wenceslas (Václav) becomes Duke of Bohemia. An enlightened ruler and a convinced Christian, concerned for the economic and spiritual wellbeing of his people, he forms a close relationship with the German kingdom. About 925 he founds on the Hradčany a church dedicated to St Vitus, a rotunda on the Ottonian model, on the site now occupied by St Wenceslas's Chapel. In 929 Wenceslas is murdered at Stará Boleslav by his brother Boleslav the Cruel. Revered after his canonisation as the patron saint of Bohemia, he (and the "crown of St Wenceslas") become the enduring symbol of the unity and independence of a country which is so frequently to suffer arbitrary foreign rule.

Bishopric

In the reign of Boleslav II, the Pious (967–999), Prague becomes the see of a bishop (*c.* 973), and thereafter the first two monasteries in the town are founded (St George's on the Hradčany in 973, Břevnov in 993).

The first kings of Bohemia

After many vicissitudes the Přemyslids gain a respected place among the princes of the German Empire. In 1086 Vratislav II (1061–92) is crowned king of Bohemia, and in 1158 Duke Vladislav II (1140–73), who had accompanied the Emperor Frederick I Barbarossa on his campaign in Upper Italy, is crowned king as Vladislav I. Vladislav builds the first stone bridge over the Vltava, the Judith Bridge, predecessor of the Charles Bridge. This convenient and safe crossing of the river ensures Prague's long predominance as the most important trading centre in Bohemia. As early as the 10th and 11th centuries Jewish, German, Italian and French merchants begin to establish themselves in the town.

In 1178 Vladislav's successor Sobeslav II (1173–78) grants German merchants certain privileges and the right to be dealt with under German law.

Municipal charter

Around 1230, by which time it has 25 churches and many stone buildings, the Old Town of Prague receives its municipal charter and is surrounded by walls.

Otakar II

In 1257 King Přemysl Otakar II (1253–78) founds the Lesser Quarter, gives it a code of laws on the model of Magdeburg and peoples it mainly with German merchants.

Around 1300 the first Prague groschens are minted.

Luxembourg dynasty

With the murder of Otakar's grandson Wenceslas (Václav) III in 1306 the Přemyslid dynasty becomes extinct.

After a period of turmoil, during which the Habsburgs first put forward a claim to the throne of Bohemia in the short reign of Rudolph I (d. 1307), Henry VIII succeeds in 1310 in securing the crown of St Wenceslas for his son John, Count of Luxembourg, through his marriage to the Přemyslid princess Elizabeth and thanks to the support of France and the Church.

Charles IV

The outstanding representative of the House of Luxembourg is John's son Charles IV (1346–78), king of Germany and Bohemia and from 1355 Emperor. French-educated, learned, artistic and pious, Charles makes his capital of Prague for half a century one of the great cultural and spiritual centres of

Europe. In 1344 he secures the establishment of an archiepiscopal see in Prague, and in 1348 founds the university which bears his name, the first in Central Europe.
Charles's reign is a period of intense building activity, the principal architect of which is Peter Parler, whom Charles summons from Germany at the age of 22. There now come into being in quick succession the great Gothic buildings which are the glory of medieval Prague. Even before coming to the throne Charles begins the construction of the Gothic royal palace and the Chapel of All Saints, following French models; in 1344 he lays the foundation stone of St Vitus's Cathedral; in 1340 the Church of Our Lady of the Snows and Karlštejn Castle are begun, and in 1357 the Charles Bridge and the Old Town Bridge Tower.
Charles's far-sighted planning is also of great importance for the future of Prague. In 1348 he founds the New Town, which is laid out on such a generous scale, with squares which even by present-day standards are spacious (Wenceslas Square, Charles Square), broad streets, harmoniously designed churches and religious houses and a wide circuit of walls which take in the rebuilt Gothic Vyšehrad, that it is able to accommodate the steadily growing population of Prague for several centuries without any major extensions.

"Rome of the North"

As a result of this activity, by about 1400 Prague, with a population of some 50,000, is one of the most beautiful and most magnificent capitals in Europe, a "Rome of the North" which attracts scholars and artists (the Prague painters' guild) from far and wide and in which trade and industry flourish. This period of splendour, however, is short-lived. Charles's successor Wenceslas IV (1378–1419) is powerless in face of a rebellion by the high nobility and rivalries in his own family, and as a result of a conflict with the Pope loses the Imperial crown. On the urging of the Reformer Jan Hus he restricts the rights of the Germans in the Charles University in favour of the Czechs, which leads some 2000 German students and many professors to leave Prague in 1409 and found the University of Leipzig.

Jan Hus

The reforming efforts – at first moderate in tone – of Jan Hus (1369–1415) and his followers, who seek to take the Christian faith back to its origins and get rid of abuses in the church hierarchy, develops into a social and national rising which makes increasingly radical demands and is given fresh impetus by Hus's steadfast death at the stake in Constance. On July 30th 1419 a mob storms the Town Hall of the New Town, frees the Hussite prisoners confined there and throws the Catholic councillors out of the window.

First Defenestration of Prague
Hussite Wars

This First Defenestration of Prague sparks off the fiercely fought 15-year-long Hussite Wars. On July 14th 1420, on Mt Vítkov (Žižkov), the Hussite leader Jan Žižka (see Famous People) inflicts an annihilating defeat on a numerically far superior army from all parts of Central Europe led by the Emperor Sigismund, and thus prevents the capture of Prague; the site is now marked by the National Memorial. With his well organised forces, inspired by religious enthusiasm, he carries the war victoriously far beyond the bounds of Bohemia. After his death the hitherto undefeated Hussite forces split up but are still able to achieve some of their demands (communion in both kinds, expropriation of church property), later revoked by the Counter-Reformation.

George of Poděbrady

After a brief period of rule by Albert of Habsburg and a 13-year vacancy of the throne a Bohemian noble of the Hussite faith, George of Poděbrady (Jiří z Poděbrad, 1420–71), with the support of the Utraquist citizens of Prague, becomes first Regent and then King of Bohemia. Under his conciliatory rule building activity in Prague, which had been interrupted by the turmoil of the Hussite Wars, is resumed and the Týn Church is built; but the town has lost its predominance as a trading centre to towns situated nearer the country's frontiers and the standing of the University has declined.

Vladislav II Jagiello

At the turn of the 15th–16th century Vladislav II Jagiello (1471–1516) builds the Vladislav Hall (in the style known as Vladislavian Gothic) on the Hradčany and rebuilds its fortifications. After his election as king of Hungary, however, he moves his capital to Budapest.

The Habsburgs

After the death of Vladislav's son Louis (Ludvík; 1516–26) in the battle of Mohács against the Turks the country passes into the hands of the Habsburgs by the election of Louis' brother-in-law, the future Emperor Ferdinand I (1526–64), as king of Bohemia. This brings the country, and Prague in particular, new rights and advantages (restoration of the archbishopric, Prague a royal and imperial residence). When the king seeks to restrict these rights a rising of the towns and the Estates breaks out in 1547 under the leadership of Prague; and after the repression of the rising Prague and many other Bohemian towns are punished by the loss of rights, privileges and income. The Jesuits, who are summoned to Prague by Ferdinand in 1555, develop a lively building activity and form a new generation of strictly Catholic nobles and burghers. These measures and the repeated attempts of the royal house to restrict the freedom of religious belief which had been guaranteed by the Compact of Basle in 1436 leads to continued conflict between the Bohemian Estates and the House of Habsburg, which also overshadow the reign of Maximilian II (1564–76).

Rudolph II

Maximilian's son Rudolph II (1576–1611) is interested only in his art collections and his scientific and astrological studies, for which he summons Tycho Brahe and Johannes Kepler to Prague. In order to repel an attack by his nephew the Archduke Leopold in 1611 he is compelled to call on the help of the Bohemian Estates and his brother Matthias (1612–19), who thereupon is crowned as king of Bohemia. During his reign there are conflicts over the interpretation of the "Letters of Majesty" issued in 1609

A section of the Langweil model of Prague about 1830

which renewed the assurance of freedom of belief for the Protestants and over the liberties which had been recovered by the towns and the Estates, and these finally lead to the Second Defenestration of Prague and spark off the Thirty Years' War.

Second Defenestration of Prague: Thirty Years' War

The battle of the White Mountain (November 8th 1620) decides the fate of the Bohemian Protestant movement led by Count Matthias von Thun which under a new constitution making Bohemia an elective monarchy has elected Elector Frederick of the Palatinate king (the "Winter King", 1619–20). The rebel leaders are executed in the Old Town Square of Prague on June 21st 1621; the Protestant nobility and the prosperous burghers are crippled by the confiscation of their property or expelled from the country; and under a new constitution in 1627 Bohemia is declared a hereditary possession of the House of Habsburg and governed from Vienna through officials appointed by the Emperor. German now becomes an official language in Bohemia alongside Czech. These harsh measures lead to the emigration of many of the educated upper classes of the population, deprive Prague of its intellectual and economic importance and cause long-lasting resentment in the remaining population.

Battle of White Mountain

Bohemia a Habsburg possession

During the Thirty Years' War the Protestant armies only twice reach Prague. In 1631 the Swedes are quickly thrown back from the town by Albrecht von Wallenstein (Valdštejn); and in 1648 they occupy the Lesser Quarter and are about to attack the Old Town when news of the Treaty of Westphalia arrives. Peace does not, however, bring the hoped-for improvement in the standing of Prague and Bohemia within the Habsburg empire. The devastated land has lost almost half of its population, and is subjected to oppressive taxation in the later wars of the Habsburgs.

Although in the course of the Counter-Reformation Prague is embellished with magnificent Baroque churches and the sumptuous palaces of the new nobility loyal to the Emperor it now finally loses its true cultural and economic importance.

Counter-Reformation

During the War of the Austrian Succession Prague is occupied by the Bavarians, Saxons and French in 1741 and by the Prussians in 1744.

War of Austrian Succession

During the Seven Years' War the town is bombarded for more than two weeks by the Prussians but is liberated by the Austrian victory over Frederick the Great in the battle of Kolín.

Seven Years' War

Under the reforming Emperor Joseph II (1765–90), who abolishes serfdom, grants freedom of worship and introduces the German system of elementary schools in Bohemia, the four separate townships of Prague are combined under a single town council.

Joseph II

In 1848, the year of revolution, a Czech nationalist rising centred on Prague collapses. František Palacký refuses to take part in the German National Assembly in Frankfurt am Main, and in the same year the Slav Congress meets. The tensions between Czechs and Germans become more acute.

1848

Since the end of the 18th century the Czech national revival movement has gradually been making headway, with the passionate involvement of intellectuals and artists in particular. In 1861, after fierce parliamentary battles, German is displaced as an official language, and thereafter the number of Germans in the population of Prague declines steadily – from 40% (almost 150,000) to under 4% in 1939 and less than 1% now.

National revival movement

The Peace of Prague in 1866 puts an end to the war between Prussia and Austria for predominance in Germany.

Peace of Prague

After the First World War Prague becomes capital of the first Czech Republic (ČSR), with Tomáš Garrigue Masaryk as President. In 1922 its area is considerably increased (to 171sq.km/66sq.miles) by the incorporation of

Capital of first Czech Republic

City Centre

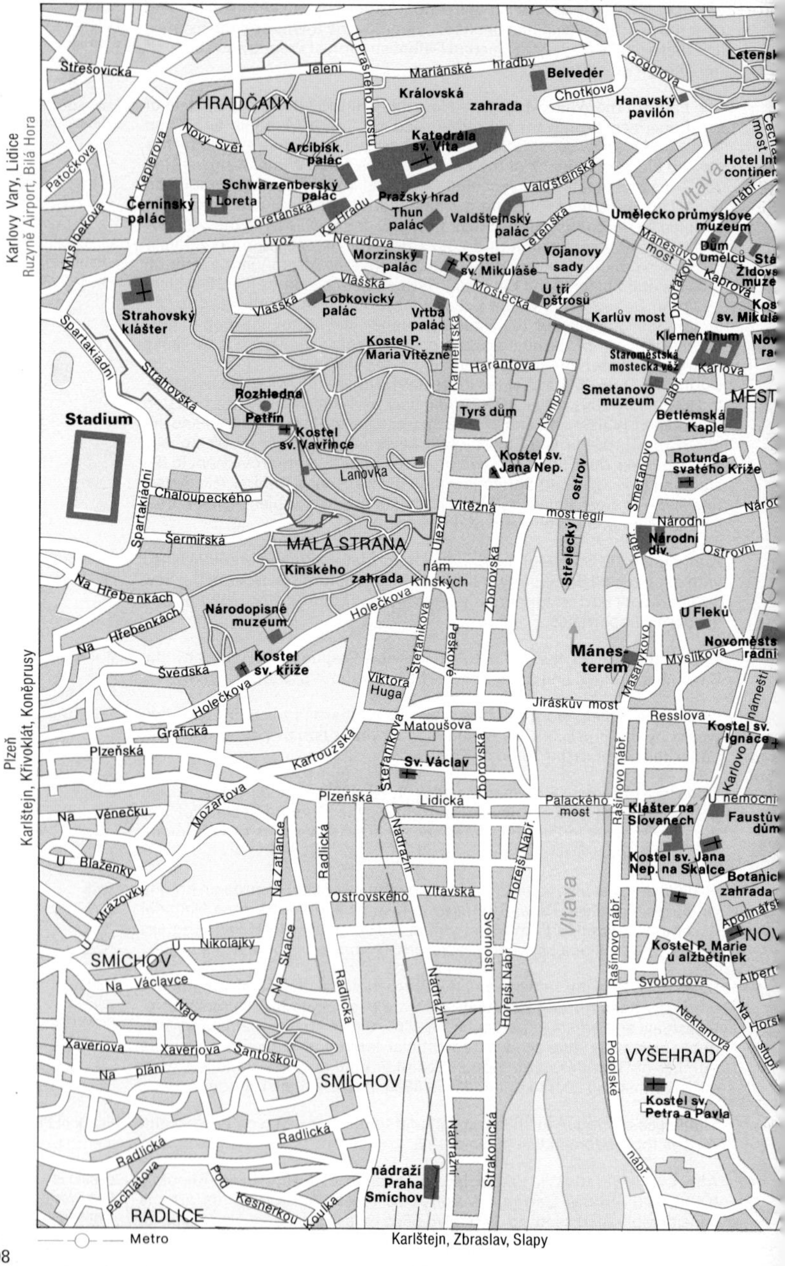

Střešovická
Jelení
U Prašného mostu
Mariánské hradby
Belvedér
Letenská
Gogolova
Královská zahrada
Chotkova
Hanavský pavilón
HRADČANY
Nový Svět
Arcibisk. palác
Katedrála sv. Víta
Čechův most
Hotel Inter-continental
Patočkova
Keplerova
Schwarzenberský palác
Valdštejnská
Vltava
nábř.
Černínský palác
Loreta
Loretánská
Ke Hradu
Pražský hrad
Thun palác
Valdštejnský palác
Letenská
Umělecko průmyslove muzeum
Mánesův most
Dům umělců
Staré Židovské muzeum
Mysbekova
Úvoz
Nerudova
Morzinský palác
Kostel sv. Mikuláše
Vojanovy sady
Dvořákovo
Kaprova
Strahovský klášter
Vlašská
Lobkovický palác
Vrtba palác
Mostecká
U tří pštrosů
Karlův most
Kostel sv. Mikuláše
Spartakiádní
Kostel P. Maria Vítězné
Karmelitská
Klementinum
Nová radnice
Staroměstská mostecká věž
Karlova
Harantova
Strahovská
Rozhledna
Smetanovo muzeum
nábř.
MĚSTO
Stadium
Petřín
Kostel sv. Vavřince
Tyrš dům
Kampa
Betlémská Kaple
Lanovka
Kostel sv. Jana Nep.
Střelecký ostrov
Rotunda svatého Kříže
Smetanovo
Spartakiádní
Chaloupeckého
Vítězná
most legií
Národní
Šermířská
MALÁ STRANA
Újezd
Národní div.
nábř.
Ostrovní
Kinského zahrada
nám. Kinských
Na Hřebenkách
Na Hřebenkách
Národopisné muzeum
Holečkova
Štefánikova
Peškova
Zborovská
U Fleků
Novoměstská radnice
Mánes-terem
Masarykovo
Myslíkova
Švédská
Kostel sv. kříže
Holečkova
Viktora Huga
Jiráskův most
Resslova
Karlovo náměstí
Matoušova
Grafická
Kartouzská
Štefánikova
Zborovská
Kostel sv. Ignáce
Plzeňská
Sv. Václav
Karlovo
Plzeňská
Lidická
Palackého most
Rašínovo nábř.
U nemocnice
Mozartova
Na Věnečku
Klášter na Slovanech
Faustův dům
Na Zatlance
Radlická
Nádražní
Hořejší Nábř.
Kostel sv. Jana Nep. na Skalce
U Blaženky
Botanická zahrada
Mrázovky
Ostrovského
Vltavská
Vltava
Apolinářská
Svornosti
Rašínovo nábř.
NOVÉ
Kostel P. Marie u alžbětinek
U Nikolajky
SMÍCHOV
Na Václavce
Na Skalce
Radlická
Nádražní
Hořejší Nábř.
Svobodova
Albertov
Nad
Na Slupi
Neklanova
Horská
Xaverova
Xaverova
Santoškou
Podolské
VYŠEHRAD
Na pláni
SMÍCHOV
Kostel sv. Petra a Pavla
Radlická
Strakonická
Nádražní
Radlická
nábř.
Pechlátova
Pod Kesnerkou
Koulka
nádraží Praha Smíchov
RADLICE
Karlovy Vary, Lidice
Ruzyně Airport, Bílá Hora
Plzeň
Karlštejn, Křivoklát, Koněprusy
Metro
Karlštejn, Zbraslav, Slapy

Letohrádek Troja

Mělnik, Kokořín
Stromovka, Výstaviště

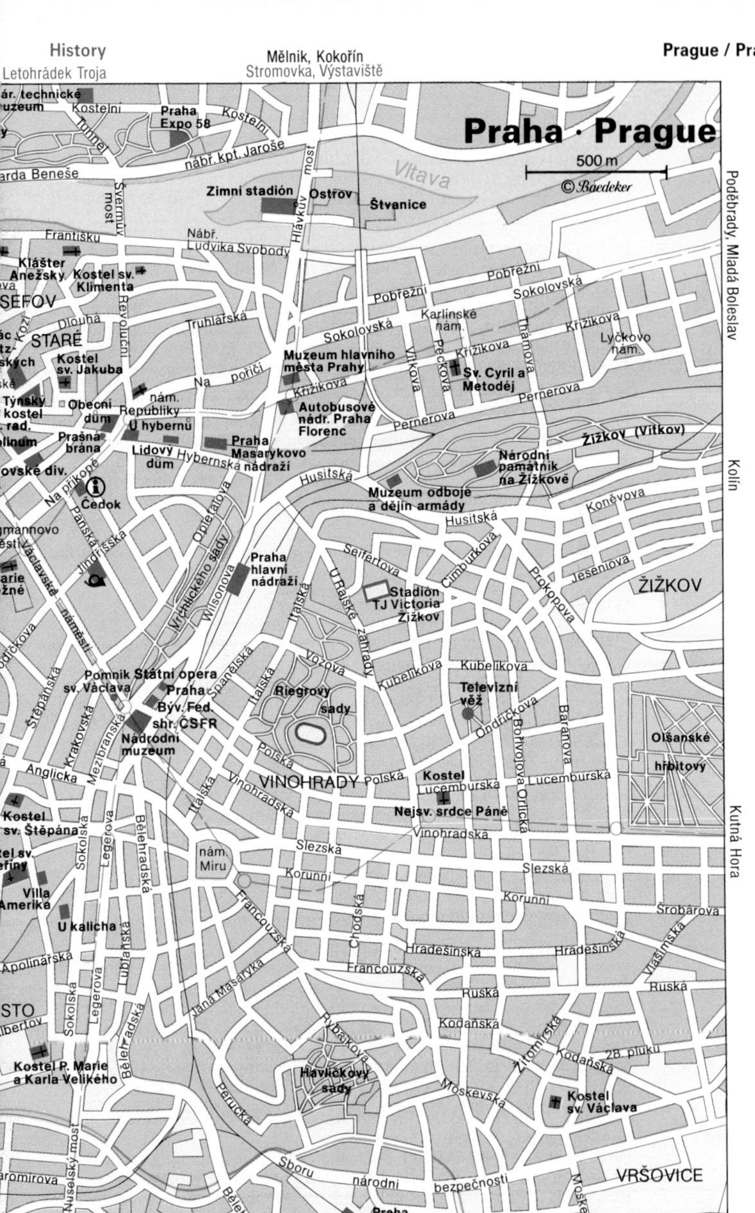

Benešov, Konopiště

neighbouring communes, and it is divided into 19 wards. The population is now 677,000.

Munich agreement

Protectorate

After the Munich agreement of 1938, under which the German-settled peripheral regions of Czechoslovakia (the Sudetenland) are incorporated in the German Reich, Hitler forces the remaining areas of Bohemia and Moravia to become a German Protectorate governed by a German-appointed "Protector".

Second World War

During a demonstration against the German occupying forces on the 20th anniversary of Czechoslovak independence (October 28th 1918) a student named Jan Opletal is fatally injured.
In the course of reprisals for the assassination of the German "Protector", Reinhard Heydrich, on June 2nd 1942 the SS massacre the population of Lidice. The rising by the people of Prague on May 5th 1945 spreads throughout the country.

Postwar period

On May 9th 1945 Soviet troops enter Prague. Edvard Beneš returns from his exile in London (May 25th) and becomes President (until his resignation on June 7th 1948) of the resurrected Czechoslovak Republic.
The seizure of power by the Czechoslovak Communist Party in 1948 is followed by the transformation of the state into a "People's Republic". Under a local government reorganisation in 1949 Prague is divided into 16 wards.

Capital of ČSSR

In 1960 Czechoslovakia becomes the Czechoslovak Socialist Republic (ČSSR), and Prague is divided into ten wards.

Prague Spring

On August 21st 1968 military intervention by Soviet, Polish and Bulgarian forces crushes the "Prague Spring", a political movement aimed at realising "socialism with a human face". In the same year Prague is enlarged by the incorporation of 21 neighbouring communes.
On January 16th 1969, in a protest against the invasion by the Warsaw Pact forces, a 20-year-old philosophy student named Jan Palach commits suicide in Wenceslas Square by pouring petrol over himself and setting fire to it. Six weeks later, also in Wenceslas Square, an 18-year-old schoolboy named Jan Zajíc follows his example.

Capital of Federation of ČSR and SSR

A new constitution in 1969 establishes a Federation of the Czech Socialist Republic (ČSR) and the Slovak Socialist Republic (SSR), with their own parliaments and governments in Prague and Bratislava and a federal parliament and government in Prague.
In 1974 the area of Prague is again considerably enlarged by the incorporation of bordering areas (mainly rural). The first line in Prague's underground system (Metro) comes into operation.

Charter 77

On New Year's Day 1977 a civil rights group headed by Jiří Háyek, a former foreign minister, the playwright Václav Havel and the philosopher Jan Patočka publish "Charter 77", which among other things calls for the freedom of opinion and of religious belief which is enshrined in the constitution.
The apostolic administrator of the archdiocese of Prague, František Tomášek (1899–1992), is created a cardinal by Pope John Paul II (June 1977), and in January 1978 is appointed archbishop of Prague (until 1991).

Fall of communism

In April 1987 the Soviet Communist Party chief, Mikhail Gorbachev, pays a goodwill visit to Prague.
On August 21st 1988, the 20th anniversary of the invasion of Czechoslovakia by Warsaw Pact forces and the crushing of the 1968 reform movement, thousands of demonstrators in Prague protest against the occupation and call for freedom, civil rights and the rehabilitation of the supporters of the Prague Spring, who have been politically discriminated against.
Demonstrations in Wenceslas Square on October 28th 1988 commemorating the establishment of the first Czechoslovak Republic in 1918 and criticising the communist regime are brutally repressed by the police.

When the West German embassy in Prague has to be closed after some 140 East German citizens have taken refuge there hundreds of others who want to escape to the West climb over the railings into the embassy grounds (August 22nd 1989). The embassy has to be closed again on October 2nd, by which time it is hopelessly overcrowded with 4500 refugees from East Germany. The East German government now issues exit permits but at the same time requires East German citizens to have visas for entry into Czechoslovakia (a requirement which is withdrawn only a month later).
The government responds to the growing discontent of the population with still harsher reprisals, culminating in the ruthless action of the state security authorities against a procession by university students on November 17th 1989 commemorating the death of Jan Opletal in 1939. This is the final impulse for the "Velvet Revolution" which leads to the collapse, without violence, of the communist regime which had held power in Czechoslovakia for over forty years.

Velvet Revolution

The first milestones on the road to a new democratic Czechoslovakia are the appointment of a "government of national understanding" and the election of the writer Václav Havel, a man committed to the cause of human rights, as President of the Republic (December 29th 1989).
The new name of the state, the Czechoslovak Federative Republic (ČSFR), which is introduced on March 29th 1990, is changed soon afterwards, at the request of the Slovaks, to the Czech and Slovak Federative Republic (with the same initials, ČSFR). Prague retains its dual role as capital of the ČSFR and of the federative Czech Republic.

Capital of ČSFR

Free parliamentary elections held on June 8th 1990 result in victory for the civic movements in both the Czech and the Slovak Republics. These groups provide the core of the "Government of National Sacrifice" which is formed on June 27th. The main objectives of the new government are the introduction of a free market economy, the privatisation of economic agencies, the restructuring of industry and the solution of urgent ecological problems.
In parliamentary elections on June 7th 1992 the Citizens' Democratic Party (ODS) in the Czech Republic and the Movement for a Democratic Slovakia (HZDS) in the Slovak Republic gain a majority of the votes.

Dissolution of ČSFR: Prague capital of independent Czech Republic

Since the dissolution of the Czechoslovak Federation into two independent states on January 1st 1993 Prague has remained only capital of the Czech Republic.
On the occasion of a state visit to the Grand Duchy of Luxembourg by the President of the ČSFR, Václav Havel, in the summer of 1992 the possibility was discussed that Prague, as the twin city of the Luxembourg capital, might share its designation as European City of Culture in 1995.

Sightseeing in Prague

Suggestions for a Brief Visit

Flying visit

The Prague Information Service (PIS) and various travel agencies regularly run city tours and walks round the principal sights (usually 1–3 hours; English-speaking guides).

Sightseeing on your own

If you have only a day or two in Prague you should concentrate on the most important sights, since with so many things to see there is a danger of doing too much, losing the overall view and tiring yourself out.
You should follow the descriptions given below, which are arranged in districts (Old Town, Josefov, New Town, Lesser Quarter, Hradčany). If time permits, it is advisable to allow a day for each district.
Since in comparison with other large cities the distances in Prague are relatively short, it is best – except in the outer districts, which have less to

offer the tourist – to do your sightseeing on foot, particularly since some of the most interesting parts of the town (e.g. in the Old Town and on the Hradčany) are pedestrian zones closed to traffic.

Principal sights

If you are particularly pressed for time you should see at least in the Old Town the Old Town Square, with the Town Hall and the Týn Church, in Josefov the old Jewish quarter with the synagogues and the old cemetery, and in the New Town the busy street called Na Příkopě and Wenceslas Square.

The left bank of the Vltava, with the Lesser Quarter, is best reached by way of the Old Town Bridge Tower in Knights of the Cross Square (Křižovnické Náměstí) and the celebrated Charles Bridge with its Baroque statues.

In the Lesser Quarter you should look into the magnificent St Nicholas's Church in Lesser Quarter Square and the gardens of the Valdštejn Palace, with the sala terrena, explore the little streets with their numerous palaces and continue up the hill, passing gardens (some of them open to the public) from which there are incomparable views of the city with its towers and spires and the river Vltava.

The high point here is the Hradčany, with the Royal Palace, St Vitus's Cathedral, the Basilica of St George, the Belvedere Palace, the Loreto complex and Strahov Monastery.

Viewpoints

Finally the observation tower on Petřín Hill will give you an excellent general view of what you have seen. There are also fine panoramic views from the new Television Tower in the eastern suburb of Žižkov.

Principal museums

Of Prague's numerous museums the most important are the National Gallery on the Hradčany, with the picture gallery in the Šternberk Palace and the collection of Bohemian art in St George's Convent, the Jewish Museum in Josefov and the Museum of Literature in the library of Strahov Monastery.

If you have more time you can see the National Museum, the art collections in St Agnes's Convent, the Náprstek Ethnological Museum, the National Museum of Technology, the collections of glass, porcelain and ceramics in the Museum of Decorative Art and the Mozart Museum in the Villa Bertramka.

Public transport

You can of course also do some of your sightseeing by taxi, or can use the city's various forms of public transport – the Metro, trams and buses.

Metro

Prague's Metro runs for the most part underground. The first section of Line C (which now runs between the Florenc and Kačerov stations, a distance of some 7km/4½ miles) was opened in 1974, and this was followed by Lines A and B. The system, including a new Line D, is due to be complete by the year 2005.

Old Town / Staré Město (detailed plan, pp. 308–309)

****Old Town Square**

The central feature of the Old Town is the spacious Old Town Square (Staroměstské Náměstí), with a series of charming old houses on the south and east sides. At No. 22 is an office of the Prague Information Service (PIS).

*Hus Monument

The north side of the square, which is usually crowded with market stalls, is dominated by the massive monument (by Ladislav Šaloun, 1915) commemorating the Bohemian Reformer Jan Hus (see Famous People).

****Town Hall**
(ill., p. 290)

On the south-west side of the square stands the Town Hall (Staroměstské Radnice), the oldest part of which consists of burghers' houses dating from the 11th century and much altered from 1338 onwards; the main building dates mainly from the 14th and 15th centuries. A neo-Gothic extension was burned down during the Prague rising in 1945.

*Astronomical clock

On the south side of the tower (built 1364, with later alterations; fine views from top; lift) is an astronomical clock (1410; perfected 1490) which shows

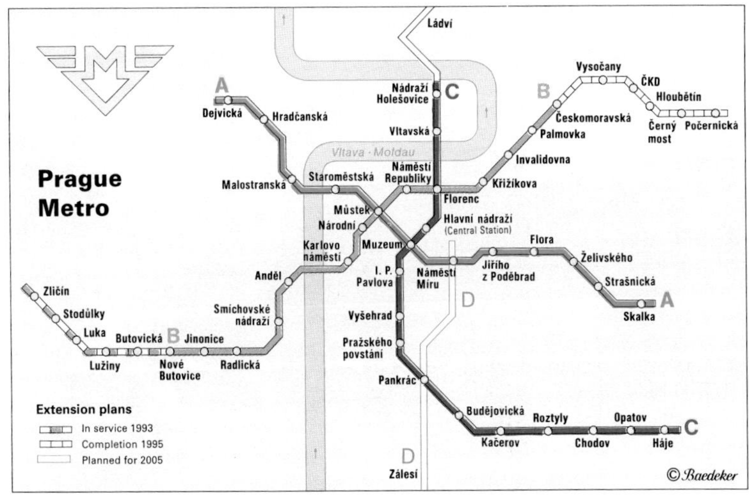

the phases of the moon and the positions of the planets. Every hour, on the hour, the clock strikes and the mechanical figures above the clock face come into action: Christ and the Apostles move slowly past two narrow windows, while in a third window higher up a cock crows. The procession of figures was a 19th century addition.

Oriel chapel

On the north-east side of the Town Hall can be seen the picturesque oriel window of a chapel (1381; restored after its destruction in the 1945 fire). Below the window, set into the wall, is a casket containing earth from the Dukla pass (eastern Slovakia), where in the autumn of 1944 Soviet and Czech forces threw back the Germans. To the right of this a tablet contains the names of the 27 leaders of the Bohemian Protestant uprising who were executed here on June 21st 1621. The site of their execution is marked in the pavement by two large white crossed swords with the Crown of Thorns, the date of execution and 27 small crosses.

Interior of Town Hall

To the left of the astronomical clock is the handsome main entrance to the Town Hall. The main features of the interior, principally used for ceremonial occasions, are the Council Chamber (1879), with a doorway of 1619, the old Council Room (15th c.), with fine carved woodwork, the Communal Room (17th c.) and the Chapel. In the cloister and on the second floor the Municipal Art Gallery puts on periodic exhibitions.

House At the Minute

On the south side of the Town Hall, projecting into the square, is the House At the Minute (Dům U Minuty), a Renaissance building (*c.* 1600) with figural sgraffito decoration and arcades on the ground floor (passage to Malé Náměstí, Little Square).

St Nicholas's Church

At the north-west corner of Old Town Square stands St Nicholas's Church (Kostel Svatého Mikuláše), built by Kilian Ignaz Dientzenhofer in 1732–37, with a handsome façade (sculpture from the workshop of Matthias Bernhard Braun von Braun) and a richly furnished interior, which requires a good light to be seen properly (under the dome is a large crystal chandelier). Originally a centre of the Utraquist movement, the church passed in 1635 to the Benedictines of the Emmaus Monastery, was used from 1870 to 1914 by the Russian Orthodox community and has belonged since 1920 to the Czechoslovak Hussite Church which was founded in that year.

Hus Monument, Old Town Square

Birthplace of Franz Kafka

To the left of St Nicholas's Church, in U Radnice Street (No. 5), can be seen the house in which the writer Franz Kafka (see Famous People) was born in 1883 (bust on the corner), Kafka's grave is in the New Jewish Cemetery in the Žižkov district (Želivského Ulice).

Goltz-Kinsky Palace

The north-east side of Old Town Square is dominated by the large Goltz-Kinsky Palace (Palác Goltz-Kinských; now State-owned), built in 1755–65 for Count Johann Arnold von Goltz by Anselmo Lurago to the design of Kilian Ignaz Dientzenhofer, with an elegant Rococo façade. The palace now houses the National Gallery's collection of graphic art.

On the ground floor, now largely unused, was the haberdashery shop of Hermann Kafka, the writer's father. Until the First World War the palace (which may have been the model for Kafka's "Castle") was occupied by the German Gymnasium (grammar school), at which Kafka and many other noted Germans were pupils. The recently founded Franz Kafka Society plans to establish a cultural centre in the palace, with a Kafka Museum, a library, a publishing house, a bookshop, a small theatre and various reatau-rants and cafés.

*House At the Stone Bell

To the right of the Goltz-Kinsky Palace is the tower-like House At the Stone Bell (Dům U Kamenného Zvonu), named after the stone bell on the corner of the building. The house, restored to its original Gothic form in 1973–87, is used for art exhibitions, concerts and lectures.

Týn School

Farther to the right, beyond Týn Street (Týnská Ulice), the old Týn School (Týnská Škola; 16th c.) has fine Renaissance gables and Gothic arcades.

***Týn Church**

A passage entered through the third arch from the left leads to the Gothic Týn Church or Church of Our Lady before Týn (Týnský Chrám, Kostel Panny Marie před Týnem; begun 1365), once the principal Utraquist church in Prague. The choir was completed in 1380; the façade with its tall pointed gable and twin towers (80m/260ft high), each with four elegant corner turrets, was built in the 1360s, during the reign of George of Poděbrady. The golden chalice and the statue of the king which were set up on the gable to commemorate his coronation were replaced after the battle of the White Mountain in 1620 by a figure of the Virgin. The original of the fine tympanum of the round-headed north doorway is now in the collection of Bohemian art in St George's Convent on the Hradčany.

Interior

The interior of the church, with its high Gothic choir and large and rather dark Baroque altars, is impressive. On the fourth pillar to the right of the main entrance is the red marble tombstone of the Danish astronomer Tycho Brahe (d. 1601; see Famous People), usually decked with a Danish flag. There are numerous other epitaphs on the surrounding walls.
On the high altar are an "Assumption" and a "Holy Trinity" (Karel Škréta). In the chapel to the left of the choir is a Gothic "Crucifixion". In the Lady Chapel to the right of the high altar is a pewter font of 1414.

Týn Court

To the rear of the Týn Church can be found the old Týn Court or Ungelt (in course of restoration), once a warehouse used by foreign merchants, who had to pay duty (*ungelt*) here on their goods. Immediately on the left is the restored Granovský House, a Renaissance building with loggias on the first floor (1560) in which the merchants lodged.

***St James's Church**

Farther east stands St James's Church (Kostel Svatého Jakuba), built in 1232 as the church of the Minorite friary (on its north side), burned down in 1366 and rebuilt in Gothic style, and finally remodelled in Baroque style between 1689 and 1739, with fine reliefs on the façade (SS James, Francis and Anthony, by Ottavio Mosto, *c.* 1700) and a richly furnished interior.
On the high altar is a painting by Wenzel Lorenz Reiner of the "Martyrdom of St James" (1739). In the north aisle is the marble monument (designed by Johann Bernhard Fischer von Erlach and executed by Ferdinand Maximilian Brokoff; 1714–16) of Count Václav Vratislav of Mitrovice (d. 1712). The church has excellent acoustics and is frequently used for recitals of church music.

*Celetná Ulice

At the south-east corner of Old Town Square is Celetná Ulice, which is lined with handsome Baroque houses.

***Estates Theatre**

300m/330yd along Celetná Ulice, on the right, we come to the Ovočný Trh (Fruit market), in which is the Estates Theatre (Stavovské Divadlo), a neoclassical building by Anton Haffenecker (1783). It was originally called the Nostitz Theatre, then the Theatre of the Estates of the Bohemian Nobility, from the mid 19th century to 1920 the German National Theatre and from 1948 to 1990 the Týl Theatre. Here on October 29th 1787 Mozart's "Don Giovanni" was given its first performance.
In 1834 the comic opera "Fidlovačka" ("The Fiddlers' Festival") by the Czech composer František Škroup, on a libretto by the Czech dramatist Josef Kajetán Týl, had its first performance here. One of the songs in this

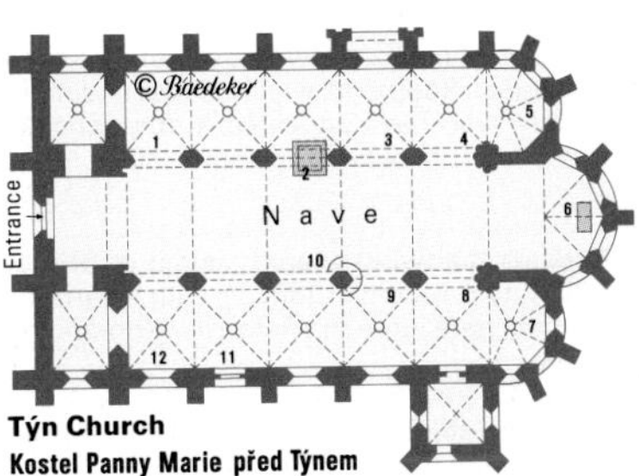

Týn Church
Kostel Panny Marie před Týnem

1 St Adalbert's Altar
2 Late Gothic baldachin, St Luke's Altar
3 St Joseph's Altar
4 Altar of Annunciation
5 Gothic Calvary
6 High altar
7 Gothic consoles, pewter font
8 St Barbara's Altar
9 Gravestone of Tycho Brahe
10 Renaissance altar
11 Gothic Virgin and Child
12 St Wenceslas's Altar

Towers of the Týn Church

opera, "Kde domov můj?" ("Where is my home?"), was adopted in 1919 as the Czech part of the Czechoslovak national anthem.

***Carolinum**

Facing the Estates Theatre, in Železná Ulice, is the Carolinum, with a Baroque façade (1718) and a Gothic oriel window on the Fruit market side. Founded in 1383, the Collegium Carolinum (Charles University) was the first university in Central Europe. The building now houses the Rector's Office, the Great Hall and the Seminar Rooms in which students defend their doctoral theses. Among those who have appeared in the principal Seminar Hall was Jan Hus; there is a statue of him (by Karel Lidický, 1959) in the courtyard.

St Gall's Church

South-west of the Carolinum stands the twin-towered church of St Gall (Kostel Svatého Havla; originally Gothic, rebuilt in 18th c.), with a Baroque interior. Among those who preached here were the Reformer Konrad von Waldhausen (1363–69) and Jan Hus.

***Powder Tower**

At the east end of Celetná Ulice the Late Gothic Powder Tower (Prašná Brána) was built in 1475 on the model of the Old Town Bridge Tower and

An imposing building in the style of the Austro-Hungarian monarchy

restored in neo-Gothic style in 1875–83. Originally part of the town's fortifications, it was used in the 18th century as a gunpowder store. A steep spiral staircase leads up to a small exhibition on the history of the tower and to the wall-walk, from which there are fine views of the town.

***Civic House**

On the north side of the Powder Tower (linked with it by a bridge at first-floor level) is the Civic House (Obecní Dům; by Antonín Balšánek and Osvald Polívka, 1906–11), a good example of the Czech Sezession (Art Nouveau) style, with function rooms, concert halls (including the richly decorated Smetana Hall, with an organ), exhibition halls, a restaurant, an artists' café (Repre) and a wine restaurant.

Hibernian House

Opposite the Civic House, to the east, is the Hibernian House (U Hibernů), with a neo-classical façade of 1810. Originally the church of an Irish Franciscan friary and later a custom house, it is now an exhibition hall.

***Little Square**

To the west of the Town Hall in Old Town Square is the Little Square (Malé Náměstí), which is partly surrounded by arcades and has an attractive fountain (iron grille of 1560) in the centre. On the south side of the square (No. 12; 1698) is a house which was once occupied by Christoph Dientzenhofer (see Famous People).

***St Mary's Square**
New Town Hall
Municipal Library

To the north-west lies St Mary's Square (Mariánské Náměstí). On the east side of the square can be seen the New Town Hall (Nová Radnice; 1909–12) and on the north side the Municipal Library (Městská Knihovna; 1928). The Library contains over 350,000 volumes and a large collection of music scores, and also houses the National Gallery's Collection of Modern Art (Sbírka Moderního Umění; mainly 20th century Czech painting).

***Clam-Gallas Palace**

At the south-east corner of St Mary's Square the Vltava Fountain has a figure by Václav Prachner (1812) familiarly known to the people of Prague

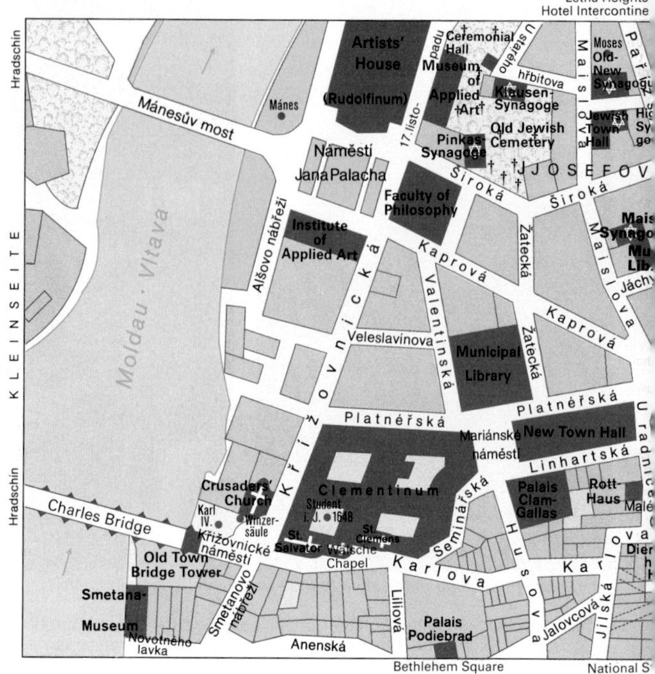

as Terezka ("Little Theresa"). In Hus Street (Husova Třída), which runs south from here, is the Clam-Gallas Palace (Palác Clam-Gallasův), which was begun by Johann Bernhard Fischer von Erlach in 1715. The statues on its two doorways and the Hercules Fountain in the first courtyard were the work of Matthias Bernhard Braun von Braun. There is a beautiful staircase hall decorated with frescoes.

State Archives

The Clam-Gallas Palace now houses the State Archives (documents from 14th c. onwards).

***Clementinum**

The end of the extensive complex of buildings known as the Clementinum flanks the west side of St Mary's Square. It is bounded on the north by Platnéřská Ulice and on the south by Karlova Ulice (Charles Street), which leads to the Charles Bridge. This former Jesuit College was begun in 1578 on a site cleared by the demolition of a whole quarter of the old town and continued in Baroque style between 1653 and 1778, with several churches and chapels, three gates and four towers.

National Library
University Library
Slavonic Library
Technical Library

In the Clementinum are the National Library (some 5.5 million volumes; numerous valuable manuscripts, including the Codex Vyšehradiensis of 1086; several thousand incunabula), the rich University Library, the Slavonic Library, the State Technical Library and an observatory with a collection of instruments.

The finest rooms in the building are the Baroque Hall (1722–27; ceiling frescoes), the Mirror Chapel (Zrcadlová Siň, 1724; now a concert hall for chamber music) and the Mozart Hall, with Rococo paintings.

The building is laid out around four spacious courtyards. In the south-west courtyard is a statue of a student of 1648 (by Josef Max, 1848).

*St Clement's Church

Karlova Ulice passes the Baroque St Clement's Church (Kostel Svatého Klimenta; 1711–13, which forms part of the Clementinum complex and is

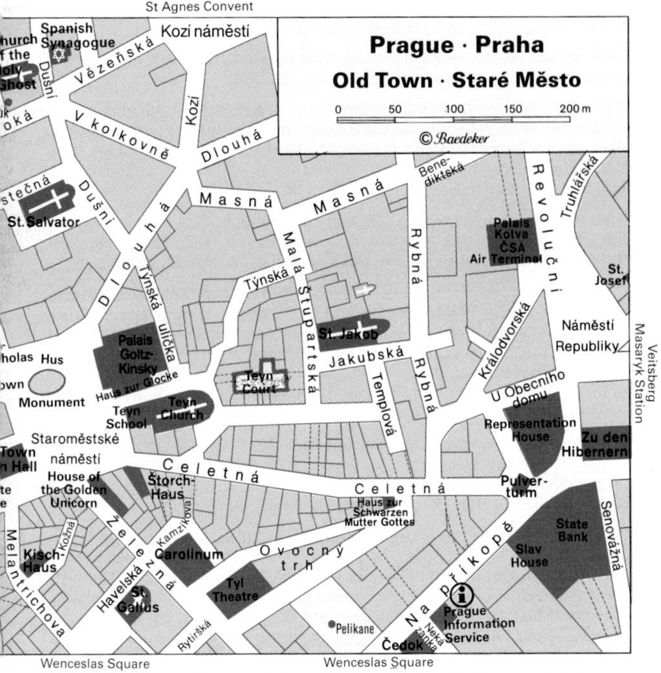

now a Greek Catholic church. Its eight figures (four Fathers of the Church and the four Evangelists) by Matthias Bernhard Braun von Braun are the finest examples of Baroque sculpture in Prague.

Italian Chapel

Karlova Ulice continues past the Italian Chapel (Vlašská Kaple; 1590–1600), dedicated to the Assumption – the church of the Italian community – to the picturesque Knights of the Cross Square, at the end of the Charles Bridge.

***Knights of the Cross Square**
***St Salvator's Church**

On the east side of Knights of the Cross Square (Křižovnické Náměstí) is the Renaissance-style St Salvator's Church (Kostel Svatého Salvátora; 1578–1602), originally a Jesuit church within the Clementinum complex. The Baroque porch was added in 1649–53 by Carlo Lurago and Francesco Caratti, with figures of saints by Johann Georg Bendl.

***Church of St Francis Seraphicus**

On the north side of the square stands the Church of St Francis Seraphicus (Kostel Svatého Františka Serafinského; by Jean-Baptiste Mathey, 1679–88), which belonged to the Order of Knights of the Cross. It has an interesting façade in the manner of the French pre-classical school, a large dome and a richly furnished interior (fresco of Last Judgment in dome, by W. L. Reiner, 1722).

Outside the church is the Vintners' Column (by J. G. Bendl, 1676), with a statue of St Wenceslas. Nearer the Charles Bridge can be seen a bronze statue of Charles IV (by Ernst Hähnel) erected in 1848 on the 500th anniversary of Prague University.

***Old Town, Bridge Tower and** ****Charles Bridge** See page 324

***Smetana Embankment**

To the south of Knights of the Cross Square the Smetana Embankment (Smetanovo Nábřeží) extends along the banks of the Vltava, offering magnificent views of the Charles Bridge and the Hradčany and ending at the

National Theatre. At the near end of the street, to the right, is an old water-tower (15th c., with later rebuilding).

Smetana Museum

West of this, on the banks of the Vltava, is the Renaissance-style Smetana Museum (1885), with mementoes of the composer.

Chapel of Holy Rood

Half-way along the Smetana Embankment, at a public garden with a neo-Gothic monument, Betlémské Ulice (Bethlehem Street) goes off on the left. Beyond this, at the west end of Konviktská Ulice, is the Chapel of the Holy Rood (Kaple Svatého Kříže; Old Catholic), a small Romanesque rotunda (*c.* 1100; restored 1865) which contains remains of Gothic wall paintings.

Náprstek Museum

Betlémská Ulice joins Betlémské Náměstí (Bethlehem Square), in which (on left) is the Náprstek Museum, an interesting ethnological museum on the cultures of East Asia, Africa, Oceania and the American Indians.

Bethlehem Chapel

On the north side of Bethlehem Square stands the Bethlehem Chapel (Betlémská Kaple), a reproduction (1950–54) of the original chapel (built 1391, demolished by the Jesuits 1786) in which Jan Hus preached between 1402 and 1413; it could accommodate a congregation of 3000. It is now a memorial to Hus.

Hus's house

In the courtyard, to the right, can be seen a reproduction of the house in which Hus lived (periodic special exhibitions).

St Giles' Church

In Hus Street (Husova Třída), which runs north-east from Bethlehem Square to St Mary's Square, is the Gothic St Giles' Church (Kostel Svatého Jiljí; 1339–71), with a Baroque interior of 1793). It has ceiling and altar paintings by W. L. Reiner, who is buried in the church.

Mánes Bridge

From Knights of the Cross Square Křižovnická Ulice (Knights of the Cross Street) runs north, passing between the former monastery of the Knights of the Cross (on left) and the Clementinum, to Jan Palach Square (Náměstí Jana Palacha), from which the Mánes Bridge (Most Josefa Mánesa or Mánesův Most; built 1911–14, renovated 1991–92) crosses the Vltava to the Lesser Quarter. At the east end of the bridge, in gardens to the right, is a monument (by Bohumil Kafka, 1947) to the Czech painter Josef Mánes.

Jan Palach Square

Rudolfinum

On the south side of Jan Palach Square, which is laid out in gardens, is the College of Decorative Art (Vysoká Škola Umělecko-Průmyslova); on the east side the University's Faculty of Philosophy (by Josef Sakař, 1927–29); and on the north side the massive Rudolfinum or Artists' House (Dům Umělců), a neo-Renaissance building (by Josef Zítek and Josef Schulz, 1876–84; major renovation 1990–92) which was originally a concert hall and art gallery, in 1919–39 and 1945–46 housed the Czechoslovak Parliament and a picture gallery (now in the Šternberk Palace) and is now the home of the Prague Philharmonic Orchestra (Dvořák Hall).

Museum of Decorative Arts

Opposite the Rudolfinum, on the west side of the Old Jewish Cemetery, stands the Museum of Decorative Arts (Umělecko-Průmyslové Muzeum; by Josef Schulz, 1897–1901), with a magnificent collection of glass, porcelain and ceramics from antiquity to the present day and rich departments of applied art (furniture of the 16th–19th centuries, 15th century parchments, goldsmiths' work of the 15th–19th centuries, small bronzes, coins, watches and clocks, bookbinding, costumes, etc.).

Josefov

To the east of the Rudolfinum extends the Josefov district (German Josefstadt), Prague's old Jewish quarter, now mainly occupied by buildings erected since the end of the 19th century. There are believed to have been Jews settled in this area as early as the 9th century, and from the 13th century they lived in an independent walled Jewish town which in the 16th century came to be known as the Ghetto. In the 17th century the town was considerably enlarged, and in 1850 it was incorporated in the city of

Prague. In 1338 and again in 1754 it was almost completely destroyed by fire. After a programme of slum clearance in 1893 only a few historic buildings of any importance were left.

***State Jewish Museum**

The old part of the former Jewish town is represented by the Town Hall, the synagogues and the State Jewish Museum (Státní Židovské Muzeum). The collections, which in 1936 comprised only 1000 items, increased during the period of German occupation to almost 200,000, when countless Bohemian, Moravian and other European synagogues unwillingly contributed to a documentation on the Jewish faith and on Jewish life which is unique in the world.

Jewish Town Hall

In the heart of the old Jewish town, at the intersection of Maislova Ulice with Červená Ulice, can be found the Jewish Town Hall (Židovská Ratnice), which was built in the 16th century and remodelled in Baroque style by Josef Schlesinger in 1765. On the north gable is a clock with Hebrew figures and hands which go anti-clockwise.

The Town Hall, with a wooden clock-tower, is the seat of the local government authority for the 1000 Jews living in Prague and of the Council of Jewish Communities in the whole of former Czechoslovakia.

High Synagogue

Adjoining the Jewish Town Hall on the east the High Synagogue (Vysoká Synagóga) is a Renaissance building which was enlarged at the end of the 17th century. It contains an exhibition of ritual fabrics.

***Old-New Synagogue**

On the north side of the High Synagogue is the Old-New Synagogue (Staronová Synagóga), the oldest synagogue in Prague, a modest Early Gothic building erected by Cistercian monks in 1273, with a gable built after the 1338 fire. It is associated with the Jewish legend of the golem, an artificially created human being brought to life by supernatural means. From the vaulting hangs a large flag presented to the Jewish community by the Emperor Ferdinand III for their valour during the Swedish siege of 1648.

Statue of Moses

In front of the synagogue is a statue of Moses by František Bílek (1872–1941).

Klaus Synagogue

From the Old-New Synagogue a short street, U Starého Hřbitova ("By the Old Cemetery"), leads west to the Klaus Synagogue (Klausova Synagóga; 1694), with a permanent exhibition, "The Life of the Jews from the Cradle to the Grave".

Ceremonial Hall

Near the Klaus Synagogue, to the right of the entrance to the Old Jewish Cemetery, can be seen the former Ceremonial Hall (Obřadní Siň; neo-Romanesque), with an exhibition of children's drawings from the Theresienstadt concentration camp (see Terezín).

****Old Jewish Cemetery**

The Old Jewish Cemetery (Starý Židovsky Hřbitov; in Hebrew Beth-Hachayim, "House of Life") extends for almost 200m/220yd between the Museum of Decorative Art on the west, Široká Ulice (Broad Street) on the south and Břehová Ulice on the north.

Gravestones

Under the elder-trees in the cemetery are some 20,000 moss-covered gravestones with Hebrew inscriptions, closely packed together, since owing to shortage of space the dead had to be buried in nine superimposed layers. The oldest stone is that of Rabbi Avigdor Karo (d. 1439); the latest dates from 1787. Some stones bear the symbol of the dead man's tribe: thus two hands raised in blessing mean the tribe of Aaron, a pot the tribe of Levi, a bunch of grapes the tribe of Israel. A sarcophagus carved with lions marks the grave of the learned and wonderworking Rabbi Jehuda ben Besalel (d. 1609), known as the Löw (= "Lion"). Other family names are also represented by symbols – Hahn (a cock), Hirsch (a stag), Karpeles (a carp),

Klaus Synagogue

Fischl (crossed fishes). The piles of stones on the graves have been laid there by friends or relatives of the dead man as a sign of respect and veneration.

Pinkas Synagogue

On the south side of the Old Jewish Cemetery is the Pinkas Synagogue (Pinkasova Synagóga; entrance from cemetery), which dates from the 11th and 12th centuries (renovated in 16th and 17th c.). It is now a memorial to the 77,297 Jews from Bohemia and Moravia who died in concentration camps. The names of the dead are listed on tablets on the walls.

Maisl Synagogue

To the east, beyond Široká Ulice, and then south along Maislova Ulice is the Maisl Synagogue (Maislova Synagóga; founded 1560, rebuilt 1893–1905), which displays a rich collection of silver from Bohemian synagogues (Torah crowns, breastplates, spice-boxes, goblets, candlesticks, etc.).
To the right of the synagogue, at Jáchymova Ulice 3, are the offices and library of the State Jewish Museum.

Spanish Synagogue

To the east of the Old-New Synagogue, beyond the broad Pařížká Třída (Paris Street; view to left of Letná Hill) and the little Gothic Church of the Holy Spirit (Kostel Svatého Ducha; 14th c., Baroquised 1689; in front of the church a statue of St John of Nepomuk by F. M. Brokoff, 1727), in Dušní Ulice, is the Moorish-style Spanish Synagogue (Španělská Synagóga; 1882–93).
It occupies the site of Prague's oldest synagogue, known as the Old School (12th c.); it takes its present name from the Jews who fled from the Inquisition in Spain and came to Prague. In later centuries the synagogue was several times burned down but was always rebuilt. After major restoration works have been completed a collection of ritual fabrics from destroyed synagogues in many countries will be displayed here.

St Salvator's Church

To the south of the Spanish Synagogue we come to the Late Gothic St Salvator's Church (Kostel Svatého Salvátora; 1611–14), which belongs to the Bohemian Brethren.

***St Agnes's Convent**

Some 500m/550yd north-east of the Spanish Synagogue, separated from the Vltava embankment only by a strip of gardens, can be found one of the oldest Christian monuments in Bohemia, St Agnes's Convent (Anežský Klášter), a convent of Poor Clares dating from the 13th century which fell into ruin after its dissolution in 1797.

The whole complex, including several churches and chapels, was completely rebuilt in the 1970s and 1980s. It now houses collections from the National Gallery (19th century Czech painting) and the Museum of Decorative Art (19th century Bohemian decorative art), and is also used for lectures and concerts.

Inter-Continental Hotel

500m/550yd west of St Agnes's Convent, in Náměští Curieových (Curie Square), is the Inter-Continental Hotel, which adds a distinctive note to the city's skyline.

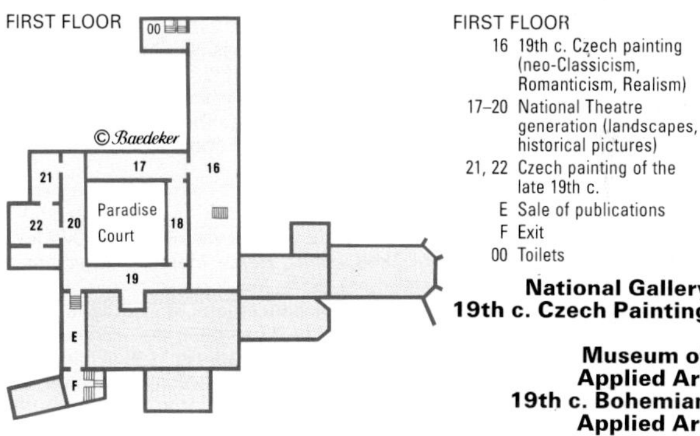

FIRST FLOOR
- 16 19th c. Czech painting (neo-Classicism, Romanticism, Realism)
- 17–20 National Theatre generation (landscapes, historical pictures)
- 21, 22 Czech painting of the late 19th c.
- E Sale of publications
- F Exit
- 00 Toilets

National Gallery
19th c. Czech Painting

Museum of Applied Art
19th c. Bohemian Applied Art

Former Convent of St Agnes
Bývalý Anežský klášter

GROUND FLOOR
- A Entrance (Anezska ulice)
- B Tickets
- C Cloakroom
- D Buffet

- 1 Entrance Hall
- 2 19th c. applied art
- 3–5 Special exhibitions
- 6, 7 19th c. applied art
- 8–12 Czech paintings of the 19th c.
- 9 St Salvator's Church
- 10 Chapter House
- 11 Chapel of St Mary Magdalen
- 12 Presbytery
- 13 Josef Mánes Hall (old nave of Church of St Francis, now a concert hall)
- 14 Concert hall (former St Barbara's Church)
- 15 Excavation finds from Přemyslid tombs (cloister of the former Minorite Convent)

New Town / Nové Město

The New Town of Prague extends around the east and south sides of the Old Town.

Na Príkope

Na Příkopě ("On the Moat"), the busiest street in Prague (pedestrian zone), runs from the Powder Tower along the south-eastern edge of the Old Town, on the line of the old moat. It is lined with offices, shops, restaurants and the stalls of street traders.

State Bank

Slavonic House

Prague Information Service

Čedok

At the near end of the street, on the left, is the Czechoslovak State Bank (Státní Banka Československá) and beyond this the Přichovský Palace (No. 22), built about 1700. From 1875 to 1945, as the German House, this was the meeting-place of the Germans in Prague, and then became the Slavonic House (Slovanský Dům; restaurant). Then follow, at the corner of Nekázanka Ulice, the Prague Infomation Service (Pražská Informační Služba, PIS; No. 20) and Čedok travel agency (No. 18).

Church of Holy Rood

Sylva-Taroucca Palace

At the corner of Panská Ulice stands the neo-classical Church of the Holy Rood (Kostel Svatého Kříže), built in 1816 for the Piarists. Beyond this (No. 10) is the Sylva-Taroucca Palace (1749), built for Prince Ottavio Piccolomini by Anselmo Lurago to the design of Kilian Ignaz Dientzenhofer, with an entrance flanked by columns, several courtyards and a beautiful staircase hall.

***Wenceslas Square**

At the south-west end of Na Příkopě, on the left, is the lower end of Wenceslas Square (Václavské Náměstí), a boulevard (750m/820yd long, 60m/65yd wide; known until 1848 as the Horse Market) rather than a square. Lined with shops, restaurants, cafés, hotels and cinemas, and with shopping arcades and underpasses for pedestrians, it is Prague's main thoroughfare and the hub of the city's life. It has been the scene of some notable events in recent political history – the deaths in 1969 of Jan Palach and Jan Zajíc, the demonstrations of 1988 and the Velvet Revolution of 1989 (memorials at St Wenceslas Monument).

St Wenceslas Monument

Near the upper end of Wenceslas Square, on a high plinth, can be seen a bronze equestrian statue (by Josef Václav Myslbek, 1912–13) of St Wenceslas, the country's patron saint.

***National Museum**

Wenceslas Square ends at the National Museum (Národní Muzeum), built in 1885–90 to the design of Josef Schulz. In the Pantheon, a two-storey domed hall in the centre of the building, are numerous bronze statues and busts of distinguished Czechs. In the side wings are the Museum's extensive prehistoric, archaeological, historical and scientific collections, including mineralogical, geological, palaeontological, zoological and botanical sections; there is also a collection of coins and medals and a section devoted to the theatre. The Museum has a rich library, with around a million books and 8000 manuscripts.

28th October Street

The continuation of Na Příkopě to the south-west is 28th October Street (Ulice 28. Října), along the left-hand side of which are arcades constructed after the Second World War. On the right is the entrance to the Old Town Market Hall (1893–94).

Jungmann Square

28th October Street joins Jungmann Square (Jungmannovo Náměstí), where a monument (by Ludvík Šimek, 1878) to the Czech philologist Josef Jungmann (1773–1847), who translated Milton's "Paradise Lost" into Czech, can be seen.

Our Lady of the Snows

Beyond the Jungmann monument, reached through a neo-classical forecourt (18th c.), is the Gothic church of Our Lady of the Snows (Kostel Panny Marie Sněžné), built between 1348 and 1397 and restored in 1611 after the collapse of the roof. The church was planned to be larger than St Vitus's Cathedral, but only the 33m/108ft high choir was completed. It has a

Wenceslas Square

Baroque high altar of 1625, the tallest in Prague, with a painting of the Annunciation by W. L. Reiner to the left.

Franciscan Garden

To the right, beyond the Jungmann monument, is the entrance to the Franciscan Garden, with two small pools. From the more southerly of the two there is a fine view of the tall choir of Our Lady of the Snows.

Shopping arcades

From Jungmann Square two long shopping arcades run north-east to Wenceslas Square and south-east to Vodičkova Ulice.

National Street

Adria Palace

On the south side of Jungmann Square and at the near end of National Street (Národní Třída), which continues the line of 28th October Street, stands the Adria Palace, built in 1923–25 for the Italian insurance company Riunione Adriatica de Sicurità, with sculpture by Jan Štursa. In the basement (entrance at No. 40) is the "Theatre Behind the Gate" (Divadlo za Bránou).

St Ursula's Church

Near the end of National Street, on the left, the Baroque St Ursula's Church (Kostel Svaté Voršily, 1704) has a richly articulated façade and a fine interior.

The former Ursuline Convent (Klášter Voršilek, 1674–78) stands to the right of the church. Part of this convent is now occupied by a wine restaurant, the Klášterní Vinárna.

***National Theatre**

At the west end of National Street, on the banks of the Vltava at the south end of the Smetana Embankment, is the neo-Renaissance National Theatre (Národní Divadlo; by Josef Zítek, 1868–81). The theatre was burned down after only one performance and was rebuilt by Josef Schulz (1883). In 1976–83 both the exterior and the richly decorated interior were completely renovated and restored to their original form. At the same time a modern annexe, the New Theatre (Nová Scéna), was built, in which the "Laterna Magika" show (a combination of film, theatre, dance, mime and musical) is presented.

New Theatre

National Museum
Národní muzeum

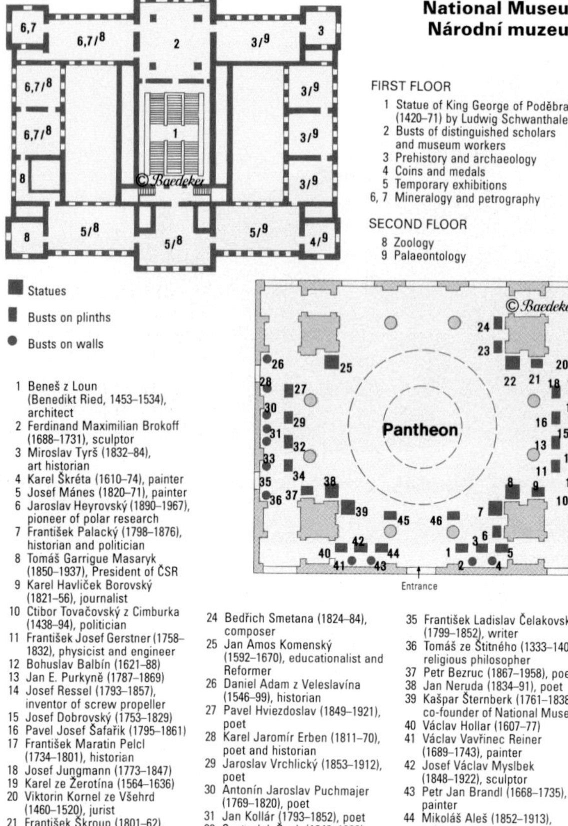

FIRST FLOOR

1 Statue of King George of Poděbrady (1420–71) by Ludwig Schwanthaler
2 Busts of distinguished scholars and museum workers
3 Prehistory and archaeology
4 Coins and medals
5 Temporary exhibitions
6, 7 Mineralogy and petrography

SECOND FLOOR

8 Zoology
9 Palaeontology

Statues

Busts on plinths

Busts on walls

1 Beneš z Loun (Benedikt Ried, 1453–1534), architect
2 Ferdinand Maximilian Brokoff (1688–1731), sculptor
3 Miroslav Tyrš (1832–84), art historian
4 Karel Škréta (1610–74), painter
5 Josef Mánes (1820–71), painter
6 Jaroslav Heyrovský (1890–1967), pioneer of polar research
7 František Palacký (1798–1876), historian and politician
8 Tomáš Garrigue Masaryk (1850–1937), President of ČSR
9 Karel Havlíček Borovský (1821–56), journalist
10 Ctibor Tovačovský z Cimburka (1438–94), politician
11 František Josef Gerstner (1758–1832), physicist and engineer
12 Bohuslav Balbín (1621–88)
13 Jan E. Purkyně (1787–1869)
14 Josef Ressel (1793–1857), inventor of screw propeller
15 Josef Dobrovský (1753–1829)
16 Pavel Josef Šafařík (1795–1861)
17 František Maratin Pelcl (1734–1801), historian
18 Josef Jungmann (1773–1847)
19 Karel ze Žerotína (1564–1636)
20 Viktorin Kornel ze Všehrd (1460–1520), jurist
21 František Škroup (1801–62), composer of national anthem
22 Jan Hus (1371–1415), Reformer
23 Antonín Dvořák (1841–1904), composer
24 Bedřich Smetana (1824–84), composer
25 Jan Amos Komenský (1592–1670), educationalist and Reformer
26 Daniel Adam z Veleslavína (1546–99), historian
27 Pavel Hviezdoslav (1849–1921), poet
28 Karel Jaromír Erben (1811–70), poet and historian
29 Jaroslav Vrchlický (1853–1912), poet
30 Antonín Jaroslav Puchmajer (1769–1820), poet
31 Jan Kollár (1793–1852), poet
32 Svatopluk Čech (1846–1908), poet and writer
33 Václav Matěj Kramerius (1753–1808), writer
34 Alois Jirásek (1851–1930), writer
35 František Ladislav Čelakovský (1799–1852), writer
36 Tomáš ze Štitného (1333–1405), religious philosopher
37 Petr Bezruc (1867–1958), poet
38 Jan Neruda (1834–91), poet
39 Kašpar Šternberk (1761–1838), co-founder of National Museum
40 Václav Hollar (1607–77)
41 Václav Vavřinec Reiner (1689–1743), painter
42 Josef Václav Myslbek (1848–1922), sculptor
43 Petr Jan Brandl (1668–1735), painter
44 Mikoláš Aleš (1852–1913), painter
45 Eliška Krásnohorská (1847–1926), poet
46 Božena Němcová (1820–62), writer

Bridge of the Legions
Marksmen's Island
Vltava Monument

From the National Theatre the Most Legií (Bridge of the Legions; 1889–1901), from which there is a fine view (to the right) of the Hradčany, crosses the Vltava by way of the Střelecký Ostrov (Marksmen's Island) to the Lesser Quarter. To the left, on the weir, is the Vltava Monument (by J. Sander and J. Pekárek, 1916).

Slavonic Island

To the south of the National Theatre lies the Slavonic Island (Slovanský Ostrov), with an attractively situated restaurant and open-air swimming pool.

Šitek Water-Tower
Mánes House of the Arts

Near the south end of the Slavonic Island are the Šitek Water-Tower (Šitkovská Věž; originally 1495, rebuilt in 18th c.) and the modern Mánes House of the Arts (exhibitions), built over the river.

Wilson Street

North-east of the National Museum extends the Vrchlický Park (Vrchlického Sady), a remnant of the old municipal park. Along its east side runs Wilson

Street (Wilsonova Třída), flanked on the left by the North–South Freeway, borne on high piers.

Federal Assembly

On the right-hand side of Wilson Street is the cube-shaped building of the old Federal Assembly of the ČSFR; its future use has not been decided.

State Opera (Smetana Theatre)

Beyond this is the Smetana Theatre (Smetanovo Divadlo), an opera house built by Ferdinand Fellner and Hermann Helmer in 1887 which has been known since 1992 as the Prague State Opera.

***Central Station**

Farther along Wilson Street we come to the Art Nouveau Central Station (Hlavní Nádraží; 1901–08), which between 1970 and 1979 was completely renovated and enlarged by the construction of a new departures hall extending to the west under street level, with a Metro station below (architects Jan Šrámek and his wife Alena Šrámková, Jan Bočan and Josef Fanda).

Hybernská Ulice

A short distance beyond the Central Station Hybernská Ulice goes off on the left towards the Powder Tower. At the near end of this street, on the right, is Masaryk Station (Masarykovo Nádraží; 1844–45; demolition planned). Farther along, also on the right, are the Kinsky Palace (17th c., rebuilt 1789) and the neo-classical Sweerts-Sporck Palace (1780–90).

St Henry's Church

Some 200m/220yd south, at the north end of Jindřišská Ulice, is the Gothic St Henry's Church (Kostel Svatého Jindřicha; 1348–51), with a Baroque interior (18th c.) and a massive separate bell-tower (originally a defensive tower of 1475; restored in neo-Gothic style in 1879).

Republic Square

Hybernská Ulice ends at the U Hybernů exhibition building and joins Republic Square (Náměstí Republiky), a hub of the city's traffic which extends north from the Powder Tower.

City Museum

From Republic Square a street (Na Poříčí) runs north-east to the Jan Šverma Park (Sady Jana Švermy), on the south side of which is the

Central Station, in Art Nouveau style

Museum of the City of Prague (Muzeum Města Prahy; by Antonín Balšánek, 1898), with a rich collection of applied art and material on the history of Prague, including the well-known model of Prague as it was around 1830 (measuring some 20sq.m/215sq.ft) by the lithographer Antonín Langweil (illustration, p. 296).

National Memorial on Mt Vítkov

In the eastern district of Žižkov, rather more than 1km/¾ mile north-east of the Central Station, can be seen the National Memorial on Mt Vítkov (Národní Památnik na Hoře Vítkově), erected in 1929–32. It is most easily reached by way of Wilsonova Třída, Husitská Třída and the street called U Památniku (At the Monument), from which a flight of steps leads up to the Memorial.

*View
Statue of Jan Žižka

Above a terrace from which there is a panoramic view of Prague and the hills to the west stands a monumental equestrian statue (by Bohumil Kafka, 1950) of the Hussite leader Jan Žižka, who won a great victory here over the Catholic forces in 1420.

Mausoleum

Behind this stands a massive Mausoleum (above, a Hall of Mourning, with a large organ; below, the mausoleum proper, with a memorial hall for the dead of the First World War). Below the statue of Žižka is the Tomb of the Unknown Soldier of the Second World War (one of those killed at the Dukla pass).

Museum of Resistance

At the foot of the hill, at the end of U Památniku, on the right, is the Museum of the Resistance and of Military History (Muzeum Odboje a Dějin Armády).

Television Tower

Some 800m/½ mile south of Mt Vítkov, in Mahler Park (Mahlerovy Sady), rises the bizarrely shaped Television Tower (Televizní Věž; 1987–90). It consists of three tubes which join to support the aerial tower, with a total height of 216m/709ft. Although this outsize modernistic structure introduces a jarring note to the Prague skyline it does at least offer magnificent views of the whole of Prague from the restaurant in the tower.

**Views

Karlov Monastery
Church of Assumption and Charles the Great

From the National Museum in Wenceslas Square Mezibranská Ulice and its continuation Sokolská Třída run south for 1.5km/1 mile to Karlov Monastery (now a Police Museum), with the Gothic Church of the Assumption and St Charles the Great (Kostel Nanebevzetí Panny Marie a Svatého Karla Velikého). The church, on an octagonal plan, was built in 1358–77 and has a Baroque interior (by Kilian Ignaz Dientzenhofer, 1720). The dome, 22.75m/75ft in diameter, has stellar vaulting of 1575 (by Bonifaz Wolmut) which ranks as one of the finest architectural achievements of its time.

*Dome

Vyšehrad

From Karlov Monastery Horská Ulice (for part of the way a stepped street) ascends to the old stronghold of Vyšehrad, at the southern tip of old Prague. It can be reached by car by way of Vratislavova Ulice on the north or the street called V Pevnosti ("In the Fortress") on the south-east.

According to legend this was the site of Libussa's castle, the cradle of Bohemian history. The first documentary reference to a castle on the site, however, is in the reign of King Vratislav I (second half of 11th c.). In the reign of Charles IV (mid 14th c.) it was an important stronghold. Destroyed in 1420, during the Hussite Wars, it was rebuilt in the late 17th century as a Baroque fort. In 1866 it was abandoned and in 1911 demolished.

Walls
St Martin's Chapel
Church of SS Peter and Paul

The outer walls of the fortress have survived (fine views from northern, western and southern bastions), together with St Martin's Chapel, a Romanesque rotunda (*c.* 1275; near the Leopold Gate, to the south-east) and, to the north-west of this, above the Vltava, the Church of SS. Peter and Paul (Kostel Svatého Petra a Pavla). SS. Peter and Paul, originally Romanesque (*c.* 1070), was converted in the 15th century into a three-aisled Late Gothic basilica and renovated in neo-Gothic style in 1885–87. It contains a panel painting of Our Lady of Rain (second half of 14th c.), whose aid was sought in times of drought.

Cemetery
Slavín

Immediately north of the church, surrounded by arcades, is the Vyšehrad Cemetery, with the Slavín (Pantheon) of 1893. Here are buried many famous Czechs, including the composers Smetana (obelisk on east wall)

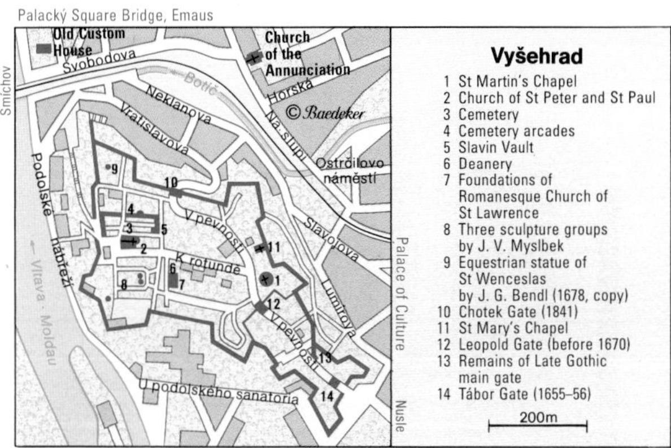

and Dvořák (bust in west arcade), the writer Božena Nemcová (d. 1862), the painter Mikoláš Aleš (d. 1913) and the sculptor Josef Václav Myslbek (d. 1922; in the Slavín).

***Palace of Culture**

On a plateau 1km/¾ mile south-east of Vyšehrad, in the Nusle district, is the monumental Palace of Culture (Palác Kultury; 1981). This multi-storied example of modern Czech architecture, with a floor area of 278,000 sq.m/ 3 million sq.ft, is used for a variety of major events, concerts, theatrical performances, entertainment programmes (including the film and stage show Laterna Magika) and exhibitions.

Vyšehrad: Church of SS Peter and Paul

St Martin's Chapel

Palace of Culture: an example of modern Prague architecture

In the centre of the building is the Great Hall (with an organ), which can be transformed into an auditorium with seating for up to 3000. There are also four smaller halls equipped with the latest technology, an exhibition hall and numerous conference rooms. Within the complex are two restaurants with views over the city and a night club.

Forum Hotel

A footbridge links the Palace of Culture with the large new Forum Hotel.

Emmaus Monastery

1km/¾ mile north of Vyšehrad, on Vyšehradská Třída (No. 49), is the Emmaus Monastery (Klášter Emauzy or Na Slovanech, "With the Slavs"), founded by Charles IV in 1347 for the Slavonic Benedictines. Burned down after an American air attack in 1945, it was restored in 1967.

Church of Our Lady

The Gothic Church of Our Lady, built in 1348–72 and remodelled in Baroque style in the 17th century, was restored in neo-Gothic style and repainted in 1880–89 by Benedictine monks who had been expelled from Germany. In 1967 further restoration work was carried out and the church was given a modern façade and two intersecting pointed concrete towers. It is now used as a concert hall.

*Frescoes

The beautiful Gothic cloister has a series of much restored 14th century frescoes in 26 panels (Old and New Testament scenes in parallel), in the manner of the "Bibles of the poor" – the finest example of the work of the Prague school of painters.

***Church of St John of Nepomuk on the Rock**

To the east of the Emmaus Monastery the Church of St John of Nepomuk on the Rock (Kostel Svatého Jana na Skalce; by Kilian Ignaz Dientzenhofer, 1730–39) is a beautiful Baroque church on a centralised plan, approached by a double staircase, with fine frescoes of 1748 in the vaulting.

Palacký Bridge

To the north-west of the Emmaus Monastery is the Palacký Bridge (Palackého Most). In the square in front of the bridge is an imposing monument (by Stanislav Sucharda, 1912) to the Czech historian František Palacký (1798–1876).

Botanic Gardens

A short distance south-east of the Emmaus Monastery are the beautiful Botanic Gardens (Botanická Zahrada), which have occupied this site since 1898. Prague's first botanic garden was established in the reign of Charles IV by a pharmacist from Florence; it lay on the site of the Head Post Office (Jindřišská Ulice 14), in the New Town.

*** Charles Square**

From the Emmaus Monastery Vyšehradská Třída runs north to the spacious Charles Square (Karlovo Náměstí; known until 1848 as the Cattle Market). This is Prague's largest square (530m/580yd by 150m/165yd), which with its gardens and monuments to Czech scientists and writers has something of the air of a park. On the south and south-east sides of the square are hospitals.

Faust's House

On the south side of Charles Square (No. 40) is "Faust's House" (Faustův Dům), the former Mladota Palace, in which Dr Faust or Faustus is said to have lived. In the 16th century it did in fact belong to an English alchemist named Edward Kelley who was employed in the service of Rudolph II. It is now the pharmacy of a polyclinic.

College of Technology

On the west side of Charles Square stands the College of Technology (České Vysoké Učení Technické; 1867).

Church of SS Cyril and Methodius

To the west, along the broad Resslova Ulice, the former Church of St Charles Borromeus (by Kilian Ignaz Dientzenhofer, 1740) has, since 1935, been the church of the Orthodox community, dedicated to SS Cyril and Methodius.

The resistance fighters (paratroopers) who killed the German "Protector" Reinhard Heydrich in June 1942 hid in the crypt of the church but were discovered and killed in a gun battle on June 18th. There is a memorial tablet in Resslova Ulice. (See Lidice).

Church of St Wenceslas in Zderaz

Diagonally opposite the Church of SS. Cyril and Methodius is the Gothic Church of St Wenceslas in Zderaz (Kostel Svatého Václava na Zderaze; 14th c.), which belongs to the Czechoslovak Hussite Church.

Church of St Ignatius

On the east side of Charles Square is the Jesuit Church of St Ignatius (Kostel Svatého Ignáce; by Carlo Lurago, 1665–70), with a porch by Paul Ignaz Bayer (1699) and a finely decorated interior (rich stucco ornament; altarpieces by Karel Škréta, Ignaz Raab and others).

The former Jesuit College now forms part of the adjoining hospital.

Old Town Hall

At the north-east corner of Charles Square stands the tower of the former Town Hall of the New Town (Novoměstská Radnice; 14th c., now in course of reconstruction), which was the scene of the First Defenestration of Prague in 1419. Some parts of the Town Hall were incorporated in a new Criminal Court building, which now serves a variety of purposes; part of it is a registry office.

St Stephen's Church

To the east of Charles Square, in Štěpánská Ulice, is the Gothic St Stephen's Church (Kostel Svatého Štěpána; built 1351–67, restored 1866–78), with a Baroque interior and a Late Gothic font of 1462.

Rotunda of St Longinus

Beyond St Stephen's Church can be found the Rotunda of St Longinus (Rotunda Svatého Longina), a 12th century Romanesque chapel.

St Catherine's Church

To the south of St Stephen's is St Catherine's Church (Kostel Svaté Kateřiny; 1737–41), now an exhibition hall.

Villa Amerika
Dvořák Museum

Farther east is the small but very elegant Villa Amerika, built by Kilian Ignaz Dientzenhofer in 1717–20 as a summer palace for Count Michna. It now houses the Dvořák Museum, with mementoes of the great Czech composer.

Charles Bridge

Statues

Lesser Quarter Bridge Towers

→ N

St Wenceslas
by J. K. Böhm, 1858

SS. Cosmas and Damian
by J. O. Mayer, 1709

SS. John of Matha, Felix of Valois and Ivan and figure of a Turk
by F. M. Brokoff, 1714

St Vitus
by F. M. Brokoff, 1714 (marble)

St Adalbert
by F. M. Brokoff, 1709 (copy, 1973)

St Philip Benizi
by M. B. Mandl, 1714

St Luitgard
by M. B. Braun, 1710

St Cajetan
by F. M. Brokoff, 1709

The **Charles Bridge** was begun in 1357 by Peter Parler, but completed only at the beginning of the 15th c. Its irregular course is probably due to the fact that after the collapse in 1342 of the first stone bridge over the Vltava (the Judith Bridge, built between 1158 and 1172), new piers were set beside the old ones but the original bridgeheads were re-used.

St Nicholas of Tolentino
by J. F. Kohl, 1706 (copy, 1969)

St Augustine
by J. F. Kohl, 1708 (copy, 1974)

SS. Vincent Ferrer and Procopius
by F. M. Brokoff, 1712

Roland Column
(originally 16th c.; copy of 1884)

St Jude Thaddaeus
by J. O. Mayer, 1708

St Francis Seraphicus
by E. Max, 1855

St Anthony of Padua
by J. O. Mayer, 1707

SS. Ludmilla and Wenceslas
workshop of M. B. Braun, *c.* 1730

St John of Nepomuk
by M. Rauchmüller and J. Brokoff, 1683; cast in bronze by W. H. Heroldt, Nuremberg, 1683

St Francis Borgia
by J. amd F. M. Brokoff, 1710 (restored by R. Vlach, 1937)

SS. Wenceslas, Norbert and Sigismund
by J. Max, 1853

St Christopher
by E. Max, 1857

St John the Baptist
by J. Max, 1857

St Francis Xavier
by F. M. Brokoff, 1711 (copy, 1913)

SS. Cyril and Methodius and three allegorical figures (Bohemia, Moravia and Slovakia), by K. Dvořák, 1938

St Joseph
by J. Max, 1854

St Anne with the Virgin and Child
by M. W. Jäckel, 1707

Pietà
by E. Max, 1859 (originally 1695)

Bronze Crucifix
cast by J. Hilger, 1629; the first piece of sculpture on the bridge, set up 1657; Hebrew inscription of 1696; figures by E. Max, 1861

SS. Barbara, Margaret and Elizabeth
by F. M. Brokoff, 1707

Virgin with SS. Dominic and Thomas Aquinas
by M. W. Jäckel, 1709 (copy, 1961)

St Ivo
by M. B. Braun, 1711 (copy, 1908)

Virgin with St Bernard
by M. W. Jäckel, 1709 (copy)

Old Town Bridge Tower

Charles Bridge, looking towards the Old Town Bridge Tower

St John of Nepomuk

The Virgin and Child and St Bernard

** Charles Bridge / Karlův Most

The Old Town and the Lesser Quarter are linked by the sixteen-arched Charles Bridge (Karlův Most). 520m/570yd long between the mighty defensive towers at each end and 10m/33ft wide, it is the oldest bridge over the Vltava in Prague.

The bridge is now closed to traffic and is usually crowded throughout the day with tourists, who are catered for by street musicians and street traders offering souvenirs of varying interest and quality.

**** Old Town Bridge Tower**

At the east end of the bridge, on the west side of Knights of the Cross Square, is the imposing Old Town Bridge Tower (Staroměstská Mostecká Věž), built in the 14th–15th century by Peter Parler (restored 1874–79), which is surely the finest tower in Prague. On the east side are the coats of arms of the countries which at one time were allied with Bohemia; above the arched gateway is a statue of St Vitus flanked by seated figures of Charles IV and Wenceslas IV, and above these are St Sigismund and St Adalbert.

**** Statues**
(see plan, p. 322)

The picturesque effect of the Charles Bridge, from which there are superb views of the many-towered Old Town and the Hradčany, is mainly due to the rich sculptural decoration, the work of many different artists since the 17th century. Most of the statues and groups which line both sides of the bridge were created between 1706 and 1714, mainly by Ferdinand Maximilian Brokoff but also by Matthias Bernhard Braun von Braun, Johann Friedrich Kohl, Johann Friedrich Mayer, Matthäus Wenzel Jäckel and others. A few less expressive figures are more recent, mainly by Josef and Emanuel Max (1853–61); the most recent is by Karl Dvořák (1938). Some statues have been replaced by copies.

Particularly fine is the bronze Crucifix by Johann Hilger (1629; third group on right). In the centre of the bridge, on the right, is a bronze statue (by Matthias Rauchmüller and Johann Brokoff, 1683; cast in Nuremberg) of St John of Nepomuk, who was canonised only in 1729 (pilgrimage day May 16th). A small marble tablet with a cross (on the wall, between the seventh and eighth piers) marks the spot where John was cast into the river on the orders of Wenceslas IV because he had sided with the archbishop against the king in a dispute over the Church's rights. (His tomb is in the ambulatory in St Vitus's Cathedral.)

Kampa Island
Little Venice

The west end of the Charles Bridge passes over Kampa Island, which is separated from the Lesser Quarter by a narrow arm of the river, the Čertovka. This is the area known as Little Venice (riverside houses in course of restoration).

Bruncvík

On the island, close to the bridge (on left), is a reproduction of a Late Gothic Roland Column (known in Czech as Bruncvík), set up here in 1884.

House At the Three Ostriches

At the west end of the bridge, lower down (on right), stands the House At the Three Ostriches (Dům U Tří Pštrosů), a Renaissance building of 1585 with carefully restored paintings on the façade (hotel and restaurant).

Lesser Quarter Bridge Towers

The Charles Bridge ends at the Lesser Quarter Bridge Towers (Malostranské Mostecké Věže), which are linked by an arch.

The higher of the two towers was built in 1464 on the orders of King George of Poděbrady, replacing an earlier Romanesque tower. Its Late Gothic architecture resembles that of the Old Town Bridge Tower, as does its sculptural decoration.

The lower tower (last quarter of 12th c.) was part of the fortifications of the old Judith Bridge, which collapsed in 1342 during a spate on the river. The Renaissance gable and the decoration of the outer wall date from 1591.

Lesser Quarter / Malá Strana

Mostecká Ulice

From the west end of the Charles Bridge Mostecká Ulice (Bridge Street) leads west, lined by handsome old houses, with the Kaunitz Palace (Kauni-

The Lesser Quarter, a district of many towers

ců̊v Palác; 1753–55) at No. 15 on the left, to Lesser Quarter Square (Malostranské Náměstí), which is partly surrounded by arcades and by charming old burghers' houses.

****St Nicholas's Church**

In the centre of the square can be seen St Nicholas's Church (Chrám Svatého Mikuláše), the finest Baroque church in Prague, originally built by the Jesuits, with a magnificent dome and a tall tower (completed in 1756 by Anselmo Lurago; restored in 1925 after a fire).

History

The foundation stone of the church was laid in 1653 and work began under the direction of Domenico Orsi. In 1704 he was succeeded by Christoph Dientzenhofer, who completed the nave in 1711. The dome and choir (1737–59) were the work of his famous son Kilian Ignaz Dientzenhofer.

Interior

The richly furnished interior owes its overpowering effect mainly to the superb frescoes with which it is decorated. The ceiling painting over the nave (by Johann Lukas Kracker, 1760–61) depicts scenes from the life of St Nicholas. The paintings in the dome, depicting the glorification of the saint and the Last Judgment, are by Franz Xaver Balko (1752–53), who together with Joseph Hager was responsible for the wall paintings in the choir. The sculpture in the nave and choir and the figure of St Nicholas on the high altar are by Ignaz Platzer the Elder, the pulpit by Richard and Peter Prachner (1765).

Trinity Column

Next to the richly articulated west front of St Nicholas's (view of St Vitus's Cathedral) is a Trinity Column (Plague Column) by Giovanni Battista Alliprandi (1715).

Liechtenstein Palace
Lesser Quarter Town Hall

On the west side of Lesser Quarter Square is the neo-classical Liechtenstein Palace (1791) and on the east side the former Lesser Quarter Town Hall, a handsome Late Renaissance building (17th c.).

St Thomas's Church

To the east of Lesser Quarter Square, in Letenská Ulice, is St Thomas's Church (Kostel Svatého Tomáše), a 14th century church which was remodelled in Baroque style by Kilian Ignaz Dientzenhofer in 1725, with ceiling frescoes by W. L. Reiner.

St Joseph's Church

To the south is the beautiful Baroque church of St Joseph (Kostel Svatého Josefa). The façade (1673–91) and the interior were the work of Jean-Baptiste Mathey.

Thun Palace

North-west of Lesser Quarter Square, at Thunovská 14 (along Nerudova, then right into Sněmovní and left into Thunovská) can be found the Thun Palace (17th c.; façade by Antonio Giovanni Lurago, 1716–27), in which Mozart and his wife stayed in 1787. It is now the British Embassy.

Valdštejn Square
Valdštejn Palace

From the north-east corner of Lesser Quarter Square Tomásská Ulice leads to the Valdštejn (Waldstein) Palace.
The palace, built for Albrecht von Wallenstein (Waldstein), Duke of Friedland, by the Milanese master builder Giovanni Battista Marini to the plans of Andrea Spezza and Giovanni Pieroni, was Prague's first Baroque palace. It now houses the Ministry of Culture and the Komenský Museum (material on the life and work of the educationist and philosopher Jan Amos Komenský, better known under the name Comenius). On the ground floor are the high palace chapel and the Banqueting Hall or Knights' Hall (concerts).

Valdštejn Gardens

In the Valdštejn Gardens (Zahrada Valdštejnského Paláce; entered from Letenská Ulice) are a number of bronze statues by the Dutch sculptor Adriaen de Vries (copies made in 1911–13; the originals, mostly dating

Sala terrena in the Valdštejn Gardens, below the Hradčany

from around 1625 and probably intended for a fountain, are in Drottningholm Palace, Stockholm. From the gardens there is a fine view of St Vitus's Cathedral and Prague Castle.

***Sala Terrena**

At the west end of the gardens is the Sala Terrena, a large open loggia with rich stucco decoration and frescoes by Baccio del Bianco (theatrical performances and concerts).

Ledebour Palace
Sala terrena

On the north side of Valdštejn Square stands the Ledebour Palace (Ledeburský Palác). In the gardens (entered from Valdštejnská Ulice) is a small sala terrena of 1716.

Palaces in Valdštejnská Ulice

In Valdštejnská Ulice, which runs along the slope of the hill on the north side of the Valdštejn Palace, are a number of handsome palaces. On the left (No. 14) is the Pálffy Palace; then at No. 12 is the entrance to the Ledebour Gardens, which communicate on both sides with other beautiful, steeply terraced gardens, with loggias and a pavilion, belonging to palaces in Valdštejnská Ulice (wide views over the city).

Farther along Valdštejnská Ulice are the Kolowrat Palace (No. 10; 18th c.) and the Fürstenberg Palace (No. 8; 1743–47), which is now the Polish Embassy (no admission to gardens).

Diagonally opposite, on the right-hand side of the street, is the former Valdštejn Riding School (Jízdárna Valdštejnského Paláce), now used for exhibitions.

Church of St Mary under the Chain

A little way south of Mostecká Ulice the Maltese Church, known as Our Lady Under the Chain (Kostel Panny Marie pod Řetežem), was originally built in the 12th century but much altered in later centuries, with Gothic towers and a beautiful Baroque interior.

Grand Prior's Square
Grand Prior's Palace

To the south of the church, fronting on to Grand Prior's Square (Velkopřevorské Náměstí), is the Palace of the Grand Prior of the Knights of Malta (Palác Maltézského Velkopřevora; by Bartolomeo Scotti, 1726–31), which, together with the Maltese Convent at Lázeňská Ulice 4, is now once more the residence of the ambassador of the Sovereign Order of the Knights of Malta.

Buquoy Palace

Opposite the Grand Prior's Palace, at No. 2, is the Buquoy Palace, built in 1628, probably to the plans of Jean-Baptiste Mathey, and altered in 1738. It is now the French Embassy.

Maltese Square
Nostitz Palace

Farther west in Maltese Square (Maltézské Náměstí) can be seen numbers of attractive Baroque houses. The south side of the square is occupied by a large Baroque building, the Nostitz Palace (Nostickí Palác), originally built in 1658–60 but much altered later, with sculpture on the façade by M. J. Brokoff and a charming courtyard. It is now the Netherlands Embassy. In the Nostitz Gallery are paintings by 17th century Dutch masters and the Prague Music Salon.

Tyrš House (Museum of Sport)

To the south of the Nostitz Palace is the Tyrš House (Tyršův Dům; originally an arsenal, later the Michna Palace), a 17th century palace which now houses the Museum of Physical Education and Sport (Muzeum Tělesné Výchovy a Sportu; entrance in Karmelitská Ulice).

Church of Our Lady Victorious

A short distance west of Maltese Square, in Karmelitská Ulice (Carmelite Street), is the Church of Our Lady Victorious (Kostel Panny Marie Vítežné), in Early Baroque style. It was built in 1611–16 as the church of a Carmelite convent, on the site of a Hussite church, and was to become a monument to the victory of the Imperial forces in the battle of the White Mountain (1620). The interior is modelled on the Gesù church in Rome. On the right-hand wall is the "Christ Child of Prague", a wax figure 50cm/20in. high, originally from Spain, which was presented to the convent in 1628 by Princess Polyxena von Lobkowitz and is still much venerated.

In the catacombs under the church (no admission) are the bodies of Carmelites and their benefactors, dried up by the circulation of air.

Vrtba Gardens

Near the north end of Karmelitská Ulice stands the Vrtba Palace (Vrtbovský Dům; No. 25). This is the entrance to the delightful Vrtba Gardens (Vrtbovská Zahrada; in course of restoration), laid out in Baroque style on the steep slopes behind the palace which were once covered with vines. There are numerous statues by the Baroque sculptor M. B. Braun von Braun. From the top of the gardens there are fine views (St Nicholas's Church, etc.).

Schönborn Palace

Lobkowitz Palace

North-west of the north end of Karmelitská Ulice is the New Market (Tržiště), in which (on the left) is the Schönborn Palace (17th–18th c.), now the United States Embassy. From here Vlašská Ulice continues to the Lobkowitz Palace (Lobkovický Palác; by Giovanni Battista Alliprandi, 1703–07), with a finely articulated garden front; it is now the German Embassy.

Hradčany

Access to the ****Hradčany**

From Lesser Quarter Square there are two routes to the Hradčany:
The shorter route runs north along Zámecká Ulice (Castle Street) and then turns left up the New Castle Steps (Nové Zámecké Schody; 205 steps); then to the right under the Paradise Garden (Rajská Zahrada).

***Nerudova Ulice**

The longer route follows Nerudova Ulice, an old-world street (many house signs) which leads west, rising gently. In this street are the Morzin Palace (on left, No. 5; built in 1670 and remodelled in 1713–14 by Giovanni Santini-Aichel; Atlas figures on façade by F. M. Brokoff, 1714), now the Romanian Embassy; the Thun Palace (on right, No. 20; by Giovanni Santini-Aichel, 1710–20; Baroque doorway with two eagles by M. B. Braun von Braun), now the Italian Embassy; and, adjoining this, the Baroque church of St Cajetan or Theatine Church (Kostel Panny Marie a Svatého Kajetánů; by Jean-Baptiste Mathey and Giovanni Santini-Aichel, 1691–

Bird's eye view of the Hradčany

1717). Then turn sharp right into the street called Ke Hradu (To the Castle), passing below the Schwarzenberg Palace (on left).

***Hradčany Square**

In the centre of the Hradčany lies Hradčany Square (Hradčanské Náměstí), a long rectangle with a Plague Column by Ferdinand Maximilian Brokoff (1725).

Archbishop's Palace

On the north side of the square can be seen the Archbishop's Palace (Arcibiskupský Palác), built by J.-B. Mathey in 1675–1684 and altered in 1764–65.

***Schwarzenberg Palace**

On the south side of the square stands the Schwarzenberg Palace (Schwarzenberský Palác; 1545–63), one of the earliest Renaissance buildings in Prague. It is in two parts: on the left is the Swiss Embassy, and in the building on the right, which has sgraffito decoration imitating faceted ashlar on the outer walls, is the Museum of Military History (Vojenské Historické Muzeum), with old cannon in the courtyard.

Toscana Palace

The Toscana Palace (Toskanský Palác; by J.-B. Mathey, 1680), at the west end of the square is now occupied by various government offices. At the south corner can be seen a vigorous Baroque sculpture of the Archangel Michael with the dragon (probably by Ottavio Mosto, *c.* 1700).

Martinitz Palace

At the north-west corner of Hradčany Square stands the Martinitz Palace (Martinický Palác), a handsome Renaissance building (late 16th c., altered in early 17th c.) which is now the office of Prague's City Architect, with carefully restored figural sgraffito decoration.

Church of St John of Nepomuk

From the Martinitz Palace Kanovnická Ulice (Canons' Street) runs north-west to the church of St John of Nepomuk (Kostel Svatého Jana Nepomuckého), Kilian Ignaz Dientzenhofer's earliest church (1720–29), with a ceiling fresco by W. L. Reiner (1717).

****Prague Castle**

The whole of the east end of Hradčany Square is occupied by Prague Castle (see p. 330).

Sternberg Palace

From the west side of the Archbishop's Palace a narrow lane leads down into the courtyard of the Sternberg Palace (Šternberský Palác; by G. B. Alliprandi, *c.* 1720), which houses the main collections of the National Gallery (Národní Galerie).

****Picture Gallery**

The National Gallery's collection, formerly displayed in the Artists' House and considerably increased by new acquisitions since the Second World War, is the finest in the country. The Sternberg Palace contains outstanding works by painters of the Italian, Dutch, Flemish and German schools and by 19th and 20th century painters from France and other European countries. The National Gallery's famous collection of Bohemian art (from Gothic to Baroque) is now housed in St George's Convent in Prague Castle, which has been restored for the purpose.
The rooms are not numbered. The pictures are arranged according to the artists' countries of origin, and chronologically within each group.
The gallery is at present closed while security measures are being carried out.

Older European art

The staircase to the right of the entrance leads to the collection of older European art (Sbírka Starého Evropského Umění).
The first rooms on the first floor are devoted to Italian painters of the 14th and 15th centuries, particularly of the Florentine school, with works by Orcagna, Giovanni d'Allemagna, Antonio Vivarini, Piero della Francesca, Sebastiano del Piombo and Palma il Vecchio.
The narrow room opening off the third room (on left) displays valuable icons.
Then follow Dutch and Flemish masters of the 15th and 16th centuries, including works by Geertgen tot Sint Jans, Gerard David, Jan Gossaert

(Mabuse: "St Luke painting the Virgin"), Cornelis Engelbrechtsz., Pieter Brueghel the Elder ("Haymaking") and Pieter Brueghel the Younger ("Arrival of the Three Kings", "Winter Landscape").
The second floor begins with Italian painters of the 16th–18th centuries, including Tintoretto ("David with Goliath's Head"), Veronese, Palma il Giovane, Bronzino, Tiepolo ("Portrait of a Venetian Gentleman") and Canaletto ("View of London").
Then come German painters of the 14th–18th centuries. The finest work here is Dürer's "Festival of the Rosary", painted in 1506 for German merchants in Venice. It shows the Virgin and Child crowned by angels and surrounded by numerous figures, including the artist himself (above, right), the humanist Konrad Peutinger, the wealthy German merchant Ulrich Fugger the Elder, the Emperor Maximilian I, Pope Julius II and a number of Venetians. There are also pictures by nameless 15th century masters, including the Master of Grossgmain, and works by Hans of Tübingen, Hans Holbein the Elder, Hans Baldung Grien, Altdorfer, Lucas Cranach the Elder and Thomas Burgkmair.
There follow 17th century Dutch and Flemish painters, including Jacob Jordaens ("Apostles"), Rubens ("Cleopatra"; "Martyrdom of St Thomas" and "St Augustine on the Seashore", both 1637–39), David Teniers the Younger ("Boon Companions"), Antony van Dyck ("Abraham and Isaac"), Frans Hals ("Portrait of Jasper Schade van Westrum", 1645), Rembrandt ("Old Scholar", "Annunciation"), Adriaen van Ostade, Gerard Dou ("Young Woman on Balcony"), Metsu, Gerard Terborch (two portraits) and Philips Wouwermann.

19th and 20th c. French art

The collection of 19th and 20th century French art (Sbírka Francouzkého Umění 19. a 20. Století) is displayed on the ground floor of the north and west wings, reached by keeping straight across the courtyard from the entrance.
The collection covers French art from the Romantic school to Cubism, arranged in chronological order according to the artists' dates of birth, with works by Delacroix, Daumier, Rousseau, Courbet, Monet, Cézanne, Renoir, Gauguin, van Gogh, Toulouse-Lautrec, Matisse, Vlaminck, Utrillo, Picasso (important works of his early Cubist period), Braque and Chagall.
There is also sculpture by Degas, Rodin, Bourdelle and Maillol.

19th and 20th c. European art

The collection of 19th and 20th century European art (Sbírka Evropského Umění 19. a 20. Století) is on the first floor of the north and west wings. It includes works by Austrian (Ferdinand Georg Waldmüller, Gustav Klimt, Oskar Kokoschka), German (Caspar David Friedrich, the "Bridge" group), Russian (Ilya Repin) and Italian (Renato Guttuso; sculpture by Manzù) artists.

****Prague Castle**

At the east end of Hradčany Square is the extensive range of buildings which make up Prague Castle (Pražský Hrad). The first building on the site was devastated by fire in 1303 and was reconstructed from 1333 onwards by Matthias of Arras (d. 1352) for the future Emperor Charles IV. There was further building and alteration in the reigns of Vladislav II (by Benedikt Ried), Louis and Ferdinand I, who after a fire in 1541 had the Castle restored by Bonifaz Wohlmut from Constance. The gatehouse, with the Matthias Gate, was the work of Giovanni Maria Philippi (1614). The last extension of the Castle, giving it a total of over 700 rooms, was carried out by Anselmo Lurago to the design of Nikolaus Pacassi in 1756–74, during the reign of Maria Theresa.

First and Second Courtyards

From the First Courtyard the Matthias Gate (from which a staircase on the right leads to the former Imperial apartments, now the reception rooms of the President of the Republic) gives access to the Second Courtyard, with a large Baroque well-house (by Francesco Torre, 1686; sculpture by Hieronymus Kohl) and two smaller fountains. To the left of the Matthias Gate is the Plečnik Hall, created in 1927–31 by the reconstruction of older buildings, which was combined with the Staircase Hall to form an entrance lobby to the Spanish Hall (on the north-west side of the Second Courtyard,

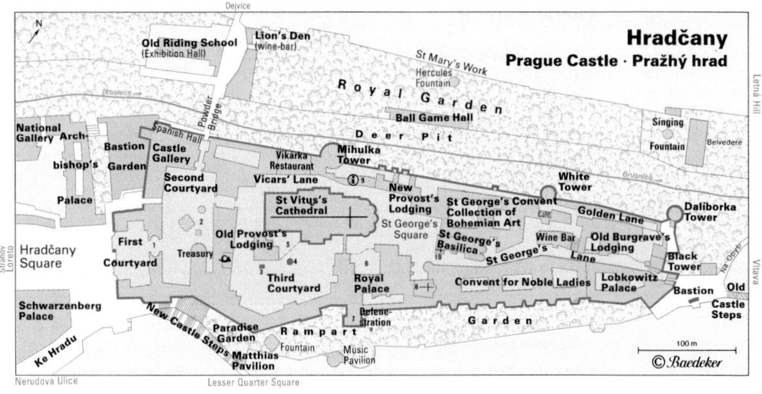

1 Matthias Gate 2 Fountain 3 Obelisk 4 St George 5 Romanesque remains 6 Palace Courtyard 7 Louis Wing 8 All Saints Chapel 9 Old Deanery (Mladota House) 10 Chapel of St John of Nepomuk

above the Castle Gallery; by G. M. Philippi, 1602–06, with later alterations) and the adjoining Rudolph Gallery in which Rudolph II had kept his art collection. All these rooms are used for ceremonial purposes and official occasions and are seldom open to the public.

Chapel of Holy Rood (Treasury)

To the right is the Chapel of the Holy Rood (Kaple Svatého Kříže; after 1753), a small building by Anselmo Lurago which now houses the Treasury (Klenotnice), with valuable liturgical utensils, reliquaries, monstrances, vestments, etc.

***Castle Gallery**

On the north side of the Second Courtyard, on the left, is the entrance to the Castle Gallery (Obrazárna Pražského Hradu).

The Gallery displays in six rooms pictures which were formerly housed in the Rudolph Gallery and elsewhere in the Castle. Among the painters represented are Hans of Aachen ("Portrait of the Emperor Matthias", *c.* 1612, in Room 1), Titian ("Young Woman at her Toilet"), Tintoretto ("Christ with the Woman Taken in Adultery"), Veronese ("St Catherine with the Angel"), and Rubens ("Assembly of the Olympian Gods", *c.* 1602, in Room 4). There is also some sculpture, including Adriaen de Vries's stucco relief, "Adoration of the Kings".

In Room 6, to the left of Room 2, are large photographs showing works from Rudolph II's collection, now dispersed, and illustrating methods of art-historical research. Behind a glass screen are the foundations, partly excavated after the Second World War, of a church dedicated to the Virgin (9th–10th c.), the oldest church within the precincts of the Castle, which had been several times destroyed and rebuilt.

From the Second Courtyard a passage leads into the Third Courtyard, in which is St Vitus's Cathedral.

Old Provost's Lodging

At the south-west corner of the Cathedral the Old Provost's Lodging (Staré Proboštství; 17th c.) has a statue of St Wenceslas (by J. G. Bendl, 1662) on the corner. Beside it is a 17m/56ft high obelisk erected in 1928 to commemorate the dead of the First World War, and beyond this, on a high plinth, a small equestrian statue of St George (copy; original in St George's Convent).

Excavations

Between here and the south wall of the Cathedral are the foundations (excavated in 1920–28 and now roofed over) of a Romanesque chapel.

****Royal Palace**

At the east end of the Third Courtyard is the Royal Palace (Královský Palác), which has several entrances.

Royal Palace Královský palác

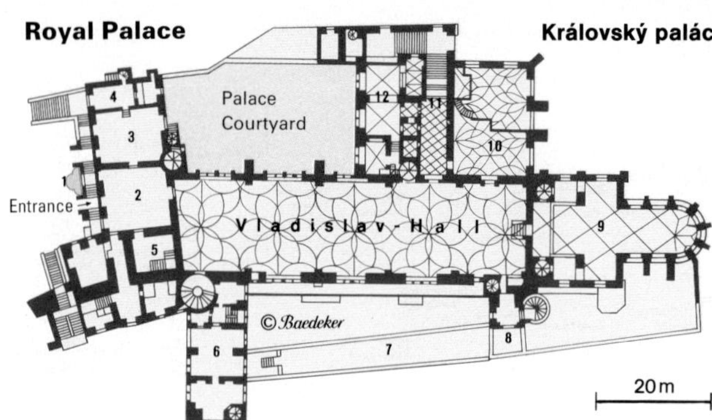

1 Eagle Fountain
2 Antechamber
3 Green Room
4 Vladislav's bedroom
5 Romanesque tower
6 Bohemian Chancellery
7 Theresian range
8 Outlook terrace
9 All Saints Chapel
10 Hall of Diet
11 Staircase (for horsemen)
12 New Appeal Court

Green Chamber

The central doorway under the balcony, to the right of the Eagle Fountain (by Francesco Torre, 1664), leads into an antechamber, with the Green Chamber to the left. From the time of Charles IV this was used as a court room. The Baroque ceiling painting (copy) depicts the Judgment of Solomon. Adjoining the Green Chamber are the so-called Vladislav Bedroom and (to the right) a small room which used to house land records.

**Vladislav Hall

From the antechamber a doorway opposite the entrance leads into the Vladislav Hall (or Hall of Homage; 62m/203ft long, 16m/52ft wide, 13m/43ft high), built by Benedikt Ried in 1493–1502, incorporating some earlier Romanesque work. With its rich Late Gothic net vaulting this is the showpiece of Prague Castle. The hall was the scene of the election of the Bohemian kings and other splendid ceremonies, and it has been used since 1934 for the election of the President of the Republic and important acts of state.

All Saints Chapel

At the east end of the Vladislav Hall a flight of steps leads into All Saints Chapel, originally built by Peter Parler in the late 14th century and rebuilt in 1579–80 after its destruction in the 1541 fire. From 1755 it belonged to the sumptuously appointed Baroque Convent for Noble Ladies adjoining the palace on the east.

Hall of the Diet

To the left of the entrance to the chapel is a doorway leading into the Hall of the Diet, built by Benedikt Ried about 1500 and rebuilt by Bonifaz Wohlmut in 1559–63 with ribbed vaulting after the collapse of the roof in the 1541 fire. Until 1847 this was the meeting-place of the Bohemian Diet. It has a Renaissance gallery and a 17th century throne, and on the walls are portraits of Habsburg rulers.

Horsemen's Staircase

Farther to the left is the Horsemen's Staircase, with wide, shallow steps up which horsemen could ride for the tournaments held in the Vladislav Hall.

Palace Courtyard

The doorway on the right at the foot of the staircase leads into St George's Square, the one on the left into the Palace Courtyard, on a lower level, with 13th century arcades along two sides. Another staircase gives access to the Gothic Palace.

Gothic Palace

In the Gothic Palace are the Room of the Old Land Records, with massive vaulting borne on two squat piers, an arcaded passage dating from the

South side of St Vitus's Cathedral, with the main tower ►

Vladislav Hall

All Saints Chapel

time of Otakar II (1245–78), the Charles Hall (with casts of busts from the triforium of St Vitus's Cathedral), the Old Registry (at one time the palace kitchen) and Wenceslas IV's Hall of Columns (with interesting vaulting from around 1400).

Romanesque Palace

From the western arcades in the Palace Courtyard a long staircase leads down to the Romanesque Palace, now underground, the oldest parts of which date from the 9th century.

Louis Wing

To the right of the central doorway of the Royal Palace is the entrance to the Louis Wing, which projects on the south side of the palace. In Early Renaissance style, it was built by Benedikt Ried in 1502–09.

Bohemian Chancellery

In the Louis Wing, on the level of the Vladislav Hall, are two rooms occupied by the Bohemian Chancellery (or Governor's Office). The second room was the scene of a heated dispute on May 23rd 1618 between Count Thun, leader of the Protestant Estates, and the hated Catholic representatives of the Emperor, Jaroslav von Martinitz and Wilhelm Slawata, who were then thrown, along with their clerk Peter Fabricius, into the castle moat (the Second Defenestration of Prague). The spot is marked by two obelisks in the moat.
From here a spiral staircase leads up to the former Chancellery of the Imperial Council, in Late Renaissance style. From the window there is a fine view of Prague.

****St Vitus's Cathedral**

St Vitus's Cathedral (Chrám Svatého Víta), the metropolitan church of the archdiocese of Prague, stands on the site of a small round chapel begun about 925 by Duke (St) Wenceslas (Václav) which was replaced in the second half of the 11th century by a three-aisled basilica.
The east end of the present Cathedral was begun in 1344 by Matthias ofArras, following the model of Narbonne Cathedral. When he died in 1352

only the lower part of the choir (74m/243ft long, 39m/128ft high) had been built; it was completed in 1356–85 by Peter Parler in rich German Gothic style. Work on the church (nave from 1392; from 1399 by Parler's sons) was suspended in 1419 on the outbreak of the Hussite Wars. After the 1541 fire Bonifaz Wohlmut restored the choir and in 1563 completed the Renaissance steeple on the south tower (103m/338ft; no ascent). Thereafter work was resumed only in 1862 under the Cathedral's masters of works Josef Kranner (d. 1871), Josef Mocker (d. 1899) and Kamil Hilbert. With the building of the two slender west towers (1892) and the westward extension of the nave (involving the transfer of the old organ gallery to the north transept) the Cathedral in its present form was completed in 1929.
Over the south doorway, the Golden Gate (Zlatá Brána), can be seen a mosaic depicting the Last Judgment (1370–71), and above this is a beautiful traceried window (by Max Švabinský, 1934), also a representation of the Last Judgment; the largest window in the Cathedral, it contains 40,000 pieces of glass. On the west front is a rose window ("Creation of the World"; 1928), made up of 27,000 pieces of glass, with an area of 100sq.m/1080sq.ft.

Interior

The interior of the Cathedral (124m/407ft long, 60m/200ft wide across the transepts, 34m/112ft high in the nave), with its soaring columns and high Gothic windows, is of profoundly impressive effect.

**Triforium gallery

In the triforium gallery are 21 busts of those who were concerned with the building of the Cathedral in the 14th century, the earliest examples of

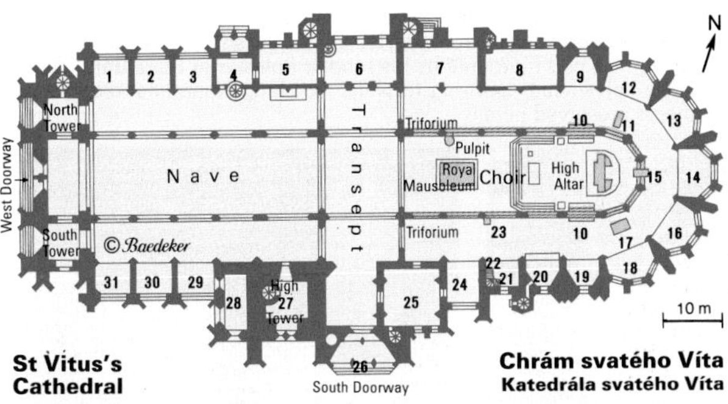

St Vitus's Cathedral

Chrám svatého Víta
Katedrála svatého Víta

1 Bartoň-Dobenín Chapel
2 Schwarzenberg Chapel
3 New Archbishop's Chapel (Hora Chapel)
4 Old Treasury (Cathedral Treasury now in Chapel of Holy Rood in Second Courtyard)
5 New Sacristy
6 Wohlmut's Choir (Organ Gallery)
7 St Sigismund's Chapel (Czernin Chapel)
8 Old Sacristy (formerly St Michael's Chapel)
9 St Anne's Chapel (Nostitz Chapel)
10 Historical reliefs
11 Statue of Cardinal Friedrich von Schwarzenberg
12 Old Archbishop's Chapel
13 Chapel of St John the Baptist (Pernstein Chapel)
14 Lady Chapel (Trinity Chapel, Imperial Chapel)
15 Tomb of St Vitus
16 Reliquary Chapel (Saxon Chapel, Sternberg Chapel)
17 Tomb of St John of Nepomuk
18 Chapel of St John of Nepomuk (St Adalbert's Chapel)
19 Waldstein Chapel (Magdalene Chapel)
20 Royal Oratory (Vladislav Oratory)
21 Chapel of Holy Rood
22 Entrance to Royal Vault
23 Monument of Count Leopold Schlick
24 Martinitz Chapel (St Andrew's Chapel)
25 St Wenceslas's Chapel (above, Crown Chamber)
26 Golden Gate
27 Hasenburg Chapel
28 Chapter Library
29 Thun Chapel
30 Chapel of Holy Sepulchre
31 St Ludmilla's Chapel (Baptistery)

medieval art in Central Europe. There are casts of the busts in the Charles Hall of the Gothic Palace and in Karlštejn Castle.

*Imperial Mausoleum

In the centre of the choir, surrounded by a beautiful Renaissance screen (by Jörg Schmidthammer, 1589), is the large marble Imperial Mausoleum. Originally begun in Innsbruck in 1564–89 by Alexander Colin of Mechlin as the tomb of Ferdinand I (1556–64) and his wife Anne of Hungary (d. 1547), it was remodelled in the reign of Rudolph II (1585–89) to accommodate Maximilian II (1564–76) as well. On top of the monument are the reclining figures of Ferdinand (centre), Maximilian (left) and Anne (right); on the sides are medallions of the kings and queens of Bohemia, all of whom are buried in the vault below the monument.

The vault is entered from the Chapel of the Holy Rood; the exit is by a flight of steps in front of the choir screen. In front, in the centre, is Charles IV (d. 1378), with George of Poděbrady (d. 1471) on the left and Ladislav Postumus (d. 1457) on the right. In the second row are Wenceslas IV (d. 1419) with his brother John of Görlitz (d. 1396) and the common sarcophagus of Charles IV's four wives. To the rear are the Empire-style sarcophagus of Maria Amalia, the widowed Duchess of Parma (d. 1804), a daughter of Maria Theresa, the pewter sarcophagus of Rudolph II (d. 1612) and a low granite sarcophagus with the remains of Charles IV's children.

Excavations

In the passages in front of the vault are excavations of Romanesque remains. On the wall can be seen a plan of the original Romanesque church.

*St Wenceslas's Chapel

The finest of the choir chapels is St Wenceslas's Chapel, beside the south door of the Cathedral, which was built by Peter Parler in 1362–67 on the site of the earlier Romanesque rotunda. It contains the shrine with the relics of the saint, who was murdered by his brother Boleslav at Stará Boleslav in 929. The lion's-head door-ring to which he clung when attacked by his brother is preserved here.

Interior of St Vitus's Cathedral

Tomb of St John of Nepomuk

The lower part of the walls is decorated with Bohemian semi-precious stones. Above this are two tiers of wall paintings, the lower row depicting scenes from Christ's Passion (by Master Oswald of Prague, 1373), the upper one the legend of St Wenceslas (studio of the Master of the Litoměřice Altar, *c.* 1509). On the east wall, below the window, is a polychrome statue of St Wenceslas by Heinrich Parler (1373). In the left-hand corner is a bronze candelabrum with a statue of St Wenceslas (by Hans Vischer of Nuremberg, 1532).
In the Crown Chamber above the south doorway (no admission) the Bohemian crown jewels have been preserved since 1625.
On the first pier opposite St Wenceslas's Chapel is the Baroque monument of Field Marshal Count Schlick (d. 1723; by Matthias Bernhard Braun von Braun, after a design by Joseph Emanuel Fischer von Erlach).

Martinitz Chapel

In the Martinitz (or St Andrew's) Chapel, next to St Wenceslas's Chapel, is the gravestone (under the window, to the left) of Jaroslav von Martinitz (1649), one of the victims of the Second Defenestration of Prague.

Chapel of the Holy Rood

In the next chapel, the Chapel of the Holy Rood (with the entrance to the imperial burial vault) can be seen a painting of the Vernicle (1369), with representations of the six patron saints of Bohemia on the frame.

Vladislav Oratory

Next to this is the Vladislav Oratory, a richly decorated Gothic chapel (1493) with a long pendant boss, which is now attributed to Hans Spiess of Frankfurt.

Waldstein Chapel
Tomb of St John of Nepomuk

Beyond the Waldstein or Magdalene Chapel (with the Waldstein family vault), in the ambulatory, is the silver tomb of St John of Nepomuk, made in Vienna in 1736 to the design of Joseph Emanuel Fischer von Erlach.
Opposite the tomb, on the altar of St Adalbert's (or St John of Nepomuk's) Chapel, are silver busts of SS Adalbert (Vojtěch), Wenceslas, Vitus and Cyril (1699).

Přemyslid tombs

The three following chapels contain tombs of the Přemyslid kings. In the Reliquary Chapel (also known as the Saxon Chapel) are the Gothic tombs of Otakar I (1197–1230; on the right) and Otakar II (1253–78; on left), by Peter Parler. In the Lady Chapel are the tombs of Bretislav I (d. 1055; right) and Spytihnev (d. 1061; left), also from the workshop of Peter Parler.

Tomb of St Vitus

Opposite the Lady Chapel, behind the high altar, can be seen the tomb of St Vitus, with a statue of the saint by Josef Max (1840).

Chapel of John the Baptist

In the Chapel of John the Baptist, to right and left, are the tombs of Břetislav II (d. 1100) and Bořivoj II (d. 1124). Also on the left is a bronze candelabrum, with a Romanesque base which came from Vladislav II's share of the booty brought back by the Emperor Frederick Barbarossa from Milan; the upper part dates from 1641.

Archbishops' Chapel

The Archbishops' Chapel next to this contains the burial vault of the archbishops of Prague. Opposite it is a bronze statue (by Josef Václav Myslbek, 1904) of Cardinal Friedrich von Schwarzenberg (d. 1885).

St Anne's Chapel

Next comes St Anne's Chapel, opposite which is the first part of a relief wood-carving (formerly attributed to Georg Bendl, more recently to Caspar Bechterle) depicting the destruction of images in the Cathedral in 1619. Its counterpart on the south side of the ambulatory, opposite the Waldstein Chapel, shows the flight of the "Winter King", Frederick of the Palatinate, after the battle of the White Mountain in 1620 (interesting view of Prague as it then was).
The Old Sacristy, which formerly housed the Treasury (now in the Chapel of the Holy Rood in the Second Courtyard), has rich stellar vaulting (no admission).

Organ gallery

In the north transept is the two-storey organ gallery (by Bonifaz Wohlmut, 1557–61), which was originally on the temporary west wall of the Cathedral. The organ (1757) has 6500 pipes.

Vikářská Ulice
Mihulka

Along the north side of the Cathedral runs Vikářská Ulice (Vicars' Lane). On the left is the Vikárka restaurant, and beyond this the Mihulka, a round tower which was originally a late 15th century artillery bastion. An old armoury has been preserved, and the tower contains an exhibition of late 16th century furniture and art.

Old Deanery (Mladota House)

The Old Deanery (also called Mladota House) farther along Vicars' Lane was, from 1483, the lodging of the Dean and the home of the cathedral choir; the original building was altered in 1590 and again in 1705. On the ground floor is the former Chapter Library, with carefully restored ceiling paintings by Jan Vodňanský (1726); it now houses an information centre and the office of the Prague Castle guide service.

***St George's Basilica**

Beyond the east end of the Cathedral, in St George's Square (Jiřské Náměstí), stands the Romanesque Basilica of St George (Bazilika Svatého Jiří), a convent church founded in 912 and rebuilt in 1142–50 after a fire, with a Baroque façade (*c.* 1670); it is now used as a concert hall. During renovation in 1897–1907 and 1959–62 it was restored to its original Romanesque form, with slender light-coloured towers and, in the interior, an alternation of piers and columns and three-arched galleries in the thick walls over the arcades. It has a fine Early Renaissance south doorway (workshop of Benedikt Ried, *c.* 1500) with a relief of St George (copy).
In the raised choir are some remains of Romanesque ceiling paintings ("Heavenly Jerusalem", after 1200). In front of the entrance to the crypt can be found the tomb of Boleslav II (d. 999), surrounded by a Baroque wrought-iron grille, and to the right of this is the painted wooden sarcophagus of Vratislav I (d. 920). In St Ludmilla's Chapel, on the south side of the choir, can be found the tomb of St Ludmilla (d. 921), from the Parler workshop (*c.* 1380).

Chapel of St John of Nepomuk

On the south side of the church is the Chapel of St John of Nepomuk (1718–22), with a statue of the saint by Ferdinand Maximilian Brokoff on the façade.

St George's Convent

On the north side of the church is the former Benedictine Convent of St George (Jiřsky Klášter), founded in 973, rebuilt after fires in 1142 and 1541 and remodelled in Baroque style in 1657–80. After the dissolution of the

St George's Basilica

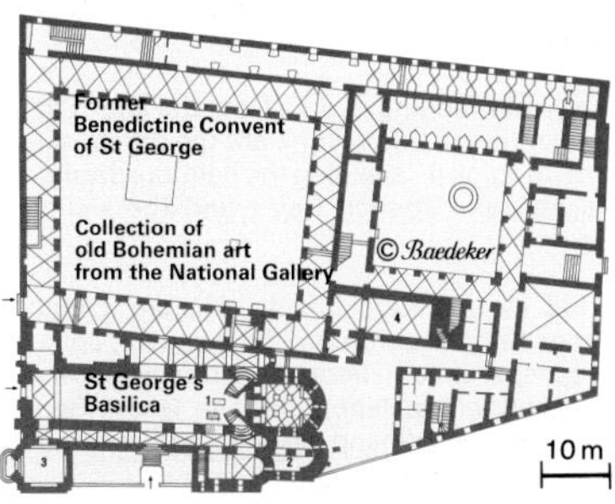

St George's Basilica and Convent

Bazilika a klášter svatého Jiří

1 Tombs of Přemyslid rulers

2 St Ludmilla's Chapel

3 Chapel of St John of Nepomuk

4 St Anne's Chapel

convent in 1782 the buildings were used for various secular purposes; then between 1963 and 1974, after thorough archaeological investigation, they were restored and adapted to house the National Gallery's Collection of Old Bohemian Art (Sbírka Starého Českého Umění).

****Collection of Old Bohemian Art**

Gothic art

The collection is arranged chronologically, beginning with Gothic art on the basement floor. Here are displayed the principal treasures of the collection; in particular the works of the Bohemian school of painting and the Prague painters' guild, which were fostered by the patronage of Charles IV but continued to flourish after his reign, are represented on a scale found nowhere else.
The long north corridor contains sculpture and architectural fragments, including a tympanum from the Church of Our Lady of the Snows (1346) and a number of beautiful Early Gothic Madonnas.

**Cycle of the Master of Vyšší Brod

A separate room is devoted to the Cycle of the Master of Vyšší Brod (Mistr Vyšebrodského Cyklu), an altarpiece of nine panels (*c.* 1330–50) from the Cistercian abbey of Vyšší Brod. Particularly impressive are the panels depicting the Nativity and Christ on the Mount of Olives.

*Statue of St George

In the adjoining corridor is the original of the bronze statue of St George (cast by Martin and George of Cluj in 1373) in the Third Courtyard of Prague Castle.

*Panels of Master Theodoric

Beyond this comes a room containing six of the panels painted by Master Theodoric (Mistr Theodorik) for the Chapel of the Holy Rood in Karlštejn Castle, depicting saints and a Pope.
Farther along are a votive image of Archbishop Jan Očko of Vlašim (by a Bohemian master, *c.* 1370) and a "Crucifixion" from the Emmaus Monastery in Prague.
The long corridor turning back towards the entrance contains fine statuary of the late 14th century.

**Cycle of the Master of Třeboň

The first room on the ground floor contains three of the panels ("Gethsemane", "Resurrection", "Entombment") painted about 1380 by the Master of the Třeboň Altarpiece (Mistr Třeboňského Oltáře) for the church of the Augustinian monastery of Třeboň. On the back of the panels are paintings from the master's workshop (only a few heads by the master himself).
A special room (entered from the north corridor) is devoted to the tympanum from the north doorway of the Týn Church, depicting three scenes from Christ's Passion (Peter Parler's workshop, 1402–10).
The paintings and sculpture displayed in the long corridor illustrate the development of Late Gothic art in Bohemia, with particular reference to the "beautiful" or "soft" style, extending to the dramatic "Crucifixion" (early 15th c.) by the Master of Rajhrad.

Renaissance

Notable among the Renaissance works in the collection are the "Trinity" by the Master of the Litoměřice Altarpiece in the cloister and the carved altar shrine by Master I.P. (known only by his initials) in the last room before the stairs leading up to the first floor.

Mannerism

On the first floor are displayed works ranging in date from the late 16th to the late 18th century. At the beginning of this section are the artists of the Mannerist school at the court of Rudolph II, including the painters Bartholomäus Spranger, Hans of Aachen and Joseph Heinz and the sculptor Adriaen de Vries.

Baroque

Painters of the Baroque period include Karel Škréta, Michael Leopold Willmann, Petr Brandl, Johannes Kupetsky (rooms of their own), Johann Christoph Lischka and Wenzel Lorenz Reiner. There are also selected works by outstanding sculptors of the period, including Johann Georg Bendl, Matthias Bernhard Braun von Braun, Ferdinand Maximilian Brokoff and Ignaz Franz Platzer.

Rococo

The transition to Rococo is shown in works by the painters Anton Kern, Norbert Grund and others.

St George's Lane

To the right of St George's Basilica is St George's Lane (Jiřská Ulice), which leads down, passing the Convent for Noble Ladies (Ústav Šlechtičen) established in the reign of Maria Theresa, to the Lobkowitz Palace (Lobkovický Palác; 16th–17th c.).

Golden Lane

From here a flight of steps descends to the picturesque Golden Lane (Zlatá Ulička; also known as the Goldmakers' Lane or Alchemists' Lane), an old-world little cul-de-sac with 24 small houses which were once occupied by castle guards, craftsmen and the poor. The alchemists employed by Rudolph II had their laboratories in the Mihulka Tower in Vicars' Lane.
The writer Franz Kafka lived in No. 22 in the winter of 1916–17 (commemorative tablet).

Golden Lane

Loreto Monastery

Old Burgrave's Lodging

At the end of St George's Lane, on the left, is the Old Burgrave's Lodging (Staré Purkrabství; in course of restoration), with fine Renaissance gables.

Black Tower
Daliborka
Bastion
*View

Through a gateway at the foot of Golden Lane we come to the Black Tower (Cerná Věž) and the Daliborka, a round tower built in the 15th century with three floors of dungeons. To the right of the Black Tower is the Bastion, from which there are fine views.
From here the Old Castle Steps (Staré Zámecké Schody; 98 steps) lead down to the street called Pod Bruskou.

Rampart Garden
Paradise Garden

To the west of the Bastion, flanking the south side of the Castle (views), is the Rampart Garden (Zahrada na Valech), with two obelisks commemorating the Second Defenestration of Prague. This leads into the Paradise Garden (Rajská Zahrada), above the New Castle Steps, with the little Matthias Pavilion (1617).

Powder Bridge
Deer-Pit
Riding School
St Mary's Work
Royal Garden
Ball Game Hall
***Belvedere**

From the Second Courtyard of the Castle a passage leads north to the Powder Bridge (Prašný Most), over the Deer-Pit (Jelení Příkop) and into a lane on the left of which is the former Riding School (Jízdárna). To the east, along St Mary's Work (Mariánské Hradby), extends the Royal Garden (Kralovská Zahrada; no admission), with the Ball Game Hall (Míčovna; by Bonifaz Wohlmut, 1568). At the far end stands the Belvedere (Belvedér, Královský Letohrádek; 1538–55), a charming little summer palace built by Ferdinand I for his wife Anne. The architect was Paolo della Stella, a pupil of Jacopo Sansovino (upper floor completed by Bonifaz Wohlmut 1564). The colonnaded hall on the ground floor has a frieze of arabesques and mythological reliefs. In the Great Hall (periodically used for exhibitions) the original decoration has been replaced by frescoes of scenes from Bohemian history by Christian Ruben (d. 1875). From the balcony there are views of the Hradčany and the city.

Singing Fountain

On the west side of the Belvedere can be found the beautiful Singing Fountain (bronze; by Tomáš Jaros, 1568).

Chotek Gardens

To the east of the Belvedere are the Chotek Gardens (Chotkovy Sady).

Loreto Square
Czernin Palace

From Hradčany Square Loretánská Ulice (Loreto Street), lined with handsome old houses, runs south-west to Loretánské Náměstí (Loreto Square), with the 150m/165yd long façade of the Czernin Palace (Černínský Palác; by Francesco Caratti, 1669–92), now occupied by the Foreign Ministry of the Czech Republic.

****Loreto**

Opposite the Czernin Palace, on the lower east side of Loreto Square, we come to the Loreto Monastery, a great Marian pilgrimage centre.
The façade (by Christoph and Kilian Ignaz Dientzenhofer, from 1721) has rich figural decoration, mostly by Johann Friedrich Kohl.

Carillon

In the tower is a famous carillon (1694; 27 bells from Amsterdam) which in summer plays the tunes of Marian hymns every hour.

Cloister
Santa Casa

In the cloister is the Santa Casa or Loreto Chapel (Svatá Chýše, Loretánská Kaple), modelled on the original Santa Casa in the Italian town of Loreto, with numerous reliefs on the outer walls.

*Treasury

The Treasury, in the upper gallery of the cloister, displays liturgical vestments and valuable 17th and 18th century monstrances, including a star-shaped monstrance with 6222 diamonds (Viennese work, 1699).

*Church of Nativity

On the east side of the cloister is the Church of the Nativity (Kostel Narození Páně), which was begun in 1717 by Christoph Dientzenhofer, continued by his son Kilian Ignaz and completed in 1735 by Georg Aichbauer. Notable features of the richly decorated and rather theatrical interior are the ceiling paintings by Wenzel Lorenz Reiner ("Presentation in the Temple", 1735–36) and Johann Adam Schöpf ("Adoration of the Shepherds" and "Adoration of the Kings", 1742).

Capuchin Friary

On the north side of Loreto Square is the former Capuchin Friary, with the Church of Our Lady (Kapucínský Klášter s Kostelem Panny Marie; 17th c.).

***"New World"**

North-east of Loreto Square can be found a picturesque little lane known as the "New World" (Nový Svět). Its small houses, once occupied by the poor, are now fashionable, with 18th and 19th century façades. Particularly notable are No. 3, At the Sign of the Golden Pear (wine bar); No. 5, At the Sign of the Black Grapes; and No. 1, At the Sign of the Golden Horn, which was occupied by Johannes Kepler about 1600 (commemorative tablet).

Pohořelec

South-west of Loreto Square is the Pohořelec, an elongated square surrounded by handsome Baroque houses, with a statue of St John of Nepomuk.

****Strahov Monastery**

Immediately south is Strahov Monastery (Strahovský Klášter), a Premonstratensian house founded in 1148. The present buildings date mainly from the 17th and 18th centuries.

Strahov Abbey

Church of the Assumption
Library
Convent
Prelature
© Baedeker

Strahovský klášter

The monastery courtyard can be entered either directly through a passage (steps) at No. 8 on the south side of the Pohořelec or, preferably, by walking up a short curving street and turning through a Baroque gateway of 1719 on the left. In the courtyard, on the left, is St Roch's Church (Kaple Svatého Rocha, 1603–11).

St Roch's Church

Church of Assumption

Straight ahead stands the Abbey Church of the Assumption (Kostel Nanebevzetí Panny Marie; 17th c.), with a richly furnished Baroque interior. In the right-hand aisle is the Pappenheim Chapel, with the tomb of Gottfried Heinrich zu Pappenheim (1594–1632), a cavalry general who was killed in the battle of Lützen.

Adjoining the church are the conventual buildings, parts of which date from the Romanesque period, with the library and the cloister (Museum of National Literature).

**Library

The core of the Library, which has now been returned to the Premonstratensians, consists of the old monastic library (entered from the cloister by a staircase to the first floor), one of the finest of the kind, with some 130,000 volumes, including 2500 incunabula, 3000 manuscripts and numerous old maps. The oldest book is the Strahov Gospel Book (9th–10th c.; in the passage between the Theological and Philosophical Libraries). The finest rooms are the Theological Library, with rich stucco decoration and paintings (1723–27) by Siard Nosecký, one of the monks, and the Philosophical Library in the neo-classical west wing (by Ignaz Palliardi, 1782–84). The dimensions of the Philosophical Library (32m/105ft long, 10m/33ft wide, 14m/46ft high) were dictated by the richly carved bookcases, which came from Louka Monastery at Znojmo in southern Moravia. The tremendous ceiling fresco (1794) by Franz Anton Maulbertsch, in the allegorical style of the Viennese Academy, depicts scenes from the intellectual history of mankind.

The cloister and adjoining rooms contain Czech literature of the pre-Hussite and particularly of the Hussite periods, and also of the period of national revival in the 19th century.

The library also has rich stocks of books from Bohemian monasteries dissolved after the Second World War.

***Petřín Hill**

From the gateway of the monastery, to the left, Strahov Street (fine views) ascends Petřín Hill (St Lawrence's Hill; 318m/1043ft), an eastern outlier of the White Mountain which is now a public park. On top of the hill is the Observation Tower (Petřínská Rozhledna), which at one time served as a

Observation Tower
**View

Theological Library, Strahov Monastery

Philosophical Library

television tower – a 60m/200ft high replica of the Eiffel Tower in Paris, built in 1891, from the upper gallery of which (384m/1260ft) there are wide views.

St Lawrence's Church

Near the Observation Tower are the Baroque St Lawrence's Church (Kostel Svatého Vavřince; 1735–70) and a pavilion containing a diorama of the "Battle of the Prague Students with the Swedes on the Charles Bridge in 1648" (by Karl and Adolf Liebscher, 1898) and a mirror maze, the Bludiště. To the south of St Lawrence's Church is the upper station of a funicular from the street called Újezd.

Observatory

Farther south-east can be found the Observatory (Hvězdárna), which is open to the public in the evening.

Stadium

Some 500m/550yd south-west of the Observation Tower, beyond the Hunger Wall (Hladová Zed'), part of the old fortifications, built by Charles IV in 1360, are various sports facilities, notably the Stadium, built for the Sokol Gymnastic Festival in 1926 and later enlarged.

Kinsky Gardens

In the Smíchov district at the foot of Petřín Hill, 500m/550yd south of the Observation Tower, are the beautiful Kinsky Gardens (Kinského Zahrada; open to the public).

Ethnographic Museum

At the south-west corner of the Kinsky Gardens, in the former Villa Kinsky, is the Ethnographic Museum, a branch of the National Museum, with models of peasant houses and interiors, pottery, traditional costumes, embroidery, etc. (at present closed for reconstruction).

Villa Bertramka (Mozart Museum)

Some 750m/820yd south-west, at Mozartova Ulice 2, is the Villa Bertramka, in which Mozart stayed in 1787 as a guest of the Dušek family and composed "Don Giovanni". The house is now a Mozart Museum.

Northern Districts

Letná Hill

North-east of the Hradčany, on the left bank of the Vltava, rises Letná Hill (Summer Hill), with a public park. From the Svatopluk-Čech Bridge stepped paths (256 steps) lead up to the viewing terrace on the massive base which once supported a 30m/100ft high statue of Stalin (removed in 1962). The statue has now been replaced by a giant metronome. From the terrace there are wide views of Prague, Petřín Hill and St Vitus's Cathedral.

***Letná Park**
Praha Restaurant

In the eastern part of Letná Park (Letenské Sady; formerly Belvedere Park) is the Praha Restaurant, which was part of the Czechoslovak section of the Brussels International Exhibition of 1958. From here too there is a good view of Prague, though the Hradčany is concealed.

***National Museum of Technology**

On the northern edge of the park, in the Holešovice district, near the north end of the road tunnel under the hill, at Kostelní Třída 42, stands the National Museum of Technology (Národní Technické Muzeum).

The Museum illustrates the development of cinematography in over 50 countries, radio and television, transport (historic cars and motorcycles) and mining. In the main hall are displayed aircraft, locomotives and the Imperial train (two carriages) of the Emperor Francis Joseph, in which the heir to the throne, Archduke Francis Ferdinand, travelled to Sarajevo in 1914. In the courtyard to the right of the Museum are a number of other aircraft.

Stromovka

To the north of Letná Hill, extending to the Vltava, lies the Stromovka, a large and beautiful park. On the south-west side of the park is a former hunting lodge (Místodržitelský Letohrádek), originally dating from the 15th century, which was rebuilt in neo-Gothic style in 1804. It now houses the newspapers and periodicals section of the National Museum.

Exhibition Grounds

On the east side of the Stromovka Park are the Prague Exhibition Grounds (Výstaviště), originally laid out for the Jubilee Exhibition of 1891 and the Ethnographic Exhibition of 1895. Since 1918 the Prague Trade Fair has been held here. In the early 1950s it became a "Park of Culture and Rest". It is now used for a variety of exhibitions (industry, agriculture, architecture, art, etc.). The large Congress Palace (Sjezdový Palác) was built for the 1891 exhibition. There are also a sports hall, a swimming stadium and other sports facilities, exhibition halls, the Lapidarium of the National Museum and a Planetarium. The Křižík Fountain (illuminated after dark) and an amphitheatre were added in 1991.

Trade Fair Palace

Near the Exhibition Grounds, at Dukelských Hrdinů 45, is the Trade Fair Palace (Veletržní Palác; by O. Tyl and J. Fuchs, 1924–28), in the Bauhaus manner, which was burned down in 1974. It is planned to use the building, after restoration, as a Museum of Contemporary Art.

***Trója Palace**

To the north of the Stromovka Park, in the Trója district beyond the Vltava, stands the Trója Palace (Letohrádek Trója), a handsome Baroque mansion built in 1679–85 by Jean-Baptiste Mathey. The magnificent Baroque staircase on the garden side was a later addition, with sculpture (the Battle of the Gods and Titans) by J. G. and P. Heermann of Dresden and the brothers J. J. and F. M. Brokoff. The finest room in the house is the Imperial Hall, with wall and ceiling paintings (1691–97) by the Dutch painter Abraham Godin. There is a permanent exhibition of European faience.

Zoo

Farther west is Prague Zoo (Zoologická Zahrada), whose attractions include a herd of Przewalski's horse.

Břevnov and the White Mountain (Bilá Hora)

Břevnov

5km/3 miles from the city centre on the Karlovy Vary road (No. 6), in the Břevnov district, beyond two small ponds on the right, we come to the Benedictine monastery of Břevnov, the oldest monastic house in Bohemia, founded by St Adalbert (Vojtěch) in 993.

The monastery courtyard is entered through a handsome doorway (1740) by Kilian Ignaz Dientzenhofer, with a statue of St Benedict by Karl Josef Hiernle.

The Baroque conventual buildings were begun by Paul Ignaz Bayer in 1708 and completed by Christoph Dientzenhofer about 1715. A notable feature of the interior is the Prelates' Hall, with a ceiling fresco (by Cosmas Damian Asam, 1727) depicting St Günther's miracle of the peacock.

St Margaret's Church

The central feature of the monastery is St Margaret's Church (Kostel Svaté Markéty; by Christoph Dientzenhofer, *c.* 1720), with ceiling frescoes by Johann Jakob Steinfels, altarpieces by Petr Brandl and a statue of St Margaret on the high altar by Matthäeus Wenzel Jäckel, who was also responsible for the sculpture on the façade. The crypt of the original Romanesque church has recently been brought to light under the choir.

White Mountain

2km/1¼ miles farther west on Road 6, on the city's western outskirts, is the White Mountain (Bilá Hora; 381m/1250ft), a bare limestone hill which was the scene of the battle of the White Mountain on November 8th 1620. The Bohemian Protestant forces, under their "Winter King" Frederick of the Palatinate, were entrenched on the hill, but Maximilian of Bavaria, head of the Catholic League, launched a violent attack with his Bavarian and Imperial forces and won a decisive victory in little more than an hour. On the hill is a pilgrimage church (with ambulatory) dating from the first half of the 18th century.

Hvězda (Star Palace)

In a former deer park on the north-western slopes of the White Mountain can be found the Hvězda (Star), a summer palace in Italian Renaissance style in the form of a six-pointed star, said to have been built by Archduke Ferdinand of Tyrol in 1555–58 for Philippine Welser, daughter of an Augsburg patrician, whom he married two years later. Later it was used as a powder magazine. It was restored in 1875 and 1890. Some charming stucco reliefs have survived from the original decoration. In the basement is an exhibition on the battle of the White Mountain.

Zbraslav Castle

Zbraslav

10km/6 miles south of Prague city centre, on the left bank of the Vltava near the inflow of the Berounka, lies Zbraslav (alt. 210m/690ft), a small town which was incorporated in Prague in 1974, with Zbraslav Castle (Zbraslavský Zámek), once a rich and important monastery.

The monastery

In the second half of the 13th century King Otakar II built a hunting lodge, with a chapel, at the junction of the Vltava and the Berounka, and in the reign of Wenceslas II this was enlarged and converted into a Cistercian monastery.

The castle

The monastery was destroyed during the Hussite Wars and was rebuilt in the early 18th century by G. Santini-Aichel and F. M. Kaňka. In 1784 the monastery was dissolved, and at the beginning of the 20th century was remodelled by D. Jurkovič as a castle with three wings round a central court. The National Gallery's collection of Czech sculpture has been housed in the castle and its park since 1976.

Collection of Czech sculpture of 19th and 20th c.

The collection of work by Czech sculptors of the 19th and 20th centuries illustrates the development of Czech sculpture from neo-classicism (V. Prachner, V. Levý, A. B. Popp, etc.) by way of Romanticism (J. V. Myslbek), Impressionism (J. Mařatka, B. Kafka) and Art Nouveau (S. Sucharda, late works) to Symbolism (F. Bílek) and more recent trends.

**Karlštejn Castle

See Karlštejn

Příbor H 3

Region: Northern Moravia
District: Nový Jičín
Altitude: 297m/974ft. Population: 13,000

Situation and characteristics

The old Northern Moravian town of Příbor, 30km/19 miles south-west of Ostrava (see entry), lies on the slopes of a hill above the valley of the Lubina. Its main industries are textiles and automobile construction.

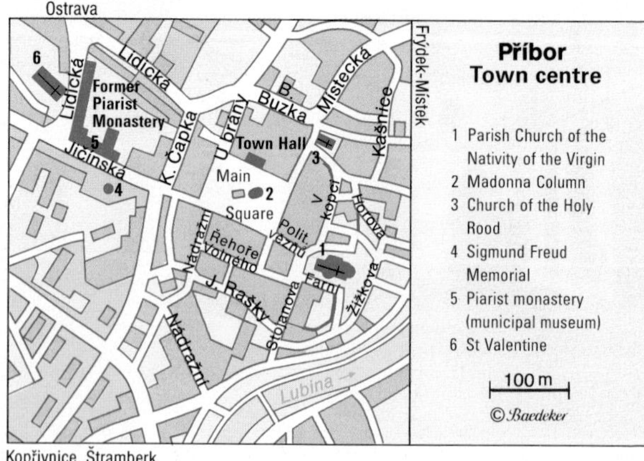

Příbor was the birthplace of the doctor and psychologist Sigmund Freud (see Famous People), founder of scientific psychoanalysis.

Sights

Town Hall

In the rectangular market square, surrounded by old arcaded houses (many of them dating from the Renaissance and Baroque periods), stands the Town Hall, a 16th century Baroque building with fine sgraffito decoration.

Parish church

South-east of the market square is the large parish church of the Nativity of the Virgin, originally a Gothic fortified church (14th c.) which was later enlarged (fine interior).

Piarist monastery

North-west of the market square is a former Piarist monastery, with St Valentine's Church (18th c.).

Freud Memorial Museum

In the conventual buildings is a Freud memorial museum and a short distance away to the south can be seen a monument to him.

Surroundings of Příbor

Kopřivnice

10km/6 miles south of Příbor by way of Lubina lies the busy industrial town of Kopřivnice (alt. 320m/1050ft; pop. 24,000), with the Tatra automobile works (lorries and private cars), in which Ferdinand Porsche (1875–1951) built the first car (the Tatraplan) powered by an air-cooled engine. The Municipal Museum has a section illustrating the history of car manufacture in the town; among the exhibits is the first Tatra President Car (1897). The Museum also displays the sporting trophies of the great Czech long-distance runner Emil Zátopek, born in Kopřivnice in 1922, who won four Olympic gold medals (10,000 metres, London, 1948; 5,000 metres, 10,000 metres and marathon, Helsinki, 1952) and established thirteen world records.

Štramberk

5km/3 miles south-west of Kopřivnice in the picturesque little town of Štramberk (alt. 418m/1371ft; pop. 4500) can be seen old wooden houses and remains of town walls. Above the town rears a round tower known as the Trúba (restored; view), a relic of a 14th century castle.

*Šipka Cave

To the south of Štramberk (15 minutes' walk) is Mt Kotouč (532m/1745ft), a limestone hill with the Šipka Cave, which contains numerous petrifactions. The jaw of a Stone Age man of Neanderthal type (some 100,000 years old) was found here.

Hukvaldy

8km/5 miles east of Příbor is the village of Hukvaldy (alt. 350m/1150ft; pop. 2000), birthplace of the Czech composer Leoš Janáček (see Famous People). The house in which he was born, the old village school, is now a memorial museum. The Janáček Musical Festival is held annually in May. Hukvaldy also has a ruined 13th century castle (300m/330yd long) which was burned down in 1792. Nearby is a large game park (fallow deer, moufflons).

Rychnov nad Kněžnou F 2

Region: Eastern Bohemia
District: Rychnov nad Kněžnou
Altitude: 321m/1953ft
Population: 11,000

Situation and characteristics

The Eastern Bohemian district town of Rychnov nad Kněžnou, in a beautiful setting at the foot of the Orlík Hills (see entry), has a long-established reputation as a clothmaking town. The main tourist attraction is its large 17th century castle.

Sights

Castle

Rychnov Castle, which belonged to the Counts Kolowrat, is a large Early Baroque building (1676–90, with 18th and 19th century alterations), notable for its picture gallery (Bohemian, Dutch, Flemish and Italian art), rich library, fine tapestries and carved woodwork.

Church

The castle church was built in 1594–1602 but was later remodelled in Baroque style and was further altered in 1843.

Clothworkers' houses

Below the castle, in the street called V Chaloupkách, are a number of old clothworkers' houses.

Surroundings of Rychnov nad Kněžnou

Vamberk

5km/3 miles south of Rychnov, the little industrial town of Vamberk (alt. 320m/1050ft; pop. 5700) has a long tradition of lace-making. The Municipal Museum illustrates the art and craft of making pillow-lace.

Doudleby nad Orlicí

6km/4 miles south of Rychnov is Doudleby nad Orlicí (alt. 281m/922ft; pop. 2000), which has a late 16th century Renaissance castle with sgraffito decoration (restored 1953–71), set in a park. It contains a permanent exhibition of objects from the Museum of Decorative Art in Prague (dressing tables, mirrors, etc., of the 16th–20th centuries).

Liberk

6km/4 miles north-east of Rychnov is the village of Liberk, with a wooden Baroque church of 1691 (panel paintings, sculpture).

Kostelec nad Orlicí

Kostelec nad Orlicí (alt. 272m/892ft; pop. 7000), a small industrial town (light industry, foodstuffs) 8km/5 miles south-west of Rychnov, has two castles (17th and 19th c.), a Baroque church (Gothic Madonna, *c.* 1500) and an English-style castle park (42 hectares/105 acres; nature reserve).

Častolovice

2km/1¼ miles west of Kostelec is Častolovice (alt. 263m/863ft; pop. 1500), with a Renaissance castle of around 1600, later remodelled in neo-Gothic style (fine period interior; collection of pictures, library); park.

Potštejn

9km/6 miles south of Rychnov, on the Divoká Orlice, is Potštejn (alt. 315m/1035ft), a popular summer holiday resort, with a Baroque castle of 1749. Above the little town can be seen a 13th century castle which fell into ruin in the 17th century.

Skalka

11km/7 miles north of Rychnov is Skalka, which has a charming Baroque castle (1736–39; Rococo interior, large chapel; museum).

Žamberk

In the little industrial town of Žamberk (alt. 418m/1371ft; pop. 6300), 15km/9 miles south-east of Rychnov, can be seen a Baroque church containing paintings by Petr Brandl. Žamberk was the birthplace of Prokop Divis (d. 1765), inventor of the lightning conductor.

Slaný D 2

Region: Central Bohemia. District: Kladno
Altitude: 290m/950ft. Population: 17,000

Situation and characteristics

The old town of Slaný, which received its municipal charter in 1305, lies in Central Bohemia on the important medieval trade route between Cheb and

Prague. It has considerable industry (textile machinery, accumulators, etc.); development of coal-mining under consideration.

Sights

Churches

St Gotthard's Church (Gothic, 14th c.); Trinity Church (1655); Chapel of the Holy Sepulchre; Franciscan friary (1651).

Piarist College

The former Piarist College (1655; beautiful Lady Chapel) is now a museum and library.

Town Hall

The Town Hall, with a tall tower, dates from 1751.

Town walls

There are considerable remains of the Gothic town walls (bastions, Velvary Gate).

Municipal Museum

The Municipal Museum has collections of material on the history of the town, folk art and traditions and archaeology.

Surroundings of Slaný

Mšecké Žehrovice

1km/¾ mile west of Slaný is Mšecké Žehrovice (alt. 420m/1380ft), with remains of a fort of the early historical period known as the "Swedes' Redoubt". A stone Celtic head of about 100 B.C. (now in the National Museum in Prague) was found here in 1943.

Zlonice

Zlonice (alt. 230m/755ft; pop. 2500), 6km/4 miles north of Slaný, has a large Baroque church designed by Kilian Ignaz Dientzenhofer. The Baroque priest's house is now a Dvořák memorial museum.

Třebíz

7km/4½ miles north-west of Slaný lies the village of Třebíz (alt. 330m/1085ft), with an open-air museum containing examples of stone-built Bohemian village architecture.

Slavkov u Brna / Austerlitz F 3

Region: Southern Moravia
District: Vyškov
Altitude: 211m/692ft. Population: 5600

Situation and historical importance

20km/12½ miles east of Brno (see entry) is Slavkov u Brna, better known under its German name of Austerlitz, scene of the "Battle of the Three Emperors" on December 2nd 1805 in which Napoleon inflicted an annihilating defeat on the allied Russian and Austrian armies. The armistice negotiations which began immediately after the battle in Austerlitz Castle led to the Peace of Pressburg (see Bratislava, in Sights from A to Z: Slovak Republic).

Sights

Castle (Museum)

The large Baroque castle of the Kaunitz family (1731–52; restored in the 1950s after suffering heavy damage in the Second World War) contains a fine collection of pictures, a library and a museum on Napoleon and the battle of Austerlitz.

Gardens

The castle gardens are laid out in the style of an English park.

The town

The town of Slavkov u Brna (spirit and sugar factories) has a number of Late Gothic and Renaissance burghers' houses and a late 16th century Renaissance Town Hall. The former synagogue is now a concert hall.

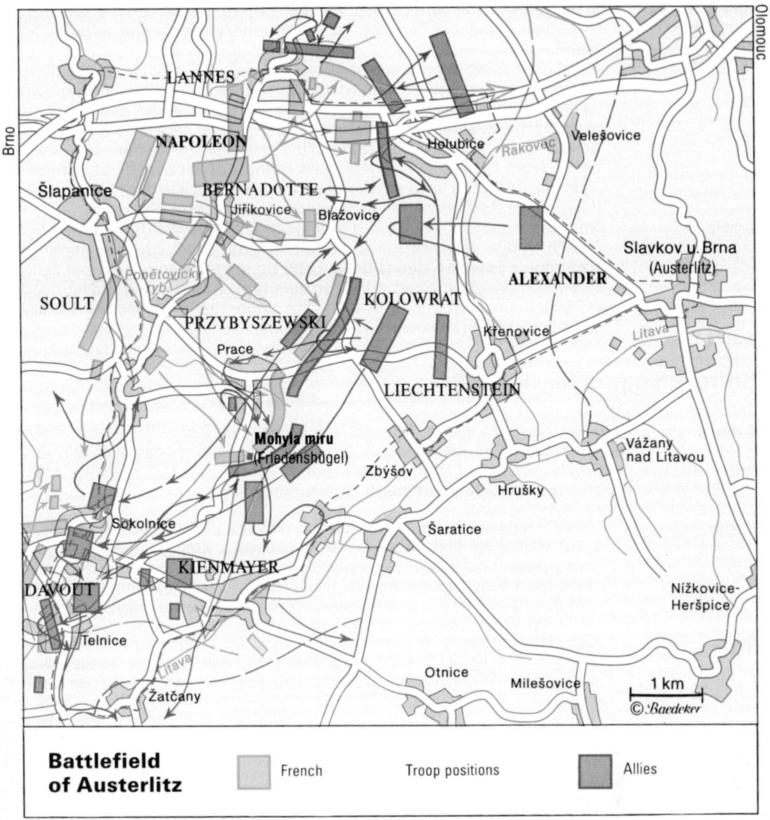

Battlefield of Austerlitz

***Austerlitz Memorial**

A road signposted to the "Mohyla Míru" (10km/6 miles) runs west from Slavkov u Brna by way of the little village of Křenovice (4km/2½ miles), headquarters of the Russian and Austrian army in 1805, to Prace (9km/6 miles; church of the Holy Rood), from which it is 1km/¾ mile south to the Pratecký Kopec or Pratzen Heights (324m/1063ft; car park), a low hill which was the scene of the fiercest fighting in the battle. On top of the hill can be seen the 26m/85ft high Austerlitz Memorial (Mohyla Míru, "Peace Memorial"; 1910–11), an Art Nouveau monument in the form of an ancient Slav tomb commemorating the soldiers who fell in the battle (some 7000 Frenchmen and 27,000 Austrians and Russians). In the base is a memorial chapel (altar of Carrara marble; ossuary; "whispering vault").

*View

From the hill there is an extensive view of the battlefield to the north.

Museums

Lower down can be found a small museum (plans, pictures, weapons, uniforms, etc; souvenir stall), with a snack bar.

There is another museum commemorating the battle at Šlapanice, 5km/3 miles north-west.

◀ *Austerlitz Memorial*

Other sites connected with the battle

In and around the surrounding villages – Újezd, Sivice, Telnice, Žatčany, Šlapanice, Sokolnice, Pozořice – are many other places connected with the battle.

Mt Žuraň

Among the most important of these is Mt Žuraň (287m/942ft), north of the village of Šlapanice, the hill on which Napoleon set up his tent, also known as the Emperor's Hill or Napoleon's Table. On top of the hill can be seen a marble table bearing the emblems of France, set up here in 1935; on it is a bronze relief showing the positions of the armies on the morning before the battle. From here there is a good view of most of the battlefield, with the Austerlitz Memorial in the background to the south. Near here 1850 burials dating from the time of the great migrations were brought to light.

Santon

Near the village of Tvarožná is a wooded hill (296m/971ft) to which the French troops gave the name of Santon, after a hill which featured in Napoleon's Egyptian campaign in 1798. On the hill stands a chapel dedicated to the Virgin, erected in 1832 on the site of an earlier chapel destroyed in 1805. In the surrounding area (now a nature reserve) traces of military positions can still be seen.

Surroundings of Slavkov u Brna

Bučovice

12km/7½ miles east of Slavkov is Bučovice (alt. 230m/755ft; pop. 4500; furniture and foodstuffs industries), with a Renaissance castle of 1567–82, now a museum of folk art; fine rooms (Imperial Hall, Hall of Venus, etc.), arcaded courtyard, gardens in contemporary style.

Vyškov

18km/11 miles north-east of Slavkov, Vyškov (alt. 254m/833ft; pop. 24,000), a district capital and industrial town (woodworking, engineering), was once the centre of a German linguistic island. It has a 17th century Baroque castle (now a local museum with a collection of ceramics of the 17th–19th centuries) and a Renaissance Town Hall (1730–43) in the market square.

Střílky

30km/19 miles east of Slavkov is Střílky (alt. 337m/1106ft; pop. 1000), with a Baroque cemetery (1730–43) laid out on a symmetrical plan. On the western outskirts of the village is a Renaissance castle remodelled in Baroque style.

Slavonice E 3/4

Region: Southern Bohemia
District: Jindřichův Hradec
Altitude: 512m/1680ft
Population: 2500

Situation and characteristics

The historic little town of Slavonice lies in southern Bohemia, near the Czech–Austrian frontier. It was founded in 1277, but developed mainly in the 15th and 16th centuries, when it was an important posting-station on the road between Vienna and Prague.

Sights

Old houses

*Sgraffito decoration

Flanking the town's two main squares, the Lower Square (Dolní Náměstí) and Upper Square (Horní Náměstí), are numbers of old houses (some Late Gothic but mainly Renaissance) with Lombard and Venetian gables and rich sgraffito decoration. A characteristic feature of the houses is the large entrance hall with diamond vaulting.
Also of interest are the church (Gothic, with a Renaissance tower; 1549) and the Town Hall (1599).
There are some remains of the town's Renaissance fortifications (in particular two 16th century gates).

Pfaffenschlag, Landstein, Český Rudolec

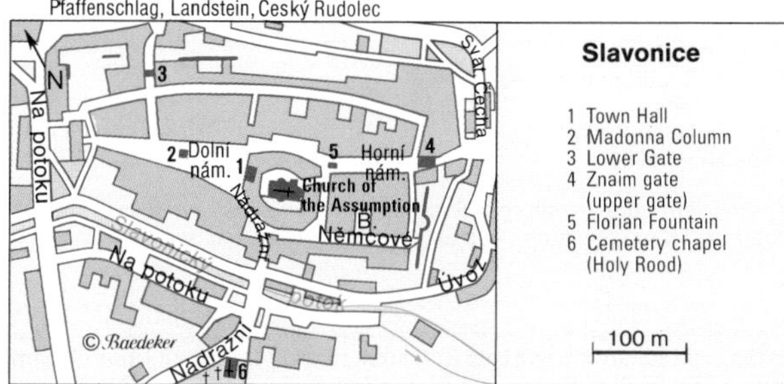

Surroundings of Slavonice

Pfaffenschlag

4km/2½ miles north-west of Slavonice lies the archaeological site of Pfaffenschlag (excavations of a medieval village).

Český Rudolec

7km/4½ miles north-west of Slavonice is the village of Český Rudolec (alt. 511m/1677ft), with a two-aisled Late Gothic church (1480) and a neo-Gothic castle of 1860.

Landštejn

10km/6 miles north-west of Slavonice, on the old frontier between Bohemia, Moravia and Lower Austria, are the extensive ruins of Landštejn Castle (alt. 649m/2129ft), founded in the early 13th century (Romanesque chapel) and later enlarged. In 1771 the castle was destroyed by fire and thereafter was abandoned; restoration is now in progress.

Richly decorated façades . . . . . . in Slavonice

Soběslav D 3

Region: Southern Bohemia
District: Tábor
Altitude: 405m/1330ft
Population: 6800

Situation and characteristics

The ancient little Southern Bohemian town of Soběslav, 16km/10 miles south of Tábor (see entry), has textile and furniture factories.

Sights

Main square

In the main square are two Late Gothic churches (14th–15th c.), one of them with a 78m/256ft high tower which is a prominent landmark, Renaissance houses of the 16th and 17th centuries, the Baroque Old Town Hall and the Municipal Museum (local costumes and folk art).

Castle

Of the medieval castle (founded in 13th c.) only a round watch-tower of the 14th century survives.

Surroundings of Soběslav

Moorland

5–10km/3–6 miles south-west of Soběslav, between patches of woodland, are extensive areas of moorland, with peat-bogs and typical flora.

Rustic Baroque

In the peripheral villages – Klečaty, Komárov, Zálší, Plástovice and particularly Vlastiboř – can be seen numerous examples of "rustic Baroque" architecture. The stone-built manor-houses frequently have enclosed courtyards and Baroque features (particularly on the gables).

Strakonice C 3

Region: Southern Bohemia
District: Strakonice
Altitude: 393m/1289ft
Population: 24,000.

Situation and characteristics

The Southern Bohemian district town of Strakonice, founded in the first half of the 13th century, lies in the most northerly foothills of the Bohemian Forest (Šumavské Podhůří) at the junction of the Volyňka with the Otava. It is a considerable industrial town, with textile factories (knitwear; felt, particularly for fezzes, manufactured since 1812) and engineering and motor vehicle plants (motorcycles). It is also noted for the making of bagpipes.

Sights

Castle (Museum)

The large Castle of the Knights of St John, originally Gothic (13th c.), was rebuilt in the 15th century. It now contains a museum (archaeology, art, gold-panning, bagpipes). The International Bagpipe Festival is held annually in the castle courtyard. The castle church of St Procopius has wall paintings.

Churches

The Renaissance church of St Margaret (16th c.) was later remodelled in Baroque style. The cemetery church of St Wenceslas, originally Romanesque, was altered in the 18th century.

Burghers' houses

There are a number of old burghers' houses in the market square.

Municipal Savings Bank, Strakonice

Surroundings of Strakonice

Rustic Baroque

To the south and south-east of Strakonice are a number of villages with examples of 19th century rustic Baroque – Miloňovice, Radošovice, Sousedovice, Strunkovice, Jiřetice, Zechovice.

Helfenburg

On a hill 13km/8 miles south-east of Strakonice are the ruins of the Helfenburg (alt. 683m/2241ft), a Gothic castle of the Rosenberg family (founded 1355) which was abandoned at the end of the 16th century.

Volyně

10km/6 miles south of Strakonice is Volyně (alt. 461m/1513ft; pop. 3000), which has an early 14th century castle (museum), a Renaissance Town Hall with sgraffito decoration and a Gothic church partly remodelled in Baroque style.

Strážnice G 4

Region: Southern Moravia
District: Hodonín
Altitude: 177m/581ft. Population: 6000

Situation and characteristics

The town of Strážnice, which first appears in the records in 1302, lies below the north-west side of the White Carpathians in the fertile wine-producing region of southern Moravia, near the frontier with the Slovak Republic (see Surroundings). Characteristic of the Strážnice region are the white stone-built houses with their brightly painted porches (*žudro*).

*King's Ride

Here and in the neighbouring villages of Vlčnov and Hluk the traditional "King's Ride", accompanied by a large folk festival, is held annually in May.

Sights

Castle (Museum)

Strážnice's Renaissance castle was altered in the mid 19th century but retains two Renaissance gates. It contains a collection of folk musical instruments and folk art (pottery).

***Open-air museum**

In the large park below the castle is an open-air museum of the traditional Moravo-Slovakian architecture of the Slovácko region. A popular festival of folk dancing and folk singing is held here annually at the end of June.

Surroundings of Strážnice

Bzenec

10km/6 miles south of Strážnice is Bzenec (alt. 183m/600ft; pop. 4000), a little Southern Moravian town famed since the 14th century for its wine (popular wine festival annually in August). It has a neo-Gothic castle with Baroque gardens and an English-style park.

Blatnice

12km/7½ miles north-east of Strážnice lies the village of Blatnice, which is noted for its folk festivals. Above the village is the well-known pilgrimage church (17th c.) of St Anthony of Padua.

Kuželov

12kmí7½ miles east of Strážnice is Kuželov (alt. 294m/965ft), an outlying part of Hrubá Vrbka, with a Hollander-type windmill of 1824 (open to visitors).

Milotice

12km/7½ miles north-west of Strážnice we come to Milotice (alt. 184m/604ft), which has a late 17th century parish church, a Baroque castle (1720–25; art collections) and a bridge decorated with sculpture.

Hodonín

14km/8½ miles south-west of Strážnice, the district town of Hodonín (alt. 167m/548ft; pop. 25,000), has food producing industries and a large power station using the modest local resources of oil, natural gas and lignite. Features of interest are the Late Baroque church (1780–86); the Marian Column (1716) in the market square; the Moravo-Slovakian Museum, with a fine collection of folk art; and an Art Nouveau art gallery.
Hodonín was the birthplace of Tomáš Garrigue Masaryk (see Famous People), first President of the Czechoslovak Republic. In the wine-

Painted Easter eggs from southern Moravia

producing country around the town there are many wine-cellars in characteristic style, e.g. at Čejkovice, Mutěnice, Petrov and Prušánky.

Kyjov

16km/10 miles north-west of Strážnice is the industrial town of Kyjov (alt. 192m/630ft; pop. 12,000), with a small Renaissance castle (most recently altered in 1911) housing a local museum. The Renaissance Town Hall dates from 1562 (reconstructed 1868).
Kyjov is the scene of an annual folk festival, the "Moravo-Slovakian Year".

Nearby Places of Interest in the Slovak Republic

Skalica

8km/5 miles south-west of Strážnice lies Skalica (alt. 186m/610ft; pop. 15,000). Features of interest are a 12th century Romanesque rotunda (built over in the 17th century); the remains of Gothic town walls; the Renaissance parish church, with a burial chapel and a charnel-house; the House of Culture (by Dušan Jurkovič, 1905); and the Záhorie Museum (Habaner pottery, Holič majolica).

Holič

16km/10 miles south-west of Strážnice can be found the little town of Holič (alt. 185m/607ft; pop. 8000), with a large Baroque and neo-classical castle (1749–54) in which, in the time of the Austro-Hungarian monarchy, members of the Habsburg family used to stay during the summer. The Empress Maria Theresa's husband, Francis of Lorraine, established a majolica manufactory here.

Stříbro — B 3

Region: Western Bohemia
District: Tachov
Altitude: 400m/1310ft
Population: 4000

Situation and characteristics

Stříbro is a little mining town above the river Mže, founded in 1240, which was granted particular privileges by the kings of Bohemia. It took its name (*stříbro* = "silver") from the zinc, lead and silver that were formerly worked here.

Sights

Features of interest are the Renaissance Town Hall, with sgraffito decoration (1543; renovated 1883–88), a Plague Column of 1725 and a gate-tower (1555–60) on a Gothic bridge spanning the river Mže.
The former Minorite friary (dissolved by the Emperor Joseph II) is now a school.
There are some well preserved stretches of the Late Gothic town walls.

Surroundings of Stříbro

Lake Hracholusky

Extending between 5km/3 miles and 25km/15 miles north-west of Stříbro is Lake Hracholusky, formed by a dam on the Mže (1964). With an area of 470 hectares/1160 acres and a length of 20km/12½ miles, it is now a popular recreation area. At the east end of the lake, near the dam, are the ruins of Buben Castle.

Kladruby

*Abbey church

5km/3 miles south of Stříbro is Kladruby, with a Benedictine abbey founded in the early 12th century. The conventual buildings, originally Romanesque and Gothic, were rebuilt in the 17th and 18th centuries. The church is

Stříbro

particularly beautiful, and the whole complex is one of the finest architectural monuments in Bohemia.

Svojšin

7km/4½ miles north-west of Stříbro is Svojšin (alt. 406m/1332ft), which has an early 13th century Romanesque church (later remodelled in Baroque style) with a very fine tower.

Přimda

On Mt Přimda (800m/2625ft), a wooded hill 30km/19 miles south-west of Stříbro, near the Czech–German frontier crossing (Rozvadov/Waidhaus), are the remains of the old frontier fortress of Přimda. This Romanesque castle, which first appears in the records in 1121, is the oldest surviving noble stronghold in Bohemia.

Sušice C 3

Region: Western Bohemia
District: Klatovy
Altitude: 435m/1425ft
Population: 11,000

Situation and characteristics

The old Western Bohemian town of Sušice is charmingly situated in a hollow in the Otava valley, at the foot of Mt Svatobor (845m/2770ft; observation tower). In early times gold was panned in the river here. Much of the town was destroyed by a devastating fire in 1707. In the mid 19th century a match-making industry developed in the town.

Sušice is a good centre from which to explore the beautiful country in the north-western foreland of the Bohemian Forest.

Sights

Museum of the Bohemian Forest

The Late Gothic Deanery (with a Renaissance attic) is now occupied by the Museum of the Bohemian Forest, which has a special exhibition of matches and matchbox labels.

An early 17th century building (No. 48) houses the Old Pharmacy and an Early Baroque building with sgraffito decoration at No. 49 is now the Fialka Hotel.

Jewish cemetery

To the south of the town is the old Jewish cemetery (17th c.).

View

From the Baroque Chapel of the Guardian Angel on a nearby hill there is a fine view of the town.

Surroundings of Sušice

Albrechtice

4km/2½ miles south-east of Sušice is the village of Albrechtice (alt. 715m/2345ft), with a 12th century church, later rebuilt, which preserves an Early Gothic doorway.

Annín

6km/4 miles south of Sušice can be found the holiday resort of Annín (alt. 530m/1740ft; camping site), with a large glassworks.

Petrovice

7km/4½ miles south-west of Sušice is the village of Petrovice (alt. 650m/2135ft), with a fine Gothic fortified church (Romanesque tower of early 13th c.).

Rabí Castle

Rabí (alt. 478m/1568ft), 10km/6 miles north-east of Sušice, has the ruins of an early 14th century castle which was later considerably enlarged and

Museum of the Bohemian Forest, Sušice

strongly fortified (restoration in progress). During the siege of the castle in 1421 Jan Žižka (see Famous People) lost his second eye.

Rejštejn

10km/6 miles south of Sušice is Rejštejn (alt. 563m/1847ft), an old mining town where gold was formerly worked. It is a good base for trips into the Vydra valley (nature reserve).

Kašperské Hory

10km/6 miles south-east of Sušice is Kašperské Hory (alt. 740m/2430ft; pop. 2000), an old mining town. Evidence of the prosperity brought by medieval gold-mining is provided by the town's Renaissance Town Hall and its Gothic church (later remodelled in Baroque style). The cemetery church (*c.* 1300) has Gothic wall paintings. Museum of the Bohemian Forest.

Kašperk Castle

To the north of Kašperské Hory can be seen the prominent ruins of Kašperk Castle (alt. 886m/2907ft), built in the 14th century by Charles IV, with two towers and remains of the residential block.

Horažd'ovice

20km/12½ miles north-east of Sušice is Horažd'ovice (alt. 427m/1401ft; pop. 6500), an old town founded before 1279. In the market square are Gothic and Baroque houses. To the north stands the three-aisled 13th century church of SS Peter and Paul, with a richly furnished interior. Gothic castle, rebuilt in Baroque style. Museum. Pearl oysters were reared in an arm of the river Otava until the beginning of the 20th century.

Tábor D 3

Region: Southern Bohemia. District: Tábor
Altitude: 437m/1425ft. Population: 34,000

Situation

The Southern Bohemian district town of Tábor lies some 90km/55 miles south of Prague on a promontory between Lake Jordán (the oldest artificial lake in the country, created in 1492) to the north and the Lužnice valley, which at some points is deeply indented, to the south. The town, named after the Biblical Mount Tabor, was founded in 1420 by the Hussite leader Jan Žižka (see Famous People) on the site of an earlier town and castle (Kotnov Castle), and soon became a stronghold of the Hussite movement, particularly of the radical sect of Taborites.

*Townscape

With its old-world streets and lanes and the remains of its fortifications the old town, to the west, has preserved the atmosphere of a small medieval settlement, while in the extensive newer part of the town to the east are the important railway station (five lines) and a variety of industrial establishments (sparking plugs, clothing, foodstuffs).

Sights

Žižka Square

In the centre of the old town is Žižka Square (Žižkovo Náměstí), with a bronze statue of Jan Žižka (by Josef Strachovský, 1884) and a charming Renaissance fountain. Under the square, and indeed under the whole of the old town, is a maze of passages (entered from the Museum) which provided the Hussites with a safe refuge.

***Old Town Hall** (Museum)

On the west side of the square stands the Old Town Hall, which was begun in 1440, completed in 1521 and subsequently much altered and rebuilt. It now houses the Municipal Museum, which is mainly devoted to the Hussite movement. The finest room in the building (on the first floor) is the Late Gothic Council Chamber (1515), with rich net vaulting and the town's coat of arms, framed by statuettes of Jan Žižka, Procopius, Jan Hus and Jerome of Prague, together with a group of Adamites (an extreme Hussite sect).

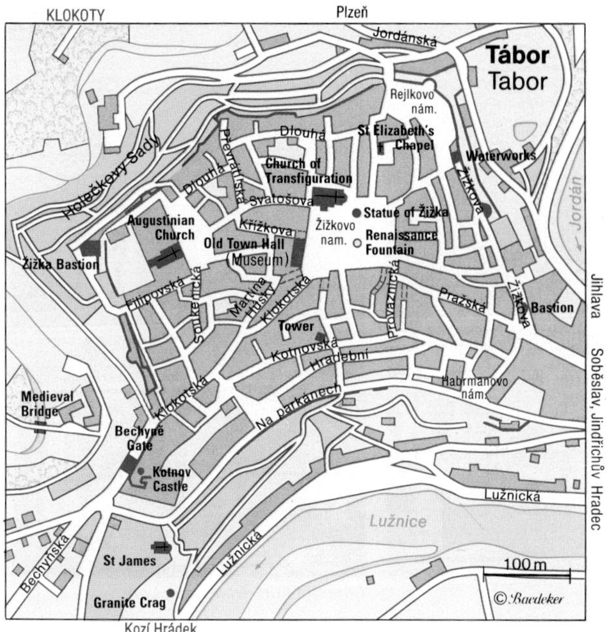

In front of the Town Hall and the Ctibor House (No. 6 in the square) are stone tables at which the Hussite Communion is believed to have been dispensed.

Church of Transfiguration

At the north-west corner of the square, the Church of the Transfiguration of Christ on Mount Tabor (Chrám Proměnění Krista Pána na Hoře Tábor), was started at the same time as the Town Hall and completed in 1512; it has a 77m/253ft high tower.

Burghers' houses

At the south-east corner of the square in Pražská Ulice (Prague Street) are a number of handsome Renaissance houses.

Augustinian Church

A little to the west of the Town Hall, in Klášterní Náměstí (Monastery Square; officially Náměstí Mikuláše z Husi), is the Augustinian Church, completed in Baroque style in 1662.

Kotnov Castle

From the south-west corner of Žižka Square Klokotská Ulice leads to the remains of Kotnov Castle (14th c.) – in fact little more than a massive round tower, now housing a section of the Municipal Museum.

Bechyně Gate

Beside the tower is the Bechyně Gate (Bechyňská Brána).

Town walls

There are still some remains, particularly on the north side of the old town, of the old town walls, with pentagonal bastions.

Surroundings of Tábor

Klokoty

In the north-western suburb of Klokoty, on the road to Plzeň, is a Baroque pilgrimage church with eight copper-sheathed onion domes (1701–30).

Kozí Hrádek

5km/3 miles south-east of Tábor, in a beautiful forest setting, are the ruins of Kozí Hrádek, a 14th century castle (destroyed 1438) in which Jan Hus (see Famous People) lived in 1412–14.

Old Town Hall

Church of the Transfiguration

Market square, Telč

There is plenty of scope for water sports on the beautiful windings of the river Lužnice, downstream from the town.

River Lužnice

Telč

E 3

Region: Southern Moravia
District: Jihlava
Altitude: 514m/1686ft. Population: 5000

Situation and characteristics

The charming little old-world town of Telč lies on the east side of the basin of the river Dyje in the undulating landscape of the southern Bohemo-Moravian Highlands (Českomoravská Vrchovina).

*Architecture

Telč, whose heyday was in the 16th century under the rule of the Lords of Hradec, ranks together with Český Krumlov (see entry) as one of the finest architectural ensembles in the whole country.

Sights

****Market square**

The great glory of the town is the market square, unique in its authenticity and unity, with its picturesque gabled houses and arcades of the Renaissance and Baroque periods. At the east end of the square are a Marian Column (1716–17) and two Baroque fountains.

Marian Column

***Castle**

The north-western end of the square is closed off by the Castle (Zámek), a handsome Renaissance building of 1553–80 (originally 14th c.) with a richly appointed interior (stucco decoration, carved ceilings) and collections of pictures, weapons and hunting trophies. To the rear are carefully tended Renaissance gardens.

St James's Church

Immediately adjoining the Castle is St James's Church, built in the second half of the 14th century and altered in Late Gothic style in 1443. From the tower there are fine views.

Jesuit Church

Close by are the Jesuit Church and the former Jesuit College (Seminary; end of 17th c.).

Ponds

The two ponds surrounding the town centre, the Štěpnický Rybník and the Ulický Rybník, formed part of Telč's medieval defences, earning the town the name of the "Water Lily".

Town walls

There are some remains of the town walls and two old gates, the Great Gate (Upper Gate) and the Little Gate (Lower Gate).

Church of Holy Spirit

Between the town walls and the market square stands the town's oldest building, the Romanesque tower (early 13th c.) of the Late Gothic Church of the Holy Spirit.

Surroundings of Telč

Recreational facilities

There are facilities for bathing in the Roštejnský Rybník (Pond; 10km/6 miles north) and the Velký Pařezitý Rybník (9km/5½ miles north-west).

Mrákotín

6km/4 miles west of Telč is Mrákotín, with granite quarries.
North-west of the village is Mt Javořice (837m/2746ft), the highest point in the Bohemo-Moravian Highlands.

Šternberk

9km/5½ miles north-west of Telč can be seen the ruins of Šternberk or Štamberk, a Gothic castle which was destroyed by the Hussites in 1423.

Roštejn

10km/6 miles north of Telč, Roštejn Castle was built in the mid 14th c., remodelled in Renaissance style from 1570, and recently reconstructed. Several rooms in the castle have fine wall paintings. There are extensive views from the tower.

Nová Říše

11km/7 miles south-east of Telč is Nová Říše (alt. 536m/1759ft; pop. 1000), with a former monastery; the church has frescoes by Johann Lukas Kracker (1766).

Dačice

12km/7½ miles south of Telč lies Dačice (alt. 577m/1893ft; pop. 4000), an old-world little town on the upper Dyje with some industry (sugar and spirit

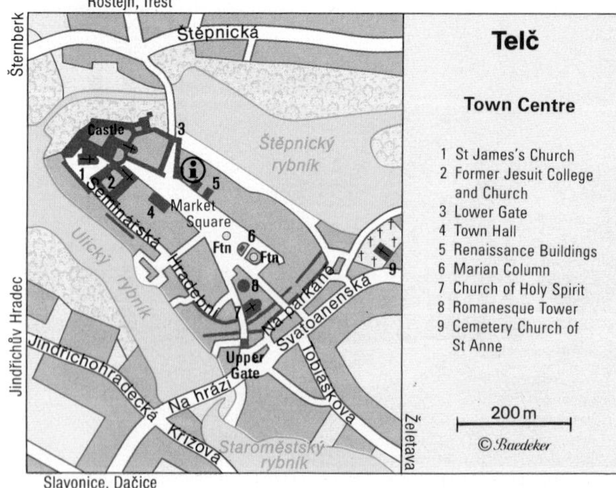

factory; woodworking). The New Castle (originally Renaissance; rebuilt in 18th and 19th c.) has a finely furnished interior (Hall of Mirrors, Library). The Old Castle, a 16th century Renaissance palace, is now the Town Hall. A former 17th century monastery (Baroque) now houses an ethnographic museum.

Želetava

16km/10 miles south-east of Telč is Želetava (alt. 578m/1896ft; pop. 1000), with St Michael's Church (Gothic, rebuilt in 17th and 18th c.).
Near the little town can be found a number of ponds; there is good bathing in the Vidlák Pond.

Teplice C 2

Region: Northern Bohemia
District: Teplice
Altitude: 228m/748ft
Population: 53,000

Situation and characteristics

The district town of Teplice (until 1945 called Teplice-Šanov; German Teplitz) lies between the Ore Mountains (Krušné Hory) and the Bohemian Massif (České Středohoří) in a wide undulating depression in the Northern Bohemian brown coal region. The oldest of the Bohemian spas, it is also an important industrial centre (textiles, ceramics, chemicals, glass).

Thermal springs

The radioactive alkaline and saline springs (28–46°C/82–115°F) emerge here from clefts in the local porphyry. The best known spring is the Pravřídlo (the Urquelle or "Original Spring").

History

The mineral springs of Teplice were already known to the Celts, but the real development of the spa began only at the beginning of the 18th century. In 1813 Tsar Alexander I of Russia, the Emperor Francis I of Austria and King Frederick William of Prussia met in Teplice and concluded the Holy Alliance against Napoleon.

Sights

Market square
Town Hall

The central feature of the old town is the market square, on the north side of which stands the Town Hall (Radnice; 1545).

Castle Square
Plague Column

From the market square the Dlouhá Ulice (Long Lane) runs south to Zámecké Náměstí (Castle Square), in the oldest part of the town. In the square a Baroque Trinity Column (Plague Column) is by Matthias Bernhard Braun (1718).

Decanal Church

On the east side of Castle Square is the Decanal Church of St John the Baptist (originally 12th c.; rebuilt in Baroque style about 1700).

Castle
(Museum)

On the south side of the square can be seen the Castle (Zámek; built 1585–1634, remodelled in Baroque style in 1751 and in Empire style in the early 19th century), which from 1666 to 1945 belonged to the Counts and Princes of Clary-Aldringen. It now houses a local museum and library.

Castle church

The castle church stands on the north side of the Castle. Nearby are the excavated remains of a Benedictine convent which was destroyed during the Hussite Wars.

***Castle Gardens**

To the south of the Castle are the extensive Castle Gardens (Zámecká Zahrada; entered through main doorway of Castle), with old trees, lakes and an open-air thermal swimming pool.

Mt Letná
*Viewpoint

To the south-east of the Castle is Mt Letná (264m/866ft; for path to top see below), with a tower from which there are fine panoramic views.

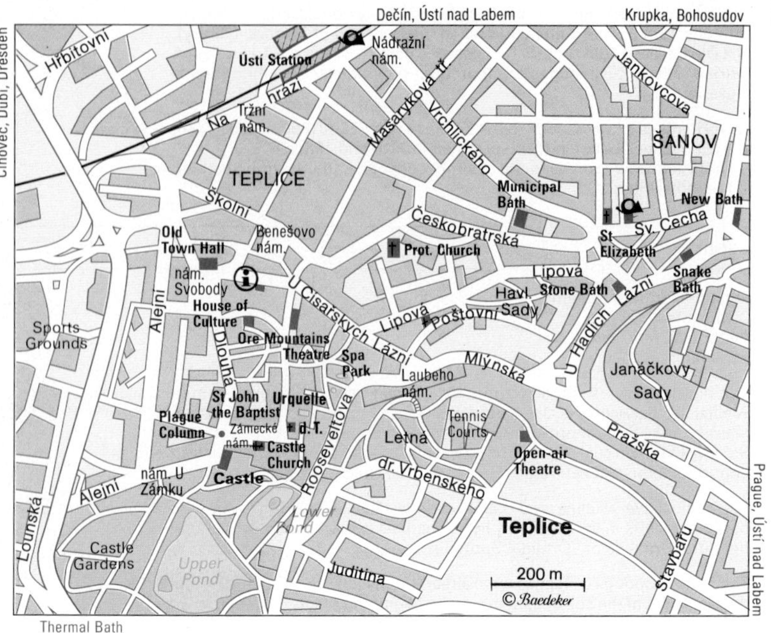

Steel Bath
Urquelle

To the north of the Decanal Church is the Steel Bath, with the Pravřídlo spring (Urquelle), whose water (42°C/108°F) is raised by a pump and is also piped to the Kurhaus, the Stone Bath and the Snake Bath (see below).

Spa Park
Kurhaus

To the north of the Steel Bath lies the Spa Park (Lázeňský Park), the centre of spa life. On its east side is the Kurhaus (Léčebny Ústav).

Path up Mt Letná

From the square behind the Kurhaus a stepped path (230 steps, then in 5 minutes bear right) leads to the top of Mt Letná.

Ore Mountains Theatre

At the north corner of the Spa Park is the Ore Mountains Theatre (Krušnohorské Divadlo; drama, opera, ballet, etc.), rebuilt in 1924 after a fire.

Šanov

From the Spa Park Lipová Třída runs east to the district of Šanov, which was incorporated in Teplice in 1894.

Stone Bath

At the end of the street, on the right, is the Stone Bath (Kamenné Lázně; 1911) with a beautiful fountain in the gardens in front.

Šanov Hill

To the south is Šanov Hill (Šanovský Vrch; 255m/837ft; 15-minute climb from south or east side), an excellent viewpoint on the east side of Teplice.

Drinking Fountain

In the gardens to the east of the Stone Bath can be found the Drinking Fountain with radioactive spring water.

Military Bath-House
Snake Bath
New Bath

East of the fountain, to the left, stands the Military Bath-House (Vojenský Lázeňský Ústav); to the right is the Snake Bath (Hadí Lázně); and straight ahead the New Bath (Nové Lázně; built 1839, restored 1927), which has its own spring.

Stone Bath, Teplice-Šanov

St Elizabeth's Church

North-west of the Military Bath-House, in Čechovova Třída (Chekhov Street), which skirts the park, is St Elizabeth's Church (1877).

Municipal Bath
Synagogue
Protestant church

At the west end of the park is the Municipal Bath (Městské Lázně). Still farther west are the Synagogue (1882) and the Protestant church.

Surroundings of Teplice

Dubí

4km/2½ miles north-west of Teplice is Dubí (alt. 389m/1276ft; pop. 9000), an industrial town (glass, ceramics) with a small spa in the northern district of Horní Dubí. The church with its campanile (1898–1906) is an imitation of the church of Santa Maria dell'Orto in Venice.

Krupka

5km/3 miles north-east of Teplice is Krupka (alt. 320m/1050ft; pop. 13,000), a mining town (tin and copper workings) founded in the 14th century which straggles northward up a valley in the Ore Mountains. The Late Gothic church dates from the 15th century.
On the west side of the town are the ruins of Krupka Castle (Hrad Krupka; alt. 375m/1230ft), from which there is a fine view of the Teplice basin.

Bohosudov

7km/4½ miles north-east of Teplice we come to Bohosudov (alt. 262m/860ft; pop. 4000), a much frequented pilgrimage centre. The church (rebuilt 1702–08) of the former Jesuit house has an image of the Virgin which is revered as wonderworking.

*Komáří Vížka

A chair-lift (2000m/2200yd long) runs up to the Komáří Vížka ("Tower of Flies"; 809m/2654ft), from which there are extensive views.

Cinovec

13km/8 miles north-west of Teplice is Cinovec (alt. 790–875m/2590–2870ft), a village in the Ore Mountains with a frontier crossing point into Germany.

Teplice and Adršpach Crags / Teplicko-Adršpašské Skály F 2

Region: Eastern Bohemia
District: Náchod
Altitude: up to 700m/2300ft

Situation and *topography

Between the Krkononoše range and the Orlík Hills (see entries), at the north-eastern tip of Bohemia, are the extensive complexes of sandstone crags known as the "rock cities".

**Rock cities

The largest of these rock cities is the 25km/15 mile long and 4km/2½ mile wide rock massif of the Teplice and Adršpach Crags (Teplicko-Adršpašské Skály), two extraordinary areas (now nature reserves) in which the formerly continuous masses of sandstone have been broken up and fissured by erosion and reduced to a host of isolated rock towers and pinnacles up to 40m/130ft high and a labyrinth of gorges.

The Adršpach Crags (270 towers), to the north, are separated from the Teplice Crags (110 towers) by the Vlčí Rokle (Wolf's Gorge).
In the Adršpach Crags it is the form of the rocks that is particularly striking, in the Teplice Crags their relationship to one another.

Surroundings of the Rock Cities

Teplice nad Metují

Teplice nad Metují (alt. 464m/1522ft; pop. 3000) is a popular holiday resort. Features of interest are the Upper Castle (Horní Zámek; Renaissance, 1599), the Baroque castle (1664) and the Baroque church (1723–27).

Dolní Adršpach

5km/3 miles north-west of Teplice nad Metují lies the village of Dolní Adršpach (alt. 518m/1700ft), with a Renaissance castle (1577–80).

Teplice Crags

Adršpach Crags

Teplice-Adršpach Crags

Skály

Skály (alt. 646m/2120ft), to the south-west, has a small Early Baroque castle (1666). On a nearby hill are the ruins of the Gothic castle of Katzenštejn or Bišofštejn (late 14th c.).

Terezín / Theresienstadt D 2

Region: Northern Bohemia
District: Litoměřice
Altitude: 155m/510ft
Population: 4000

Situation, history and characteristics

The fortified town of Terezín (German Theresienstadt), built by the Empress Maria Theresa, from whom it takes its name, and Joseph II, lies on the lower course of the Ohře a few kilometres above its junction with the Labe (Elbe) at Litoměřice. The town, built within a period of less than ten years (1780–87), is a textbook example of a planned town in the Empire and neo-classical manner of the late 18th century. The massive fortifications designed by General Pellegrini were abandoned in 1887, and Terezín remained merely a garrison town. It now has some industry (canning plants, pharmaceuticals).
The Little Fort (Malá Pevnost) to the east of the town was used from the mid 19th century as a state prison; among those confined here by the Austro-Hungarian authorities were the Greek freedom fighter Alexander Ypsilanti (d. 1828) and Gavrilo Princip (d. 1918), who assassinated Archduke Francis Ferdinand at Sarajevo in 1914.

Theresienstadt ghetto and concentration camp

During the Second World War Theresienstadt gained tragic celebrity when the town became a ghetto into which Czech Jews were herded and the Little Fort, at first used as a police prison by the Prague Gestapo, became one of the most ill-famed of the German concentration camps. From 1940

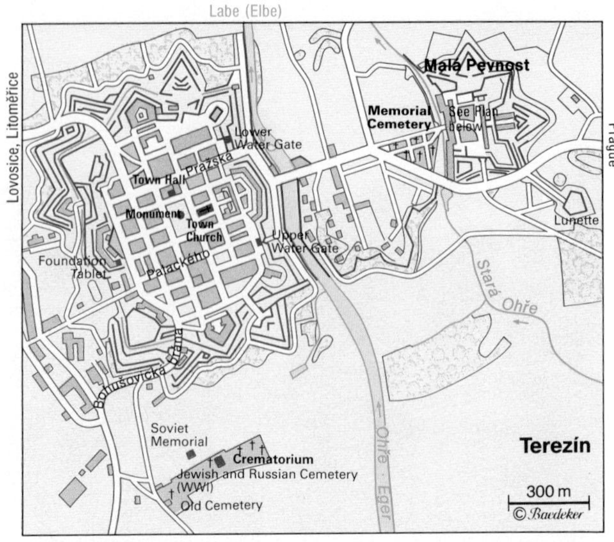

onwards an estimated total of over 150,000 Jews from all over Europe were sent to this camp, from which regular convoys went to the extermination camps, mainly to Auschwitz (Oświęcim in Poland).

Theresienstadt Memorial / Památník Terezín

Concentration Camp Museum

Since the end of the Second World War the Little Fort has been an anti-fascist memorial, a concentration camp museum (conducted tours, with English-speaking guides).

Cemetery

Outside the entrance to the Little Fort is a large cemetery with the graves of some 26,000 victims of the Nazis.

Theresienstadt Memorial · Malá Pevnost · Little Fort

1 Entrance
2 Administrative area
3 Registry
4 Guardroom
5 Commandant's office
6 Clothing store
7 Gate with the motto "Arbeit macht frei" ("Labour makes man free")
8 Medical treatment room
9 Individual cells
10 Bathroom
11 Sick bay
12 Barber's room
13 Hospital
14 Underground passage
15 Mortuary
16 Place of execution
17 Cinema
18 Shared cells
19 Memorial room
20 Museum
21 Mansion

I,II,III,IV = Prison Yards

© Baedeker

On the southern outskirts of the town, near the old municipal cemetery, is the former crematorium (open to the public). Here too are Jewish and Russian cemeteries of the First World War.

Crematorium

On the spot where the ashes of over 20,000 cremated Jews were scattered in 1944 is the conspicuous Menorah Memorial (in the form of a Jewish seven-branched candlestick).

Menorah Memorial

Třebíč E 3

Region: Southern Moravia
District: Třebíč
Altitude: 406m/1332ft
Population: 37,000

Situation and characteristics

The old town of Třebíč in the south-eastern Bohemo-Moravian Highlands was founded in the 12th century close to a Benedictine monastery. It is now chief town of its district, with several technical colleges and a variety of industry (engineering, footwear, hosiery).

Sights

Church of St Procopius

The Church of St Procopius, a three-aisled Romanesque and Gothic basilica, was originally a monastic church, built in the 13th century (*c.* 1240–60) and remodelled in the 18th. It has a crypt containing the tombs of the founders of the monastery and a beautiful Romanesque north doorway, the "Gate of Paradise" (13th c.).

"Gate of Paradise"

Western Moravian Museum

The original monastery was rebuilt as a Renaissance castle, which was renovated in the 17th century. It now houses the Western Moravian Museum, with interesting Christmas cribs (Nativity groups), a collection of pipes and other exhibits.

St Martin's Church

The 13th century parish church of St Martin was remodelled in Baroque style in the 18th century.
Beside the church is a square tower with a gallery round the top and the largest clock in the country (7m/23ft in diameter).

Burghers' houses
Synagogues
Jewish cemetery

Other features of interest in Třebíč are its Gothic, Renaissance and Baroque burghers' houses (many with sgraffito decoration), two synagogues and an old Jewish cemetery (16th c.).

Surroundings of Třebíč

Kožichovice

3km/2 miles south of Třebíč is the village of Kožichovice (pop. 400), birthplace of the skiing pioneer Mathias Zdarsky (1856–1940).

Jaroměřice nad Rokytnou

12km/7½ miles south of Třebíč lies Jaroměřice nad Rokytnou (alt. 430m/1410ft; pop.3000), with a large and well preserved Baroque castle of the Karolyi family, built in the first half of the 18th century, perhaps to the design of J. L. von Hildebrandt (fine furniture and pictures).

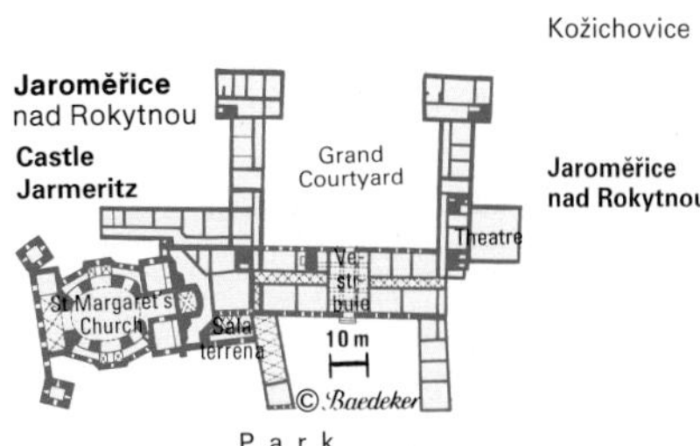

Church of St Procopius, Třebič

Within the castle complex are St Margaret's Church, with two towers and a large dome, a sala terrena, a small theatre, a French-style garden and a park containing statues of figures from classical mythology.
During the summer months there are concerts of 18th century music in the castle.

Velké Meziříčí

16km/10 miles north-east of Třebíč we come to Velké Meziříčí (alt. 425m/1395ft; pop. 15,000), an old town on the river Oslava, with light industry and engineering plants. The castle (16th c., altered in 18th and 19th c.) is now occupied partly by a rest home and partly by a museum (mementoes of the assassination of Archduke Francis Ferdinand in Sarajevo in 1914). Also of interest are the Renaissance Town Hall and remains of the town walls (three gates).

Moravské Budějovice

17km/10½ miles south of Třebíč is Moravské Budějovice (alt. 390m/1280ft; pop. 6000), an old-world little town with some industry (woodworking, foodstuffs, engineering). The Renaissance castle (17th c.) now houses the Western Moravian Museum. Other features of interest are a 16th century church (remodelled in 19th c.), with a charnel-house, and remains of the town walls. In the old Butchers' Stalls is an exhibition on the development of craft production.

Náměšť nad Oslavou

The little town of Náměšť nad Oslavou (alt. 365m/1200ft; pop. 4500), 18km/11 miles east of Třebíč, has a large and well preserved Renaissance castle (1565–78) on a steep hill above the Oslava, surrounded by beautiful terraced gardens. The river is spanned by a stone bridge with 20 Baroque statues (1730–40).

The most notable features of the castle are a collection of 24 18th and 19th century tapestries from leading European manufactories, the fine ceiling paintings, the Armoury and the Library.

Here in the 16th century the Bohemian Brethren installed an (illegal) printing press in which the first Czech grammar was printed in 1533. The press was later transferred to the little town of Kralice nad Oslavou, 4km/2½ miles east, where between 1579 and 1593 the first Czech translation of the Bible was written and printed (Bible Museum, with over 3500 pieces of type found buried in the surrounding area).
The castle belonged from 1752 to 1945 to the Counts von Haugwitz. A member of the family, until recently in exile in Vienna, has now returned to the castle, where she hopes to revive the musical tradition of the past: in earlier centuries well-known composers, including Gluck, Haydn, Salieri and Johann Strauss, lived and worked in the castle.

Dukovany

24km/15 miles south-east of Třebíč, at Dukovany, is a nuclear power station.

Třeboň D 3/4

Region: Southern Bohemia
District: Jindřichův Hradec
Altitude: 434m/1424ft
Population: 9500

Situation and characteristics

Třeboň lies some 25km/15 miles east of České Budějovice (see entry) in an extensive district of fish-ponds (the Třeboň basin and the boggy valley of the river Lužnice), between the Zlatá Stoka (Golden Canal) and the Rybník Svět ("World" Pond). Under the art-loving Rožmberk (Rosenberg) family which ruled here from 1366 the town flourished, developing into the main centre of the Bohemian fish-farming industry. In recent years it has also become an important poultry-breeding centre.

Spa treatment

Třeboň now also operates as a spa, offering among other treatments mud baths.

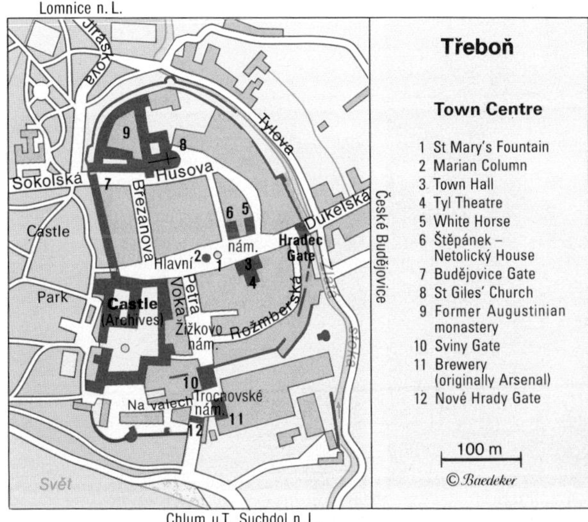

*Fish-farming

In the 16th century Štěpánek Netolický (d. 1523) and his successor Jakub Krčín of Jelčany (1535–1604) constructed artificial fish-ponds in the marshy surrounding country, and these still yield considerable harvests of fish (particularly carp) in autumn.

Golden Canal

From the same period dates the Golden Canal (Zlatá Stoka; 1505–20), which branches off the river Lužnice to the south of Chlum u Třeboně and after a course of 48km/30 miles rejoins the river at the Horusický Rybník, linking up with many fish-ponds on the way.

Sights

Square

In the centre of the town is the main square (Hlavní Náměstí), surrounded by charming Renaissance and Baroque houses. In the square are a fountain of 1569 and a Baroque Marian Column (1780).

Town Hall

On the south side of the square stands the Town Hall (Radnice; built 1566, rebuilt 1802–20), with a tower of 1638.

Burghers' houses

On the north side of the square, opposite the Town Hall, is a handsome Renaissance house, U Bilého Konička ("At the Sign of the White Horse"; 1544), now an inn. A little to the west (No. 89) can be seen a house once occupied by Štěpánek Netolický.

Hradec Gate

In the street which runs east from the square is the Hradec Gate (Hradecká Brána) and immediately beyond it the Golden Canal.

Castle

At the south-west corner of the square is the entrance to the Castle, built by the Rožmberks in the 15th and 16th centuries on the site of a 14th century Gothic fortified castle and rebuilt in Renaissance style by the Schwarzen-

Marian Column and Town Hall

Bastion in the town's fortifications

bergs in the 17th and 18th centuries, with several courtyards and a handsome staircase hall. Most of the Castle is now a hospital, but some rooms are open to the public.

*Archives

The castle contains one of the largest and oldest collections of archives in the Czech Republic, with valuable documents and manuscripts from the 12th century to the present day. In the Heraldic Hall (open to the public) are displayed photocopies of the most important documents. There is also an exhibition on the fish-farming practised in the area. Two other notable features of the Castle are the Courtiers' Hall and a corridor 108m/118yd long.

Castle Park

The beautiful Castle Park (Zámecký Park) extends to the west of the Castle.

Sviny Gate

From the square a street runs south, passing the Tyl Theatre (1835) on the left, to the Sviny Gate (Svinenská Brána). Beyond this, to the left, is the Brewery (Pivovar; producing the well-known Regent beer); it was built in 1379 as the town's Arsenal and remodelled in Baroque style in 1699–1712.

Nové Hrady Gate

Farther south is the Nové Hrady Gate (Novohradská Brána).

Town walls

Beyond the Nové Hrady Gate extends part of the old town walls, with the Water Bastion (Vodácká Bašta). Altogether seven bastions and three gates have been preserved.

Svět (World) Pond

To the south of the town can be found the Svět (World) Pond (over 2km/1¼ miles long; area 210 hectares/520 acres), created by Jakub Krčín of Jelčany in 1571–73. On the north side of the pond is the Svět Hotel, and near the hotel is a sanatorium which uses the local peat (containing sulphur and iron) for medical treatment. On the south side of the pond is an open-air swimming pool.

Schwarzenberg Burial Church

To the south of the Svět Pond stands the neo-Gothic Schwarzenberg Burial Church (1875–77), with the imposing tomb of Prince Johann Schwarzenberg (1793).

In the pond country, Třeboň

Budějovice Gate

From the west side of the main square Březanova Ulice, lined by arcaded houses of the 16th–18th centuries, runs north into Husova Třída (Hus Street). Along this on the left is the Budějovice Gate (Budějovická Brána).

St Giles' Church

On the north side of Hus Street is the town's principal church, the former Augustinian church of St Giles (Chrám Svatého Jiljí), built in the 14th century and rebuilt in 1871 after a fire. It has Gothic wall paintings, the Madonna of Třeboň (a Gothic sculpture of 1390) and fine Baroque altars.

During Baroque alterations in 1781 the famous altarpiece by the Master of Třeboň was removed and the panels were distributed among churches in the surrounding area. Three of them are now in the National Gallery in Prague.

Augustinian monastery

On the west side of the church is the former Augustinian monastery to which it belonged (founded 1367). It has a cloister of 1369 with frescoes (including scenes from the life of St Sigismund; 14th–15th c.).

Surroundings of Třeboň

***Ponds**

3km/2 miles north of Třeboň lies the largest pond in Bohemia, the Rožmberský Rybník (490 hectares/1210 acres), with a dam 2.5km/1½ miles long, constructed by Jakub Krčín of Jelčany in 1584–90. 6km/4 miles north of Třeboň is the Velký Tisý (320 hectares/790 acres). This and the neighbouring Malý Tisý (26 hectares/64 acres) are now a bird sanctuary and bathing is prohibited. Bathing is, however, permitted in the Staňkovský Rybník (240 hectares/600 acres), one of the most popular and most frequented of the ponds, at Staňkov (alt. 470m/1540ft), 4km/2½ miles north-east of Chlum u Třeboně; part of this pond is in Austria.

Lomnice nad Lužnicí

11km/7 miles north-west of Třeboň is the holiday resort of Lomnice nad Lužnicí (alt. 424m/1391ft; pop. 2900). 8km/5 miles farther north can be found the Horusický Rybník, the third largest pond in the country (415 hectares/1025 acres).

Chlum u Třeboně

12km/7½ miles south-east of Třeboň is Chlum u Třeboně (alt. 492m/1614ft; pop. 1800), a popular summer resort, with the Hejtman pond (80 hectares/200 acres; good bathing). Features of interest in the town are the Baroque castle (1710), with its park, and a glassworks making Bohemian crystal (Český Křištal').

Suchdol nad Lužnicí

Suchdol nad Lužnicí (alt. 454m/1490ft; pop. 3400), 14km/8½ miles south-east of Třeboň, has a 14th century Gothic church with later alterations. Suchdol is a good base for canoeing and boating trips on the Lužnice.

Trutnov E 2

Region: Eastern Bohemia
District: Trutnov
Altitude: 414m/1358ft
Population: 31,000

Situation and characteristics

The district town of Trutnov, situated on the river Úpa below the south-east side of the Krkonoše range, is a railway junction and the main centre of the Northern Bohemian flax-spinning industry. Coal and iron ore are mined in the surrounding area.

Trinity Column in market square, Trutnov

Sights

Market square

The market square is surrounded by historic old arcaded houses, and there are more of them in the adjoining streets.
In the square are an 11m/36ft high Trinity Column (1704) and a fountain with a statue of Rübezahl, the legendary spirit of the Krkonoše.

Museum

Trutnov has an interesting Folk Museum.

Surroundings of Trutnov

Horní Staré Město

5km/3 miles north of Trutnov is the village of Horní Staré Město (alt. 438m/1437ft), birthplace of the pioneer aircraft constructor Igo Etrich (1879–1967).

Žacléř

13km/8 miles north of Trutnov lies the little mining town of Žacléř (alt. 612m/2008ft; pop. 4000). Bordering the market square are handsome wooden arcaded houses, and above the town is a castle (rebuilt in 18th and 19th c.). Jan Amos Comenius, expelled from Bohemia in 1628, went into exile from here.

Rýchory Hills

Žacléř is a good base for walks and climbs in the Rýchory Hills (1033m/3389ft), a nature reserve with some remnants of natural beech forest.

Hostinné

18km/11 miles west of Trutnov is Hostinné (alt. 351m/1152ft; pop. 5000; papermaking factory), which has handsome arcaded houses in the market square, a Gothic church (with later alterations; fine interior), a Renaissance Town Hall (1570–1600), with two giant figures of a baker and a butcher, and a Museum of Ancient Art.

Turnov

E 2

Region: Eastern Bohemia
District: Semily
Altitude: 260m/855ft
Population: 14,000

Situation and characteristics

The Eastern Bohemian town of Turnov lies on the river Jizera on the northern edge of the Bohemian Paradise (see entry). It has been noted since the 17th century for the cutting of semi-precious stones (Bohemian garnets), and also has glassworks (imitation precious stones, optical glass) and textile factories.

Sights

Town Hall
Churches

In the market square are the Old Town Hall and the monastic church of St Francis (1650; renovated 1822–42). Nearby stands the Church of Our Lady (Gothic; rebuilt 1825–53). The 14th century St Nicholas's Church was remodelled in Baroque style in 1722.

Museum of Bohemian Paradise

The Museum of the Bohemian Paradise has a large collection of semiprecious stones.

Surroundings of Turnov

Hrubý Rohozec

On a steep-sided crag 2km/1¼ miles north of Turnov, set in a beautiful park, can be found the Late Gothic castle of Hrubý Rohozec (16th c., later remodelled in Renaissance style; collections).

Turnov

Dolánky

3km/2 miles north-east of Turnov is the village of Dolánky (alt. 264m/866ft), which has some fine examples of traditional local architecture, notably Dlaskův Statek (1716), a timber-built farmstead.

Suché Skály

5km/3 miles north-east of Turnov, on the left bank of the Jizera, can be seen the "rock city" of Suché Skály, with rugged and much-fissured sandstone formations which have been called the "Dolomites of the Bohemian Paradise".

Malá Skála

6km/4 miles north of Turnov is Malá Skála (alt. 262m/860ft), a village in the Jizera valley with typical wooden houses.

In the surrounding area there are numerous rock formations, making this part of the Bohemian Paradise a good area for rock climbing. There are also a number of ruined castles.

Sychrov
*Castle

The village of Sychrov (alt. 384m/1260ft) lies 8km/5 miles north-west of Turnov. The large neo-Gothic castle which belonged to the Princes de Rohan was built in 1847–62 on the site of an earlier castle belonging to the Valdštejn (Wallenstein) family. The castle, lavishly appointed and decorated (finely carved ceilings, walls and doors), contains a collection of French portraits (of the Rohan family) which is the largest of its kind outside France.

The composer Antonín Dvořák lived in the castle for some years during the summer months, and a musical festival is held here annually in his honour.

Mt Kozákov

8km/5 miles east of Turnov rises Mt Kozákov (744m/2441ft), a hill of volcanic origin which affords far-ranging views. This is a good area for finding semi-precious stones (garnets, agates, amethysts, etc.), which are cut and polished locally.

Železný Brod

10km/6 miles north-east of Turnov is Železný Brod (alt. 287m/942ft; pop. 7000), a little industrial town on the Jizera which is also a popular holiday resort. Its principal product is ornamental glass (moulded, blown and cut). There are a small museum of glass and the glass industry and a technical college for the training of glassworkers. Iron was worked in the surrounding area until the 17th century.

In the town and surrounding area there are fine examples of traditional timber-built architecture.

Uherské Hradiště G 3

Region: Southern Moravia
District: Uherské Hradiště
Altitude: 185m/605ft
Population: 26,000

Situation and characteristics

The old industrial town of Uherské Hradiště, chief town of its district, lies on the left bank of the Morava in south-eastern Moravia. It is the main centre in northern Moravian Slovakia (Moravské Slovácko), with canning, furniture and engineering factories and numbers of craft workshops. In the Kunovice district is an aircraft construction plant.

Sights

Churches

Uherské Hradiště has two notable churches, a 15th century Franciscan church (remodelled in Baroque style) and a 17th century Jesuit church.

Town Hall
Pharmacy

In the market square are the Late Gothic Town Hall and a Rococo pharmacy with ceiling paintings of 1754.

Town walls

There are some remains of the town's 14th century walls.

Arsenal

The former Arsenal (Baroque, 1721–26) now houses the Municipal Art Gallery.

Museum of Moravian Slovakia

In Smetana Park is the interesting Museum of Moravian Slovakia (Slovácké Muzeum), with collections of folk art and archaeological material and a picture gallery.

Wine-cellars

In the Maratice district is a long and continuous series of wine-cellars.

Surroundings of Uherské Hradiště

Staré Město u Uherského Hradiště

Staré Město u Uherského Hradiště is an old town on the right bank of the Morava with a variety of industry (sugar factory; chemicals, textiles, engineering). The numerous important archaeological finds made here (burials, metal jewellery and ornaments, foundations of churches) suggest that in the 9th century this was the site of the town of Veligrad, capital of the Great Moravian Empire, to which Cyril and Methodius, the Apostles of the Slavs, may have come in the course of their missionary journey.

Sady

2km/1¼ miles south-east of Uherské Hradiště is the village of Sady, with other important archaeological sites where excavations have brought to light material ranging in date from prehistoric times to the Great Moravian Empire.

Velehrad monastery church

A window in the church

Velehrad

7km/4½ miles north-west of Uherské Hradiště lies the pilgrimage centre of Velehrad (alt. 219m/719ft; pop. 1000). The present Baroque buildings of the large Cistercian monastery founded in the early 13th century date from the 18th century. The twin-towered church dedicated to SS Cyril and Methodius, an 86m/282ft long basilica, has a sumptuous interior (stucco-work by the Italian artist Baldassare Fontana, 1719; wall and ceiling paintings by two Brno painters, J. J. Etgens and F. I. Eckstein, 1720–30; finely carved choir-stalls; elegant organ). Parts of the original monastery buildings (chapterhouse, etc.) and Romanesque crypts containing burials have been brought to light under the church. Velehrad was formerly thought to have been the capital of the Great Moravian Empire and the starting-point of Cyril and Methodius's mission; and although this is now known to be an error a pilgrimage is still held annually on July 5th. The town was visited by Pope John Paul II in 1990.

Modrá

1km/¾ mile east of Velehrad is Modrá, where the foundations of a small church dating from the first half of the 9th century, first discovered in 1911, were excavated in 1953.

Buchlovice

8km/5 miles north-west of Uherské Hradiště is the little town of Buchlovice (pop. 2500), with an interesting early 18th century Baroque castle set in a beautiful park (exotic trees).

***Buchlov Castle**

10km/6 miles north-west of Uherské Hradiště stands the large castle of Buchlov (13th c., enlarged in 15th and 16th c.), which contains rich collections of weapons, glass, porcelain and pewter. From the castle there are fine views of the surrounding densely wooded hills. On the nearest hill to the north-east is a church dedicated to St Barbara (1672–73).

Ústí nad Labem — C/D 2

Region: Northern Bohemia
District: Ústí nad Labem
Altitude: 218m/715ft
Population: 106,000

Situation and characteristics

Ústí nad Labem, the largest town in northern Bohemia, with various government offices, a Faculty of Education and a theatre, is situated at the mouth (Czech *ústí*) of the Bílina as it joins the Labe (Elbe), which here breaks through the Bohemian Massif (České Středohoří). It lies on the eastern edge of the northern Bohemian lignite region, and the coal is shipped from its port (the largest on the Elbe after Hamburg). It is predominantly an industrial town (large chemical plants producing edible fats, cosmetics, medicines, etc.; engineering, glass manufacture).

Sights

Peace Square

The central feature of the town, most of which lies on the left bank of the Labe, is the market square, officially Peace Square (Náměstí Míru; pedestrian zone). On the west side of the square can be found the birthplace of the 18th century painter Raphael Mengs (memorial plaque), on the east side a statue of St Anthony of Padua (1708). To the north-west, higher up, is the House of Culture, an example of modern architecture.

House of Culture

Church of Assumption

From the south-west corner of the square a street runs south to the Church of the Assumption, which was destroyed by the Hussites in 1426 and subsequently rebuilt and restored (pulpit of 1574; beautiful winged altarpiece).
As a result of an air raid in 1945 the tower of the church is almost 2m/6½ft off the vertical.

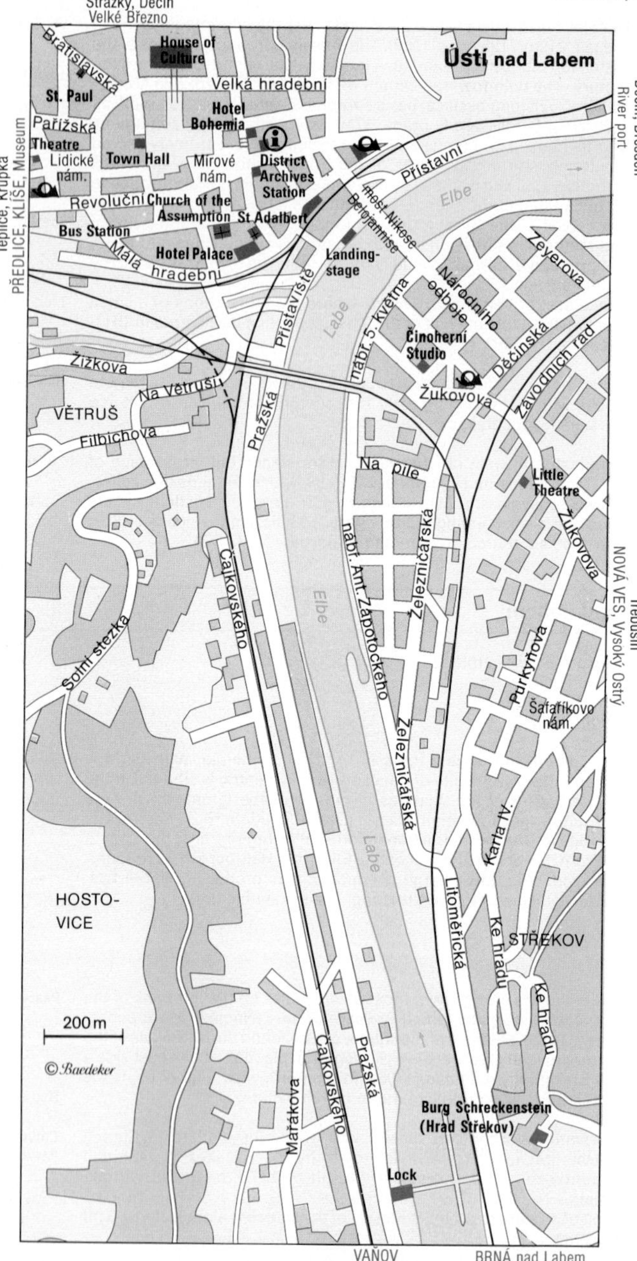
Ústí nad Labem
Strážky, Děčín
Velké Březno
Děčín, Dresden
River port
Teplice, Krupka
PŘEDLICE, KLÍŠE, Museum
NOVÁ VES, Vysoký Ostrý
Trebušín
VAŇOV
Lovosice, Prague
BRNÁ nad Labem
Sebuzín, Litoměřice
House of Culture
Bratislavská
St. Paul
Velká hradební
Hotel Bohemia
Pařížská
Theatre
Lidické nám.
Town Hall
Mírové nám.
District Archives
Station
Revoluční
Church of the Assumption
St Adalbert
Bus Station
Hotel Palace
Malá hradební
Přístavní
Elbe
most Nikose Belojannise
Landing-stage
Přístaviště
Labe
Zeyerova
Národního odboje
nábř. 5. května
Činoherní Studio
Děčínská
Závodních rad
Žukovova
Žižkova
Na Větruši
VĚTRUŠ
Filbichova
Pražská
Na pile
Little Theatre
Čajkovského
nábř. Ant. Zápotockého
Železničářská
Solní stezka
Purkyňova
Šafaříkovo nám.
Karla IV.
Litoměřická
Ke hradu
STŘEKOV
HOSTO-VICE
200 m
© Baedeker
Mařákova
Burg Schreckenstein (Hrad Střekov)
Lock

Ludwig Richter, "Crossing the Elbe at Schreckenstein Castle" (1837)

St Adalbert's Church

A little way east of the Church of the Assumption stands the 13th century Dominican church of St Adalbert (Vojtěch; remodelled in Baroque style in 18th c.), now used for concerts and exhibitions.

Ferdinandshöhe

From the Church of the Assumption a street runs south, crossing the railway line and the Bílina; then at the bridge over the Labe a road on the right leads up to the Ferdinandshöhe (208m/682ft), from which there is a good view of the city, its industrial and residential districts reaching out far beyond the bounds of the old town.

Surroundings of Ústí nad Labem

Střekov

2km/1¼ miles from the town centre, on the right bank of the Labe, is the district of Střekov, from which it is a 20-minute climb to the ruins of Střekov Castle, 85m/280ft above the river on a phonolite crag (alt. 246m/807ft; wide view of Labe valley).

*Střekov Castle

Střekov Castle (in German Schreckenstein), built about 1318 and abandoned in the 18th century, is said to have given Wagner the inspiration for "Tannhäuser". Since the construction of a dam on the Labe below the castle, with locks and a hydro-electric station (1928–36), little is left of the romantic atmosphere of Ludwig Richter's well-known painting.

Vysoký Ostrý

From Střekov a path to the south-east (1½ hours) ascends the Vysoký Ostrý (585m/1919ft), from which there are far-ranging views.

Mt Vrkoč

4km/2½ miles south of Ústí nad Labem rises Mt Vrkoč (250m/820ft), a rocky hill on the left bank of the Labe with basalt columns radiating in a star shape.

Mt Běhání

5km/3 miles west of Ústí nad Labem, at the village of Hrbovice, is Mt Běhání (207m/679ft), a flat-topped hill which was the scene in 1426 of one of the greatest battles of the Hussite Wars (monument erected 1926).

Chlumec

7km/4½ miles north-west of Ústí nad Labem is Chlumec (alt. 235m/770ft; pop. 3000), with a neo-Romanesque and neo-Gothic church. On nearby Horka Hill can be seen a monument commemorating a battle in 1813 in which Napoleon's forces were defeated by the combined Austrian, Prussian and Russian armies. 1km/¾ mile south-west is a Russian monument; 3km/2 miles north-east, at Varvažov, are Prussian and Austrian monuments.

Nakléřov Hill

3km/2 miles farther north-east, at the village of Nakléřov, is Nakléřov Hill (701m/2300ft), from which there are extensive views.

Velké Březno

8km/5 miles east of Ústí nad Labem, on the right bank of the Labe, is Velké Březno (alt. 139m/456ft; pop. 3000), with the New Castle, an Empire-style villa (1842) which now houses the Chotek Gallery.

Stadice

8km/5 miles south-west of Ústí nad Labem, in the village of Stadice, is a monument (1841) to Přemysl the Ploughman, founder of the Přemyslid dynasty, who according to the legend was sought out here by the emissaries of Princess Libussa (Libuše).

Zubrnice

The village of Zubrnice (alt. 260m/855ft), 12km/7½ miles east of Ústí nad Labem, has an open-air museum of the traditional architecture of the Bohemian Massif.

Kalich

12km/7½ miles south-east of Ústí nad Labem in the village of Kalich ("Chalice") are the ruins of a castle built by the Hussite leader Jan Žižka on Mt Kalich (538m/1765ft). The castle keep has the form of a chalice. From the top of the hill there are far-ranging views.

Valašské Meziříčí G 3

Region: Northern Moravia
District: Vsetín
Altitude: 305m/1000ft
Population: 28,000

Situation and characteristics

Valašské Meziříčí is an old town, a rail and road junction situated at the confluence of the Horní or Světínská Bečva and the Dolní or Rožnovská Bečva, with a variety of industry, including chemicals, electrical engineering, glass, woodworking, the manufacture of carpets and tapestries (technical college founded in 1900) and hat-making.

Moravian Wallachia

The region to the east and south-east of Valašské Meziříčí is known as Moravian Wallachia (Valašsko), in which a dialect resembling Slovak is spoken, showing the influence of Carpathian shepherds.

Sights

Castle

In the main part of the town, south of the Dolní Bečva, stands the 16th century Castle.

Town Hall

The Town Hall dates from 1677, but was altered in 1865.

Old Pharmacy

In the market square can be seen an old pharmacy with a Rococo façade, "At the Sign of the Red Eagle".

Parish church

The late 14th century Gothic parish church has a Renaissance tower (1532).

Trinity Church

Also of interest is the wooden Trinity Church (much altered).

Wallachian Folk Museum

The Wallachian Folk Museum has an interesting collection of folk art.

Krásno nad Bečvou

To the north of the Dolní Bečva lies the district of Krásno nad Bečvou (until 1923 an independent town), with a Renaissance Town Hall (1580) and an

Empire-style castle. In the castle park, which is laid out in the English style, is a monument to the dead of Austerlitz (see Slavkov u Brna).

Surroundings of Valašské Meziříčí

Lake Bystřička

8km/5 miles south-east of Valašské Meziříčí is Lake Bystřička, an artificial lake which is a popular recreation area. In the little town of Velká Lhota (alt. 540m/1770ft), to the north of the lake, stands a wooden church of 1783 (Protestant) without a tower. In Malá Lhota can be seen a wooden bell-tower of 1687 which is due to be moved to the Wallachian Open-Air Museum (see below).

Hustopeče nad Bečvou

9km/5½ miles north-west of Valašské Meziříčí is Hustopeče nad Bečvou (alt. 275m/900ft; pop. 2200), with a Renaissance castle (1580–1600) built on the site of a medieval fortified castle. The castle park has old beeches and lime-trees.

Rožnov pod Radhoštěm

12km/7½ miles east of Valašské Meziříčí, on the Dolní Bečva, we come to Rožnov Radhoštěm (alt. 375m1/1230ft; pop. 17,000). In the past mainly a

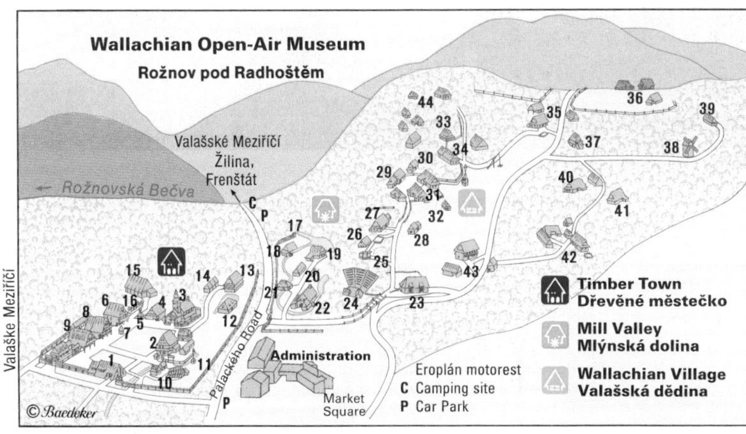

Timber Town
Dřevěné Městečko

1 Entrance (tickets, kiosk, toilets)
2 Steward's house from Velké Karlovice
3 Church from Větřkovice
4 Bills House
5 Bell-tower from Dolní Bečva
6 Town Hall
7 Well from Horní Lideč
8 Vašek's Inn
9 Inn at the Sign of the Last Groschen
10 Open-air theatre
11 Bell-tower from Horní Bečva
12 Landlord's barn from Prostřední Bečva
13 Landlord's barn from Heřmanice
14 Weavers' sheds from Štramberk
15 Jeník's shed
16 Beehives

Mill Valley
Mlýnská Dolina

17 Entrance (tickets, toilets)
18 Fuelling shop from Velké Karlovice
19 Mill from Velké Karlovice
20 Sawmill from Velké Karlovice
21 Oil-press from Brumov
22 Hammer Mill

Wallachian Village
Valašská Dědina

23 Steward's barn from Hodslavice (entrance, tickets, snack bar)
24 Open-air theatre on hillside
25 Shed from southern Wallachia
26 Mountain shepherd's hut from Černá Hora
27 Logger's house from Velké Karlovice
28 Peasant house from Leskovec
29 Gelder's house from Studlov
30 Fruit-drying kiln from Seninka
31 Farmhouse from Horní Bečva
32 Bell-tower from Lužná
33 Fruit store from Seninka
34 Mališ's farmhouse from Lužná
35 Farmhouse from Velké Karlovice
36 Woodcutter's house from Velké Karlovice
37 Smithy from Lutonina
38 Windmill
39 House from Prlov
40 Farmhouse from Valašská Polanka
41 House from Nový Hrozenkov
42 Matocha's house from Velké Karlovice
43 Steward's house from Lidečko
44 Place of assembly from Rákošové

In the Wallachian Open-Air Museum

spa and holiday resort, it is now also an industrial town (electrical engineering).

***Wallachian Open-Air Museum**

A major attraction of this area is the Wallachian Open-Air Museum (Valašské Muzeum v Přírodě), with characteristic examples of the traditional architecture of the region. Altogether there are 90 buildings from all over Wallachia, including a small wooden church, Rožnov's wooden Town Hall, an inn, a smithy, a steward's house, mountain shepherds' huts, etc. The buildings contain traditional furniture and furnishings, tools and clothing. Every year in July and August a variety of folk events are presented here.

Holiday centres

To the east is the picturesque and densely settled valley of the Dolní Bečva, with the well-known holiday resorts of Dolní Bečva (alt. 427m/1401ft; pop. 3600), Prostřední Bečva (470m/1542ft; pop. 1500) and Horní Bečva (504m/1654ft; pop. 300), all on the banks of the river.

Mt Radhošt'

Rožnov pod Radhoštěm is a good base for excursions in the wooded country around Mt Radhošt' (1129m/3704ft), 7km/4½ miles north-east. A narrow hill road, with many bends as it climbs, takes off in Prostřední Bečva and comes in 8km/5 miles to the upland meadows of Pustevny (1018m/3340ft), with good mountain huts and a hotel which are frequented both in summer and by winter sports (chair-lift, ski-lifts).

From here there is a rewarding ridge walk (1 hour), passing a modern statue of the pagan god Radhošt', to the summit of the legendary Mt Radhošt' (wooden chapel with a Wallachian Madonna; statues of SS Cyril and Methodius). From here it is another 11km/7 miles down to Frenštát pod Radhoštěm (see below).

Vsetín

15km/9 miles south of Valašské Meziříčí is the district town of Vsetín (alt. 342m/1122ft; pop. 31,000; mechanical and electrical engineering). In the Upper Square (Horní Náměstí) stands a Renaissance castle (rebuilt in Baroque and Empire style) with a 55m/180ft tower, now a museum. Other notable features are the Old Town Hall of 1721 (now housing archives), the Early Baroque parish church, the Baroque Maštaliska (Stables; 1710) and the Salt-House. There are two Protestant churches which recall the religious conflicts of the past, the Lower Church for the Augsburg Confession and the Upper Church for the Helvetic Confession.

Velké Karlovice
Rat'kov

To the north-east extends the beautiful valley of the Vsetínská Bečva, with many wooden buildings in traditional style, particularly in the Leksové, Podt'até, Jezerné and Bzové side valleys. The finest are to be seen in Velké Karlovice (alt. 510m/1675ft; pop. 3000), the largest numbers in Rat'kov.

Frenštát pod Radhoštěm

18km/11 miles north-east of Valašské Meziříčí is Frenštát pod Radhoštěm (alt. 401m/1316ft; pop. 11,000), an industrial town (electric motors, textiles). In the neo-Renaissance Town Hall (1890) is a museum (linen- and cloth-weaving; Wallachian folk art and traditions).
South-west of the town is a new coalfield which is still being developed (four pits).

Horečky

To the west lies the holiday resort of Horečky, with a Wallachian restaurant and a skiing area (synthetic surface for summer skiing). This is a good base from which to climb Mt Radhošt' (1129m/3704ft) and also the Velký Javorník (918m/3012ft) and Ondřejník (Skalka, 964m/3163ft).

Velké Losiny — G 2

Region: Northern Moravia
District: Šumperk
Altitude: 406m/1332ft
Population: 2000

Situation and characteristics

The Northern Moravian altitude resort and spa of Velké Losiny lies below the south-west side of the Praděd range (Hrubý Jeseník; see Jeseníky), a few kilometres from the river Desná. Its hot sulphurous springs (24–29°C/75–84°F) are used to relieve rheumatic pain.
Velké Losiny also has a long tradition in the production of hand-made paper: the paper factory was founded by the Žerotín family in 1515.

Sights

Castle

The Castle, which formerly belonged to the Liechtenstein family, is an imposing Renaissance building of 1580–89 (late 17th c. Baroque wing), with a beautiful arcaded courtyard, a Baroque chapel of 1742 and a richly appointed interior (furniture, pictures, etc.). It acquired a macabre celebrity as the scene of the 17th century witch trials which led to the deaths of many innocent people.

Paper Museum

The old-established paper factory has an interesting Paper Museum.

Surroundings of Velké Losiny

Maršíkov

2km/1¼ miles east of Velké Losiny is Maršíkov (alt. 434m/1424ft), with an early 17th century wooden church and a number of examples of traditional local architecture (19th c.).

Bludov

4km/2½ miles south-west of Velké Losiny is the spa of Bludov (alt. 306m/1004ft; pop. 2500) with sulphurous springs and a children's rehabilitation home. The Late Renaissance castle was remodelled in Baroque style in 1708 as was the Gothic church which contains the burial vault of the Žerotín family (1838).

Šumperk

8km/5 miles south-west of Velké Losiny, situated in the wide valley of the Desná just above its junction with the Morava, lies the district town of Šumperk (alt. 315m/1035ft; pop. 30,000), an industrial centre (heavy engineering, textiles). There are remains of late 15th century town walls. The parish church, originally Gothic, was later remodelled in Baroque style. There is also an Early Baroque church which belonged to a Dominican friary. In the market square can be seen a Baroque Plague Column. The little castle of the Chiari family now houses a local museum (flora and fauna of the Praděd range).

Šumperk was the birthplace of the singer Leo Slezak (1873–1946).

Rýmařov

18km/11 miles east of Velké Losiny, in the foreland of the Moravian Uplands (Nízký Jeseník: see Jeseníky), is Rýmařov (alt. 590m/1936ft; pop. 7000), an important silk-manufacturing town. It has a fine 17th century Town Hall in the market square. The Baroque pilgrimage church of V Lipkách ("In the Lime-Trees") has frescoes by the Moravian Baroque painter Johann Handke (1694–1774). The priest's house, which has a 16th century tower, was originally a mint.

Vimperk C 3

Region: Southern Bohemia
District: Prachatice
Altitude: 696m/2284ft
Population: 7000

Situation and characteristics

The old Southern Bohemian town of Vimperk lies on the southern fringe of the Bohemian Forest (Šumava) in the wooded valley of the Volyňka. Once a staging-point on the "Golden Road" (see Prachatice), it is now a popular summer holiday and winter sports resort. It has a crystal factory established in 1841 and one of the oldest printing houses in Bohemia, founded in 1484, producing not only books but calendars, religious texts and even miniature Korans.

Sights

Castle (Museum)

The old castle of the Schwarzenbergs, originally Gothic (13th c.), was rebuilt in the 18th and 19th centuries. It now houses a museum with exhibits illustrating the history of the Bohemian Forest, glass-making, match manufacture and printing.

Church

The town's principal church, originally Early Gothic (14th c.), was altered about 1500. It has a free-standing bell-tower.

Town walls

A stretch of the old town walls survives.

Surroundings of Vimperk

Primeval forest

Vimperk is the starting-point of trips into the area of primeval forest (48 hectares/120 acres) around Mt Boubín (1362m/4469ft), 7km/4½ miles south of the town. Other possible excursions are to the mountain village of Kubova Hut' (alt. 960m/3150ft), with the highest railway station in Bohemia (995m/3265ft), or to the village of Zátoň (615m/2675ft), slightly farther

Vimperk Castle

south. The area of primeval forest has been protected as a nature reserve since 1858 (nature trail).

Sudslavice

4km/2½ miles north of Vimperk in the village of Sudslavice (alt. 610m/2000ft) can be seen an ancient lime-tree, a botanical curiosity with a girth of almost 12m/40ft.

Mařský Vrch

5km/3 miles north-east of Vimperk is the Mařský Vrch (907m/2976ft), with an observation tower.

Maří

The nearby village of Maří has a fine Gothic church.

Lenora

The village of Lenora (alt. 765m/2510ft; pop. 600), 18km/11 miles south of Vimperk in the valley of the Teplá (Warm) Vltava, has a small glassworks, a covered wooden bridge and the Packmen's Bridge (Soumarský Most) on the Golden Road (see Prachatice).

River Vltava / Moldau C/D 2–4

Bohemia's principal river
Regions: Southern and Central Bohemia
Length: 440km/275 miles
Catchment area: about 30,000sq.km/11,600sq.miles

Description of the River

Source streams

The Vltava (German Moldau), a left-bank tributary of the Labe (Elbe), is formed in the Bohemian Forest (Šumava) by the confluence of the Teplá (Warm) Vltava, which rises to the north-east of Mt Lusen (1373m/4505ft), with the Studená (Cold) Vltava, which rises in Bavaria, to the south-east. It flows at first in a south-easterly direction, and then at Vyšší Brod (see entry) turns north, carving a narrow passage through the "Devil's Wall".

Tributaries

The Vltava's principal tributaries are the Malše, Lužnice and Sázava on the right bank and the Otava and Berounka on the left bank.

Towns on the Vltava

After passing the towns of Rožmberk nad Vltavou (alt. 527m/1729ft), Český Krumlov (509m/1670ft), České Budějovice (384m/1260ft) and Týn nad Vltavou (356m/1168ft) and flowing through Prague (187m/614ft), where it is spanned by numerous bridges and is now navigable by medium-sized cargo vessels, the Vltava (with a lateral canal running parallel) flows into the Labe (Elbe) at Mělník.

Dams and artificial lakes

In the upper course of the Vltava there are several dams forming artificial lakes which power hydro-electric stations. The largest of these lakes are at Orlík (see entry), Lipno and Slapy (see below).

Smetana's "Vltava"

The great Czech composer Bedřich Smetana gave one section of his symphonic cycle "Ma Vlast" ("My Fatherland") the title "Vltava".

Moldavites

Moldavites are a type of tektite (small pieces of glassy rock) which are found in the Vltava (Moldau) area and are thought to have come from a giant crater caused by the fall of a meteorite near Nördlingen in Bavaria.

*Lake Lipno / Údolní Nádrž Lipno C/D 4

Situation and characteristics

The largest of the Vltava dams, the Lipno Dam (Lipenská Přehrada; 250m/275yd long and 25m/80ft high) in the southern Bohemian Forest (Šumava), was completed in 1959. It has formed the irregularly shaped and much indented Lake Lipno (Údolní Nádrž Lipno; alt. 727m/2385ft; 40km/25 miles long and up to 16km/10 miles wide; area 4660 hectares/11,500 acres), surrounded by forest. The water stored in the lake is conveyed in a 3.5km/2 mile long tunnel to the underground hydro-electric power station 170m/560ft lower down, near the small compensating basin above Vyšší Brod (see entry). As a result the picturesque rapids at the "Devil's Wall" (Čertova Stěna) now have only a very scanty flow of water.

Recreation area

In addition to its use as a supplier of electric power the lake is also a popular and well equipped recreation area (hotels; auto-camps at Černá v Pošumaví, Frymburk, Horní Planá–U Pláže, Horní Planá–Karlovy Dvory and Lipno; bungalow villages; camping sites; boat rental). There are boat services calling in at several places on the lake and at Lipno (680m/2230ft), near the dam.

Places around Lake Lipno

Černá v Pošumaví

The old village of Černá v Pošumaví (alt. 728m/2389ft; pop. 500), on the east side of the lake, is now a holiday centre. The church dates from the end of the 18th century. A brewery founded by Jakub Krčín in 1568 now produces soda water. There are large deposits of graphite in the surrounding area.

Frymburk

Frymburk (alt. 740m/2430ft; pop. 1300), on the narrow south-eastern tip of the lake, was founded by the Rožmberks in the 13th century. The Gothic parish church (1277) was remodelled in Late Gothic style in the 16th century. The fountain dates from 1676, the pillory from about 1651. There is a car ferry to the opposite side of the lake. Two hours' walk south-west is the ruined castle of Vítkův Hrádek (alt. 1032m/3386ft), from which there are extensive views.

Lake Lipno

Horní Planá

The ancient little town of Horní Planá (alt. 726m/2382ft; pop. 2000) was the birthplace of the German novelist Adalbert Stifter (1805–68); the house in which he was born is now a memorial museum, and there is a statue of him in the park. The Gothic church (13th c., with much later alteration) has a 15th century Gothic Madonna.

Hořice na Šumavě

The little town of Hořice na Šumavě (alt. 674m/2211ft), 14km/8½ miles south-west of Český Krumlov (see entry), has a 13th century Gothic church (altered in Late Gothic style 1483–1513), a pillory of 1549 and seven stone fountains. Before the Second World War the town was famed for its Passion play on the model of the Oberammergau play, which was filmed by the Lumière brothers in 1897.

Nová Pec

The village of Nová Pec (alt. 737m/2418ft), 7km/4½ miles north-west of Horní Planá, is the only holiday resort on the west side of the lake. Timber-working plays a major part in the village's economy. There are remains of the Schwarzenberg Canal (1789–1822), 44km/27 miles long, on which logs were floated down to Zwettelbach in Austria.

*Lake Slapy / Vodní Nádrž Slapy D 3

Situation and characteristics

Lake Slapy, a long straggling sheet of water with numerous inlets, surrounded by wooded hills, is one of the favourite holiday and recreation areas of the people of Prague. The Slapy Dam (Slapská Přehrada; alt. 280m/920ft), 5km/3 miles east of the village of Slapy and 30km/19 miles south of Prague, was constructed in 1949–54. 260m/285yd long and just under 70m/230ft high, it has formed a lake 44km/27miles long, with an area of some 1400 hectares/3500 acres, which stores around 270 million cubic metres (60 billion gallons) of water for the production of electric power.

Lake Slapy

Recreation area

The lake, which in summer can be reached from Prague by boat, offers abundant facilities for all kinds of water sports, for angling and for round trips on the Vltava boats, which call near the dam and at Nová Rabyně. The two principal tourist centres on the lake are Nová Rabyně and Živohošt'. There is good bathing at Ždáň, Živohošt' and Cholín on the west side of the lake and Rabyně, Nová Živohošt' and Měřín on the east side.
For archaeological enthusiasts there is a Celtic oppidum of the 1st century B.C. to be seen at Hrazany.

Places around Lake Slapy

Křečovice

35km/22 miles south of Prague is the village of Křečovice (alt. 365m/1200ft), birthplace of the composer Josef Suk (1874–1935). There is a memorial museum in the old schoolhouse in which he was born.

Dobříš

40km/25 miles south-west of Prague, in a beautiful forest setting, is Dobříš (alt. 371m/1217ft; pop. 8500; glove manufacture), with a Rococo castle of 1745–65 (now a meeting-place for writers); French-style gardens and large game park. 3km/2 miles south-east of Dobříš, on the shores of the Strž Pond, is a villa in which the writer Karel Čapek (see Famous People) lived in 1935–38; memorial museum.

Příbram

55km/34 miles south-west of Prague is the district town and industrial centre of Příbram (alt. 502m/1647ft; pop. 37,000). Silver was mined in this area from the 13th century (now uranium). Above the town rises the Svatá Hora (Sacred Mount; 586m/1923ft), with a much-visited Baroque pilgrimage church (17th c.).
6km/4 miles south of Příbram, near the village of Milín, can be seen on the road to Slivice a memorial commemorating the last shots fired in Bohemia in the Second World War (on May 11th 1945).

Volary

C 4

Region: Southern Bohemia
District: Prachatice
Altitude: 757m/2484ft
Population: 4000

Situation and characteristics

The little Southern Bohemian town of Volary, a popular summer resort, lies 16km/10 miles south-west of Prachatice (see entry) in a pleasant valley in the Bohemian Forest (Šumava). Formerly a staging-point on the "Golden Road", the old trade route between Passau in Bavaria and Prachatice, it now has a large wood-processing plant. The local type of house, timber-built, with broad balconies and saddle roofs weighed down by stones, was introduced in the 15th century by settlers from the Alps.

Surroundings of Volary

Jelení

10km/6 miles south of Volary, in the village of Jelení, is a tunnel on the old Schwarzenberg Canal. 2km/1¼ miles north is a monument marking the spot where the last bear in the Bohemian Forest was killed in 1856.

Plöckenstein
Mt Plechý
Třístoličník

15km/9 miles south of Volary, between the Plöckenstein (1362m/4469ft) in Bavaria and its Bohemian counterpart Mt Plechý (1378m/1378m/4521ft), rises the Třístoličník ("Three Countries Peak"; 1320m/4331ft), the highest peak in the Bohemian Forest, where the frontiers of Bohemia, Bavaria and Austria have met since 1765 (3 hours' climb from Jelení).

Lake Plöckenstein

To the south-east, below the Plöckenstein, is Lake Plöckenstein (Plešné Jezero; alt. 1090m/3576ft), which features in the stories of the 19th century German writer Adalbert Stifter.

Vrchlabí

E 2

Region: Eastern Bohemia
District: Trutnov
Altitude: 477m/1565ft
Population: 13,000

Situation and characteristics

The Eastern Bohemian holiday resort of Vrchlabí (walking and climbing in summer, skiing in winter) straggles for some 5km/3 miles along both sides of the young Labe (Elbe) as it emerges from the Krkonoše (see entry). The original village, founded in the 13th century, was raised to the status of a royal mining town in 1533. The mines were closed down in the 18th century, and the town's economy is now centred on the production of motor vehicles and the textile industry.

*Tourist centre

Vrchlabí is the main base, both in summer and in winter, for excursions into the Krkonoše from the south.

Sights

Town Hall
Church
*Arcaded houses

In the town's main street are the Town Hall (1581; remodelled in Baroque style in 1735), the neo-Gothic town church (1888) and a number of old arcaded wooden houses of the 17th and 18th centuries.

Krkonoše Museum

In the Baroque buildings (1705–25) of a former monastery is the Krkonoše Museum, with a large collection of material on the natural history, history and culture of the region.

Houses in Vrchlabí (left, the Krkonoše Museum)

Castle

South-west of the church stands the four-towered castle of the Czernin-Morzin family (1546–1614; rebuilt 1894), which now houses the administration of the Krkonoše National Park (KRNAP).

Park

The castle is surrounded by a park in the English style, with an arboretum and a small botanical and zoological garden (mountain flora and fauna).

Surroundings of Vrchlabí

To the east

Černý Důl

At Černý Důl (alt. 684m/2244ft) is a limestone quarry.

Svoboda nad Úpou

The little hill town of Svoboda nad Úpou (alt. 515m/1690ft; pop. 2500; paper factory), a popular winter sports resort, has a number of handsome old wooden houses.

Rudník

The village of Rudník (alt. 411m/1348ft) has a fine Gothic church (with later alterations).

Janské Lázně

Janské Lázně (alt. 630m/2065ft; pop. 800), situated below the south side of the Černá Hora ("Black Mountain", 1299m/4262ft; 3000m/3300yd long cabin cableway; aerial tower 80m/260ft high), is a spa (founded 1677) with 30 radioactive thermal springs, and now also a holiday resort and winter sports centre. The spa colonnade, in Art Nouveau style, dates from 1893.

To the west

Jilemnice

Jilemnice (alt. 451m/1480ft; pop. 4500) is a little hill town with some industry (textiles, sports articles) which is also a popular winter sports centre. The Castle (originally Renaissance; rebuilt in the late 19th century) houses a Krkonoše Museum (old skis, Christmas cribs, etc.). Many old wooden houses in the Zvědavá Ulička.

Vítkovice

Vítkovice (alt. 683m/2241ft), a little hill town with a weaving mill, is a favourite place for a restful holiday.

Vysoké nad Jizerou

The little town of Vysoké nad Jizerou (alt. 692m/2270ft; pop. 1700), founded in the 14th century, has an interesting local museum.

Jablonec nad Jizerou

Jablonec nad Jizerou (alt. 450m/1475ft; pop. 2200), a little hill town in the Jizera valley, has a number of old wooden houses of log cabin type.

Vyšší Brod D 4

Region: Southern Bohemia
District: Český Krumlov
Altitude: 571m/1873ft
Population: 2800

Situation and characteristics

Vyšší Brod is an ancient little town on the young Vltava, 30km/19 miles south of Český Krumlov (see entry) and only 7km/4½ miles north of the Czech–Austrian frontier. Its main attraction is its Cistercian monastery.

Sights

*Monastery

The Cistercian monastery of Vyšší Brod, enclosed by a circuit of walls, was founded in 1259 by Petr Vok Rožmberk (Rosenberg) and contains the

Vyšší Brod Monastery

Madonna of Vyšší Brod

Rožmberk family burial vault. The oldest part of the monastery is the east wing, with the chapterhouse (1285); the cloister dates from the 14th and 15th centuries, the refectory from the late 14th century. Particularly notable are the church (13th–15th c.), with a slender tower, the Gothic cloister and the library (70,000 volumes, manuscripts and incunabula). The picture gallery contains mainly works by Dutch masters of the 17th and 18th centuries; the famous cycle of panel paintings by the Master of the Vyšší Brod Altarpiece is now in the National Gallery in Prague.

Postal Museum

There is also an interesting Postal Museum.

Surroundings of Vyšší Brod

Devil's Wall

4km/2½ miles north-west of Vyšší Brod can be found the "Devil's Wall" (Čertova Stěna) nature reserve, above the now almost dry valley of the

Vltava, filled with great granite blocks, many of them hollowed out by the action of the water; water is now directed into the "Devil's Rapids" (Čertovy Proudy) only on the occasion of white-water races. Smetana based an opera ("The Devil's Wall", 1882) on the legend about the creation of the huge rock wall.

Loučovice

6km/4 miles west of Vyšší Brod is Loučovice (alt. 663m/2175ft; pop. 2200), with a paper and cardboard factory established in 1894.

***Rožmberk nad Vltavou**

6km/4 miles north-east of Vyšší Brod is the old village of Rožmberk nad Vltavou (alt. 528m/1732ft; pop. 300), picturesquely situated in a bend on the upper Vltava. On a high promontory above the river is the ancient castle of the Rožmberk and later the Buquoy family. The two-storey Lower Castle, with a square tower, was originally built in the 14th century but was much altered and rebuilt in the 16th, 17th and 19th centuries. It contains fine furniture, pictures, weapons, objets d'art, coffered ceilings, etc. Between 1840 and 1857, when the castle was remodelled in pseudo-Gothic style, the New Castle was also built. Of the 13th century Upper Castle, the ancestral seat of the Rožmberk family, which was destroyed by fire in the 16th century, there survives only the slender tower known as the Jakobínka.

On the left bank of the Vltava stands the 15th century Church of Our Lady, on the site of an earlier 13th century church; it has beautiful net vaulting. There are also some remains of the old town walls.

Žatec C 2

Region: Northern Bohemia
District: Louny
Altitude: 240m/785ft
Population: 22,000

The Northern Bohemian town of Žatec (German Saaz), 20km/12½ miles west-south-west of Louny and the same distance east-south-east of Kadaň (see entries), lies in the Žatec basin on a hill ridge on the right bank of the Ohře. It is the centre of the Bohemian hop-growing region, with numerous oast-houses.

History

The medieval writer known as Johannes von Saaz or Johannes von Tepl, author of "Der Ackermann aus Böhmen" ("The Ploughman from Bohemia"), a work showing early traces of humanism, lived in Žatec as town clerk and notary from 1378 to 1411.
Thomas Müntzer, a Reformer and leading figure in the German Peasant War, lived in Žatec for a time in 1521.

Sights

Market square
Town Hall

In the market square, which is surrounded by arcaded houses with charming gables, is the Town Hall (1559) with a richly sculptured Trinity Column in front of it.

Parish church

To the north of the Town Hall stands the large parish church of the Assumption (14th c.).

Castle
(Brewery)

At the north end of the old town is the Hrad (Castle), now occupied by a brewery.

Town walls

There are considerable stretches of the Late Gothic town walls, with two gates, the Kněžská Brána amd the Libočanska Brána.

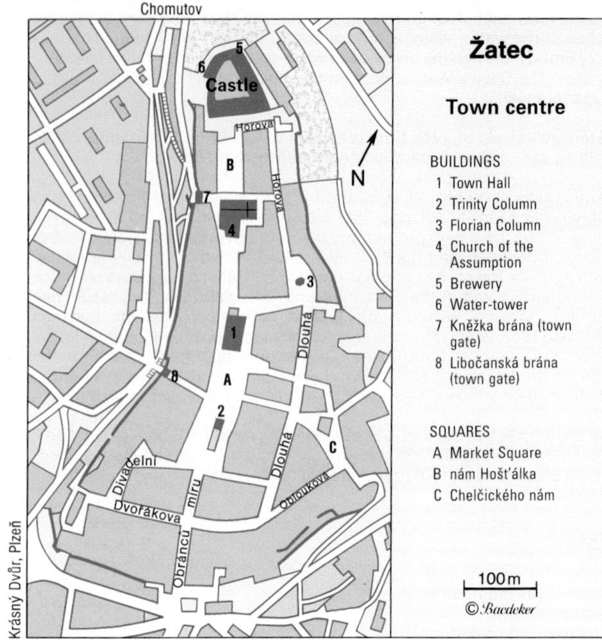

Surroundings of Žatec

Krásný Dvůr

15km/9 miles south-west of Žatec, in a large English-style park, is the Baroque castle of Krásný Dvůr, in which Goethe once stayed.

Žd'ár nad Sázavou E 3

Region: Southern Moravia
District: Žd'ár nad Sázavou
Altitude: 580m/1905ft
Population: 27,000

Situation and characteristics

The Southern Moravian district town of Žd'ár nad Sázavou lies on the southern fringes of the Žd'ár Hills (Žd'árské Vrchy), in which are the highest peaks in the central part of the Bohemo-Moravian Highlands (Českomoravská Vrchovina). The town's economic life centres on industry (engineering, foundries).

Sights

***Monastery**

The town's principal tourist attraction is its Cistercian monastery, which was destroyed during the Hussite Wars but enjoyed a new heyday in the 18th century.

Trinity column, Žatec

Parish church

Museums

The Baroque conventual buildings dating from that period (by Giovanni Santini) now house the Museum of the Book, which illustrates the development of writing and printing.
Also of interest are the Art Gallery and the District Museum.
In the renovated stables is an exhibition devoted to the architect Giovanni Santini (1677–1723).

Buildings by Giovanni Santini

Other fine works by Giovanni Santini in the town and surrounding area are the monastery cemetery (with Baroque sculpture); the Lyra farmstead on the outskirts of the town; a Baroque church on a pentagonal plan on the Zelená Hora, perhaps the finest example in the whole country of the style known as "Baroque Gothic"; churches at Obyčtov (10km/6 miles south-east) and Netín (20km/12½ miles south); and an inn in Ostrov nad Oslavou (10km/6 miles south).

Surroundings of Žd'ár nad Sázavou

Velké Dářko

8km/5 miles north of Žd'ár nad Sázavou lies the Velké Dářko Pond (alt. 617m/2024ft; area 200 hectares/500 acres; bathing facilities). Near here is the source area of the river Sázava.

Nové Město na Moravě

8km/5 miles east of Žd'ár nad Sázavou, below the Žd'ár Hills, is the town of Nové Město na Moravě (alt. 594m/1949ft; pop. 12,000), which is noted for the manufacture of skis and as the cradle of tourism (particularly winter sports) in the Bohemo-Moravian Highlands.

Fryšava

10km/6 miles north-east of Žd'ár nad Sázavou we come to the holiday village of Fryšava (alt. 708m/2323ft), near which are the Medlov and Sýkovec Ponds, in a beautiful setting dominated by two hills, Devět Skal (836m/2743ft) and Žákova Hora (810m/2658ft).

Baroque buildings in Žd'ár nad Sázavou . . . *. . . and surroundings*

Hlinsko

22km/14 miles north of Žd'ár nad Sázavou is Hlinsko (alt. 580m/1905ft; pop. 11,000), an industrial town (electrical appliances) on the western edge of the Žd'ár Hills. It has a Baroque church (1730–45) and a Town Hall of 1792.

Open-air museum

8km/5 miles west, the new open-air museum of Veselý Kopec or Vysočina has examples of traditional buildings from the region.

Železná Ruda C 3

Region: Western Bohemia
District: Klatovy
Altitude: 754m/2474ft
Population: 1500

Situation and characteristics

Železná Ruda is beautifully situated in the Bohemian Forest (Šumava) at the junction of the river Řezne and the Železný Potok, near the Czech–German frontier (crossing Železná Ruda–Bayerisch Eisenstein). It is a popular resort both in summer and for winter sports (ski-lifts) and a good base from which to explore the Bohemian Forest.

History

Železná Ruda was founded in the 14th century as a staging-point on a much used trade route through the Bohemian Forest. In the 16th–18th centuries iron was mined in the area, but the pits are now in a state of decay. Later a glass-making industry developed (window glass, mirror glass).

Parish church

The parish church with its large octagonal onion dome (1732) is a prominent feature of the town.

Surroundings of Železná Ruda

Špičácké Sedlo

3km/2 miles north of Železná Ruda is the Špičácké Sedlo (1000m/3280ft), a saddle on the watershed between the Danube and the Labe (Elbe).

Parish church, Železná Ruda

Devil's Lake

Black Lake

It is a 30–45 minutes' walk north-west through lonely primeval forest to the dark Devil's Lake (Čertovo Jezero; 1030m/3380ft; area 11 hectares/ 27 acres; up to 35m/115ft deep) or to the Black Lake (Černé Jezero; 1008m/3307ft; area 19 hectares/47 acres; up to 40m/130ft deep), two glacier lakes below the sheer rock face of the Jezerní Stěna (1343m/4406ft).

Mt Pancíř

**Views

From the Špičácké Sedlo it is an hour's climb (or by chair-lift) to the summit of Mt Pancíř (1214m/3983ft; mountain hut). From the observation tower on the top there are magnificent views in all directions, extending in clear weather as far as the Alps.

Mt Špičák

4km/2½ miles north of Železná Ruda rises Mt Špičák (1202m/3944ft), a popular winter sports area with several ski-lifts and good pistes.

Hojsova Stráž

11km/7 miles north of Železná Ruda is the village of Hojsova Stráž (alt. 890m/2920ft), a popular summer and winter resort with several small hotels.

Nýrsko

18km/11 miles north-east of Železná Ruda is the little town of Nýrsko (alt. 452m/1483ft; pop. 5000), below the northern foothills of the Bohemian Forest. It has a Baroque church (originally Gothic) and a Baroque Town Hall (1684).

Zadov-Churáňov

20km/12½ miles south-east of Železná Ruda, on the northern edge of the plateau, is Zadov-Churáňov (alt. 1119m/3671ft), a popular tourist centre with several lifts and excellent skiing facilities, particularly langlauf trails.

Moorland

6km/4 miles south-west of Zadov-Churáňov, near the villages of Kvilida and Modrava (alt. about 1000m/3280ft), are several expanses of moorland, with rare moor flora.

Třijezerní Slad'

There is a waymarked trail over the Třijezerní Slad' (Moor of the Three Lakes).

Vydra and Křemelná valleys

To the west of Zadov are the Vydra and Křemelná valleys, with delightful walking country.
The beds of the rivers are littered with large boulders, many of them hollowed out by the action of the water into "giants' punchbowls".

Zlín G 3

Region: Southern Moravia
District: Zlín
Altitude: 230m/755ft
Population: 87,000

Situation and characteristics

The district town of Zlín (known from 1949 to 1989 as Gottwaldov, after the communist politician Klement Gottwald, 1896–1953) lies in the beautifully wooded valley of the Dřevnice, a left-bank tributary of the Morava.

The "shoe town"

Zlín has long been known as the "shoe town". It owes its fame to Tomáš Bat'a, a native of the town, who from 1894 onwards developed the small family shoemaking business, by introducing progressive and efficient production methods and worker participation in profits, into one of the largest shoe factories in the world and gave Bat'a shoes an international reputation. The headquarters of the firm are now in Canada.

A modern industrial town

Zlín's original industries of shoemaking, leather-working and hosiery were later followed by the chemical industry (Barum tyres, plastics, etc.) and by engineering and aircraft production, leading to a considerable expansion of the town, with new modern factories and extensive housing areas. Well-known architects including Le Corbusier and Josef Kotěra were involved in the development of the modern town with its museums, theatre, film studios and airport at Holešov.

Sights

Town centre

In the centre of the town are Labour Square (Náměstí Práce) and Peace Square (Náměstí Míru).

Castle (Museum) **Art Gallery**

The Castle (Renaissance, remodelled in Baroque style) is now occupied by the Regional Museum of South-Eastern Moravia. It has an English-style park. The Bohemian Gallery of Painting and Sculpture is housed partly in the castle and partly in the House of Art.

Shoe Museum

There is an interesting Shoe Museum in the Svit factory.

Film studios

3km/2 miles south of the town centre, in the Kudlov district, are the film studios which produce the well-known Czech animated cartoons, puppet films and shorts.

Surroundings of Zlín

Štípa

6km/4 miles north-east of Zlín is the outlying district of Štípa (alt. 267m/876ft), with a Baroque pilgrimage church (Gothic Madonna). On a nearby hill (20 minutes' walk south-east) is a stone-built windmill (1860).

Lešná

Lešná, 7km/4½ miles north-east of Zlín, has a neo-classical castle (early 19th c.) which was remodelled in Romantic style at the end of the 19th century. The Austrian dramatist Franz Grillparzer was a tutor in the castle in 1812–13. Beautiful park; Zoo.

Lukov

10km/6 miles north-east of Zlín are the ruins of Lukov Castle (13th c.). In the village of Lukov is an Art Nouveau villa, "Tusculum", belonging to the Seiler family.

Napajedla

12km/7½ miles south-west of Zlín, on the left bank of the Morava, lies the little town of Napajedla (alt. 200m/655ft; pop. 6000; chemical factory, diesel engine plant), with a famous stud farm. Other features of interest are the Late Baroque castle (1764–69), the castle park, the town church (1712; Renaissance doorway) and the local museum (archaeological collections).

Znojmo F 4

Region: Southern Moravia
District: Znojmo
Altitude: 289m/948ft
Population: 39,000

Situation and *townscape

The Southern Moravian district town of Znojmo, finely situated on a hill 75–95m/245–310ft above the river Dyje, has largely preserved its old-world aspect.

Founded about 1266, Znojmo is the market town of an extensive agricultural area (stock farming, fruit and vegetable growing: Znojmo gherkins are famous), with a variety of industry (food-canning, ceramics, footwear manufacture, engineering, tanning).

Vintage festival

A great vintage festival, with a parade, is held here annually in autumn.

Sights

Castle (Museum)

The Baroque castle, originally a stronghold of the Margraves of Moravia (11th c.). now houses the Museum of Southern Moravia.

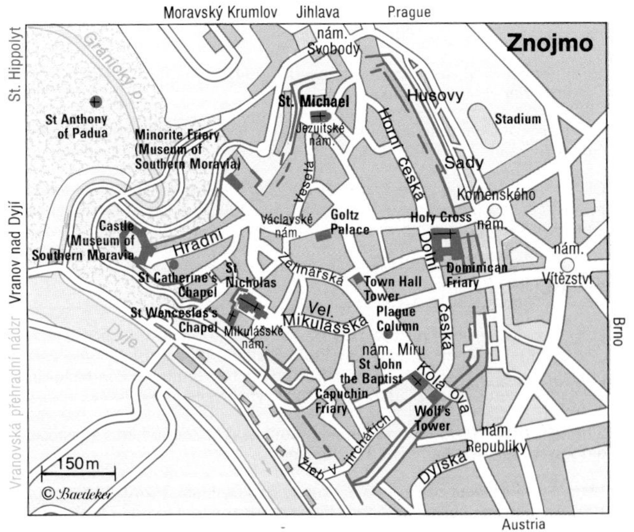

Vranov Castle

*St Catherine's Chapel

The castle chapel, a Romanesque rotunda dedicated to St Catherine, has fine wall paintings of 1134 (cycle of the Přemyslid dynasty; several times restored, most recently in 1949).

Churches

Znojmo has two notable churches – St Nicholas's, a Gothic hall-church of 1338–1440 (Baroque interior; tower of 1848) and, to the south of this, St Wenceslas's Chapel, a 16th century double church.

Town Hall tower

Of the Town Hall, which was destroyed in 1945, only the 80m/260ft high Gothic tower (1448) remains.

Town walls

There are considerable remains of the old town walls, in particular the Late Gothic bastions.

Louka monastery

Outside the town, on the banks of the Dyje, is the Louka ("Meadow") monastery, a Cistercian house founded in 1190. The Late Romanesque church has largely been preserved.

Surroundings of Znojmo

Přímětice

2km/1¼ miles north of the town centre is Přímětice (alt. 324m/1063ft), now incorporated in Znojmo, with large wine cellars. Prokop Diviš, who was priest here from 1746 to 1765, constructed the first lightning conductor in 1754 (commemorative plaque on presbytery).

Slup

Slup (alt. 191m/627ft), 14km/8½ miles south-east of Znojmo, has a historic old water-mill (first half of 17th c.; museum).

Vranov nad Dyjí
Vranov Castle

18km/11 miles west of Znojmo is Vranov nad Dyjí (alt. 312m/1024ft; pop. 1000), a popular summer resort. Picturesquely situated on a high crag

Bítov Castle

above the village is a Baroque castle (built in 11th–13th c.; remodelled in 17th and 18th c., partly to plans by J. B. Fischer von Erlach). Notable features of the castle are the twin-towered chapel, the oval Hall of Ancestors (frescoes) and a collection of ceramics and porcelain.

***Lake Vranov**

1km/¾ mile north of Vranov lies Lake Vranov (Vranovská Přehradní Nádrž; alt. 350m/1150ft), formed in 1930–33 by the construction of a dam on the river Dyje. 30km/19 miles long, surrounded by fine forests, the lake offers a range of recreational facilities (bathing, camping sites, boat rental, fishing). During the summer there are boat services between Vranov and Vítov (pop. 250), at the north-western end of the lake.

***Bítov Castle**

A short distance away is Bítov Castle, founded in the 11th century; the present buildings date from the 15th and 16th centuries and were remodelled in the 19th century in neo-Gothic style. The castle contains collections of weapons, arts and crafts and natural history.

Cornštejn Castle

Near Bítov are the ruins of Cornštejn Castle (14th c.).

Moravský Krumlov

26km/16 miles north-east of Znojmo is Moravský Krumlov (alt. 255m/835ft; pop. 7000), with a large Renaissance castle of 1557–62. In the chapel is a famous cycle of paintings, "The Slav Epic" (1910–28), by the Art Nouveau painter Alfons Mucha (1860–1939).
The celebrated 16th century doctor Paracelsus stayed in the castle in 1537.

Privatisation and Restitution

These are the great slogans so much discussed in the Federal Republic of Czechoslovakia after the overthrow of the communist regime and in the two independent Republics established in 1993, which are now gradually beginning to be put into effect.

In the economic field there has been both small-scale and large-scale privatisation. Under the arrangements for small-scale privatisation many small enterprises have passed into private hands, either through the acquisition of privatisation coupons by citizens of the Republic or through sale to foreign investors. Large-scale privatisation has involved the transformation of mainly State-owned enterprises into private joint-stock companies.

Restitution means the handing back to the original owners of properties expropriated and land nationalised after 1948. This applies particularly to innumerable castles and manor-houses, monasteries and other church properties, together with the estates belonging to them (forests, arable land, pastureland, vineyards, etc.). Thus the old Bohemian princely house of Lobkowitz (Lobkowicz) has received back from the State sixteen castles and some 15,000 hectares (37,500 acres) of land.

As a result of these transfers references in the descriptive part of this guide to the "former" owners of castles, etc., may no longer be apt.

Autumn in the High Tatras: the Lomnický Štít ▶

Sights from A to Z: Slovak Republic

Banská Bystrica I 4

Region: Central Slovakia
District: Banská Bystrica
Altitude: 362m/1188ft
Population: 85,000

Situation and characteristics

The Central Slovakian district town of Banská Bystrica is beautifully situated at the confluence of the Hron and the Bystrica, between the Low Tatras and Slovakian Ore Mountains to the east and the High Tatras and Kremnica Hills to the west. The cultural centre of its region, it has a number of higher educational establishments, a theatre and a symphony orchestra. Its principal industries are engineering, textiles, woodworking and the manufacture of building materials.

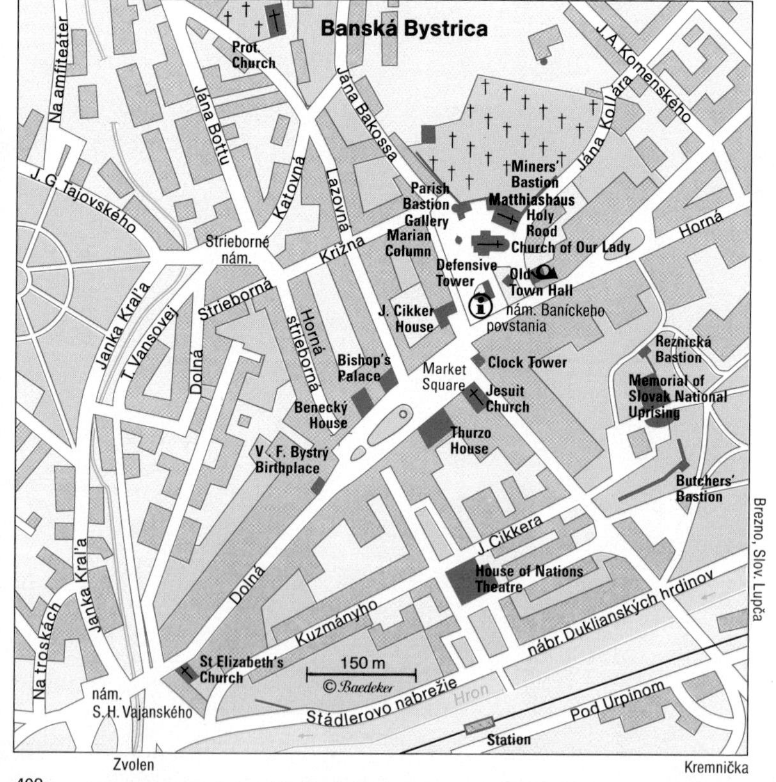

History

The town – which still preserves many medieval buildings – owed its early prosperity to the silver which was worked here from the 13th century and the copper (at the village of Špania Dolina) which was worked in the 14th–16th centuries. It was granted the status of a free royal mining town in 1255. In the 16th century, under the rule of the Thurzo family, it took a leading place in the European silver and copper trade. In the late 18th century and mid 19th century it was a centre of the Slovak national movement (Slovak grammar school founded 1850). On August 29th 1944 the Slovak National Uprising was proclaimed in Banská Bystrica.

Sights

Market square

Thurzo House (Central Slovak Museum)

In the centre of the town is the elongated market square (officially Square of the Slovak National Uprising, Námestie Slovenského Národného Povstania), surrounded by handsome Renaissance burghers' houses. On the east side of the square is the Thurzo House, a Renaissance building with fine sgraffito decoration which now houses the Central Slovakian Museum (Stredoslovenské Museum; history of the town, ethnography).

Historical plan of the Castle Church of Banská Bystrica

Theatre

Protestant church

Clock-Tower

Adjoining the Museum to the left is the Theatre, and farther along, at the corner of Moyzesova Ulica, the neo-classical Protestant church (1807). At the north-east end of the square is the free-standing Clock-Tower (Hodinová Veža, 1552).

Citadel area

The market square leads into another long square to the north-east, the Námestie Baníckeho Povstania. To the left of this square, rising gradually towards the north, is the citadel area.

Castle

Matthias House

Just above the square are the 15th century Castle, with a massive keep, and the Matthias House (Matejov Dom; 1479), once the residence of King Matthias of Hungary.

Old Town Hall

To the right of the Matthias House is the Old Town Hall or Praetorium (originally Gothic, remodelled in Renaissance style 1564–65), with a Renaissance loggia on the first floor, now housing the District Art Gallery. Across the street is the Head Post Office.

Churches

To the rear of the Castle can be found the Church of Our Lady (13th–15th c.), and beyond it the Gothic Church of the Holy Rood, also known as the Slovak Church. Adjoining are an artillery bastion and a town gate with a barbican. Other features of interest are the Gothic St Elizabeth's Church (14th c. carved altar) and the Baroque Bishop's Palace (18th c.).

***Memorial of National Uprising**

The town is dominated by the modern Memorial of the Slovak National Uprising (with museum).

Near the Memorial are two bastions which formed part of the town's fortifications.

Memorial of the Slovak National Uprising, Banská Bystrica

Surroundings of Banská Bystrica

Sásová

Sásová, on the northern outskirts of the town, has a beautiful Gothic church.

Kremnička

6km/4 miles south of Banská Bystrica, at Kremnička (alt. 337m/1106ft), can be seen a monument marking the mass grave of 747 resistance fighters.

Panský Diel

6km/4 miles north of Banská Bystrica is a prominent hill, Panský Diel (1100m/3610ft), from which there are fine panoramic views.

Špania Dolina

10km/6 miles north of Banská Bystrica is Špania Dolina (alt. 728m/2389ft), with traces of mining activity, old miners' houses and a covered wooden bridge.

Slovenská Lupča

Slovenská Lupča (alt. 378m/1240ft; pop. 3000), 10km/6 miles north-east of Banská Bystrica, has a castle which first appears in the records as a medieval fortified castle in 1250. In the course of its history it has been much altered and rebuilt but has remained continuously inhabited. The town's principal church dates from the 14th century.

Izbica Cave

16km/10 miles north-west of Banská Bystrica, in the Harmanec valley, is the stalactitic Izbica Cave (alt. 828m/2717ft).

Banská Štiavnica H 4

Region: Central Slovakia. District: Žiar nad Hronom
Altitude: 550–800m/1805–2625ft. Population: 9000

Situation and characteristics

The old mining town of Banská Štiavnica, on the slopes of the Štiavnica Hills (Štiavnické Vrchy), has a variety of industry (woodworking, textiles, tobacco-processing). The possibility of reviving the old mining industry by the recovery of non-ferrous metals from ores in the surrounding area is being examined.

The old town centre is a conservation area.

History

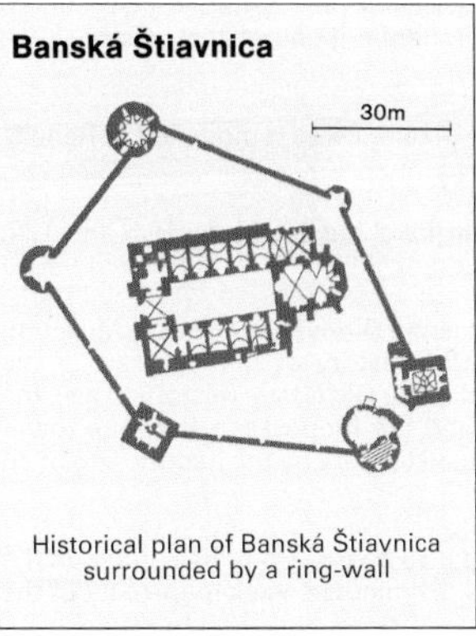

Historical plan of Banská Štiavnica surrounded by a ring-wall

The town, founded in the 12th century by German miners, on a site which is first mentioned in the records in 1075, was granted the privileges of a free royal town in 1217. Its heyday was in the 14th–16th centuries, when large quantities of gold and silver were mined here. In the reign of Ferdinand I the mining rights were held by the Fuggers, the great merchant family of Augsburg. The Hussite Wars and Turkish attacks led to the decline of the town. In 1735, however, the first school of mining was established here, and in 1763 this became the Academy of Mining and Ironworking (and later also of Forestry), which existed until 1918.

1 St Catherine's Church 2 Town Hall 3 Marian Column 4 Sember House

Sights

*Old Castle

At the west end of the town is the picturesque Old Castle, originally built in the 13th century as a church but rebuilt and fortified in the 16th century as a Renaissance fortress directed against the Turks.

New Castle

To the south of the Old Castle stands the New Castle (Nový or Panenský Zámok), built in 1564–71 as a stronghold against the Turks.

Churches

Banská Štiavnica has three notable churches – St Nicholas's Cathedral (Late Romanesque; altered in neo-classical style), St Catherine's Church (Gothic, 15th c.; fine interior) and the Frauenberg Church (Late Gothic, with beautiful vaulting).

Old Town Hall

The Gothic Old Town Hall dates from 1488 but was remodelled in Renaissance style in the 16th century.

Market square

In the market square are many old burghers' houses of the 16th and 17th centuries and a Baroque Plague Column of 1764.

*Mining Museum

In the 16th century Hellenbach House is the Dionýz Štúr Mining Museum, with interesting exhibits illustrating the history of mining. Part of the Slovak Mining Museum is also housed in the Old Castle (history of art), the New Castle (battles with the Turks) and the Klopačka, a Baroque tower (1681) from which the miners were called to work by the hammering of an oak mallet on a wooden panel.

Calvary

The best view of the surrounding area is to be had from the church on the hill of Calvary (Kalvária; 727m/2385ft), 20 minutes' walk to the east of the town.

Arboretum

Still farther east lies an arboretum, with exotic trees and shrubs.

Surroundings of Banská Štiavnica

Mt Sitno

A rewarding excursion (2 hours) is to Mt Sitno (1009m/3311ft), the highest peak in the Štiavnica Hills. Below the west side of the hill is a mountain lake, the Počúvadlianské Jazero.

Antol

6km/4 miles south-east of Banská Štiavnica is the village of Antol (alt. 449m/1473ft; pop. 1500), with a Baroque and neo-classical castle which belonged to the Dukes of Coburg. It now houses a museum of forestry, timber-working and hunting.

Hontianske Nemce

Hontianske Nemce (alt. 224m/735ft; pop. 1000), 20km/12½ miles south of Banská Štiavnica, has a Romanesque church and some fine examples of local traditional architecture.

Krupina

20km/12½ miles south-east of Banská Štiavnica we come to Krupina (alt. 280m/920ft; pop. 10,000), an old mining town (originally German) with a Romanesque church remodelled in Late Baroque style. There are remains of town walls and a watch-tower, the Vartovka (1564), built for protection against Turkish attacks.

Nová Baňa

20km/12½ miles south-west of Banská Štiavnica is the old mining town of Nová Baňa (alt. 224m/735ft; pop. 7000), with a 14th century Gothic church and a local museum.

Dicine

The village and spa of Dicine (alt. 139m/456ft), 32km/20 miles south of Banská Štiavnica, has modern treatment facilities. The travertine rocks in the surrounding area are now a landscape reserve.

Banská Štiavnica

Levice

34km/21 miles south-west of Banská Štiavnica lies the district capital and industrial town of Levice (alt. 163m/535ft; pop. 19,000), with the ruins of a medieval castle, Renaissance and Baroque buildings which now house a museum and three neo-classical churches.

Margita-Ilona

6km/4 miles east of Levice are a municipal recreation area and the spa of Margita-Ilona.

Bardejov L 3

Region: Eastern Slovakia
District: Bardejov
Altitude: 271m/889ft
Population: 30,000

Situation and characteristics

The old-world town of Bardejov lies on the river Topl'á in eastern Slovakia. Originally founded by German settlers, mostly weavers, it developed into an important trading town (from the late 14th century a free royal town under the Hungarian crown), dealing particularly in linen (with a monopoly in the bleaching of linen) and wine, on the trade route between Hungary and Poland. It was also an important cultural centre for the Šariš region, with a grammar school and two printing houses.

Sights

***Town walls**

The old town of Bardejov, the best preserved medieval town centre in Slovakia, is surrounded by fortifications of the 14th–16th centuries – walls and a moat, with bastions and three gates (the Upper Gate, with a barbican, the Powder Tower and the Lower Gate).

Market square

The spacious market square, sloping gently down from south to north, is surrounded by burghers' houses. At its lower end is the handsome Gothic

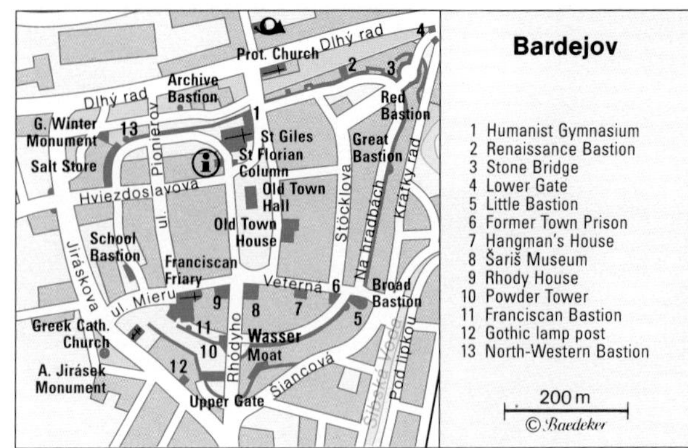

St Giles' Church
*Altars

church of St Giles, a three-aisled hall-church of the 15th century (restored at the end of the 19th century) with eleven Late Gothic carved winged altars (1460–1510), finely carved 15th century choir-stalls, a brass font (first half of 16th c.), a carved "Crucifixion" over the crossing, perhaps by Veit Stoss, and a richly decorated Gothic tabernacle of 1464 (lower part restored 1957).

***Old Town Hall**
(Museum)

To the south of the church stands the Old Town Hall (now the Šariš District Museum), a Late Gothic building (early 16th c.) with a Renaissance staircase and oriel (1505–08) on the east side and steeply pitched gables decorated with figures.

*Icon collection

The Museum has the largest collection of icons in Slovakia.

Market Square, Bardejov (left, the Old Town Hall)

The burghers' houses round the market square, originally dating from the 16th century, were mostly rebuilt after a fire in 1878. Among those which survived the fire was No. 13 (1566). Particularly notable is the Rhody House (1660; restored) in Rhody Street, with arcading borne on four columns, which now houses part of the Šariš Museum. There are other fine old houses in Veterná Ulica and Stöcklova Ulica.

Burghers' houses

Surroundings of Bardejov

Orthodox churches

In the villages to the south and north-west of Bardejov are a number of historic old Orthodox churches:

Frička: 16th century church with a Renaissance bell of 1697 and an altar of 1716.
Hervartov: Church of 1593–96 with fine wall paintings.
Krivé: Church of 1826 with good icons.
Lukov: Church of 1708 with beautiful wall paintings.
Tročany: Church of 1739 with a large collection of icons.

Bardejovské Kúpele

6km/4 miles north of Bardejov, in a wooded valley, is the little spa of Bardejovské Kúpele (alt. 350m/1150ft; acidic chalybeate springs, mud baths). It has an interesting open-air museum with 30 wooden buildings typical of the Šariš district, including a little Orthodox church (18th c.; collection of icons) from Zboj (10km/6 miles south of the point where the Slovak, Polish and Ukrainian frontiers meet) and another 18th century church from the nearby village of Mikulášová.

Zborov

Zborov (pop. 2000), 10km/6 miles north of Bardejov, has a Renaissance castle. To the south of the little town, on a wooded hill (nature reserve), are the ruins of Zborov Castle (13th c.; destroyed 1684).

Svidník

25km/15 miles north-east of Bardejov, at the confluence of the Ondava and the Ladomirka, is the district town of Svidník (alt. 220m/720ft; pop. 11,000; clothing industry, engineering). The town was destroyed during the fighting for the Dukla pass in 1944 and was rebuilt after the war. Features of interest are the Late Baroque Greek Catholic church (second half of 18th c.), a neo-classical church of 1800, an open-air museum and the Ukrainian Regional Museum.

Annually in June a Ukrainian folk festival is held in Svidník's open-air theatre.

War memorial

On the road which runs north-west from Svidník to Zborov and Bardejov (on right) is a large war memorial to those who fell in the battle for the Dukla pass.

***Wooden churches**

From Svidník a road leads north-east up the wide valley of the Ladomirka to the villages of Ladomirová (6km/4 miles), with a wooden Orthodox church of 1742, Potoky (8km/5 miles north-east) and Hunkovce (10km/6 miles), which also has a little wooden church (above the village to the left). 2km/1¼ miles north of Potoky we come to Korejovce, with a wooden church of 1761 (restored 1947).

13km/8 miles farther on, at Krajná Pol'ana, a road branches off on the right to the villages of Bodružal (2km/1¼ miles south-east) and Mirol'a (5km/3 miles south-east), with interesting wooden churches of 1658 (restored 1902) and 1770.

Dukla Pass Open-Air Museum

Farther north, beyond Krajná Pol'ana, is the Dukla Pass Open-Air Museum (Prírodné Múzeum na Dukle), in which the various stages in the battle for control of the pass in the autumn of 1944 between German and combined Soviet and Czechoslovak forces are graphically represented.

After passing through an entrance gate the road comes in 1.5km/1 mile to the village of Nižný Komárnik (pop. 300). To the left are a Soviet fighter plane, guns and a viewing platform with a panoramic sketch of the battlefield. Farther on, to left and right of the road, are field guns. In another

Wooden church in Svidník open-air museum

War memorial on Dukla Pass

6km/4 miles, below the road on the right, is a car park, and farther to the right, in front of a military cemetery, a memorial to the soldiers of the First Czechoslovak Army Corps who were killed here. The Soviet army lost 80,000 men, the Czechoslovaks 6500.

Dukla pass

A few hundred metres farther north is the Dukla pass (Slovak Dukelský priesmyk, Polish Przełęcz Dukielska; 502m/1647ft; frontier crossing), the lowest pass through the Carpathians, which was also the scene of bitter fighting between Austrian and Russian forces in the First World War. (Warning: There is an old minefield here: keep to the marked paths).

Belianske Tatras / Belianské Tatry K 3

Region: Eastern Slovakia
District: Poprad

Situation and *topography

The limestone hills of the Belianske Tatras (Belianské Tatry) lie immediately east of the main ridge of the High Tatras (see entry), reaching their highest point in Mt Havran (2152m/7061ft). The crests of the range are under strict protection as a nature reserve (the Tatras National Park), and the old Tatras Trail (Magistrala) no longer crosses this area.

Places in the *Belianske Tatras

Freedom Road

The "Freedom Road" runs from south-east to north-west, linking the villages and spas on the east and north sides of the hills.

Kežmarske Žlaby
Tatranská Kotlina

From Kežmarske Žlaby (alt. 902m/2959ft) the road goes 6km/4 miles north-east to Tatranská Kotlina (alt. 760m/2495ft). 20 minutes' walk to the west is

In the Belianske Tatras

the Belianská jaskyňa, a stalactitic cave, 1000m/1100yd of which are open to visitors.

***Ždiar**

From Tatranská Kotlina it is 7km/4½ miles to Ždiar (alt. 904m/2966ft; pop. 2000), a village populated by Gorals (a mountain people with some Polish blood), who still preserve their old customs and way of life (traditional costumes, fortified farmsteads, painted wooden houses with shingle roofs). The best examples of their houses are to be seen at the northern end of the village, around the Antosovský Vrch and in the Bachledová and Blaščatská valleys. In one of the old farmhouses is an ethnographic museum. Ždiar is also a popular winter sports resort (2000 beds in private houses; excellent skiing facilities for beginners).

Spišska Magura

The best views of the Belianske Tatras range are to be enjoyed from the easily accessible ridge of the Spišska Magura.

Javorina

Beyond Ždiar the road crosses the Sedlo pod Prislobum (1081m/3547ft), a pass between the Spišska Magura to the north-east and the Belianske Tatras to the south, and after passing through Podspády (alt. 919m/3015ft) comes in 11km/7 miles to Javorina (alt. 1000m/3280ft), at the foot of Mt Muráň (1882m/6175ft), with a hunting lodge which belonged to the Princes of Hohenlohe. From there it is another 2km/1¼ miles to the Polish frontier at Lysa Polana.

From the frontier it is 20km/12½ miles to Zakopane (alt. 837m/2746ft), the Polish gateway to the Tatras.

Bojnice H 4

Region: Central Slovakia
District: Prievidza
Altitude: 298m/978ft
Population: 4000

Situation and characteristics

The Central Slovakian spa of Bojnice lies on the upper course of the river Nitra, surrounded by forests. The thermal springs (temperatures up to 47°C/117°F) are used in the treatment of rheumatism and nervous diseases.

***Castle**

Bojnice Castle, which formerly belonged to the Counts Pálffy, was sumptuously rebuilt in 1888–1910 in the style of the French châteaux. It now houses a museum and art gallery.

*Park

In the castle park, one of the most beautiful in Slovakia, is a zoo. Below the castle is a dripstone cave, the Prepoštská jaskyňa.

Surroundings of Bojnice

Prievidza

5km/3 miles east of Bojnice is the district capital and industrial town (coal-mining, woodworking) of Prievidza (alt. 280m/920ft; pop. 41,000). In the market square can be seen burghers' houses in Renaissance and Baroque style. There are two notable churches, the Late Romanesque cemetery church (1260) and the Gothic parish church (end of 14th c.), both with later alterations.

Nitrianské Rudno

8km/5 miles west of Bojnice is the former mining town of Nitrianské Rudno (alt. 318m/1043ft), now a holiday centre on Lake Nitrica, formed by a dam on the river of that name.

Nitrianské Pravno

10km/6 miles north of Bojnice is the ancient little mining town of Nitrianské Pravno (alt. 348m/1142ft), with a Gothic church which was enlarged in neo-Gothic style in 1915.

***Cičmany**

22km/14 miles north of Bojnice is the interesting village of Cičmany (alt. 655m/2150ft; pop. 1000), with painted wooden houses decorated with

Bojnice Castle

carved ornament. The villagers still wear colourful and richly embroidered traditional costumes on days of festival.

Bratislava

G 4

Capital of the Slovak Republic
Region: Western Slovakia
Administratuve unit: Bratislava City Region
Altitude: 127–514m/417–1686ft
Area: 368sq.km/142sq.miles
Population: 450,000

General

The old frontier town of Bratislava (formerly known under its German name of Pressburg; Hungarian Pozsony), is the largest city in Slovakia and the political, economic and cultural centre of the Slovak Republic, the seat of the Slovak parliament and government, with a University and a Technical University, the Slovak Academy of Sciences, Colleges of Economics, Education, Art, Music (the Conservatoire) and the Theatre and several technical schools. In addition it has the Slovak National Museum and other museums, the Slovak Art Gallery and other art galleries, several libraries, other cultural institutions including the Matica Slovenská, film, radio and television organisations, several publishing houses, a busy theatrical and musical programme (Slovak National Theatre, Slovak Philharmonic Orchestra), a variety of sports facilities, a Botanic Garden and a Zoo. Bratislava is also a city of festivals and trade fairs.

Situation

Bratislava lies in latitude 48°10′ north and longitude 17°10′ east on the extreme south-western borders of Slovakia, a few kilometres north-west of

Panoramic view of Bratislava

the point where the frontiers of Slovakia, Austria and Hungary meet. The city extends in the form of a fan along the left bank of the swiftly flowing Danube (Dunaj), which here emerges from the narrow defile of the "Porta Hungarica" (Devínská Brána), between the Little Carpathians (see entry) and the Leitha Hills, into the Little Hungarian Plain. At Bratislava the Danube is up to 300m/330yd wide, with an average flow of 2000 cubic metres (440,000 gallons) per second. Within the city it is spanned by four bridges, a combined motorway and railway bridge and three road bridges.

Area

Bratislava forms a separate city region within the Slovak Republic, with an area – since the incorporation of some neighbouring communes in 1971 – of just under 368sq.km/142sq.miles. It is divided into 17 wards or districts.

Townscape

Even since the construction of the boldly engineered high-level road bridge which spans the Danube, linking the south bank with the old town centre, the dominating landmark of Bratislava is still the square bulk of the Castle with its four corner towers on the hill above the town. The urban motorway which sweeps up from the bridge has cut a broad swathe through the town (involving the demolition of the old Jewish quarter), passing close to Bratislava's other major landmark, St Martin's Cathedral. The pattern of the old town is still largely determined by the Late Baroque style of the reign of the Empress Maria Theresa (1740–80).

The extensive modern districts and suburbs of Bratislava, with their housing areas and large industrial installations, now spread from the foot of the

Little Carpathians to the banks of the Danube and into the plain to the east, and in recent years the city has reached out on to the south bank of the Danube with the huge blocks of flats in the suburb of Petržalka.

Economy

Bratislava's varied pattern of industry includes petro-chemicals (natural gas pipeline from the Ukraine since 1962), metalworking (engineering, automobile parts), electrical engineering and electronic appliances, tyres, glass, cosmetics, leather goods, woodworking, machinery for the production of building materials, graphic trades, furniture, textiles and foodstuffs (canning factories, bakeries, dairy products, chocolate, sweets, brewing, wine-making). Vines and vegetables are intensively cultivated in the surrounding area. Together with the services sector (banking and insurance, commerce, tourism), industrial production, the construction industry and trade in industrial products and the agricultural produce of the city's hinterland form the basis and the central element in the economic life of the whole of Slovakia.

Transport

Although situated at one end of the country, Bratislava lies at the meeting-place of important long-distance routes (railway junction; motorways via Brno to Prague and into the middle Váh valley; E 58 to Vienna, 65km/40 miles west-north-west; E 75 to Budapest, 195km/121 miles east-south-east; Ivánka international airport). The city's river port on the Danube has long been of importance for shipping on the middle and lower Danube and

to the Black Sea, and its importance will be even greater after the completion of the Main–Danube Canal and the creation of a continuous waterway between the North Sea and the Black Sea (the Rhine–Main–Danube Waterway). In addition to the cruise ships and local excursion ships which ply on the Danube there is also the hydrofoil "Raketa" which runs a shuttle service between Vienna and Budapest, calling in at Bratislava.

History of Bratislava

Early settlement

Archaeological finds have shown that the site of Bratislava was settled as early as the Neolithic period, and there is much evidence of occupation during the Bronze Age and Iron Age (La Tène phase). In the 1st century B.C. there was a settlement of the Boii (a Celtic tribe) on the site, and between the 1st and 4th centuries A.D. the Danube at this point marked the northern frontier of the Roman Empire, the Limes, which was reinforced by a chain of military bases. Later the Goths and the Huns pressed over this frontier into the Empire. The Slavs are believed to have arrived in the region in the 5th century, and at the end of the 6th century they came under the rule of the Avars.

A regional centre in the Great Moravian Empire

In the 9th century the Great Moravian Empire, of which Slovakia formed part, was established. On the castle hill there grew up a cultural and ecclesiastical centre, evidenced by remains of the foundations of a basilica. The nearby castle of Devín at the junction of the Morava with the Danube, on a site which was already fortified in Roman times, appears in the annals of Fulda monastery (864) as the mighty frontier fortress of Dowina.

Name of the town

The first written reference to the town, under the name Brezalauspurc, is in the annals of Salzburg for the year 907, when it was the scene of a heavy defeat of the Bavarian army of Margrave Luitpold (who was killed in the battle) by the Magyars. Thereafter it became a frontier stronghold of the Magyar kingdom which was then in process of formation. In the early medieval period various other names are found – the Latinised Bratslaburgum, the German forms Braslavespurc, Preslawespurch, Brezespurch and Pressburch (hence the modern German form Pressburg; earlier Slovak Prešpork or Prešporek) and the Slavonic Bratslavov Hrad (no doubt the origin of its present Slovak name). The late Latin form Posonium gave rise to the Hungarian name Pozsony.

Chief town of Hungarian komitat

Around the year 1000 King Stephen I of Hungary (St Stephen) makes the market town which has grown up under the castle the chief town of a komitat (referred to on coins as "Breslava Civitas") and brings in settlers from Bavaria.
In 1052 the Emperor Henry III occupies the town and the castle.

Emperor Barbarossa St Elizabeth

In 1189 the Emperor Frederick I Barbarossa assembles his army in Bratislava for the Third Crusade (from which he does not return). Here in 1207 is born Elizabeth, daughter of King Andrew II of Hungary, who marries the Landgrave of Thuringia and after his death devotes herself to a life of poverty and charity, for which she is canonised in 1235.

Charter

In 1217 the town is granted a charter on the German model.
In the winter of 1241–42 the Tatars devastate the surrounding country but are unable to capture either the castle or the town which is under its protection.
King Otakar II of Bohemia (who had married a grand-daughter of King Bela IV of Hungary) repeatedly captures and devastates the town. King Stephen V of Hungary calls in German settlers to rebuild it.

Peace of Pressburg (1271)

Under the Peace of Pressburg concluded by Stephen V of Hungary and Otakar II of Bohemia Stephen gives up Styria, Carinthia and Carniola, while Otakar gives up his conquests in Hungary with the exception of western Slovakia (including Pressburg).

◀ *View of Bratislava from the south-west (in the foreground the SNP Bridge)*

Municipal privileges

In 1291 King Andrew III of Hungary grants the town extensive privileges (self-government, administration of justice, freedom of trade, etc.) which promote its future development.
In 1302, during the conflict for the Hungarian throne, the town is occupied by Archduke Rudolph of Austria.

Regulation of guilds

In 1376 the town council promulgates a first ordinance on the regulation of guilds.

A free royal town

Under the Hungarian kings Louis I, the Great (1342–82), Sigismund of Luxembourg (1387–1437) and above all Matthias I Corvinus (1458–90) the town enjoys a period of rising prosperity. In 1405 Sigismund grants it the status of a free royal town under the Hungarian crown. In 1428–29 it withstands an attack by a Hussite army; it strengthens its walls, and in 1420 is granted the right to coin money. In 1465 Matthias establishes in the town the Academia Istropolitana, the first institute of higher education in Hungary, at which many German humanists teach.

Academia Istropolitana

Peace of Pressburg (1491)

Under the Peace of Pressburg (1491) Vladislav II of Bohemia (from 1471) and Hungary (from 1490) makes over to the Habsburgs the succession to the thrones of Bohemia and Hungary.

16th century

The 16th century is the period of the Turkish wars. After the Hungarian defeat in a decisive battle in 1526, in which King Louis II is killed, the Hungarian Diet, meeting in the Franciscan friary in Pressburg, elects Ferdinand of Habsburg hereditary king of Hungary.

Capital of Habsburg Hungary

After Buda (part of what was to become Budapest) falls to the Turks the capital of Habsburg Hungary is transferred to Pozsony (Pressburg), a strongly fortified town. It remains capital from 1536 to 1784, and from 1563 (coronation of Maximilian II) until 1830 is the place of coronation of the Habsburg kings of Hungary. The Hungarian archbishops of Esztergom, whose chapter is based in Nagyszombat (Slovak Trnava) from 1541 to 1820, have two residences in Pressburg. Until 1848 the Hungarian Diet meets here.

It is recorded in the annals of Pressburg that a baker named Veit Bach, a forebear of Johann Sebastian Bach, has acquired a vineyard "outside the gates" of the town.

17th century

By around 1600 Pressburg has a population of some 5000.
In the first half of the 17th century there are repeated rebellions by the Protestant Hungarian nobility against the Catholic Habsburgs. In 1606 Pressburg is besieged by Prince Stephen Bocskay of Transylvania. From 1619 to 1621 it is occupied by Prince Gabriel Bethlen. In 1626 Archbishop Peter Pázmány summons Jesuits to Pressburg to strengthen Catholic influence in the town.
In 1687 the Hungarian Council of State, meeting in Pressburg, recognises the hereditary succession to the Hungarian throne in the male line of the Habsburgs. In 1698 Tsar Peter the Great visits the town. In 1699 the first merchant guild in Pressburg is established.

18th century

In 1704 Prince Eugene of Savoy saves Pressburg from the forces of the rebellious Hungarian magnate Francis II Rákóczi, who devastates the outlying districts of the town. An estimated 3860 citizens die in the cholera epidemic of 1710–11. The town's first newspeper, the "Nova Posoniensia", appears in 1721. In 1722 the Hungarian Council of State adopts the Pragmatic Sanction, under which the heir to the Austrian throne becomes king of Hungary. In 1741 the Empress Maria Theresa is crowned as queen of Hungary in St Martin's Cathedral in Pressburg.

Reign of Maria Theresa

During the reign of Maria Theresa the town enjoys a cultural and social flowering and there is much building activity (noble palaces, patrician houses; demolition of town walls) and economic development (craft and factory production). A German-language newspaper, the "Pressburger Zeitung", begins to appear in 1764. In 1776 the Theatre of the Estates is opened.

A centre of Slovak national movements

During the reign of the Emperor Joseph II (1780–90) Pressburg declines in political importance. In 1783 the capital of Habsburg Hungary is transferred to Buda. Meanwhile the ideas of the Enlightenment make increasing headway, and Prešporok (Pressburg) gradually develops into a major centre of Slovak national movements and a focal point of Slovak cultural life. In 1783 the first newspaper in the Slovak language, the "Presspúrske Nowiny", begins to appear. In 1784 the Academy of Law moves from Trnava to Pressburg. From 1787 two Catholic seminarists, Anton Bernolák and Juraj Fándly, seek to create a Slovak written language.

19th century Napoleonic wars

Peace of Pressburg (1805)

During the Napoleonic wars of the early 19th century, in 1805, French troops reach Pressburg. After the Battle of the Three Emperors at Austerlitz (Slavkov u Brna in Moravia) Francis II of Austria and Napoleon sign the Peace of Pressburg on December 26th 1805 in the Hall of Mirrors of the Primatial Palace. In 1809 the town is again besieged and captured by Napoleon, and during their withdrawal the French blow up the frontier fortress of Devín.

In 1811 Pressburg Castle is devastated by a great fire. After a period of decline due to war the town's economy and trade begin to recover; new factories (textiles, sugar, spirits) are established; in 1818 a steamship sailing on the Danube, the "Caroline", puts in at Pressburg for the first time.

In 1830 Ferdinand is crowned as king of Hungary in Pressburg – the last coronation in the town.

In 1840 a horse-drawn railway (15km/9 miles long) begins to run between Pressburg and the wine-producing town of Sankt Georgen (Hungarian Szentgyörgy; Slovak Svätý Jur, now Jur pri Bratislave).

In 1843 a Slovak priest, L'udovít Štúr, sets about codifying the Slovak written language.

March Laws

A stormy session of the Hungarian Diet in 1847–48 is the last to be held in Pozsony (Pressburg). On April 11th 1848 the Emperor Ferdinand I signs the "March Laws", abolishing serfdom, in Pressburg. In the same year the first train drawn by a steam engine comes to Pressburg.

Between 1850 (when the town has a population of some 23,000 Germans, 9500 Slovaks and 3000 Hungarians) and the economic crisis of 1873 Pressburg enjoys a period of rapid economic development, in which some foreign investors are involved (Nobel explosives, Stollwerck confections).

On July 22nd 1866 the last battles of the Austro-Prussian War are fought in the Pressburg suburb of Blumenau (Lamač) and on the Gemsenberg (Mt Kamzík).

An Austro-Hungarian frontier town

After the Ausgleich (Compromise) of 1867, under which the Austrian Empire is transformed into the Austro-Hungarian Dual Monarchy, the proportion of Hungarians in the population of Pozsony (Pressburg) increases. While the Hungarian and Austrian nobility play the leading part in the town's social life (in particular developing a rich musical culture), the German-speaking middle classes (63% of the population in 1880, 49% in 1907) are predominant in trade and industry. For the people of Vienna, only 65km/40 miles away, Pressburg tends to be seen as a pleasant wine-drinking resort in the Carpathians, a kind of "suburb beyond the Danube". Until the fall of the Dual Monarchy it is the chief town of a komitat within the province of Upper Hungary.

Landmarks in the development of the town in the late 19th and early 20th centuries are the introduction of electric street lighting in 1884, the opening of the new Municipal Theatre (now the opera house of the Slovak National Theatre) in 1886, the building of the first bridge over the Danube in 1891, the first electric trams in 1895 and the completion in 1914 of the electric railway between Vienna and the Pressburg suburbs of Audorf and Engerau (Petržalka), which continues to operate until the 1940s. (The possibility of reopening this railway, the rails of which are still in place, has recently been under consideration.)

Hungarian University

From 1914 to 1919 Pozsony (Pressburg) is the seat of the Hungarian Elizabeth University, successor to the Academia Istropolitana founded by King Matthias Corvinus in 1465.

20th century
First World War

Towards the end of the First World War, on October 10th 1918, the Slovak National Council for Bratislava and the surrounding area is established. Contrary to the intention to give this area extra-territorial status, the town is occupied on December 31st 1918, on orders from Prague, by the Czech Legion; and this action is given retrospective authority by the treaty of Trianon (June 4th 1920), under which the komitats of Upper Hungary, including Pozsony (Pressburg), are assigned to the first Czechoslovak Republic proclaimed on October 28th 1918. Bratislava now considers itself as the *de facto* capital of Slovakia, though in law it is merely the administrative centre of Slovakia, a region within the newly founded Czechoslovak state.

Bratislava: a regional centre in the first Czechoslovak Republic

In 1919 the town (pop. 83,200) is officially renamed Bratislava. The Slovak Comenius University (named in honour of the 17th century educationist Jan Amos Komenský) is founded.
During the twenties and thirties Bratislava develops into the economic and cultural centre of Slovakia. This is reflected in the foundation of the Slovak National Theatre in 1920, the establishment of the first radio studio in 1926, increased building activity (banks, department stores, housing, etc.), the development of the town's port on the Danube (1920–32; oil port, 1927), the foundation of the Czechoslovak Danube Shipping Company (1922) and the trade fairs now regularly held in the town. In 1930 Bratislava has a population of 123,000 or, including its suburbs, 142,000 (including 39,600 German-speakers).

Seat of government of autonomous Slovakia

In view of the external political problems of the Czechoslovak Republic and internal tensions between the Czechs, who favour a centralised government, and the Slovaks who (under the leadership of the Catholic priest Andrej Hlinka, founder of the Slovak People's Party) want independence, Slovakia is finally granted self-government. On October 8th 1938 Bratislava becomes the seat of the autonomous Slovak government headed by another Catholic priest, Jozef Tiso (one of the founders of the Slovak People's Party).

Second World War
Capital of first Slovak state

On March 14th 1939, the day after German forces enter Prague, Slovakia becomes an independent state under the "protection" of Germany, with Tiso as President. Until the end of the Second World War Bratislava is capital of the first Slovak Republic. During this period, after the proclamation of "Slovak National Socialism" on July 30th 1940, a third of the city's Jews (some 20,000 in 1938) are deported to Poland and murdered in German extermination camps.
In order to crush the Slovak National Uprising, proclaimed on August 29th 1944 in the central Slovakian town of Banská Bystrica, the German army, for whose help the Slovak government has appealed, establishes a command centre in Bratislava and builds a defensive wall round the city. After the German withdrawal Soviet forces enter Bratislava as "liberators" on April 4th 1945.

Postwar period

In May 1945 the Slovak National Council moves from the eastern Slovakian town of Košice to Bratislava and declares the "solidarity of the Slovak and Czech peoples". Soon afterwards Slovakia is returned to the control of the re-established Czechoslovak government. Jozef Tiso, taken prisoner by the Americans, is condemned to death and hanged in Bratislava on April 18th 1947.

In April 1946 the neighbouring communes of Rača, Vajnory, Dúbravka and Lamač are incorporated in Bratislava, bringing the city's population to more than 191,350.
During the Presidency of Edvard Beneš Germans are expelled not only from the former Sudeten territories but also from Bratislava, including the remaining Jews who had declared themselves to be Germans in the last prewar census. Most of the Magyars are deported to Hungary, and many representatives of the Slovak middle-class intelligentsia are thrown into prison. Empty houses are taken over by Slovaks, who now stream into the city from country areas, so that Bratislava can now call itself, for the first time, a predominantly Slovak city.

A district town in the ČSR

The internal political conflicts of the early postwar years culminate in Bratislava in the seizure of power on February 25th 1948 by the Communist Party of Slovakia, which soon afterwards is compelled to amalgamate with the Communist Party of Czechoslovakia. A new constitution introduced on May 9th 1948, based on the complete identity of interest between the Communist Party and the state, establishes a "People's Democracy", a unified Czechoslovak Republic of two formally equal peoples, the Czechs and the Slovaks. Within the ČSR Bratislava is now only one district town among many.
Among notable events of the 1950s are the foundation of the Slovak Academy of Sciences, the beginning of restoration work on Bratislava Castle (1953) and the coming of television in 1956.

A district town in the ČSSR

The concessions made to the Slovaks in a constitutional amendment of 1956 are withdrawn when the Czechoslovak Republic becomes the Czechoslovak Socialist Republic (ČSSR), on the Soviet model, in the summer of 1960. Bratislava remains merely a district town, with a population in 1961 of 241,796 (including some 1200 of German origin).
During the sixties and seventies the socialist authorities embark on a vast building programme in Bratislava. In the outer districts of the city great industrial complexes, huge satellite towns using prefabricated methods of construction and numerous sports stadia are built, while in the central area large-scale road improvements use up much land, leading for example to the destruction of the whole of the old Jewish quarter and leaving the venerable old Cathedral standing on the very edge of a new urban motorway. Many old town houses which have come down in the world are demolished.
From 1962 the Slovnaft petro-chemical plant is supplied with oil by a pipeline from the Ukraine.

Crushing of the Prague Spring

After disputes within the Communist Party between "orthodox" communists and "reformers" (advocates of "socialism with a human face") the "Prague Spring" of 1968, led by the Slovak Alexander Dubček, is crushed by Warsaw Pact forces from the Soviet Union, Poland and Bulgaria on August 20th 1968.

Capital of the Federative Slovak Socialist Republic

On October 30th 1968 a law establishing a new federal Czechoslovakia is signed in Bratislava Castle, and on January 1st 1969 Bratislava becomes capital of the Slovak Socialist Republic (SSR).
After the incorporation in 1971 of the adjoining communes of Čuňovo, Devínska Nová Ves, Jarovce, Podunajské Biskupice, Vrakuňa and Záhorská Bystrica the city has a population of 302,119.
On August 26th 1972 the city's second bridge over the Danube, a high-level road bridge (Bridge of the Slovak National Uprising) is opened to traffic. By 1973 the population has risen to 400,000. In 1985 a third bridge is built over the Danube, a combined rail and motorway bridge in the port area.

Political change

The first intimations of a political change, which soon spreads to the whole of the Eastern bloc, are visible in Bratislava in 1988, with demonstrations in March against the government's religious policy. These first demonstrations are ruthlessly repressed.

In the following year – Bratislava now has 435,700 inhabitants, including some 800 Jews – there are increasingly frequent public protests, which on November 27th 1989 culminate in a general strike in support of the "Citizens against Violence" movement, Civic Forum and the students. These demonstrations, together with the subsequent mass rallies, give the final impulse to the "Velvet Revolution" which ends in the overthrow, without violence, of the communist regime which has ruled the country for forty years.

Velvet Revolution

The first milestones on the road to a new democratic Czechoslovakia are the appointment of a "Government of National Understanding" and the election as President of the Republic of Václav Havel, a writer committed to the cause of human rights (December 29th 1989).

Capital of the Federative Slovak Republic

The new name of the state, the Czechoslovak Federative Republic (ČSFR), introduced on March 29th 1990, is soon afterwards, on Slovak insistence, changed to the Czech and Slovak Federative Republic (with the same initials). Bratislava is now capital of the Federative Slovak Republic.

In free parliamentary elections held on June 8th 1990 the civic movements in the Czech and Slovak Republics are victorious. These groups provide the core of the "Government of National Sacrifice" formed on June 27th. The new government's main objectives are the introduction of a free market economy, the privatisation of the main economic agencies, the restructuring of industry and the solution of urgent ecological problems.

Papal visit

An important event, particularly for Catholics, is the first visit of a Pope to Slovakia. On April 22nd 1992 Pope John Paul II arrives in Bratislava and celebrates a Papal mass at Ivanka Airport.

In parliamentary elections on June 7th 1992 the Movement for a Democratic Slovakia (HZDS) in the Slovak Republic and the Democratic Citizens' Party (ODS) in the Czech Republic win a majority of the votes.

On July 17th the sovereignty of the Slovak Republic is proclaimed in the Slovak Parliament – an act intended to be seen as a first official step on the road to Slovakia's full independence from the rest of Czechoslovakia.

Capital of the independent Slovak Republic

After the dissolution of the Czechoslovak Federation into two independent states on January 1st 1993, as agreed by the Slovak prime minister Vladimír Mečiar and his Czech counterpart Václav Klaus at a meeting in Brno on August 27th 1992, Bratislava is capital of the Slovak Republic.

On September 1st 1992 the Slovak Parliament adopts a new constitution for the Slovak Republic.

Sightseeing in Bratislava

Central Area (plan, p. 435)

SNP Square

One of the main hubs of the city's traffic is the Square of the Slovak National Uprising (Námestie Slovenského Národného Povstania, or SNP for short), the old market square, which lies to the north-west of the older bridge over the Danube, immediately outside the line of the old town walls.

Calvinist Church

Convent of Brothers Hospitallers

At the upper (north-western) end of this elongated square is the neo-Romanesque Calvinist Church (Kalvínský Kostol; 1913). Facing it, to the east, is the imposing Baroque façade of the Church, Convent and Hospital of the Brothers Hospitallers (Kostol, Kláštor a Nemocnica Milosrdných Bratov; 17th c.).

On the south side of the square, on the site of the town moat (which was filled in at the end of the 18th century), are the Head Post Office (No. 39; 1912) and the former Tatrabank (No. 33; 1923–25), now television studios.

Manderla House

At the lower (south-eastern) end of the square Manderla House, Bratislava's first tower block (12 floors; 1935) was named after its one-time owner. A little to the south is the State Bank (Štátna Banka).

In the centre of the square can be seen a large group of statuary erected in 1974 on the 30th anniversary of the Slovak National Uprising.

Elizabethine Church

In Špitálska Ulica, which runs north-east from SNP Square in the direction of Trnava, stands the beautiful Church of the Elizabethines (Kostol Alžbětínok), built by the Viennese architect F. A. Pilgram in 1739–43 in the purest Baroque style, with ceiling frescoes by P. Troger and altarpieces by F. X. Palko.

Aspremont Palace

Farther along Špitálska Ulica, on the right (No. 24), can be seen the Aspremont Summer Palace (Aspremontov Letný Palác; 1770), now the Dean's Office of the medical faculty of the Comenius University, with a large garden which was formerly laid out in the French style.
Špitálska Ulica finally joins Americké Námestie (America Square), which is laid out in gardens.

Šafárik Square
University

From SNP Square Štúrova Ulica (named after L'udovít Štúr: see Famous People) runs south-east to Šafárik Square (Šafárikovo Námestie). To the right is the massive building occupied by the Comenius University (Univerzita Komenského; 1936). The University was re-established by Hungary in 1914 as the successor to the old Academia Istropolitana and became Slovak in 1919. Its name commemorates the preacher and educationist Jan Amos Comenius (Komenský: see Famous People).

Duck Fountain

In the gardens opposite the University is the charming Duck Fountain (Kačacia Fontána; by R. Kühmayer, 1914).

St Elizabeth's Church

To the north of Šafárik Square, in Bezručova Ulica (named after the Czech poet Petr Bezruč, 1867–1958), stands St Elizabeth's Church (Kostol Sv. Alžběty), known as the "Little Blue Church" (Modrý Kostolík), built by O. Lechner (1910–13) in Sezession style (the Viennese version of Art Nouveau).

Red Army Bridge

From Šafárik Square Viedenská Cesta (the Vienna Road) runs south, together with the railway, on to the old bridge over the Danube (originally built 1891, replacing an earlier ferry), now officially named Red Army Bridge (Most Červenej Armády). After its destruction in 1945 the bridge was rebuilt with the aid of the Soviet Army in lattice girder technique, borne on six stone piers. On the far side of the Danube, here 300m/330yd wide, is the suburb of Petržalka.

Petržalsky Park

Immediately beyond the bridge lies Petržalsky Park (21 hectares/52 acres), which has been a public park since 1775; it is now known as the Janko Král' Park (Sad Janka Král'a), after the revolutionary Slovak poet Janko Král' (1822–76). In the park are over-lifesize statues of Janko Král' and the hero of Hungarian independence Sándor Petőfi (1823–49) and the "Franziskare", the tip of a Gothic tower from the Franciscan church in Františkánské Námestie (see below).
To the east, near the Danube, is the Lído, an open-air swimming pool.

Vajansky Embankment
Slovak National Museum

To the west of Šafárik Square extends the Vajanský Embankment (Vajanského Nábrežie), named after the Slovak writer Svetozár Hurbán-Vajanský (1847–1916). On the left (No. 2) is the Slovak National Museum (Slovenské Národné Múzeum), with various scientific collections. The Museum's extensive collections on the natural history of Slovakia are now in Bratislava Castle.
In front of the Museum, on the Danube, can be found the landing-stage used by passenger boats on the river. Farther along is L'udovít Štúr Square (Námestie L'udovíta Štúra), from which Mostová Ulica (Bridge Street), on the right, leads to Hviezdoslav Square (Hviezdoslavovo Námestie).

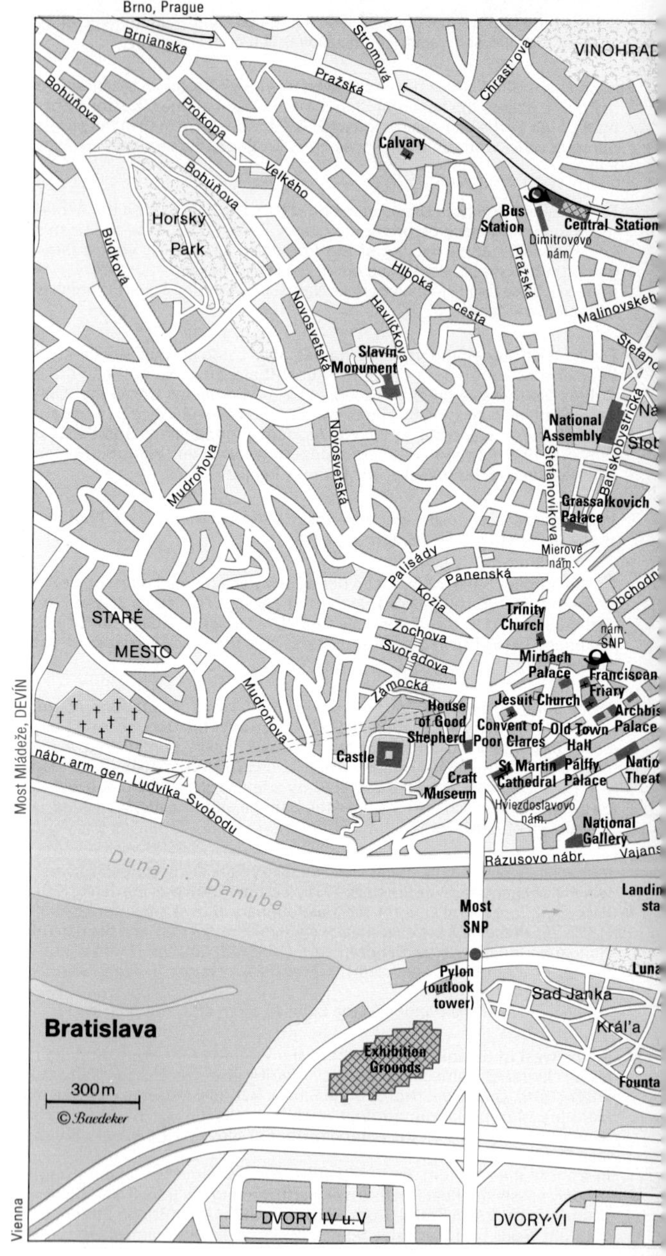
Brno, Prague
Brnianska
Stromová
Chrasťova
VINOHRAD
Pražská
Bohúňova
Prokopa
Calvary
Velkého
Bohúňova
Horský
Park
Búdková
Bus
Station
Central Station
Dimitrovovo
nám.
Pražská
Hlboká
cesta
Malinovského
Havlíčkova
Novosvetská
Slavín
Monument
Štefano
National
Assembly
Banskobystrická
Slob
Novosvetská
Mudroňova
Štefanovikova
Grassalkovich
Palace
Mierové
nám.
Palisády
Panenská
Kozia
Obchodná
STARÉ
MESTO
Zochova
Trinity
Church
nám.
SNP
Svoradova
Mirbach
Palace
Franciscan
Friary
Zámocká
Mudroňova
House
of Good
Shepherd
Jesuit Church
Convent of
Poor Clares
Old Town
Hall
Archbis
Palace
Castle
St Martin
Cathedral
Pálffy
Palace
Natio
Theat
nábr. arm. gen. Ludvíka Svobodu
Craft
Museum
Hviezdoslavovo
nám.
National
Gallery
Most Mládeže, DEVÍN
Rázusovo nábr.
Vajans
Dunaj · Danube
Landin
sta
Most
SNP
Pylon
(outlook
tower)
Luna
Sad Janka
Král'a
Bratislava
Exhibition
Grounds
Founta
300 m
© Baedeker
Vienna
DVORY IV u.V
DVORY VI

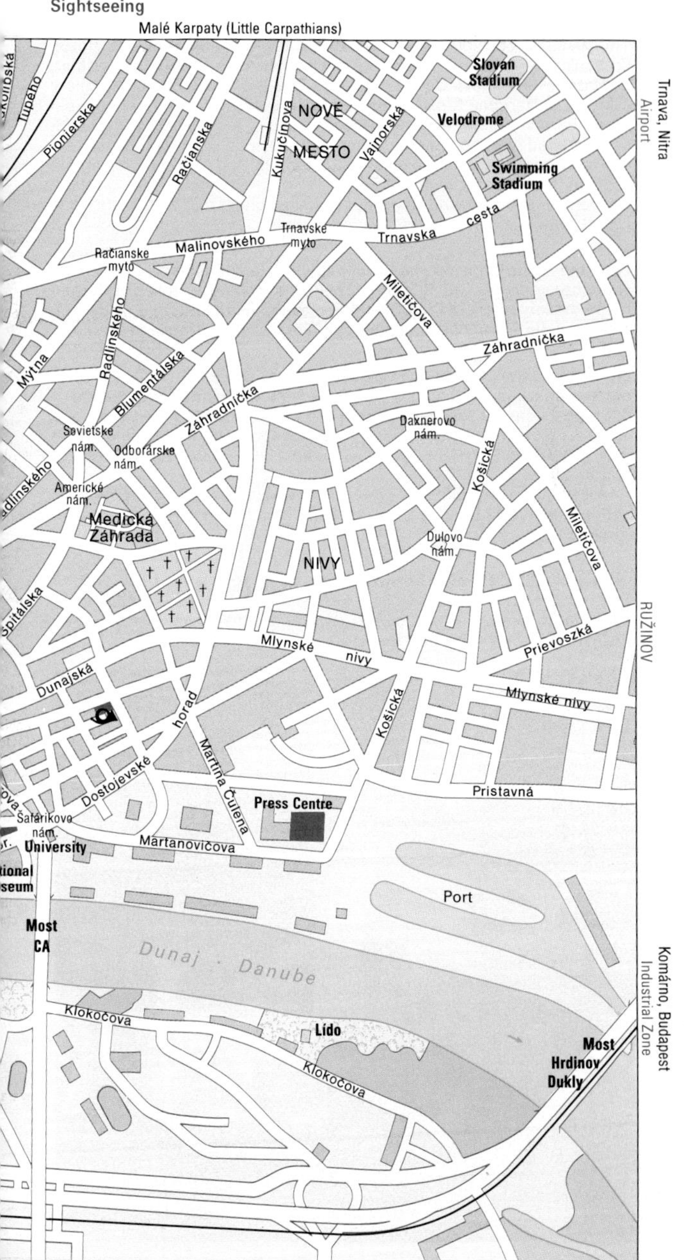
Malé Karpaty (Little Carpathians)
Trnava, Nitra
Airport
Slovan Stadium
Velodrome
Swimming Stadium
NOVÉ MESTO
Tupého
Pionierska
Račianska
Kukučinova
Vajnorská
Trnavské mýto
Trnavská cesta
Račianske mýto
Malinovského
Miletičova
Záhradnícka
Radlinského
Mýtna
Blumentálska
Daxnerovo nám.
Sovietske nám.
Odborárske nám.
Americké nám.
Košická
Medická Záhrada
Dulovo nám.
NIVY
Špitálska
RUŽINOV
Mlynské nivy
Prievozská
Dunajská
Karadžičova
Martina Čulena
Dostojevského
Pristavná
Press Centre
Šafárikovo nám.
University
Martanovičova
Port
Most CA
Dunaj · Danube
Komárno, Budapest
Industrial Zone
Klokočova
Lído
Most Hrdinov Dukly
PETRŽALKA, Racecourse

Rázus Embankment
***Slovak National Gallery**

The western continuation of the Vajanský Embankment, the Rázus Embankment (Rázusovo Nábrežie), was named after the Slovak poet Martin Rázus (1888–1937). On the right (No. 2) is the Slovak National Gallery (Slovenská Národná Galéria), housed in the surviving rear part of the old Water Barracks, a three-storey Baroque building of 1759–63 with round-headed windows and open arcading. It displays painting, graphic art and sculpture by native and foreign artists of the 19th and 20th centuries; there are also periodic special exhibitions.
Farther along the Rázus Embankment, on the right, is the large Devín Hotel (1954), with a terrace café.

Park of Culture and Recreation

From the Rázus Embankment the beautifully laid out riverside promenade continues under the SNP Bridge (see below) and along the foot of the castle hill to the large Park of Culture and Recreation (Park Kultúry a Oddychu), with gardens, an amusement park, a sports hall and a House of Culture.

Rabbis' Tombs

Before the entrance to the road tunnel under the castle hill, on the site of an old Jewish cemetery (established 1660; destroyed by the construction of the tunnel), can be seen a catacomb-like vault containing the tombs of a number of leading rabbis of the local Jewish community, including that of the "Wonderworking Rabbi" Chatham Sofer (1762–1839), still the object of pilgrimages.

Jewish cemeteries

On the slopes of the hill to the right of Žižkovo Ulica, which continues west above the riverside road, are the Orthodox and the Reform Jewish cemeteries.

Mestská Reduta

On the right-hand side of Mostová Ulica, which runs north from L'udovít Štúr Square, stands the Mestská Reduta (1913–19), an imposing neo-Baroque building with rich stucco decoration, the home of the Slovak Philharmonic Orchestra (restaurant).

Slovak National Gallery

Hviezdoslav Square

Mostová Ulica joins Hviezdoslav Square (Hviezdoslavovo Námestie), an elongated open space laid out in gardens with an over-lifesize statue of the Slovak writer Pavol Országh, known as Hviezdoslav (see Famous People), after whom the square is named.

Slovak National Theatre

On the north side of the square is the Slovak National Theatre (Slovenské Národné Divadlo), built by the Viennese architects Fellner and Helmer in 1884–86 on the site of the earlier neo-classical Theatre of the Estates (restored 1969–71). It is now used for opera and ballet.

Ganymede Fountain

In front of the Theatre can be seen the Ganymede Fountain (Ganymedova Fontána; by Viktor Tilgner, 1888).

From the Theatre Hviezdoslav Square, a tree-lined avenue rather than a square, laid out in the 19th century on the site of the old moat, extends south-west to Rybné Námestie (Fish Square), flanked on either side by handsome buildings. Among them, on the left, are the Carlton Hotel (No. 2; restaurants and cafés) and the Csomo Palace (Csomov Palác, No. 6; 1778), and on the right the Pálffy Palace (Pálffyho Palác, No. 18; 1885), now the Rector's Office of the College of Art.

Csomo Palace
Pálffy Palace

Hummel Monument

Near the end of Hviezdoslav Square, where Paulinyho Ulica (named after the Slovak writer Víliam Pauliny-Tóth, 1826–77) comes in on the left, we find the Hummel Monument, with a bust (by Viktor Tilgner, 1887) of the Bratislava-born composer Johann Nepomuk Hummel (whose birthplace is at Klobúčnicka Ulica 2). Here too, on the left (No. 2), is the Rococo Illésházy Palace (Illésházyho Palác; 1769).

Illésházy Palace

Rybné Námestie

At the south-west end of Hviezdoslav Square is Rybné Námestie (Fish Square), which now serves, after much demolition of older buildings, as a means of access to the SNP Bridge.

Plague Column

The last relic of the original square is a Baroque Plague Column of 1713.

Slovak National Theatre

St Michael's Gate (p. 441)

***SNP Bridge**

The striking SNP Bridge (Bridge of the Slovak National Uprising), Bratislava's second road bridge over the Danube and a new city landmark, was built in 1967–72. It is 430m/470yd long and 21m/69ft wide. In the 85m/280ft high tower, secured by steel cables, on the south bank, is the Bystrica Café (magnificent views).

Staromestská Ulica

Since the redevelopment of part of the old Židovská Ulica (Jews' Lane) Staromestská Ulica (Old Town Street), which runs north to Peace Square (Mierové Námestie), has become an important traffic artery. In this street are some remains of the old town walls, with the New Bastion (Nová Bašta), St Martin's Cathedral and the Bird Bastion (Ptačí Bašta) opposite St Nicholas's Church.

Žižka Street

The large-scale redevelopment of the riverside area made necessary by the building of the SNP Bridge also altered the aspect of Žižkovo Ulica (Žižka Street), the most important street in the district below the Castle.

Trinity Church

A few interesting old buildings have survived around the little Baroque Church of the Trinity (1738).

Old houses

Particularly charming are the Rococo Guild-House of the Fishermen and Boatmen (Dom Cechu Rybárov a Lodníkov; No. 1), built about 1760 and recently restored (Rybársky Cech restaurant), and two Renaissance houses, the Kamper House (No. 4; second half of 16th c.) and the Brämer House (No. 10; early 17th c.).

Podhradie
Rudnayovo Námestie

The construction of the road from the SNP Bridge into the city centre led to the demolition of much dilapidated old property in the Podhradie, the area below the Castle. Among surviving buildings are St Martin's Cathedral (see below) and Rudnayovo Námestie, a square laid out on the site of an old cemetery which remained in use until 1778. In the square can be seen a monument to Anton Bernolák (1762–1813), who set out to codify a literary Slovak language, and busts of the 18th century sculptor George Raphael Donner and of Franz Liszt, who conducted his "Coronation Mass" in St Martin's Cathedral in 1884.

***St Martin's Cathedral**

St Martin's Cathedral, a Gothic hall-church (14th–15th c.) built on the site of a Romanesque church of St Salvator, was from 1563 to 1830 the coronation church of the Habsburg kings of Hungary. Topping its 85m/280ft high tower (steeple renewed 1835–47) is a stone cushion supporting a gilded copy of St Stephen's Crown, symbolising the place of coronation.

Interior

The three-aisled interior contains a few surviving Gothic features (a font of 1403, a monstrance and a number of panel paintings on the south wall of the presbytery) and important works by the Viennese sculptor Georg Raphael Donner (1693–1741), who worked in Bratislava between 1728 and 1739 for Archbishop Emmerich Esterházy, Primate of Hungary.

*Statue of St Martin

At the west end of the south aisle is an equestrian statue of St Martin in Hungarian dress by G. R. Donner (1735), the centrepiece of a three-figure group from the old high altar.

Chapel of St John the Almsgiver

Adjoining the north aisle we find the Chapel of St John the Almsgiver (1734), decorated by Donner in Baroque style, with a kneeling marble figure of the founder, Bishop Esterházy.

St Anne's Chapel

Built on to the north aisle is St Anne's Chapel, with a delicate relief of the Trinity (early 14th c.) over the doorway and the recess tomb of Provost Georg von Schomburg, Vice-Chancellor of the Academia Istropolitana (1470).

Town walls

Opposite the north doorway of the Cathedral are some remains of the old town walls.

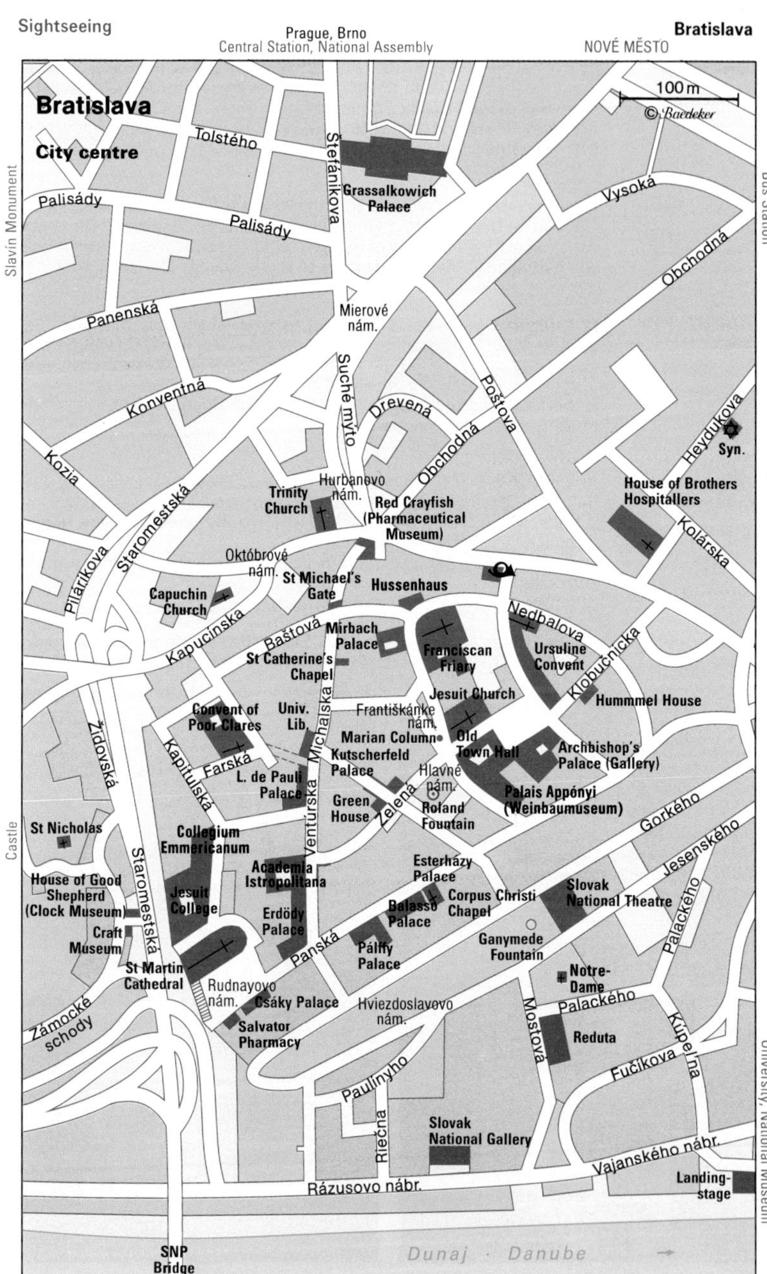
Prague, Brno
Central Station, National Assembly
NOVÉ MĚSTO
Bratislava
City centre
100 m
© Baedeker
Slavín Monument
Bus Station
Castle
University, National Museum
Tolstého
Štefánikova
Grassalkowich Palace
Palisády
Vysoká
Obchodná
Mierové nám.
Panenská
Suché mýto
Konventná
Drevená
Poštova
Heydukova
Syn.
Kozia
Staromestská
Hurbanovo nám.
Trinity Church
Red Crayfish (Pharmaceutical Museum)
House of Brothers Hospitallers
Kolárska
Pilárikova
Októbrové nám.
St Michael's Gate
Hussenhaus
Capuchin Church
Kapucínska
Baštova
Mirbach Palace
Nedbalova
Franciscan Friary
Ursuline Convent
St Catherine's Chapel
Klobučnícka
Jesuit Church
Hummel House
Convent of Poor Clares
Univ. Lib.
Františkánke nám.
Marian Column
Old Town Hall
Archbishop's Palace (Gallery)
Židovská
Kapitulská
Farská
Michalská
Kutscherfeld Palace
Hlavné nám.
L. de Pauli Palace
Ventúrska
Green House
Zelená
Roland Fountain
Palais Appónyi (Weinbaumuseum)
Gorkého
St Nicholas
Collegium Emmericanum
Esterházy Palace
Jesenského
Academia Istropolitana
Corpus Christi Chapel
Slovak National Theatre
House of Good Shepherd (Clock Museum)
Jesuit College
Balassa Palace
Palackého
Erdödy Palace
Craft Museum
Panská
Pálffy Palace
Ganymede Fountain
St Martin Cathedral
Notre-Dame
Rudnayovo nám.
Csáky Palace
Hviezdoslavovo nám.
Palackého
Mostová
Zámocké schody
Salvator Pharmacy
Reduta
Kúpeľná
Fučíkova
Paulínyho
Riečna
Slovak National Gallery
Vajanského nábr.
Rázusovo nábr.
Landing-stage
SNP Bridge
Dunaj · Danube
Vienna, Budapest

Jesuit College

At the corner of Kapitulská Ulica (Chapter Street) is the Early Baroque Jesuit College (Jezuitské Kolégium), built in the time of Archbishop Peter Pázmány (1628–35) by the Roman architect Jacopo Rava. It later became an Academy of Law, and from 1658 to 1833 was a pharmacy; it now houses the (Roman Catholic) SS Cyril and Methodius Faculty of Theology.

Provost's Palace

Opposite the Jesuit College stands the Provost's Palace (Prepoštsky Palác; 1632). In the front garden is a monument (1907) to St Elizabeth of Thuringia, daughter of King Andrew II of Hungary, who was born in Bratislava in 1207 and betrothed to Margrave Ludwig of Thuringia only four years later.

Esterházy Palace

In Kapitulská Ulica, the course and form of which date from the 13th century, is the Renaissance palace of the Esterházy family, in which Josef Haydn was employed as kapellmeister. The palace is at present in course of restoration to house the municipal archives.
A short distance south, on the way to the SNP Bridge, can be seen some remains of the old town walls.

***House of the Good Shepherd**

At the near end of Beblavého Ulica (Židovská Ulica 1) is a charming little Rococo house, the House of the Good Shepherd (Dom U Dobrého Pastiera; *c.* 1760), with rich stucco decoration and elegantly curving window grilles. It contains a small clock museum.
Opposite is a Late Baroque mansion (late 18th c.) with an exhibition of arts and crafts.

St Nicholas's Church

A little higher up, in St Nicholas's Street (on left), is the little Baroque Church of St Nicholas (Kostol Sv. Mikuláša; Russian Orthodox) of 1661–64,

House of the Good Shepherd

Roland Fountain (p. 439)

*Bratislava Castle

Access on foot

The castle can be reached on foot from the south-east by way of an old stepped lane which climbs up the hill, passing two wine bars. The houses in the lane were occupied by castle servants.

Sigismund Gate

The lane leads to the Sigismund Gate (Žigmundova Brána) which gives access to the eastern esplanade (view) within the extensive area enclosed by the castle walls.

Access by car

The castle can be reached by car from the north or west by way of Zámocká Cesta or Modroňova Ulica, which lead to a car park below the south-west side of the castle.

Vienna Gate

From the car park the Vienna Gate (Viedenská Brána; 1712) gives access to the western esplanade, 74m/243ft above the Danube.

History

The castle (alt. 212m/696ft) was originally a frontier stronghold of the Great Moravian Empire, probably built in the 9th century (first documentary reference in 907) on a site previously occupied by a Slav hill fort which was later taken over by the Hungarians. The Emperor Sigismund enlarged the castle about 1430, and it remained an important stronghold, regarded as impregnable, until the 16th century. When Hungary was incorporated in the Habsburg Empire the castle gained renewed importance as a defence

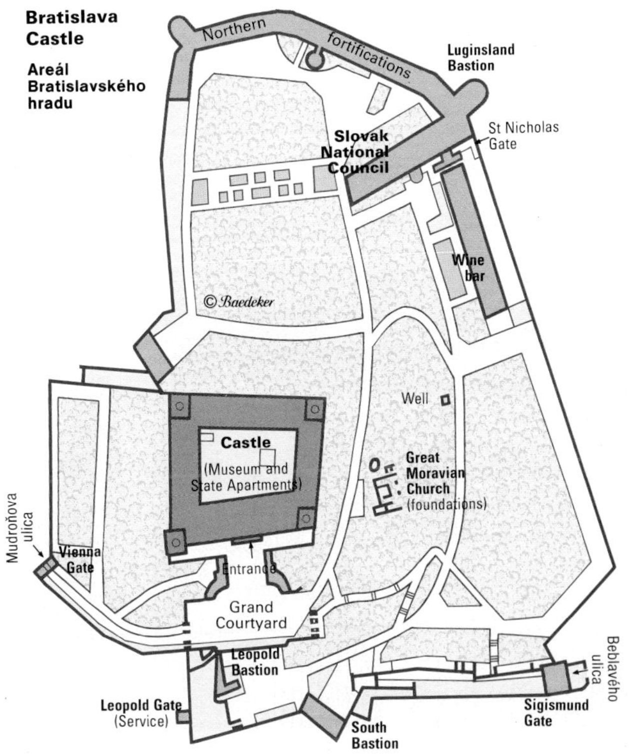

against Turkish attacks. It underwent much alteration in later years and was given its present appearance (popularly likened to an upturned bed) in 1635–49. From 1572 to 1784 the Hungarian crown jewels were kept in the south-western tower, the Crown Tower (Koruna Veža), which originally dated from the 11th century.

The strategic importance of the castle declined after the Turks were thrown back, and in the 1760s the Empress Maria Theresa, who frequently stayed in the castle, had it converted into a sumptuous royal residence. The castle proper was surrounded by new buildings and gardens, and on the east side was built the Theresianum, a palace for the Empress's son-in-law Duke Albert of Sachsen-Teschen (Saxony-Těšín), then Regent of Hungary. Here he assembled a large collection of pictures, later to form the core of the Albertina collection in Vienna. Thereafter the castle was occupied for a time by a seminary for the training of priests, and later became a barracks. In 1811 it was almost completely destroyed in a devastating fire and the ruins were abandoned for more than 140 years. Restoration work began only in 1953, and was completed with the rebuilding of the four corner towers in 1968. During the reconstruction particular importance was attached to the restoration of the surviving architectural features.

***Castle (Hrad)**

From the Grand Courtyard below the south front of the castle a ramp leads up between two guard-houses to the main entrance.

Inner courtyard

In the paving to the left of the inner courtyard are marked the outlines of a tower of 1245 and a residential building of the 12th century. Here too is the entrance to the underground part of the castle, with an 82m/270ft deep well of 1436.

Interior

The castle contains the natural history collections of the Slovak National Museum. Some apartments are also used for receptions and other ceremonial purposes.

Outer Ward

To the north of the castle is a section of a Gothic wall. The area once occupied by the French-style gardens still awaits restoration. Along the

Bratislava Castle

north side of the outer ward is a range of Baroque buildings which were spared by the 1811 fire; some of them are used by the Slovak National Council. In a building to the right is the castle wine bar.
In the grass-covered area to the east of the castle can be seen the foundations of a church dating from the time of the Great Moravian Empire (9th c.).

**View

From the terrace below the castle there is a superb view of much of the city, with the modern bridge over the Danube; to the east can be seen the many-towered old town.

Old Town (plan, p. 435)

Part of the Old Town (Staré Město), many of the buildings in which are protected as national monuments and have been restored, is closed to motor traffic. It is better, therefore, to do your sightseeing on foot, exploring the narrow lanes and passages and looking into the typical balconied courtyards.

Main Square

The central feature of the Old Town is the Main Square (Hlavné Námestie), in which the market was formerly held.

***Roland Fountain**

In the centre of the square is the Roland Fountain (Rolandova Fontána; by Andreas Luttringer, 1572), symbolising municipal authority. The original purpose of the fountain was to supply water for firefighting.

Old Town Hall

The east side of the square is dominated by the Old Town Hall (Stará Radnica), a 14th century Gothic building (enlarged in 15th–16th c.) with a Baroque tower of 1734 (in summer concerts of classical music by trumpeters). A Gothic gateway (1457) leads into an inner courtyard with Renaissance arcades (north side 1581, others restored 1912).

Appónyi Palace
Municipal Museum

Along with the Appónyi Palace (Appónyiho Palác; 1761–62) which adjoins it on the south, the Old Town Hall now houses the Municipal Museum (Mestské Múzeum; history of the town, legal history, wine-making).

Jesuit Church

Facing the Old Town Hall, to the north, is the Jesuit Church (Kostol Jezuitov; 1636–38) or St Salvator's Church, in Late Renaissance style. Originally built for German Protestants, it was taken over by the Jesuits in 1672. It has a sumptuous Baroque interior (18th c.).

Marian Column

Outside the church is a Marian Column of 1675.

Primatial Square

On the east side of the Old Town Hall is Primatial Square (Primaciálne Námestie).

New Town Hall

On the north side of the square is the New Town Hall (1949–52).

***Primatial Palace**
(Municipal Art Gallery)

Opposite the New Town Hall stands the imposing neo-classical Primatial Palace (Primaciálny Palác), built by Melchior Hefele in 1778–81 as the winter residence of the Archbishop of Esztergom, the highest church dignitary in Hungary, with the style of Prince-Primate. The allegorical figures on the attic storey are by J. Kögler and F. Prokop, the decorative vases by J. A. Messerschmidt. The palace now houses the Municipal Art Gallery (Městská Galéria).

Hall of Mirrors

Within the palace a handsome staircase leads up to an entrance hall on the first floor. To the left is the Hall of Mirrors, in which the Peace of Pressburg was signed by the Emperor Francis II of Austria and Napoleon on December 26th 1805, after Napoleon's victory at Austerlitz. The hall contains Gothic and Baroque art by native artists.

*Tapestries

To the right are the former state apartments, now containing paintings and sculpture by Italian, Spanish, Flemish and other masters and a cycle of six tapestries ("Hero and Leander"; *c.* 1630). The tapestries (measuring 280–310cm/110–122in. by 250–420cm/98–165in.), based on cartoons by the Rostock painter Francis Cleyn, were woven in the royal manufactory at Mortlake, near London, for Cardinal Mazarin and were later acquired by

Archbishop Batthyányi of Esztergom. During the Napoleonic wars they were concealed behind wallpaper and rediscovered only during restoration work in the early 20th century, after the palace had become the property of the city.

Hummel Memorial Museum

In Klobučnicka Ulica, which runs east from Primatial Square to the Square of the Slovak National Uprising (SNP Square), in the courtyard of No. 2 (commemorative plaque), is a little house in which the composer Johann Nepomuk Hummel was born in 1778 (museum).

Ursuline Church

A little way north of the Primatial Palace, where Nedbalova Ulica joins Ursulínska Ulica, is the Ursuline Church (Kostol Uršulíniek), originally built in 1659 for Slovak and Hungarian Protestants and handed over to the Ursuline order in 1675; interior redecorated in the 18th century. The conventual buildings date from 1677–87.

Franciscan Square

On the north side of the Main Square is the tree-lined Franciscan Square (Františkánské Námestie).

***Franciscan Church**

At the upper end of the square, on the right, is the Franciscan Church (Kostol Františkánov), the oldest building in the old town centre, originally Early Gothic (1280–97), partly remodelled in Baroque style. On the north side is the High Gothic burial chapel of St John the Evangelist (1361), one of the finest Gothic buildings in Slovakia (entrance from transept, on the left). The present tower dates only from the 19th century; the original Gothic steeple is now in Janko Král' Park.

Remains of Franciscan friary

Of the friary of the 14th–15th centuries there remain only the cloister (entrance to right of church entrance), with Baroque sculpture and epitaphs, and the chapel of St Rosalia (entered from cloister).

Mirbach Palace (Art Gallery)

Opposite the church, at No. 11 in the square, is the Mirbach Palace (Mirbachov Palác), a handsome Rococo building (1768–70) which now houses the Municipal Art Gallery (pictures and sculpture of 17th–19th c., 20th c. Slovak art).

Wine bar

In the adjoining house (No. 10) is a well known wine bar, the Vel'kí Františkáni, which is first recorded in 1347.

Ventúrska Ulica

From the west corner of the Main Square either Zelená Ulica or Sedlárska Ulica (on the left, at No. 1, the Bratislava Information Office, BIPS) leads to Ventúrska Ulica and its northward continuation Michalská Ulica.

Marshal Pálffy's Palace

Zelená Ulica, a short street, forms a right-angled junction with Ventúrska Ulica, which is lined with old noble palaces. At the junction, to the left (No. 10), stands Marshal Pálffy's Palace (Palác Maršála Pálffyho), a Baroque mansion of the first half of the 18th century, with a handsome doorway.

Academia Istropolitana

Opposite the junction (No. 3) is the Academia Istropolitana ("Academy of the City on the Danube"; Greek Istros = Danube), the city's first University, founded in 1465 by King Matthias Corvinus of Hungary (closed down 1490).

Leopold de Pauli Palace

Turning right from Zelená Ulica along Ventúrska Ulica, we pass on the left (No. 11) Leopold de Pauli Palace (Palác Leopolda de Pauliho), birthplace of the versatile Hungarian scholar Farkaš Wolfgang von Kempelen (1734–1804), famous in his day as the inventor of chess-playing automata and a "speaking machine". Franz Liszt performed in this house as a child. It now contains part of the University Library.

At No. 17 is a vaulted passage (Ulica Podjazd) leading to the Church of the Poor Clares (see below).

Michalská Ulica

From the junction with Sedlárska Ulica (on the right, coming from the Main Square) the lively Michalská Ulica continues the line of Ventúrska Ulica.

House of the Estates (University Library)

On the left (No. 1) is the former House of the Estates, a large Baroque palace (1753–56; enlarged 1772) built by G. B. Martinelli for the Royal Chamber, in which the Hungarian Estates met from 1802 to 1848 (Palác Uhorskej Kráľovskej Komory). After being occupied for a time by the Supreme Court it now houses the University Library (Univerzitná Knižnica; about 900,000 volumes).

St Catherine's Chapel

Farther along, on the right (No. 8), can be seen the plain neo-classical façade (1840) of St Catherine's Chapel (1311).

Segner House

On the opposite side of the street (No. 7) is the Segner House (Segnerova Kúria), built in 1648 for Andreas Segner, a well-to-do burgher. In Northern Renaissance style, it has two double-storey oriels. It was the birthplace of the physicist and mathematician Johann Segner (1704–77), inventor of the turbine engine.
Adjoining the Segner House is the narrowest house in Bratislava (No. 10).

***St Michael's Gate**

Michalská Ulica leads to St Michael's Gate (Michalská Brána), Bratislava's only surviving town gate. It was built in the 14th century and reinforced in 1445 by the addition of a barbican. The finely worked cornerstones on the Gothic tower show that it was originally lower: the octagonal upper part was added in 1511–13 and the copper-sheathed Baroque roof with the figure of St Michael in 1758. On the four upper floors of the tower is an exhibition on the development of Bratislava's fortifications (plans, documents, weapons); from the gallery on the top floor there are fine panoramic views of the city.

Convent of Poor Clares

To the left of St Michael's Gate is the narrow Baštová Ulica, which leads into Klariská Ulica (passage from Ventúrska Ulica), named after the old Convent of Poor Clares at No. 5 (founded by Cistercian nuns in 12th–13th c.; rebuilt 1637–40).
The Gothic Church of the Poor Clares (Kostol Klarisiek) was built in the 14th century but much altered in later centuries. The tower (with a neo-Gothic steeple of 1900) is set on the church walls without foundations of its own. The conventual buildings now house the Slovak Educational Library (about 120,000 volumes).

***Pharmacy At the Sign of the Red Crayfish** (Pharmaceutical Museum)

St Michael's Gate is the northern exit from the old town. Just outside the gate, to the right (Michalská Ulica 28), can be found the old Pharmacy At the Sign of the Red Crayfish (Lekáren U Červeného Raka), now a Pharmaceutical Museum (Farmaceutické Múzeum).

Town moat

From here, passing through the barbican and following a street which curves round to the right, we cross a bridge flanked by statuettes of St John of Nepomuk (on right) and the Archangel Michael (on left) over the town moat, which is still visible at this point (to the right, lower down, remains of town walls), into Hurban Square.

Hurban Square

Hurban Square (Hurbanovo Námestie), named after the Slovak politician Jozef Miloslav Hurban (1817–88), is the north-western continuation of the Square of the Slovak National Uprising (SNP Square; see above).

Trinitarian Church

At the western corner of Hurban Square, on the site of a church dedicated to St Michael which was demolished in 1528 in preparation for a Turkish attack, stands the Trinitarian Church (Kostol Trinitárov; 1721–25), a Baroque building on an elliptical plan with two squat towers. In the dome is a perspectivist painting by Antonio Galli da Bibbiena (1700–74).

October Square
Župný Dom

South-west of the Trinitarian Church is the 18th century Župný Dom (Komitat House), whose façade dominates the north side of October Square (Októbrové Námestie). Originally a monastery, it was adapted in 1844 to house the administrative offices of the Hungarian komitat; it is now occupied by various government agencies.

Pharmacy at the Sign of the Red Crayfish, now the Pharmaceutical Museum

Plague Column

In the centre of October Square rises a Plague Column of 1723.

Capuchin Church

At the south-west corner of the square is the Capuchin Church (Kostol Kapucínov), a Baroque building of 1717 with a façade of 1861. From here Kapucínska Ulica runs towards the Cathedral and the Castle.

To the North of the Old Town

Protestant Grammar School

From Hurban Square Konventná Ulica runs north-west to the former Protestant Grammar School (Evanjelické Lyceum), now occupied by the Slovak Academy's Institute of Slovak Literature. No. 15 dates from 1783, No. 13 from 1854–55.

Protestant churches

Beyond the former Grammar School we come to the Great Protestant Church (Vel'ký Evanjelický Kostol; entrance through No. 15), on a rectangular plan, which was built in 1776, with special permission from the Empress Maria Theresa, for German-speaking Protestants.
Immediately adjacent, in the angle between Lycejná Ulica and Panenská Ulica, is the Little Protestant Church (Malý Evanjelický Kostol; 1776), for Slovak and Hungarian Protestants.

Peace Square
***Grassalkowich Palace**

From Hurban Square a street called Suché Mýto leads north to Peace Square (Mierové Námestie), the whole of the north side of which is occupied by the Grassalkowich Palace (Grassalkovičov Palác). This Rococo palace (ornamental fountain; beautiful wrought-iron garden gates and railings), built about 1760 for Prince Anton Grassalkowich, became a favourite meeting-place of the Hungarian aristocracy. Within the palace a magnificent triple staircase leads up to the state apartments, with delicate stucco decoration, on the first floor.
To the rear of the palace lies a park (entrance in Štefánikova Ulica) which was originally laid out in the French style. In the park can be seen a monument to the composer Johann Nepomuk Hummel.

Freedom Square

North-east of Peace Square is the spacious Freedom Square (Námestie Slobody; formerly Esterházy Square), laid out in gardens. In recent years there has been much new building round this square: on the south and east sides administrative offices and institutes of the Slovak University of Technology (Slovenská Vysoká Škola Technická), on the north side the ten-storey headquarters of the Post Office.

University of Technology

Archbishop's Summer Palace

On the west side of Freedom Square stands the former Archbishop's Summer Palace (Letný Palác Primasov), a long, low range of buildings originally erected in the 17th century, remodelled in Rococo style in 1761–65 and renovated in 1940–42. It is now occupied by government offices.

Sports grounds

To the north-east of the town, in the Tehelné Pole and Pasienky areas, which lie between the Vajnory and Trnava roads, are extensive sports grounds, with the Slovan Stadium (seating 55,000 spectators), tennis courts, a cycle race track, an open-air swimming pool, a skittle alley, an unconventionally designed sports hall and the Winter Stadium (ice rink).

Pistorius Palace

From Peace Square Štefánikova Ulica runs north, passing on the right the park of the Grassalkowich Palace. On the left of the street (No. 21A) is the Pistorius Palace (second half of 19th c.), with a richly decorated façade.

Central Station

The Central Station (Hlavná Stanica or Hlavné Nadražie) is on the northern edge of the inner city.

Slavín

North-west of the city centre, on one of the foothills of the Little Carpathians, can be found the Slavín (Hall of Fame; alt. 252m/827ft; best approached from Peace Square by way of Palisady, Šulekova, Timravina and Mišikova Ulica), a memorial erected in 1960 to the Soviet soldiers killed in the battle for Bratislava at the end of the Second World War. This monumental complex consists of three parts – a grand staircase, a cemetery and a memorial hall with two bronze sculptures.

**Views

From the broad terrace round the memorial there are magnificent panoramic views: to west and north the vine-clad slopes and wooded summits of the Little Carpathian foothills (Mt Kamzík, with telecommunications tower), to the east, lower down, the buildings round Freedom Square and, farther away, the new residential and industrial districts extending into the Danube depression, and to the south the old town, with the Cathedral, the SNP Bridge and the massive bulk of Bratislava Castle.

Surroundings of Bratislava

Zlaté Piesky

On the north-eastern outskirts of the city, on the road to Senec, lies the lake of Zlaté Piesky (50 hectares/125 acres), with good facilities for bathing and water sports.

Botanic Garden

On the west side of Bratislava, near the newest bridge over the Danube, is the Botanic Garden (Botanická Zahrada) of Comenius University.

Železna Studienka

On the north-western outskirts of the city, in the Vydrica valley, is the former spa of Železna Studienka (alt. 220m/720ft). From here there is a chair-lift up Mt Kamzík (440m/1445ft; telecommunications tower), with fine views of Bratislava and the vine-clad slopes of the Little Carpathians (see entry).

Koliba

From Železna Studienka a waymarked path leads to Koliba (film studios).

***Devín**

8km/5 miles west of Bratislava is Devín (alt. 212m/696ft), with a ruined castle above the junction of the Morava with the Danube. There was a

Ruins of Devín Castle

Roman fort on the site, and the castle is referred to in 864 as the seat of a ruler of the Great Moravian Empire. In 1809 it was blown up by French troops. Following a successful excavation of the site it has been conserved and partly reconstructed. From the top there are fine views.

Malacky

36km/22 miles north-west of Bratislava is Malacky (alt. 160m/525ft; pop. 15,000), a regional centre in the Záhorie area. It has a fortified Franciscan friary (1653) and a castle of 1624 (remodelled in neo-classical style in 1808).

Vel'ké Leváre

Vel'ké Leváre (alt. 170m/560ft; pop. 5000), 41km/25 miles north-west of Bratislava, has a 17th century castle, a twin-towered Baroque church and old houses of the Habaners, members of an Anabaptist sect formerly living in this area, most of them potters. Particularly notable is a settlement of 35 houses of rammed clay (now protected as a national monument).

High Tatras / Vysoké Tatry I/K 3

Region: Eastern Slovakia
District: Poprad

Situation

The High Tatras (Vysoké Tatry), in the Western Carpathians, are the only high mountain region in Slovakia. They extend along the Slovak–Polish frontier area, broadly bounded by four rivers – on the north the Polish river Dunajec, on the west the Orava (see entry), on the south the Váh and on the east the Poprad.

**Winter sports

The High Tatras have long been a popular winter sports region, offering good snow and excellent facilities. Slovakia is putting forward an application to host the Winter Olympic Games here in 2002.

Summer in the High Tatras

Structure

The chain of the High Tatras, some 75km/45 miles long and 15–35km/9–22 miles across, falls into three parts which differ geologically and morphologically.

Western Tatras

The Western Tatras (Slovak Západne Tatry, Polish Tatry Zachodnie) or Liptov Tatras (Liptovské Tatry) are composed of granites and crystalline schists and for the most part have rounded forms. The highest peak is Mt Bystra (2250m/7382ft).

***High Tatras**

The central part of the range is the High Tatras proper (Slovak Vysoké Tatry, Polish Tatry Wysokie), which rise to a height of 2655m/8711ft between the L'aliové Sedlo (Lily Pass, 1947m/6388ft) in the west and the Kopské Sedlo (Kopa Pass, 1756m/5761ft) in the east.

Belianske Tatras

Beyond the Kopa Pass, at an angle to the High Tatras, are the Belianske Tatras (Belianské Tatry; Mt Havran, 2154m/7067ft), which consist of Jurassic dolomites and limestones, with a rich flora which is very different from that of the other Tatras.

Characteristics

****High Tatras**

The most magnificent and the wildest part of the whole Tatra range is the High Tatras, which extend along the Slovak–Polish frontier. Their highest point is the Gerlachovský Štít (2655m/8711ft), the highest peak not only in Slovakia but in the whole of the 1200km/750 mile long arc of the Carpathians.

Rising abruptly, like a gigantic wall, out of the Spiš basin (Spišská kotlina) to the south and the Podhale basin to the north, the High Tatras – the world's

High Tatras

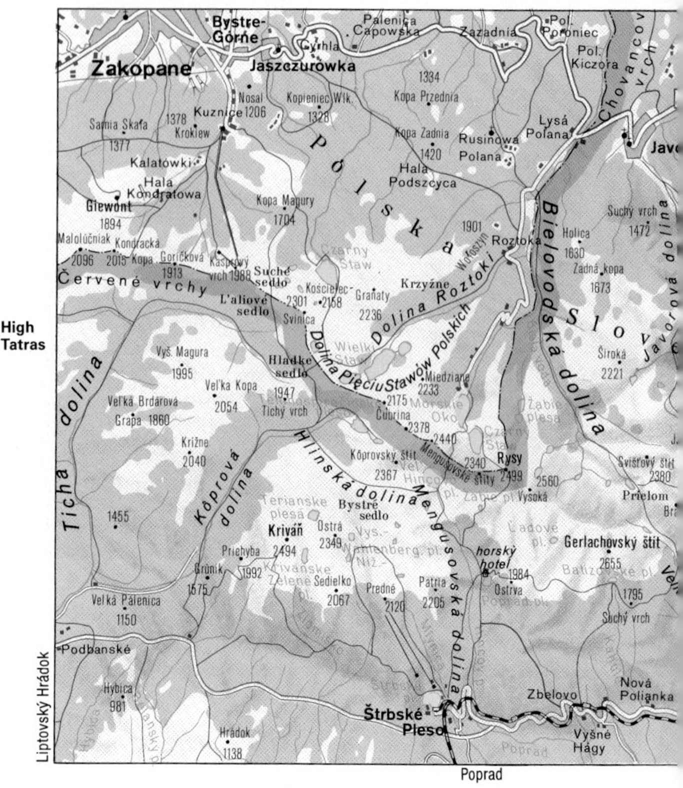

smallest mountain range, with an area of only 260sq.km/100sq.miles, a length of 26km/16 miles and a greatest width of 17km/10½ miles – are remarkable for their variety of form and their extreme wildness. They fall short of a fully alpine effect, however, in having no glaciers.

Corries

Evidence of glacier action during the ice ages is provided by the corries, hemmed in by jagged arêtes and sheer rock walls and frequently filled by lonely mountain lakes, which are characteristic of the range. The barren upper reaches of the valleys are filled with huge masses of detritus.

Lakes

The larger lakes in the wooded valleys at lower levels are the result of the damming of rivers by ice age moraines. They are referred to, particularly in the Polish part of the range, as "eyes of the sea", since it used to be thought that they were connected with the sea by underground channels.
Altogether there are more than a hundred lakes (Slovak *pleso,* Polish *staw*) in the High Tatras. The largest is the Wielki Staw (Great Lake), with an area of almost 35 hectares/85 acres, and the deepest the Czarny Staw (Black Lake) – both in Poland. The largest Slovak lakes are the Velké Hincovo Pleso (20 hectares/50 acres) and the Štrbské Pleso (20 hectares).

Highest peaks

In addition to the Gerlachovský Štít the highest peaks – from west to east – are the legendary Mt Kriváň (2494m/8183ft), in a south-westerly offshoot of

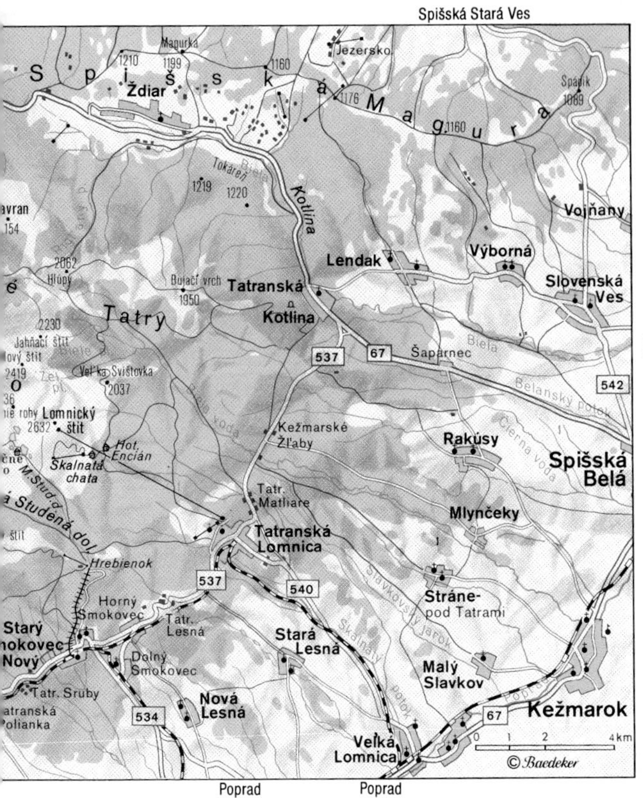

High Tatras

the range; Mt Rysy (2499m/8199ft), the highest peak in Poland; Vysoká (2560m/8399ft); the Slavkovský Štít (2432m/7979ft), in a subsidiary range to the north-west of Starý Smokovec (see entry); the L'adovy Stít (2628m/8622ft); and the Lomnický Štít (2632m/8636ft; cableway).

Caves and waterfalls

There are also numbers of impressive caves (Belianská Jaskyňa, etc.) and waterfalls (Skok, Obrovský Vodopád, Kmet'ov Vodopád, etc.) in the High Tatras.

Flora and Fauna of the High Tatras

Vegetation zones

The upper limits of the vegetation zones in the High Tatras are some 500m/1650ft lower than in the ancient rocks of the Alps, thanks to their more northerly latitude and continental climate. From the foot of the hills to an altitude of about 1550m/5100ft extend forests of spruce, sometimes including larches and, particularly in the eastern part of the range, deciduous trees. On the tree line there are frequently picturesque groups of stone pines and Carpathian birches. Above this, to about 1800m/5900ft, is the zone of dwarf pines, and above this again, up to about 2300m/7550ft,

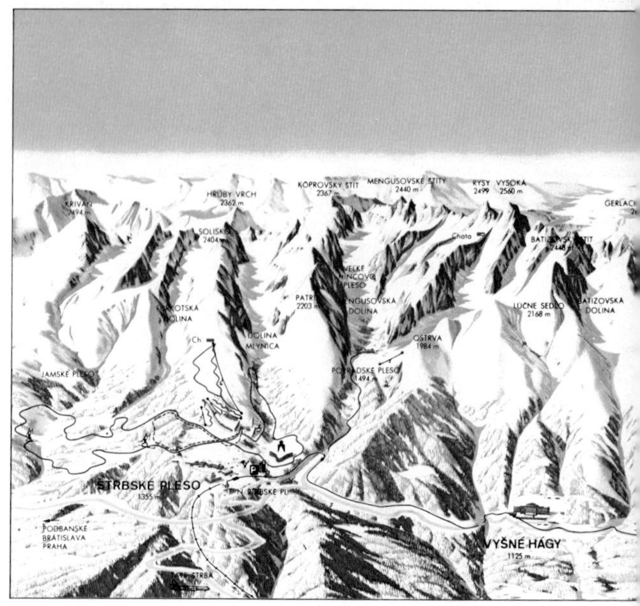

are alpine meadows, with a profusion of flowers in spring and early summer.

At the highest level is the subniveal zone, with patches of grass and ferns and modest mosses and lichens. In the rocky regions (only in the Belianske Tatras) there are also edelweiss and other strictly protected mountain plants.

Fauna

There is relatively little animal life in the High Tatras – only an estimated 700 red deer, 400 roe deer, 500 chamois (plus 150 on the Polish side), 1000 marmots, 90 wild pigs, 25 lynxes and 15 bears. The only animals which can be shot are wolves, which are a danger to other game.

***High Tatras National Park**

In order to protect the flora and fauna of the High Tatras an area of 51,125 hectares/197sq.miles on the Slovak side was designated in 1949 as a National Park, managed by the National Park Administration (TANAP) in Tatranská Lomnica. In 1955 a National Park (21,546 hectares/83sq.miles) was established on the Polish side, with its headquarters in Zakopane. In 1987 the Slovak National Park (which includes the Belianske Tatras) was enlarged by the inclusion of a further area in the Western Tatras.

TANAP maintains an extensive network of waymarked paths and routes to mountain huts and summits, including the Magistrala, a magnificent trail along the southern slopes of the range from Podbánské by way of the Štrbské Pleso, Lake Poprad, the Hrebienok moraine and the Skalnaté Pleso to the old Kežmarok hut.

Restrictions on visitors

The considerable increase in the number of visitors in recent years has made it necessary to impose certain restrictions. An area of some 1000 hectares/2500 acres can be visited only with special permission from the National Park Administration, and the crest ridges of the Belianske Tatras are completely closed to visitors. Moreover visitors must keep to the marked paths, and in winter they are confined above the tree-line to the paths leading to the official mountain huts.

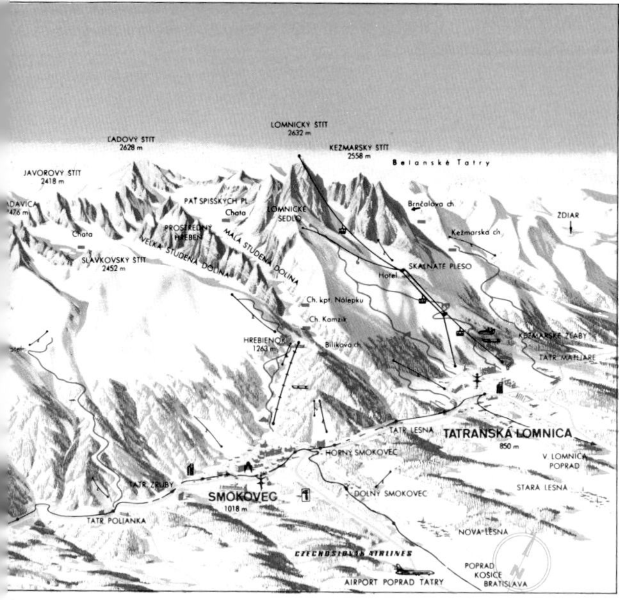

Considerable restrictions have also been imposed in recent years on traffic on the Cesta Slobody ("Freedom Road") which runs along the edge of the mountains.

Tourist Centres under the High Tatras

The main tourist centres, altitude resorts and winter sports areas on the Slovak side of the High Tatras are Tatranská Lomnica and Starý Smokovec (see entries) to the east and Štrbské Pleso (see entry) to the west. In additions to hotels of all categories (advance booking advisable in main holiday season) there are numerous holiday homes and rest homes, and in recent years accommodation has also become available in private houses. Outside the main centres there are large sanatoria.

Transport

All the little towns and villages below the south and east sides of the High Tatras are linked by the Cesta Slobody (Freedom Road) between Štrbské Pleso and Lysa Pol'ana.
Narrow-gauge electric railways: Poprad–Starý Smokovec and Tatranská Lomnica–Starý Smokovec–Štrbské Pleso.
Rack-railways: Štrba–Štrbské Pleso and Starý Smokovec–Hrebienok.
Cableways, etc.: see descriptions of principal towns.

Humenné

L 4

Region: Eastern Slovakia
District: Humenné
Altitude: 156m/512ft
Population: 30,000

Situation and characteristics

The district town of Humenné in the Upper Zemplín area of eastern Slovakia is first mentioned in the records in 1322. It is now a busy industrial town (chemicals, polyamide fibres).

Sights

Castle (Museum)

Humenné's moated castle, originally Gothic, was remodelled in Renaissance style in 1610. Rebuilt after being twice destroyed by fire (in the 18th century and in 1946), it now houses a local museum.

Churches

There are two churches of interest, a 14th century Gothic church (much altered in later centuries; re-Gothicised at the end of the 19th century) and a Greek Catholic church (1777) in Baroque and neo-classical style.

***Open-Air Museum**

In the nearby park is an open-air museum with examples of traditional building from the Carpathian region, including a wooden church (1754) from Nová Sedlica.

Surroundings of Humenné

Lake Domaša

16km/10 miles north-west of Humenné is Lake Domaša (14km/8½ miles long; area 14sq.km/5½sq.miles), formed by a dam on the river Ondava. On the south side of the lake lies a recreation area.

Nature Reserve

North-east of Humenné is the Eastern Carpathian Nature Reserve (area 668sq.km/258sq.miles), with great expanses of unspoiled natural forest. In this remote region bears, lynxes, wild cats, wolves, golden eagles and other rare animals are still to be found.

***Wooden churches**

Within easy reach of Humenné are a number of villages with interesting old Orthodox wooden churches:

Kalná Roztoka — Late 18th century church (26km/16 miles east).
Hrabová Roztoka — Mid 18th century church (27km/17 miles east).
Ruská Bystrá — Church of 1730 (29km/18 miles east).
Inovce — Church of 1836 (34km/21 miles south-east).
Topol'a — Church of second half of 17th century (34km/21 miles north-east).
Ruský Potok — Church of 1740 (36km/22 miles north-east).
Ulïcské Krivé — Church of 1718 (38km/24 miles north-east).

Medzilaborce (Andy Warhol Museum of Modern Art)

40km/25 miles north of Humenné, near the Polish frontier, is the Carpathian village of Medzilaborce, with a Museum of Modern Art (Múzeum Moderného Umenia) dedicated to the world-famous American pop artist and film director Andy Warhol (originally Andrej Varchola; 1928–87). Andy Warhol's parents – his father was a miner – left their home village of Mikova (15km/9 miles north-west of Medzilaborce) after the First World War and emigrated to America.

Kežmarok K 3

Region: Eastern Slovakia
District: Poprad
Altitude: 626m/2054ft
Population: 20,000

Situation and characteristics

The ancient little town of Kežmarok in north-eastern Slovakia, chief place of the Upper Spiš region (see Spiš), is beautifully situated on the river Poprad.

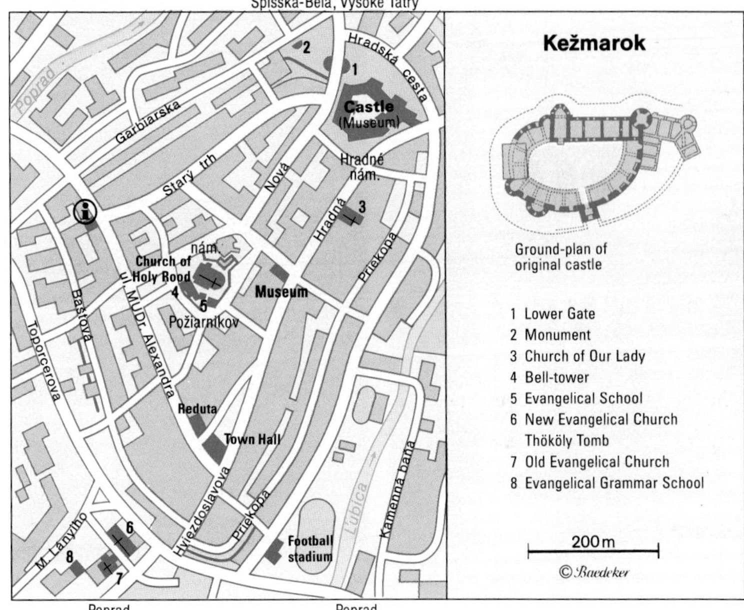

It was strongly fortified in the 16th and 17th centuries. Until 1944 a third of the population was German-speaking.
Kežmarok now has textile and woodworking industries.

Sights

*__Old town__
Church of Holy Rood

The core of the old town is now a conservation area. Its central feature is the parish church (R.C.) of the Holy Rood, a 15th century Gothic hall-church (magnificent carved altar, sculpture by Master Pavol of Levoča) with a separate Renaissance bell-tower of 1586–91.

Evangelical (Protestant) churches
Old Town Hall

In the southern part of the town are the Old Evangelical Church (early 18th c.; now a museum), which is wholly constructed of wood; the New Evangelical Church (1892), in neo-Byzantine style, with the tomb of Count Imre Thököly (d. 1705); and the Old Town Hall (1461; rebuilt in neo-classical style 1799).

Reduta
Lyceum

Other features of interest are the neo-classical Reduta (1818) and the Lyceum (a former Protestant grammar school; 1775), now part of the Municipal Museum.

Wooden houses

In Hradná Ulica (Castle Street) can be seen a number of characteristic old wooden houses with shingle roofs and arched entrances.

*__Castle__
(Museum)

At the north end of the old town is the castle of the Thököly family, a 15th century Late Gothic fortified castle which was rebuilt in Renaissance style in 1628. It was burned down in 1741 and again in 1787, and during the 19th century fell into ruin. It was rebuilt in the 20th century and since the 1960s has housed the Municipal Museum.

A Renaissance tower in Kežmarok

Church of the Holy Rood

Town walls

Kežmarok has preserved considerable stretches of its old town walls.

Lubica

In the south-eastern district of Lubica is an Early Gothic church with a Renaissance bell-tower.

Surroundings of Kežmarok

Strážky

5km/3 miles north-east of Kežmarok we come to the old village of Strážky (alt. 635m/2085ft), with a Gothic church (bell-tower of 1629) and a recently restored Renaissance castle (1570) set in an old park at the junction of the Čierna Voda with the Poprad; it now contains interesting collections belonging to the Slovak National Gallery (restaurant).

Spišská Belá

8km/5 miles north of Kežmarok is the ancient little town of Spišská Belá (alt. 631m/2070ft; pop. 5000; cigarette factory), with an Early Gothic church (R.C.) of the 13th century (altered in 15th c.; bell-tower of early 17th c.). Spišská Belá was the birthplace of Josef Max Petzval (1807–91), inventor of the photographic lens. The house in which he was born now contains a museum of photographic optics.

Vyšné Ružbachy

22km/14 miles north-east of Kežmarok lies the village of Vyšné Ružbachy (alt. 615m/2020ft; pop. 1000), with a pool (20m/65ft in diameter, 3km/10ft deep) formed by a spring in a travertine crater. In the nearby travertine quarry is a permanent natural gallery of sculpture.
In a wooded park on the western outskirts of the village is a popular spa with nine hot carbonated mineral springs (used in the treatment of nervous conditions and depression; public mineral bath).

Stará Lubovňa

34km/21 miles north-east of Kežmarok, in the romantic Poprad valley, is the district town of Stará Lubovňa (alt. 545m/1790ft; pop. 8000). In the market

Strážky Castle

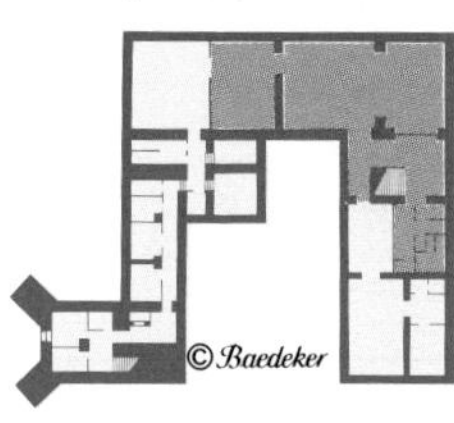

LOWER FLOOR

Restaurant

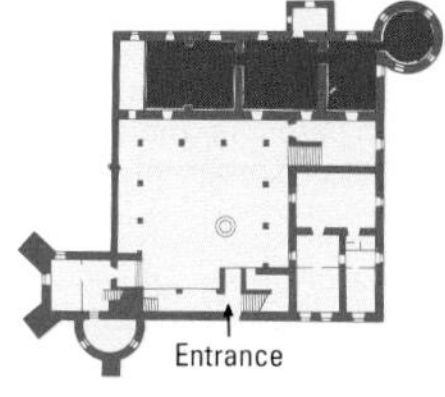

GROUND FLOOR

Historical portraits from Slovakia (17th–19th c.)

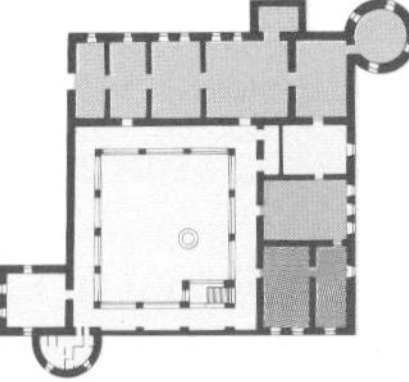

FIRST FLOOR

Arts and crafts (17th–19th c. furniture, interior objects, porcelain, liturgical vessels from Zips)

Humanist library (16th–20th c.)

Exhibition of "Ladislav Mednyánszky" and his time (1852–1919)

Collections and exhibitions of the Slovakian National Gallery

square are an Early Gothic church (*c.* 1280; later remodelled in Baroque style), with a fine interior (Madonna of about 1300, Late Gothic font, etc.), and a number of old burghers' houses with open arcades.

Castle

Above the town are the ruins of a 13th century castle (alt. 648m/2126ft). The lower residential block and the chapel have been restored and now house the local museum.

Open-air museum

Below the castle is an open-air museum of the traditional architecture of north-eastern Slovakia.

Komárno H 5

Region: Western Slovakia
District: Komárno
Altitude: 112m/367ft
Population: 38,000

Situation and characteristics

The district town of Komárno (Hungarian Komárom) lies on the Slovak–Hungarian frontier at the junction of the Váh with the Danube. It is an important traffic junction with an old-established port on the Danube (shipyards), the most important in Slovakia. The population of the town is mainly Hungarian, and it has a Hungarian Regional Theatre. A road bridge links Komárno with the Hungarian town of Komárom on the south bank of the Danube.

History

Originally a fortified town situated at the eastern tip of the Žitný Ostrov, an island formed by two arms of the Danube, Komárno prospered in the 15th and 16th centuries and successfully withstood Turkish attacks. In 1763 the town was destroyed by an earthquake.

Komárno was the birthplace of the famous operetta composer Franz (Ferenc) Lehár (1870–1948; commemorative plaque on the house in which he was born) and the writer Móric Jókai (1825–1904).

Sights

Fortress

The only relics of the town's more distant past are some remains of its underground fortress (originally medieval) and the old town walls (restored in 19th c.).

Churches
Trinity Column

Notable features of the town are the Baroque Orthodox church (1754–70; fine interior), the Roman Catholic church (1756) and a Trinity Column of 1715.

Danubian Museum

The Danubian Museum (Podunajské Múzeum) has an interesting collection, including in particular material from the Roman legionary camp at Iža (5km/3 miles east of Komárno) and the Roman settlement of Celemantia.

Surroundings of Komárno

Hurbanovo

Hurbanovo (alt. 115m/375ft; pop. 7000), 14km/8½ miles north of Komárno, has an astrophysical and meteorological observatory established in 1863.

Nové Zámky

28km/17 miles north of Komárno is the district town of Nové Zámky (alt. 120m/395ft; pop. 33,000; electrical engineering), founded in 1571 as a fortress against Turkish invasion. In the town is the grave of the Slovak language reformer Anton Bernolák (1762–1813).

Košice L 4

Region: Eastern Slovakia
District: Košice
Altitude: 205m/675ft
Population: 232,000

Situation and characteristics

Košice, Slovakia's second largest city (after Bratislava) and a regional capital, lies on the right bank of the river Hornád and on a lateral canal, on the eastern fringes of the Slovakian Ore Mountains (see entry). It is the see of a Roman Catholic bishop and the cultural centre of eastern Slovakia, with a University, a Technical College and other institutes of higher education, a theatre (with three companies) and a Philharmonic Orchestra. The city's economic life is centred on a variety of industry (iron and steel works, engineering, foodstuffs).

History

Košice was granted the status of a free royal city in 1347, and by the end of the 15th century had become the third largest city in Hungary. Particularly in the 14th and 15th centuries, but also in later centuries, a large proportion of the population was German. Lying only 25km/15 miles from the present Hungarian frontier, Košice belonged to Hungary until 1918 and again between 1938 and 1945, when it was the chief town of a strip of territory along the frontier predominantly inhabited by Magyars.
On April 5th 1945, soon after the establishment of a provisional government of Czechoslovakia in the town, the "Košice Programme" of the National Front of Czechs and Slovaks – providing the basis for a new Czechoslovak constitution – was proclaimed in Košice.

Sights

Main Square

The central feature of the city is the Main Square (Hlavné Námestie), laid out in gardens and flanked on east and west by the Main Street (Hlavná Ulica), which runs through the whole of the central area from north to south.

State Theatre

On the north side of the square is the neo-Renaissance State Theatre (Štátne Divadlo; 1898), which also serves as an opera house.

St Elizabeth's Cathedral ▶

Plan of town centre

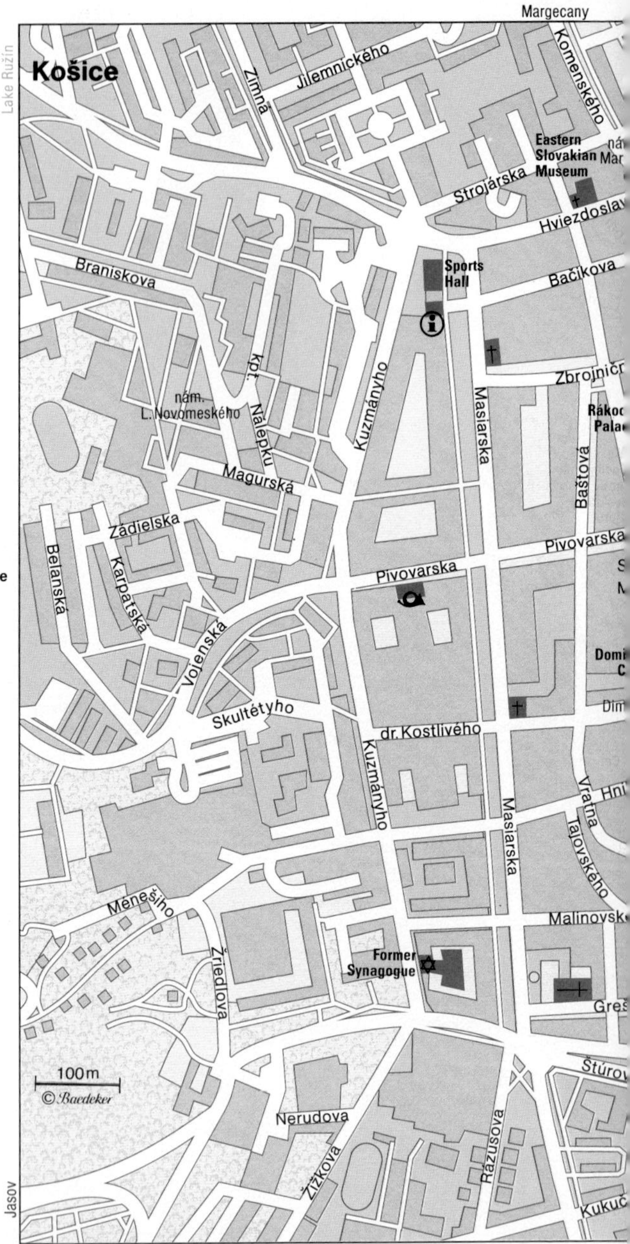

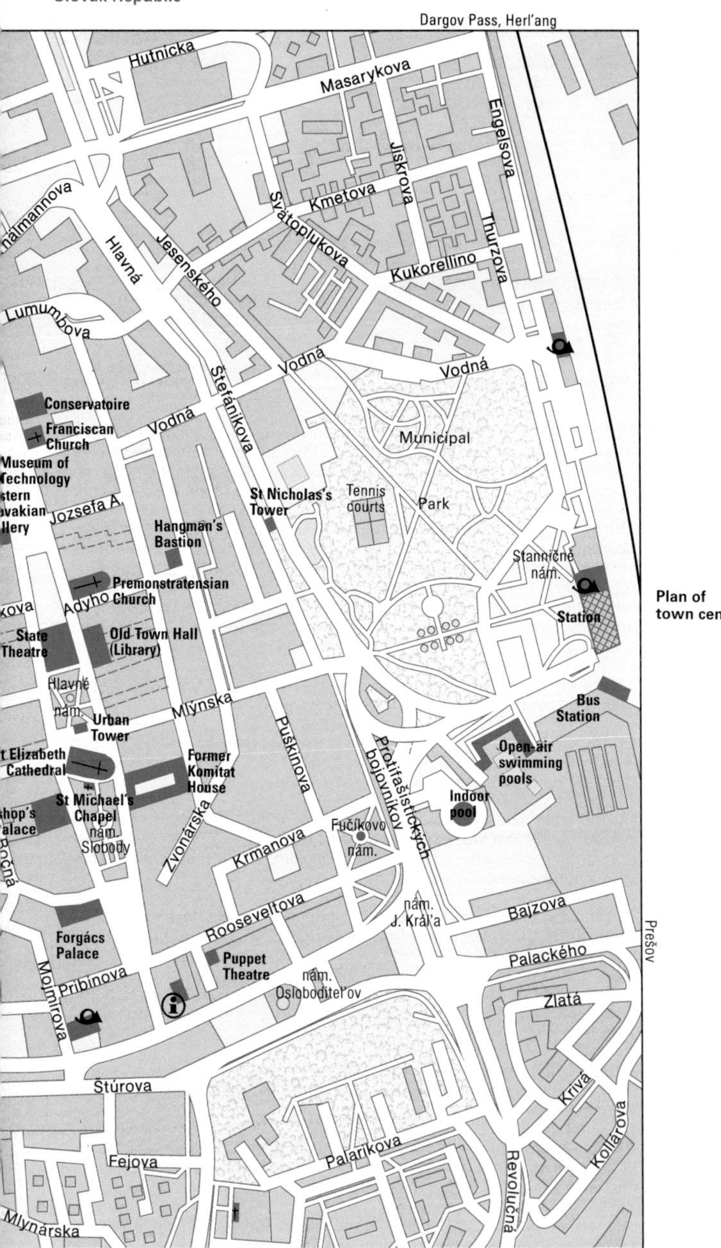

Plan of town centre

St Elizabeth's Cathedral
Dóm sv. Alžbety

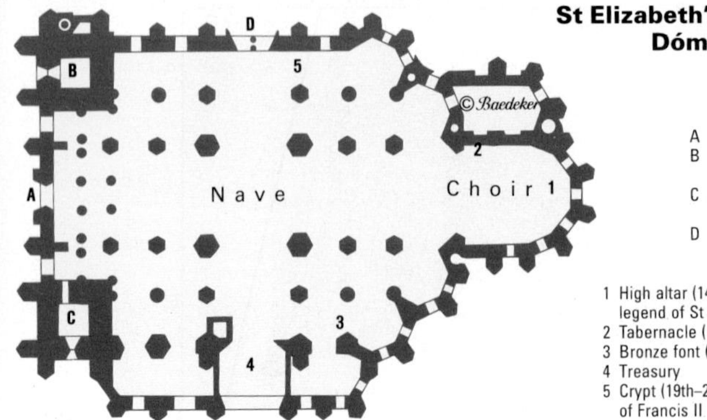

A West doorway
B North-west tower
C South-west tower (unfinished)
D North doorway (Porta Aurea, 1460)

1 High altar (1474–77; legend of St Elizabeth)
2 Tabernacle (1462–77)
3 Bronze font (14th c.)
4 Treasury
5 Crypt (19th–20th c; tomb of Francis II Rákóczy, 1676–1735)

***Cathedral** On the south side of the square stands the Gothic St Elizabeth's Cathedral (Dom Sv. Alžbety), the largest church in Slovakia, with two west towers (the north tower 59m/194ft high, the south tower unfinished). In the tympanum of the north doorway can be seen a representation of the Last Judgment.

Interior The interior of the Cathedral is harmonious and richly furnished. It has a beautifully carved Late Gothic high altar, 11m/36ft high, with four panels and 48 paintings on a gold ground (1474–77; legend of St Elizabeth); a monstrance 1m/40in. high; and (on the north wall of the choir) a 16m/52ft high tabernacle with rich openwork decoration (1462–77). Particularly fine are St Stephen's Chapel (to the left, beside the sacristy) and St John's Chapel (to the rear, on right).

Urban Tower To the north of the Cathedral is the free-standing Urban Tower (1628; restored 1909), with beautiful arcades at the base.

Freedom Square
St Michael's Chapel On the south side of the Cathedral, in the tree-planted Freedom Square (Námestie Slobody), is St Michael's Chapel (1260), the place of worship of the German Catholic community between the two world wars.

Bishop's Palace
Komitat House On the west side of Freedom Square stands the 18th century Bishop's Palace, on the east side the New Komitat House (Nový Župný Dom; 1779), the former headquarters of the Hungarian *komitat* (county) administration, with a handsome façade.

Dominican Church To the west of Freedom Square, in Dominikánske Námestie (Dominican Square), is the Dominican Church (originally Gothic; remodelled in Baroque style about 1700).

Town Hall Facing the State Theatre, to the east, is the neo-classical Town Hall (Radnica; 1782), in which the new government's programme was proclaimed in 1945 (see History).

Marian Column
Premonstratensian Church In the square to the north of the State Theatre can be seen a beautiful Marian Column. On the east side of the square is the 16th century Premonstratensian Church.

Hangman's Bastion A little way east of the Premonstratensian Church is the Hangman's Bastion (Katova Bašta; 13th c.), a relic of the town's fortifications; it now contains a museum.

St Nicholas's Tower Still farther east stands the little St Nicholas's Tower (Miklušova Veznica), which was once a prison, complete with torture chambers.

Station

Some 500m/550yd east of St Nicholas's Tower, on the east side of the Municipal Park, is the Station (Stanica).

Eastern Slovakian Gallery

An old palace with a beautiful arcaded courtyard on the west side of the Main Street, opposite the Premonstratensian Church, houses the Eastern Slovakian Gallery (Východoslovenská Galéria), a branch of the Eastern Slovakian Museum.

***Museum of Technology**

Farther north, on the left of the Main Street, which now becomes narrower, is the richly stocked Museum of Technology (Technické Múzeum), in the former headquarters (1654) of the Town Commandant.

Franciscan Church

Opposite the Museum, on the east side of the street, is the 15th century Franciscan Church.

Square of the Peace Marathon

At the north end of the Main Street is the Square of the Peace Marathon (Námestie Maratónu Mieru), commemorating this annual Košice sporting event. In the square is a statue of a marathon runner.

***Eastern Slovakian Museum**

On the west side of Peace Marathon Square can be found the Eastern Slovakian Museum (Východoslovenské Múzeum), with a fine collection of folk and decorative art.

Botanic Garden

From Peace Marathon Square Ulica J. A. Komenshého (Comenius Street) runs north through a spaciously planned new district, mostly developed after the Second World War, on the north-western outskirts of which is the beautiful Botanic Garden (Botanická Zahrada).

Calvary
*View of city

1km/¾ mile west of Peace Marathon Square is Calvary Hill (Kalvária), from which there is a superb view of the city.

Open-air theatre

South-west of Calvary Hill, beyond a large open-air theatre, is Šafárikova Trieda (Šafárik Street), which runs 1km/¾ mile south to the Nové Mesto

Urban tower

Fountains in Main Square

(New Town) district, which, like the new northern district, is spaciously planned.

Surroundings of Košice

Dargov pass

20km/12½ miles east of Košice we come to the Dargov pass (Dargovský priesmyk, 473m/1552ft), an important means of passage through the forest-covered Slanské Vrchy (up to 1092m/3583ft). In the winter of 1944–45 this was the scene of bitter fighting between German forces and the Soviet Army, which lost some 22,000 men. The dead are commemorated by a "Rose-Garden of Gratitude".

Herl'any
*Geyser

25km/15 miles north-east of Košice is Herl'any (alt. 365m/1200ft), with a geyser which shoots a jet of cold water 30–40m/100–130ft into the air at intervals of 32–34 hours.

Jasov

Jasov (alt. 280m/920ft; pop. 2500), 25km/15 miles west of Košice, has a Premonstratensian monastery and church probably founded at the end of the 12th century. After their destruction by the Tatars they were rebuilt in Baroque style on the original foundations in 1750–66. They contain fine frescoes (by J. L. Kracker) and altarpieces and a rich library.
Behind the monastery lies a Baroque garden in the French manner. The hothouse is in a style transitional between Rococo and neo-classicism.

Jasov Cave

To the south of Jasov is the Jasov Cave (Jasovská jaskýna). On the crag above the cave are the ruins of the 14th century Jasov Castle (alt. 350m/1150ft).

Lake Ružín

25–40km/15–25 miles north-west of Košice is Lake Ružín (alt. 310m/1015ft; area 600 hectares/1500 acres), an artificial lake formed by a dam on the river Hornád, with a wide range of recreational facilities.

Kremnica H 4

Region: Central Slovakia
District: Žiar nad Hronom
Altitude: 550m/1805ft
Population: 6500

Situation and characteristics

The old Central Slovakian mining town of Kremnica, still surrounded by well preserved 15th century walls, was formerly in the centre of a German linguistic island. It has retained its historic role as a mint town and also has a variety of industry (ceramics, lace, tanning).

History

Kremnica was founded in the 12th century by settlers from Silesia and Thuringia and in 1328 was granted the privileges of a free royal town. The rich deposits of gold and silver in the area brought the town great prosperity in the Middle Ages. From 1335 gold ducats and silver groschen were minted in the Kremnica mint – still the only one in the country producing gold coins and medals.

Sights

Old Castle

Commandingly situated above the town, which is built on the slopes of a deeply indented valley, is the Old Castle, from which there is a fine view of the town.
An underground passage leads down from the castle into the town.

***St Catherine's Church**

The castle church of St Catherine, originally the keep, was rebuilt in Late Gothic style in 1468–85 and restored in 1886. It has some remains of 15th century frescoes.

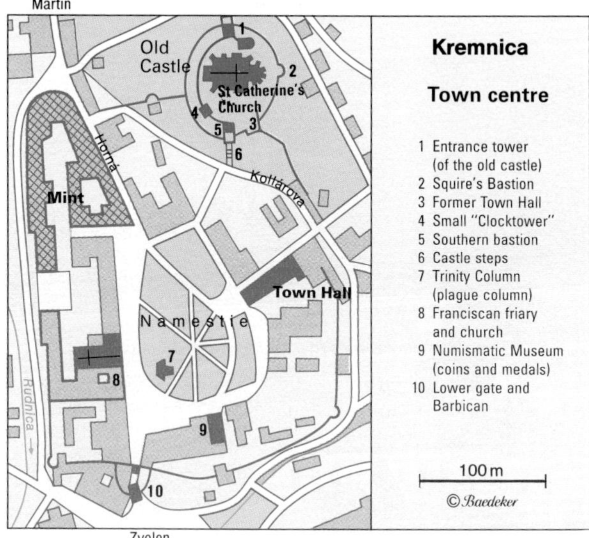

St Andrew's Chapel, a Romanesque rotunda, dates from the 13th century. The castle area is surrounded by a double ring of walls up to 12m/40ft high, with a moat between the two.

***Town walls**

The walls of the castle link up with the 15th century town walls. Of the original circuit there survive four towers and the Lower Gate.

Square
Town Hall
Museum
Trinity Column

In the main square are numerous fine Gothic patrician houses (15th–16th c.), the Town Hall (No. 1), the Municipal Museum and a Trinity Column (1765–72) richly decorated with figures.

St Elizabeth's Church

The Gothic St Elizabeth's Church (formerly a hospital church) dates from the late 14th century.

Mint

The State Mint, in Horná Ulica, can be visited on application.

Surroundings of Kremnica

Kremnica Hills

From Kremnica there are rewarding trips into the Kremnica Hills (Kremnické Pohorie), which also offer good skiing in winter.

Žiar nad Hronom

13km/8 miles south of Kremnica is the district town of Žiar nad Hronom (alt. 226m/742ft; pop. 18,000), with an aluminium plant (reddish slag-heaps). It has a handsome Renaissance castle (16th c., renovated in 1678) and a Baroque church.

Handlová

44km/27 miles north-west of Kremnica is the old mining town of Handlová (alt. 416m/1365ft; pop. 15,000), around which lignite is mined. The Gothic church (1360) was badly damaged during the Second World War and was restored in 1958.

Kremnica, with St Catherine's Church rising above it

Levoča K 3

Region: Eastern Slovakia
District: Spišská Nová Ves
Altitude: 573m/1880ft
Population: 13,000

Situation and characteristics

The Eastern Slovakian town of Levoča lies 26km/16 miles east of Poprad (see entry) below the south side of the Levoča Hills (Levočské Vrchy).
In the 17th century the town was an important cultural centre of the Reformed faith (printing press established 1624) and in the 19th century of the national revival movement under the leadership of L'udovít Štúr (see Famous People).
The town's main source of income is the textile industry.

History and **townscape

In 1721 Levoča became the headquarters of the League of the 24 Free Cities of Spiš (see entry). It is the best preserved medieval town in Slovakia, with an almost complete circuit of town walls of the 14th and 15th centuries, some 250 Renaissance burghers' houses, a magnificent Renaissance Town Hall amd a unique Late Gothic carved altar in St James's Church.

Sights

***Town Square**

The central feature of the town is the large Town Square, surrounded by numerous handsome Renaissance buildings.

***Town Hall**

In the centre of the square is the Town Hall, with arcading at street level, a loggia on the first floor and a bell-tower. Originally Gothic, it was rebuilt in Renaissance style after a fire in 1550 (completed 1615).

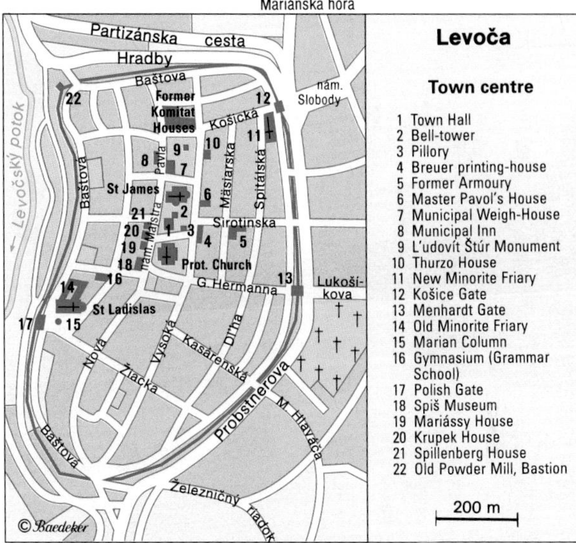

The Town Hall has a handsome council chamber and contains the interesting Spiš Museum (Spišské Múzeum), which is mainly devoted to the history of the town and the Spiš district.

Pillory

On the south side of the Town Hall is an iron pillory of the Renaissance period (Klietka Hanby, the "Cage of Shame").
Adjoining is a Soviet war memorial.

Protestant Church

To the west of the Town Hall stands the Empire-style Protestant Church (1825).

***St James's Church**

To the east of the Town Hall is the Gothic church of St James (Chrám Sv. Jakuba), built in the 14th century and renovated in the 15th (illustration, p. 91).

Interior
**High altar

In the richly furnished interior is a Late Gothic high altar (by Master Pavol of Levoča, probably a pupil of Veit Stoss; 1508–17). 18m/59ft high by 6m/20ft wide, it is one of the largest Gothic carved altars known, with rich sculptural decoration, particularly on the predella. To the left of the altar is a delicately carved Late Gothic tabernacle.
In the north aisle and the choir are wall paintings of the 14th and 15th centuries, with German inscriptions which are still legible.
Other notable features are the altar of St Catherine (*c.* 1460), the Corvinus Altar (*c.* 1485), the pulpit, the font, the organ (16th c.) and tombs of the Thurzo family, some of whom were Archbishops of Breslau.

***Burghers' houses**

On the north side of the square are a number of fine old burghers' houses, some of them with handsome Renaissance courtyards, like No. 55, the Spillenberg House (No. 45) and the Máriássy House (No. 43), with a beautiful Renaissance doorway and courtyard.
On the west side of the square is the Thurzo House (Turzov Dom; No. 7), a handsome Renaissance building which was remodelled in neo-classical style in 1824; the sgraffito façade dates from the 1900s.

Town Hall, Levoča

Evangelical Church

Gymnasium Church

South-west of the square, just inside the town walls at the Polish Gate (Polská Brana), are the Gymnasium (Grammar School) Church (1310–20) and the former Minorite friary to which it originally belonged, with a Gothic cloister.

Minorite Church

At the Košice Gate (Košická Brana), a plain structure near the north-east corner of the old town is the New Minorite Church (Baroque) which has a richly furnished interior.

Surroundings of Levoča

Dravce

7km/4½ miles west of Levoča is the village of Dravce (alt. 648m/2126ft; pop. 500), which has a 13th century Gothic church with 13th and 15th century frescoes.

Spišská Kapitula

8km/5 miles east of Levoča is Spišská Kapitula, the old spiritual centre of the Spiš district, now part of the little town of Spišské Podhradie (see below).
The twin-towered St Martin's Cathedral was begun in 1245 in Romanesque style and rebuilt at the end of the 15th century as a Late Gothic hall-church. Over the north doorway can be seen a wall painting of 1317. Built on to the south side of the church is the Gothic funerary chapel of the Zápolya family (1493). The ten canons' houses adjoining the Cathedral date from the Baroque period.
The town preserves its old circuit of walls and two gates.

Spišské Podhradie

9km/5½ miles east of Levoča lies the old-world little town of Spišské Podhradie (alt. 435m/1425ft; pop. 3500), with a 13th century Late Romanesque church which was renovated in the 19th century.

****Spiš Castle**
(plan p. 467)

10km/6 miles east of Levoča, on a bare travertine hill in the commune of Žehra, are the imposing and well preserved remains of Spiš Castle (Spišsky Hrad; alt. 634m/2080ft), the largest in Slovakia.
The castle, founded in the 12th century, enlarged between the 13th and 16th centuries and destroyed by fire in 1780, gave its name to the Spiš district (see entry). It has been in course of restoration since 1970 and has been opened to the public in stages from 1983 onwards. From the castle there are far-ranging views, extending to the High Tatras.

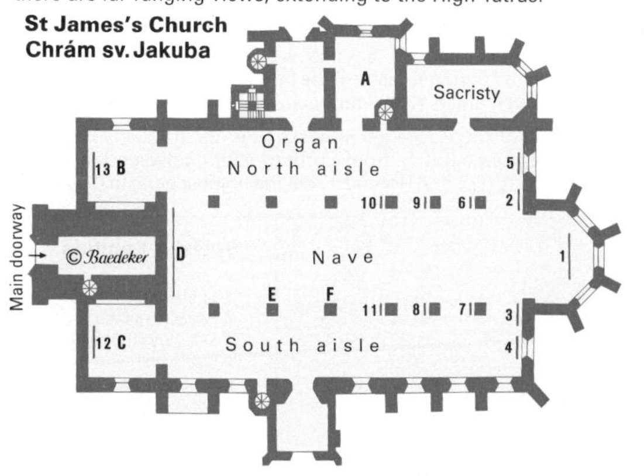

A St George's Chapel
B Chapel of the Nativity
C Baptistery (bronze Gothic font; tombs of Thurzo family)
D Senators' bench
E Renaissance pulpit
F Epitaph of Alexis II Thurzo

ALTARS
1 High altar of St James
2 Altar of the four SS John
3 Altar of SS Peter and Paul
4 Altar of the Man of Sorrows
5 Altar of Our Lady of the Snows
6 Altar of St Nicholas
7 Altar of St Anne
8 Altar of St Catherine
9 Altar of the fourteen Auxiliary Saints
10 Altar of the Good Shepherd
11 Altar of the Archangel Michael
12 Altar of St Elizabeth
13 Altar of the Nativity

Spiš Castle

Žehra

3km/2 miles south of Spiš Castle is the little town of Žehra (alt. 442m/1450ft). In the Church of the Holy Rood (1275) are Gothic wall paintings uncovered in 1954.

Spišsky Štvrtok

The ancient little town of Spišsky Štvrtok (alt. 570m/1870ft; pop. 1500), 9km/5½ miles south-west of Levoča, has an early 14th century Gothic church which preserves some Romanesque work. Built on to the church, which was remodelled in Baroque style in 1693 and 1747, is the beautiful Zápolya Chapel (1473).

Betlanovce

18km/11 miles south-east of Levoča is Betlanovce (alt. 546m/1791ft; pop. 1000), with a Renaissance castle of 1564–68 (restored 1955–60).

Bijacovce

20km/12½ miles north-east of Levoča we come to Bijacovce (alt. 562m/1844ft), with the Baroque castle of the Counts Czaky (1780–85), a 14th century Gothic church and a 13th century charnel-house.

Branisko Hills

22km/14 miles east of Levoča are the Branisko Hills (up to 1200m/3900ft), a forest-covered ridge which runs from north to south between the upper valleys of the rivers Torysa and Hornád. From the highest point in the range

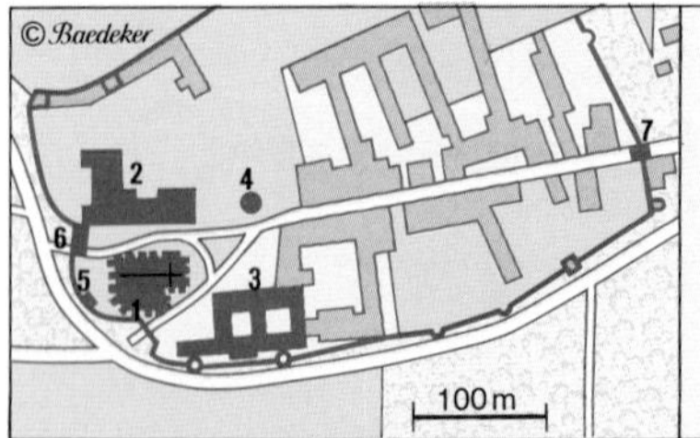

Spišská Kapitula

1 St Martin's Cathedral
2 Episcopal palace
3 Seminary building
4 Clockwriter
5 St John of Nepomuk
6 Upper gate
7 Lower gate

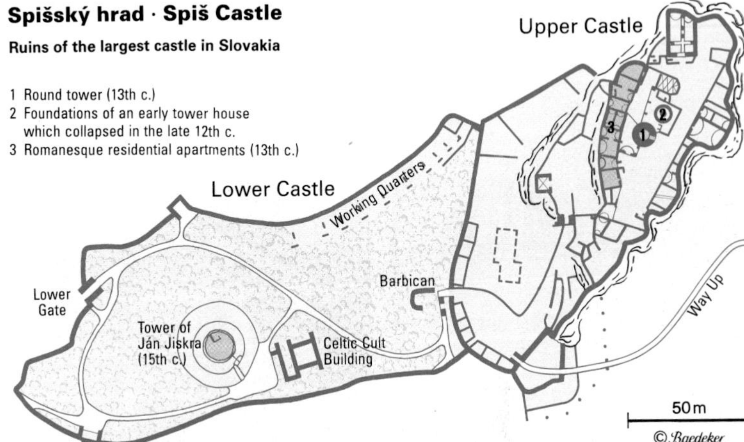

there are superb views of Spiš Castle above the valley to the west, with a distant view, in clear weather, of the High Tatras.

Fričovce

30km/19 miles east of Levoča, at Fričovce (alt. 462m/1516ft; pop. 1200), is a Renaissance castle (1623–30), with coats of arms on the attic and figural sgraffito decoration (temporarily closed for restoration).

Liptovský Mikuláš

I 3

Region: Central Slovakia
District: Liptovský Mikuláš
Altitude: 576m/1890ft
Population: 29,000

Situation and characteristics

The Central Slovakian district town of Liptovský Mikuláš (formerly Liptovský Svätý Mikuláš), on the right bank of the Váh (see entry), is a good base from which to visit the Low Tatras (see entry) and Western Tatras (Západné Tatry). It has a variety of industry (tanning, woodworking, textiles, foodstuffs).

History

Liptovský Mikuláš was granted its municipal charter in the second half of the 13th century. In 1713 the folk hero Juraj Jánošík (born in 1688 at Terchová in the Little Fatra: see entry) was condemned to death and executed here. In the 19th century the town developed into an important centre of Slovak national and political life in the Liptov area. On May 10th 1848 the first Slovak revolutionary programme was formulated here, and from here on May 1st 1918 the call went out for the establishment of a common Czech and Slovak state.

Sights

St Nicholas's Church

The Gothic parish church of St Nicholas (13th c.; renovated 1943–46) has three beautiful Late Gothic altars.

Museum of the Slovakian Karst

In a former monastery at Školská Ulica 4 is the Museum of the Slovakian Karst (Múzeum Slovenského Krasu), with a geological and speleological

Gymnasium, Liptovský Mikuláš

St Nicholas's Church

collection (explanations of the caves in the Demänova valley in the Low Tatras: see entry).

Literary Museum Picture Gallery

Also of interest are the Janko Král' Literary Museum (named after the Slovak poet of that name, 1822–76, a native of the town), in the Selig House, a Renaissance mansion of 1713, and the Petr Bohúň Picture Gallery (after the Slovak painter, 1821–79), both containing works by local artists.

Okoličné

In the Okoličné district are a former monastery and church (15th c.) and a small Renaissance castle (17th c.).

Surroundings of Liptovský Mikuláš

Liptovská Mara Lake

3km/2 miles west of Liptovský Mikuláš is the artificial lake of Liptovská Mara (area 21.6sq.km/8½sq.miles; hydro-electric station). On the northern shores of the lake are the holiday centres of Liptovský Trnovec and Bobrovník.

Liptovský Ján

The spa of Liptovský Ján (alt. 634m/2080ft; pop. 1000), 8km/5 miles south-east of Liptovský Mikuláš, has hot springs (up to 26.6°C/79.9°F; containing calcium, sulphur and carbonic acid); thermal swimming pool. There are many old castles and churches in the surrounding area.

Liptovský Hrádok

10km/6 miles south-east of Liptovský Mikuláš is the industrial town of Liptovský Hrádok (pop. 8000; woodworking, engineering, boatbuilding), a good base from which to explore the Western Tatras, the Low Tatras and the High Tatras. On the northern outskirts of the town are the ruins of a 14th century Gothic moated castle. Nearby, in a fortified Renaissance castle (1600–03), is the Liptov Folk Museum. In the field of industrial archaeology there are a weigh-house and a bell-tower belonging to a blast furnace of 1792.

Lazisko

20km/12½ miles south-west of Liptovský Mikuláš we come to the village of Lazisko, with one of the largest wooden churches in Central Europe (1774), from a village submerged by the Liptovská Mara reservoir.

Western Tatras

The Western Tatras (Západné Tatry), the second highest range of hills in Slovakia (Mt Bystrá, 2248m/7376ft), extend north-east from Liptovský Mikuláš for some 40km/25 miles. The most striking peaks are the Roháče massif (2084m/6838ft), Ostrý Roháč (2084m/6838ft), Banikov (2178m/7146ft) and Mt Trikopy. Particularly beautiful is the Roháčská dolina (valley), with a number of moraines and mountain lakes. All this area offers magnificent scope for climbers and winter sports enthusiasts.
The best approaches are from the village of Zuberec on the west, and on the south from Liptovský Mikuláš by way of the Žiarská dolina.

Demänova valley

A few kilometres south of Liptovský Mikuláš is the Demänova valley (see Low Tatras).

***Prosiecka valley**

20km/12½ miles north-west of Liptovský Mikuláš lies a beautiful dry karstic valley, the Prosiecka dolina (nature reserve; special equipment necessary).

Kvačianska dolina

A new road follows the east side of the Kvačianska dolina, a romantic canyon 5km/3 miles long.

Pribylina

20km/12½ miles north-east of Liptovský Mikuláš is the village of Pribylina (alt. 765m/2510ft; pop. 1500), with the interesting Open-Air Museum of the Liptov Village.

Važec

The village of Važec (alt. 792m/2599ft; pop. 4000), 26km/16 miles east of Liptovský Mikuláš in the upper Liptov basin (Liptovská kotlina), was devastated by a fire in 1931. It has an interesting ethnographic museum, the Važecká Izba.

Stalactitic cave

On the south-western outskirts of the village can be found a 400m/440yd long stalactitic cave (230m/250yd open to visitors).

Východná

29km/18 miles east of Liptovský Mikuláš is the village of Východná (alt. 775m/2545ft; pop. 3000; woodcarving, embroidery, traditional costumes), with handsome old wooden houses. This is now a popular holiday resort. Folk festival annually at the beginning of July in an open-air theatre.

Štrba

32km/20 miles east of Liptovský Mikuláš lies Štrba (alt. 829m/2720ft; pop. 2500) which has fine examples of traditional architecture. Within easy reach is Lake Štrba (Štrbské Pleso; alt. 1345m/4415ft; electric rack railway).

Little Carpathians / Malé Karpaty G 4

Region: Western Slovakia
Districts: Bratislava and Trnava

Situation and characteristics

The Little Carpathians (Malé Karpaty), the most westerly outlier of the great arc of the Carpathians, extend north-east from Bratislava (see entry) for some 90km/55 miles, with a breadth of around 10km/6 miles and heights of up to 768m/2520ft (Mt Záruby), between the broad valleys of the Morava and the Váh (see entries). Some 655sq.km/253sq.miles of this forest-covered upland region are now a nature reserve. On the south-eastern slopes of the hills and in the foreland region are vineyards which produce excellent wine from different varieties of grapes.

Excursions in the *Little Carpathians

Jur pri Bratislave

13km/8 miles north-east of Bratislava is the old-world little wine-making town of Jur pri Bratislave (alt. 180m/590ft; pop. 5000), with characteristic 17th century wine-makers' houses and remains of its town walls. There is a Renaissance castle with an arcaded courtyard, originally built in 1609 and altered in 1746.

The Early Gothic Upper Church (R.C.), originally 13th century, was altered in the 14th century; it has a separate wooden bell-tower. The former Piarist monastery dates from 1654.

Biely Kameň
Něstich

North-west of the town (1 hour's walk) are the ruins of Bielý Kameň, a 13th century castle, and the Slav fortified site of Neštich.

Pezinok

21km/13 miles north-east of Bratislava is Pezinok (alt. 152m/499ft; pop. 19,000), a former free royal town still partly surrounded by walls; vine-growing, pottery manufacture. Its most notable features are the 14th century Town Church (altered in 15th c.; fine vaulting; R.C.); the Lower Church (formerly Protestant, now also R.C.), a Renaissance building of 1659 which was later remodelled in Baroque style; the Capuchin Church (1718); the Town Hall (*c.* 1600); typical 17th century wine-makers' houses; and remains of the old town walls. The 17th century castle (wine cellars, wine bar) developed out of a medieval moated stronghold. There is an interesting Wine Museum (Vinohradnické Múzeum). Every other year (alternating with Modra) a Vintage Festival is held in September.

Pezinok was the birthplace of the portrait painter Ján Kupecký (1667–1740); there is a memorial museum in the house in which he was born (Kupeckého Ulica 39).

Pezinok is a good base for walks and climbs in the Little Carpathians (13km/8 miles to the Na Babe mountain hut).

Pottery from Modra

Modra

29km/18 miles north-east of Bratislava can be found the old town of Modra (alt. 160m/525ft; pop. 8000), which first appears in the records in 1158 and became a free royal town under the Hungarian crown in 1607. Modra is the largest wine-producing commune in Slovakia; every other year (alternating with Pezinok) a Vintage Festival is held in September. Pottery manufacture; craft products.
The town is surrounded by walls, mostly well preserved, with several bastions and three gates. Notable features are the Gothic cemetery church (with a Renaissance bell-tower) and a number of Renaissance houses. The former synagogue now houses an exhibition of craft pottery and majolica (Slovenská ludová majolika).
The Slovak writer and language reformer L'udovít Štúr (see Famous People) lived in Modra and died in the town in 1856. There is a monument to him in the market square and a memorial museum at Štúrova Ulica 80; his grave is in the town cemetery.
From Modra there is a minor road to the Zochova Chata (mountain hut).

Častá

34km/21 miles north-east of Bratislava is the old mining town of Častá, with a 15th century Catholic church (wall paintings) and a Jewish cemetery (gravestones of 17th and 18th centuries).

*Červený Kameň (Museum)

The village of Červený Kameň (alt. 248m/814ft), 2km/1¼ miles south-west of Častá, was a well preserved frontier stronghold originally founded in the 13th century and developed between 1523 and 1537 into a powerful fortress with four circular corner bastions. The interior was remodelled in Early Baroque style in 1670–80. Notable features are the sala terrena, with rich stucco vaulting, frescoes and an artificial grotto, and a deep well constructed for the wealthy Fugger merchant family. The castle is now open to the public as a museum (period furniture, majolica, pictures, tapestries, arms and armour; torture chamber). There are huge sequoias in the park.

Smolenice

52km/32 miles north-east of Bratislava, Smolenice (alt. 242m/794ft; pop. 2000) has a Renaissance church (1622–24) and a 17th century pillory. Above the village to the north, on the site of a medieval castle (first mentioned in the records in 1390), is a modern castle (1880–90), now occupied by the Slovak Academy of Sciences, which is still surrounded by 14th century walls and a bastion. From the tower (open to public) there are extensive views of the Váh depression.

Driny Cave

Half an hour's walk south-west is the Driny stalactitic cave (alt. 400m/1300ft; open to public).

Little Fatra / Malá Fatra H/I 3

Region: Central Slovakia
Districts: Žilina and Martin

Situation and *topography

The Little Fatra (Malá Fatra), a range of hills in north-western Slovakia, is a region much favoured by climbers and winter sports enthusiasts. The hills, built up of granite, sandstone and dolomite, range in height between 1500 and 1700m (4900 and 5600ft; highest point Vel'ky Fatranský Krivaň, 1709m/5607ft) and have a varied flora (temperate to sub-alpine) and fauna. The scenery is magnificent, with jagged peaks, bizarre rock formations, gorges and dolines; panoramic views from the summits.
Half way along the range the Váh cuts through the main ridge in a narrow valley (see Žilina, Strečno).

***Little Fatra National Park**

The Little Fatra National Park (area 200sq.km/77sq.miles) occupies the north-eastern part of the range. The main tourist area is the Vrátna valley. In the southern part of the range (the Martinské Hole area) the principal

Vel'ký Rozsutec, in the Little Fatra

attractions are the Turčianská kotlina (to the east: see Martin) and the Rajčanka valley (to the west: see Žilina, Rajecké Teplice). The highest peak is the Vel'ká Lúka (1476m/4843ft), from the summit of which there are far-ranging views.

Excursions in the *Little Fatra

Terchová

The summer holiday resort and winter sports centre of Terchová (alt. 514m/1686ft) in the north of the Little Fatra was the birthplace of the legendary robber-chief and Slovak folk hero Juraj Jánošík (1688–1713), who was executed at Liptovský Mikuláš (see entry).

Vel'ký Rozsutec

5km/3 miles south-east of Terchová is Vel'ký Rozsutec (1610m/5282ft; views), a jagged dolomitic peak, with bizarre rock formations, swallowholes and a varied flora.

***Vrátna valley**

5km/3 miles south of Terchová lies the beautiful Vrátna valley (Vrátna dolina), a large depression (36sq.km/14sq.miles) which attracts walkers and climbers in summer and winter sports enthusiasts in winter. It is reached by way of the rocky Tiesňavy gorge. At the head of the valley is the lower station (750m/2460ft) of a chair-lift to the Snilovské Sedlo (1520m/4987ft), a saddle between Vel'ky Fatranský Krivaň (1709m/5607ft) and Mt Chleb (1646m/5401ft).
A folk festival, "Jánošík Week", is held annually in the Vrátna valley.

Zázrivá

10km/6 miles north-east of Terchová is the commune of Zázrivá (alt. 600m/2000ft), which consists of eleven villages. This is an area of pastoral agriculture with some fine examples of traditional local architecture. It is also a popular holiday area and a good base for walkers and climbers.

Low Tatras / Nízke Tatry I/K 3/4

Regions: Central and Eastern Slovakia
Districts: Banská Bystrica, Liptovský Mikuláš and Poprad

Situation and *topography

The Low Tatras (Nízke Tatry) lie in the heart of Slovakia, between the valleys of the Hron to the south and the Váh to the north. The highest parts of the 80km/50 mile long main ridge are markedly mountainous in character, offering visitors both great natural beauty and some testing climbs. The long subsidiary ridges which branch off the main ridge are lower and are often bare of vegetation.

Morphology

The main massif of the Low Tatras consists of granites and schists, while some of the subsidiary ridges and their valleys are of limestones and dolomites, with fine caves and rock formations hewn by Ice Age glaciers. The principal attractions are the "Rock Window" on Mt Ohniště (1539m/5049ft) and the Vrbické Pleso (1113m/3652ft; area 7 hectares/17 acres), a mountain lake in the Demänova valley.

***Low Tatras National Park**

Some 800sq.km/300sq.miles of the range now form the Low Tatras National Park.

The Hron and Váh valleys are linked by a road over the Čertovica pass (1238m/4062ft).

Excursions in the **Low Tatras

Main Ridge (from the North)

***Caves in *Demänova valley**

Near Liptovský Mikuláš a side road branches off into the wild and romantic Demänova valley (Demänovská dolina; nature reserve). In 9km/5½ miles a road on the left leads to the Demänova Ice Cave (Demänovská L'adová Jaskyňa) or Dragon Ice Cave (Dračia L'adová Jaskyňa; 815m/2675ft), a karstic cave referred to as early as the 13th century, with rich ice formations (open May–September; conducted visits). The bones of a primeval cave bear were found here. 2km/1¼ miles along the valley, on the left (a few minutes' walk from the car park), is the Demänova Freedom Cave (Demänovská Jaskyňa Slobody), a limestone cave system on several levels, with large chambers, halls and galleries, and colourful stalactites and stalagmites (open throughout the year; conducted visits).

***Jasná valley**

The road continues to climb the Jasná valley (Jasná dolina; 1236m/4055ft), an attractive and popular summer holiday and winter sports area, and ends in 5km/3 miles near the Družba Hotel (1200m/3940ft), below the lower station of a chair-lift which runs up Mt Chopok (2024m/6641ft; see below), with an intermediate station at Luková. From Mt Chopok there is a rewarding ridge walk (1½ hours) to Mt Ďumbier (2043m/6703ft; see below).
The chair-lift continues south into the Bystrá valley (see below).

Main Ridge (from the South)

***Bystrá valley**

The main ridge of the Low Tatras is reached from the south from either Podbrezová or Brezno on the road which cuts through the hills. In 10km/6 miles the road comes to the village of Bystrá (small karstic cave), now part of the commune of Mýto pod Ďumbierom, to the north of which is the beautiful Bystrá valley (Bystrá dolina). A narrow road ascends the valley, following the little river Bystrianka, to below the main ridge.

Tále

3.5km/2 miles from Bystrá on the road through the hills, on the left, is the holiday centre of Tále (alt. 750m/2460ft; ski-lift), amid a large expanse of upland meadows.

A cave in the Demänova valley

In another 7.5km/4½ miles the road ends at the Srdiečko Hotel, near the lower station (1242m/4075ft) of a chair-lift which runs up Mt Chopok (2024m/6641ft), with an intermediate station at Juh (1600m/5250ft; Kosodrevina Hotel).
The chair-lift then continues north into the Jasná valley (see above).

Highest Peaks in the Low Tatras

***Mt Ďumbier**

Mt Ďumbier (2043m/6703ft), the highest peak in the Low Tatras, falls steeply down on the north in a 500m/1640ft high rock wall with corries gouged out by glaciers. In good weather there are magnificent views from the summit, particularly of the High Tatras. To the south-east of the summit is the Mountain Hut of the Slovak National Uprising (Chata Hrdinů SNP; 1740m/5710ft).

***Mt Chopok**
(illus. p. 476)

Mt Chopok (2024m/6641ft) is the second highest peak in the Low Tatras and another magnificent viewpoint. It offers excellent skiing, particularly on the northern slopes.

Králova Hol'a

Králova Hol'a (1948m/6391ft) is the highest peak in the eastern Low Tatras. On the summit is a telecommunications tower.
To the north-west is the interesting mountain village of Liptovská Teplička (alt. 900m/2950ft).

Tourist Resorts in the Low Tatras

Brezno

The industrial town of Brezno (alt. 498m/1634ft; pop. 14,000), in the south of the Low Tatras, is the economic centre of the Horehronie (Hron valley), with an interesting Regional Museum.

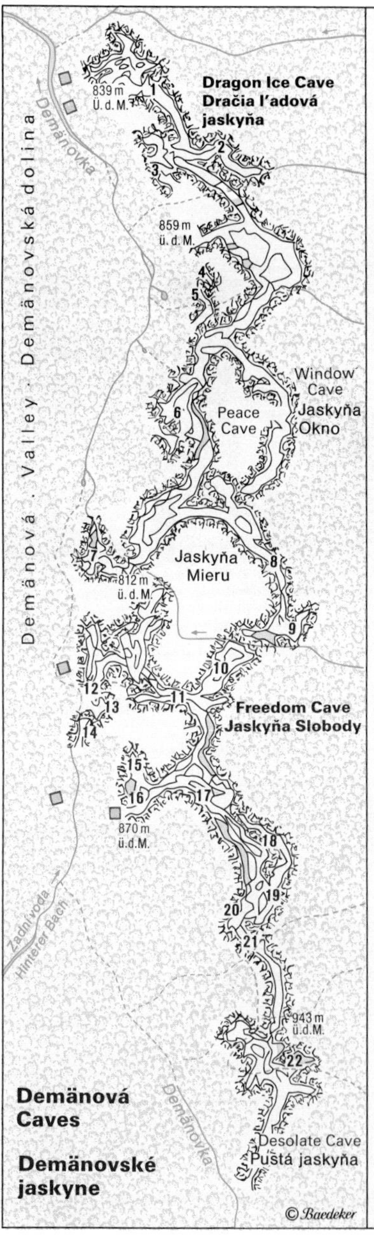

DRAGON ICE CAVE
DRAČIA L'ADOVÁ
JASKYŇA

The Dragon Cave gets its name from the bones of a cave bear that were discovered here. In this cave and the adjoining Freedom Cave a labyrinth of 8355m/9138yds of passages on four levels has been surveyed, some 800m/875yds of which can be walked through. The very old stalactitic formations in these caves have a tendency to die off. The tour of the cave takes about 40 minutes.

1 Kmet'ov Hall
2 Beník Cave
3 Gateway (Brána)
4 Rams' Cave (Barania Jaskyňa)
5 Tunnel Cave (Tunelová J.)
6 Robbers' Cave (Zbojnická J.)
7 Karstic Spring Cave (Vyvieranie)
8 Rose Gallery (Ružová Galéria)
9 Concert Hall (Koncertný Sál)

FREEDOM CAVE
JASKYŇA SLOBODY

The Freedom Cave was formed through the erosion of the rock by the river Demänovka and its tributary streams. In the cave system, which is on five levels, there are great numbers of stalactites and stalagmites, varied in form and brilliant in colour, underground lakes and waterfalls. The tour of the cave takes about 1¾ hours.

10 Dry Passage (Suchá Chodba)
11 Marble Riverbed (Mramorové Riečisko)
12 Gorge at Björnson Hut
13 Cave under Reef (Jaskyňa pod Útesom)
14 Valley Cave (Údolní Jaskyňa)
15 Spherical Hall (Gulový Dom)
16 Deep Hall (Hl'boký Dom)
17 Maiden's Passage (Panenská Chodba) Jánošík Cave
18 Chambers of Wonders (Zázračné Siene)
19 Violet Hall (Fialový Dom)
20 Rose Chamber (Ružová Sieň)
21 Feather Passage (Brková Chodba)
22 Agate Hall (Achátný Dom)

On Mt Chopok, a popular winter sports area

The villages of Polomka, Hel'pa, Pohorelá and Šumiac in the surrounding area have good examples of traditional local architecture and have preserved old customs.

Boca, Nižná, Vyšná

The old mining villages of Boca, Nižná (alt. 850m/2790ft) and Vyšná (1000m/3280ft) are now summer holiday resorts and winter sports centres (ski-lifts), which also preserve fine examples of traditional local architecture. A short distance to the north we come to the Čertovica pass, which carries the road over the main ridge of the Low Tatras.

Nemecká

20km/12½ miles north-east of Banská Bystrica (see entry) is the large commune of Nemecká (alt. 440m/1445ft). Near here some 900 Slovaks and Jews were murdered in January 1945 (memorial and small museum).

Záhradky

At the foot of Mt Chopok, at the head of the Demänova valley, is the popular skiing centre of Záhradky.

Lučenec

I 4

Region: Central Slovakia. District: Lučenec
Altitude: 189m/620ft. Population: 25,000

Situation and characteristics

The Central Slovakian district town of Lučenec lies in a boggy depression to the west of the river Ipel', only some 10km/6 miles north of the Slovak–Hungarian frontier. It is an important railway junction and industrial town (engineering, textiles).

History

In the 16th century the town played an important part in the Hussite wars. An epidemic of plague in 1719 carried off 60% of the population.

Sights

Sights

Gothic Calvinist church (renovated 1849); Town Hall (1892); burghers' houses in Art Nouveau style.

Surroundings of Lučenec

Lúčenský Kúpele

To the west of the town is the spa of Lúčenský Kúpele.

Lake Ladovo

To the north-west lies the little artificial lake of Ladovo.

Halič

7km/4½ miles north-west of Lučenec is Halič (alt. 274m/899ft), with a 17th century castle which was remodelled in Baroque style in the 18th century. Some of the rooms are open to the public.

Fil'ákovo

The old town of Fil'ákovo (alt. 198m/650ft; pop. 7000; engineering, chalybeate springs), 15km/9 miles south-east of Lučenec, has a local museum housed in a former monastery and a ruined 13th century castle on a basalt crag.

Divín

20km/12½ miles north-west of Lučenec is Divín (alt. 265m/870ft; pop. 2500), with a ruined 13th century castle (destroyed 1683) on a hill above the little town. At the foot of the hill is a Renaissance castle (1670) which belonged to the Counts Zichy. There is a Baroque church of 1657 within Renaissance fortifications. To the south-east is the Ružiná reservoir (area 200 hectares/500 acres; good bathing).

Rimavská Sobota

25km/15 miles north-east of Lučenec, on the river Rimava, is the district town of Rimavská Sobota (alt. 208m/682ft; pop. 20,000; canning factories). The town, founded in the 13th century, was granted a royal charter in 1334 and later succeeded Plešivec as the chief place in the Gemer region. Features of interest are the neo-classical parish church (1774–90); the Town Hall (1801) and the former Komitat House (1798; now the headquarters of the District Council), on the south side of the main square. In the side streets are numbers of small wooden houses dating from the 15th–18th centuries. There is an interesting Gemer District Museum (founded 1852).

Vel'ký Krtiš

30km/19 miles south-west of Lučenec is the district town of Vel'ký Krtiš (alt. 193m/633ft; pop. 7000; lignite mining). The neo-classical church (fine interior) preserves some Baroque features. There is a 17th century fortress, later twice rebuilt.

Modrý Kameň

4km/2½ miles north of Vel'ký Krtiš lies Modrý Kameň (alt. 308m/1011ft; pop. 2000), with the ruins of a Gothic castle. In the lower part of the town is a Baroque fortress of 1730.

Vel'ký Bih

35km/22 miles north-east of Lučenec is Vel'ký Bih (alt. 216m/709ft; pop. 2000), with a castle, originally Rococo, which was remodelled in Empire style in 1817–22, set in a large English-style park.
On the northern outskirts of the little town are remains of a 14th century castle.

Šafárikovo

The industrial town of Šafárikovo (formerly Tornal'a; alt. 183m/600ft; pop. 7000; engineering, textiles), 50km/31 miles north-east of Lučenec, was named after the Slovak literary historian and antiquarian Pavol Jozef Šafárik (see Famous People). The Gothic church (15th c.) has a fine coffered wooden ceiling of 1768. There is a mineral spring (19°C/66°F).

Martin H 3

Region: Central Slovakia. District: Martin
Altitude: 394m/1293ft. Population: 65,000

Situation and characteristics

The old Central Slovakian district town of Martin (formerly Turčiansky Sväty Martin) lies in a wide basin between the Little Fatra (see entry) and the Great Fatra (Vel'ka Fatra). In recent years it has developed into a considerable industrial centre (engineering – formerly the main producer of tanks for the Warsaw Pact countries – papermaking, printing, railway workshops).

History

Martin was granted its municipal charter in 1340. In the 19th century, with the foundation of the Matica Slovenská, an institution designed to promote Slovak culture, in 1853 and the Slovak Museum Society in 1893, the town gained increased cultural and political importance. On October 30th 1918 representatives of the Slovak people signed the Martin Declaration, rejecting any link with Hungary and calling for the establishment of a new state of the Czechs and Slovaks. In August 1944 Martin was a centre of the Slovak National Uprising (SNP).

Sights

St Martin's Church
Protestant Church

The town's principal church, St Martin's, a Gothic church originally built in 1270–80, was enlarged in the 16th century and altered in the 19th and 20th centuries. The Protestant Church dates from 1784.

***Slovak national institutions**

Martin has a number of national institutions and buildings associated with the 19th century national revival: the former Slovak Gymnasium (Grammar School; 1865); the former House of the Slovak Nation (1888), now a theatre; the Slovak National Museum (Slovenské Národné Múzeum), with

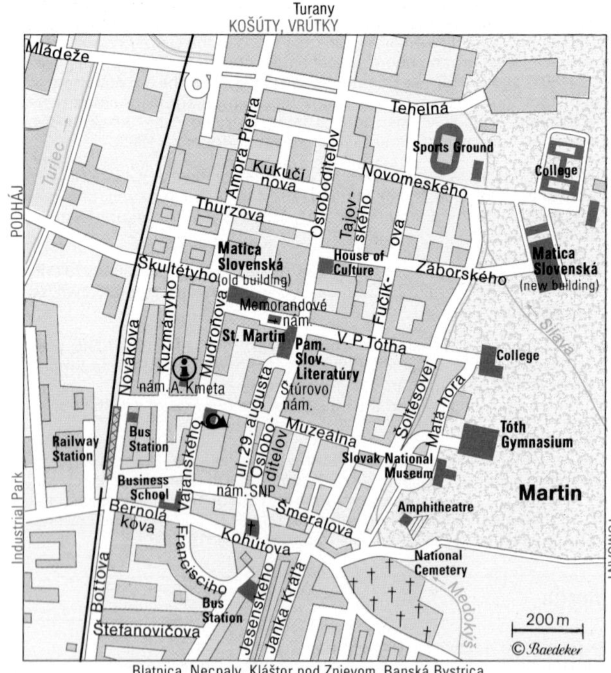

a rich collection of material on Slovak history and traditions (old building 1906–08, new building 1932); the Slovak National Library (Slovenská Národná Knihovna), with over 1 million volumes; and the Matica Slovenská (old building 1869–75, new building 1925).

Monuments

All over the town are monuments and commemorative tablets for distinguished Slovaks.

***National Cemetery**

In the National Cemetery can be found the graves of over sixty noted Slovak figures, including the poets Svetozár Hurban-Vajanský (1847–1916) and Janko Jesenský (1874–1945) and Viliam Pauliny-Tóth (1826–77), a politician who concerned himself particularly with cultural and educational matters.

Surroundings of Martin

Turany

12km/7½ miles north-west of Martin is the little town of Turany (alt. 406m/1332ft; pop. 5000), which has an Early Gothic church (with later alterations). Turany was the birthplace of the physicist and philosopher Ernst Mach (1838–1916).

Necpaly

12km/7½ miles south-east of Martin lies the hamlet of Necpaly (alt. 515m/1690ft; pop. 100), at the mouth of the Necpaly valley, with four country houses (17th and 18th c.) and a Gothic church (12th c.; fine frescoes).

Kláštor pod Znievom

16km/10 miles south of Martin we come to Kláštor pod Znievom (alt. 480m/1575ft; pop. 1500), a little town which first appears in the records in 1113. A Premonstratensian monastery was founded here in 1521, and one of the first three grammar schools in Slovakia was established in the town in 1869. There are an Early Gothic church and a later one which was remodelled in Baroque style in 1728. Above the town are the ruins of a 13th century castle. There are some examples of traditional local architecture in the Lazany district.

Blatnica

17km/10½ miles south of Martin, picturesquely situated near the Gäderská dolina and the Blatnická dolina in the Great Fatra, is Blatnica (alt. 500m/1640ft). In the village is a castle dating from the first half of the 18th century (exhibition of work by the photographer Karel Plicka), and above it, to the north-east, are the ruins of a 13th century castle.

Turčianske Teplice

22km/14 miles south of Martin is the spa of Turčianske Teplice (alt. 520m/1705ft; pop. 6000), one of the oldest in Slovakia, with hot mineral springs (42°C/108°F) and a large park.

Diviaky

In the Diviaky district is a Renaissance castle (second half of 17th c.) which now houses the archives of the Matica Slovenská.

Michalovce L/M 4

Region: Eastern Slovakia
District: Michalovce
Altitude: 115m/375ft
Population: 35,000

Situation and characteristics

The Eastern Slovakian district town of Michalovce, on the river Laborec, is the cultural and economic centre of the Lower Zemplín region. Its principal industries are textiles, ceramics and foodstuffs.

Folk festival

An old-established folk festival is held annually in Michalovce.

Sights

Castle (Museum)

The fine 17th century castle of the Counts Szatáray, built on the foundations of a medieval moated stronghold, now houses a local museum.

Churches

The town's principal church, originally Gothic, was remodelled in Baroque style in the 18th century. There are also an early neo-classical church of 1772 and a neo-Byzantine Orthodox church.

Surroundings of Michalovce

Pozdišovce

4km/2½ miles south-west of Michalovce in the village of Pozdišovce (alt. 123m/404ft; pop. 1500), can be seen a Renaissance castle which was rebuilt in the Gothic style in the 19th century. Pozdišovce has a tradition of ceramic and pottery manufacture going back to the 15th century.

Zemplínska Šírava

6km/4 miles north-east of Michalovce, between the town and the Vihorlat Hills, lies the Zemplínska Šírava, an artificial lake (area 33.5sq.km/ 13sq.miles) formerly known as the Vihorlat Reservoir or Lake Vinna, with recreational and bathing facilities.

Viniansky Hrad

8km/5 miles north-east of Michalovce, on a conspicuous conical hill, are the ruins of Viniansky Hrad, a 14th century castle from which there are extensive views.

Nearby is the Vinianské Jazero, a small lake (8 hectares/20 acres) with facilities for bathing.

Vihorlat Hills

16–26km/10–16 miles north-east of Michalovce are the forest-covered volcanic Vihorlat Hills (up to 1076m/3530ft), with stands of ancient beeches which have the aspect of a primeval forest (nature reserve).

*Eye of the Sea

Below the Sninský Kameň (1005m/3297ft), at an altitude of 618m/2028ft, lies the Morské Oko ("Eye of the Sea"), a beautiful mountain lake (area 14 hectares/35 acres; max. depth 74m/243ft). It is reached by a 2-hour walk through the forest.

Nitra G/H 4

Region: Western Slovakia
District: Nitra
Altitude: 190m/625ft
Population: 89,000

Situation and characteristics

The Western Slovakian district town of Nitra lies below the south side of the Tribeč range on both banks of the river Nitra. A regional centre and the sea of a Roman Catholic bishop, it has a college of agriculture, a teachers' training college and a theatre. Its main industries are chemicals and foodstuffs.

*Townscape

Nitra is a charming town, with its medieval core (much of it a conservation area) merging harmoniously into the newer districts (with some high-rise blocks of flats), all dominated by the castle on its hill.

History

There is much archaeological evidence of very early settlement in this area. In the time of the Great Moravian Empire (9th c.) Nitra was an important centre of the Christian mission to the Slavs. The first church was con-

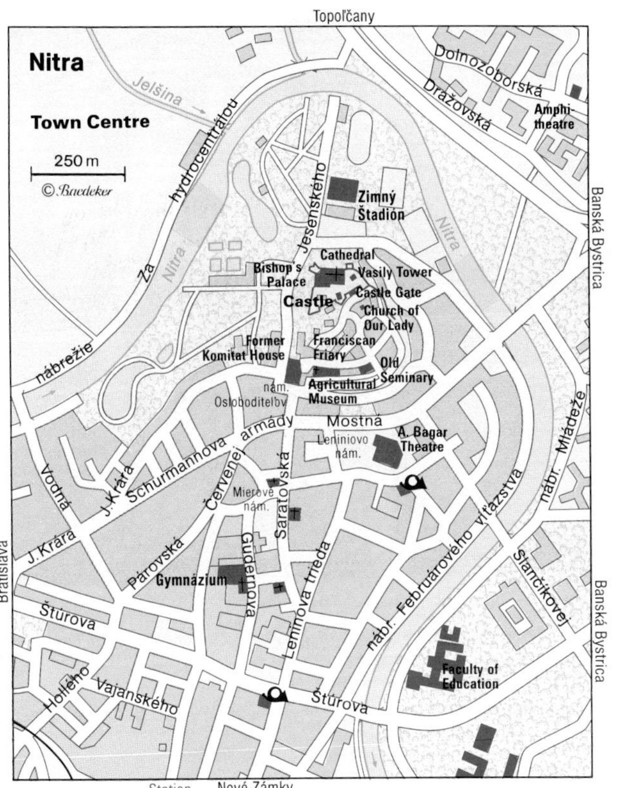

secrated here in 830, during the reign of Prince Pribina, and the bishopric (which still exists) was founded in 880.

Events

A harvest festival and an agricultural show (Agrokomplex) are held here annually in August.

Sights

Castle

On a hill above the right bank of the Nitra stands Nitra Castle, founded in the 11th century and continually altered down to the 17th century. It is now occupied by the Archaeological Institute of the Slovak Academy of Sciences.

Plague Column

In front of the entrance to the castle is a Plague Column of 1750.

Cathedral

Within the castle walls, built in the 17th century to repel Turkish attacks, can be found the Gothic Cathedral (originally 13th–14th c.; remodelled in Baroque style and enlarged in 17th c.).

Archbishop's Palace

Immediately adjoining the Cathedral are the Archbishop's Palace (originally Gothic, later remodelled in Baroque style), with floors levelled from the native rock, and various offices.

Nitra Castle

Figure of Hercules

Old town

Notable features of the old town are the Piarist Church (1701; fine interior), on higher ground; the former Franciscan Church (1630), now the Agricultural Museum; and numerous Renaissance houses.

Párovce

In the outer district of Párovce, in the little Romanesque church of St Stephen (11th–12th c.), can be seen remains of frescoes.

Surroundings of Nitra

Mt Zobor
*View

6km/4 miles north of Nitra is Mt Zobor (588m/1929ft; cableway), the most southerly outlier of the Tribeč range, its slopes covered with forest and vineyards. From the summit there are views extending to the Danube plain. Traces of occupation by prehistoric man have been found in this area.

Mlyňany Arboretum

16km/10 miles east of Nitra lies the Mlyňany Arboretum (60 hectares/150 acres), with some 1600 exotic trees and shrubs.

Jelenec

16km/10 miles north-east of Nitra is the popular summer resort of Jelenec (alt. 192m/630ft), with the ruins of Gýmeš Castle (13th c.; views).

Kostol'any pod Tribečom

18km/11 miles north-east of Nitra, in Kostol'any pod Tribečom (alt. 245m/805ft), can be found an Early Romanesque church (altered in 13th c.), with Romanesque frescoes and a stone font, also Romanesque.

Zlaté Moravce

24km/15 miles north-east of Nitra, on the upper Žitava, we come to the little town of Zlaté Moravce (alt. 196m/643ft; pop. 15,000; engineering), with a Renaissance castle and Renaissance houses. In the cemetery is the grave of the Slovak poet Janko Král' (1822–76).

***Topol'čianky Castle**

At the little town of Topol'čianky (alt. 220m/720ft; pop. 5000), 28km/17 miles north-east of Nitra, stands the handsome castle of Topol'čianky, which once belonged to the Habsburgs and under the first Czechoslovak Republic was the summer residence of the President. Originally built in 1660, it has a later front wing in neo-classical style. The castle is set in a landscaped park, with a large game park (12,000 hectares/30,000 acres; bison, red deer, wild pig, moufflon; stud).

Topol'čany

35km/22 miles north of Nitra, in the valley of the Nitra, is the district town of Topol'čany (alt. 174m/571ft; pop. 35,000), with a Baroque church of 1740. 18km/11 miles north-west of Topol'čany, at Závada, are the ruins of Topol'čany Castle (views).

Topol'čany Castle

Hronský Beňadik

35km/22 miles east of Nitra, on the river Hron, lies Hronský Beňadik (formerly Svätý Beňadik; alt. 192m/630ft), with a former Benedictine monastery (founded in 11th c.; rebuilt in Renaissance period). The monastery church (14th–15th c.) contains several pieces of Gothic sculpture.

Orava Region

I 3

Region: Central Slovakia
District: Dolný Kubín

Situation and *topography

The Orava region, which takes its name from the Orava, a right-bank tributary of the Váh, lies between the Little Fatra (see entry) in the west and the Slovak–Polish frontier on the north and east. It takes in the Middle or Slovakian Beskyds (Stredné Beskydy, Slovenské Beskydy; max. height 1725m/5660ft) in the north and the Oravská Magura (highest point Kubinská Hol'a, 1346m/4416ft; skiing area) to the south. Under the south-east side of the Oravská Magura is the valley of the Orava, one of the most beautiful in Slovakia. The upper course of the river is dammed to form a large artificial lake, the Oravská Priehradná Nádrž; the lower course offers excellent facilities for water sports.

Rural architecture

This was formerly a poor and backward region of Slovakia, which preserved much of its distinctive character into the mid 20th century. In the northern villages there are still many typical old wooden houses and churches (Oravská Lesná, Párnica, Podbiel, Rabča, Zábřež, Zázrivá, Zubrohlava) with thatched or shingled roofs. Particularly fine examples are to be seen in the open-air museum at Zuberec-Brestová, on the road to the Roháče Hills.

Excursions in the *Orava Region

Dolný Kubín

The district town of Dolný Kubín (alt. 468m/1536ft; pop. 20,000; electronic industry), on the lower Orava, is the chief town in the Orava region. Features of interest are the Roman Catholic and the Protestant church (neo-Gothic) and the former Komitat House (Župný Dom; 1868), now an art gallery.

Vyšný Kubín

4km/2½ miles south of Dolný Kubín we come to Vyšný Kubín (alt. 626m/2054ft), birthplace of the Slovak poet Pavol Országh, who wrote under the name of Hviezdoslav (see Famous People).

Choč Hills

From here a road runs through the Choč Hills (Chočské Pohorie; Vel'ky Choč, 1611m/5286ft; waymarked trails, rare limestone flora) to Ružomberok (see entry), in the Váh valley.

Veličná

5km/3 miles west of Dolný Kubín is Veličná (alt. 462m/1516ft; pop. 1000), the oldest commune in the Orava valley (traditional architecture), birthplace of the Slovak painter Petr Bohúň (1822–79).
The village of Zábrež, on the other bank of the Orava, had a fine 16th century church, now in the open-air museum at Zuberec-Brestová.

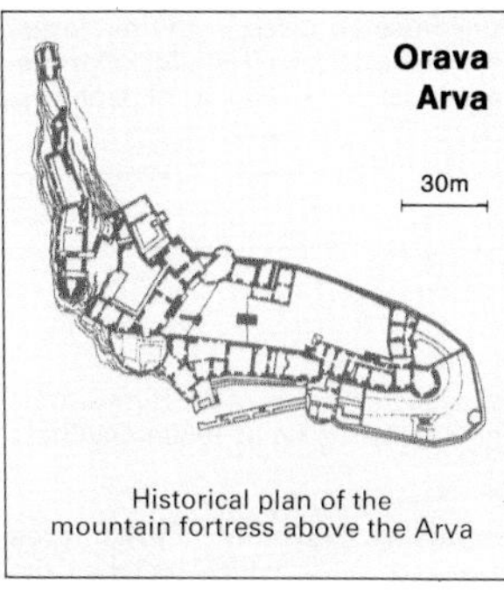

Historical plan of the mountain fortress above the Arva

***Orava Castle**

10km/6 miles north-east of Dolný Kubín, at the village of Oravský Podzámok (alt. 511m/1676ft; pop. 700; neo-classical houses of 1792 onwards, 19th century Old Post House), is Orava Castle (Oravský Hrad; alt. 623m/2044ft), picturesquely perched on a 112m/367ft high limestone crag in the middle of the Orava valley. First mentioned in 1267 as Castrum Arva, the castle was enlarged in the 15th and 16th centuries and much altered and renovated in later centuries. The castle was built in stages on three terraces, and the largest and oldest part is reached by a flight of almost 900 steps. Below the castle were found traces of an early settlement of about 1100 B.C.

Orava Regional Museum

The castle contains a museum on the history of the whole Orava region. From the watch-tower there are magnificent views of the surrounding hills.

***Lake Orava**

30km/19 miles north-east of Dolný Kubín lies Lake Orava (Oravská Priehradná Nádrž; alt. 603m/1978ft), an artificial lake created between 1948 and 1963. The lake, which has an area of 35sq.km/13½sq.miles and extends northward into Poland, pounds the water of the White Orava (Biela Orava), which rises in the Oravská Magura, and the Black Orava (Czarna Orawa), coming from Poland, to power a hydro-electric station below the dam.

The lake, which is up to 38m/125ft deep and well stocked with fish, is a popular holiday area. On its southern and south-eastern shores, fringed by areas of woodland, are a number of hotels, auto-camps and other camping sites, bungalow villages and other holiday accommodation. There are cruises on the lake from the little port of Ůstie nad Priehradou.

Slanica Island of Art

In the lake is the island of Slanický Ostrov Umenia (Slanica Island of Art; boat service from Slanická Osada), with a Baroque church (collection of folk art), a relic of the village of Slanica which was submerged by the lake.

Oravice

South-east of the Orava Dam we come to the charmingly situated village of Oravice (alt. 790m/2590ft), an old woodcutters' settlement which is now a popular holiday centre.

*Juráňova valley

From Oravice it is an hour's walk to the Juráňova valley (Juráňova dolina), one of the most beautiful in Slovakia – a 2km/1¼ mile long limestone canyon through which runs a path hewn from the rock.

Tvrdošín

24km/15 miles north-east of Dolný Kubín, to the south of Lake Orava, is Tvrdošín (alt. 570m/1870ft; pop. 5000), a little town in the Orava valley with a Late Gothic wooden church dating from the second half of the 15th century (wall paintings in popular style).

Trstená

6km/4 miles north-east of Tvrdošín lies Trstená (alt. 607m/1992ft; pop. 4000), a little town founded by German settlers in 1371.

Slovakian Beskyds

The Slovakian or Middle Beskyds (Slovenské Beskydy, Stredné Beskydy), a range of hills between 1000m/3280ft and 1700m/5580ft in height, extends for some 100km/60 miles along the Slovak–Polish frontier in the districts of Žilina and Dolný Kubín.

The western part of the range, the Kysuca uplands, reaches a height of 1236m/4055ft in the Vel'ká Rača and offers excellent skiing conditions in winter. In the eastern part, to the north of Lake Orava, is the Babia Hora (1725m/5660ft), from which there are fine panoramic views.

◀ *Orava Castle*

Hornà Orava Nature Reserve

The Horná Orava (Upper Orava) Nature Reserve takes in the extensive forests (mainly spruce) on the Babia Hora and Mt Pilsko (remains of primeval forest), the area around Lake Orava and several expanses of peat-bog.

Pieniny Hills K 3

Region: Eastern Slovakia
Districts: Poprad and Stará L'ubovňa

Situation and characteristics

The Pieniny Hills are a small limestone massif north-east of the High Tatras, in the border area between Slovakia and Poland, rising to 1050m/3445ft in the Vysoké Skalky.

Pieniny National Park
*Dunajec Canyon

The Pieniny National Park (Pieninský Národný Park; area 21sq.km/8sq.miles) takes in that part of the range which includes the impressive canyon of the Dunajec, the river marking the frontier with Poland. Rock walls up to 300m/985ft high flank this narrow defile, which at some points is no more than 100m/330ft wide.

Raft trips on Dunajec

Raft trips are organised on the 9km/5½ mile long stretch of the Dunajec between Červený Kláštor and Lesnica. A waymarked footpath runs along the banks of the river.

Excursions in the Pieniny Hills

Červený Kláštor

In Červený Kláštor ("Red Monastery"; alt. 465m/1525ft) is a Carthusian monastery founded in 1315 and abandoned at the end of the 18th century. Restored in 1956–66, it now houses a museum with historical, ethnographic and pharmaceutical collections.

Lesnica

The village of Lesnica (alt. 485m/1590ft), on the northern edge of the Pieniny National Park, preserves a number of examples of traditional wooden architecture. There are others in the villages of Haligovce and Vel'ká Lesná, south of Lesnica.

Haligovské Skaly

On the southern edge of the National Park are the Haligovské Skaly, a much eroded complex of limestone crags with scree-covered slopes and numbers of caves (Aksanitka).

Piešt'any G 4

Region: Western Slovakia
District: Trnava
Altitude: 162m/532ft
Population: 33,000

Situation and *importance

The Western Slovakian spa of Piešt'any, whose reputation extends beyond the bounds of Slovakia, lies on the right bank of the Váh, between the Little Carpathians (see entry) in the west and the Inovec Hills which rise immediately east of the town. On the southern outskirts of the town is Lake Slňava (water sports), formed by a dam on the Váh.
Although there is an airfield to the north of the town, most foreign visitors to Piešt'any come from Bratislava (see entry) by bus (motorway, 80km/50 miles).

Piešt'any's reputation as a spa depends on the radioactive sulphurous springs (69°C/156°F; 4 million litres/880,000 gallons daily) on an island in the Váh and on sulphurous mud from a dead arm of the river, which is used

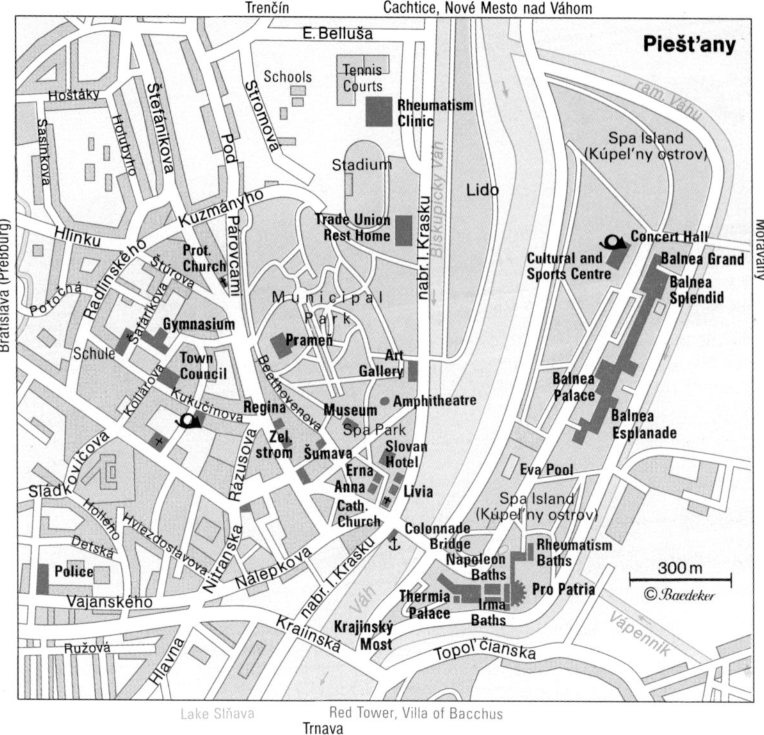

in the treatment of rheumatism (particularly rheumatism of the joints), gout and sciatica, and recently also in organic nervous diseases and the follow-up treatment of injury resulting from an accident.

Sights

Spa Park
Slovan Hotel
Municipal Museum

The life of the spa centres on the large Spa Park (Municipal Park). At the southern end of the park is the Slovan Hotel, and just to the north of this the Municipal Museum (Mestské Múzeum), among the exhibits are displays of colourful traditional costumes which are still worn in the surrounding area and a collection of crutches left by patients who had been cured.

Theatre
Open-air theatre

To the east of the Museum are the Theatre (Divadlo) and the Amphitheatre, an open-air theatre in which performances are given during the Piešt'any Musical Summer.

Protestant Church

On the western edge of the Spa Park stands the Protestant Church.

Colonnade Bridge

To the south of the Slovan Hotel, just beyond the Catholic Church, is the Colonnade Bridge (Kolonádný Most; shops), at the near end of which is the figure of a man breaking his crutches in two – the emblem of the spa.

Spa Island

The Colonnade Bridge crosses the main arm of the Váh to the Spa Island (Kúpelný Ostrov), on which are the largest and most modern of the spa

Piešt'any, on the banks of the Váh

establishments (Balnea Palace, with winter garden; Balnea Grand; Balnea Esplanade). At the south end of the island is the Thermia Palace, with the Irma Baths, and to the east of this the Pro Patria; to the north are the Napoleon Baths (Napoleonské Kúpele).

Thermal swimming pools

Still farther north can be found the Eva Pool, an open-air thermal swimming pool, with an adjoining covered pool.
Also on the island are a golf course and a racecourse.

Krajinský Bridge

To the south of the Colonnade Bridge is the Krajinský Bridge, which spans the main arm and a side arm of the Váh. From the east end of the bridge a footpath leads up in a few minutes to the Red Tower (Červená Veža), from which there is an attractive view of the town.

Villa of Bacchus

A little farther south (15 minutes' walk), surrounded by vineyards, is the Villa of Bacchus, in which Beethoven stayed several times.

Surroundings of Piešt'any

Lake Slňava

Immediately south of the town is Lake Slňava (area 500 hectares/1250 acres), with a bathing beach and two thermal swimming pools.

Brunovce

12km/7½ miles north of Piešt'any, set in a landscaped park, stands the four-towered Renaissance castle of Brunovce (1695–97; in course of restoration).

Čachtice

14km/8½ miles north of Piešt'any is Čachtice (alt. 180m/590ft; pop. 4000), with a Late Gothic fortified church (15th c.) and a Renaissance castle (17th c.). Above the town are the conspicuous ruins of the legendary Čachtice Castle (alt. 375m/1230ft; 13th–17th c.; burned down in 1708), once the seat of Elizabeth Báthory, who was alleged to have had many young girls

murdered so that she might rejuvenate herself by bathing in their blood – for which she was condemned in 1611 to imprisonment for life.
In the karstic terrain of the surrounding area can be found a number of dripstone caves and springs.

Tematín

14km/8½ miles north-east of Piešt'any is Tematín (alt. 525m/1725ft), with the ruins of a 13th century castle. On the slopes of the limestone hills is a nature trail.

Nové Mesto nad Váhom

20km/12½ miles north of Piešt'any lies Nové Mesto nad Váhom (alt. 195m/640ft; pop. 19,000; engineering, foodstuffs industry), an old-world little town with a hydro-electric power station. On higher ground, on the site of an earlier Romanesque church of which the tower survives, is the Gothic parish church, on an octagonal plan (1414–23; remodelled in Baroque style in 1667). There is an interesting local museum. To the east of the town, around the Zelená Voda (Lake), is a recreational area.

Mt Bradlo

25km/15 miles north-west of Piešt'any is Mt Bradlo, with a monument commemorating General Milan Rastislav Štefánik, a close associate of T. G. Masaryk who was killed in an air crash here in 1918.

Poprad

K 3

Region: Eastern Slovakia
District: Poprad
Altitude: 675m/2215ft
Population: 51,000

Situation and characteristics

The Eastern Slovakian district town of Poprad, on the river Poprad, is an important road and rail junction, the "Gateway to the Tatras". It has a variety of industry (engineering, woodworking, foodstuffs).

History

Poprad was one of the 24 "free cities of the Spis" (see entry) founded by German settlers in the 12th and 13th centuries.

Sights

St Giles' Church

In the long market square is the Early Gothic church of St Giles (13th c.; altered in 15th and 18th c.), with Gothic frescoes. The free-standing bell-tower dates from 1658.

Tatras Museum

The Tatras Museum (Podtatranské Múzeum), founded in 1886 as the Carpathian Museum, has an interesting ethnographic collection and the Tatras Art Gallery.

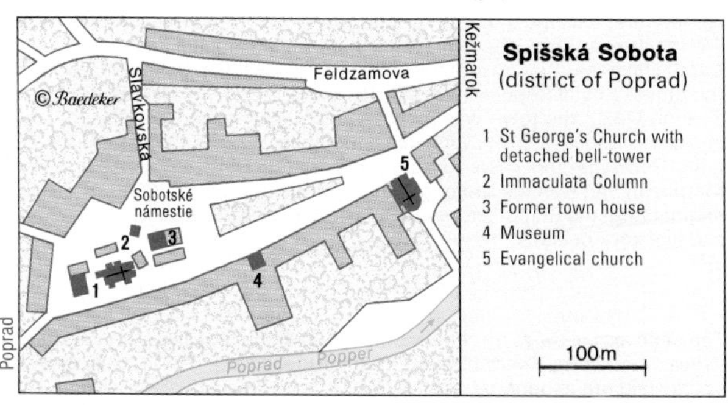

Winter Stadium

Poprad has a Winter Stadium (ice rink).

*Spišská Sobota

2km/1¼ miles north-east is Spišská Sobota (alt. 638m/2093ft), now designated as a conservation area, which was incorporated in Poprad in 1945. First recorded in the 13th century under the name of Forum Sabathi, it has preserved its original character as a medieval craft workers' town. It has an attractive market square with Renaissance and Baroque burghers' houses.

In the market square stands St George's Church (originally Romanesque; altered in the 15th century in Gothic style and later remodelled in Baroque style), with a fine high altar by Master Pavol of Levoča (1516). The Renaissance bell-tower (1598) was also rebuilt in Baroque style in 1728.

Surroundings of Poprad

Gánovce

5km/3 miles south-east of Poprad is Gánovce (alt. 650m/2135ft; pop. 500), with a thermal spring (swimming pool, open only in summer).

The impression of the skull of a primitive man of Neanderthal type, estimated to be 120,000 years old, was found in a quarry near the town.

Svit

7km/4½ miles west of Poprad is Svit (alt. 763m/2503ft; pop. 10,000), a young industrial town (artificial fibres, hosiery),

Tatry Airport

with Poprad's Tatry Airport, now regularly used by scheduled services.

Prešov L 3/4

Region: Eastern Slovakia
District: Prešov
Altitude: 250m/820ft
Population: 87,000

Situation and characteristics

The Eastern Slovakian district town of Prešov, on the river Torysa (a tributary of the Hornád), is the political, cultural and ecclesiastical centre of the Šariš region and of the Carpatho-Ukrainian minority of some 70,000 Ruthenians living in the extreme east and north-east of Slovakia. It is the see of a Catholic and a Ruthenian Uniate bishop; based in the town are the faculties of philosophy and education of the University of Košice (see entry); and in addition to the Slovak Theatre it has the Ukrainian National Theatre.
Since the Second World War Prešov has developed into a regional industrial centre (engineering, clothing, graphic trades, foodstuffs), and the old town centre (declared a conservation area) is now surrounded by modern buildings.

History

The town, situated on an important trade route between the Black Sea and the Baltic, was founded by German settlers at the beginning of the 13th century and became a free royal town under the Hungarian crown in the 14th century. In 1687, after a Protestant rising, the Imperial general Antonio Caraffa held the "bloody tribunal of Prešov" in the town. On June 16th 1919 the Slovak Soviet Republic was proclaimed in Prešov. Under the Treaty of Trianon (1920) the town was incorporated in the newly established Czechoslovak Republic. In 1921 it had a population of 17,580 Slovaks, Hungarians, Germans and Jews (Synagogue of 1888, with decoration by A. Martinelli) and was the see of a Protestant bishop. Its industries included engineering, the manufacture of stoves, schnapps distilleries, mills, grain and livestock dealing.

Sights

Street of the Slovak Soviet Republic

The main axis of the town centre is the Street of the Slovak Soviet Republic (Ulica Slovenskej Republiky Rád), which opens out into an elongated square laid out in gardens.

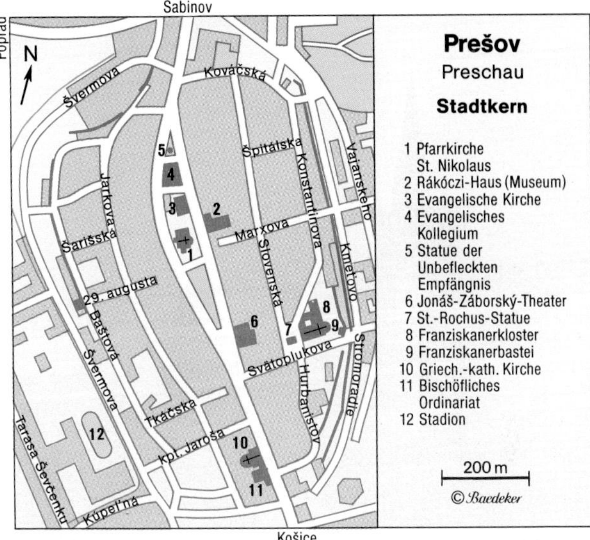

Prešov has numbers of burghers' houses in a Renaissance style which still shows Gothic influences, many of them with richly decorated façades. A notable example is the handsome Rákóczi House, now occupied by a museum. — Burghers' houses

Also in the main street are a Marian Column of 1687, the 19th century Neptune Fountain and an obelisk honouring the Soviet Army. — Marian Column, Neptune Fountain

Prešov has a number of notable churches: the Roman Catholic parish church of St Nicholas (Sv. Mikuláš, 1330–1505, with later alterations, most recently in the 18th century), the Baroque Protestant church (1637–42), the Late Gothic Uniate church (15th c., altered in 18th c.) and the Franciscan church (14th c., rebuilt 1709). — ***Churches**

The bastions and moats of the old fortifications are partly preserved, including the "Caraffa Prison", named after General Antonio Caraffa, who held the notorious "bloody tribunal" of Prešov in 1687. — **Fortifications**, Caraffa Prison

The town's sports facilities include an indoor swimming pool, an outdoor pool and an ice rink. — Sports facilities

In the Nizná Šebastová district, 4km/2½ miles north-east of the town centre, is a Renaissance castle with corner towers. — Nizná Šebastová

In the Solivar district, 3km/2 miles east, is a salt-works which was in operation from the late 16th to the early 19th century. It is now an open-air museum. — **Solivar**

In the Haniska district, on Mt Furča (305m/1001ft), can be seen a monument commemorating one of the last peasant risings, in 1831. — Haniska

There are beautiful recreation areas at Dúbrava (forest park), 4km/2½ miles north, Borkút (4km/2½ miles south) and Cemjata (4km/2½ miles west), a former spa. — Recreation areas

St Nicholas's Church, Prešov

Surroundings of Prešov

Vel'ký Šariš

6km/4 miles north-west of Prešov, Vel'ký Šariš (alt. 269m/883ft; pop. 5000) has an Early Gothic church (13th c.; altered in 17th–18th c.) and a Baroque cemetery chapel (17th c.). Of the Renaissance castle in which Ferenc II Rákoczi (1676–1735) plotted the last great rising of the Hungarian nobility against the House of Habsburg at the beginning of the 18th century there remains only the Gothic chapel (originally 14th c.). The rest of the castle was destroyed by fire.

Šariš Castle

On a hill north-west of Vel'ký Šariš (572m/1877ft; nature reserve) are the ruins of Šariš Castle (13th c.; burned down 1687), which gave its name to the area.

Brežany

10km/6 miles west of Prešov, in the commune of Brežany, can be seen a wooden church, built in 1727 on the model of the church at Hervartov.

Sabinov

Sabinov (alt. 324m/1063ft; pop. 6000), 15km/9 miles north-west of Prešov, has remains of 15th–16th century fortifications on the south side of the town and a 14th century Gothic church (fine interior). In the market square is a bell-tower of 1657. Local museum.

Hanušovce nad Topl'ou

23km/14 miles north-east of Prešov is Hanušovce nad Topl'ou (alt. 190m/625ft; pop. 2500), a little town on the right bank of the Topl'a with an early 18th century Baroque castle (local museum).

Krompachy

25km/15 miles south-west of Prešov we come to Krompachy (alt. 380m/1245ft; pop. 6000), an old mining town in which a steelworks with several blast furnaces and a power station were established at the beginning of the 20th century.
The town has preserved a number of burghers' houses as well as the Town Hall and a mansion, both in Baroque/neo-classical style.

Rožňava K 4

Region: Eastern Slovakia
District: Rožňava
Altitude: 314m/1030ft
Population: 22,000

Situation, history and characteristics

The Eastern Slovakian district town of Rožňava lies in a basin on the river Slaná, between the Slovakian Ore Mountains (see entry) to the north and the Slovakian Karst (see entry) to the south. This old mining town, founded by German settlers in the 13th century (now the see of a bishop, with a large Hungarian population) has an iron and steel works using ore worked in the surrounding area (mainly iron; only small quantities of non-ferrous ores).

Sights

Churches

There are three notable churches: the former cathedral (originally Gothic, 13th–14th c.; altered in 15th and 16th c.) in the market square, the former Premonstratensian church (mid 17th c.) and the Franciscan church (18th c.). In the market square is a Late Renaissance tower (1643–57), from which there are extensive views.

Bishop's Palace
Old Mint
Mining Museum

Other features of interest are the Bishop's Palace (Empire style, late 17th c.), the Old Mint (17th c.) and the informative Mining Museum.

Surroundings of Rožňava

Brzotín

5km/3 miles north of Rožňava is the old mining town of Brzotín (alt. 267m/876ft; pop. 1500), now incorporated in Rožňava, where gold was worked in the Middle Ages. Features of interest are two churches, a castle and the ruins of a medieval stronghold.
To the south of the town are the Brzotín Crags, falling steeply down to the Silická plain.

Betliar

5km/3 miles north-west of Rožňava is Betliar (alt. 320m/1050ft; pop. 1500), with a 16th century hunting lodge, formerly the property of the Counts Andrássy, which was remodelled in 1880 in the style of a French château. It is now a Museum of Interior Design (furniture, porcelain, pottery, hunting trophies, clocks, pictures, library; exotica). The house is surrounded by a beautiful English-style landscaped park.

Krásna Hôrka Castle

5km/3 miles east of Rožňava, above the little town of Krasnohorské Podhradie (alt. 350m/1150ft; pop. 2000; parish church of 1460, altered 1590–1620), stands the well preserved castle of Krásna Hôrka (alt. 500m/1640ft), originally built in the 13th century, enlarged and strengthened in 1578–83 as a stronghold against Turkish attacks and finally converted into an imposing noble residence from 1676 onwards. After restoration in 1905 it became the family museum of the Counts Andrássy; it is now a branch of the Betliar museum.

*Andrássy Mausoleum

In a small park on the road to Košice can be found the mausoleum built by Count Dionysius Andrassy for his wife Franziska (d. 1902). The pantheon-like interior of this sandstone building in Art Nouveau style, the work of German and Italian artists, is richly decorated with coloured marbles from many countries in the world and polychrome mosaics. The mausoleum is now a section of the Betliar museum.

Štítník

14km/8½ miles west of Rožňava is the former mining town of Štítník (alt. 286m/938ft; pop. 1500), where iron ore was mined from the 12th century.

The fine Gothic church (14th–15th c.), with a massive tower, has Gothic frescoes (14th–16th c.) and the oldest organ in Slovakia (1792). Other features of interest are the ruins of a moated castle, part of which was converted in the 19th century into church offices, and a number of examples of Slovak traditional architecture.

Plešivec

15km/9 miles south-west of Rožňava is Plešivec (alt. 218m/715ft; pop. 2500), formerly the chief town of the Gemer district. At one time lead and zinc were mined in the area. The principal church (14th c.) has remains of Gothic wall paintings; the tower was a 19th century addition. There are also the ruins of a 13th century moated castle.

Jelšava

22km/13½ miles south-west of Rožňava is Jelšava (alt. 258m/846ft; pop. 3500), an old mining town with a former Town Hall in Rococo style (1781) and an Empire-style mansion (1796–1801) in the market square.

Ružomberok

I 3

Region: Central Slovakia
District: Liptovský Mikuláš
Altitude: 486m/1595ft
Population: 29,000

Situation and characteristics

The old mining town of Ružomberok in the Liptov region lies on the left bank of the Váh and on both sides of its tributary the Revúca. To the south-west are the Great Fatra (Vel'ká Fatra) uplands, to the north-east the Choč Hills.
The town's principal industries are now woodworking, paper and cellulose manufacture and textiles.

Sights

St Andrew's Church

In the main square stands the town's principal church, St Andrew's (14th c., with later alterations), which has an early 16th century Gothic font.

SNP Obelisk

Close by is an obelisk commemorating those who died in the Slovak National Uprising (SNP) of 1944.

Town Hall

Other features of interest are the neo-Baroque Town Hall and a number of 18th century craftsmen's houses.

Liptov Museum

The Liptov Museum has a large collection of material on the mining and folk traditions of the surrounding area and a gallery of pictures by the Slovak painter L'udovít Fulla (1902–80).

Piarist monastery

The Late Baroque Piarist monastery (end of 18th century) has an early 19th century church in Empire style.

Castle

Near the railway station is a 14th century Gothic castle (with much later alteration).

Open-air museum

In the Vlkolínec district of the town is an open-air museum with good examples of Slovak traditional architecture.

Surroundings of Ružomberok

Likava Castle

4km/2½ miles north of the town are the ruins of Likava Castle (14th–17th c.).

Lúčky Lázně

12km/7½ miles north-east of Ružomberok is Lúčky Lázně (alt. 616m/2021ft), a spa founded in 1761. Between the town and the spa establishment are large outcrops of travertine.

A decorative 19th-century façade in Ružomberok

Mt Salatín

12km/7½ miles south-east of Ružomberok is Mt Salatín (1630m/5348ft). The ascent (from Ludrová) of this isolated hill is worth while not only for the sake of the interesting limestone flora to be seen on the way up but also for the magnificent panoramic views, taking in almost all the ranges of hills in Slovakia, to be enjoyed from the summit.

**Views

L'ubochňa

12km/7½ miles west of Ružomberok is L'ubochňa (alt. 445m/1460ft), a climatic resort which also provides a water cure.

The L'ubochňa valley (L'ubochianská dolina) extends south for some 25km/15 miles into the Great Fatra (Vel'ká Fatra; narrow-gauge railway). In the valley are seven areas designated as nature reserves, including the dolomitic hill of Čierný Kameň.

Magurka

18km/11 miles south-east of Ružomberok we come to Magurka (alt. 1036m/3399ft), a mining settlement founded in the 13th century. A few abandoned gold and silver workings can still be seen.

Magurka is now a quiet holiday resort, a good base for hill walks and climbs in the western part of the Low Tatras (see entry) – for example to Mt Chabenec (1955m/6414ft; 3½ hours), a hill, offering extensive views, which featured in the Slovak National Uprising (SNP) of 1944.

3km/2 miles north-west of Magura is Železnô, a little summer resort with a children's holiday home.

Donovaly

25km/15 miles south of Ružomberok lies Donovaly (alt. 960m/3150ft; cableway up Mt Zvolen, 1402m/4600ft; ski-lifts), a tourist centre which is particularly busy in winter.

Korytnica Kúpele

North-east of Donovaly is the spa of Korytnica Kúpele (alt. 847m/2779ft), whose mineral springs were already known in the 16th century and are now used for internal complaints.

Kalište

The commune of Kalište (alt. 900m/2950ft), south of Donovaly, was a centre of the Slovak National Uprising of 1944. The village was burned down by the Germans and the inhabitants murdered (commemorative monument).

Great Fatra

The Great Fatra (Veľ'ká Fatra) uplands occupy an area of some 1200sq.km/465sq.miles between the towns of Ružomberok, Banská Bystrica and Martin (see entries), rising to a height of 1592m/5223ft in Mt Ostredok. It is a region of great scenic beauty but so far with little in the way of tourist infrastructure. Most of the main ridge, except the northern section, is treeless, but some 90% of the range as a whole is covered with beech and spruce forests; there are also large numbers of yews.

On the west side of the range wild and beautiful valleys with karstic formations (for example the Gäderská dolina) extend up into the hills. Access from the north is facilitated by a cabin cableway from Ružomberok (Hrabovo-Máliné, 1209m/3967ft), from the south by a cableway from Turecká, to the north of Banská Bystrica. There is a good footpath from Harmanec through the Bystrická dolina to the hotel below the Král'ovna Studňa (1384m/4541ft).

Slovakian Karst / Slovenský Kras — K 4

Region: Eastern Slovakia
Districts: Rožňava and Kosice-Vidiek

Situation and *topography

The Slovakian Karst (Slovenský Kras), the largest area of karstic terrain in Slovakia, extends south-west and south-east of the district town of Rožňava, near the Slovak–Hungarian frontier.

The meaning of the term "plain" (*planina*) in this karstic region can be seen from the examples of the Plešivská planina south-west of Rožňava and the Silická planina to the south of the town, which make up the greater part of the Slovakian Karst and show typical karstic features such as rock caves and ice caves, bizarre rock formations, gorges and deep canyons cut by watercourses through the 300–500m/980–1640ft deep limestone strata. The pattern is similar to some extent in the eastern outliers of the karstic terrain, the hills of the Turnianská planina (on which are the ruins of a medieval castle).

Features in the **Slovakian Karst

Brázda Gorge

The Brázda Gorge, 10km/6 miles south of Rožňava, is one of the deepest in the country (180m/590ft).

Silická Ice Gorge

Near the village of Silica, 10km/6 miles south-west of Rožňava, is the impressive Silická L'adnica, an ice gorge 85m/280ft deep, with a 12m/40ft high ice-fall.

Gombasek Cave

Near the village of Gombasek (alt. 249m/817ft), 11km/7 miles south-west of Rožňava, is the Gombasek dripstone cave (Gombasecká jaskyňa), with thin stalactites up to 3m/10ft long and reddish waterfalls on the walls. The "Marble Hall" is used in the relief of asthma and allergies.

Ochtina Cave

18km/11 miles west of Rožňava, on the western edge of the Slovakian Karst, is the Ochtina aragonite cave (alt. 660m/2165ft), with exceptionally delicate crystal formations (mostly in the form of "flowers").

***Domica Cave**

The Domica Cave (Jaskyňa Domica), 26km/16 miles south of Rožňava, is a large limestone cave system with numerous chambers, halls, domes, columns and colourful stalactitic formations, in which traces of occupation by prehistoric man were found.

***Aggtelek Cave**

An underground stream known as the Styx links the Domica Cave with the still larger Aggtelek Cave in Hungary. Boat trips operate between the two caves from June to October.

The Ochtina Cave in the Slovakian Karst

The whole cave system with its various ramifications has a total length of 21km/13 miles, of which 7km/4½ miles are in the Domica Cave. The tour of the caves (including boat trips) takes 1½–2 hours.

Zádiel canyon

The Zádiel canyon (Zádielska dolina), with a great variety of limestone formations and a number of waterfalls, begins at the village of Zádiel (alt. 236m/774ft), 22km/13½ miles east of Rožňava. The canyon, traversed by the little river Blatnica, is some 3km/2 miles long and at many points only 10m/33ft wide, with rock walls rising vertically to a height of up to 400m/1300ft.

Slovakian Ore Mountains / Slovenské Rudohorie I–L 4

Region: Eastern Slovakia
Districts: Banská Bystrica, Rožňava and Košice-Vidiek

Situation and characteristics

The Slovakian Ore Mountains (Slovenské Rudohorie) are a range which extends westward from Košice (see entry) for some 145km/90 miles.
During the Middle Ages the area, which is mostly forest-covered, attracted German settlers with its rich mineral resources (precious metals, iron). Thanks to its remoteness it has remained relatively unspoiled and there is little tourist traffic.

Excursions in the Slovakian Ore Mountains

Volovec
Kojšovská Hol'a

The most easterly part of the Slovakian Ore Mountains, with the peaks of Volovec (1284m/4213ft) and Kojšovská Hol'a (1246m/4088ft), is the most visited. It offers excellent conditions both for summer holidays and for winter sports.

A woodman's house in the Slovakian Ore Mountains

Muránska Planina

Farther west is the Muránska planina (Kl'ak, 1409m/4623ft), a plateau with more than 100 karstic caves.

Under the south-east side of the plateau is Muráň (alt. 394m/1293ft; pop. 1500), with the imposing ruins of a medieval castle (alt. 938m/3078ft;; originally 13th c., rebuilt in 16th c.).

Mt Stolica

20km/12½ miles east of Muráň rises the highest peak in the Slovakian Ore Mountains, Mt Stolica (1476m/4843ft).

Pol'ana

At the west end of the range is the Pol'ana massif (1458m/4784ft). Below the south-east side of the hills is Čierny Balog (alt. 550m/1805ft; pop. 6000), where traditional costumes are still frequently worn. In the surrounding area are numerous shepherds' and woodcutters' settlements. To the south of Čierny Balog are areas of primeval forest (Dobročský prales), now protected as nature reserves.

A narrow-gauge railway 11.5km/7 miles long, opened in 1909, runs between Hronec, Čierny Balog and Vydrovská Dolina.

Slovakian Paradise / Slovenský Raj K 3/4

Region: Eastern Slovakia
Districts: Spišská Nová Ves, Rožňava and Poprad

Situation and *topography
***Slovakian Paradise National Park**

The region known as the Slovakian Paradise (Slovenský Raj) lies in the northern Slovakian Ore Mountains (see entry), and within this region an area of 140sq.km/54sq.miles has been designated as a National Park. This limestone plateau, abraded and eaten away by erosion, shows not only typical karstic features such as dolines and caves but also numerous deep, narrow canyons, gorges and waterfalls and a varied flora and fauna.

Convenient bases from which to explore the region are Dobšiná to the south and Spišská Nová Ves to the east. For water sports enthusiasts the gorge of the river Hornád offers a challenge.

Excursions in the **Slovakian Paradise

Dobšiná

Charmingly situated towards the south of the Slovakian Paradise is the little mining town of Dobšiná (alt. 468m/1536ft; pop. 4500), founded in the first half of the 14th century (old iron and copper workings).

Dedinky

Dedinky (alt. 790m/2590ft), 13km/8 miles north of Dobšiná, another little town founded in the 14th century, lies below the sheer rock walls of the Gačovská Skala (1106m/3629ft). It has become an increasingly popular holiday resort since the damming of the river Hnilec to form a lake, the Palcmanská Masa (1956). This is a good base for walks and climbs on the Geravy karstic plateau (cableway; hotel).

Stratená

Stratená (alt. 860m/2820ft; pop. 500), 11km/7 miles north-west of Dobšiná on a pass road, originally a mining village, is a good base for walks in the Stratenská dolina and the ascent of the Havrania Skala (1157m/3796ft), one of the finest viewpoints in the Slovakian Paradise. At the foot of the south-eastern face of the hill is a sporadically active spring, the Občasný prameň (alt. 920m/3020ft).

***Dobšiná Ice Cave**

17km/10½ miles north-west of Dobšiná is a car park, from which it is a half hour's climb on an attractive forest path to the entrance to the Dobšiná Ice Cave (Dobšinská L'adová Jaskyňa; alt. 969m/3179ft).

The cave, discovered in 1870, has a total area of some 8800sq.m/10,500sq.yd (of which 7000sq.m/8400sq.yd are ice-covered) and a total length of about 1400m/1530yd (of which 475m/520yd are accessible for visitors). The very striking formations are of the purest crystallised ice. In the lower part of the cave, which can be entered only in summer, the temperature falls as low as −7°C/+19°F (warm clothing and stout footwear advisable). A tour of the cave takes about an hour.

Town Hall, Spišska Nová Ves

Mlynky

Mlynky (alt. 739m/2425ft), an old mining village in the Hnilec valley, on the south-eastern edge of the Slovakian Paradise, is now the leading winter sports centre in the region.

Vernár

The village of Vernár (alt. 778m/2553ft), on the western edge of the Slovakian Paradise, has typical examples of traditional architecture.

Švermovo

Švermovo (formerly called Telgárt; alt. 881m/2891ft; pop. 2500) is the highest commune in the Hron valley (carbonated springs). The village was completely destroyed during the fighting in 1944 and was rebuilt after the war.

Spišská Nová Ves

Spišská Nová Ves (alt. 458m/1503ft; pop. 37,000) is an important district town (woodworking, ore-mining) in the valley of the Hornád. It was granted its municipal charter in 1407; from 1412 to 1772 it was under Polish rule; and thereafter it succeeded Levoča (see entry) as "capital" of the autonomous Spiš region (see entry).

In the market square are the neo-classical Town Hall (1780–1820) and the Reduta (1900–05) in Sezession style (the Viennese version of Art Nouveau). Other features of interest are the Gothic parish church (second half of 14th c.; neo-Gothic tower 86m/282ft high; "Calvary" by Master Pavol of Levoča) and several Renaissance and neo-classical burghers' houses.

On the right bank of the Hornád is the Šestnáctka district (*šestnáct* = 16), with the houses of the representatives of the 16 (originally 24) free cities of the Spiš.

Čingov

Čingov (alt. 420m/1380ft) is a popular holiday centre on the north-eastern edge of the Slovakian Paradise National Park. Within easy reach are the Hornád gorge and the rock terrace (viewpoint) of Tamášovsky Výhlad.

Kláštorisko

Kláštorisko (alt. 744m/2441ft), the only tourist resort in the heart of the Slovakian Paradise, can be reached only on foot. This is another good base from which to reach the Hornád gorge.

Podlesok

The holiday resort of Podlesok (alt. 550m/1805ft) lies on the north-western edge of the Slovakian Paradise. It is a good base from which to visit the Suchá Belá canyon.

Markušovce

6km/4 miles south-east of Spišská Nová Ves, on the left bank of the Hornád, is the little town of Markušovce (alt. 445m/1460ft; pop. 3000), with a Renaissance castle of 1643 (later remodelled in Rococo style; museum of historic furniture). In the little summer palace of Dardanely is a museum of historic keyboard instruments. There are also the ruins of a late 13th century castle.

Spiš

K 3/4

Historic territory
Region: Eastern Slovakia

The Spiš (German Zips, Hungarian Szepes) is a historic territory taking in the area below the south-east side of the High Tatras (the Upper Spiš), the upper valleys of the Poprad and the Hornád (the Spiš Basin) and the mining area of the Slovakian Ore Mountains (see entry) around Gelnica (the Lower Spiš). The cultural centre of the territory was the town of Kežmarok (see entry).

History

In the 12th century the Hungarian kings settled peasants from central Germany and Silesia in the Upper Spiš; then in the 13th century they brought in German miners and craftsmen to seven towns in the Lower

Spiš. In 1370 24 "cities" of the Upper Spiš were granted autonomy under their own counts and their own code of law. The two largest towns, Kežmarok and Levoča, became free royal towns under the Hungarian crown. In 1412 the Emperor Sigismund pledged 13 of the 24 towns and three other "crown towns" to Poland, and in 1769 these 16 towns were united with Hungary (county of Szepes). In 1876 they lost their autonomy. During the 19th century the position of the German population of the Spiš was threatened by the emigration of Germans, the moving in of Slovaks and the Hungarian government's policy of Magyarisation. The incorporation of the Spiš in the first Czechoslovak Republic in 1918–19, when there were still 37,000 Germans in the territory, made possible a revival of the German schools; but after the Second World War the German population was expelled, and there are now only a few German-speakers left in the Spiš.

Starý Smokovec K 3

Region: Eastern Slovakia
District: Poprad
Altitude: 1017m/3337ft
Population: 1000

*Situation and *characteristics

Starý Smokovec, the main Slovak tourist centre below the High Tatras (see entry), lies in a sheltered situation amid coniferous forests at the foot of the Slavkovský Štít (2452m/8045ft; 5 hours' climb). It is a popular summer holiday resort (festival programme) but is particularly busy as a winter sports centre (good skiing area, toboggan run). The exhibitions in the Tatras Art Gallery provide an additional attraction.

Transport

Starý Smokovec lies only 12km/7½ miles north of the district town of Poprad (see entry; Tatry Airport) and is connected with it by a narrow-gauge electric railway, which runs west to Štrbské Pleso and east to Tatranská Lomnica (see entries).

Surroundings of Starý Smokovec

Funicular to Hrebienok

Just above the Grand Hotel, to the north, is the lower station (Smokovecký Výstup, 1025m/3365ft) of a 2km/1¼ mile long funicular (Pozemná Lanovká) which reaches in 11 minutes the morainic ridge of Hrebienok (1280m/4200ft; ski-lift).

Walks and climbs

From the Hrebienok there are a variety of rewarding walks and climbs of only moderate difficulty – for example north-west through beautiful forest and rock country, passing two waterfalls on the Studený Potok, and then either north-west into the 7km/4½ mile long Vel'ká Studená Dolina or, more steeply, north up the terraced Malá Studená Dolina in about 3 hours to the Five Spiš Lakes (Pät' Spišských Plies) at the head of the valley (mountain hut; 2015m/6610ft), in a magnificent landscape enclosed by the rock walls of the Lomnický Štít (2632m/8636ft) and the L'adový Štít (2628m/8622ft).

***Five Spiš Lakes**

Freedom Road

Nový Smokovec

Immediately west of Starý Smokovec on the "Freedom Road" (Cesta Slobody; Starý Smokovec to Štrbské Pleso) is the altitude resort of Nový Smokovec (alt. 992m/3255ft; pop. 1200), with several sanatoria and holiday homes.

Tatranská Polianka

Farther west are Tatranské Sruby (pop. 100) and Tatranská Polianka (alt. 1003m/3291ft), an altitude resort in the forest.

Slezský Dům

Two hours' walk north of Tatranská Polianka is the Slezský Dům (Silesian House; alt. 1663m/5456ft), at the south end of a little lake, the Velické Pleso.

Grand Hotel, Starý Smokovec

**Gerlachovský Štít

From here it is a 5-hour climb (guide essential; last section difficult) up the Velická dolina (rich Alpine flora) to the summit of the Gerlachovský Štít (2655m/8711ft), the highest peak in the High Tatras, from which there are superb panoramic views.

Vyšné Hágy

6km/4 miles beyond Tatranská Polianka on the "Freedom Road" is the charmingly situated altitude resort of Vyšné Hágy (alt. 1072m/3517ft).

Štrbské Pleso K 3

Region: Eastern Slovakia
District: Poprad
Altitude: 1350m/4430ft
Population: 400

*Situation and *characteristics

The village of Štrbské Pleso below the south side of the High Tatras (see entry), on the watershed between the rivers Váh and Poprad, is the highest commune in Slovakia. Situated amid extensive forests on the shores of the lake from which it takes its name (area 20 hectares/50 acres), it is widely famed as an altitude resort, a summer holiday place (open-air swimming pool, boat hire) and a winter sports centre.

**Views

From the lake there are magnificent views northward of the Tatras peaks, from Mt Kriváň to the Slavkovský Štít, and from the railway station side southward of the Váh, Poprad and Hornád valleys, with the chain of the Low Tatras (see entry) beyond.

Transport

Štrbské Pleso lies 23km/14 miles north-west of Poprad (see entry; Tatry Airport), with which it is connected by a narrow-gauge electric railway via Starý Smokovec.

Štrbské Pleso, at the foot of the High Tatras

Surroundings of Štrbské Pleso

Skiing area

At the mouth of the Mlynická dolina lies an extensive skiing area (two ski-jumps, langlauf trails; chair-lift up Mt Solisko, 1830m/6004ft; ski-lifts).

Mengusovská dolina
***Lake Poprad**

There is a rewarding walk (1½ hours) on a path which runs up the beautiful Mengusovská dolina to Lake Poprad (Popradské Pleso; 11513m/4964ft; area 7 hectares/17 acres). On the south side of the lake is a climbers' cemetery with a chapel.

Mt Ostrva
****Mt Rysy**

From Lake Poprad it is 1½ hours' walk east to Mt Ostrva (1984m/6510ft; extensive views) and 3 hours' walk north to Mt Rysy (2499m/8199ft; mountain hut), one of the most rewarding climbs in the whole of the Tatras, with magnificent views.

***Mt Kriváň**

From Štrbské Pleso it is a 5–6 hours' climb of no great difficulty to the summit of Mt Kriváň, to the west of the main ridge of the High Tatras.

Tatranská Lomnica K 3

Region: Eastern Slovakia
District: Poprad
Altitude: 849m/2786ft
Population: 1500

*Situation and
*characteristics

Tatranská Lomnica is a magnificently situated resort, commanding wide views, which attracts visitors both in summer and in winter. It ranks with Starý Smokovec and Štrbské Pleso (see entries) as one of the leading tourist centres in the Slovakian High Tatras.

Autumn in Tatranská Lomnica

TANAP

In Tatranská Lomnica are the offices of the Tatras National Park (Tatranský Národný Park, TANAP) and the Guide and Mountain Rescue Service. The TANAP Museum displays the flora and fauna and illustrates the history and way of life of the High Tatras, and also has a showroom selling local craft products.

Transport

Tatranská Lomnica lies 18km/11 miles north of Poprad (see entry; Tatry Airport), with which it is connected by a narrow-gauge electric railway (via Starý Smokovec).

Auto-camp

On the Poprad–Vel'ká Lomnica–Tatranská Lomnica road is a well equipped auto-camp, Eurocamp FICC (the largest in the country).

Surroundings of Tatranská Lomnica

****Lomnický Štít**

At the Grand Hotel Praha, above the town on the north, is the lower station (989m/3245ft) of a 5847m/6395yd long cableway, the Visutá Lanovka (in high season seats must be reserved in advance), which climbs in 23 minutes by way of the intermediate Štart station (1150m/3775ft) to the Encián Hotel near the observatory on the Skalnaté Pleso (1750m/5740ft; good skiing, mountain hut; chair-lift to Lomnický Hrebeň, 2200m/7220ft). From the Skalnaté Pleso another cableway runs up in 11 minutes to the Lomnický Štít (2632m/8636ft), the second highest peak in the High Tatras, with superb near and distant views.

Walk to the ***Green Lake**

From the Tatranské Matliare district (alt. 896m/2940ft) it is 3km/2 miles north-east up the valley of the Biela Voda (White Water), passing on the right the Stežky (1530m/50020ft), a morainic ridge, to the Šalviový Prameň (Spring; alt. 1200m/3940ft; 45 minutes). From here, after crossing a bridge to the right bank of the stream, it is a 90 minutes' walk to the Green Lake

(Zelené Pleso, 1545m/5070ft; mountain hut) in a grandiose setting at the head of the valley, enclosed by the sheer rock walls of the Vel'ká Svišt'ovka (2037m/6683ft), the Kežmarský Štít (2558m/8393ft), the Lastovičia Veža (2625m/8613ft), the Vyššia Barania Strážnica (2526m/8288ft), the Kolový Štít (2418m/7933ft) and the legendary sugarloaf-shaped Jastrabia Veža (2137m/7011ft).
In winter this is also a very rewarding trek for experienced langlauf skiers.

Trebišov L 4

Region: Eastern Slovakia
District: Trebišov
Altitude: 109m/358ft
Population: 15,000

Situation and characteristics

The district town of Trebišov, some 50km/30 miles east-south-east of Košice (see entry) beyond the Slanské Vrchy, is the chief place of the Zemplín region in the Eastern Slovakian Plain (Východoslovenská Nižina), near the Slovak–Hungarian frontier.

Sights

Castle

Trebišov Castle, a Baroque structure of 1786, now houses a local museum.

Andrássy Mausoleum

In the castle's English-style landscaped park can be seen the neo-Gothic Mausoleum (1893) of the great Hungarian noble family of the Andrássys.

Pavič Castle

Archaeological excavations are in progress on the site of Pavič Castle (1254), now in ruins.

Monastery and church

Also of interest are a monastery founded in 1529 and its church (originally Late Gothic, remodelled in the Baroque period).

Surroundings of Trebišov

Král'ovský Chimec

30km/19 miles south-east of Trebišov and only some 10km/6 miles west of the point where the frontiers of Slovakia, Hungary and the Ukraine meet is the little town of Král'ovsky Chimec (alt. 130m/425ft). Features of interest are the largest Slav cemetery in Eastern Slovakia, the remains of a medieval castle and a Gothic church remodelled in Baroque style.

Trenčín H 4

Region: Western Slovakia
District: Trenčín
Altitude: 211m/692ft
Population: 57,000

Situation and characteristics

The Western Slovakian district town of Trenčín lies on the left bank of the Váh, on the south-eastern fringe of the White Carpathians (Bíle Karpaty), along the crest of which extends the Slovak–Czech frontier (the former frontier between Hungary and Moravia). Trenčín is an important road and rail junction and an industrial town (engineering, textiles, foodstuffs).

Sights

***Castle**

Above the town, on a massive crag, loom the imposing ruins of a castle which was founded in the 11th century, rebuilt and strengthened in the 13th

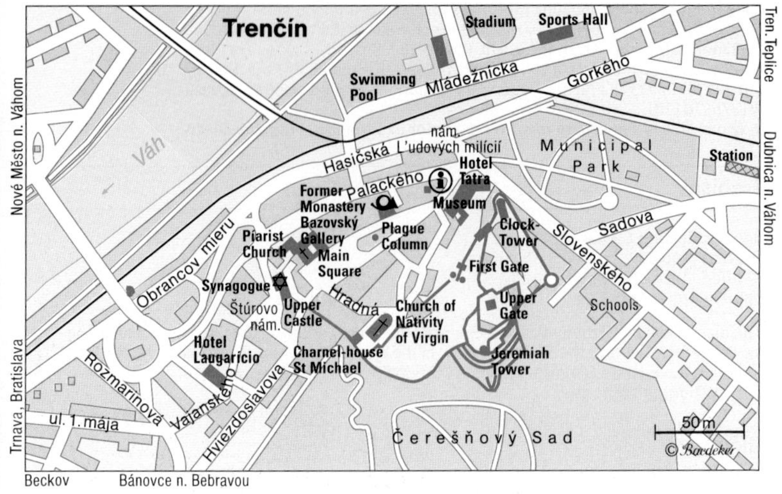

century to defend the middle Váh valley (the 33m/108ft high keep dates from this period) and considerably enlarged in the 15th and 16th centuries. In 1790 the castle was burned down and thereafter was abandoned. Since 1954 it has been in course of restoration, and part of the District Museum is now installed in the restored buildings. In the courtyard of the castle is the "Lovers' Well", which according to the legend was dug by a Turkish prince in the 15th century as the ransom for his bride, who was held prisoner by the lord of the castle. A Latin inscription of A.D. 179 on the castle rock (thought to be the oldest writing on the soil of Slovakia) records a victory of the Roman legion stationed here in the fort of Laugaricio over a Germanic tribe, the Quadi.

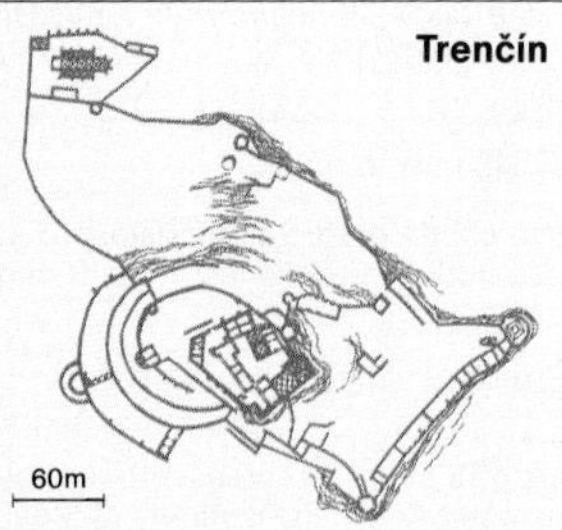

Historical plan of the Castle of Trenčin (a summit fortress with many ranges, extensive outworks, and an adjoining fortified church)

View

From the castle there are extensive views of the Váh valley.

Parish church

Built against the castle rock is the Gothic parish church of the Nativity of the Virgin (14th c.; altered 1528), with a magnificent alabaster altar (perhaps by G. R. Donner) in the Illéshazy Chapel.

Piarist Church

In the long market square is the twin-towered Baroque Piarist Church (early 18th c.).

Burghers' houses
Town walls
Plague Column
Synagogue

Other features of interest in the town are a number of Renaissance and Baroque houses, some well preserved remains of the old town walls (including a 16th century town gate), a Plague Column of 1712 and a large synagogue.

Trenčín Castle

Surroundings of Trenčín

Trenčianské Teplice

12km/7½ miles north-east of Trenčín is the spa of Trenčianské Teplice (alt. 268m/879ft; pop. 4000), picturesquely situated on the river Teplička in a wooded upland region. The town has several sulphurous springs at temperatures of up to 40°C/104°F. A striking feature of the spa is the Moorish-style Sina Baths. There is also a thermal swimming pool, the Zelená Žába ("Green Frog"). The "Musical Summer" is an annual musical festival.

Dubnica nad Váhom

13km/8 miles north-east of Trenčín is the industrial town of Dubnica nad Váhom (alt. 242m/794ft; pop. 19,000; engineering plants), with a castle (16th and 17th c.) surrounded by a park and a pillory of 1728.

Beckov
*Castle

15km/9 miles south-west of Trenčín lies the little town of Beckov (pop. 2000), above which rear the picturesque ruins of Beckov Castle (13th–15th c.; burned down in 1729).
Notable features of the town are the Baroque buildings of a former Franciscan friary (late 17th c. church), a Gothic church of the late 14th century, five ecclesiastical buildings and remains of the town walls.

Ilava

18km/11 miles north-east of Trenčín is Ilava (alt. 255m/835ft; pop. 5000), with an old castle (occupied by a monastery in the 17th century, later a prison).

Pruské

On the opposite bank of the Váh (hydro-electric station; bridge over river and canal) is Pruské, with a former Franciscan friary (18th c.) and a Renaissance castle which belonged to the Counts of Königsegg.

Vršatec Castle

7km/4½ miles north-west of Ilava, on a steep-sided rocky crag, are the ruins of Vršatec Castle (13th c.). Nearby are bizarrely shaped rock walls.

Beckov Castle

Trnava G 4

Region: Western Slovakia
District: Trnava
Altitude: 146m/479ft. Population: 72,000

Situation and characteristics

The historic old town of Trnava, a district town and a regional centre in south-western Slovakia, lies 55km/34 miles north-east of Bratislava (motorway) on the river Trnávka, which flows down from the Little Carpathians (see entry). It is an important road and rail junction and an industrial town (engineering, foodstuffs), with a teachers' training college and a theatre.

History

In 1238 Trnava became the first royal town under the Hungarian crown in Slovakia. From 1541 to 1820 it was the seat of the chapter of Esztergom Cathedral and for a time the residence of the Primate of Hungary. From 1635 to 1777 it had a University, which was then transferred to Budapest. Trnava's numerous churches earned it the name of the "Rome of Slovakia".

Sights

***St Nicholas's Cathedral**

The Gothic St Nicholas's Cathedral, founded in 1389 (interior renovated 1906), has two massive towers added in the 18th century.

Jesuit Church

The Baroque Jesuit Church (rich stucco decoration in interior), once the University Church, dates from 1637.

◀ *St Nicholas's Cathedral, Trnava*

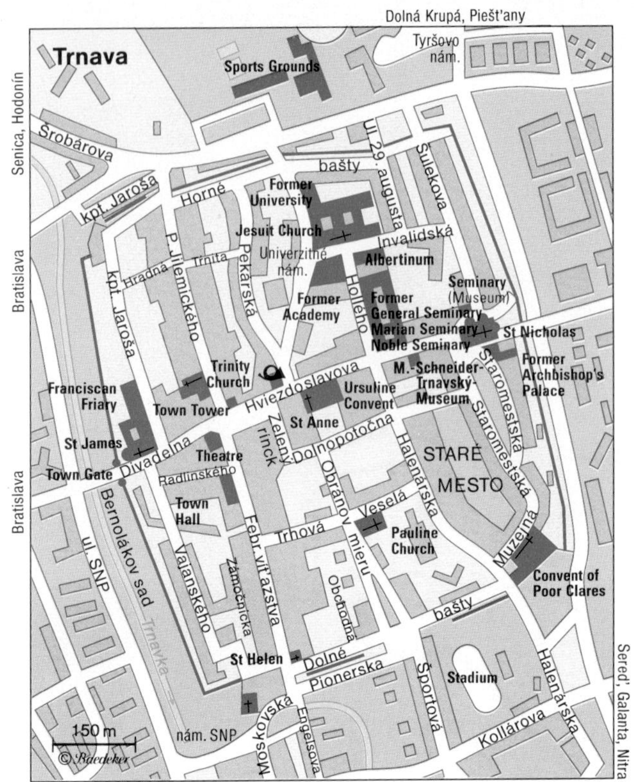

Franciscan Church The Franciscan Church (originally Gothic) was built in the 14th century and remodelled in Baroque style in the 17th century.

Secular buildings Trnava also has a number of notable secular buildings – the Baroque buildings (17th and 18th c.) of the former University in Univerziné Námestie (University Square); the former Archbishop's Palace (1562); the Renaissance-style Town Tower (later Baroquised) in the long main square; numerous old burghers' houses; and considerable remains of the town's fortifications (13th–14th c.).

Municipal Museum The Municipal Museum has a collection of material illustrating the history of the town and surrounding area.

Schneider-Trnavský Museum In Seminarská Ulica is the birthplace of the Slovak composer Mikuláš Schneider-Trnavský (1881–1958), now a memorial museum.

Surroundings of Trnava

Dolná Krupá 11km/7 miles north of Trnava is the little town of Dolná Krupá (alt. 192m/630ft; pop. 2500), with a late 18th century neo-classical castle (Musical Museum) and a beautiful park (exotic trees). Beethoven stayed in the Beethoven Pavilion on various occasions between 1803 and 1809.

Leopoldov Fort

12km/7½ miles north-east of Trnava, on the right bank of the Váh, stands the star-shaped Leopoldov Fort (alt. 146m/479ft), built in 1665–69 as a defence against the Turks. From 1854 it was used as a prison.

Hlohovec

16km/10 miles north-east of Trnava, on the left bank of the Váh, is the town of Hlohovec (alt. 156m/512ft; pop. 17,000; furniture manufacture, textiles, pharmaceuticals, wireworks). Above the town is an 18th century Baroque castle which belonged to the Erdödy family (with an Empire-style theatre of 1802 in the park). The parish church (originally Gothic, with much later alteration) dates from the 15th century. Other features of interest are the Town Hospital, with a mid 14th century church (remodelled in neo-classical style in the late 18th century), and a Franciscan church of 1465 (remodelled in Renaissance style in the 16th century).

Sereď

16km/10 miles south-east of Trnava is Sereď (alt. 130m/425ft; pop. 16,000), an industrial town (nickel plant), with an Empire-style castle (1840; originally Baroque; in course of restoration) which belonged to the Esterházy family. The town is famed for its basketwork.

Galanta

32km/20 miles south-east of Trnava, in the little district town of Galanta (alt. 122m/400ft; pop. 5000), stands the ancestral castle of the Esterházy family, a Tudor-style mansion which replaced an earlier Renaissance castle; it now houses a local museum. There is also a Baroque parish church (1805; fine interior).

Žilina — H 3

Region: Central Slovakia
District: Žilina
Altitude: 344m/1129ft
Population: 96,000

Situation and characteristics

The district town of Žilina lies in north-western Slovakia near the junction of the Kysuca and the Rajčianka with the Váh, ringed by the Javorníky range on the north-west, the Kysuca uplands on the north, the Little Fatra (see entry) on the south-east and the Stražovská Hornatina on the south-west. It is an important road and rail junction, with a variety of industry (woodworking, cellulose, engineering, chemicals, etc.), a College of Transport and Communications and other technical colleges.

History

The town was founded in the 13th century at the intersection of a number of trade routes and built up by German settlers at the turn of the 13th–14th centuries. It has retained its medieval core and preserves the famous Book of Žilina (Žilinská Kniha) of 1378, a collection of legal precedents, originally in German but from the mid 15th century also in Slovak. Žilina's development into an industrial town began with the construction of the railway line between Bohumín and Košice in 1871.

Sights

Market square

At the south-west corner of the market square (Dukla Square), which is surrounded by old arcaded houses, can be found a former Jesuit house, with a church of 1743.

Parish church

North-east of the market square is the imposing parish church (originally Romanesque; rebuilt in Early Gothic style about 1400), with an additional free-standing tower in Renaissance style built in 1540.

Municipal Theatre

Facing the parish church, to the south-east, is the Municipal Theatre.

Burghers' houses

In Holdžova Ulica and Radničná Ulica, which leave the north-east and south-east corners of the square, are a number of Renaissance burghers' houses.

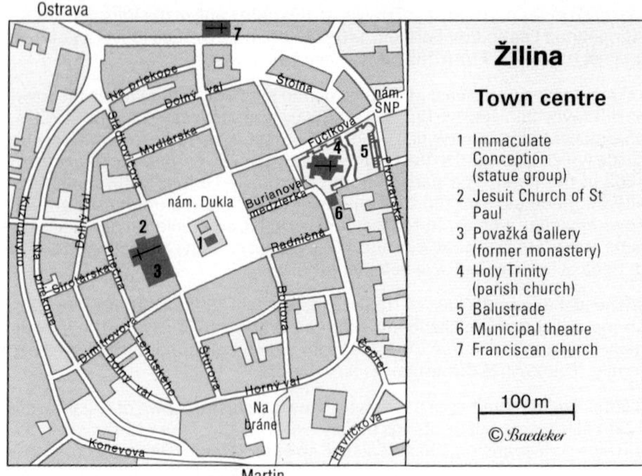

Franciscan Church

On the northern edge of the old town is the Franciscan Church (1723–30).

Town walls

There are some remains of the old town walls.

Fortified church in Závodie

In the north-western suburb of Závodie (1km/¾ mile from the market square) is the little Late Romanesque fortified church of St Stephen (13th c.), with fine frescoes.

Trnové

In the Trnové district (south-east of the town centre) are a 16th century wooden church and some examples of traditional Slovak architecture.

Sports facilities

North-east of the town, on the left bank of the Váh, are a stadium, an ice rink, a swimming pool and other sports facilities. To the south, outside the town, is a covered swimming pool.

Surroundings of Žilina

Budatín Castle

2km/1¼ miles north of the old town, at the confluence of the Kysuca with the Váh, stands Budatín Castle, originally a toll-collecting post built in the mid 12th century, enlarged in the 15th and 16th centuries and restored in 1922–23; it preserves a 13th century tower. The castle now houses the Váh Valley Museum (Považské Múzeum): local crafts (wire-making, woodcarving, etc.), arms and armour, pictures.

Strečno

9km/5½ miles east of Žilina is Strečno (alt. 360m/1180ft), situated at the mouth of a defile cut by the Váh through the Little Fatra (see entry) which was the scene of heavy fighting during the Second World War. Above the town, in the direction of Žilina, rises Mt Zvonica, with a monument to the Frenchmen killed in the partisan fighting here.

Strečno Castle

On a steep-sided crag to the south of Strečno are the ruins of Strečno Castle (mid 14th c.), which was destroyed in 1698, leaving only the outer walls and a tower; it is now in course of restoration. From the walls of the castle there are far-ranging views.

Starhrad Castle

To the east of Strečno the road follows a narrow bend in the river, with the railway taking a shorter route through a tunnel. At the highest point on the

A Renaissance building in Žilina

Parish church

road, on the far side of the river, can be seen the ruins of the 13th century Starhrad Castle (alt. 475m/1560ft), which was abandoned in the 18th century.

Lietava Castle

6km/4 miles south of Žilina is Lietavská Lúčka (6km/4 miles), to the west of which, on a high crag, are the imposing ruins of Lietava Castle (13th c.).

Rajecké Teplice

8km/5 miles farther on is the picturesquely situated spa of Rajecké Teplice (alt. 415m/1360ft; pop. 1000), with thermal springs (up to 39°C/102°F) containing alum.

Kunerád Castle

7km/4½ miles south-east, in the wooded valley of the Bystrička, stands Kunerád Castle, built in the 16th century as a hunting lodge (rebuilt in 1910; destroyed by fire in 1944), which for a time during the Second World War was the headquarters of a Slovak partisan brigade; it is now a sanatorium.

Rajec

6km/4 miles beyond this, in the Rajčanka valley, is the old-world little town of Rajec (pop. 4000; furniture-making, textiles), where the railway line from Žilina ends. The little church of St Ladislas has a Romanesque core (13th c.), with much later alteration. In the surrounding villages, in which traditional costumes are still worn, are many charming wooden houses.

Bytča

Bytča (alt. 308m/1011ft; pop. 12,000; engineering, manufacture of sports equipment) is situated 14km/8½ miles west of Žilina in the Váh valley. It has a Renaissance castle built in 1571–74 on the site of a medieval moated castle (once the seat of the Thurzo family) which now houses the State Archives. The Wedding Palace (1601–06; sgraffito-decorated façade) has fine wall paintings in the arcaded inner courtyard.

Považská Bystrica

31km/19 miles south-west of Žilina is the district town of Považská Bystrica (alt. 282m/925ft; pop. 31,000), an industrial centre (heavy engineering) with a 14th century Gothic church (much altered in later centuries).

Strečno Castle

In the Považské Podhradie district (on the opposite side of the Váh) are a Late Renaissance castle of 1631, a Baroque castle (1750–75) and the imposing ruins of a 15th century castle, Považsky Hrad (fine view).
In the Orlové district is a Baroque castle of 1773, now containing a local museum.
At Považská Bystrica is the Youth Dam (Priehrada Mládeže), forming a lake on the river Váh.
The Manin Gorge (Maninská Úžina) is a limestone canyon enclosed by high rock walls which at some points is only a few metres wide.

Kysuce Nature Reserve

The Kysuce Nature Reserve (area 654sq.km/253sq.miles) in north-western Slovakia takes in part of the Javorníky range and of the Slovakian Beskyds. It has preserved its original landscape pattern of widely scattered farmsteads on cleared forest country (*kopaniny*). Until the Second World War this was one of the poorest parts of Slovakia. The valley of the river Kysuca is now a popular holiday area.

Čadca

The industrial centre of the Kysuce area is the district town of Čadca (alt. 420m/1380ft; pop. 20,000; Tatra Automobile Works, woodworking, textiles), 31km/19 miles north of Žilina. Regional Museum in Palárikova Ulica.

24km/15 miles south-east of Čadca, at Vychylovka, is an open-air museum of traditional local architecture.

Zvolen

I 4

Region: Central Slovakia
District: Zvolen
Altitude: 292m/958ft
Population: 42,000

Situation and characteristics

The Central Slovakian town of Zvolen lies at the confluence of the Hron and the Slatina, surrounded by the Kremnica Hills (Kremnické Pohorie) on the north-west, the Pol'ana massif (see Slovakian Ore Mountains) on the north-east, the Javorie Hills on the south-east and the Štiavnica Hills (Štiavnické Pohorie) on the south-west.
Once the chief town of a Hungarian komitat, Zvolen is now a district town and industrial centre (woodworking, foodstuffs, large brickworks) with a College of Forestry.

History

The history of Zvolen was closely bound up with that of the castle built by Louis I of Hungary in the second half of the 14th century as a royal residence. In the 15th century it was a favourite residence of King Matthias Corvinus.

Sights

***Castle**

Above the banks of the Slatina rises Zvolen's massive Renaissance castle (16th c.; originally a fortified castle built between 1360 and 1382). After

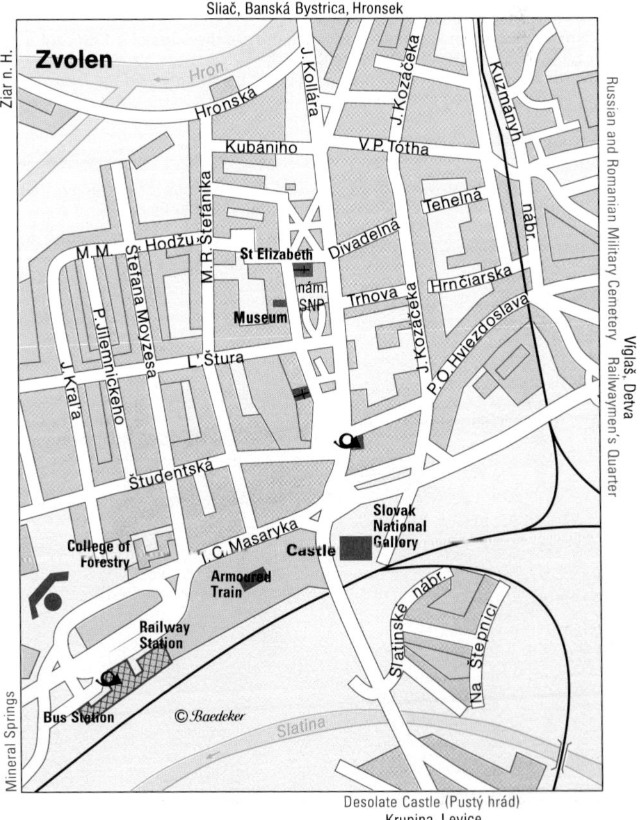

much alteration and renovation (most recently in 1967) it now houses a section of the Slovak National Gallery (medieval and modern art, Slovak Gothic art). The Royal Hall is used for periodic concerts and a summer festival.

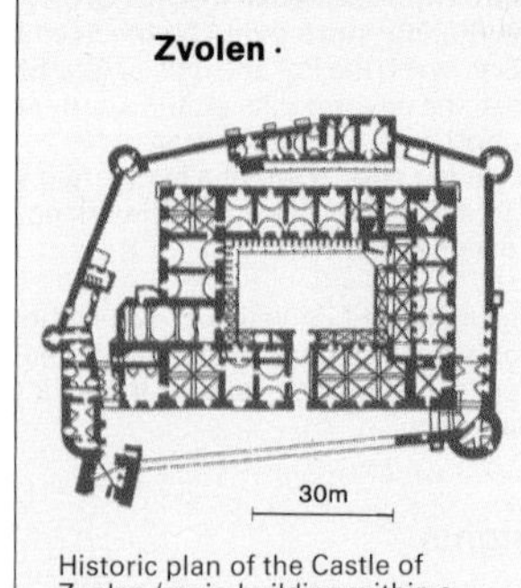

Historic plan of the Castle of Zvolen (main building within a five-cornered outer ward)

Parish church

In the long town square (Námestie SNP) stands the Gothic parish church of St Elizabeth (1390).

Theatre

The Theatre is in Blažovského Ulica.

Burghers' houses

The town has a number of Gothic, Renaissance and Baroque burghers' houses.

Military cemeteries

On the north-western outskirts of the town are Russian and Romanian military cemeteries.

Ruined castle

On a wooded hill (500m/1640ft) 3km/2 miles south-west of the town centre are the ruins of a 13th century castle, the Pustý Hrad ("Desolate Castle").

Mineral springs

North-west of the castle, at the junction of the Slatina and the Hron, are several carbonated mineral springs.

Surroundings of Zvolen

Kováčová

5km/3 miles north-west of Zvolen lies the little spa of Kováčová (alt. 320m/1050ft), with thermal springs (45–49°C/113–120°F).

Zvolen Castle

Sliač

5km/3 miles north of Zvolen is Sliač (alt. 350m/1150ft; pop. 3000), a commune formed by the amalgamation of the villages of Hájniky, Rybáre and Sliač Kúpele.

In Hájniky, on the right bank of the Hron, are a 14th century church (originally Romanesque, later rebuilt in the Gothic style; bell of 1313) and a Renaissance castle.

Sliač Kúpele

2km/1¼ miles east, beautifully situated on a wooded hill above the Hron valley, is the spa of Sliač Kúpele, first recorded about 1245 and known in the 16th century as Teplicae. Its five springs (12.5–33°C/54.5–91°F), which emerge from clefts in the rock at an altitude of 373m/1224ft, are used mainly in the treatment of heart conditions and circulatory disorders. The spa establishment is surrounded by a carefully tended park. There is an open-air thermal swimming pool. Summer festival, with international artistes.

Hronsek

10km/6 miles north of Zvolen is the village of Hronsek (alt. 312m/1024ft), with a charming wooden church of 1726.

Víglaš

12km/7½ miles east of Zvolen is Víglas (alt. 345m/1130ft; pop. 1500), above which is a 15th century castle (burned down during the Second World War), a hunting lodge of King Matthias Corvinus of Hungary.

Detva

20km/12½ miles east of Zvolen lies Detva (alt. 400m/1300ft; pop. 15,000; metalworking industry), where old crafts (woodcarving), costumes and traditions (folk singing and dancing) are preserved. Old houses with finely carved gables and doorways; carved wooden headstones in the form of crosses in the cemetery.

In the park, Sliač Kúpele

Cemetery, Detva

FORUM

Practical Information from A to Z

Following the division of Czechoslovakia into the independent Czech and Slovak Republics at the beginning of 1993 further changes in the two new states are to be expected. **N.B.**

Telephone numbers in Prague are in the process of being changed. If difficulty is experienced contact Directory Enquiries (see Telephone).

Air Travel

Airports

International flights

Air services to and from the Czech and Slovak Republics are flown by ČSA (Czechoslovak Airlines) and by numerous foreign airlines.
The Czech Republic has two international airports, Prague's Ruzyně Airport and Brno's Tuřany Airport. The Slovak Republic's international airport is Bratislava-Ivanka.

Czech Republic

In the Czech Republic there are regular flights, with varying frequencies, between Prague, Brno, Karlovy Vary (Karlsbad), Ostrava and Zlín.

Slovak Republic

In the Slovak Republic there are airports at Bratislava, Banská Bystrica (Sliač), Košice, Piešt'any, Prešov and Poprad (Tatry).

Airlines

ČSA

ČSA (Československé Aerolinie, Czechoslovak Airlines; since 1992 associated with Air France) fly domestic services in the Czech and Slovak Republics and also many routes in Europe and overseas.

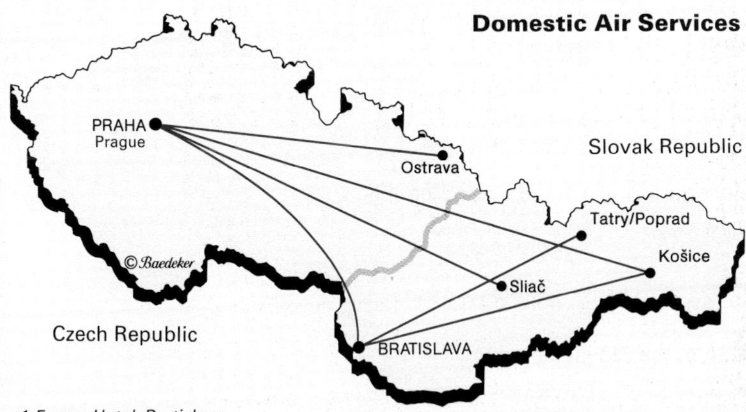

◀ *Forum Hotel, Bratislava*

ČSA Airtours

The ČSA Airtours travel agency, established by ČSA in 1989, caters for both individual travellers and groups, offering a programme which includes trips to Prague, tours in the two republics, cultural and sporting visits and much else besides.

Tours and accommodation can be booked through all ČSA offices and branches of ČSA Airtours.

ČSA Offices Abroad

United Kingdom

72/3 Margaret Street
London W1N 7HA. Tel. (071) 255 1898

Olympic House
Manchester Airport. Tel. (061) 498 8840

United States

545 Fifth Avenue
New York NY 10017. Tel. (212) 682 5833

35 East Wacker Drive
Chicago IL. Tel. (312) 201 1781

Canada

401 Bay Street
Suite 1510, Toronto, Ont. M5H 2Y4
Tel. (416) 363 3174

2020 University Street
Montréal, Qué. H3A 2A5. Tel. (514) 844 6376

ČSA in the Czech Republic

Prague

Head office, information and ticketing:
Revoluční 1
CZ-11000 Praha 1 (Nové Město)
Tel. (02) 24 21 01 32
Flight information (domestic and international): tel. (02) 2 31 73 95

Ruzyně Airport

Tel. (02) 3 36 78 14

Brno

Nádražni 4
Tel. 422 106 89

Karlovy Vary

Mírové 2
Tel. (017) 2 57 60 and 2 78 55

Ostrava

Nádražní 7
Tel. (069) 23 31 64 and 23 37 65
At Mošnov Airport: tel. (069) 5 82 16

Zlín

Dlouhá 4228
Tel. (067) 2 43 91

Foreign Airlines in the Czech Republic

British Airways

Štěpánská 63, Prague 1
Tel. (02) 2 36 03 53

Delta

Pařížska 11
Tel. (02) 2 32 47 72

ČSA in the Slovak Republic

Banská Bystrica

Partyzánská Cesta 4
Tel. (088) 4 19 75

Bratislava

Dom Gorkého 5
Tel. (07) 33 07 88 and 33 07 90
Štúrova 13
Tel. (07) 31 12 17

Košice

Pribinova 4
Tel. (095) 2 25 78 and 2 25 77

Piešt'any

Nalepkova 1825/2
Tel. 2 61 84 and 2 29 50

Prešov

Hlavná Ulica 26
Tel. 3 32 35

Antiques

Since the export of certain antiques may be either prohibited or subject to high export duties, it is advisable to consult the foreign trade organisation TUZEX before making any purchases. TUZEX has salerooms and agencies throughout the country.

Banks

See Currency

Beer

Beer is the national drink of the Czechs and Slovaks, and they produce some of the best beer in the world. They are exceeded only by the Germans and Belgians in consumption of beer per head of the population. There are over a hundred breweries in the two countries – the majority of them in the Czech Republic – producing light-coloured (*světlé*) and dark (*tmavé*) beers, almost exclusively bottom-fermented. Czech and Slovak beers owe their international reputation to the fortunate circumstance that the three basic ingredients are all available locally and of excellent quality. In the first place there are hops, the growing of which in Bohemia is recorded in chronicles as early as the 9th century; and by the 12th century supplies of hops were being shipped to Hamburg on the rivers Vltava and Labe (Elbe). For centuries the export of hop seedlings was prohibited on pain of death. Nowadays "red Žatec hops" or "Bohemian hops" are grown in northern Bohemia, around Žatec, Roudnice, Úštěk and Dubá, and exported to many countries.
The other essential ingredients are the exceedingly soft water and the high quality malt, produced solely from barley grown in central Bohemia.

History

The first documentary reference to brewing in Bohemia is in the foundation charter of the church of SS Peter and Paul on the Vyšehrad in Prague in the 11th century; but it is certain that beer was being brewed throughout the country well before that date. The kings of Bohemia granted all their subjects the right to brew beer. On the basis of this privilege the towns of Plzeň (Pilsen), České Budějovice and Prague – still the most famous brewing towns in the Czech and Slovak Republics – had their own breweries by the 13th century. In the course of time many of the peasant farmers growing hops and barley gave up their right to brew their own beer and sent their crops to the breweries, receiving in return a supply of beer which they consumed themselves or sold. Around the middle of the 16th century Bohemian beer – flavoured not only with hops but also with juniper, laurel or nutmeg and mainly top-fermented, using a proportion of wheat malt – was famed throughout Europe and appeared on the tables of the great ones of the world. The traditional method of brewing was maintained until the first decades of the 19th century, when František Poupě introduced the bottom-fermented technique. In 1842 the Plzeň brewery, using this method, produced for the first time a clear golden beer which was left to mature longer – the prototype of the present-day Pilsner (Pils). The new type of beer became fashionable throughout Europe; but since the brewers omitted to register the name as a trade mark Pilsener-type beer was soon being brewed in many towns and many countries.

Types of Beer

Strength

The strength of a beer as shown in degrees on the label does not relate to its alcoholic content but to its density (i.e. the proportion of fermentable substances used in the production of the beer). The alcohol content by weight is about a third of the number of degrees. On this basis beers are classified into draught beers, with a density of not more than 10° (3–4% alcohol by volume); lagers, with a density of between 10° and 12° (5% alcohol); and special beers, with a density of 13° or over.

Draught beers
Gambrinus
Staropramen
Pražanka
Starovar
Dalila

Light draught beers, mainly light-coloured, with a density between 7° and 10°, are popular as low-alcohol thirst-quenchers. The best known are the Gambrinus (10°) of Plzeň, Staropramen (7°) from Prague-Smíchov and Pražanka (10°) from the Holešovice brewery in Prague. Others are the Starovar (10°) of Žatec and the Dalila (10°) of České Budějovice, which ranks as one of the best.

Lagers

Lager beers (11–12°), usually golden in colour, are noted for their full taste and almost cream-like head. The most famous of all Bohemian beers, of

Pilsner

course, is Pilsner Urquell (Plzeňský Prazdroj), which tastes even better in its country of origin than in the export version. The bouquet, with the bitterness of the hops, and the full taste come from the Žatec hops and from the oak casks in which the beer is left to mature for several months.

Budweiser

Less famous than Pilsner is the beer produced in České Budějovice in southern Bohemia, the original Budweiser, which is smoother and slightly more sweetish than Pilsner.

Staropramen
Braniker

The Staropramen brewery in Prague, the largest in the country, produces a 12° lager. Also brewed in Prague is Braniker, another 12° lager, of which there are both light-coloured and dark versions.

Velkopopovický
Kozel
Starobrno
Radhošt'
Tatran

Other popular beers of this type are Velkopopovický Kozel from Velké Popovice in central Bohemia, very light in colour, with a delicate hop flavour and a firm head; dark Starobrno; Radhošt', from the Nosovice brewery in northern Moravia; and Tatran, from the Slovakian town of Poprad, at the foot of the High Tatras.

Special beers
Krakonoš
Martinský
Porter

The choice of special beers ranges from the sweetish, light-coloured Krakonoš (14°) from Brno to the heavy Martinský Porter (20°) from Martin in the Slovak Republic.

U Fleků
Velkopopovický
Braniker

In between are specialities like the dark beer from the U Fleků brewery, the only privately owned brewery in Prague, the dark Velkopopovický and the light Braniker, all with a density of 14°.

Ondraš
Tatran
Diplomat

Among stronger beers are Ondraš (16°) from Ostrava, the dark version of Tatran (16°) and Diplomat (18°) from the Gambrinus brewery in Prague.

Business Hours

Banks

See Currency

Castles, museums, galleries

Usually open Tue.–Sun. 10am–5pm.
Closed on Mondays and on the days following statutory public holidays (see entry). Some museums are open on Monday and close instead on Saturday. It is advisable to check opening times locally. Castles are also closed on official public holidays and usually from November to March.

Chemists

See entry

Museums

See under individual museums in "Sights from A to Z" section

Shops

Food shops: Mon.–Fri. 6am–6pm, Sat. to noon.
Other shops: Mon.–Fri. 8.30 or 9am to 6pm.
Department stores are open on Thursday until 8pm and on Saturday until 2pm. Small shops close at lunch-time for 1–2 hours between noon and 3pm, and on Saturday after noon.
Cake shops and souvenir shops are also open on Sunday, when all other shops are closed, until 6pm or even later.

Spa establishments

See Spas

Bus Services

Both the Czech and the Slovak Republic are served by a dense network of bus services. Practically every town and village in both countries can be reached by bus.
Under the system established by the previous regime all bus services were run by the State Transport Authority (Československá Státní Automobilova Doprava, ČSAD). This is now being reorganised.

Information

In Prague: Pod Výtopnou 10, CZ-18000 Praha 8, tel. (02) 22 86 42–9
In Bratislava: tel. (07) 6 32 13 and 21 22 22

Timetables

Hitherto the timetables of bus services have been published annually in ten volumes covering the different regions of Czechoslovakia, with an eleventh volume for long-distance and international services.

Tickets

Tickets can be bought from automatic machines, newsagents' and tobacconists' shops and other specially indicated sales points. For journeys outside normal business hours you should buy your tickets in advance.

Bus stops, bus stations

There are usually bus stops (*zastávky*) close to railway stations. In the larger towns there are special bus stations.

Coach tours

Coach tours (sometimes combined with a steamer trip on the Vltava in the Czech Republic or the Danube in the Slovak Republic: see Shipping Services) are organised by branches of Čedok (see Information), ČSA Airtours (see Air Services) and other operators.

International coach services

During the summer there are also international coach tours. Information from Bohemiatours, CZ-11000 Praha 1, tel. (02) 2 31 25 89, and other travel agencies.
See also Getting There, By Coach

Camping and Caravanning

There are several hundred camping sites (some of them with simple cabins or chalets which can be rented) all over the territory of the Czech and Slovak

	Republics, signposted "Autocamp". They are usually closed during the winter.
Reservation	During the main holiday season it is advisable to book a place in advance.
Camping carnet	Possession of an international camping carnet (obtainable through national motoring organisations) simplifies the formalities of registration at a camping site. At some sites only campers with a carnet will be admitted, and there may also be reduced charges for holders of carnets.
Classification	Camping sites are classified in two categories, A and B.
Wild camping	"Wild" camping (camping outside official camping sites) was formerly prohibited but is now tolerated. The owner or tenant of the land should always be asked for permission.
List of sites	A list of camping sites, with addresses and telephone numbers, categories and opening times, can be obtained from Čedok (see Information).

Car Rental

	The various car rental firms have offices in the centre of the larger towns and desks at airports.
Tariffs	Rates vary according to the type of car and length of rental. In addition to the daily or weekly charge there will be a charge per kilometre. As a rule a deposit will be asked for. Some rental firms include the insurance premium in the charge, others invoice it separately. You should always ask about possible reduced rates, since information may not be volunteered, for example, about weekend reductions. If you are renting a car for at least a week or for several weeks you can expect to get a better rate. It is advisable to book in advanece.
Driving licence	National driving licences are accepted.
Information	Further information can be obtained from the firms listed below or from Čedok offices (which usually work with Sixt/Budget Rent-a-Car).
Luxury limousines	Individual visitors can rent, through Čedok, luxury limousines (with English-speaking drivers), e.g. for transfers between Prague and Bratislava.

Rental Firms

AVIS In Czech Republic	Head office in Prague: Tel. (02) 31 55 15
Europcar In Czech Republic	Pářížská Náměstí 26 Prague Tel. (02) 51 12 90
Hertz In Czech Republic	In Prague: Karlovo 28, tel. (02) 29 14 82 Ruzyně Airport, tel. (02) 12 07 17 Atrium Hotel, tel. (02) 84 20 47 Forum Hotel, tel. (02) 19 12 13 Hertz also has branches in a number of other towns in the Czech Republic.

Bratislava-Ivanka Airport, tel. (07) 29 14 82

In Slovak Republic

Also branches in a number of other towns in the Slovak Republic.

Eurocar
In Slovak Republic

Bratislava-Ivanka Airport, tel. (07) 22 02 85

Sixt/Budget
In Czech Republic

Ruzyně Airport, tel. (02) 3 34 32 53
Inter-Continental Hotel, tel. (02) 31 95 95

Mobile homes, motor caravans

Some of these firms (e.g. Europcar) also have mobile homes and motor caravans available for hire.

Casinos

There are casinos in a number of towns in the Czech Republic and in Bratislava in the Slovak Republic, most of them opened only quite recently. They are usually in the larger hotels used by foreign visitors.
The games played are roulette and blackjack.
There is usually a restaurant or night club associated with the casino.

Casinos in the Czech Republic

Central Bohemia

There are casinos in the Forum, Palace, Ambassador and Park Hotels in Prague; also –
Casino Admiral, in Palace of Culture, Ulice 5.Května 65, Praha 4
Casino de France, in Atrium Hotel, Pobřežní 3, Praha 8
Casino in Diplomatic Club, Karlova 21, Praha 1
Casino in Savarin Palace, Náměstí Republiky, Stará Celnice, Praha 1

Western Bohemia

In Karlovy Vary:
Casino 777, in Bath-House I
Casino in Grand Hotel Pupp

In Plzeň:
Casino in Continental Hotel

Eastern Bohemia

In Hradec Králové:
Casino in Černigov Hotel

In Pardubice:
Casino in Labe Hotel

Northern Bohemia

A casino has recently been opened in Teplice. There is also a casino in the Bohemia Hotel in Ústí nad Labem.

Southern Bohemia

In České Budějovice:
Casino, Náměstí Otokara II

Northern Moravia

In Ostrava:
Casino in Palace Hotel

Southern Moravia

In Brno:
Casinos in Grand Hotel and International Hotel

In Zlín:
Casino in Moskva Hotel

Castles

There are about 3000 castles in the Czech and Slovak Republics, ranging from fortified medieval castles to splendid Renaissance, Baroque and

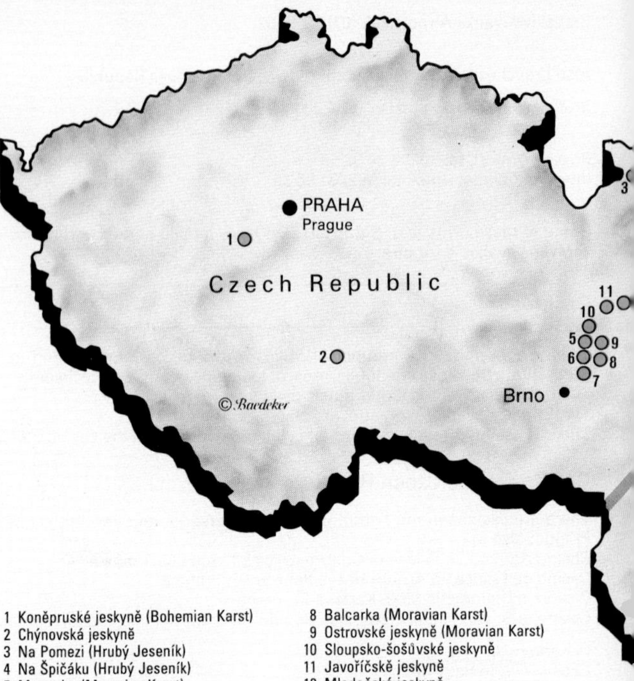

1 Koněpruské jeskyně (Bohemian Karst)
2 Chýnovská jeskyně
3 Na Pomezi (Hrubý Jeseník)
4 Na Špičáku (Hrubý Jeseník)
5 Macocha (Moravian Karst)
6 Punkevní jeskyně (Moravian Karst)
7 Kateřinská jeskyně (Moravian Karst)
8 Balcarka (Moravian Karst)
9 Ostrovské jeskyně (Moravian Karst)
10 Sloupsko-šošůvské jeskyně
11 Javoříčske jeskyně
12 Mladečské jeskyně
13 Zbašovské aragonitové jeskyně
14 Šipka

neo-classical buildings which are palaces rather than castles. Many of them contain valuable collections and specialised museums, and they are often surrounded by beautiful parks and gardens.

Organised tours

Between April and October Čedok (see Information) runs a series of tours lasting several days and visiting castles in Bohemia and Moravia, and also day trips from Prague to castles within easy reach. A brochure giving details of tours, with departure times and prices, is available from Čedok.

Caves

There are numbers of extensive cave systems in the Czech and Slovak Republics which have been explored and mapped and are now open to the public. The most important of these caves, most of which have stalactites and stalagmites or the rarer aragonite formations, are described in the "Sights from A to Z" section of this guide and are shown on the map above.

Chemists

Pharmacies in the Czech and Slovak Republics (*lékárna* in Czech, *lekáreň* in Slovak) stock both Czech/Slovak and foreign medicines.

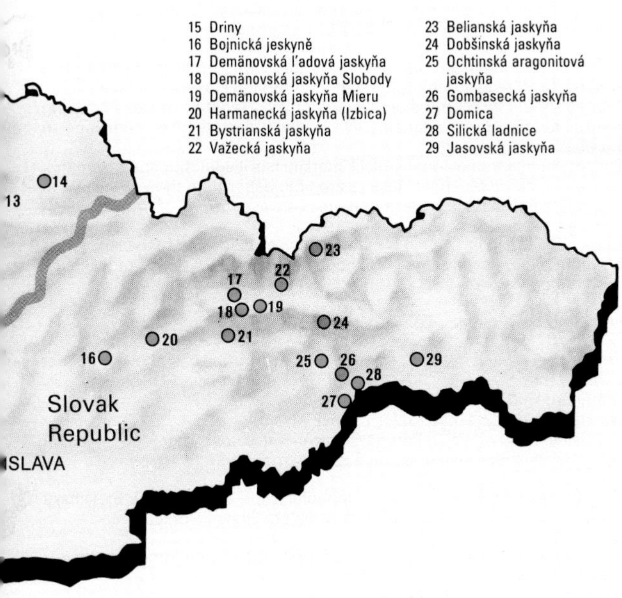

Normally Mon.–Fri. 8am–6pm, Sat. 8am–noon.

Opening times

All chemists' shops display a sign giving the address of the nearest pharmacy providing an out-of-hours service. In large cities such as Prague and Bratislava there are pharmacies open day and night.

Out-of-hours service

See Medical Aid, Emergencies

Further information

Currency

Since the division of the Czechoslovak Republic the two successor states have introduced their own currencies, the **Czech crown** (koruna česká, or kč for short) and the **Slovak crown** (koruna slovenská, ks). After a period during which both old and provisional new coins and banknotes were in circulation only the new notes and coins are now valid. In both the Czech and the Slovak Republic there are now coins in denominations of 1, 2, 5, 10 and 50 crowns and banknotes for 20, 50, 100, 200, 500 and 1000 crowns. The heller, of which there were once 100 to the crown, has disappeared without trace.

The new Czech and Slovak currencies are, strictly speaking, valid only in their own country. Since the Czech crown has a rather better exchange rate against western currencies than the Slovak crown, you should beware, when in the Czech Republic, of getting change in Slovak money. Czech money is welcomed in Slovakia.

Currency regulations

You may export and import an amount of up to 100 crowns.
It is advisable to declare western currency at the borders of both republics, and to obtain a receipt from the bank when exchanging any currency. This will facilitate changing crowns back to western currency.

Changing money

There is no longer any obligation, as there was under the communist regime, to change a minimum amount of foreign currency per day.
Money should be changed only in authorised exchange offices (including banks, hotels, travel agencies, etc.), which are steadily increasing in number.
Do not change money on the black market. It is illegal; but apart from that the rates offered by street dealers are little better than those available in legitimate exchange offices, and there is always the risk of fraud.

Eurocheques

Eurocheques can be cashed at state banks (see below) up to the equivalent of about £150. Restaurants and shops bearing the EC (EU) sign will also cash them.

Banks
Opening times

Usually Mon.–Fri. 9am–2pm

The principal bank in the Czech Republic (with branches in every district town) is the
Státní Banka Česká (Czech State Bank)
Na Příkopě 28, CZ-11000 Praha 1 (Nové Město)
This is the head office, in Prague city centre. It is open later Mon.–Fri. than other banks and is also open on Saturday morning.

The principal bank in the Slovak Republic is the Štátna Banka Slovenská (Slovak State Bank) in Bratislava, at Dunajská 24 and Gorkého 14.

The leading commercial bank with an international department is the
Komerční Banka
Na Příkopě 28, CZ-11003 Praha 1
Tel. (02) 4 22 21 22–1111
which also has an exchange desk.

Foreign banks in Prague (Praha 1):
Deutsche Bank, Národní Třída 10
Dresdner Bank, in Palace Hotel, Panská 12
Bank der Österreichischen Sparkassen, Ovocný Trh 15
Crédit Suisse/First Boston, V Jámě 1

Exchange offices

Exchange offices in the larger towns and in hotels are usually open throughout the day.

Credit Cards

The following credit cards are accepted: Access, American Express, Carte Blanche, Diners Club, Eurocard/Mastercard, Bank Americard/Visa, JCB.

Customs Regulations

The Czech and Slovak Republics are still joined in a customs union and plan to establish a free trade zone providing for the free movement of goods, capital, services and labour.
The import (into the Czech or Slovak Republic) or export (from the Czech or Slovak Republic) of Czech or Slovak currency is prohibited.
Although petrol or diesel fuel in cans may be taken into either of the republics it may not be taken out.

In any matter of importance regarding imports or exports it is advisable to seek advice from a Czech or Slovak embassy or consulate or from a customs official at the frontier. The customs authorities issue a leaflet listing items the export of which is prohibited or is subject to special permission and the payment of duty.

Entry

The following may be taken in duty-free: personal effects; 250 cigarettes or 250 grams of other tobacco goods; 2 litres of wine and 1 litre of spirits; and gifts up to a value of 3000 crowns. (These limits may be subject to change). Objects of value (cameras and video cameras, valuable watches and jewellery, all kinds of electronic aparatus, etc.) and items which are not part of personal baggage must be declared on entry and must be re-exported. The loss or theft of any such items must be reported immediately to the police and to the customs authorities.
For information about the import of sporting guns and ammunition, CB radio and car telephones apply to Čedok.

Exit

The following may be taken out without payment of duty: souvenirs up to a value of 1000 crowns; requirements for the journey to an appropriate amount; 2 litres of wine and 1 litre of spirits; and 250 cigarettes or an equivalent amount of other tobacco goods.
Particular regulations apply to lead crystal, children's articles and antiques (see entry). All goods which can be shown (by production of the receipt) to have been bought for hard currency in a Tuzex or Artia shop can be exported duty-free. (Tuzex shops will also arrange for the despatch of purchases to your home address).

Distances

The table on page 530 shows the distance (in kilometres) between selected towns in the Czech and Slovak Republics.

Electricity

The power supply in the Czech and Slovak Republics is normally 220 volts AC. In the older parts of towns and in country areas it may occasionally be 120 volts.
In the larger hotels at least the normal continental type of plug (with an adaptor for British and other visitors with other types of plugs) can be used for electric razors, etc.; elsewhere a special adaptor may be necessary.

Embassies and Consulates

Czech and Slovak Embassies

United Kingdom

Czech Embassy
26–30 Kensington Palace Gardens
London W8 4QY. Tel. (071) 743 1115

Slovak Embassy
25 Kensington Palace Gardens
London W8 4QY. Tel. (071) 243 0803

United States

Czech/Slovak Embassy
3900 Linnean Avenue NW
Washington DC 20008
Tel. (202) 363 6315

Distances

Distances by road (in kilometres) between selected towns in the Czech and Slovak Republics

	Banská Bystrica	Bratislava	Brno	České Budějovice	Domažlice	Zlín	Hradec Králové	Jeseník	Jihlava	Karlovy Vary	Košice	Liberec	Luhačovice	Mariánské Lázně	Nitra	Olomouc	Opava	Ostrava	Pardubice	Piešťany	Plzeň	Poprad	Praha	Prešov	Strážnice	Špindlerův Mlýn	Tábor	Teplice	Ústí nad Labem	Žilina
Banská Bystrica	•	205	273	463	587	206	413	331	360	625	214	514	191	630	120	259	251	216	417	179	565	124	499	208	216	298	434	589	586	117
Bratislava	205	•	138	322	452	170	285	309	225	490	418	386	164	495	85	213	270	277	282	82	430	329	364	413	118	370	299	454	451	202
Brno	273	138	•	190	314	98	147	173	87	352	475	248	104	357	176	77	151	168	144	146	292	355	226	439	76	232	161	316	313	212
České Budějovice	463	322	190	•	142	288	214	338	117	216	665	257	294	202	366	267	341	358	200	346	137	545	148	629	266	283	60	238	235	402
Domažlice	587	452	314	142	•	412	246	406	227	136	796	254	418	77	490	391	465	482	248	460	57	676	145	760	380	284	153	182	199	533
Zlín	206	170	98	288	412	•	217	159	185	443	378	318	23	455	153	63	118	126	214	109	390	258	317	342	52	302	259	408	401	109
Hradec Králové	413	285	147	214	246	217	•	160	114	227	559	101	240	263	323	154	207	242	22	293	189	439	101	523	223	85	154	191	184	296
Jeseník	331	309	173	338	406	159	160	•	214	387	477	261	182	423	309	96	80	115	182	248	349	357	261	441	191	235	286	351	348	214
Jihlava	360	225	87	117	227	185	114	214	•	265	562	189	191	270	263	164	238	255	92	233	205	442	139	526	163	195	74	229	226	299
Karlovy Vary	625	490	352	216	136	443	227	387	265	•	785	213	456	47	528	380	434	469	229	498	79	665	126	749	428	257	210	105	122	522
Košice	214	418	475	665	796	378	559	477	562	785	•	660	384	821	320	405	397	362	556	383	747	128	659	36	418	644	636	749	746	263
Liberec	514	386	248	257	254	318	101	261	189	213	660	•	341	260	424	255	308	343	119	394	197	540	109	624	324	83	197	109	99	397
Luhačovice	191	164	104	294	418	23	240	182	192	456	384	341	•	461	131	86	124	132	237	82	396	264	330	348	48	325	265	420	417	121
Mariánské Lázně	630	495	357	202	77	455	263	423	270	47	821	260	461	•	533	416	470	505	265	503	74	708	162	785	433	301	196	152	169	558
Nitra	120	85	176	366	490	153	323	309	263	528	320	424	131	533	•	201	236	261	320	49	468	244	402	328	124	408	337	492	489	164
Olomouc	259	213	77	267	391	63	154	96	164	380	405	255	86	416	201	•	74	99	151	152	342	285	254	369	95	239	238	344	341	142
Opava	251	270	151	341	465	118	207	80	238	434	397	308	124	470	236	74	•	35	211	205	396	277	308	361	152	282	312	398	395	134
Ostrava	216	277	168	358	482	126	242	115	255	469	362	343	132	505	261	99	35	•	246	212	431	242	343	320	178	317	329	433	426	99
Pardubice	417	282	144	200	248	214	22	182	92	229	556	119	237	265	320	151	211	246	•	290	191	436	103	520	220	103	140	193	190	293
Piešťany	179	82	146	346	460	109	293	248	233	498	383	394	82	503	49	152	205	212	290	•	438	263	372	347	75	378	307	462	459	120
Plzeň	565	430	292	137	57	390	189	349	205	79	747	197	396	74	468	342	396	431	191	438	•	627	88	711	368	227	131	125	142	484
Poprad	124	329	355	545	676	258	439	357	442	665	128	540	264	708	244	285	277	242	436	263	627	•	539	84	298	524	516	629	626	143
Praha	499	364	226	148	145	317	101	261	139	126	659	109	330	162	402	254	308	343	103	372	88	539	•	623	302	139	88	90	87	396
Prešov	208	413	439	629	760	342	523	441	526	749	36	624	348	785	328	369	361	320	520	347	711	84	623	•	382	608	600	713	710	227
Strážnice	216	118	76	266	380	52	223	191	163	428	418	324	48	433	124	95	152	178	220	75	368	298	302	382	•	308	237	392	389	155
Špindlerův Mlýn	298	370	232	283	284	302	85	235	195	257	644	83	325	301	408	239	282	317	103	378	227	524	139	608	308	•	223	190	182	381
Tábor	434	299	161	60	153	259	154	286	74	210	636	197	265	196	337	238	312	329	140	307	131	516	88	600	237	223	•	178	175	373
Teplice	589	454	316	238	182	408	191	351	229	105	749	109	420	152	492	344	398	433	193	462	125	629	90	713	392	190	178	•	17	486
Ústí nad Labem	586	451	313	235	199	401	184	348	226	122	746	99	417	169	489	341	395	426	190	459	142	626	87	710	389	182	175	17	•	483
Žilina	117	202	212	402	533	109	296	214	299	522	263	397	121	558	164	142	134	99	293	120	484	143	396	227	155	381	373	486	483	•

Canada

Czech/Slovak Embassy
50 Rideau Terrace
Ottawa, Ont. K1M 2A1
Tel. (514) 849 4495

Embassies in the Czech and Slovak Republics

United Kingdom

Embassy
Thunovská 14
CZ-12550 Prague 1
Tel. (02) 53 33 47, 53 33 40 and 53 33 70
Consular section: tel. (02) 53 67 37

United States

Embassy
Tržiště 15
CZ-12548 Prague 1
Tel. (02) 53 66 41 and 53 66 46

Canada

Embassy
Mickiewiczova 6
Prague 6
Tel. (02) 3 12 02 51

Emergencies

Emergency calls from anywhere in the Czech and Slovak Republics:

Police: dial 158
Doctor: dial 155
Fire: dial 150

On all motorways there are emergency telephones for calling assistance in the event of accident or breakdown.

Events and Festivals

Information

Detailed information about events and festivals can be obtained from Čedok offices (see Information).

Public holidays

See entry

A Selection of Events in Bohemia, Moravia and Slovakia

Prague

Prague has a full programme of cultural events (concerts, theatre, etc.) during the winter months.

Bratislava

There are also numerous cultural events in Bratislava. The concerts by the Slovak Philharmonic Orchestra and the opera and ballet performances of the Slovak National Theatre are world-famed. The State Puppet Theatre is also a very popular show.

January
Brno

Go (an annual Tourism Fair)

January 6th
Many places

The end of the Christmas season is celebrated, particularly in country areas, with a parade of the Three Kings.

Events and Festivals

End January Liberec	Ski Marathon (50km/30 miles) in the Jizera Hills
February Prague	Opera Ball in the State Opera House (Smetana Theatre) Holiday World Trade Fair (Exhibition Grounds) Matthias Fair (Exhibition Grounds)
Brno	Salima (Food Fair) Janáček Festival
February/March Many places	Carnival, with parades in carnival costume on last Sunday in Shrovetide. The best parades are in southern Bohemia, in the Hlinsko area in the Bohemo-Moravian Highlands, in a number of villages in Moravian Slovakia and in Uherský Brod (Southern Moravia). Carrying out of the death goddess Morena, the symbol of winter.
March Karlovy Vary	Jazz Festival
March/April Many places	"Easter Switching" Switches woven from young willow (or in Wallachia juniper) branches are sold before Easter, and if young girls and women are struck with these "Easter switches" this is supposed to make them younger and more beautiful.
March/May Luhačovice	Luhačovice Musical Spring
April Prague	Pragomedica (Medical Show) Intercamera (International Audiovisual Technology Show)
Mid April Brno	International Consumer Goods Show
May Many places	Maypoles are set up
Mariánské Lázně	International Musical Festival
Prague	International Book Fair (Palace of Culture)
Last Sunday in May Vičnov and elsewhere in S. Moravia	"King's Ride" on last Sunday in May or at Whitsun A boy dressed in girl's clothing rides on a richly decorated white horse, with a white rose in his mouth. During the ride, which lasts several hours, he must not speak. He is accompanied by two adjutants armed with sabres and by heralds, who announce the king's arrival and ask for money.
May/June Prague	"Prague Spring" (musical festival; opera and ballet performances and concerts by internationally famed orchestras, conductors and soloists)
May–August Luhačovice	International Musical Summer
Mid May to mid September	In Karlovy Vary: Colonnade Concerts (Tue.–Sun.)
May–October	Church patronal festivals in many places
June Bratislava	Incheba (Chemical Trade Fair)
Brno	Transport Show
Karlovy Vary	Dvořák Competition for Singers

Event	Month / Place
Kmoch's Brass Band Festival	Kolín
International Brass Band Festival	Poděbrady
"Golden Prague" International Television Festival "Prague June" (international musical festival)	Prague
Shostakovich Festival	Teplice
"Concertino" (concerts by young musicians)	Třeboň
Janáček Festival	**June/July** Luhačovice
Music in the Castle	**June–September** Teplice
Puppet Festival	**July** Chrudim
International Film Festival (alternate years: 1994, 1996, etc.)	Karlovy Vary
International Musical Festival	Mariánské Lázně
Wallachian Festival	Rožnov pod Radhoštěm
International Folk Festival	Strážnice
Prague Cultural Summer (concerts, theatre, folk events, exhibitions, etc.)	**July/August** Prague
Třeboň Cultural Summer	Třeboň
"Round Brno" car race	**August** Brno
Chod Festival	Domažlice
"Young People on the Platform" (series of concerts)	Karlovy Vary
Chopin Festival	Mariánské Lázně
Čedok Open Grand Prix (tennis tournament)	Prague
Musical and Cultural Festival in Valtice Castle	Valtice
Agricultural Show	**August/Sept.** České Budějovice
International Engineering Show	**September** Brno
Dvořák Autumn Festival	Karlovy Vary
"Garden of Bohemia" (fruit, vegetable and flower show)	Lutoměřice
Speedway races for the "Golden Helmet"	Pardubice
Bagpiping Festival (alternate years: 1994, 1996, etc.)	Strakonice
Musical Festival	**Sept./October** Bratislava
Harvest Thanksgiving, Hop Harvest and Vintage Festival (frequently with humorous plays); church patronal festivals Particularly popular is the harvest festival at Žatec, in the middle of a hop-growing area in northern Bohemia.	Many places in country

Teplice	Beethoven Festival
October Brno	International Musical Festival
Jáchymov	Musical Festival
Pardubice	Grand Pardubice Steeplechase (annually since 1874), one of the most difficult steeplechases in Europe (7km/4½ miles; 39 jumps, some of them extremely daunting)
Prague	International Jazz Festival
November Prague	Čedok Musical Festival
December Eastern Moravia	December 5th: St Nicholas procession, with "devils"
Many places	December 6th: "Christmas begging" from house to house Christmas trees, illuminated and decorated, in large squares in towns; Christmas markets; Christmas cribs (Nativity groups) in churches.
New Year's Eve Many places	Celebrations in many hotels, with gala dinners and floor shows

Food and Drink

Food

Bohemia and Moravia

Bohemian cuisine

Bohemian cuisine is substantial and tasty, with a predominance of meat and dumplings.

Soups

Among the best known soups are the potato soup of the Bohemian Forest and the *kyselo* (sour soup) of the Krkonoše.

Meat dishes

On special occasions the usual roast pork gives place to a crisply roasted goose or duck.

Bohemian game dishes are excellent (venison, or perhaps a larded hare, which may be served in a cream sauce).

Among the most popular specialities are steamed beef, boiled pork, loin roast and various kinds of sausages.

In many towns there are street sausage stalls selling bacon sausages, the delicate Prague sausages, pork sausages and strongly spiced frankfurter-type sausages.

The juicy Prague boiled ham is widely famed.

A common dish in northern Bohemia is Liberec roulade (pork with onions, bacon and sausages).

Fish

Fish appears less commonly on the menu, but few families are without the traditional carp at Christmas – usually coated with breadcrumbs, but also roasted, boiled or in aspic.

In addition to carp the most favoured kinds of fish are pike from the fish ponds of southern Bohemia and trout from the country's many streams.

Dumplings

Dumplings and noodles feature prominently in the main meal of the day. Popular types are potato or bread dumplings with roast pork or smoked meat and bacon dumplings with cabbage, spinach or roasted onions.

A particular speciality is the fruit dumpling, made from yeast dough and filled with plums, apricots, apples, cherries or bilberries. The dumplings are sometimes sprinkled with grated hard quark or poppy seeds or topped with melted butter, and are eaten while they are still hot.

Barley broth

A traditional Christmas dish in the Krkonoše is barley broth served with mushrooms (*houbový kuba*).

Sauces

Great importance is attached to sauces, ranging from spicy gravy to more delicate cream-based sauces. A white sauce flavoured with marjoram or caraway seeds is served both with meat and with vegetables.

Vegetables, salads, mushroom dishes

Vegetables and salads play a relatively small part in the menu. Mushroom dishes are a speciality of the Bohemian Forest.

Cheese

Homolský sýr is a cheese made from sour milk, *oštěpek* a ewe's-milk cheese which keeps well, *parecina* a rather sharp ewe's-milk cheese.

Desserts

There is a tempting range of sweets, including applestrudel and a variety of small cakes and doughnuts; but best of all, perhaps are *palačinky* – pancakes filled with quark, jam or chocolate which are not so thin as French pancakes but no less tasty.
Other favourite deserts are plum jam cake (*povidlový koláč*), jam-filled buns (*buchty*) and the wafers, light as air, of Karlovy Vary.

Moravian cuisine

Favourite items on the Moravian menu are excellent poultry and game dishes and roast pork.

Vegetables

Particular specialities, in season, are the delicate asparagus of southern Moravia and the cucumbers of Znojmo.

Cheese

The sour-milk cheese of Olomouc has a very characteristic aroma.

Slovakia

Slovakian cuisine is strongly influenced by Hungarian, and shows a preference for more highly spiced dishes than Czech cuisine.

Meat dishes

The commonest meat dishes are goulash, mutton and various kinds of meat roasted on the spit.

Vegetables, etc.

Meat dishes are accompanied by potatoes, dumplings and paprika pods.

Cheese

Tasty cheeses are produced on the upland pastures of the Low Tatras. The well known Liptov cheese (*Liptovská bryndza*) is made from ewe's milk (with a proportion of cow's milk) flavoured with red paprika. Ewe's-milk cheeses are often cut into slices and fried.

Gastronomic Vocabulary

(The Slovak term is shown only when it differs from the Czech word).

English	Czech	Slovak
restaurant	restaurace	reštaurácia
café	kavárna	kaviareň
breakfast	snídaně	raňajky
lunch	obed	
dinner	večeře	večera
eat	jísti	jest'

Food and Drink

English	Czech	Slovak
drink	píti	pit'
much	mnoho	
little	málo	
knife	nůž	nôz
fork	vidlička	
spoon	lžíce	lyžica
plate	talíř	tanier
cup	šálek	šálka
glass	sklenice	pohár
napkin	ubrousek	servítka
corkscrew	vývrtka	
bill	účet	
tip	spropitné	prepitné
waiter	vrchní	čašník
pay	platiti	platit'
at once	hned	hned'
menu	jidelní listek	jedalny listok
soup	polévka	polievka
dumpling	knedlík	knedl'a
meat	maso	mäso
beef	hovězí	hovädzí
boiled pork	ovar	obar
goulash	guláš	
mutton	skopové	škopovo
pork	vepřová	bravčové
roast	pečeně	pečienka
sausage (small)	klobása	
schnitzel	řízek	rezeň
smoked meat	uzené	údeniny
veal	telecí	tel'ací
poultry	drůbež	hydina
chicken	kohoutek	kohútik
duck	kachna	kačica
goose	husa	hus
pheasant	bažant	
game	zvěřina	divina
hare	zajík	zajac
roedeer	srnec	
venison	jelen	jeleň
sausage (large)	sálam	saláma
ham	šunka	
tongue	jazyk	
fish	ryba	
carp	kapr	kapor
pike	štika	šťuka
trout	pstruh	
vegetables	zelenia	

English	Czech	Slovak
cauliflower	karfiol	
cucumber	okurka	uhorka
lettuce	hlávkový salát	hlávkový šalát
mushrooms	houby	huby
onion	cibule	cibul'a
potatoes	brambora	zemiak
red cabbage	červené zelí	červena kapusta
sauerkraut	kyselé zelí	kyslá zelina
spinach	špenát	
tomato	rajske jablíčko	paradajka
ice	zmrzlina	
cheese	sýr	syr
ewe's-milk cheese	brynza	bryndza
compote	kompot	kompót
pancake	palačinka	palacinka
fruit	ovoce	ovocie
apple	jablko	
apricot	meruňka	marhul'a
bilberry	borůvka	čučoríedka
cherry	třešně	čerešňa
grapes	hrozen	hrozno
lemon	citrón	
orange	pomeranče	pomaranč
peach	broskev	broskyňa
pear	hruška	
plum	slíva, švestka	slivka
drinks	nápoje	
apricot brandy	meruňkovice	
beer	pivo	
brandy	pálenka	
corn schnapps	režná	kořolka
juniper schnapps	borovička	
plum brandy	slivovice	slivovica
coffee	káva	
lemonade	limonáda	
milk	mléko	mlieko
mineral water	minerálka	
tea	čaj	
water	voda	
wine	víno	
red wine	červené víno	
white wine	bilé víno	
bread	chléb	chlieb
bun	buchta	
cake	koláč	
croissant	rohlík	rožok
roll	chlebiček	
wafer	oplatka	

English	Czech	Slovak
butter	máslo	maslo
honey	med	
jam	marmeláda	
eggs	vejce	vajce
hard-boiled	vejce na tvrdo	vajce na tvrdo
soft-boiled	vejce na měkko	vajce na měkko
fried eggs	sázená vejce	volské oko (sing.)
noodles	nudle	rezance
rice	rýža	
salt	sůl	sol'
sugar	cukr	cukor
vinegar	ocet	ocot
oil	olej	

Drink

Beer See entry

Wine See entry

Spirits

Among the best known spirits are the slivovice (plum brandy) of Moravian Slovakia, meruňkovice (apricot brandy), žitná or režná (corn schnapps) and jalovcová or borovička (juniper schnapps, resembling gin). After a hearty meal many people swear by the becherovka of Karlovy Vary, an excellent bitter herb liqueur.
In Slovakia there is a popular hot drink made from honey and various fruit liqueurs.

Coffee

Coffee is usually made in the Turkish fashion, the ground coffee being boiled with the water. Italian-style espresso coffee and Viennese coffee with whipped cream can also be had.

Other non-alcoholic drinks include Czech and Slovak mineral waters, orange or grapefruit juice (the English word "juice" is used), tea and milk.

Getting to the Czech and Slovak Republics

By Air

There are numerous scheduled flights from European and American cities to Prague and Bratislava, as well as charter flights during the holiday season.

Information: from ČSA and other international airlines.

By Car

The journey by car from Britain to the Czech and Slovak Republics is a long and strenuous one. From the Channel ports to Prague by the shortest route (via Cologne, Frankfurt and Nuremberg, entering the Czech Republic at the Waidhaus–Rozvadov frontier crossing) it is at least two days' hard driving. If the journey through Germany is regarded as part of the holiday and rather more time is allowed for it, there are possible alternative routes via Dresden, Leipzig, Bayreuth, Regensburg, Munich and other towns.

The most suitable route can be selected with the help of the following list of frontier crossings from Germany (which are normally open 24 hours a day).

Frontier Crossings from Germany

Görlitz or Bautzen–Česká Lípa–Mělník–Prague (Road 9):
frontier crossing Seifhennersdorf–Varnsdorf.

Dresden–Děčín–Ústí nad Labem–Litoměřice–Prague (E 442, E 55/Road 8):
frontier crossing Schmilka–Hřensko.

Dresden–Ústí nad Labem–Litoměřice–Prague (E 55/Road 8):
frontier crossing Bahratal–Petrovice.

Dresden–Teplice–Terezín–Prague (E 55/Road 8):
frontier crossing Zinnwald–Cínovec (heavy goods traffic).

Leipzig–Chomutov–Louny–Prague (Road 7):
frontier crossing Reitzenhain–Hora Svatého Šebestiána.

Leipzig–Chemnitz–Karlovy Vary–Prague (Roads 25 and 13, E 48/Road 6):
frontier crossing Oberwiesenthal–Boží Dar.

Plauen–Cheb–Karlovy Vary–Prague (E 49):
frontier crossing Bad Brambach–Vojtanov.

Bayreuth–Cheb–Karlovy Vary or Plzeň–Prague (E 49, E 48 or Road 21 and E 50):
frontier crossing Selb–Aš.

Bayreuth–Cheb–Karlovy Vary–Prague (E 49, E 48/Road 6):
frontier crossings (extremely busy) Schirnding–Pomezí nad Ohří or Waldsassen–Svatý Kříž.

Bayreuth–Mariánské Lázně–Plzeň–Prague (Road 21 and E 50):
frontier crossings Mähring–Broumov or Bärnau–Tachov.

Nuremberg–Stříbro–Plzeň–Prague (Road 5/E 50):
frontier crossing Waidhaus–Rozvadov (very busy).

Regensburg or Munich–Domažlice–Plzeň–Prague (Road 26, then E 50):
frontier crossings Waldmünchen–Lisková, Furth im Wald–Folmava, Eschlklamm–Všeruby or Bayerisch Eisenstein–Železná Ruda.

Munich or Salzburg–Klatovy–Plzeň–Prague (Road 27, then E 50):
frontier crossing Bayerisch Eisenstein–Železná Ruda.

Passau–Strakonice–Dobříš–Prague (Road 4):
frontier crossings Philippsreuth–Strážný or Haidmühle–Stožec.

By Coach

There are direct coach services from London to Prague several times a week, run by Kingscourt Express and Eurolines. The journey takes between 21 and 28 hours.

Information

Kingscourt Express
15 Balham High Road
London SW12 9AJ
Tel. (081) 673 7500

Eurolines
164 Buckingham Palace Road
London SW1. Tel. (071) 730 0202

By Rail

The journey from London to Prague by rail takes just over 24 hours, changing twice in Germany. Alternatively it is possible to travel via Paris, from which (Gare de l'Est) there are through coaches to Prague; this takes about 8 hours longer.

Information

British Rail European Travel Centre
Victoria Station
London SW1. Tel. (071) 834 2345

Eurotrain
52 Grosvenor Gardens
London SW1. Tel. (071) 730 3402

Help for the Disabled

There is little accommodation in the Czech and Slovak Republics specially suited to the needs of the disabled. One hotel with suitable facilities is the Club Hotel at Průhonice, 12km/7½ miles from Prague city centre on the D 1 motorway (Prague–Brno).

Detailed information can be obtained from Čedok (see Information).

Hotels

Categories

Alongside the official categories A* de luxe, A*, B* (usually very good), B (good) and C (modest) – mainly still applied to older establishments – a new classification is increasingly coming into use, ranging from five stars (*****) for a luxury hotel down to one star for hotels of modest pretensions.

Reservation

Advance reservation, either direct or through Čedok (see Information), is necessary, particularly in Prague, Bratislava and Brno, the spa towns and the large holiday resorts in the mountains.

Other accommodation

Other accommodation is available in motels, inns, mountain huts (*bouda, chata)*, student residences, youth hostels and camping sites.

Private rooms

Increasing numbers of private rooms are now available, though the facilities may sometimes be rather basic. The price should be agreed in advance.

Hotels in the Czech Republic

Abertamy Plečivec, C, 93 beds

Aš Lev, B, 74 b.

Babylon Čerchov, B, 85 b.; Praha, B, 217 b.

Bavorov Šumava, C, 35 b.

Lužnice, C, 40 b.	**Bechyně**
U Radnice, C, 21 b.	**Bělá** pod Bezdězem
Karbo, B, 72 b.	**Benátky** nad Jizerou
Žalý***; Hančova Bouda, B and C, 45 b.; Súca, C, 50 b.	**Benecko**
Motel Konopiště***, 80 b.; Pošta, B, 72 b.; Zimní Stadión, C, 49 b.	**Benešov**
Černá, C, 39 b.	**Benešov** nad Černou
Jelen, B, 50 b.	**Benešov** nad Ploučnicí
Český Dvůr, C, 36 b.; Litava**, 137 b.	**Beroun**
Ebeka, B, 72 b.	**Bílá** (Frýdek-Místek)
Praha, C, 19 b.; Vyhlídka, C, 26 b.	**Bílina**
Dukla, B, 144 b.; Macocha, B, 52 b. ; Panoráma***, Češkovice	**Blansko**
Beránek, C, 29 b.	**Blatná**
Panský Dům, C, 16 b.	**Blovice**
Grand, B, 50 b.; Národní Dům, C, 32 b.	**Bohumín**
Hvězda, C, 14 b.; Nový Světlov Castle, C	**Bojkovice**
Národní Dům, C, 22 b.	**Bor**
Velen, B, 81 b.; Slavia, C, 26 b.	**Boskovice**
Bouzov, B, 34 b.	**Bouzov**
Praha, C, 66 b.; Zelený Dům, C, 42 b.	**Boží Dar**
Jiříčka, B, 25 b.	**Brandýs** nad Orlicí
Grand, B, 49 b.; Slávie, B, 58 b.; Zimní Stadión, B, 72 b.	**Břeclav**
Městský Pívovar, B, 31 b.; Vlčava, C, 24 b.	**Březnice**
Racek, C, 33 b.; Srdičko, C, 18 b.	**Brná** nad Labem
Continental****, Kounicová 20, 564 b.; Slavia****, Solniční 15–17, 157 b.; Grand Hotel, Benešova 18–20, A*, 184 b.; International, Husova 16, A*, 435 b.; Voroněž I, Křížkovského 47, A*, 947 b.; Voroněž II, Křížkovského 49, B*, 322 b.; Avion, Česká 20, B*, 62 b.; Slovan, Lidická 23, B*, 207 b.; U Jakuba, Jakubské Náměstí 6, B*, 65 b.; Metropol**, Dornych 5, 120 b.; Morava**, Novobranská 3, 160 b.; Evropa, Náměstí Svobody 13, B, 98 b.; Korzo, Kopečná 10, B, 55 b.; Merkur, Rostislavovo Náměstí, B, 49 b.; Společenský Dům, Horova 30, 40 b.	**Brno**
Městský, B, 68 b.; Praha, C, 43 b.	**Broumov**

Brumov-Bylnice	U Nádraží, Bylnice, C, 27 b.
Bruntál	Společenský Dům, B, 10 b.
Brusno (Banská Bystrica)	Brusno, B, 32 b.
Bučovice	Hvezda, C, 23 b.
Bystřice pod Hostýnem	Podhoran, C, 86 b.; In Chavalšov: Říha, C, 29 b.
Bystřička (Vsetín)	Klenov, B, 41 b.
Bzenec	Lidový Dům, C, 48 b.
Čáslav	Bílý Kůň, B, 51 b.; Grand, C, 28 b.
Černá Hora (Janské Lázně)	Horský, B, 88 b.; Sokolská Bouda, B, 103 b.
Černá v Pošumaví	Racek, B, 63 b.
Červenohorské Sedlo	Červenohorské Sedlo, C, 42 b.; Dlohé Stráně, C, 40 b.
Červený Kostelec	Hvězda, C, 30 b.
Česká Kamenice	Slávie, C, 85 b.
Česká Lípa	Merkur, B, 94 b.; Kahan, C, 223 b.; U Nádraží, C, 30 b.
Česká Skalice	Na Rozkoši, C, 95 b.
Česká Třebová	Moskva, C, 56 b.
České Budějovice	Gomel****, 469 b.; Zvon, A* and B, 104 b.; Vltava***, 140 b.; Malše, B, 83 b.; Slunce, B, 64 b.
České Velenice	Konzul**, 39 b.
Český Brod	Slavoj***, 112 b.; Sport, C, 24 b.
Český Dub	Koruna, C, 22 b.
Český Krumlov	Krumlov, B*, 53 b.; Růže, B*, 44 b.; Vyšehrad, B*, 128 b.
Český Šternberk	Pod Hradem, C, 23 b.
Český Těšín	Slezský Dům, B*, 52 b.; Piast, B, 100 b.
Chabařovice	Slávie, B, 18 b.
Cheb	Hvězda, B*, 88 b.; Hradní Dvůr, B, 46 b.; Slávie, B, 66 b.; Chebský Dvůr, C, 35 b.
Chlum v Třeboňe	Společenský Dům, B; Panská, C, 43 b.
Chlumec nad Cidlinou	Astra, C, 58 b.
Chocerady	Ostende, C, 33 b.

Horský, B, 32 b.; Royal, B, 90 b.; Třetí Mlýn, B, 60 b.; Zimní Stadión, C, 41 b.	**Chomutov**
Vysočina, B, 63 b.	**Chotěboř**
Družstevní Dům, C, 122 b.	**Choustník**
Ječmínek, C, 43 b.	**Chropyně**
Družba, B, 100 b.	**Chrudim**
Churáňov, B, 156 b.; Sporthotel Olympia, B, 127 b.	**Churáňov** (Bohemian Forest)
Pomezí, B, 55 b.	**Cínovec**
Jednota, B, 33 b.	**Čkyně**
Sever, C, 23 b.	**Cvikov**
Dyje, B, 35 b.; Stadión**, 37 b.	**Dačice**
Pivovar, B, 41 b.; U Topolů, C, 70 b.	**Davle**
Grand, B*, 144 b.; Radnice, C, 29 b.; Sever, C, 49 b.; Sport, C, 39 b.	**Děčín**
Chata U Můstku, C, 39 b.	**Desná**
Národní Dům, B*, 49 b.; Orlice, B, 40 b.; Květa, C, 42 b.	**Deštné** v Orlických Horách
Motel, on Prague–Brno motorway, B, 40 b.	**Devět Krízu**
Pohostinství, B, 40 b.	**Dobronice**
Heinz, C, 32 b.	**Dobříš**
Grand, B, 106 b.; Bezděz, C, 17 b.; Pasáž, C, 46 b.; Sport, C, 29 b.	**Doksy**
Morava, C, 45 b.	**Dolní Dvůr**
Družba, B, 120 b.; Chodský, B, 32 b.; Koruna, B, 25 b.; Slavia, C, 32 b.	**Domažlice**
Slavia, C, 55 b.	**Dubá**
Motel Halda, B, 45 b.	**Dubenec**
Sport, C, 47 b.	**Dubí**
Městský Hotel, C, 22 b.	**Duchcov**
Dvoračky, C, 38 b.	**Dvoračky** (Krkonoše)
Central, C, 44 b.; Květen, C, 30 b.	**Dvůr Králové** nad Labem
Monti (sanatorium), A, 67 b.; Bajkal, B, 108 b.; Slovan, B, 42 b.; Ztíší, B and C, 87 b.; Tatran, C, 72 b.	**Františkovy Lázně**
Vlčina, B*, 64 b.; Radhošt', B, 38 b.; Sport, B, 34 b. Mountain hotels: Tanečnica, Pustevny, B, 120 b.; Radhošt', Skalikova Louka, B, 37 b.	**Frenštát** pod Radhoštěm
Beskyd, B, 83 b.; Centrum***	**Frýdek-Místek**
Valdštyn, C, 22 b.	**Frýdlant**

Hotels

Frýdlant nad Ostravicí	Motel Panoráma, B, 123 b. Mountain hotel: Solárka, C, 60 b.
Frymburk	Vltava, B, 55 b.
Fulnek	Zlatý Kříž, C, 23 b.
Gruň (Beskýds)	Mountain hotel: Charbulák, C, 66 b.
Harrachov	Hubertus, B*, 48 b.; Hubertka, B, 22 b.; Juniorhotel Fit & Fun***, 354 b.; Sporthotel Skicentrum***; Chata Diana, C, 14 b.; Krakonoš, C, 40 b.; Ryžoviště, C, 189 b. Mountain hotel: Vosecká Bouda, C, 51 b.
Havířov	Merkur, B*, 233 b.
Havlíčkův Brod	Slunce***, 102 b.; Černý Orel, C, 49 b.
Hejnice	Perun, B, 108 b.
Herálec	Žákova Hora, C, 33 b.
Heřmanuv Městec	Heřman, B, 56 b.; Obora, C, 10 b.
Hluboká nad Vltavou	Parkhotel, B, 100 b.
Hodonín	Grand, B, 56 b.; Sportklub, B, 42 b.; Central, C, 44 b.
Hojná Voda	Hojná Voda, C, 28 b.
Hojsova Stráž (Bohemian Forest)	Bílá Strž, C, 78 b.; Na Stráži, C, 35 b.; Vyhlídka, C, 38 b.
Holešov	Slavia, C, 27 b.; Sokolský Dům, C, 23 b.
Holice	U Krále Jiřího, C, 43 b.
Holoubkov	Plzeň, C, 38 b.
Horažd'ovice	Modrá Hvězda, C, 46 b.; Zlatý Jelen, C, 37 b.
Hořice	Beránek, C, 50 b.
Horní Bečva	Valaška, C, 50 b.
Horní Blatná	Modrá Hvězda, C, 45 b.
Horní Mísečky (Krkonoše)	Cáchovna, Hořec, Kleč, C, 220 b.
Horní Planá	Smrčina, B, 35 b.
Hořovice	Zelený Strom, B*, 50 b.
Horšovský Týn	Dělnický Dům, C, 39 b.
Hostinné	Městský Hotel, B, 46 b.
Hostivice	Chmelový Keř, C, 48 b.
Hošt'ka	Tichý, C, 24 b.

Černigov, A*, 592 b.; Alessandria, B*, 203 b.; Bystrica, B*, 171 b.; Zimní Stadión, B*, 92 b.; Paříž, B, 44 b.	**Hradec Králové**
Zámecký, B and C, 58 b. and 35 b.	**Hradec** nad Moravicí
Sokolovna, B, 30 b.; Brno, C, 25 b.	**Hranice**
Hrazany, B, 56 b.	**Hrazany** (Lake Slapy)
Hukvaldy, B, 80 b.; Labe, C, 46 b.	**Hřensko**
Radnice, C, 68 b.	**Hronov**
Central, C, 40 b.	**Hulín**
Orlík, B, 24 b.; Rekrea, B, 48 b.	**Humpolec**
Na Knižecí, C, 29 b.	**Husinec**
Hotel, B, 49 b.	**Hustopeče**
Praha, B, 34 b.	**Hvězdonice**
Černý Lev, B, 16 b.; Besední Dům, C, 17 b.	**Ivančice**
Merkur***; Zlatý Jelen, B**, 208 b.; Corso, B*, 73 b.; Praha, B, 62 b.; Zlatý Lev, B and C, 43 b.	**Jablonec** nad Nisou
U Černého Mědvěda, B, 37 b.	**Jablonné** nad Orlicí
Hvězda, C, 29 b.	**Jablonné** v Podjěstědí
Jablunkov, C, 19 b.	**Jablunkov**
Klínovec, C, 149 b.; Slavia, C, 57 b.	**Jáchymov**
Praha, B, 55 b.; Lesná Dům, C, 53 b. Mountain hotel: Horský**	**Janské Lázně**
Praha, C, 21 b.	**Jaroměř**
Opera, B, 60 b.	**Jaroměřice** nad Rokytnou
Terasa, B, 35 b.	**Jedovnice**
Mir*** (spa hotel); Priessnitz*** (spa hotel); Morava, B, 57 b.; Slovan, B, 70 b.; Mýtinka**; Jeseník, C, 51 b.; Slunný Dvůr, C, 47 b.; Stařič, C, 40 b.; Zlatý Chlum, C, 58 b.	**Jeseník**
Mountain hotel: Ještěd, A, 24 b.	**Ještěd** (Liberec)
Jevany, B, 50 b.	**Jevany**
Morava, C, 21 b.	**Jevíčko**
Astra, B, 46 b.; Start, B, 123 b.; Praha, C, 32 b.	**Jičín**
Grand****, 65 b.; Jihlava***, 172 b.; Zlatá Hvězda***, 60 b.	**Jihlava**
Cedron**, 30 b.; Česká Bouda, C, 46 b.; Grand, C, 35 b.	**Jilemnice**

Hotels

Jince	Kratochvil, B, 32 b.
Jindřichův Hradec	Grand, B, 55 b.; Vajgar, B, 68 b.
Jiřetín pod Jedlovou	Slovan, C, 80 b.
Jiříkov	Beseda, C, 35 b.
Jirkov	Praha, C, 37 b.
Josefův Důl	Pošta, C, 30 b.
Kadaň	Zelený Strom, B*, 200 b.; Svoboda, B, 40 b.; Bílý Beránek, C, 23 b.
Kamenice nad Lipou	Lípa, B, 45 b.
Kandlův Mlýn (Prachatice)	Kandlův Mlýn, C, 46 b.
Kaplice	Sport, C, 29 b.; Zlatý Kříž, C, 24 b.
Kařez (Rokycany)	Bouchalka, B, 40 b.
Karlova Studánka	Džbán, B, 28 b. Mountain hotels: Barborka, C, 131 b.; Kurzovní Chata, C, 180 b.
Karlovy Vary	Bristol, A*, 58 b.; Grand Hotel Pupp, A*, 337 b., and Villa Margareta, 16 b.; Imperial (spa hotel), A*, 367 b.; Park, A*, 295 b.; Dvořák****, 76 rooms and 3 suites; Ohře, B*, 26 b.; Adria, B, 66 b.; Atlantik, B, 88 b.; Central***, 114 b.; Jizera, B, 65 b.; Juniorhotel Alice, B, 189 b.; Národní Dům, B, 230 b.; Otava, B, 155 b.; Slavia, B, 120 b.; Turist, B, 42 b.; Beseda, C, 46 b.; Brix, C, 52 b.; Motel Gejzír Park, C, 51 b.

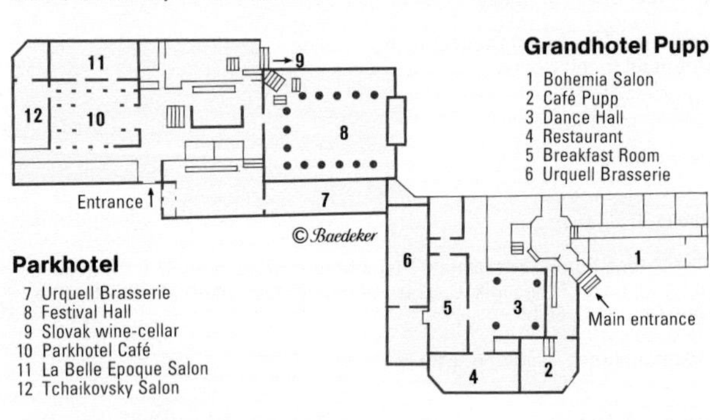

Karviná	Jelen, B*, 56 b.; Darkov, C, 24 b.; Sport, C, 46 b.
Kašperské Hory	Bílá Růže, B, 52 b.; Kašperk, C, 65 b.
Kdyně	Bílý Lev, B, 39 b.
Kladno	Kladno, B*, 254 b.; Lidový Dům, B, 43 b.; Sport, C, 55 b.

Place	Hotels
Klášterec nad Ohří	Slavia, B, 23 b.
Klášterec nad Orlicí	U Mostu, C, 19 b.
Klatovy	Beránek, B, 51 b.; Bílá Růze, B, 58 b.; Central, B, 115 b.
Klenčí pod Čerchovem	Výhledy, B, 68 b.; Haltrava, C, 44 b.
Klínovec (Ore Mountains)	Horský, C, 95 b.
Kojetín	Pivovar, C, 15 b.
Kokořín	Dolina, B, 44 b.; U Grobiána, C, 54 b.
Kolín	Savoy, B, 73 b.; Zimní Stadión, B and C, 29 and 27 b.
Koloděje nad Lužnicí	Lužnice, C, 25 b.
Komárov	Krumphanzl, C, 28 b.
Komorní Lhotaka	Goduala, C, 26 b.
Konopiště	Myslivna, B, 93 b.; Zámecký, C, 72 b.
Konstantinovy Lázně	Jitřenka, B, 46 b.; Tvorba, C, 31 b.
Kopřivnice	Stadión, B, 49 b.; Tatra***, 162 b.
Kořenov	Sport, C, 30 b.
Kost	Podkost, C, 42 b.
Kostelec (Jihlava)	Horal, B, 52 b.
Kostelec pod Černými Lesy	Závist, C, 26 b.; Zelený Dům, C, 35 b.
Kovářská (Ore Mountains)	Central, C, 65 b.
Králíky	Beseda, C, 19 b. Městský Dvůr, C, 47 b.; Zlatá Labut', C, 20 b.
Kralovice (Plzeň)	Prusík, C, 14 b.
Kralupy nad Vltavou	Praha, B, 26 b.; Sport, B, 100 b.
Kraslice	Praha, B, 66 b.
Krásná (Frýdek-Místek)	Mountain hotel: Visalaje, B, 136 b.
Krásná Lípa	Beseda, C, 55 b.
Křemešník	Křemešník, C, 46 b.
Křivoklát	Křivoklát, C, 46 b.

Hotels

Krnov	Morava, B*, 32 b.; Slezský Domov, B, 71 b.
Kroměříž	Haná, B, 139 b.; Straka, C, 35 b.
Krupka (Teplice)	Komáří Vížka, C, 36 b.
Kunštát	Rudka, B, 61 b.
Kupařovice	Zámek, B, 92 b.
Kutná Hora	Mědinek, B*, 164 b.
Kyjov	Slavia, C, 51 b.
Kynšperk nad Ohří	Bílá Labut', C, 54 b.
Lanškroun	Společenský Dům, B, 54 b.; Slavia, C, 60 b.
Lázně Bělohrad	Bohumilka, C, 32 b.
Lázně Kynžvart	Kynžvartský Dvůr, B, 28 b.
Lázně Libverda	Park, C, 48 b.
Ledeč nad Sázavou	Sázava, C, 15 b.; Stadión, C, 14 b.
Lednice	Zámecký, B, 28 b.
Letohrad	Orlice, C, 14 b.
Letovice	Koupaliště, C, 140 b.; Svitavice (Larinov), C, 50 b.
Liberec	Imperial, B*, 150 b.; Zlatý Lev, B*, 114 b.; Praha, at Town Hall, 60 b.; U Jezírka, B, 57 b.; Česká Beseda, C, 66 b.
Libochovice	Černý Orel, C, 28 b.
Lipník nad Bečvou	Lípa, B, 42 b.
Lipno nad Vltavou	Lipno, C, 102 b.
Lipová Lázně	Lípa, C, 17 b.
Litoměřice	Hotelový Dům, B*, 60 b.; Labut', B and C, 39 b.
Litomyšl	Dalibor, B, 140 b.; Slezák, C, 32 b.; Zlatá Hvězda, C, 25 b.
Litoval	Záložna, C, 38 b.
Litvínov	Radniční Sklípek, B, 17 b.
Loket	Bílý Kůn, B, 159 b.
Lomnice nad Popelkou	Praha, C, 13 b.
Loučeň	Otomanský, C, 17 b.
Loučovice	Lesní Krčma, B, 37 b.

Louny
Union, B*, 85 b.; Podniková Ubytovna, C, 144 b.

Lovosice
Lev, B, 36 b.

Luby
Nový Hotel, C, 28 b.

Luhačovice
Alexandra, B*, 73 b.; Litovel, C, 115 b.; Miramare, C, 41 b.

Lukov (Zlín)
Na Pivovarě, C, 32 b.

Lysá nad Labem
Polabí, B, 44 b.

Lysice
Lidový Dům, C, 37 b.

Malá Morávka
Na Rychtě, C, 46 b.; Praděd, Karlov, C, 15 b.

Malá Škála
Jizera, C, 70 b.; U Nádraží, C, 38 b.

Malá Úpa
Devětsil, C, 31 b.; Honzíček**; Rusalka, C, 47 b.

Manětín
Manětín, B, 47 b.

Mariánské Lázně
Golf, A* de luxe, 52 b.; Palace Praha, A*, 95 b.; Royal (sanatorium), B*, 47 b. (incl. 3 apts); Excelsior, B*, 173 b.; Atlantic, B, 108 b.; Corso, B, 67 b.; Cristal, B, 192 b.; Esplanade***, 267 b.; Juniorhotel Krakonoš, B, 228 b.; Kamzík, B, 36 b.; Park, B, 53 b.; Sporthotel Slunce, B, 63 b.; Haná, C, 20 b.

Měděnec
Praha, C, 52 b.

Mělník
Ludmila, B, 203 b.; U Nádraží, C, 30 b.; Zlatý Beránek, C, 18 b.

Mezná (Děčín)
Mezní Louka, B, 73 b.

Mikulášovice
Střelnice, C, 24 b.

Mikulčin Vrch (Uherské Hradiště)
Mikulčin Vrch, C, 40 b.

Mikulov
U Nádraží, C, 25 b.; Zámecký, C, 29 b.

Milevsko
Modrá Hvězda, B, 72 b.; Stadión**, 108 b.

Miličín
Česká Sibiř, C, 45 b.

Mladá Boleslav
Auto Škoda, B, 148 b.; Věnec, B, 76 b.; Hvězda, C, 45 b.

Mladá Vožice
Záložna, B, 50 b.

Mnichovo Hradiště
U Hroznu, B, 42 b.; U Nádraží, C, 25 b.

Modrava
Zlatá Stezka, C, 24 b.

Mohelnice (Šumperk)
Slavia, C, 42 b.

Moldava (Ore Mountains)
Hranice, C, 56 b.

Morávka (Frýdek-Místek)
Morávka, C, 31 b.; Partyzán, C, 25 b.
Mountain hotel: Visalaje, B, 136 b.

Moravská Třebová	Slavia, B, 50 b.; Morava, C, 33 b.
Moravské Budějovice	Komják, C, 69 b.
Moravský Beroun	Národní Dům, C, 35 b.
Moravský Krumlov	Jednota, B, 53 b.
Most	Murom***, 490 b.
Mosty u Jablunkova	Beskyd, C, 20 b.
Mšeno	Zlatý Lev, C, 12 b.
Náchod	Beránek, B, 67 b.; Zimní Stadión***; Hron, C, 45 b.; Itálie, C, 47 b.; Vyhlídka, C, 33 b.; Zámecká Restaurace, C, 45 b.
Náměšť nad Oslavou	Fontana, C, 16 b.
Nejdek	Krásná Vyhlídka, B, 18 b.; Pošta, C, 42 b.
Nepomuk	U Nádraží, C, 25 b.
Neratovice	Srdíčko, C, 17 b.
Neznašov	Na Soutoku, C, 28 b.
Nižbor	Praha, C, 40 b.
Nová Paka	Centrál, B*, 57 b.
Nova Pec (Prachatice)	U Nádraží, B, 67 b.
Nová Ves (Mladá Boleslav)	U Jezera, B, 60 b.
Nové Hrady (Č. Budějovice)	Maj, C, 43 b.
Nové Město na Moravě	Ski, B, 126 b.; Skalský Dvůr, Lisek, B, 100 b.
Nové Město nad Metují	Metuje, C, 59 b.
Nové Město pod Smrkem	Dělnický Dům, C
Nové Strašecí	Sport, C, 47 b.
Nový Bor	Grand, B, 98 b.
Nový Bydžov	Lev, B, 59 b.
Nový Jičín	Kalač, B*, 143 b.; Praha, B*, 70 b.; Krytý Bazén, B, 14 b.; Salaš, B, 31 b.; U Nádraží, C, 41 b.
Nymburk	Praha, B, 54 b.; Záložna, C, 21 b.; Zimní Stadión, C, 46 b.

Radnice, B, 30 b.; Koruna, C, 20 b.	**Nýrsko**
Flora, B*, 340 b.; Národní Dům, B*, 102 b.; Praha, B*, 80 b.; Sigma***, 191 b.; Morava, B, 102 b.; Haná, C, 42 b.	**Olomouc**
Koruna***, 220 b.; Orient, B, 102 b.; Zimní Stadión, B, 40 b.; Park**, 80 b.	**Opava**
Zámecký, B, 55 b.; Holub, C, 44 b.	**Opočno**
Slunce, C, 52 b.	**Osečná**
Horník, C, 21 b.	**Oslavany**
U Nádraží, C, 25 b.; Imperial, A*, 140 b.; Palace, B*, 309 b.; Beseda, B, 47 b.; Chemik***, 60 b.; Moravia, B, 78 b.; Odra, B, 114 b.	**Ostrava**
Na Mýtě, C, 53 b.; Ostravice, C, 46 b.; Smrk, C, 24 b.	**Ostravice**
Krušnohor, B, 67 b.	**Ostrov** (Karlovy Vary)
Společenský Dům, B, 180 b.	**Otrokovice**
Na Panské, C, 14 b.	**Pacov**
Nádraží****, 67 b.; Grand, B, 81 b.; Zimní Stadión, B, 40 b.; Zlatá Štika, B, 77 b.	**Pardubice**
Koruna, C, 50 b.; Pecka, C, 44 b.	**Pecka**
U Karla IV, B, 28 b.	**Pecký** (Nymburk)
Horizont, B*, 354 b.; Hořec, B, 44 b.; Děčín, C, 87 b. Large mountain hotels: Luční Bouda and Výrovka	**Pec** pod Sněžkou
Vysočina, B*, 130 b.; Grand, B, 20 b.; Slavie, B, 41 b. Sportovní Hala, C, 46 b.; U Nádraží, C, 10 b.	**Pelhřimov**
Perninský Dvůr, C, 44 b.; Zelené Údolí, C, 32 b.	**Pernink**
Meran, C, 28 b.; Potočná, C, 58 b.	**Perštejn** (Chomutov)
Otava, B*, 94 b.; Bílá Růze, B, 58 b.; Sport, B, 40 b.; U Tří Korun, B, 33 b.; Zimní Stadión, C, 144 b.	**Písek**
Motorest, B, 43 b.; Hejtman, C, 30 b.	**Planá** nad Lužnicí
Plešivec, C, 23 b.	**Plešivec** (Ore Mountains)
Continental, A*, 83 b.; Central, B*, 133 b.; Škoda, B*, 154 b.; Plzeň, B, 90 b.; Slovan, B, 210 b.	**Plzeň**
Lidový Dům, C, 56 b.	**Poběžovice** (Domažlice)
Modrá Hvězda, C, 18 b.	**Počátky**
Slunce, B, 35 b.; Národní Dům, C, 12 b.; Růže, C, 14 b.	**Podbořany**
Hubert, B*, 60 b.; Praha, B*, 32 b.	**Poděbrady**

Hotels

Podhradí nad Dyjí (Znojmo)	Zátiší, C, 32 b.
Pohořelice	Morava, B*, 148 b.
Polička	Opus, B, 42 b.; Poličan, C, 23 b.; U Pošty, C, 10 b.
Potštejn	Praha, C, 25 b.
Prachatice	VTS, B*; Národní Dům, B, 30 b.; Zlatá Stezka, B, 26 b.; Kandlův Mlýn, C, 28 b.
Prachov	Skalní Město, B, 62 b.
Prague ***** hotels	Alcron, Štěpánská 40, Praha 1, 194 b. (under renovation); Esplanade, Washingtonova 19, Praha 1, 98 b.; Inter-Continental, Nám. Curieových, Praha 1, 732 b.; Jalta, Václavské Nám.; 45, Praha 1, 127 b.; Palace, Panská 12, Praha 1, 147 b.
**** hotels	Ambassador, Václavské Nám. 5, Praha 1, 212 b.; Atlantik, Na Poříčí 9, Praha 1, 131 b.; Atrium, Pobřežní 1–3, Praha 8, 780 rooms; Diplomat, Evropská 15, Praha 6, 860 b.; Evropa, Václavské Nám. 25, Praha 1, 184 b.; Forum, Kongresová 1, Praha 4, 1093 b.; International, Nám.; Družby 35, Praha 6, 483 b.; Olympik I, Invalidovna, Praha 8, 515 b.; Panorama, Milevská 7, Praha 4, 864 b.; Paříž, U Obechního Domu 1, Praha 1, 162 b.; Park, Veletržní 20, Praha 7, 391 b.; President, Nám. Curieových 100, Praha 1, 194 b.; Villa Voyta (elegant, quiet), K Novému Dvoru 124/54; U Páva (small; view), U Lužického Semináře 36; Club Hotel Průhonice, at Průhonice Castle (12km/7½ miles from city on D 1 motorway; beautiful setting, recreational facilities; shuttle bus service from Metro), CZ-25243 Průhonice, 190 b.
*** hotels	Flora, Vinohradská 121, Praha 3, 361 b.; Globus, Horní Roztyly, Praha 4, 300 b.; Karl Inn (200m from Křižíkova Metro), Praha 8, 168 b.; Olympik II (no rest.), Invalidovna, Praha 8, 426 b.; Splendid, Ovenecká 33, Praha 7, 79 b.
No restaurant	Apollo, Kubišova 23, Praha 8, 65 b.
Botels	Good accommodation is also available in botels (hotel ships) moored on the banks of the Vltava: Admiral, Hořejší Nábřeží, Praha 5, 180 b.; Albatros, Nábřeží Ludvíka Svobody, Praha 1, 166 b.; In Praha-Východ district: René**, CZ-25001 Nechánice, tel. (02) 99 26 91, 20 b.
Pražmo (Frýdek-Místek)	Travný, C, 55 b.
Přelouč	Sport, B, 25 b.
Přerov	Grand, B, 83 b.; Přerov, B, 118 b.
Přeštice	Lidový Dům, C, 16 b.; Zemědělský Dům, C, 10 b.
Příbor	Letka, B, 100 b.; U Nádraží, B, 27 b.
Příbram	Kulturní Dům, B*, 110 b.; Plavecký Bazén, B, 14 b.; Zimní Stadión, B, 36 b.; Horymír, C, 40 b.
Přibyslav	Délnický Dům, C, 21 b.; Mladý Požárník, C, 92 b.
Příchovice	Motorest Beseda, B, 50 b.
Příhrazy	Příhrazy, B, 66 b.
Proseč	Hornička, C, 24 b.

Avion, B, 28 b.; Grand, B, 73 b.; Hlavní Nádraží, B, 24 b.; Tří Králů, B, 62 b.	**Prostějov**
U Chudých, C, 20 b.	**Protivín**
Club Hotel Průhonice (see under Prague); Tulipán, B, 28 b.	**Průhonice**
Motorest, C, 13 b.	**Rabí**
Park, B, 250 b.	**Rabyně** (Lake Slapy)
Račín, C, 31 b.	**Račín** (Žd'ár nad Sázavou)
Horník, B, 32 b.	**Radnice**
Jednota, C, 32 b.	**Rajnochovice** (Kroměříž)
Družba****, 174 b.	**Rakovník**
Řeka, C, 47 b.	**Řeka**
Berounka, C, 39 b.	**Řevnice**
Morava, C, 37 b.	**Říčany**
Český Dvůr, B, 22 b.	**Rokycany**
Krakonoš, B, 99 b.; Národní Dům, C, 15 b.	**Rokytnice** nad Jizerou
Orličan, C, 43 b.; Společenský Dům, C, 34 b.	**Rokytnice** v Orlických Horach
Koruna, B, 65 b.; Sporthotel Pod Lípou, B and C, 120 b.	**Roudnice** nad Labem
Český Raj, C, 15 b.	**Rovensko** pod Troskami
Maximiliánka, C, 48 b.	**Roztoky** (nr Prague)
U Mostu, C, 14 b.	**Rožmberk** nad Vltavou
Odborový Dům, C, 18 b.; Slávie, C, 17 b.	**Rožmitál** pod Třemšinem
Tesla, B*, 124 b.; Koruna, C, 24 b.; Rožnov, C, 40 b.	**Rožnov** pod Radhoštěm
Lužan, B*, 90 b.	**Rumburk**
Labut', C, 26 b.; Panoráma, C, 33 b.	**Rychnov** nad Kněžnou
Mír, C, 47 b.; Praděd, C, 24 b.	**Rýmařov**
Modrá Hvězda, B, 14 b.	**Sadská**
Vltavan, B, 80 b.	**Sedlčany**
Český Merán, C, 27 b.	**Sedlec-Prčice**

Semily	Okresní Dům, C, 39 b.
Senohraby	Hrušov, B, 54 b.
Šerlich (Orlík Hills)	Šerlišsky Mlýn, B, 65 b. Mountain hotel: Šerlich, C, 16 b.
Škrdlovice	Pensión, C, 36 b.
Slaný	Grand, B, 82 b.; Sportovní Hala, B, 64 b.
Slavkov u Brna	U Nádraží, C, 36 b.
Slavonice	Alfa, B, 39 b.
Slušovice	Všemina, B, 120 b.
Smržovka	Park, C, 41 b.
Sněžné	Sněžné, B, 48 b.
Soběslav	Slunce, C, 42 b.
Sobotka	Pošta, C, 24 b.
Sokolov	Ohře, B*, 154 b.
Špičák (Železná Ruda)	Hrnčíř, B, 37 b.; Sirotek, B, 43 b.
Špindlerův Mlýn	Montana, A*, 180 b.; Alpský, B, 58 b.; Praha, B, 45 b.; Sněžka, B, 52 b.; Westend, B, 63 b.; Astoria, C, 35 b.; Hvězda, C, 41 b. Mountain hotels: Freud***; Arnika***; Horal***, 315 b.; Savoy***, 104 b.; Labská Bouda, B, 150 b.; Martinova Bouda, C, 38 b.; Moravská Bouda, C, 51 b.; Central*
Srní (Bohemian Forest)	Šumava, B*, 99 b.
Stachy	Modrá Hvězda, C, 26 b.
Stará Boleslav	Houšt'ka, B, 21 b.; Praha, C, 26 b.
Stará Ves (Bruntál)	Anenská Hut', B, 68 b.
Staré Hamry (Beskýds)	Ostravacka, C, 23 b. Mountain hotel: Charbulák, C, 66 b.
Staré Město pod Sněžníkem	Národní Dům, C, 45 b.
Štěchovice	Peškov, C, 28 b.
Šternberk	Šternberský Dvůr, B
Štětí (Litoměřice)	Hotelový Dům, B, 57 b.
Stochov	Slovanka, B, 48 b.
Strakonice	Švanda Dudák, B, 63 b.; Bílý Vlk, C, 40 b.
Štramberk	Šipka, C, 25 b.

Kulturní Dům, B, 46 b.	**Strašice**
Černý Orel, B*, 77 b.; Strážnice***, 92 b.	**Strážnice**
Evropa, B, 45 b.	**Stříbro**
Komorník, B, 50 b.	**Strmilov**
Ondava, B, 35 b.; Tokajík, B, 42 b.	**Stropkov**
Javořice, C, 40 b.	**Studená** (Jindřichův Hradec)
Lužnice, C, 26 b.	**Suchdol** nad Lužnicí
Turistická Chata, C, 31 b.	**Suchý Vrch** (Hrubý Jeseník)
Grand, B, 95 b.; Moravan, B, 72 b.; Sport, B, 18 b.; Praha, C, 33 b.	**Šumperk**
Fialka, B, 54 b. Mountain hotel: Svatobor, C, 51 b.	**Sušice**
Česká Koruna, C, 19 b.; U Nádraží, C, 15 b.	**Světlá** nad Sázavou
Městský Dům, C, 32 b.; Národní Dům, C, 28 b.; Slavia, C, 53 b.	**Svitavy**
Mánes, C, 52 b.	**Svratka**
Palcát***, 184 b.; Slávie, B*, 103 b.; Jordán, B, 132 b.; Slovan, B, 61 b.; Sportovní Hala, C, 31 b.	**Tábor**
Lidový Dům, B, 42 b.	**Tachov**
Koruna, B, 43 b.	**Tanvald**
Černý Orel, B*, 50 b.	**Telč**
Družba, C, 45 b.; Jiskra, C, 48 b.	**Telnice**
Flóra, B, 35 b.	**Teplá** (Karlovy Vary)
De Saxe, B*, 156 b.; Thermia, B*, 209 b.; Radnice, B, 151 b.; Stadión, B, 48 b.; Varšava, C, 47 b.	**Teplice** (N. Bohemia)
Orlík, C, 39 b.; Sokol, C, 26 b.	**Teplice** nad Metují
Park, C, 45 b.	**Terezín**
Květnice, B, 53 b.	**Tišnov**
Praha, C, 23 b.	**Toužim**
Alfa, B, 26 b.; Slavia, B, 107 b.; Zlatý Kříž, B, 52 b.; Sportovní Hala, C, 40 b.; U Nádraží, C, 39 b.	**Třebíč**
Bílý Koníček, B, 26 b.; Svět, B, 116 b.	**Třeboň**
Společenský Dům, C	**Třešť**
U Dvou Čápů, B, 40 b.	**Trhové Sviny**

Třinec	Slovan, B, 51 b.
Tři Studně	Tři Studně, C, 40 b.
Trojanovice (Beskýds)	Beskyd, B*, 82 b.; Ráztoka, C, 44 b.
Trutnov	Horník**, 216 b.; Varšava, C, 38 b.
Turnov	Sport, B, 23 b.
Týnec nad Labem	Racek, B, 40 b.
Týn nad Vltavou	Zlatá Lod', B*, 39 b.; Vltava, C, 54 b.
Týniště nad Orlicí	Orlice, C, 35 b.
Uherské Hradiště	Grand, B, 56 b.; Morava, B, 128 b.
Uherský Brod	Javořina, B, 100 b.
Uničov	Národní Dům, C, 43 b.
Úpice (Trutnov)	Pod Lány, C, 30 b.
Ústí nad Labem	Bohemia, A*, 359 b.; Maj***; Vladimir***; Palace, B, 150 b.
Ústí nad Orlicí	Poprad***, 72 b.; Praha, C, 22 b.
Úvaly	Sport, C, 51 b.
Valašské Klobouky	Ploština, B, 81 b.
Valašské Meziříčí	Apollo, B*, 90 b.; Panáček, C, 25 b.
Valtice	Hubertus, B*, 72 b.
Varnsdorf	Panorama, B, 51 b.; Praha, C, 50 b.; Sport, C, 48 b.
Vejprty	Praha, C, 60 b.
Velichovky	Jednota, C, 20 b.
Velká Bíteš	Družba, C, 25 b.
Velké Karlovice	Razula, B*, 96 b.; Javorník, C, 65 b.; Potocký, C, 40 b.; U Kratochvilů, C, 12 b.
Velké Losiny	Praděd, C, 44 b.
Velké Meziříčí	Horácko, C, 33 b.; Sport, C, 30 b.; Zlatý Lev, C, 34 b.
Veselí nad Lužnicí	Zvon, C, 25 b.
Veselí nad Moravou (Hodonín)	Rozkvět, B, 72 b.
Vimperk	Vltava, B, 54 b.; Zlatá Hvězda, B, 69 b.
Vítkov (Opava)	Růže**, 28 b.
Vizovice	Lidový Dům, C, 32 b.

Vorlina, B, 34 b.	**Vlašim**
Blanice, B, 33 b.	**Vodňany**
Bobík, B*, 57 b.; Turistická Chata, B, 36 b.	**Volary**
Na Nové, C, 21 b.	**Volyně**
Modrá Hvězda, C, 32 b.	**Votice**
Dyje, C, 96 b.; Klatovka, C, 70 b.; Zámecký, C, 128 b.	**Vranov** (Znojmo)
Morava, B, 49 b.	**Vrbno** pod Pradědem
Labuť, B, 44 b.	**Vrchlabí**
Vsacan, B*, 137 b.	**Vsetín**
Karossa, B, 80 b.; Slávia, C, 46 b.	**Vysoké Mýto**
Morava, C, 41 b.; Větrov*** (villa)	**Vysoké** nad Jizerou
Dukla, B*, 210 b.; Šumavan, C, 46 b.	**Vyškov**
Bzlet, B, 46 b.; Šumavan, C, 46 b.	**Vyšší Brod**
Praha, C, 39 b.	**Vyžlovka** (Kolín)
Beseda, C, 53 b.	**Zábřeh**
Chr Ňov, B, 156 b.; Sporthotel Olympia, B, 127 b.	**Zádov** (Prachatice)
Pošta, C, 21 b.	**Zahrádky** (Česká Lípa)
Společenský Dům, C, 38 b.	**Žamberk**
Bílý Lev, B*, 100 b.; Fit, B, 56 b.; Tálský Mlýn, B, 45 b.; Na Smíchově, C, 31 b.	**Žd'ár** nad Sázavou
Družba, B, 42 b.; Zlatý Lev, B, 62 b.; Zlatý Anděl, C, 45 b.	**Žatec**
Vltava, C, 39 b.	**Zbraslav**
Šumava, B*, 71 b.	**Zdíkov**
Javor, B*, 108 b.; Slávie, B, 48 b. Mountain hotel: Pancíř, C, 36 b.	**Železná Ruda**
Crystal, B*, 80 b.; Dům Stavbařů, C, 150 b.	**Železný Brod**
Kocanda, C, 36 b.	**Želiv**
Národní Dům, B, 51 b	**Židlochovice**
Perala, B, 18 b.	**Žirovnice**
Sporthotel, B, 66 b.	**Živohošť**
Moskva, A*, 418 b.; Družba, B*, 146 b.	**Zlín**

Žlutice	Beseda, C, 19 b.
Znojmo	Družba, B*, 128 b.; Dukla***, 300 b.; Znojmo, B, 50 b.; Černý Medvěd, C, 46 b.
Zruč nad Sázavou	Společenský Dům, B*, 101 b.
Zvíkovské Podhradí	Zvíkov, B, 103 b.; Pensión, C, 24 b.

Hotels in the Slovak Republic

Baba (Bratislava-Vidiek)	Mountain hotel: Baba, B, 93 b.
Bánovce nad Bebravou	Bebrava, C, 27 b.; Spartak Club, C, 47 b.
Banská Bystrica	Lux, B*, 179 b.; Národný Dom, B*, 48 b.; Juniorhotel, B, 112 b.; Urpín, B, 99 b.
Banská Štiavnica	Grand, B, 40 b.; Sitno, B, 30 b.
Bardejov	Dukla, B, 51 b.; Lesná Reštaurácie, B, 90 b.; Topla, C, 43 b.
Bardejovské Kúpele	Minerál, B*, 165 b.
Batizovce	Guía, C, 46 b.
Belušské Slatiny (Banská Bystrica)	Marianum, B, 48 b.
Bojnice	Regia, B*, 118 b.
Bratislava	Devín*****, Riečna 4, SQ-81102 Bratislava, 102 b.; Forum****, Mierove Nám.; 2, SQ-81625 Bratislava, 452 b.; Kyjev****, Rajská 2, SQ-81448 Bratislava; Bratislava***, Urxova 9, SQ-82663 Bratislava; Carlton***, Hviezdoslavovo Nám. 2, SQ-81609 Bratislava, 434 b.; Club Hotel***, Ulica Odbojárov 3, SQ-83104 Bratislava, 60 b.; Dukla***, Dulovo Nám. 1, SQ-82108 Bratislava, 116 b.; Florá***, Zlaté Piesky, SQ-82104 Bratislava; Juniorhotel Sputnik***, Drieňová Ulica 14, SQ-82663 Bratislava, 241 b.; Krym***, Šafárikovo Nám. 7, SQ-81102 Bratislava, 90 b.; Sporthotel Rapid***, Teločvičná Ulica 11, SQ-82105 Bratislava, 90 b.; Tatra***, Nám. 1. Mája 7, SQ-81106 Bratislava, 190 b.; Spoločenský Dom Vlčie Hrdlo**, 40 b.; Palace, Poštová 1, SQ-89404 Bratislava, 128 b.; Sporthotel TJ Trnávka, B
Brezno	Ďumbier, B, 40 b.; Sokolovňa, B, 33 b.; Hron, C, 24 b.
Brusno (Banská Bystrica)	Brusno, B, 32 b.
Bumbálka (Čadca)	Bumbálka, C, 54 b.
Bytča	Bytča, C, 23 b.; Zámok, C, 20 b.
Bzenec	Lidový Dom, C, 48 b.
Čadca	Lipa, B, 59 b.; Tatra, C, 18 b.; Husárik, B, 70 b.
Čaňa (Košice-Vidiek)	Pláž, C, 56 b.
Čertovica	Na Čertovici, C, 74 b.; Športhotel, C, 44 b.
Čičmany	Kaštiel, C, 20 b.; Unimo, C, 80 b.

Úsvit, B, 50 b.	**Čierna** nad Tisou
Flóra, B, 62 b.; Tatran, C, 32 b.	**Čingov**
Priehrada, B, 50 b.	**Dedinky**
Družba***, 30 b.; Juniorhotel Jasna***; Liptov***, 153 b.; Bystrina**, 76 b.; Studničky, B	**Demänovská Dolina**
Detva, B*; Janošík, C, 75 b.	**Detva**
Jasná, C, 90 b.	**Diakovce** (Galanta)
Dobšinská L'adová Jaskyňa, C, 108 b.; Jas, B; Ruffinya, B	**Dobšiná**
Motel Orava***, 63 b.; Severan, B, 95 b.	**Dolní Kubín**
Športhotel, B, 52 b.	**Donovaly**
Lysanka, B, 50 b.	**Drienica** (Prešov)
Zlatý Páv, B, 56 b.	**Drienovce** (Košice-Vidiek)
Filagor, B; TJ Spartak, Stadión, B	**Dubnica nad Váhom**
Smaragd*** (spa hotel); Minerál B	**Dudince**
Dunaj, B*, 76 b.; Bihari, B	**Dunajská Streda**
Sputnik, B; Kúpalisko, C, 17 b.	**Filakovo**
Družba, B, 49 b.	**Galanta**
Mier, C, 45 b.	**Ganovec** (Poprad)
Baní, C, 19 b.	**Gelnica**
Baník, C, 86 b.	**Handlová**
Hel'pa, C, 64 b.	**Hel'pa**
Gejzir, B*, 60 b.	**Herl'any**
Jeleň, B, 30 b.; Športhotel, C, 40 b.	**Hlohovec**
Mraznica, B, 103 b.	**Hnilčík** (Spišská Nová Ves)
Robotnícky Dom, C	**Hnúšt'a** (Rimavská Sobota)
Zlatý Klas, C, 25 b.	**Holčikovce**
Kriváň, C, 47 b.	**Holič**
Merkur, B*	**Hôrka** (Michalovce)
Karpatia, B*, 83 b.; Podskalka, B; Vihorlat, C	**Humenné**

Hotels

Hurbanovo	Centrál, B, 25 b.
Ilava	Vršatec, B, 16 b.; Park, B*
Jablonica (Senica)	Záhoran, B, 55 b.
Jankov Vršok (Topolčany)	Partizán, B, 70 b.
Jasná	Liptov, B*; Družba, B*, 30 b.; Mikulášská Chata, C
Jelšava	Kúpele, B, 28 b.
Kalinovo	TJ Baník, C, 40 b.
Kamenný Mlyn	Kamenný Mlyn, B, 82 b.
Kežmarok	Lipa, B*, 132 b.; Start Lesopark, B, 64 b.; Sport, C, 21 b.; Tatra, C, 15 b.
Kokošovce (Prešov)	Sigord, B, 33 b.
Kolárovo	Váh, B, 26 b.
Komárno	Európa, B*, 100 b.; Spoločenský Dom, B, 80 b.; Centrál, C, 65 b.
Košice	Slovan, A*, 300 b.; Hutník, B*, 406 b.; Imperiál, B*, 68 b.; Club, B, 69 b.; Európa, B, 90 b.; Metál, Šaca, B, 72 b.; Športhotel, C, 56 b.; Štadión TJ Lokomotiva, B, 47 b.; Tatra, C, 40 b.
Košické Hámré	Ružín, B; Sivec, B
Kováčov (Nové Zámky)	Modrá Ryba, C
Kováčová	Jednota, C, 41 b.
Králová Studňa	Mountain hotel, C, 119 b.
Královský Chlumec	Lipa, B, 18 b.
Kremnica	Veterník, B, 36 b.
Krompachy	Európa, B, 22 b.
Krupina	Minerál, B; Slovan, C, 32 b.
Kysucké Nové Město	Kysuce, B*; Závodný Klub, B, 75 b.; Mýto, C, 24 b.
Lednické Rovné (Považská Bystrica)	Krištál', B, 21 b.
Levice	Onyx, B*; Rozkvet, B*, 120 b.; Atóm, B; Lev, C, 48 b.
Levoča	Družba, B, 37 b.; Biela Pani, C, 29 b.
Lipany (Prešov)	Lipa, B, 26 b.
Liptovský Hrádok	Smrek, 81 b.
Liptovský Jan	Poludnica, C, 38 b.

Jánošík, B*, 128 b.; Bocian, B, 78 b.; Europa, B, 50 b.; Športhotel, B; Tri Studničky, B; Dynamoklub, C, 50 b.; Kriváň, C, 46 b.; Lodenica, C, 46 b.	**Liptovský Mikuláš**
Družstevný Klub, B; Športklub, B	**Lisková** (Liptovský Mikuláš)
Magnezit, B, 20 b.	**Lubeník** (Rožňava)
Fatra, B, 82 b.	**L'ubochna**
Novohrad, B*; Pelikán, B*; Slovan, B, 38 b.; Tatran, B, 40 b.	**Lučenec**
Kriváň, C, 52 b.	**Lučivná**
Pol'ana, C, 36 b.	**Makov**
Záhoran, B*, 140 b.; Tatra, C, 19 b.	**Malacky**
Malina, C	**Mâliné**
Turiec, B*, 183 b.; Slovan, B, 94 b.; Podstráne, C, 66 b.; Strojár, C, 25 b.	**Martin**
Laborec, B*, 107 b.	**Medzilaborce**
Jalta, B*, 64 b.; Družba, B; Park, B, 32 b.; Zemplín, C, 26 b.	**Michalovce**
Slalom, B, 57 b.; Geravy, B, 40 b.	**Mlýnky**
Modra, B, 30 b.; Zlaté Hrozno, B, 41 b.	**Modra**
Hrad, B	**Modrý Kameň**
Spoločenský Dom, B*, 62 b.	**Moldava** nad Bodvou
Spoločenský Dom, C	**Myjava**
Magma, C, 30 b.	**Námestovo**
Nitra, B*, 270 b.; Olympia, B; Tatra, B, 17 b.; Zobor, B, 102 b.; Slovan, C, 65 b.; Šport, C	**Nitra**
Vyšehrad, B, 46 b.	**Nitrianské Pravno**
Radar, B, 30 b.	**Nizná** (Dolný Kubín)
Išla, B	**Nizná Šebastová** (Prešov)
Hron, C	**Nová Baňa** (Žiar nad Hronom)
Luník, B*, 28 b.	**Nová Dubnica**
Javorina, B, 102 b.	**Nové Město** nad Váhom
Korzo, B, 259 b.; Partizán, B, 62 b.; Športhotel, C; Tatra, C, 36 b.	**Nové Zámky**
Park, B*, 144 b.; Tokajík, B*, 28 b.; MS 70, B, 65 b.; Bytrina, C, 92 b.	**Nový Smokovec**
Motel Slanica, A, 90 b.; Goral, B, 58 b.; Šport, C, 58 b.	**Lake Orava**

Oravský Podzámok	Odboj, C, 27 b.
Palúdzka (Liptovský Mikuláš)	Bocian, B, 70 b.
Partizánske	Spoločenský Dom, B, 67 b.
Patince (Komárno)	Prameň, B, 70 b.
Pezinok	Grand, B*, 140 b.
Piešt'any	Magnólia, A*, 198 b.; Eden, B*, 64 b.; Lipa, B, 62 b.; Slňava***, 490 b.; Victória Regia, B, 60 b.; Kominár, C, 18 b.; Športhotel, C, 421 b.
Plešivec	Planina, C, 54 b.
Podbanské	Kriváň, B*, 105 b.
Podbrezová	Podbrezovan, C, 58 b.
Poprad	Európa, B*, 96 b.; Gerlach, B*, 197 b.; Zimný Štadión, B, 30 b.
Portáš	Mountain hotel
Považská Bystrica	Grand, B*, 195 b.; Spoločenský Dom, B, 41 b.; Štadión, B, 36 b.; Motel FIM, B, 58 b.
Prešov	Dukla, B*, 195 b.; Šariš, B*, 150 b.; Išla, B, 16 b.; Savoy, B, 44 b.; Vrchovina, B, 30 b.; Motel Stop, Haniska, B, 30 b.
Pribylina	Esperanto, B, 60 b.
Prievidza	Magura, B, 54 b.; Hviezda, C, 56 b.; Šport Motel, B, 112 b.
Púchov	Šport, B*, 120 b.; Štadión, B, 24 b.; Javorník, C, 30 b.
Rájec	Kl'ak, C, 27 b.
Rajecké Teplica	Vel'ká Fatra, B, 145 b.; Encián, C, 12 b.
Revúca	Jednota, B, 96 b.
Rimavská Sobota	Slovan, B*, 82 b.; Tatra, B, 62 b.; Astra, C
Rožňava	Kras, B*, 82 b.; Šport, B*, 74 b.; Gemer, B, 46 b.; Kúpele, B, 80 b.
Ružomberok	Hrabovo, B*, 62 b.; Kultúrny Dom, B, 61 b.; Liptov, B, 31 b.; Malina, C, 84 b.; Papiernik, C, 100 b.
Šafárikovo	See Tornal'a
Šahy	Blankyt, B, 32 b.; Ipel', B, 15 b.
Šala	Centrál, B, 47 b.
Šamorín	Kormorán, B
Šantovka (Levica)	Prameň, B, 34 b.
Sečovce (Trebišov)	Gambrinus, B
Senec	Amur, B, 92 b.; Lúč, B, 40 b.

Slovan, B, 85 b.; Branč, C, 34 b.	**Senica**
Hutník, B, 59 b.	**Sereď**
Sigord, B*	**Sigord** (Prešov)
Tatran, C, 21 b.	**Skalica** (Senica)
Hron, C, 98 b.	**Sliač**
Družba, B, 27 b.	**Snina**
Morské Oko, B, 62 b.	**Sobrance** (Michalovce)
Belan, C	**Spišská Belá**
Metropol, B*, 152 b.; Športhotel, B, 56 b.	**Spišská Nová Ves**
Spiš, C, 50 b.	**Spišské Podhradie**
Srdiečko, B, 64 b.	**Srdiečko** (Banská Bystrica)
Park, C, 21 b.	**Stakčín** (Humenné)
Vrchovina, B*	**Stará L'ubovňa**
Lipa, B, 39 b.	**Stará Turá**
Grand Hotel, A*, 156 b.; Úderník, B, 70 b.	**Starý Smokovec**
Patria, A*, 156 b.; Panoráma, B*, 160 b.; FIS, B*, 118 b.	**Štrbské Pleso**
Ondava, B, 35 b.; Tokajík, B, 42 b.	**Stropkov**
Park, B*	**Stupava**
Dunaj, C, 25 b.; Športhotel, C	**Štúrovo**
Športový Dom, C, 111 b.	**Sučany**
Jednota, B	**Súl'ov**
Luník, B, 28 b.	**Šurany**
Telgárt, B, 60 b.	**Švermovo**
Dukla, B*, 62 b.; Pobeda, B	**Svidník**
Spoločenský Dom, B*	**Svit**
Partizán, B*, 181 b.	**Talé**
Grand Hotel Praha, A* and B*, 162 b.; Slovan, B*, 149 b.; Horec, B, 60 b.; Lomnica, B, 32 b.; Mier, C, 52 b.	**Tatranská Lomnica**
Sokolovo, C, 43 b.	**Tatranská Štrba**
Grúň, C, 30 b.; Jánošík, C, 146 b.	**Terchová**

Hotels

Tisovec	Centrál, C, 49 b.
Topol'čany	Tríbeč, B*, 54 b.; Zimný Stadión, B*, 32 b.; Club, B, 29 b.
Topol'čianky	Národný Dom, C, 24 b.; Tatran, C
Tornal'a	Spoločenský Dom, B; Centrál, C, 21 b.
Trebišov	Tokaj, B, 50 b.; Zemplín, B; Športhotel, C
Trenčianské Teplice	Jalta, B*, 164 b.; Dea, C, 32 b.; Miramare-Corfu, C, 100 b.; Salvator, C, 40 b.; TJ Slovan, C
Trenčín	Laugaricio, B*, 144 b.; Tatra, B, 124 b.; Trenčan, C, 23 b.
Trnava	Karpaty, B, 124 b.; Koliba Kamenný Mlyn, C, 36 b.; Park, C, 29 b.
Trstená	Oravica, B, 42 b.; Roháč, B, 51 b.
Turčianské Teplice	Vyšehrad, C, 46 b.
Turzovka	Centrum, B, 18 b.
Tvrdošín	Limba, B*, 92 b.
Valaská	Perla, C, 56 b.
Važec	Kriváň, B; Važec, C, 78 b.
Vel'ká Domaša	Dobrá, C; Nová Kelča, C; Pol'ana, C; Šport, Valkov, C
Vel'ká Lomnica	Agroclub, B; Tatran, C, 50 b.
Vel'ká Rača	Rača, C
Vel'ké Kapušany	Družba, B, 40 b.
Vel'ký Krtíš	Dolina, B, 53 b.
Vel'ký Meder	Termal, C
Vel'ký Slavkov	Slavkov, B
Vráble (Nitra)	Žitavan, B, 33 b
Vranov nad Topl'ou	Rozkvet, B; Tatra, C, 44 b.
Vrátna	Boboty, B*, 120 b.
Vrbov (Kežmarok)	Flipper, B, 60 b.
Vyšná Boca	Baník, C, 32 b.; Športhotel, C
Vyšné Ružbachy	Kráter, C, 57 b.; Magura, C, 60 b.
Žarnovica (Žiar nad Hronom)	Motel Partizán, B, 24 b.
Zemplínska Širava	Merkur, Medvedia Hora, B*, 66 b.
Žiar nad Hronom	Luna, B*, 85 b.
Žilina	Polom, B*, 120 b.; Slovakia, B*, 340 b.; Grand, B, 52 b.; Metropol, B, 95 b.; Slovan, B, 29 b.; Športhotel, B, 65 b.; Dukla, C, 70 b.

Zlaté Moravce
Inovec, C, 32 b.

Zochova Chata (Bratislava)
Hotel, B*, 75 b.

Zvolen
Pol'ana, B*, 121 b.; Grand, B, 53 b.; Rates, B

Information

Čedok Offices Abroad

United Kingdom
49 Southwark Street
London SE1 1RU. Tel. (071) 378 6009

United States
10 East 40th Street
New York NY 10016. Tel. (212) 609 9720

Čedok in the Czech Republic

There are Čedok offices in all the larger towns in the Czech Republic.

In Prague
Head office
Na Příkopě 18, CZ-11135 Praha 1
Tel. (02) 2 12 71 11
Information of all kinds, reservations of rail, bus and air tickets, exchange office, etc.

Branch for information and room reservations on arrival in Prague:
Panská 5, CZ-11000 Praha 1 (Nové Město)
Tel. (02) 2 12 75 52–57

Branch for seat reservations (city tours, excursions, tickets for cultural events); also departure point for city tours and excursions in the surrounding area:
Bílkova 6 (opposite Inter-Continental Hotel)
CZ-11000 Praha 1 (Staré Město), Tel. (02) 2 31 88 55 and 2 31 66 19

Branch in Wenceslas Square (also departure point for morning tours of "Historic Prague" and day trips, and meeting-place for guided walks in Prague):
Václavské Náměstí 24, CZ-11000 Praha 1 (Nové Město)
Tel. (02) 2 35 63 56

Čedok Intertravel Bureau
Incoming Product Department
Na Příkopě 18, CZ-11135 Praha 1 (Nové Město)
Tel. (02) 21 27–284, –682 and –564

Čedok in the Slovak Republic

Čedok, which has branches in all the larger towns in the Slovak Republic, is due to be replaced during 1994 by the Slovak Travel Bureau (SCK).

In Bratislava
Štúrova 13
SQ-81000 Bratislava 1
Tel. (07) 5 20 02 and 5 28 34 (accommodation)

Jesenského Ulica 5
SQ-81000 Bratislava 1
Tel. (07) 5 26 45 and 5 27 23 (tickets for foreign travel)

Námestie SNP 14
SQ-81000 Bratislava 1
Tel. (07) 5 01 68 and 5 40 07 (travel within Slovakia)

Other Sources of Information and Services

In the Czech Republic

CKM (Youth Travel Bureau)	CKM (Cestovná Kanceláría Mládeže) Žitná 10, CZ-12105 Praha 2 Tel. (02) 29 99 41 Booking of accommodation in hotels and youth hostels, excursions, work camps, living in families, sports training courses, rail and air tickets, etc.
ČSA Airtours	ČSA Airtours Národní Třída 27, CZ-11000 Praha 1 Tel. (02) 2 35 83 41, 2 35 83 22 and 2 35 26 71 Travel agency (air tickets, etc.).
Lost property, Prague	Bolzanova 5, CZ-11000 Praha 1 Tel. (02) 2 36 88 87
Ministry of Trade and Tourism	Ministry of Trade and Tourism of the Czech Republic Staroměstské Náměstí (Old Town Square) 6 CZ-11000 Praha 1. Tel. (02) 2 31 79 00
Chamber of Commerce	ČSOPK Argentinská 38, CZ-17005 Praha 7 Tel. (02) 8 72 48 96
PIS (Prague Information Service)	Pražská Informační Služba (PIS) Na Příkopě 20, CZ-11135 Praha 1 (Nové Město) Tel. (02) 54 44 44 Staroměstské Náměstí (Old Town Square) 22 CZ-11000 Praha 1 Tel. (02) 22 44 52 Letenská 1, tel. (02) 53 42 55 Panská 4, tel. (02) 22 34 11
Pragotur	Pragotur U Obecního Domu 2, CZ-11121 Praha 1 Tel. (02) 2 32 72 81, 2 81 72 00 Travel agency offering a variety of services (room reservation, tickets for events, city tours, boat trips; sale of Bohemian glass; exchange office).

In the Slovak Republic

BIPS (Bratislava Information and Publicity Service)	Bratislavská Informačná a Propagačná Služba (BIPS; Bratislava Information and Publicity Service) Laurinská Ulica 1, SQ-81000 Bratislava 1 Tel. (07) 33 37 15, 33 43 25 and 33 43 70 City tours: Ulica Červenej Armády 7, tel. (07) 5 97 64 Cinema tickets: Nedbalova Ulica, tel. (07) 33 40 59 Sale of periodical "Kam v Bratislave?" ("Where to in Bratislava?"): BIPS shop at No. 9
CKM (Youth Travel Bureau)	CKM (Cestovná Kanceláría Mládeže) Hviezdoslavovo Námestie 16 SQ-81000 Bratislava 1 Tel. (07) 33 16 07 (foreign travel) and 33 24 74 (travel within Slovakia)

Booking of accommodation in hotels and youth hostels, excursions, work camps, living in families, sports training courses, rail and air tickets, etc.

DCK Tatratour

Travel agency (travel within Slovakia and abroad, holiday arrangements, spa treatment)
Dibrovovo Námestie 7
SQ-81000 Bratislava 1
Tel. (07) 33 55 36

Exchange office:
Námestie 4. Aprila 2
81000 Bratislava 1
Tel. (07) 33 38 78

Interpreter and translation service

Timočnícka a Prekladatel'ská Služba
Laurinská Ulica 1
SQ-81000 Bratislava 1
Tel. (07) 33 44 15

Guide service

Sprievodcovská Služba
Ulica Červenej Armády 7
SQ-81000 Bratislava 1
Tel. (07) 5 97 64
Multilingual guides to the sights of Bratislava

Ministry of Trade and Tourism

Ministry of Trade and Tourism of the Slovak Republic
Urxova 1
SQ-82623 Bratislava 2
Tel. (07) 23 95 82

Chamber of Commerce

ČSOPK
Gorkého 9
SQ-81603 Bratislava 1
Tel. (07) 5 45 96 and 33 36 46

Slovakoturist Travel Agency

Slovakoturist Travel Agency
Volgogradská Ulica 1
SQ-81615 Bratislava 1
Tel. (07) 33 50 78

Language

Official languages

The official languages of the Czech and Slovak Republics are respectively Czech and Slovak, both of which belong to the Western Slavonic language group.

Czech, Slovak and Other Languages

According to the 1991 Census, the population of Czechoslovakia as it then was included, in addition to 9.8 million Czechs and 4.8 million Slovaks, minorities of 600,000 Hungarians along the Hungarian frontier, 60,000 Poles in the Česky Těšín area and, in Eastern Slovakia, 20,000 Ukrainians and 20,000 Carpatho-Russians (Rusíni).

The languages of the minority groups are of importance only in their areas of settlement, in which signs and inscriptions are usually bilingual. There are also Hungarian and Ukrainian National Theatres.

Romany (Roma)

Official statistics put the number of gypsies speaking Romany (Roma) at 120,000. It is estimated, however, that in reality there are about 200,000 in the Czech Republic and 300,000 in the Slovak Republic.

Language

Germans

Whereas until 1945 there were more than 3.5 million Germans living in the territory of former Czechoslovakia, the 1991 Census recorded only 53,000, some of whom had moved into the interior of Bohemia. There are many Germans in the area between Karlovy Vary, Sokolov and Cheb and around Liberec and Trutnov in the Czech Republic, and around Bratislava and in the Spiš in the Slovak Republic.

Many young Czechs and Slovaks now speak English; the older generation are more likely to have German as their second language.

Pronunciation of Czech and Slovak

Stress

In Czech the strongest stress is always, and in Slovak mainly, on the first syllable. The letters l and r, as semi-vowels, can bear the stress even if there is a following vowel (as in Vltava, Brno); and r can also carry the stress in vowelless words like prst, "finger".

Vowels

Both Czech and Slovak make a sharp distinction between long and short vowels. Long vowels are indicated by an accent – á, é, í and ý, in Slovak also ú, ó and ô, and in Czech ů. Y is always pronounced like i. E with a háček (ě) is pronounced ye.
Slovak also has the letter ä, pronounced like the short e in "net".

Diphthongs

Diphthongs formed with j or u as the second element (aj, áj, ej, etc.; au, ou) are pronounced with the stress on the first element and the second element clearly distinguished as a semi-vowel (as in kraj, "land", auto, "car", Olomouc).

Consonants

The following consonants have roughly the same pronunciation as in English: b, d, f, g, h (also sounded before a consonant and at the end of a word, as in hrad, "castle", and kruh, "circle"), k, l, m, n, p, r (slightly rolled), s, t, v, z. C is pronounced ts, ch as in "loch".
Characteristic of Czech and Slovak are the diacritics which modify the pronunciation of certain consonants. With the háček (ˇ) c is pronounced ch as in "char", ř (not in Slovak) as rzh, š as sh, ž as zh. The apostrophe combined with d, t and, in Slovak, l (d', t', l') adds a consonantal y after the consonant (roughly as in "due", "tune", "million").

Vocabulary

In the following lists the Slovak term is given only where it differs from the Czech one.

Numbers

Number	Czech	Slovak
1	jeden, jedna, jedno	jeden, jedna, jedno
2	dva, dvě, dvě	dva, dve, dvaja
3	tři	tri, traja
4	čtyři	štyri
5	pět	pät'
6	šest	šest'
7	sedm	sedem
8	osm	osem
9	devět	devät'
10	deset	desat'
11	jedenáct	jedenást'
12	dvanáct	dvanást'
13	třinact	trinást'
14	čtrnáct	štrnást'
15	patnáct	pät'nást'

English	Czech	Slovak	
16	šestnáct	šestnásť	
17	sedmnáct	sedemnásť	
18	osmnáct	osemnásť	
19	devatenáct	devätnásť	
20	dvacet	dvadsať	
30	třicet	tridsať	
40	čtyřicet	štyridsáť	
50	padesát	päťdesiat	
60	šedesát	šesťdesiat	
70	šedmdesát	šedemdesiat	
80	osmdesát	osemdesiat	
90	devadesát	deväťdesiat	
100	sto	sto	
1000	tisíc	tisíc	
1 million	milión	milión	
1st	první	prvý	Ordinals
2nd	druhý	druhý	
3rd	třetí	tretí	
½	půl	pol	Fractions
⅓	třetina	tretina	
Do you speak . . . ?	mluvíte . . . ?	rozprávate . . . ?	Useful words and phrases
. . . English?	. . . anglicky?	. . . po anglicky?	
. . . French?	. . . francouzsky?	. . . po francúzsky?	
. . . German?	. . . německy?	. . . po nemecky?	
Great Britain	Velká Británie		
England	Anglie		
Scotland	Skotsko		
Wales	Wales		
Ireland	Irsko		
United States	Spojené Státy		
Canada	Kanada		
British	britský		
English	anglický		
American	americký		
Czech lands	České Země		
Slovakia	Slovensko		
Czech	český		
Slovak	slovenský		
yes	ano	áno, hej	
no	ne	nie	
please	prosím		
thank you	děkuji	ďakujem	
excuse me	promiňte		
I beg your pardon	prepáčte		
good morning	dobré jitro	dobré ráno	
good day	dobrý den	dobrý deň	
good evening	dobrý večer		
good night	dobrou noc	dobrú noc	
goodbye	na shledanou	do videnia	
Mr	pán		
Mrs	paní		
Miss	slečna		

	English	Czech	Slovak
	where is . . . ?	kde je . . . ?	
	. . . Street	Třida . . . , Ulice . . .	Ulica . . .
	the road to . . .	cesta do . . .	
	. . . Square	Náměstí . . .	Námestie . . .
	travel agency	cestovní kancelář	cestovná kancelária
	bank	banka	
	exchange office	směnárna	zmenáreň
	railway station	nádraží	nádražie, stanica
	church	kostel	kostol
	cathedral	chrám	dóm
	museum	muzeum	múzeum
	castle	zámek	zámok
	when?	kdy?	kedy?
	open	otevřeno	otvoreno
	closed	zavřeno	zavreto
	hotel	hotel	hotel
	I should like . . .	chtěl bych	chcel bych
	(feminine form)	chtéla bych	chcela bych
	room	pokoj	izba
	single room	jednolůžkový pokoj	jednopostel'ová izba
	double room	dvoulůžkový pokoj	dvoijpostel'ová izba
	key	klíč	kl'úč
	toilet	záchod	toaleta
	bath	koupelna	kúpel'
	inn	hostinec	
	doctor	lékař	lekár
	chemist's	lékárna	lekáreň
	right	napravo,vpravo	
	left	nalevo, vlevo	nal'avo
	straight ahead	přímo	priamo
	above	nahoře	hore
	below	dole	dolu
	old	starý	
	new	nový	
	what does it cost?	co stojí?	čo stojí?
	too dear	příliš drahé	příliš drahé
	is this seat free?	je toto místo volné?	je toto miesto vol'né?
	wake me . . .	vzbud'te mě . . .	zobud'te ma . . .
	. . . at six	. . . v šest hodin	. . . o šestej hodine
	what time is it?	kolik je hodin?	kol'ko je hodín?
	what is the name of . . .	jak se jmenuje . . .	ako sa povie . . .
	. . . this church?	. . . tento kostel?	tento kostol?
Food and drink	See Food and Drink		
Months	January	leden	január
	February	únor	február
	March	březen	marec
	April	duben	april
	May	květen	máj
	June	červen	jún
	July	červenec	júl
	August	srpen	august
	September	září	september
	October	říjen	október
	November	listopad	november
	December	prosinec	december

English	Czech	Slovak	
Sunday	neděle	nedel'a	Weekdays
Monday	pondělí	pondelok	
Tuesday	úterý	utorok	
Wednesday	středa	streda	
Thursday	čtvrtek	štvrtok	
Friday	pátek	piatok	
Saturday	sobota		
holiday	svátek	sviatok	Holidays
New Year	Nový rok		
Easter	Velikonoce	Vel'ka noc	
Whitsun	Svatodušní	svátky	
Christmas	Vánoce	Vianoce	
post office	pošta		At the post office
stamps	známky		
envelopes	obálky		
letter	dopis	list	
postcard	dopisnice	karta	
registered	doporučený	doporučený	
by airmail	letadlem	leteckou	
poste restante	poste restante		
No thoroughfare	Průjezd zakázán		Traffic signs
One-way street	Jednosměrny provoz		
Diversion	Objížd'ka		
Caution	Pozor		
accelerator	pedál plynu		Motoring terms
air	vzduch		
axle	osa	os	
battery	baterie		
charge battery	nabíjet baterii		
bicycle	kolo	bicykel	
bolt	šroub	skrutka	
bonnet	kapota		
brake	brzda		
check brakes	přezkoušet brzdy		
breakdown	porucha		
bus	autobus		
car	auto		
car park	parkoviště	parkovisko	
carburator	karburator		
clutch	spojka		
cylinder	válec	cylinder	
driver	ridic	vodić	
driving licence	řidičský průkaz	vodičský preukaz	
engine	motor		
exhaust	výfuk		
filling station	benzínová stanice		
footbrake	nožní brzda		
fuse	pojistka	poistka	
garage	garáž		
gasket	ucpávka		
gear change	řazenírychlostí	zapojenie	
grease (v.)	vazati		
headlamp	reflektor		
horn	houkačka		
sound horn	houkat		
hospital	nemocnice	nemocnica	

English	Czech	Slovak
ignition	zapalování	
inner tube	duše	
insurance	pojištění	poistenie
jack	zdvihák	
key	klíč	
light	lampa	
litre	litr	
lubricating oil	mazací olej	
magneto	magnet	
motorcycle	motocykl	
number (plate)	číslo	značka
nut	matice	
oil	olej	
change oil	vyměnit olej	
park (v.)	parkovat	
parking place	parkoviště	parkovisko
petrol	benzín	
piston	píst	
puncture	defekt pneumatiky	
radiator	chladič	
rear light	odrazové sklíčko	zadné svetlo
rear-view mirror	zpětné zrcátko	
repair (v.)	spravit	opravit'
repair garage	dílna, správkárna	dielňa, opravovňa
reverse gear	zpáteční chod	
scooter	skútr	
screwdriver	šroubovák	skrutkovač
shock absorber	tlumič	
spanner	klíč	kl'úč
spare part	náhradní díl	náhradný diel
spark plug	svička	
speed limit	nejvyší rychlost	
speedometer	tachometr	
spring	pero	
starter	startér	
steering wheel	volant	
tank	nádrž na benzín	
tool	nářadí	
tow away	vzíti do vleku	
tyre	pneumatika	
repair tyre	spravit pneumatiku	
tyre pressure	tlak	
check tyre pressure	přezkoušet tlak	
valve	ventil	
wheel	kolo	koleso
change wheel	vyměnit kolo	
windscreen	sklo	
windscreen wiper	utěrák	

Topographical terms

Czech	Slovak	English
brána	brána	gate
brod	brod	ford
cesta	cesta	road
dolina	dolina	valley
důl		pit; valley
dům	dom	house
dvůr	dvor	court(yard)
hora	hora	hill, mountain
hrad	hrad	castle

Czech	Slovak	English
jeskyně	jaskyňa	cave
jezero	jazero	lake
klášter	kláštor	monastery
kostel	kostol	church
kotlina	kotlina	valley, basin
lázně	kúpele	baths, spa
les	les	forest
město	mesto	town
mlýn	mlyn	mill
most	most	bridge
nábřeží	nábrežie	embankment
nádraží	nadražie	railway station
nádrž	nádrž	reservoir
náměstí	námestie	square
nižina	nižina	plain, lowlands
pahorkatina		hilly country, hills
planina	planina	plain, plateau
pleso	pleso	mountain lake
plošina		plateau
pohorí	pohorie	range of hills, mountains
pramen	prameň	spring
přehrada	priehrada	dam
propast	priepast'	chasm, abyss
průsmyk	priesmyk	pass
radnice	radnica	town hall
rovina	rovina	plain
rybník	rybník	(fish)pond
sedlo	sedlo	saddle
soutěska		defile, gorge
štít	štít	peak
trh	trh	market
třída	trieda	street
tržiště	tržište	market (square)
údolí	údolie	valley
ulice	ulica	street
věž	veža	tower
vodopád	vodopád	waterfall
vrch	vrch	hill
vrchovina	vrchovina	highlands
zahrada	záhrada	garden
zámek	zámok	castle, country house

Medical Aid

In the event of illness the hotel reception or the representative of the tour operator should be informed.

Emergency doctor

Dial 155 (from anywhere in the Czech or Slovak Republic).

Hospital treatment

A foreign tourist suffering from a serious illness will be treated either in an outpatient department, in hospital (Czech *nemocnice,* Slovak *nemocnica*) or in a special clinic. Emergency treatment is free for visitors from abroad, and further treatment is free for British citizens under reciprocal arrangements between governments.

Insurance

Since in some circumstances a case of serious illness or accident may entail considerable expense – for example if a patient has to be brought home by air ambulance – it is advisable, before leaving home, to take out short-term insurance covering such risks.

Motoring

N.B.

Before entering the Czech or Slovak Republic motorists should note the following points:

- Any damage to the coachwork of a car must be recorded at the frontier entry point, since the car will not be permitted to leave the country without police confirmation of any damage it has suffered either before entry or in the Czech or Slovak Republic.
- Studded tyres are prohibited.
- A warning triangle must be carried. In the event of a breakdown the car must be pulled off the road and the warning triangle set up some distance in advance of its position.

Roads

The road network of former Czechoslovakia has a total length of just under 75,000km/46,600 miles.

Motorways

There is a trunk motorway linking Prague and Brno in the Czech Republic with Bratislava in Slovakia, together with shorter stretches of motorway running east from Prague to Poděbrady, south-west from Prague towards Plzeň (completed to about half way) and north-east from Brno to Vyškov in the Czech Republic and north-east from Bratislava via Piešt'any to shortly before Trenčín in the Slovak Republic.
Stopping and parking on motorways is prohibited except in designated parking places.

Distances

Distances (in kilometres) between selected towns in the Czech and Slovak Republics are shown in the table on p. 530 of this guide.

Traffic Regulations

General

Traffic regulations in the Czech and Slovak Republics are in line with those of most other European countries.
Children under 12 must sit in the back of the car.
Traffic travels on the right, with overtaking on the left.
Infringements of traffic regulations attract heavy fines.

Road signs

Road signs are in accordance with international standards, with directions, where necessary, in Czech or Slovak.

Alcohol

There is an absolute ban on driving after drinking even the smallest amount of alcohol.

Seat belts

The wearing of seat belts is obligatory.

Motorcyclists

Motorcyclists and their passengers must wear crash helmets and must not smoke.

Lights

In poor visibility dipped headlights must be used, and fog-lamps in the event of fog.

Speed limits

In built-up areas: 60km/37 miles an hour for cars, motorcycles and buses.
On the open road: 90km/56 miles an hour for cars, 80km/50 miles an hour for cars with trailers and for motorcycles, 70km/43 miles an hour for buses.
On motorways: 110km/68 miles an hour for cars and buses, 80km/50 miles an hour for motorcycles.
Within 30m/33yd of a level crossing, on either side: 30km/18½ miles an hour.

When towing another vehicle: 60km/37 miles an hour.
There are heavy fines for exceeding the speed limit.

Trams

Trams pulling out from tram stops or turning left have priority. Cars must not park within 3.5m/11½ft of a tram stop.

Parking

Stopping or parking is prohibited on bridges; within 15m/50ft on either side of level crossings, tunnels and underpasses; on continuous or broken yellow lines; on or near blind curves; before, on or after hills; and on or within 5m/16½ft on either side of zebra crossings and road intersections.

In Prague it is advisable to park in one of the large car parks in Náměstí Gorkého, at the Central Station, or preferably outside the city centre, since Wenceslas Square and surrounding streets are closed to all traffic except buses, cars belonging to residents in hotels on and around the square and delivery vehicles.

Fuel

There are no longer special tourist vouchers for the purchase of petrol, diesel fuel and oil, which are freely available at filling stations and paid for in Czech or Slovak currency.

Filling stations

Some filling stations in district towns, on main roads and on motorways are open day and night. In less frequented areas they may be closed on Saturday and Sunday.

Filling stations do not sell tyres, inner tubes or other spare parts.

Lead-free petrol

Lead-free petrol ("Natural"; 95 octane) is available at the larger filling stations.

Leaded petrol and diesel fuel

Leaded petrol is sold in "Super" (96 octane) and "Spezial" (91 octane) grades. Diesel fuel is also available.

Fuel in cans

Up to 10 litres (just over 2 gallons) of fuel in cans may be brought into the Czech and Slovak Republics, but the export of fuel in cans is prohibited.

Automobile Club

Ústřední Automotoclub (UAMK)
Mánesova 20, CZ-12000 Praha 2, tel. (02) 74 74 00

Breakdown Assistance

Motorway telephones

There are emergency telephones at short intervals along motorways in the Czech and Slovak Republics from which help can be called for in the event of breakdown or accident.

Towing

Where a car has to be towed away there is a speed limit of 60km/37 miles an hour.

Cost of breakdown assistance

Breakdown assistance must be paid for. Vouchers issued by the AA and other motoring organisations are accepted.

Breakdown Assistance in the Czech Republic

For emergency breakdown assistance dial 154.

Motoring

Police	Dial 158.
Emergency doctor	Dial 155.
Fire	Dial 150.
Road Service (Silniční Služba)	The Road Service (Silniční Služba) operates from bases throughout the Czech Republic. A brochure giving their telephone numbers is available at the frontier.
Headquarters of Road Service in Prague	Silniční Služba Opletalova 21, CZ-11000 Praha 1 Tel. (02) 22 49 06 and 22 86 07
Emergency telephone in Prague	Tel. (02) 123 (24 hour service)
Tow-away service in Prague	Tel. (02) 77 34 55 or 154

Breakdown Assistance in the Slovak Republic

For emergency breakdown assistance dial 154.

Police	Dial 158.
Emergency doctor	Dial 155.
Fire	Dial 150.
Road Service (Silniční Služba)	The Road Service (Silniční Služba) operates from bases throughout the Slovak Republic. A brochure giving their telephone numbers is available at the frontier.
Accident service in Bratislava	Tel. (07) 5 63 00
Tow-away services in Bratislava	Autoturist, Halašova 3, tel. (07) 21 54 59 and 24 40 13 Drudop, Bajkalská 31, tel. (07) 22 14 74 Communal Towing Service, Viedenská Cesta, tel. (07) 5 63 00

Repair Garages

There are repair garages in almost all towns in the Czech and Slovak Republics. During the main holiday season many of them are open on Saturdays and Sundays as well as on weekdays.

In the Event of an Accident

In the event of an accident the police should be called at once, and pending their arrival nothing should be changed at the scene of the accident. Any damage to the vehicles involved must be recorded by the police, who will give a copy to the owner of the car. This must be produced at the frontier when leaving the country. (Any damage sustained before entering the country must also be recorded on arrival at the frontier.)

Any damage should also be reported to the Czech Insurance Institute, Spálená 14–16, CZ-11000 Praha, tel. (02) 24 09 21 11 or to the branch of the Institute nearest the scene of the accident.

Museums

The principal museums in the Czech and Slovak Republics are described in the "Sights from A to Z" section of this guide. In addition to the art museums in the larger towns and the open-air museums (see entry) there are numerous specialised museums.

Opening times

See Business Hours

National Parks and Nature Reserves

There are a number of National Parks and numerous nature reserves in the Czech and Slovak Republics, established with the object of preserving and protecting the native flora and fauna. The situation of the various National Parks and nature reserves is shown on the map above.

Nature trails

In some of the National Parks and nature reserves nature trails have been laid out. They are waymarked by square white signs with a diagonal green strip and have explanatory notes at intervals along the trail.

National Parks

Czech Republic

1 Krkonoše
2 Šumava (Bohemian Forest)
3 Podyjí (Dyje depression)

Slovak Republic

4 Tatranský Národní Park (Tatras)
5 Nízké Tatry (Low Tatras)
6 Malá Fatra (Little Fatra)
7 Slovenský Raj (Slovakian Paradise)
8 Pieninský Národní Park (Pieniny Hills)

Nature Reserves

Czech Republic

9 Slavkovský Les (Slavkov Forest)
10 Křivoklátsko (Křivoklát area)
11 Český Kras (Bohemian Karst)
12 České Středohoří (Bohemian Massif)
13 Labské Pískovce (Elbe Sandstone Hills)
14 Lužicke Hory (Lusatian Hills)
15 Jizerské Hory (Jizera Hills)
16 Kokořínsko (Kokořín area)
17 Český Ráj (Bohemian Paradise)
18 Orlické Hory (Orlík Hills)
19 Jeseníky (Mt Praděd and Moravian Uplands)
20 Žd'árské Vrchy (Bohemo-Moravian Highlands)
21 Blaník
22 Třeboň (pond country round Třeboň)
23 Moravský Kras (Moravian Karst)
24 Pálava (Pavlov Hills)
25 Moravskoslezské Beskydy (Moravo-Silesian Beskyds)
26 Bílé Karpaty (White Carpathians, in Moravia)

Slovak Republic

27 Bielé Karpaty (White Carpathians, in Slovakia)
28 Kysuce
29 Horná Orava (Upper Orava area)
30 Eastern Carpathians
31 Vihorlat Hills

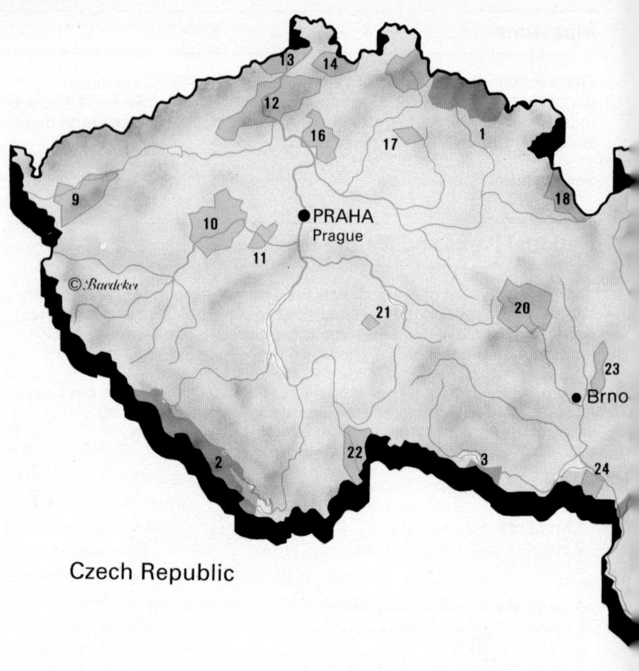

32 Slovenský Kras (Slovakian Karst)
33 Muránská Planina
34 Pol'ana
35 Vel'ká Fatra (Great Fatra)
36 Štiavnické Vrchy (Štiavnica Hills)
37 Ponitrie (with Tribeč range)
38 Malé Karpaty (Little Carpathians)

Newspapers and Periodicals

A good selection of international newspapers and periodicals can be found at kiosks in major cities and in the large hotels catering for foreign visitors. British newspapers are usually a day late, though the "Guardian" and "Financial Times", as well as the "International Herald Tribune", are available on the day of publication in Prague and Bratislava.

In Prague there is the English-language "Prague Post", published weekly.

In Bratislava there is a useful publication, "Kam v Bratislave?" ("Where to in Bratislava?"), listing what's on in the Slovakian capital.

National Parks and Nature Reserves

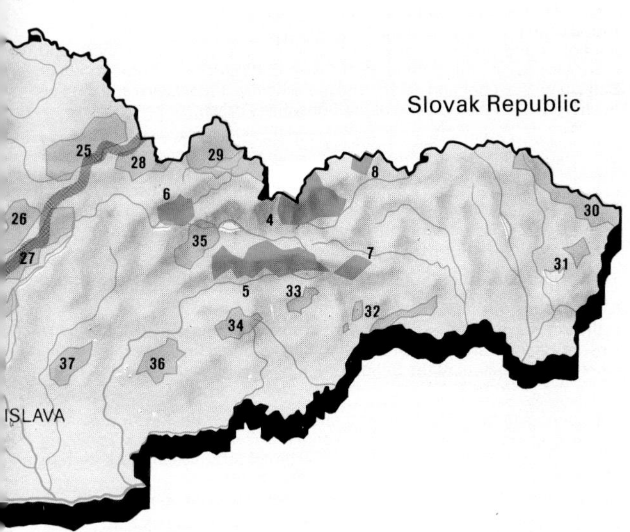

Open-Air Museums

In the Czech and Slovak Republics there are numerous well preserved examples of traditional architecture which give an impression of the life of earlier generations.

Skansens

The traditional architecture of the different regions can be seen in numerous open-air museums, known by the Scandinavian name of skansen.

During the summer some of the skansens (e.g., in the Czech Republic, Veselý Kopec: see below) are occupied by temporary inhabitants who practise various crafts (basketwork, woodcarving, painted wooden articles) in traditional working clothes and in the traditional way and on festival occasions wear special traditional costumes.

Wallachian Open-Air Museum

The Wallachian Open-Air Museum at Rožnov pod Radhoštěm (see below) is also inhabited during the summer, and puts on various interesting presentations.

Czech Republic

Stone architecture of Central Bohemian villages

Třebíz (north-west of Prague) has an open-air museum in the Baroque farmhouse of Cífkův Statek (No. 1), with 16th century objects.

Přerov nad Labem (north of the Prague–Poděbrady road) has examples of the traditional architecture of the Labe (Elbe) depression; museum (opened 1967) centred on the house at No. 19.

In Kouřim (south of the Prague–Kolín–Kutná Hora road) a skansen has been built up since 1972 on the banks of the Ždánický Potok. It includes buildings from outside Central Bohemia.

Wooden architecture of Central Bohemian villages

This type of traditional architecture has been preserved mainly on the middle course of the river Berounka (north-west of the Plzeň–Prague motorway). e.g. in Skryje (Nos. 4, 7, 13), Týřovice, Kublov, Hudlice (birthplace of the philologist and poet Josef Jungmann), Žloukovice and Bošín (in Nymburk district, east of Prague; Nos. 2, 4, 10 and 16).

Stone farmhouses of Southern Bohemia ("Rustic Baroque")

There are numbers of farmhouses in "Rustic Baroque" style (mainly built round courtyards, with Baroque features both on the gables of the dwelling-house and on the farm buildings) in the villages of Holašovice and Plástovice (west and north-west of České Budějovice), in Komárov (near Soběslav), Vlastiboř and Záluží; and in Zechovice, Předslavice and Jiřetice (near Volyně, in the foreland of the Bohemian Forest).

Wooden houses in Bohemian Forest

Only a few wooden houses in the style of the Alpine countries survive at Volary in the Bohemian Forest.

Half-timbered houses in Western and Northern Bohemia

In Western and Northern Bohemia, ranging from Cheb by way of the Ore Mountains, the Bohemian Massif and the Bohemian Paradise into the Krkonoše foreland, are numbers of half-timbered houses (usually two-storied), mainly built by German settlers.

There is an interesting skansen at Zubrnice (near Ústí nad Labem): see particularly Nos. 15, 27, 61, 74 and 82.

Wooden architecture of Bohemo-Moravian Highlands

In the skansen of Veselý Kopec (part of Vysočina, in Chrudim district), to the west of Hlinsko, are the best preserved, very interesting examples of the wooden architecture of the Bohemo-Moravian Highlands, with traditional crafts and customs.

Houses in Southern Moravia

Typical of Southern Moravia are houses of unfired brick with a painted doorway (*žudro*) gay with flowers. There are several examples (including wine-makers' houses) in the village museum of Strážnice in south-eastern Moravia.
Houses of similar type are found farther east in the Danube lowlands.

Wooden houses of Northern Moravia

In the Wallachian Open-Air Museum at Rožnov pod Radhoštěm, the oldest skansen in the Czech Republic, are a group of wooden buildings of "log cabin" type, including Rožnov town hall (1779).
There are fine examples of this type of architecture in Štramberk (Jičín district), Hodslavice (near Rožnov; birthplace of the Czech historian František Palacký) and the Bečva valley. There are also a number of little wooden churches, e.g. in Hodslavice (1551), Guty (1563), Sedlište (1624) and Nýdek (1576).

Slovak Republic

Wooden houses

Examples of wooden houses are to be seen in the museum of the Kysuca region in Nová Bystrica-Vychylovka (south-east of Čadca) and the museum of the Orava region in Zuberec-Brestová (near Lake Orava). On the south-eastern outskirts of the town of Martin is the Museum of the Slovakian Village, with examples of wooden buildings from all over Slovakia.
There are also examples of traditional wooden houses in the Little Fatra, in Terchová (30 buildings), Podbiel (Orava region; 74 buildings), Vlkolínec (Ružomberok district; 40 buildings) and Čičmany (Žilina district; 140 buildings).

Wooden architecture in North-Eastern Slovakia

There are many well preserved examples of traditional wooden architecture in north-eastern Slovakia. They can be seen, for example, in the oldest Slovakian museum of traditional architecture at Bardejovské Kúpele, in the skansen (still in course of development) below Stará L'ubovňa Castle, in the commune of Ždiar (eastern High Tatras) and in Jezersko (Zamagurie region).

In Eastern Slovakia, particularly in the Bardejov, Humenné, Michalovce, Stará L'ubovňa, Prešov and Svidník districts, are 27 little wooden churches of the 16th–18th centuries, some of them richly decorated with wall paintings.

Wooden churches in Eastern Slovakia

Opening Times

See Business Hours

Photography

See Social Conduct

Post, Telegraph

Post (*Pošta*)

Information

Ministère des Postes et Télécommunications
Division Internationale
Olšanská 5
CZ-12502 Praha 2

Opening times

Head Post Office in Prague:
Jindřišská 14
CZ-11000 Praha 1 (Nové Město)
Tel. (02) 26 41 93
Open 24 hours

Other post offices are usually open Mon.–Fri. 8am–6pm, Sat. 8am–noon. Some small post offices are open only Mon.–Fri. 8am–1pm.

Stamps

Stamps (*známky*) can be bought in tobacconists', at kiosks and in some hotels as well as in post offices.

Mail takes about a week to reach countries in Western Europe.

Telegrams

Telegrams can be handed in at post offices or in hotels. They can also be telephoned (dial 127 in both the Czech and Slovak Republics).

Public Holidays

January 1st (New Year's Day)
Easter Monday
May 1st (Labour Day)
May 8th (Liberation from Fascism, 1945)
July 5th (SS Cyril and Methodius's Day)
October 28th (Republic Day, commemorating the foundation of the first Czechoslovak Republic in 1918)
December 24th (Christmas Eve)
December 25th and 26th (Christmas)

In the Czech Republic:
July 6th (Jan Hus Day, commemorating his death at the stake in 1415)

In the Slovak Republic:
November 1st (Day of Reconciliation)

Radio and Television

Radio

The BBC World Service can now be picked up from most major cities in the Czech and Slovak Republics.

Television

The third television channel transmits CNN at certain times of the day and night. The more expensive hotels have pay TV with programmes in foreign languages.

Railways

The railway system of the Czech and Slovak Republics (see map below) is still run by the Czechoslovak State Railways (České Státní Dráhy, ČSD), which celebrated its 150th anniversary in 1989. The system has a total

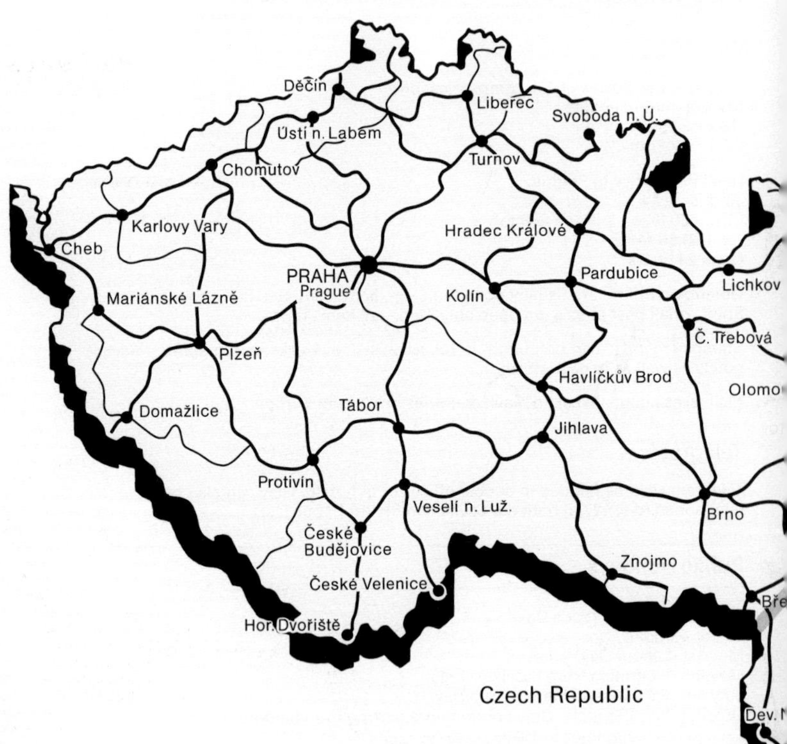

length of 13,000km/8000 miles, of which over a quarter is electrified. It is of standard gauge apart from a few sections which are still narrow-gauge or broad-gauge.

Timetables

The railway timetables of the Czech and Slovak Republics are published in Czech and Slovak versions. There are also various regional timetables.

Classes

In stopping trains there is only second (*druhá*) class. In other trains there is also first (*prvná/prvá*) class.

Tickets and seat tickets

The sale of tickets and booking of seats is now automated, with terminals in railway stations and travel agencies.

Where a seat ticket (*místenka/miestenka*) is required on a particular train this is shown in the timetable by the letter R in a square box; where reservation is recommended but not obligatory this is shown by the letter R without a box.

Railways

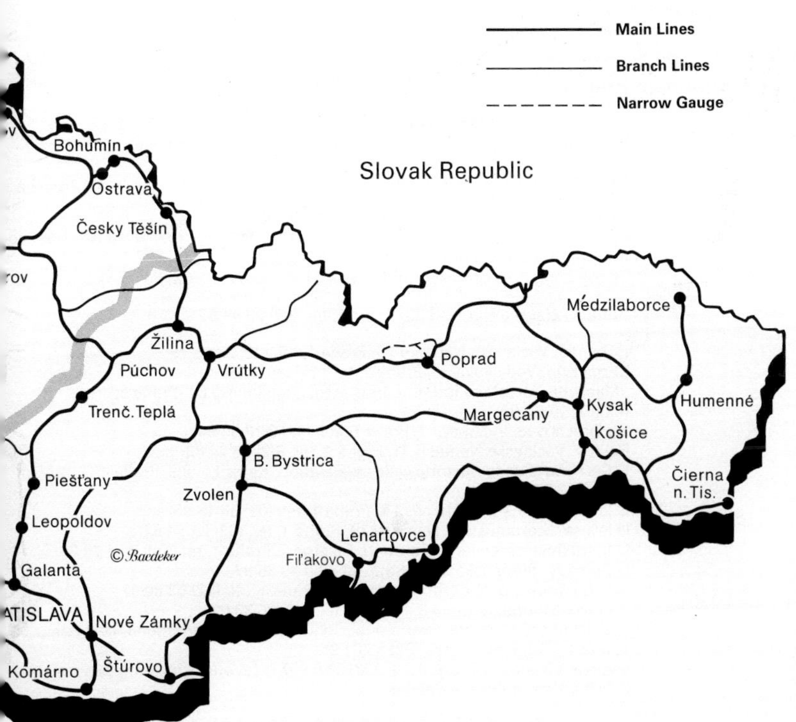

Information

ČSD information

Prague: tel. (02) 2 44 44 41 and 26 49 30
Bratislava: tel. (07) 4 69 45 and 4 82 75

ČSD Travel Agency

Passage Sevastopol
CZ-11000 Praha 1, tel. (02) 2 36 53 32 and 21 61 70 84

Tickets and information, including information about reduced fares (e.g. the Euro-Domino fare), can also be obtained from Čedok offices (see Information).

Restaurants

Restaurants are classified on the basis of quality, amenity and price in five categories, ranging downwards from I to V. The category of a particular restaurant is shown on its menu.
In addition to hotel restaurants and other restaurants, wine and beer restaurants and various kinds of snack bars and buffets there are also excellent restaurants ("motorests") in service areas on the most important European highways in the Czech and Slovak Republics.

"Speciality months"

During "speciality months" the menu in a restaurant will include special dishes such as game, fish, foie gras and fondues.

See Food and Drink

Restaurants in Prague

Prague has over 2000 restaurants, bars and cafés of all kinds. The following is a selection of restaurants offering particular types of cuisine.

Argentinian

Pampa, Karlovarská 1/4, Praha 6, tel. (02) 3 01 77 31

Asian

Asia, Letohradská 50, Praha 7, tel. (02) 37 02 15
Činská Restaurace (Chinese), Vodičkova 19, Praha 1, tel. (02) 26 26 97
Peking (Chinese), Legerova 64, Praha 2, tel. (02) 29 35 31
Thang Long (Vietnamese), Šimáčkova 21, Praha 7, tel. (02) 80 65 41

Balkan

Sofia, Václavské Náměstí 33, Praha 1, tel. (02) 26 49 86

Bohemian

Bohemia, Václavské Náměstí 29, Praha 1, tel. (02) 22 45 79
Černý Kun, Vodičkova 36, Praha 1, tel. (02) 26 26 97
*Myslivna (forester's lodge; game, etc.), Jagellonská 21, Praha 3, tel. (02) 27 62 09
Na Orechovce, Vychodní 7, Praha 6, tel. (02) 3 12 35 94
Rostov, Václavské Náměstí 21, Praha 1, tel. (02) 26 24 69
U Černého Slunce (historic cellar restaurant), Kamziková 9, Praha 1, tel. (02) 2 36 57 69
U Lorety, Loretánské Náměstí 8, Praha 1, tel. (02) 53 13 95
U Prince, Staroměstské Náměstí 29, Praha 1, tel. (02) 22 54 62
U Sixtů (historic cellar restaurant), Celetná 2, Praha 1, tel. (02) 2 36 79 80
U Šumavy, Štěpánská 3, Praha 2, tel. (02) 29 85 97
*U Tří Pštrosů, Dražického Náměstí 12, Praha 1, tel. (02) 53 60 07
*U Zlaté Studně, Karlova 3, Praha 1, tel. (02) 26 33 02
*Valdštejnská Hospoda (traditional Bohemian and international cuisine), Tomášská 16, Praha 1, tel. (02) 53 61 95
Vikárka, Vikářská 6, Praha 1, tel. (02) 53 64 97 (a favourite meeting-place of Czech artists in Prague Castle)

Caribbean

Habana, V Jámě 8, Praha 1, tel. (02) 26 01 64

French

Obecní Dům, Náměstí Republiky 5, Praha 1, tel. (02) 2 31 97 54

German

Alex, Revoluční 1, Praha 1, tel. (02) 2 31 44 89
Nürnberger Stub'n (Bavarian cuisine), Vinohradská 6, Praha 2

Indian

*Mayur, Štěpánská 61, Praha 1, tel. (02) 2 36 99 22

International

Divadelní Restaurace, Národní Třída 6, Praha 1
Hanavský Pavilon (with terrace), Letenské Sady 173, Praha 7, tel. (02) 32 57 92
Pelikan, Na Příkopě 7, Praha 1, tel. (02) 22 07 82
*Praha Expo 58 (view of Prague; terrace restaurant in summer), Letenské Sady 1500, Praha 7, tel. (02) 37 45 46
Rybárna (fish specialities), Václavské Náměstí 43, Praha 1, tel. (02) 22 78 23
U Zlatého Rožně, Československé Armady 22, Praha 6, tel. (02) 3 12 10 32

Italian

Peklo (in cellars of Strahov Monastery), Strahovské Nádvoří 1/130, Praha 1, tel. (02) 53 32 77
Trattoria Viola, Národní Třída 7, Praha 1, tel. (02) 26 67 32

Russian

Berjozka, Železná 24, Praha 1, tel. (02) 22 38 22
Gruzia, Na Příkopě 29, Praha 1, tel. (02) 26 27 74

Garden and terrace restaurants

Adria, Národní Třída 40, Praha 1, tel. (02) 26 26 37
Barrandov, Barrandovská 171, Praha 5, tel. (02) 54 53 09
Lví Dvůr, U Prašného Mostu 51, Praha 1, tel. (02) 53 53 89
Praha Expo 58 (see above, International cuisine)
Slovanský Dům, Na Příkopě 10, Praha 1, tel. (02) 22 48 51
U Fleků (see below, Beer restaurants)
U Tří Grácií, Novotného Lavka, Praha 1, tel. (02) 26 54 57

Wine bars and restaurants

Most of these establishments serve food as well as wine.
Blatnice, Michalská 8, Praha 1, tel. (02) 22 47 51
Klášterní Vinárna, Národní Třída 8, Praha 1, tel. (02) 29 05 96
*Lobkovická Vinárna, Vlašská 17, Praha 1, tel. (02) 53 01 85
Nebozízek (*view of Prague; reservation advisable), Petřínské Sady 411, Praha 5, tel. (02) 53 79 05
*Opera Grill, Karoliny Světlé 35, Praha 1, tel. (02) 26 55 08
*Parnas (view of Hradčany), Smetanovo Nábřeží 2, Praha 1, tel. (02) 26 50 17
*Rôtisserie, Mikulandská 6, Praha 1, tel. (02) 20 39 31 and 20 68 26
Svatá Klára, U Trojského Zámku 9, Praha 7, tel. (02) 84 12 13
*U Červeného Kola, Anežská 2, Praha 1, tel. (02) 23 18 94
U Kolovrata, Valdštejnská 18, Praha 1, tel. (02) 53 69 90
U Labutí, Hradčanské Náměstí 11, Praha 1, tel. (02) 53 94 76 and 53 16 84
*U Malířů (established 1543), Maltézské Náměstí 11, Praha 1, tel. (02) 53 18 83
*U Markyze, Nekázanka 8, Praha 1, tel. (02) 22 42 89
*U Mecenáše (reservation advisable), Malostranské Náměstí 10, Praha 1, tel. (02) 53 38 81
U Pantáty (Art Nouveau interior), Francouzská 76, Praha 10, tel. (02) 25 41 66
U Patrona, Drazického Náměstí 4, Praha 1, tel. (02) 53 16 61
*U Pavouka, Celetná 17, Praha 1, tel. (02) 2 32 10 37
U Sedmi Andělů, Jilská 20, Praha 1, tel. (02) 26 63 55
U Zelené Žáby, U Radnice 8, Praha 1, tel. (02) 26 28 15
*U Zlatého Jelena, Celetná 11, Praha 1, tel. (02) 26 85 95
*U Zlaté Hrušky, Noví Svět 3, Praha 1, tel. (02) 53 11 33
U Zlaté Konvice, Melantrichova 20, Praha 1, tel. (02) 26 01 28
*Valdštejnská Hospoda (see above, Bohemian cuisine)
Znojemská Vinárna, Václavské Náměstí 7, Praha 1, tel. (02) 2 14 36 19

"Wine evenings"

During the summer there are "wine evenings" (wine tasting, folk shows, specialities, competitions) in the Račianska Vinàreň wine restaurant in the International Hotel, Náměstí Družby 1, Praha 6, tel. (02) 3 31 98 55.

Restaurants

Beer-houses

U Dvou Koček, Uhelný Trh 10, Praha 1, tel. (02) 26 77 29
*U Fleků, Křemencova 11, Praha 1, tel. (02) 29 32 46
*U Kalicha, Na Bojišti 12–14, Praha 2, tel. (02) 29 19 45
U Kocoura, Nerudova 2, Praha 1, tel. (02) 53 89 62
U Medvídků, Na Perštyně 7, Praha 1, tel. (02) 2 35 89 04
U Pinkasů, Jungmannovo Náměstí 15, Praha 1, tel. (02) 26 18 04
U Schnellů, Tomašská 2, Praha 1, tel. (02) 53 20 04 and 53 32 18
U Supa, Celetná 22, Praha 1, tel. (02) 22 30 42
U Svatého Tomáše, Letenská 12, Praha 1, tel. (02) 53 00 64 and 53 34 92
*U Zlatého Tygra, Husova 17, Ptaha 1, tel. (02) 26 52 19

"Beer evenings"

At weekends from mid May to the end of September there are "beer evenings" (unlimited supplies of beer, Bohemian brass band, folk shows, specialities, competitions) in the Great Hall of the International Hotel.

Cafés

City, Vodičkova 38, Praha 1
Columbia, Mostecká 3, Praha 1
*Evropa (Art Nouveau interior), Václavské Náměstí 29, Praha 1
Jalta, Václavské Náměstí 45, Praha 1
Obecní Dům, Náměstí Republiky 5, Praha 1
Savarin, Na Příkopě 10, Praha 1
*Slávia (artists' rendezvous), Národní Třída 1, Praha 1
U Týna, Staroměstské Náměstí, Praha 1
*U Zlatého Hada, Karlova 18, Praha 1
Velryba (artists' café), Opatovická, Praha 1

Restaurants in Bratislava

Alžbetka, Kollárovo Námestie 11, tel. (07) 5 32 03
Ázia, Riečna 4, tel. (07) 33 08 51
Bajkal, Bajkalská, tel. (07) 63 46 64
Bratislava, Súmračná 3, tel. (07) 22 47 03
Centrál, Steinerova 74, tel. (07) 6 42 42
Devín, Slovanské Nábrežie, tel. (07) 33 08 51
Dukla, Dulovo Námestie 1, tel. (07) 6 34 15
Florá, Senecká Cesta, tel. (07) 21 40 00
Jadran, Nevádzová 6, tel. (07) 23 08 09
Kamzík, on Mt Kamzík, tel. (07) 4 20 74
*Mad'arská Reštaurácia (Hungarian cuisine), Hviezdoslavovo Námestie 20, tel. (07) 33 48 83
Panoráma, Borská 1, tel. (07) 32 02 11
Pivovarská Reštaurácia (beer-house), Steinerova 26, tel. (07) 6 52 46
Perugia, Zelená 3, tel. (07) 33 15 55
Pod Machnáčom, Nábrežie L. Svobodu, tel. (07) 31 45 80
Pólo, Trnavská 42, tel. (07) 6 96 52
Pol'ovnícka Reštaurácia, Duklianska 4, tel. (07) 5 24 15
Reduta, Mostová, tel. (07) 33 08 06
*Rybársky Cech (fish specialities), Žižkova 1, tel. (07) 31 30 49
*Slovenská Reštaurácia, Štúrova 15, tel. (07) 5 28 81
Smíchovský Dvor, Heydukova 33, tel. (07) 5 95 90
Snežienka (view), Železná Studnička, tel. (07) 37 39 02
Štadión, Vajnorská 44, tel. (07) 2 11 22
Stará Sladovňa, Cintorínska 32, tel. (07) 5 62 79
Terno, Dom Odievania, Námestie SNP, tel. (07) 33 47 92
U Zlatého Kapra, Prepoštská 6, tel. (07) 33 16 12
Zelený Dom, Zelená 5, tel. (07) 33 17 95
Železná Studnička, Cesta Mládeže, tel. (07) 37 30 70
Zlatá Lipa, Talichova 1, tel. (07) 36 14 40

Wine restaurants

Bulharská Vináreň, Zámočnícka 3, tel. (07) 33 28 38
*Hradná Vináreň (Castle wine cellar), Castle, tel. (07) 31 16 84

Kláštorná Vináreň, Pugačevova 1, tel. (07) 33 04 30
Malí Františkáni, Laurinská 19, tel. (07) 5 49 74
Puszta, Hviezdoslavovo Námestie 20, tel. (07) 33 48 83
Tramín, Kadnárova 65, tel. (07) 28 21 69
U Modrej Hviezdy, Beblavého 14, tel. (07) 33 27 47
U Zbrojnoša, Zámočnícka 3, tel. (07) 33 38 28
*Vel'kí Františkáni, Dibrovovo Námestie 10, tel. (07) 33 30 73
Vínny Restaurant, Dunajská 18, tel. (07) 5 00 80
Vysoká 44, Vysoká 16, tel. (07) 5 71 67
Wolkrova, Wolkrova 5, tel. (07) 33 28 44
Zlatá Lipa, Talichova 1, tel. (07) 36 14 40

Cafés

Bystrica (*view), in pylon of SNP Bridge
Danubius, Fajnorovo Nábrežie 16
Lýra, Jiráskova 2
Dukla, Dulovo Námestie 1
Grand, Námestie SNP
Horský Park, Prokopa Hollého 1
Iskra, Steinerova 7
Korzo, Hviezdoslavovo Námestie 11
Luxor, Štúrova 15
Malý Muk, Obchodná 17
*Roland, at the Roland Fountain

Shipping Services

The Czech Republic is linked with the North Sea by the Elbe (Labe). The Slovak Republic is linked with the Black Sea by the Danube (Dunáj). During the summer there are excursion boats on the Elbe and Danube, other large rivers and various lakes.

Czech Republic

Landing-stage in Prague

The landing-stage in Prague for passenger boats on the Vltava is at the Palacký Bridge (Palackého Most).

Cruises on Vltava

During the summer there are regular cruises on the Vltava, offering good views of Prague from the water.

Evening cruises

From July to September, several times a week, there are cruises on the Vltava in the historic old paddle-steamer "Vyšehrad" (music, dancing, restaurant).

Combined excursions

Čedok (see Information) runs combined coach and boat excursions, for example to Lake Orlík and Lake Slapy (with a picnic on the shores of the lake).

Slovak Republic

Landing-stage in Bratislava

The landing-stage (Osobný Prístav) in Bratislava for excursions on the Danube is on the Fajnorovo Nábrežie (No. 2).

Information

ČSPD, tel. (07) 5 95 27, 5 95 18 and 5 95 16

Vienna–Bratislava–Budapest

Between May and September there are regular services by boat and hydrofoil between Vienna, Bratislava and Budapest. Information from Erste Donau-Dampfschiffahrts-Gesellschaft, Handelskai 265, A-1021 Vienna, tel. (01) 2 17 50–0, or from ČSPD in Bratislava.

Bratislava–Grabčikovo–Bratislava

On summer weekends the Slovak shipping company Blue Danube Travel runs trips (5–9 hours) down the Danube and through the new canal to the large hydro-electric station at Gabčikovo, a project which has aroused much criticism on ecological grounds.

Shopping, Souvenirs

There are a great variety of things that visitors like to bring back from a holiday in the Czech and Slovak Republics – books, audio cassettes and discs, jewellery, toys, sports articles, local drinks (beer, the bitter liqueur becherovka, slivovice, borovička, a juniper brandy), a variety of foodstuffs (Karlsbad wafers, Pardubice gingerbread, sausages, Prague ham or Znojmo's high-quality gherkins) and much else besides. The following is a selection of popular souvenirs.

Ceramics

Bohemian porcelain has long been famous. Other pottery products are figures from Modra and Stupava (in western Slovakia) and a wide range of jugs, vases and dishes, much of it from the Chod country in southern Bohemia.

Embroidery

Blankets, towels, table runners, traditional costumes, etc., often have superb embroidered decoration.

Glass and crystal

Bohemian glass and crystal are world-famed. They offer a variety of artistic designs and magnificent colours.
Čedok (see Information) runs excursions to Harrachov in the Krkonoše to see one of the world's oldest glassworks, the Jablonec Glass and Jewellery Museum and the Glass Museum and chandelier factory in Kamenický Šenov (glass souvenirs on sale).

Jewellery and ornaments

Bohemian garnet jewellery is a popular souvenir. Pewter costume jewellery (including buttons, clasps and belt buckles) with imaginative ornament go equally well with traditional costumes and modern dress styles.

Lace

Pillow-lace in a variety of interesting designs is found in many forms – tablecloths, towels, collars, etc.

Leather, fur

Leather, fur and sheepskin jackets, sometimes with embroidered decoration, belts, boots and handbags with metal fittings are also very popular souvenirs.

Textiles

Attractive textiles are available in variety – cushions, table runners, carpets, etc.
Characteristic products are tablecloths in traditional cotton prints.

Woodcarving

Woodcarving has a long tradition behind it, particularly in Slovakia. In the past the shepherds used to carve the implements and utensils they needed (wooden axes with metal mountings, milk jugs, cheese shapes, ladles, salt-boxes, butter churns), and carved articles of all kinds are still among the most popular souvenirs.

Craft products

Among typical products of traditional crafts are wooden furniture, basketwork, toys made in a variety of materials, Christmas cribs (Nativity groups) and decorative cakes (e.g. for Christmas). Products of this kind are sold in special Úluv shops in the larger towns and tourist centres.

Social Conduct

Photography

The photographing and filming of objects of military importance (bridges, ports, railway installations, airports and airfields, buildings with a military guard, frontier posts, etc.) is prohibited.

Forms of address

Importance is attached to the use of professional and other titles in addressing people, either orally or in writing, and in introducing them to others.

Conversation

Since the Czechs and Slovaks are among the world's leading sporting nations (tennis, ice hockey, figure skating) and many of them are music-lovers and interested in culture, there is no shortage of subjects of conversation with them.

Appointments

Appointments should be settled in advance and punctually observed.

Gifts

Small gifts – flowers, drinks, sweets, etc. – are appreciated between friends, and are normally offered if you are invited to someone's house.

Drink and driving

There is an absolute ban on the consumption of alcohol by drivers.

Changing money

Changing money on the black market is a punishable offence.

Tipping

See entry

Spas

The Czech and Slovak Republics are abundantly supplied with mineral springs whose water is used at many places for drinking or bathing cures and bottled as table water. At some spas the local peat or mud is also used for treatment purposes.

The principal spas in Czech and Slovak Republics are shown on the map on page 590.

The spas are open throughout the year apart from the week between Christmas and New Year. The main season is from the beginning of May to the end of September, the off-seasons from the beginning of March to the end of April and from the beginning of October to mid November, and the winter season from mid November to the end of February.

A stay of at least three weeks for treatment is recommended. Medical reports should be brought with you.

Information

Information about spas and spa treatment can be obtained from Čedok (see Information).
More detailed information about spas in the Czech Republic can be obtained from
Balnea
Pařížská 11
CZ-11001 Praha 1
Tel. (02) 2 32 37 67

For detailed information about spas in the Slovak Republic, apply to
Slovakotherma
Radlinského 13
SQ-81289 Bratislava
Tel. (07) 5 81 80

Selected Spas in the Czech Republic

Karlovy Vary
(Karlsbad)

The Czech Republic's principal spa.
Alt. 380m/1245ft; western Bohemia
Recommended for: diseases of the digestive tract and metabolic disturbances; plastic surgery.

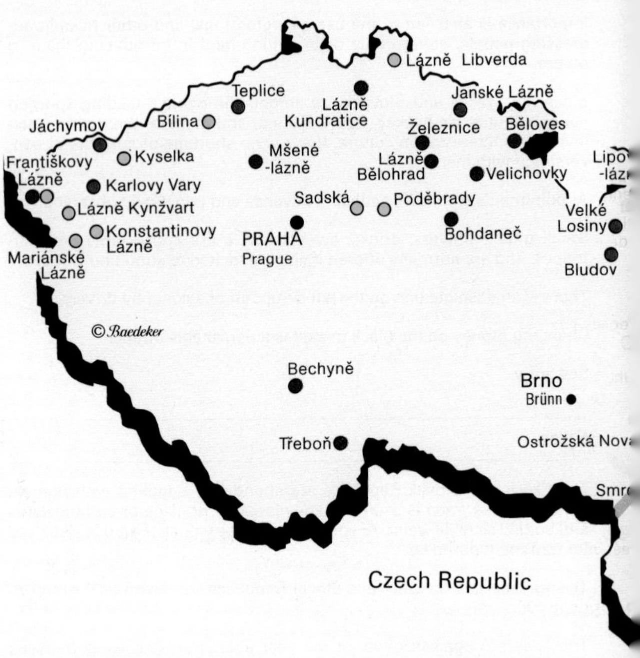

Facilities: sanatorium (concerts and dancing in the evening) and thermal swimming pool, other treatment establishments (some providing acupuncture, staged oxygen therapy, etc.), Kurhotel; golf, minigolf, riding, tennis; walking, excursions; casinos (see entry); festivals (see Events).

Mariánské Lázně (Marienbad)

The second largest spa in the Czech Republic.
Alt. 628m/2060ft: western Bohemia.
Recommended for: diseases of the respiratory tracts, kidneys and urinary tract; disorders of the locomotor apparatus; metabolic disturbances (gout, diabetes); managerial stress; rehabilitation and training of sportsmen.
Facilities: various treatment establishments and sanatoria; golf, tennis, walking; concerts, dancing, cinema; Chopin Festival (see Events).

Jáchymov

The first radium spa in the world.
Alt. 650m/2135ft; western Bohemia
Recommended for: disorders of the locomotor apparatus, nervous complaints, metabolic disturbances.
Facilities: various treatment establishments; park, with monument to Marie Curie and her husband; dances and cultural events; excursions; sport, winter sports.

Františkovy Lázně

Alt. 580m/1905ft; western Bohemia
Recommended for: gynaecological conditions, disorders of the locomotor apparatus.
Facilities: various treatment establishments (function rooms); park with bandstand; many paths for walking.

Spas

Teplice v Čechách

The oldest spa in the Czech Republic.
Alt. 220m/720ft; northern Bohemia
Recommended for: disorders of the locomotor apparatus, vascular troubles.
Facilities: treatment centre and other treatment establishments; casino; park, with beautiful paths for walking; sports grounds, open-air swimming pool; numerous social and cultural events (see Events).

Janské Lázně

Alt. 615m/2020ft; northern Bohemia
Recommended for: poliomyelitis; diseases of the respiratory tract in children; sequelae of disorders of the locomotor apparatus after accidents.
Facilities: children's sanatoria, with own bathing facilities; treatment establishment for adults.

Poděbrady

Alt. 188m/617ft; central Bohemia
Recommended for: heart conditions and circulatory disorders.
Facilities: spa establishments in a beautiful park; polyclinic; open-air swimming pool; tennis, golf, riding.

Třeboň

A biological reserve since 1978.
Alt. 430m/1410ft; southern Bohemia
Recommended for: disorders of locomotor apparatus; rehabilitation and training courses for oarsmen.
Facilities: various sanatoria, spa establishment with library and treatment rooms; concerts and dancing; "Cultural Summer" (see Events); carriage trips.

Spas

Luhačovice The largest spa in Moravia.
Alt. 250m/820ft; southern Moravia
Recommended for: diseases of the respiratory tracts, metabolic and digestive disturbances, diabetes.
Facilities: sanatorium, spa establishment; park; beautiful paths for walking; swimming pool on lake, tennis courts; Janáček Festival (see Events).

Jeseník Alt. 650m/2135ft; northern Moravia
Recommended for: nervous disorders, diseases of respiratory tracts; anti-stress courses for managers.
Facilities: several sanatoria; beautiful paths for walking; open-air swimming pool; toboggan run nearby.

Lipová Lázně Lipová is part of the Jeseník spa complex. Recommended for diabetes, obesity, etc.

Teplice nad Bečvou A small spa on the beautiful river Bečva, surrounded by forest.
Alt. 262m/860ft; northern Moravia
Recommended for: heart conditions and circulatory disorders.
Facilities: sanatorium; park; open-air swimming pool in town.

Selected Spas in the Slovak Republic

Piešt'any The leading Slovakian spa for the treatment of disorders of the locomotor apparatus.
Alt. 162m/532ft; south-western Slovakia
Recommended for: disorders of the locomotor apparatus, arthritis, arthroses, rheumatism, gout, follow-up of accidents, nervous disorders.
Facilities: spa centre with sanatoria and park; open-air thermal swimming pool; cafés, with music, club and function rooms.

Trenčianské Teplice Alt. 272m/892ft; western Slovakia
Recommended for: disorders of the locomotor apparatus, rheumatism, gout and nervous disorders.
Facilities: various spa establishments; park; promenade concerts and other cultural and social events, including the annual "Musical Summer"; facilities for various sporting activities, good walking.

Štrbské Pleso An altitude resort in the western High Tatras.
Alt. 1351m/4433ft; northern Slovakia
Recommended for: bronchial asthma
Facilities: various spa establishments, including a children's sanatorium; open-air swimming pool; beautiful lake, boating; various sports facilities in area.

Sliač Kúpele Alt. 373m/1224ft; central Slovakia
Recommended for: heart conditions and circulatory disorders.
Facilities: spa establishment with park; open-air thermal swimming pool.

Dudince Alt. 140m/460ft; southern Slovakia
Recommended for: circulatory disturbances and disorders of locomotor apparatus, follow-up of accidents, nervous disorders.
Facilities: various spa establishments.

Nový Smokovec An altitude resort in the central High Tatras.
Alt. 1010m/3315ft; north-eastern Slovakia
Recommended for: diseases of the respiratory tract, pneumonia, follow-up of operations on the lungs, metabolic disturbances.
Facilities: spa establishment.

Bardejovské Kúpele Alt. 325m/1065ft; north-eastern Slovakia
Recommended for: metabolic and digestive disturbances, non-specific diseases of the respiratory organs.
Facilities: spa establishment and various sanatoria; two bathing stations on lake; tennis and volleyball courts.

Sport

Among the most popular sports in the Czech and Slovak Republics are tennis, figure skating, motor sport and the various water sports and winter sports, and accordingly visitors will find a great range of sporting facilities at their disposal.

Čedok (see Information) can book sport and fitness holidays and obtain tickets for sporting events.
Training courses for young people in various sports can be arranged through CKM, the Youth Travel Bureau (see Information).

Roudnice nad Labem sports complex

At Roudnice nad Labem, 38km/24 miles north of Prague and 45 minutes from Prague's Ruzyně Airport, is a large sports complex with superb facilities for a variety of sports.
A multi-purpose hall with seating for 600 spectators is suitable for basketball, handball, volleyball, table tennis and gymnastics. There are tennis courts, football pitches (with floodlighting) and a hockey pitch, a well equipped fitness centre, a 25-metre indoor swimming pool and a 50-metre open-air pool. The nearby Račice Canal is used for rowing contests (world championship, 1993) and for canoeing and sailing.
The sports complex also includes special coaching rooms with audio-visual equipment, a restaurant (with bar and wine-bar) and a three-star hotel.

For information on the Roudnice complex and to book a stay there, apply to:
ČSA Airtours
Národní Třída 27
CZ-11121 Praha 1
Tel. (02) 2 35 83 41 and 2 35 17 73

Selected Sports

Angling

Anglers will find plenty of opportunity to practise their sport in the Czech and Slovak Republics. Among the principal species of fish are trout, catfish, carp, pike, pike-perch and eels.
Information about types of fishing, fishing waters, fishing permits, seasons, species of fish and minimum sizes can be obtained from branches of Čedok (see Information). Information will also be supplied by the Czech Angling Association:
Český Rybářský Svaz
Žitná 13
CZ-11000 Praha 1 (Nové Město)

Canoeing and kayaking

See Water Sports, below

Climbing

From spring to autumn there are ideal conditions for hill walking, climbing and rock-climbing in the hills and mountains of the Czech Republic and Slovakia. Details from Čedok.

Cycling

See Walking and Cycling, below

Dancing

There are arrangements for dancing in the spa towns (see Spas), Prague and other towns. On New Year's Eve in particular many hotels have gala dinners followed by dancing.
The traditional Opera Ball was held in February 1992, for the first time for almost 60 years, in Prague's Smetana Theatre, the largest and finest opera-house in the Czech Republic. It can be expected that this will again become a regular event.

Sport

Figure skating	The world figure skating championship was held in Prague in March 1993.
Flying	There are sightseeing flights (and also ascents in hot-air balloons) from various airports, particularly Prague. Information from Čedok.
Football	There are numbers of well-known football grounds in the Czech and Slovak Republics. In Prague, for example, there are: Dukla Praha, Praha 6 (Dejvice), Na Julisce 28 Sparta Praha, Praha 7, Letná, Milady Horákoré Tickets are relatively cheap. Most matches are on Sunday mornings.
Golf	Golfers will find the cost of playing very reasonable. Most of the golf courses are in the Czech Republic. There are good 18-hole courses (open all year round) at the Western Bohemian spas of Mariánské Lázně (Marienbad) and Karlovy Vary (Karlsbad), on which national championships are played. There is an 8-hole course at Poděbrady (53km/33 miles east of Prague) and another in the Motol district of Prague (Praha 5). Information on courses, hire of clubs and coaching from Čedok.
Horse-racing	The Grand Pardubice Steeplechase, one of the toughest courses in Europe (7km/4½ miles; 39 jumps of great difficulty), has been run annually in October at Pardubice (Czech Republic) since 1874. There are also racecourses at Prague and in other towns.
Ice hockey	Ice hockey is one of the most popular team sports in the Czech and Slovak Republics. There are, for example, ice-hockey stadiums in Bratislava and in Prague (where the world ice hockey championship was staged in April–May 1992) and a fine ice rink at Mariánské Lázně (Marienbad).
Minigolf	There are minigolf courses, for example, at Jáchymov and Jeseník in the Czech Republic and at Trenčianské Teplice in the Slovak Republic.
Motor sport	An event of international standing is the Motorcycle Grand Prix, run annually in August on the Masaryk Ring outside Brno. The international Speedway Race for the Golden Helmet of Pardubice takes place at Pardubice (Czech Republic) in September.
Riding	There are facilities for riding at many places in the Czech Republic, including Karlovy Vary (Karlsbad), Luhačovice, Poděbrady (where there is a riding school) and Třeboň. During the main holiday season riding horses can be hired at the Club Hotel in Průhonice (12km/7½ miles south-east of Prague city centre).
Rowing	See Water Sports, below
Sailing	See Water Sports, below
Shooting	There are numerous species of game in the Czech and Slovak Republics, including hares, red deer, roe deer, moufflons, wild pig, pheasants and wild duck. In Slovakia there are occasional bears. Detailed information about shooting in the Czech Republic and about shooting holidays (third party insurance required, import of guns and ammunition, etc.) can be obtained from Čedok. Shooting permits can be obtained from Čedok or at any frontier crossing point. In general the prospects of good shooting are better in Slovakia than in the Czech Republic. Visitors interested in hunting trophies will want to see the collection of trophies in Konopiště Castle (40km/25 miles south-east of Prague).
Skittles	There are skittle alleys in the Czech Republic at Prague (Forum Hotel; Club Hotel, Průhonice, 12km/7½ miles south-east of city centre), Karlovy Vary (Karlsbad), Jáchymov and Poděbrady.

Squash

Squash is less popular in the Czech and Slovak Republics than in some other countries. There are, however, some places where it can be played, for example in the Club Hotel, Pruhonice (12km/7½ miles south-east of Prague city centre).

Swimming

See Water Sports, below

Table tennis

Table tennis is a popular sport in the Czech and Slovak Republics. Some hotels, particularly in the spa towns, have games rooms in which table tennis and other games can be played.

Tennis

Many hotels in the Czech and Slovak Republics, particularly large new hotels, have their own tennis courts, either outdoor or indoor.
Particularly favoured by tennis-players are the Pavel Složil Tennis Camp (indoor and outdoor courts, coaching, fitness centre, hotel) at Svítkov, near Pardubice (Czech Republic), and the Club Hotel (indoor and outdoor courts, coaching, video installation; many other recreation facilities) at Průhonice (12km/7½ miles south-east of Prague city centre).
Tennis can also be played on the island of Štavnice in the Holešovice district of Prague, in the Czech spas – Františkovy Lázně, Jáchymov, Jeseník, Luhačovice, Karlovy Vary (Karlsbad), Mariánské Lázně (Marienbad), Poděbrady, Teplice nad Bečvou, Teplice v Čechách, Třeboň, etc.) – and in the spa of Bardejovské Kúpele in the Slovak Republic.

Walking and Cycling

Walking

The Czech Tourist Club (Klub Českých Turistů), founded in Prague in 1888, is responsible for the waymarking and maintenance of over 48,000km (30,000 miles) of hiking paths and trails and for the planting of trees. It also organises numerous events for walkers (some of international standing) throughout the year.

There are particularly attractive walks in the various spa towns and in the National Parks and nature reserves. On some routes in the National Parks walkers must be accompanied by a guide. Care should be taken not to drop any rubbish: in the High Tatras National Park in particular wolves, lynxes, eagles and occasionally bears may follow in the tracks of walkers who leave remains of food.
A popular starting-point for walks in magnificent country in Slovakia is Jasná pod Chopkom (alt. 1500m/4900ft) in the Low Tatras, with numerous waymarked paths.
In many of these areas – for example in the Moravian Beskyds (Czech Republic) – walkers will find accommodation at very reasonable prices indeed.

Cycling

Bicycles can be hired in many sporthotels and juniorhotels (see Hotels). During the main holiday season they can also be hired at the Club Hotel, Průhonice (12km/7½ miles south-east of Prague city centre), and elsewhere in the Czech and Slovak Republics.
Mountain bikes can be hired at some sporthotels and juniorhotels in the mountain and upland regions.

Water Sports

General

There are ample opportunities for bathing and surfing on artificial lakes, ponds and rivers in the Czech and Slovak Republics.

Information about facilities for all kinds of water sports can be obtained from Čedok (see Information).

Swimming pools

Many tourist resorts have swimming pools, outdoor and/or indoor, and many hotels have their own pools.

Areas for water sports and bathing beaches

There are excellent facilities for water sports and good bathing beaches at many places in the Czech Republic, for example on Lake Mácha, Lakes Slapy and Orlík (formed by dams on the Vltava), Lake Lipno (Bohemian Forest), Lake Vranov (South Moravia) and the Luhačovice reservoir in Moravia.

Another attractive area for water sports is the beautiful winding course of the river Lužnice downstream from Tábor (60km/37 miles south of Prague).

In the Slovak Republic there are popular bathing beaches on Lake Orava, the artificial Slnečné Jazerá (Sunny Lakes; sandy beaches) at Senec (26km/16 miles east of Bratislava), Lake Slňava at Piešt'any and the Zemplínska Širava (the "Slovakian Sea").

Wind-surfing

Particularly favoured by wind-surfers are Lake Domaša in eastern Slovakia (Vranov nad Topl'ou district; wind-surfing school at Holčíkovce) and the Slnečné Jazerá (Sunny Lakes) at Senec, east of Bratislava.

Sailing, rowing, canoeing, kayaking

There is good sailing on the Danube at Komárno (southern Slovakia).

Sailing and rowing are permitted in most of the areas for water sports mentioned above. A sailing, towing, canoeing and kayaking paradise is Lake Slňava (at Piešt'any in western Slovakia), on which water-skiing is also possible.

Sailing, rowing and canoeing on the Račice Canal near Roudnice nad Labem: see the beginning of this section.

There are facilities for the rehabilitation and training of oarsmen at the spa of Třeboň on the Svět Pond (southern Bohemia).

Winter Sports

See entry

Taxis

Taxis are available in all the larger towns in the Czech and Slovak Republics. They can be picked up at taxi ranks or called by telephone.

It is advisable before taking a taxi to enquire about the fare and check that the meter is switched on.

There is usually an additional charge at night.

Telephone

International telephone calls can be made from post offices, hotels and public telephones marked accordingly (grey telephones; yellow and blue telephones are for local calls only).

International dialling codes

From the United Kingdom to the Czech or Slovak Republic: 010 42
From the United States or Canada to the Czech or Slovak Republic: 011 42
From the Czech or Slovak Republic to the United Kingdom: 00 44
From the Czech or Slovak Republic to the United States or Canada: 00 1

Directory Enquiries

Numbers in Prague and Bratislava: dial 120
Numbers elsewhere in the Czech and Slovak Republics: dial 121

Numbers in Prague are in the process of being changed. In case of difficulty contact Directory Enquiries

Time

The Czech and Slovak Republics observe Central European Time (one hour ahead of Greenwich Mean Time).

Summer Time (two hours ahead of GMT) is in force from the end of March to the end of September. The exact dates are given on radio and television and in the newspapers.

Tipping

A service charge is included in hotel and restaurant bills, but an additional tip (5–10% of the bill) may be given for attentive service.

Travel Documents

Personal Papers

Passport

For citizens of most European countries, the United States and Canada a full passport, valid for at least three months after entry, is all that is required to enter the Czech or Slovak Republic.

Visa

For citizens from Albania, Cyprus and Turkey a visa is required for entry to the Czech and Slovak Republics.

Car Papers

National driving licences and vehicle registration documents are accepted and must be carried.

An international insurance certificate (green card) is advisable.

Visiting motorists must fill in a registration form at the frontier and will be given a copy of the form, which they must be able to produce on demand.

If the owner of the vehicle is not travelling the driver must have the owner's written permission.

No customs documents are required for pleasure boats (with or without a motor), camping cars or trailers.

Lost documents

There is an enquiry office for lost documents at Olšanská 2, Praha 3.

When to Go

General

While the towns of the Czech and Slovak Republics with their manifold attractions can be visited at any time of year, the best time to visit the country areas is from May to September.

Most of the castles are open to the public from the beginning of April to the end of October (see Business Hours).

When to Go

For the season in the spas, see Spas.

Spring

In the fruit-growing areas (e.g. in the Bohemiam Massif and the Vltava valley round Prague) the blossom is at its most beautiful from about mid April.

"Prague Spring" and "Prague June" (musical festivals): see Events

Summer

During the main holiday season hotels and camping sites tend to be overcrowded and prices are higher. Advance booking is advisable.
There are numerous festivals and other events during this period (see Events).

At higher altitudes in the Slovakian Ore Mountains the winter sports season lasts into July. Ski trekking is possible between July and September only in the High Tatras.

At the height of summer there may be sudden thunder showers.

Autumn

In autumn with its brilliant colouring and often long-continuing periods of fine weather the upland regions of mainly deciduous forest and the beautiful river valleys retain their charm until the end of October.

Winter

There are magnificent opportunities for winter sports enthusiasts in the hills surrounding Bohemia on the north and west and the Hrubý Jeseník range in Moravia from January to the end of March; and, in the Slovak Republic, in the Western Beskyds, the High and Low Tatras, the Great and Little Fatra and the Slovakian Ore Mountains from December onwards (until May and at the highest altitudes until July).

Weather

See Facts and Figures, Climate

Wine

Bohemia

In addition to the internationally known wines the wine restaurants and wine bars of Prague mainly serve Bohemian wines, in particular the famous Ludmila brand from the slopes above the Labe (Elbe) at Mělník and the Žernosecky and Primatorské brands.

Moravia

The best Moravian wines come from the Znojmo, Mikulov and Valtice areas in southern Moravia.

Slovakia

The wines from the slopes of the Little Carpathians and those produced in eastern Slovakia are well made and aromatic.

A Selection of Wines

White wines	**Name**	**Character**	**Goes with . . .**
	Bzenecká Lipka (S. Moravia)	delicate bouquet, riesling-like	grilled meat
	Pálavské (S. Moravia)	full, balanced	duck, pheasant
	Rulandské	full-bodied, aromatic	warm hors d'œuvres, veal, poultry
	Rulandské Šedé	delicate aroma	cold dishes

Name	Character	Goes with . . .
Ryzlink Rýnský	full, balanced, elegant	cold hors d'œuvres, fish
Ryzlink Vlašský	fresh, balanced	cold dishes
Sylvanské Zelené	full-bodied	foie gras, poultry
Veltínské Zelené	spicy to heavy	cold dishes
Zlatý Hrozen	slightly spicy	cold dishes, fish
Frankovka	delicately fruity	duck, grills, roast meat
Rulandské	full-bodied	grills, game, pheasant
Vavřinecké	smooth, lively	game, grills

Red wines

Winter Sports

Winter sports holidays can be booked through Čedok (see Information) or a travel agency.

During the winter season there are likely to be queues at cableways and ski-lifts.

The following is a selection of good skiing areas in the Czech and Slovak Republics. The figures in brackets give (1) the altitude of the winter sports centre, (2) the altitude range of pistes for downhill skiing, and the length of langlauf trails.

Selected Skiing Areas in the Slovak Republic

There are a number of major winter sports resorts in the High and Low Tatras and the Little and Great Fatra.

High Tatras

The highest mountains in Slovakia are the Tatras, which lie along the Slovak–Polish frontier. Finest of all are the High Tatras, which rise to a height of 2655m/8711ft in the Gerlachovský Štít.

Major winter sports centres:
Tatranská Lomnica (850m/2790ft); Starý Smokovec (1020m/3345ft); Nový Smokovec (1000m/3300ft); Štrbské Pleso (1355m/4445ft), where the international Nordic skiing championships were held in 1970.

Facilities:
Ski passes at reasonable prices; ski schools (children and adults); numerous ski-lifts and pistes; cableway from Tatranská Lomnica to the Skalnaté Pleso (lake) and the summit of the Lomnický Štít (2634m/8642ft), the second highest mountain in the Slovak Republic.

A narrow-gauge electric railway runs between Štrbské Pleso (ski stadium and many other sports facilities), Starý Smokovec and Tatranská Lomnica.

Low Tatras

The highest peak in the Low Tatras is Dumbier (2043m/6703ft). The largest winter sports centre is Jasná (950m/3115ft), on the northern slopes of Mt Chopok (2024m/6641ft) in the Demänova valley.

Facilities:
Pistes for beginners and more advanced skiers; many langlauf trails; numerous ski-lifts and cableways.

Pistes and Langlauf Trails

High Tatras
Pistes

Štrbské Pleso (1350m/4430ft; 1915–1350m/6285–4430ft)
Smokovec (850m/2790ft; 1480–800m/4855–2625ft)
Tatranská Lomnica (850m/2790ft; 2180–860m/7155–2820ft)
Ždiar (800m/2625ft; 1180–800/3870–2625ft)

Langlauf

Štrbské Pleso (2 × 5, 7 and 10km/3, 4½ and 6 miles)

Low Tatras
Pistes

Jasná, northern slopes of Mt Chopok (950m/3115ft; 2005–950m/6580–3115ft)
Srdiečko, southern slopes of Mt Chopok (600m/1970ft; 2005–600m/6580–1970ft)
Čertovica and Boca valley (850m/2790ft; 1450–850m/4755–2790ft)

Langlauf

Jasná (5, 10 and 15km/3, 6 and 9 miles)

Little Fatra
Pistes

Vrátna (620m/2035ft; 1500–620m/4920–2035ft)
Martinské Hole (1200m/3935ft; 1440–650m/4725–2135ft)

Great Fatra
Pistes

Máliné (550m/1805ft; 1350–550m/4430–1805ft)
Turecká (580m/1905ft; 1610–580m/5280–1905ft)
Donovaly (860m/2820ft; 1360–780m/4460–2560ft)

Langlauf

Donovaly (3, 5 and 10km/2, 3 and 6 miles)

Selected Skiing Areas in the Czech Republic

The four main skiing areas in the Czech Republic are the Krkonoše, the Jizera Hills, the Ore Mountains (Krušné Hory) and the Bohemian Forest (Šumava).

Krkonoše

The Krkonoše, lying along the Czech–Polish frontier, is the highest range in north-eastern Bohemia and the most popular winter sports region in Bohemia. The highest peak is Sněžka (1602m/5256ft).

Major winter sports centres:
Špindleruv Mlýn (700m/2300ft), Pec pod Sněžkou (700m/2300ft), Harrachov (660–720m/2165–2360ft), Rokytnice nad Jizerou (520–850m/1705–2790ft) and Janské Lázně (615m/2020ft).

Facilities:
Pistes, langlauf trails and circuits; numerous cableways, chair-lifts and ski-tows; giant ski jump at Harrachov; ski schools.

Jizera Hills

The ridge of the Jizera Hills in northern Bohemia marks the frontier with Poland. The highest peaks on Czech territory are Smrk (1124m/3688ft) and Jizera (1112m/3648ft). The gentler slopes on the south side of the hills (particularly at Severák-Loučky) are particularly suitable for less experienced skiers and children.

Major ski centres:
Bedřichov (600m/1970m) and Severák-Loučky (600m/1970m), below Mt Severák (804m/2638ft).

Facilities:
Ski-lifts and ski-tows; ski school; ski jumps; langlauf trails; toboggan run; racing pistes on slopes of Mt Špičák (724m/2375ft), near Tanvald. Above Liberec is one of the finest viewpoints in Bohemia, Mt Ještěd (hotel, restaurant), which can be reached in 4 minutes by cable railway.

Ore Mountains

The highest peak on the Czech side is Klínovec (1244m/4082ft).

The largest and best known skiing region in the Bohemian Ore Mountains is the Jáchymov–Klínovec–Boží Dar area (672–1244m/2205–4082ft), to the north of Karlovy Vary (Karlsbad).

Facilities:
Pistes and langlauf trails; many chair-lifts and ski-lifts; ski jumps. The area round Boží Dar is also suitable for beginners.

Šumava (Bohemian Forest)

The ridges and plateaux of the Bohemian Forest extend along the western border of Bohemia for 125km/80 miles. The highest peak on Czech territory is Plechý (1378m/4521ft).

The highest skiing centre is the town of Železná Ruda (754m/2474ft). Another popular centre is Zadov-Churáňov (800–1100m/2625–3610ft), with langlauf trails which are among the best in the Czech Republic.

Facilities:
Pistes, langlauf trails and circuits; cableway, ski-tows and ski-lifts.

Pistes and Langlauf Trails

Krkonoše Pistes

Pec pod Sněžkou (700m/2300ft; 1300–700m/4265–2300ft)
Rokytnice nad Jizerou (520m/1705ft; 1300–1650m/4265–5415ft)
Špindlerův Mlýn (700m/2300ft; 1300–700m/4265–2300ft)

Langlauf

Horní Mísečky (1, 2, 3, 4, 5, 7, 10 and 15km/¾, 1¼, 2, 2½, 3, 4½, 6 and 9 miles)
Benecko (1, 2, 3, 4, 5, 7 and 10km/¾, 1¼, 2, 2½, 3, 4½ and 6 miles)

Šumava (Bohemian Forest) Pistes

Železná Ruda–Špičák (750m/2460ft; 1210–780m/3970–2560ft)

Langlauf

Zadov-Churáňov (1, 2, 3, 4, 5, 7, 10 and 15km/¾, 1¼, 2, 2½, 3, 4½, 6 and 9 miles)

Ore Mountains Pistes

Klínovec and Boží Dar (1244m/4082ft; 1244–710m/4082–2330ft)

Langlauf

Nové Město (1, 2, 3, 4, 5, 7 and 10km/¾, 1¼, 2, 2½, 3, 4½ and 6 miles)

Jizera Hills Pistes

Bedřichov, Severák (600m/1970ft; 810–700m/2660–2300ft
Špičák (808m/2651ft; 808–530m/2651–1739ft)
Mt Ještěd (1012m/3320ft; 1012–660m/3320–2165ft)

Langlauf

Bedřichov, with the Jizera Trail.

Bohemo-Moravian Highlands Langlauf

Nové Město na Moravě (3, 5, 10 and 15km/2, 3, 6 and 9 miles)

Orlík Hills Pistes

Deštně (650m/2135ft; 850–650m/2790–2135ft)

Jeseníky Pistes

Karlov pod Pradědem (650m/2135ft; 936–700m/3071–2300ft)
Ramzová (759m/2490ft; 1300–730m/4265–2395ft)

Langlauf

Ovčárna (1, 2, 3 and 5km/¾, 1¼, 2 and 3 miles)
Nová Ves u Rymařova (1, 2, 3, 5 and 10km/¾, 1¼, 2, 3 and 6 miles)

Beskýds
Pistes | Portáš (960m/3150ft; 955–690m/3135–2265ft)
Pustevny-Radhošt' (1018m/3340ft; 1100–700m/3610–2300ft)

Langlauf | Pustevny (1, 2, 3, 5, 7 and 10km/¾, 1¼, 2, 3, 4½ and 6 miles)

Young People's Accommodation

A variety of reasonably priced accommodation is available for young people in the Czech and Slovak Republics: youth hostels (e.g. CKM "junior hotels"), student residences and lodgings, mountain huts (*bouda* or *chata,* for example in the Krkonoše in the Czech Republic and the High Tatras in Slovakia; information from Čedok or Slovakoturist in Nový Smokovec), hikers' hostels (*turistická ubytovna;* very simple accommodation, with bunk beds and cold water) and camping sites (see Camping and Caravanning).

Booking

Advance booking is advisable both for groups and for individuals.

Opening times

Youth hostels are usually open between 6am and 10pm; the dormitories are normally closed from 9am to 5pm (though this does not apply to hostels without a day room or in bad weather).

Student residences

Student residences in the large university towns are available in July and August to provide accommodation for foreign students (and non-students).

Information

The International Youth Hostel Federation publishes a "Guide to Budget Accommodation", Volume I of which covers Europe and the Mediterranean, with a chapter on former Czechoslovakia.

Youth Travel Bureau

The Youth Travel Bureau (CKM, Cestovní Kancelář Mládeže in Czech, Cestovná Kanceláría Mládeže in Slovak) finds accommodation for young people in youth hostels and hotels, and will arrange for them to stay with a family or in a work camp or to take part in a sport training course. It also gets rail and air tickets, books sightseeing tours and provides information on cultural events and guiding services.

Addresses:

Prague

CKM
Žitná 12, CZ-12105 Praha 2, tel. (02) 29 99 41
Open Mon.–Fri. 8am–4.30pm

Brno

CKM
Ceská 11, CZ-65704 Brno, tel. (05) 2 36 41

Bratislava

CKM
Hviezdozlavovo Námestie 16, SQ-81416 Bratislava, tel. (07) 33 16 07

Index